Buddhism

Introducing the Buddhist Experience

THIRD EDITION

Donald W. Mitchell
Purdue University

Sarah H. Jacoby
Northwestern University

New York Oxford
OXFORD UNIVERSITY PRESS

Oxford University Press is a department of the University of Oxford.
It furthers the University's objective of excellence in research,
scholarship, and education by publishing worldwide.

Oxford New York
Auckland Cape Town Dar es Salaam Hong Kong Karachi
Kuala Lumpur Madrid Melbourne Mexico City Nairobi
New Delhi Shanghai Taipei Toronto

With offices in
Argentina Austria Brazil Chile Czech Republic France Greece
Guatemala Hungary Italy Japan Poland Portugal Singapore
South Korea Switzerland Thailand Turkey Ukraine Vietnam

For titles covered by Section 112 of the US Higher Education Opportunity Act, please visit www.oup.com/us/he for the latest information about pricing and alternate formats.

Published by Oxford University Press.
198 Madison Avenue, New York, NY 10016
www.oup.com

Library of Congress Cataloging-in-Publication Data
Mitchell, Donald W. (Donald William), 1943-
Buddhism: introducing the Buddhist experience / Donald W. Mitchell,
Sarah H. Jacoby.—Third edition.
pages cm
Previously published: 2008.
Includes bibliographical references and index.
ISBN: 978-0-19-986187-3
1. Buddhism—History. I. Jacoby, Sarah. II. Title.
BQ266.M48 2013
294.3—dc23

2013031737

Printing number: 9 8

Printed in Canada
on acid-free paper.

To Buddhist friends in dialogue

Table of Contents

Boxes, Figures, and Maps

BOXES

FIGURES

MAPS

Preface

This third edition of *Buddhism: Introducing the Buddhist Experience* includes a number of revisions and new elements. First, Donald Mitchell has invited Sarah Jacoby to join him as co-author. Sarah Jacoby was one of the Buddhist Studies scholars Oxford University Press asked to review the previous edition of the book. Based on her review comments, her sensitivity to the style and goal of the book, and on our complementary areas of expertise, we have joined forces to collaborate on this and future editions.

SIGNIFICANT CHANGES TO THE THIRD EDITION

Our co-authorship has led to three primary changes in the book. The first is a reconceived notion of Buddhism as a globalized set of traditions encompassing a multiplicity of cultural forms. We move away from earlier concepts of Buddhism as divided into two primary categories including "Eastern," meaning Asian, and "Western," usually meaning First World or industrial and capitalist countries and often only referring to Europe, North America, and Australia. To showcase the increasingly international cross-currents of influence shaping the development of Buddhist traditions around the globe, we have reframed the final chapter of this book from its former focus on "Buddhism in the West" to "The Globalization of Buddhism." Along with this title change comes a wider lens on Buddhist developments that includes New Zealand and countries in Latin America and Africa. We have also given an enriched attention to contemporary issues facing Buddhist communities around the globe, including second- and third-generation Buddhist youth, and the central role of the Internet in the globalization of Buddhism.

The second change we have made is to remove the penultimate chapter in the previous editions titled "Modern Buddhism in Asia," which was a compilation of new Buddhist movements in nine different Asian countries. We have not deleted any of this highly relevant material from the book, but rather we have returned this information to the respective chapters dealing with these various cultural contexts. For example, information about new Buddhist movements in India, Sri Lanka, Tibet, China, Korea, Japan, and so on, can be found in the chapters focusing on these regions. We believe that this will make this new edition more user friendly for both students and instructors.

When courses reach the contemporary situation of Buddhism, this book now presents an introduction to the newest forms of Buddhist movements and most recent figures from around the globe.

Third, our collaboration has led to a rewriting of Chapter 6, "Tibetan Experiences of Buddhism." Given Sarah's specialization in this area, she took the lead and has produced a more robust and accessible chapter with new photographs and map. Indeed, we have updated all chapters with the most recent scholarship, new pictures, and a new map focused on the area of India traveled by the Buddha. We have also added new subtitles to better guide students through the chapters. These updates add to the strengths of previous editions.

WHAT MAKES THIS TEXTBOOK UNIQUE

Aspects that set *Buddhism: Introducing the Buddhist Experience* apart from other textbooks introducing Buddhism are its emphasis on the diversity of cultural contexts in which Buddhism developed over more than two millennia, its balance between the historical and contemporary significance of Buddhist philosophy and practice, and its focus on Buddhism as an aspect of everyday life for people from around the globe. To convey an inkling of the diversity of what it means to be Buddhist in different countries today, each chapter concludes with an essay written by a noted Buddhist scholar-practitioner from that chapter's cultural region. These include Ven. Dr. Mano Mettanando Laohavanich, famous monastic teacher and now president of the Hospice Foundation of Thailand; Geshe Damdul Namgyal, Drepung Loseling College, Bodhgaya, India; Dedong Wei, Institute of Buddhism and Religious Theory, Renmin University, Beijing, China; Jongmyung Kim, Academy of Korean Studies, Seoul, Korea; Tomonobu Shinozaki, former president of Gakurin Buddhist Seminary, Tokyo, Japan; and Dharma Master Rev. Dr. Heng Sure, director of the Berkeley Buddhist Monastery, Berkeley, California.

Another aspect of this book that sets it apart from others is the many quotations from Buddhist texts throughout the book, as well as gender-balanced original boxed contributions written by some of the most famous male and female Buddhist scholars and practitioners from around the world. These include Chatsumarn Kabilsingh, formerly at Thammasat University, Bangkok, and now one of the first fully ordained nuns in Southeast Asia, Dhammananda Samaneri; David W. Chappell, formerly at the University of Hawaii; Nichiko Niwano, president of the Risshō Kōsei-kai lay Buddhist movement; Judith Simmer-Brown at the Naropa Institute; Sylvia Boorstein, American Buddhist teacher and author; Ven. Dr. Vajiragnana, London Buddhist Vihara; Virginia Straus Benson, Ikeda Center for Peace, Learning and Dialogue; Alfred Bloom, formerly at the University of Hawaii; Zoketsu Norman Fischer, Zen Master at the San Francisco Zen Center; Stephanie Kaza, University of Vermont; Jeffrey Hopkins, formerly at the University of Virginia; Tenzin Gyatso, the Fourteenth Dalai Lama; Master Sheng Yen, founder of Dharma Drum Mountain Buddhist movement; Ven. Dr. Yifa, nun in the Fo Guang Shan Buddhist movement; Sung Bae Park, SUNY at Stony Brook; Ven. Chung Ok Lee, nun and representative of Won Buddhism to the United Nations; Kenneth Tanaka, Shin priest and professor at Musashino Joshi University, Tokyo; Robert Aitken, Zen Master and founder of the Diamond Sangha; Sulak Sivaraksa, director of the Santi Pracha Dhamma Institute, Bangkok; Dharma Master Cheng Yen, nun and founder of Tzu Chi Buddhist Compassion Relief Foundation; Zenkai Blanche Hartman, Zen Master at the San Francisco Zen Center; and Rita M. Gross, formerly at the University of Wisconsin—Eau Claire.

Acknowledgments

Considering the three editions of this book, we would like to thank the following scholars who contributed to this work: Paul J. Griffiths (University of Illinois, Chicago), Sallie B. King (James Madison University), Sung Bae Park (SUNY, Stony Brook), George Bond (Northwestern University), David J. Kalupahana and David Chappell (University of Hawaii), Jeffery Hopkins and Bryon Phillips (University of Virginia), John Keenan (Middlebury College), Charles Jones (Catholic University of America), Rita Gross (University of Wisconsin at Eau Clare), Geshe Lhundup Sopa (University of Wisconsin), Robert E. Buswell, Jr. (UCLA), Taitetsu Unno (Smith College), Steven Heine (Florida International University), Judith Simmer-Brown (Naropa University), Stephanie Kaza (University of Vermont), Geshin Tokiwa (Hanazono University), Masao Abe (Nara University), Ryusei Takeda (Ryukoku University), and Kenneth K. Tanaka (Musashino Joshi University). Along with these scholars, we would also like to thank the following Buddhist leaders for their assistance: A. T. Ariyaratne, Samu Sunim, Jinwol Sunim, Joseph Goldstein, Sharon Saltzberg, Geshe Lobsang Tenzin, Ven. Havanpola Ratanasara, and Ven. Henopola Gunaratna.

Special thanks also to the reviewers of the second edition selected by Oxford University Press: Catherine Benton (Lake Forest College), Daniel S. Breyer (Illinois State University), Jeffrey L. Broughton (California State University, Long Beach), Christopher Key Chapple (Loyola Marymount University), Diana Dimitrova (Michigan State University), Sarah Jacoby (Northwestern University), Russell Kirkland (University of Georgia), Laurie Hovell McMillin (Oberlin College), Daniel Veidlinger (California State University, Chico), and Kevin Vose (College of William and Mary).

Also from Oxford University Press, we want to thank Robert Miller, Liam Dalzell, and Kristin Maffei. In preparing the manuscript, we want to thank Shin Kim, Elaine Klemme, Erik Hanson, Ann Mitchell, and Antonio Terrone. Finally, we would like to thank our students, who have pushed us to deepen our understanding of Buddhism and to present it more clearly.

Donald W. Mitchell
Purdue University

Sarah H. Jacoby
Northwestern University

Pronunciation Guide

Although most of the Buddhist texts from India were written in either Pali or Sanskrit (or rather Buddhist Hybrid Sanskrit), we have preferred always to use the Sanskrit version of Indian Buddhist terms for the sake of consistency throughout this book. Where particular terms play important roles in Theravāda Buddhism, which relies on Pali, we have placed the Pali equivalents in parentheses. Because both Pali and Sanskrit have more than twenty-six letters, to write them in the Roman alphabet necessitates the use of diacritical marks. However, where terms have become part of the English language, we have left them unitalicized and without diacritical marks. For Chinese terms, we have used the Pinyin system but have included the Wade-Giles system for present-day Chinese Buddhist organizations and persons that use Wade-Giles. For Tibetan, we have used the Tibetan and Himalayan Library Simplified Phonetic Transcription of Standard Tibetan by David Germano and Nicolas Tournadre. The following are a few guidelines to aid in pronunciation for these and other languages.

SANSKRIT AND PALI

Unmarked vowels:	*Marked vowels:*
a as in "hut"	**ā** as in "father"
i as in "bit"	**ī** as in "beat"
u as in "put"	**ū** as in "rule"
e as in "bed"	
o as in "boat"	
Unmarked consonants:	*Marked consonants:*
c as in "cheap"	**ś** or **ṣ** as in "ship"
ph as in "cup-handle"	**ṛ** as in "rip"
	ñ as in "canyon"
	ṃ as *ng* in "sing"

TIBETAN

Unmarked vowels:
a as in "hut"
i as in "hit" or "reel"
e as in "say" or "help"
o as in "note"

Marked vowels:
ö roughly like "foot"
ü as in "rue" or roughly like "cute"
é as in "play"

CHINESE: PINYIN

Initials:
b as in "pit"
d as in "stop"
c as in "ca**ts**"
g as in "kiss"
h as in "lock"
j as in "search"
q as in **"chew"**
w as in "way'
x as in **"shoe"**
y as in "yes"
z as in "su**ds**"

Finals:
a as in "father"
e as in "mud"
an as in "fan"
ai as in **"eye"**
ei as in "hey"
ao as in "cow"
ou as in "toe"
en as in "broken"
er as in "bar"
i as in "tea"
ia as in "yard"
ie as in "yet"
iao as in "meow"
ian as in "ben"
uai as in **"why"**
ui as in **"way"**
uang as in **"you long"**
ong as in **"looking"**
iong as in "**tee long**"
o as in "dong"
u as in "lung"
ai as in "high"
ao as in "how"
ei as in "they"
ou as in "go"
u as in "good"
ui as "way"

CHINESE: WADE-GILES

Initial consonants:
ch or **ch'** as in "cheap"
hs as in "she"
ts/**tz** or **ts'**/**tz'** as in "its"

Vowels:
a as in "father"
e as in "change"
i as in "sing"

KOREAN

Unmarked vowels:	*Marked vowels:*
ae as in "ape"	**ŏ** as in "soap"
ai as in "gap"	**ŭ** as in "soup"
e as in "let"	**ŭi** as in "movie"

JAPANESE

Vowels with macrons, **ō** or **ū**, are simply sounded longer than those without macrons.

Introduction

Buddha—meaning "Awakened"—has inspired and fascinated people for 2,500 years. What does "Awakened" mean? Awakened from what? The Buddha taught that we are unawakened due to certain causes and conditions. When those causes and conditions are extinguished by following the Path he taught, we too can awake. To what? Nirvana—another word that has caught the imagination of people since it was preached by the Buddha. What is Nirvana?

The questions continue and the answers taught, sought, and lived tell the story of Buddhism. This story is extraordinary and multifaceted, made up of peoples' journeys of religious discoveries spanning centuries, continents, and cultures. Each story is of an experience, of a religious quest that includes practice and insight, struggle and growth, transformation and realization, and philosophical reflection and artistic expression.

Buddhism: Introducing the Buddhist Experience is the story of these religious journeys from the experience of the historical Buddha in ancient India to the experiences of Buddhists around the world today. Gautama Buddha first taught a Path that leads to Awakening through the cultivation of morality, meditation, and wisdom in the fifth century B.C.E. Over the centuries, Buddhist disciples recorded a wealth of teachings about this religious quest and the profound goal to which it leads. Religious practices and cultural forms emerged all around Asia that enriched and expressed the breadth and depth of Buddhism. Each Buddhist civilization and historical period has adapted the Buddha's message in new and culturally specific ways, creating diverse "Buddhisms" that cohere under the umbrella term *Buddhism.* The ten chapters of this book unfold the historical developments, cultural adaptations, and contemporary movements that comprise this vibrant religion from its ancient Indian inception to its current globalized forms.

Before we begin to tell this compelling story, it is important to note that only in recent centuries has the term *Buddhism* been used to name this religion. This name was coined by Western scholars and eventually became accepted by Buddhists themselves. Previously, the religion was often referred to as the Buddha's *teaching* or *message,* and the Buddha's *way* or *path.* These words from within the tradition indicate the central importance of doctrine and practice, of insight and transformation, to the experiences of what is now called Buddhism.

To attempt to capture the wholeness of the Buddhist way, we will at times use a Western term, namely, *spirituality*. By this we mean to denote specific paths to religious goals that include teachings and practices, moral and communal life, ontological and psychological foundations, as well as transformative experiences and cultural expressions. Spiritualities open one to insights into truths, to liberation from attachments, and to overcoming blockages to religious realizations. In Buddhism itself, the closest equivalent is *bhāvanā*, meaning "cultivation" and "producing," or, in a broader sense, "the process of religious cultivation." It is in this sense we use the term *spirituality*.

The first five chapters of our story of Buddhism focus on India, on the root from which all other forms of Buddhism have grown. The ideas and practices of Indian Buddhism provide a common heritage for the traditions that emerged in other parts of Asia. In Chapter 1, we introduce the religious world of India at the time of the historical Buddha and its influence on the Buddha's life and message. We take the story of the life of the Buddha primarily from the early Pali texts, while also referencing later famous biographies that present popular legends developed over the centuries after the passing of the Buddha. Chapter 1 presents what the original texts say about his early life, his religious quest, and the nature of his experience of Awakening and attainment of Nirvana. We then follow the Awakened One in his mission to preach the Dharma (Teaching) and to create his Saṅgha (Community) up until the last moments of his life.

Chapter 2 emphasizes the core teachings of the historical Buddha that explain his experience of the dissatisfactory human condition we all share, its causes and conditions, the opportunity to reach a truly liberated condition of living by extinguishing these negative aspects of life, and the path that leads to that liberated state, namely, Nirvana. In relating these foundations of the Buddha's Dharma, we present a translation of what is referred to as the Buddha's First Sermon, letting the early tradition speak for itself. We also discuss the Buddha's teachings concerning cosmology, karma and rebirth, the dependent arising of all things, and the nature of Nirvana.

In Chapter 3, we trace the development of early Buddhism in India after the passing of the Buddha. We explore the composition of what would become the first scriptures of Buddhism, the early councils that guided the growing Saṅgha, and the different philosophies that emerged during the first centuries. The second part of the chapter is devoted to one of the branches of early Buddhism, Theravāda, that eventually spread south of India into Sri Lanka and parts of Southeast Asia, where it has remained until today. A classic experience of Theravāda is captured in a famous text written by Buddhaghosa called *The Path of Purification*. We examine all three sections of this masterpiece of monastic spirituality from the discipline of moral development, through the practice of meditation, to the insights that generate the different stages of the experience of Nirvana. Finally, we look at new Buddhist movements in Southeast Asia as well as Theravāda outside the monastery today as practiced by laypersons in the Buddhist culture of Thailand.

In Chapter 4, we move from the early forms of Buddhism to the second major current of Buddhist life, namely, Mahāyāna Buddhism. Here we find the bodhisattva path leading to the attainment of what is called "Buddhahood," in order to remain in the world to benefit others. To help the reader understand this new ideal of Buddhist life, we look at selections from a number of its primary *sūtras* that characterize aspects of Mahāyāna experience. We quote the full text of the *Heart Sūtra* and analyze it to help the reader appreciate the new kind of language that Mahāyāna introduces into the Buddhist tradition. Central to Mahāyāna are the Six and Ten Perfections and the Ten Stages of the bodhisattva path. We present key passages from the *Daśabhūmika Sūtra* that guide the reader through each of the Ten Stages and Perfections to the goal of Buddhahood.

Chapter 5 is devoted to the philosophies of India. These philosophies from early Buddhism to the later systems of Mahāyāna Buddhism play key roles in the spread, development, and eventual enculturation of Buddhism outside India. We focus on the philosophies of emptiness and of consciousness, both of which express the Mahāyāna experience of the ultimate nature of existence and its relationship to the world in which we live. We also introduce the notion of Buddha-nature, a concept that plays such an important role in East Asian Buddhism, as well as in the more technical forms of later Buddhist philosophy that attempt to define the limits of our ordinary experience. Finally, we introduce a modern Buddhist movement in India that has given a new face to Buddhism in the country of its birth.

In Chapter 6, we present the story of the spread of Buddhism to Tibet. We introduce the rise of Tantra and Vajrayāna Buddhism, exploring aspects of the major contemplative practices, concepts, and key scriptures that characterize Vajrayāna Buddhism in Tibet. We also present the major schools of Tibetan Buddhism, their founders, and some of their distinguishing practices. In so doing, we quote writings from some of the major Tibetan figures about their own experiences. We conclude with an overview of recent events in Tibet along with the response of new Tibetan Buddhist movements, particularly those spearheaded by the fourteenth Dalai Lama Tenzin Gyatso, followed by a discussion of the cultural experience of Buddhism in the lives of many Tibetan people today.

Chapter 7 brings us to the fascinating story of Buddhism's spread to China and the ways that this spread defined much of East Asian Buddhism. We see how Chinese Buddhists first reproduced forms of the traditional kinds of Indian Buddhism, and then adapted them into Chinese forms of Buddhism focused on the interrelatedness and harmony of this life, and Awakening to the inner essence of Buddhahood. These specifically Chinese kinds of Buddhism captured the spirit of East Asia. To convey this spirit, we quote profound passages about ultimate reality and its relationship to our world from Tiantai and Huayan masters. We also present in some detail the highly intuitive Chan (Zen) tradition, as well as the more devotional Pure Land tradition. We conclude with a presentation of new Buddhist movements in Taiwan that have spread around the world, and the cultural experience of Buddhism in China today.

Chapter 8 takes us to the Korean experience of Buddhism. Their experience originated with the entry of Chinese Buddhism into Korea, but the richness and uniqueness of Korean Buddhism comes from the great innovators whose writings continue to inspire monastics and laypersons alike. We present passages from these writings that demonstrate the depth of Korean scholarship, insight, and devotion, as well as the Korean genius for unifying the diverse forms of Buddhism that came from China. Selections from Chinul, the greatest Korean reformer and unifier, introduce readers to the richness of the Korean experience that has continued to serve as a model down to today. We also present a new Buddhist movement in Korea that has become popular, mention the recent growth of Christianity in Korea, and describe the cultural experience of Buddhism as practiced by laypersons in Korea today.

In Chapter 9, we introduce a variety of Japanese Buddhist paths to the realization of the Dharma that emerged over the centuries in Japan. While versions of Chinese Buddhism first developed in Nara, Japan, the two classically Japanese schools of Tendai and Shingon were founded later in Kyōto, where they became pillars of Buddhist scholarship and practice. We also present the famous later reformers and innovators—Honen, Shinran, Dōgen, and Nichiren—who founded the traditions of Pure Land, Zen, and Nichiren Buddhism that have had strong influence on Japanese culture and society. We conclude with presenting new Buddhist movements in Japan that have become global, and a description of the cultural practices of Buddhism in Japan today.

In Chapter 10, we turn to the globalization of Buddhism. Globalization has brought Buddhism from Asian to non-Asian countries around the world, thus giving us a glimpse into the beginning of a new and more global chapter in the story of Buddhism. We begin with the colonialist encounter with Buddhism in Asia, and early Buddhist scholarship in Europe. Then we examine the flows of Asian forms of Buddhism into selected non-Asian countries on all continents. We have also chosen to spotlight the United States as a site to examine the spread of Asian Buddhist traditions and modern Asian movements outside of Asia because of its large number and diversity of Buddhist institutions. Finally we look at various key issues that are arising in the globalization of Buddhism, including gender equality, identity, interreligious dialogue, social engagement, and youth and the media, as well as the practice of Buddhism in American culture today.

SUGGESTIONS FOR FURTHER READING

Bechert, Heinz, and Richard Gombrich, eds. *The World of Buddhism: Monks and Nuns in Society and Culture.* London: Thames and Hudson, 1984.

Buswell, Robert E., Jr., and Robert M. Gimello, eds. *Paths to Liberation: The Marga and Its Transformations in Buddhist Thought.* Honolulu: University of Hawaii Press, 1992.

Conze, Edward. *Buddhist Texts through the Ages.* New York: Harper & Row, 1964.

de Bary, Wm. Theodore, ed. *The Buddhist Tradition in India, China, and Japan.* New York: Random House, 1972.

Gethin, Rupert. *The Foundations of Buddhism.* Oxford, UK: Oxford University Press, 1998.

Harvey, Peter. *An Introduction to Buddhist Ethics: Foundations, Values and Issues.* Cambridge, UK: Cambridge University Press, 2000.

Kalupahana, David J. *A History of Buddhist Philosophy: Continuities and Discontinuities.* Honolulu: University of Hawaii Press, 1992.

Kitagawa, Joseph, and Mark Cummings, eds. *Buddhism in Asian History.* New York: Macmillan, 1989.

LaFleur, William R. *Buddhism: A Cultural Perspective.* New York: Prentice Hall, 1997.

Lopez, Donald S., Jr., ed. *Buddhist Hermeneutics.* Honolulu: University of Hawaii Press, 1992.

———, ed. *Buddhism in Practice.* Princeton, NJ: Princeton University Press, 1995.

Reynolds, Frank E., and Jason A. Carbine, eds. *The Life of Buddhism.* Berkeley: University of California Press, 2000.

Silk, Jonathan A. *Wisdom, Compassion, and the Search for Understanding: A Buddhist Studies Legacy.* Honolulu: University of Hawaii Press, 2000.

Strong, John S. *The Experience of Buddhism: Sources and Interpretations.* Belmont, CA: Wadsworth, 1995.

Takeuchi, Yoshinori, ed. *Buddhist Spirituality I: Indian, Southeast Asian, Tibetan, Early Chinese.* New York: Crossroad, 1995.

———, ed. *Buddhist Spirituality II: Later China, Korea, Japan and the Modern World.* New York: Crossroad, 1999.

Tsomo, Karma Lekshe. *Buddhist Women across Cultures: Realizations.* Albany: SUNY Press, 1999.

Williams, Paul, Anthony Tribe, and Alexander Wynne. *Buddhist Thought: A Complete Introduction to the Indian Tradition, Second Edition.* London: Routledge, 2012.

1

The Life of Gautama Buddha

Siddhārtha Gautama (Pali: Siddhattha Gotama) is the person the world has come to know as the *Buddha,* the "Awakened One." Gautama was born during a historical epoch when the Indian culture was open to his religious message of enlightenment, compassion, and peace. The religious, social, and cultural world into which he was born had been evolving for centuries. The Indus Valley Civilization in the western part of the Indian subcontinent began around 3000 B.C.E. It included some of the great urban centers of the ancient world like Harappa and Mohenjo-daro. From what we know of their religion, it involved a belief in many deities and the practice of ritual worship, both of which played a role in the tradition that contributed to what would later develop into Hinduism. The roots of the Hindu religious tradition began around 1500 B.C.E. with the migration into India of Indo-European tribes collectively called Āryans ("Nobles"). The Āryans came from west and north of the Caspian Sea and brought their own religion that would develop into Vedic Brahmanism, named for the Four Vedas that are the early sacred scripture of the later Hindu tradition.

Vedic Brahmanism involved the worship of many gods (*devas*) and a complex ritual system. The Four Vedas contained hymns to the *devas* along with ritual materials and teachings used in daily life. The Āryans also created the caste system into which Gautama was born as a member of the second caste, the noble or warrior caste. At about 800 B.C.E., a new religious literature developed called the Upaniṣads. The Upaniṣads were more mystical and focused on the practice of yoga as a means to liberation, or *mokṣa,* from karma (Pali: *kamma*) and rebirth. Karma was thought to be a subtle form of moral energy, good and bad, that results from one's good and evil actions. This karmic energy was believed to determine what kind of rebirth one would experience after death. To gain liberation from karma and the cycle of birth and death, the Upaniṣads taught that it is not enough to worship *devas;* one has to destroy one's karma and attain spiritual realization of Ultimate Reality through yogic practice. This liberation meant a union of the Soul, Ātman, with Ultimate Reality, namely, the divine Brahman that is the one eternal source of all beings including the *devas.*

By the sixth century B.C.E., when Gautama lived, these newer ideas and practices had led to the development of different philosophies and ways of life. It was a century of social and religious change. New monarchies were established as empires and were carved out by ambitious warrior kings. There was a growth of new and larger cities that replaced smaller tribal societies. Increase in trade also led to a richer money economy and the emergence of a well-to-do and powerful merchant class. With these changes, not only were the older social structures and cultural customs coming under question but also the traditional religious viewpoints and institutions that were associated with them.

Both the Vedic ritualism and the yogic practices of the Upaniṣads clashed with the materialism found in the large cities and enjoyed by the newly rich merchant class. But, more important, some people became disillusioned by urban materialism and were instead attracted to the ideal of liberation. However, they were also suspicious of the spiritual integrity of the learned Hindu priests and sages, who, for the most part, were married and making a living from their teaching and ritual celebrations. So a number of people were open to new liberation movements. These movements were called *śramaṇa* (Pali: *samaṇa*), or "striver" for liberation. They were often wandering ascetics who lived in poverty and begged for what they needed. One group of such strivers were the Jains. Jainism was founded around the time of Siddhārtha Gautama by Vardhamāna Jnātṛputra, known as *Mahāvīra,* the "Great Hero." This group taught that all beings have a "life principle" (*jīva*). This *jīva* is like an individual soul that is bound by karma and rebirth to the material world. The only way that one can free the *jīva* from this bondage is by severe asceticism.

Another group of strivers were the Ājīvakas, meaning "lifeless ones," most likely a derogatory term given them by others. The Ājīvakas believed in rebirth, but not in the power of karma to effect the condition of one's rebirth. One's life is determined by fate, not by any moral or spiritual striving. Each life is fated as to how it will work itself out. One can find peace by accepting one's life in whatever form it might take. A third group were the Materialists, who denied both karma and rebirth. They believed that there is nothing besides matter so when one dies, one's self is annihilated. Therefore, the Materialists taught that contentment can only be found in the pleasures of a balanced life that includes enjoyable relationships with others. Finally, there were the Skeptics who avoided the confusion that was caused by all these different viewpoints by simply withholding judgment. In this skeptical avoidance of the problems that so concerned others, they found a certain peace of mind.

As we shall see, on his spiritual quest Gautama joined a small group of *śramaṇas* for a time. However, in his teachings after his Awakening, he rebuked the shortcomings of the views and practices of the *śramaṇa* groups. He was opposed to the Jains' rather mechanical notion of karma and their extreme asceticism. He felt that the Ājīvakas' fatalism discouraged the vigor and effort needed to attain Awakening. The Materialists, he believed, were deluded in thinking that lasting happiness can be found in temporary

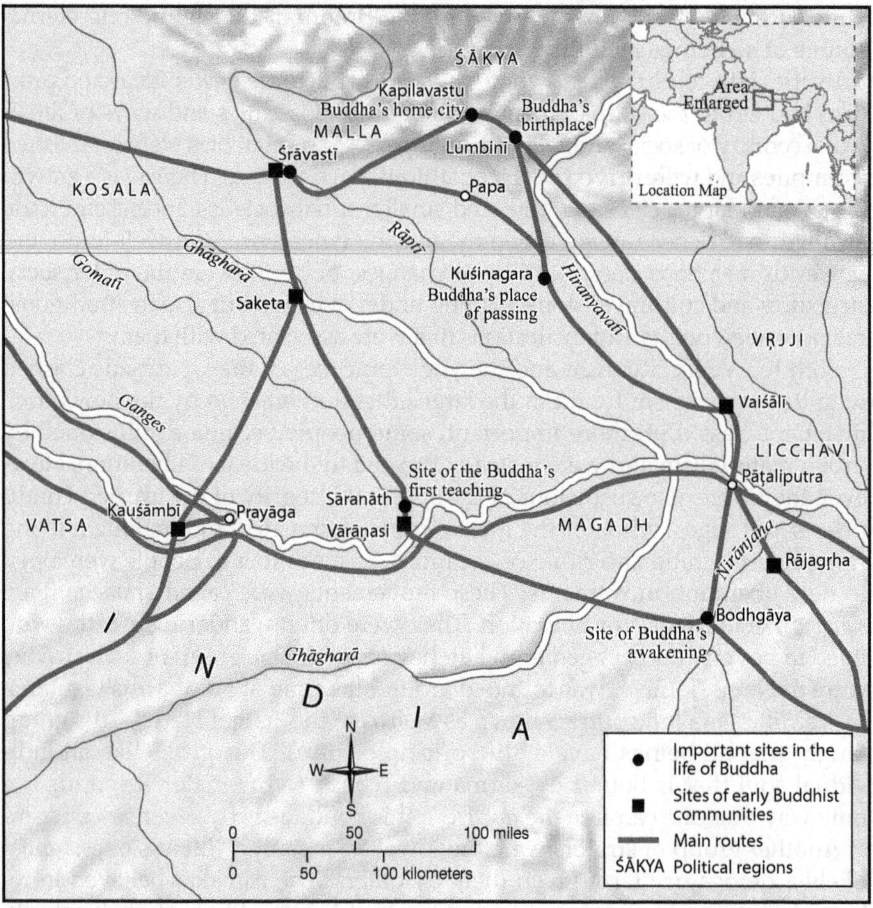

MAP 1. Early Buddhist sites.
Note: This map is taken from: *The Oxford Atlas of the World's Religions* by Ninian Smart, p. 56.

enjoyments. And the Skeptics were simply wrong in doubting all views because some viewpoints can be proven true by meditative insight. Gautama also thought that one needs a certain "faith" that the spiritual life can lead to liberation to have the necessary commitment to attain that liberation.

THE EARLY LIFE OF SIDDHĀRTHA GAUTAMA

It was into this world of religious and cultural transition that Siddhārtha Gautama was born. The exact date of his birth is a matter of contention among scholars. Different Buddhist sources claim that Gautama died either 100 years or 218 years before the consecration of King Aśoka. As that consecration can be plausibly dated anywhere between 280 and 267 B.C.E., and because Gautama is said in all Buddhist sources to have lived for eighty years, the date of his birth using these sources could be put between 578 and 447 B.C.E. On the other hand, scholars point out that the 100- and 218-year figures can also be seen as ideal numbers, hence the lack of consensus. Until recently most modern scholars have accepted the earlier dating for Gautama's life. But today, many scholars place his life fully in the fifth century B.C.E.

Scholars also point out that not only the date of Gautama's birth but also stories about his life must be questioned in terms of historical accuracy. The complete biographies of Gautama's life were written hundreds of years after his death and include legends not found in earlier texts. These later biographies include the *Mahāvastu* ("Great Story") from the first century C.E.; the *Lalitavistara* ("Graceful Description"), also from the first century C.E.; and the famous *Buddhacarita* ("Acts of the Buddha") written by Aśvaghoṣa in the second century C.E. These later narratives were also written for Buddhist communities that had their own perceptions and interests. On the other hand, the older sections of Buddhist scriptures, called the *Nikāyas* or *Āgamas*, do not contain a full biography of his life, but only fragmentary references. Also, scholars point out that we have no historical evidence concerning the Buddha's life to use to judge the value of even these earlier writings. However, it seems reasonable at least to tell the story of the Buddha's life based on the earlier writings, with occasional mention of the more popular legends that appear in the later biographies. What follows applies this approach, noting when early scriptures and later biographies are used. For sites related to the life of Gautama Buddha, see Map 1.

Birth

The earlier Buddhist scriptures say that the historical Buddha was born to the warrior-caste Gautama family of the Śākya clan in the state of Kosala. In the later tradition, the Buddha is given the title "Śākyamuni," or "sage of the Śākya clan." A personal name for the Buddha was not given in the earlier texts but appears in later texts as *Siddhārtha*, meaning "one who has achieved his goal." In early texts, Gautama's father is named *Śuddhodana*, meaning "pure rice." This seems appropriate since the Śākya clan resided between the Ganges plains and the foothills of the Himalayas, a region in which rice is cultivated. Śuddhodana is referred to in the earlier texts as one of the council of rulers of the Śākya clan and leader of the town of Kapilavastu, where the family lived. Later biographies of the Buddha claim that Śuddhodana was actually a king.

Early texts report that Gautama's mother, Māyā, was in the garden of Lumbinī near Kapilavastu when she gave birth to her son. Buddhists celebrate the birth of Siddhārtha Gautama on the full moon of Vaiśākha (April–May), which is the fourth month of the Indian calendar. An early text records a prophecy made by a hermit named Asita at the time of Gautama's birth:

> Holding the bull child of the Śākya tribe, he . . . examined him, and with joy in his mind raised his voice saying, "This is the supreme man, foremost among men. . . . This prince will reach the heights of true Awakening; he will see the

> utmost purity and benefit many because of his compassion; he will turn the wheel of the Dhamma [Teaching] and his pure actions will be widely spread. (*Suttanipāta*, 679–700)

Later biographies relate the tragic story that seven days after giving birth to Gautama, Māyā died. In this account, Śuddhodana later married Māyā's younger sister, whose name was said to be Prajāpatī. Prajāpatī is also said in this story to have raised Gautama along with his half-brother, Nanda.

Youth

All Buddhist texts agree that Gautama grew up enjoying the luxuries of an aristocratic life. Reflecting on those days, he is reported in an earlier text to have said:

> I was comfortable, extremely comfortable, incomparably comfortable. My father's mansion had lotus pools of blue, red and white all for my benefit. . . . Day and night a white canopy was held over me to protect me from the cold, heat, dust, chaff or dew. I had three palaces, one for winter, one for summer and one for the rainy season. During the rainy season, I was at the palace suited for the rains surrounded by female entertainers, and was never left alone. (*Anguttara-nikāya*, I, 145 ff.)

In later biographies, this luxury was explained with a legend concerning the conception of Gautama. In that legend, it is said that when he was conceived, his mother dreamed that a white elephant with a white lotus in his trunk entered her body (see Figure 1.1). The astrologers interpreted this dream to mean that if Gautama married and remained a householder, he would be a great warrior and perhaps unite all of India, something that had not been accomplished up until that time. However, if he would leave the householder state and retreat into the forest like the *śramaṇa* were doing, he would be a great religious leader. Śuddhodana, who was certainly influenced by the fact that during his day many nobles were creating great empires throughout India, told the astrologers that he wanted Gautama to remain a warrior and not to wander off to follow the religious life. They responded that to ensure that Gautama would not pursue the religious life, his father should surround him with sensual pleasures and hide from him anything that might make him dissatisfied with his householder life. This story is important to Buddhists today because it defines the major distractions in daily life that keep a person from undertaking the spiritual quest: attachment to worldly pleasures and the security that wealth seems to offer.

Despite the many pleasures and luxuries Gautama enjoyed in his youth, he was disturbed by certain negative aspects of the human condition that he could not avoid. After giving the previously quoted description of his comfortable life, the Buddha goes on to say that he could not help "observing old age in another person." And when he would observe old persons as

FIGURE 1.1. Māyā's dream; *stūpa* railing bas relief detail, Amarāvatī; second century B.C.E., India. Government Museum, Madras, India.

well as diseased persons and even corpses, he would feel "annoyed, ashamed and disgusted." In other words, these sights would disturb the enjoyment of his riches and pleasures. However, this feeling of annoyance led him to feel ashamed because all persons, including himself, share the weaknesses of the human condition. In the end, he felt disgusted and despondent about his being subject to, and about his reaction to, human suffering and finitude.

Another early text indicates that once Gautama did happen upon a possible spiritual avenue to a deeper form of peace and happiness that is neither dependent on fleeting pleasures nor limited by the suffering human condition:

> I remember well when my father was performing his duties and I sat under the shade of the Jambu tree along the path to the field. Separated from desires and from unwholesome affairs, I achieved the first stage of meditation. This entailed the joy produced by these separations, and is accompanied by initial and discursive thought. I believed that certainly this was the way to Awakening. (*Majjhima-nikāya*, I, 246)

In due time, Siddhārtha Gautama married a young woman named Yaśodharā, and eventually they had a son, who was named Rāhula; the name *Rāhula* means "fetter." Some interpret this name to mean that Gautama considered the birth of his son to be an obstacle to his pursuit of the religious life. Others point out that while this may be true, there is every indication in the texts that Gautama loved his family very much. So Rāhula was not so much an unwanted responsibility for Gautama but was the cause of another bond of love to his family. In any case, the naming of Rāhula certainly indicates that Gautama was struggling with his love for home and family on the one hand and the spiritual impulse to the religious life on the other. In the end, this latter impulse to find Awakening and answers to his questions about life became so strong that at the age of twenty-nine, he decided he must follow this impulse by leaving home and family to undertake a spiritual quest. Reflecting back, he would later say, "In this spring of my life, despite the tears shed by my parents, I shaved my head, put on robes, renounced my home, and became a homeless monk" (*Majjhima-nikāya*, I, 163).

The Four Sights

Gautama's struggle with the householder life and the religious quest noted in the early texts would later be woven into the story of the Four Sights. In this legend, as he approached his thirtieth birthday, Gautama found himself in the grips of a very painful struggle between his attachment to his "home," with everything his family meant to him, and his attraction to the "homeless" religious life, with its spiritual quest. This crisis was said to have been precipitated by Four Sights. It seems that one day while on a chariot ride, he passed beyond the area around his home that was secured by his father from anything upsetting. It is said that for the first time he saw a decrepit old man. When he asked his charioteer about this person's sad condition, the charioteer answered that the ills of old age are the fate of all people. Returning to the palace, Gautama fell into melancholy and could no longer find any enjoyment in the pleasures of his princely life.

On a second ride, it is said that for the first time Gautama saw a severely diseased man, and he understood more deeply that disease is not kept at bay by worldly power. Returning to the palace, Gautama's melancholy deepened. On his third trip, for the first time he saw a corpse, and again he was faced with the ultimate fate of all humankind from which no amount of worldly security can keep one safe. Deeply depressed about the plight of the human condition, Gautama set off on a fourth trip and saw a religious hermit practicing meditation. The charioteer told Gautama that this person had left the material comforts of the householder life to seek spiritual liberation from the ills of the human condition.

Through these Four Sights, it is said that Gautama understood that the impermanent pleasures he had been enjoying were passing, that they could not provide a permanent happiness that the ills of life, represented by old age, illness, and death, could not destroy. He also understood that if he wanted to find that kind of lasting inner peace, he must follow the religious life. This is a lesson that all Buddhists are taught to apply to their own lives. As with Gautama, the nature of our shared human condition includes suffering. When faced with honesty and courage, it presents one with a fundamental reason for following the religious journey to spiritual freedom and peace. In Gautama's case, his despondency is said to have lifted as he realized in the sight of a religious hermit that there is a solution to the dissatisfaction he found with his ordinary life.

The story then goes on poignantly to recount the deeply emotional parting of Gautama from his beloved family and home when he finally made the decision to pursue the religious quest for liberation. In the middle of the night, with firm resolve and motivated by a higher spiritual sense of duty, Gautama gazed for one last time at his cherished wife and son. Then with his charioteer, he left the city on horseback. Reaching the banks of a river, Gautama dismounted, shaved his head, and exchanged clothes with a passerby. Finally, it is said that Gautama sent his charioteer back to his father with a message explaining his actions, and then he set off on his spiritual quest called the "Great Renunciation."

THE GREAT RENUNCIATION

It is important to view the story of Siddhārtha Gautama's departure from his home in the social context of the sixth century. We must take into account that at that time the extended family, especially a well-to-do family like Gautama's, shared the responsibility of caring for all family members. So when Gautama set off on his pilgrimage to liberation, his wife and child would be cared for by his extended family. This certainly is not to deny the sense of loss that each member of the family must have felt because of Gautama's departure. However, his decision was not taken lightly, and he surely felt the pain of separation as he traveled on foot away from his home and loved ones. But he believed firmly that he was responding to a higher spiritual calling—a calling that he could no longer resist. He had to go out to meet his destiny with total commitment.

According to the early scriptures, Siddhārtha Gautama journeyed south from Kapilavastu, across the Ganges River to the city of Rājagṛha, the capital of the state of Magadha. Magadha was south of the state of Kosala where Gautama had lived. It is said that in Rājagṛha, Gautama begged for alms and inquired as to where the religious seekers in the area were living. Being told that they resided in the eastern foothills of Mt. Paṇḍava, he went and stayed there for some time. While there, he is said to have been visited by King Bimbisāra, who tried to persuade him to give up his spiritual quest and return to the worldly life. Some scholars say that perhaps King Bimbisāra was seeking an alliance with the Śākya clan against Kosala, Magadha's rival state. In any case, Gautama restated his decision to pursue Awakening and lasting peace, and later left the Rājagṛha area.

Spiritual Teachers

In what is referred to in some of the later texts as "a short distance away," Gautama found some ascetics and joined them for a time. However, he decided that they were "practicing a wrong path," and then went to the hermitage of Ārāḍa Kālāma, a teacher of meditation. The early texts say that Ārāḍa taught his disciples how to attain "the state of non-existence" in meditation. Gautama attained this state and was even asked by Ārāḍa to help him teach in his community. However, Gautama responded, "This Dharma (Teaching) does not lead to avoidance, to separation from desire, to cessation, to peace, to wisdom, to true Awakening, to Nirvana (Pali: *nibbāna*). It merely makes us attain the state of non-existence" (*Majjhima-nikāya*, I, 165). In other words, the meditation taught by Ārāḍa produced a high state of absorption in which all forms of existence disappear. But when one emerges from that trancelike state, his or her life is still lacking in peace, wisdom, selflessness, and true Awakening.

After Gautama studied with Ārāḍa, he went to stay with Udraka Rāmaputra, another teacher of meditation. Udraka taught Gautama the attainment of "neither perception nor non-perception." Again, Gautama reached this highest state of meditative absorption but found that it too did not produce the freedom from desires, inner peace, wisdom, Awakening, and Nirvana that were the goals of his spiritual quest. Although Gautama left Udraka as he had Ārāḍa, it seems that he was influenced by both of these teachers. Early Buddhism included both of these types of formless absorbing meditation among its practices to foster an encouraging meditative "taste" of Nirvana.

Asceticism

After leaving Udraka, Gautama journeyed east to the area of Uruvelā, later named Bodhgāya. Early texts state that Gautama practiced asceticism in that area for many years, during which time he seems to have struggled with Māra, a tempter spirit who seeks to entrap spiritual seekers to keep them in this world where he can influence their lives. In an ancient account of these temptations, Māra is said to have suggested that Gautama turn from his more spiritual "endeavor" and pursue doing good works along with making Vedic sacrificial offerings to accumulate good karma. In fact, this was a temptation to give up the search for Awakening because, in Buddhist thinking, moral behavior and ritual actions alone cannot produce the state of Awakening and Nirvana. Another early passage suggests that during his ascetic period, Gautama had to combat certain inner states of mind that are not conducive to the attainment of Nirvana, and also physical conditions that discourage spiritual advance. The text attributes these temptations and trials to Māra: "Your first army is desire, your second army is discontent, your third army is hunger and thirst, your fourth army is ceaseless clinging. Your fifth army is laziness and sleep, your sixth army is fear, your seventh army is doubt, your eighth army is pretense and stubbornness" (*Sutta-nipāta*, 436, 437).

The early texts state that it was at this time that five ascetics joined Gautama because they were so impressed with the degree to which he practiced self-mortification in hopes of spiritual freedom and Awakening. However, after several years of ascetic practice, Gautama was still unable to attain Awakening and Nirvana. He finally realized that the ascetic path was not the true way to the spiritual life he was seeking and decided to give it up. But what was the true way?

Facing this question, Gautama remembered the meditative state he had entered when he was a young boy sitting under a shady tree while his father was working. In that tranquil repose, his mind had attained a deep state of meditation that brought him a great joy and freedom from worldly desires and immoral thoughts. Overcoming his ascetic aversion to anything pleasant, Gautama considered turning to a more moderate way of spiritual practice that naturally welled up within him. Later, he would call this path the "Middle Way" because on the one hand it rejects the sensual indulgence he had enjoyed as a young man, and on the other hand it rejects the mortification of the flesh that he had practiced as an ascetic. The former ignores the spiritual journey, and the latter inhibits its progress by destroying the health of the body, thus negatively affecting the mind that is important for spiritual advancement.

Since his extreme fasting had left him emaciated, Gautama accepted some milk offered by a village girl, thus abandoning his extreme asceticism. But when his five companions saw that he had given up his fasting, they concluded that he had also abandoned his striving endeavor, and so they left his company in disgust. However, Gautama with renewed resolve then sat under what is called the *Bodhi* Tree ("Tree of Awakening") near Bodhgāya, vowing to remain in that place until he attained Awakening. Later legends narrate his abandonment of asceticism and acceptance of sustenance differently. It is said that when Gautama gave up his asceticism, he sat under a sacred tree. While he was sitting there, a woman named Sujāta arrived at the tree and gave him a bowl of rice and milk. Sujāta, honoring a vow, had come to the sacred tree intending to place an offering under it.

THE AWAKENING OF THE BUDDHA

After regaining his strength, Gautama remained in seclusion on the banks of the Nairānjana River near Bodhgāya. The opposite shore was a popular place for ritual practices and ascetic sacrifices offered by both priests and ascetics. Symbolically turning his attention away from both of those types of religious activities, Gautama began practicing meditation to seek liberation within himself. He sat under the *Bodhi* Tree, faced east, and vowed not to move from that place until he attained Awakening.

In later biographies, it is said that it was at this point that Māra appeared and presented Gautama with his temptations. According to these stories, Māra sends his armies that include such trials in the spiritual life as sensuality, discontent, doubt, fear, and so on. In some accounts, Māra sends his three daughters—Discontent, Delight, and Desire—to tempt Gautama. It is also

FIGURE 1.2. Earth-witnessing posture of the Buddha; Gangaramaya Temple, Colombo, Sri Lanka.

said that when these temptations failed, Māra then questioned Gautama's merit to become the Buddha, the Awakened One. While Gautama was protected from this temptation of self-doubt by his great merit, he had no one with him to bear witness to this fact. So Gautama touched the earth asking for its witness that he was indeed worthy to become the Buddha. This action is represented by the earth-witnessing posture of the Buddha often depicted in Buddhist art (see Figure 1.2). In response to Gautama's request, there was an earthquake and the earth goddess appeared. This goddess wrung a flood of water from her hair that had accumulated when Gautama had done ritual water-pouring after doing meritorious deeds in past lives. With the earthquake and flood, and as the sun was setting, Māra and his armies fled.

Buddhists see an important lesson in this legend, namely, that when one makes a sincere commitment to the true path of spirituality, there arise certain trials that test one's resolve. There are trials that cause fear; one fears what might lie ahead in the journey, for example. There are trials of self-doubt wherein one feels unable to go ahead or unworthy of the ideal one is seeking. And there are the temptations that arise from one's attachments to the world and the many sensual pleasures one finds in that world. One must have the faith or confidence to go ahead in the holy path despite these obstacles.

Enlightenment

Sitting under the *Bodhi* Tree at Bodhgāya on the night of the full moon during the month of Vaiśākha, Gautama attained Awakening, The early texts say that he did so by ascending what are called the Four Meditations (*dhyāna;* Pali: *jhāna*). The first meditation is one of concentration free from sensual pleasure and base thoughts but with discursive reflection, elation, and deep joy. This is what he had experienced in his youth. The second meditation sets aside any discursive reflection for a deeper and more unified mental tranquillity. The third meditation negates emotional elation, which is a hindrance to equanimity and clarity of mind. The fourth meditation transcends even joy so that its opposite, dejection or sorrow, is also transcended into a complete state of mindful equanimity. The mind, being purified at this point, is said to become stable, yet "soft and workable."

Having reached this state of meditative clarity, Gautama chose not to "work" his mind into the higher meditative absorptions that he had learned from Ārāḍa and Udraka. Rather, he purposely focused his contemplation into a penetrating insight into the truth about existence itself. In this manner, he is said to have ascended to the highest level of Awakening (*bodhi*) through three stages. During the first watch of the night (evening), Gautama saw all of his own previous lives, one by one. During the second watch of the night (midnight), he saw the rebirth of others according to their karma, and the whole of existence appeared to him "as if in a mirror." During the third watch (late night), he destroyed all mental and emotional impurities, selfish desires, false views, and ignorance. With pure and penetrating insight, some early passages say, he realized the dependent arising (*pratītya-samutpāda*) of all existence, how all tilings dependency come to be what they are. Other passages say that he was able to realize (1) the dissatisfactory nature of existence (*duḥkha*), (2) the cause of its arising, (3) the cessation of its arising, (4) and the path that leads to that cessation. Later, Gautama would call these the Four Noble Truths. By dawn, all ignorance had been extinguished, as Gautama's Awakening was complete. He was now Gautama Buddha, Gautama the Awakened One.

With this description of his Awakening, we can better understand an early text's presentation of the following words attributed to Gautama Buddha:

> I truly made effort and endeavor, my thought was firm and undistraded, my body was tranquil and passive, and my mind was concentrated. I was free of desires and unwholesome thoughts, and though I still had initial thought and discursive thought, I had arrived at the first meditation with the joy created by such a separation. . . . [Having attained the second, third and fourth meditations,] in this manner my mind became concentrated, purified, cleansed, without

> defilement, pliable, flexible, established and immovable. I then directed my mind to wisdom raising the recollections of my past lives . . . recalling numerous past lives along with each individual appearance and detailed conditions. . . . This was the first light of wisdom attained during the early part of the night. . . . I then directed my mind towards the knowledge of the birth and death of all living beings. . . . I observed living beings die and be born . . . following the results of their karma. . . . This was the second light of wisdom attained during the middle of the night. . . . Then, I directed my mind towards the knowledge of the wisdom that eliminates ignorance. At that time, I realized [the truth about] the dissatisfactory condition of life [its nature, cause, cessation and path to its cessation]. . . . When I realized this, my mind was freed from the defilement of desire, my mind was freed from the defilement of ignorance, and as I became free, I realized that I was free. . . . This was the third wisdom attained at the end of the night. (*Majjhima-nikāya,* I, 21ff.)

Nirvana

According to the early texts, the Buddha engaged in deepest meditation for four or more weeks in the vicinity of the *Bodhi* Tree. There, he enjoyed the Nirvana that he had attained by his Awakening. During that time, two merchants, Trapuśa and Bhallika, came from a nearby village and venerated him. After this offering, they asked to be received as lay followers, and the Buddha accepted them. However, in this case, the Buddha did not preach the Dharma (Pali: Dhamma), or his Teaching, to them. In fact, the Buddha wondered if humankind, given its attachment to the worldly life, could ever understand what he had realized. In one early account, it is said that he reflected: "How can I teach what I have realized through painful toil? For those who suffer from craving and ignorance, this Dharma is not easy to understand. It is contrary to the current of this world, profound and exceedingly subtle. . . . [I]t will be impossible to be seen by those clinging to greed and covered with ignorance" (*Saṃyutta-nikāya,* I, 136).

In response to this hesitation of the Buddha, Sahampatī Brahmā, said to be the most important god worshiped at that time, came to the Buddha and asked him to teach the Dharma to the world. He told the Buddha: "With eyes of wisdom . . . observe the people who are submerged in the sorrow of birth and death. Please teach the Dharma, there will be some who can become Awakened" (*Saṃyutta-nikāya,* I, 137). So, with his wisdom eyes, the Buddha surveyed the entire world and saw that in fact there were some people who would understand his teaching. Out of compassion, he decided to preach the Dharma to the world. Then, the Buddha is said to have used his eyes of wisdom to determine whom he should teach. At first, he thought of his teachers, Ārāḍa and Udraka. But then he realized by his spiritual vision that they had both died. Next, he turned his vision toward the group of five ascetics with whom he had lived and discovered that they were residing at Deer Park at Sārnāth near the city of Benares. The Buddha then realized that they had the discipline necessary to understand the Dharma. So he left Bodhgāya and traveled 130 miles to Sārnāth.

THE MISSION OF THE BUDDHA

By all accounts, the Buddha found his former companions in the Deer Park at Sārnāth. At first the five ascetics resolved to shun him because he had abandoned their severe ascetic life. However, when the Buddha approached them, given his appearance, "they were unable to follow their own agreement." The Buddha was then able to convince them that he had not returned to a lavish lifestyle, and the five ascetics decided to listen to his words. In the early texts, it is said that the Buddha taught them for a period of time. He would teach some of the ascetics while the others begged for alms. Eventually, the five came to understand the hindrances to Awakening and peace that are associated with this transient world. Then searching for emancipation from all hindrances, they found wisdom, Awakening, and Nirvana. Early texts record what has become known as the Buddha's First Sermon. This First Sermon, as presented in the early texts, is most likely a formalized presentation of the kinds of things the Buddha did teach to his first disciples. We will look at these teachings in detail in the next chapter. For now it is enough to note that whatever the Buddha taught his five new disciples, it brought them all to the attainment of Awakening and Nirvana. The Buddha referred both to himself and to these enlightened disciples as *arhats* (Pali: *arahants*), meaning "worthy ones."

The Three Refuges

Through the Buddha's instruction, the five ascetics attained enlightenment and received admission as celibate monks (*bhikṣu;* Pali: *bhikkhu*) into the Buddha's new spiritual order, which he referred to as the *Saṅgha*, or "Community." It is said that from the beginning of the Saṅgha, those who entered it as celibate members and those who associated with it as lay followers all took what came to be called the "Three Refuges." A Buddhist takes "refuge" in (1) the Buddha, (2) the Dharma, and (3) the Saṅgha. These Three Refuges are also called the "Three Jewels," because by seeking refuge in the Buddha, Dharma, and Saṅgha, one receives these three treasured gifts. The Saṅgha, in the narrow sense, includes just the ordained celibate monastics. However, in the expanded sense, the Saṅgha consists of all, including lay followers, who take the Three Refuges and have penetrated and lived the Dharma to the point that they can teach it to others.

In the Indian culture at the time of the Buddha, taking refuge was a formal act of submission to a person or god. One promised with this action to be a faithful follower of a being who could offer protection and benefits. The formal words of refuge-taking in Buddhism are as follows: "I go for refuge to the Buddha. I go for refuge to the Dharma. I go for refuge to the Saṅgha." So the word "refuge" here also carries the connotation of protection and help. In other words, in taking these refuges, one shows confidence that the Buddha, Dharma, and Saṅgha can protect one from the dissatisfactory human condition of life and can help one reach the truly satisfactory attainment of Nirvana.

In the words attributed to the Buddha by an early text, by taking the Three Refuges, one professes "clear confidence hi the Buddha . . . the Fully Awakened One . . . perfect in knowledge and conduct . . . clear confidence in the Dharma taught by the Exalted One . . . that brings one near that which should be known by the wise . . . clear confidence in the Saṅgha of the followers of the Exalted One on the direct right path . . . without defects, which brings freedom" (*Dīgha-nikāya,* II, 93). Elsewhere in the same text, the Buddha makes clear that turning to him for refuge and help implies living in conformity with his Dharma: "He who, having entered on the course, lives in conformity with the Dharma . . . pays reverence to the Tathāgata [a title for the Buddha]" (*Dīgha-nikāya,* II, 138). It is also this living together of the Dharma that is at the heart of true refuge in the Saṅgha.

Important Conversions

According to the early texts, the next convert to the Saṅgha after the five ascetics was a wealthy young man from Benares named Yaśa. Yaśa, "disillusioned" with his luxuries and his indulgence in sensual entertainment, came to the place where the Buddha was staying. Later, Yaśa's father, missing his son, came in search of him. The Buddha consoled Yaśa's father, and in the end the father took the Three Refuges. Hearing the instruction the Buddha gave his father, Yaśa attained Awakening. Thus, Yaśa became the sixth ordained disciple of the Buddha, and his father became his first official lay disciple. The two merchants who gave homage to the Buddha at Bodhgāya did not receive the Dharma or enter the Saṅgha. Yaśa's mother and wife, who also came in search of him, both took the Three Refuges and thereby became the first women lay followers of the Buddha. Lay followers of the Buddha, both men and women, did not want to enter the celibate Saṅgha but sought to benefit spiritually from the Buddha and his teachings by their association with the community of monks. Also, it is said that fifty-four of Yaśa's friends were converted and attained Awakening under the guidance of the Buddha. This brought the number of enlightened members of the monastic Saṅgha to sixty-one, including the Buddha himself. Once the Buddha had these sixty disciples, he sent them out to preach the Dharma.

After living in nearby Benares for some time, early texts say that the Buddha returned to the Uruvelā area where he had attained his own Awakening. Then he is said to have gone to Rājagṛha, where he converted King Bimbisāra of Magadha. This was an important event because it led to many people in the Magadha area joining the Buddha. Also while the Buddha was in Rājagṛha, another major event in the early Saṅgha took place when two of the disciples of a noted Skeptic converted to the Buddha and brought with them 250 of their followers. These two converts were Śāriputra and Maudgalyāyana, who became two principal disciples. Śāriputra was known for his wisdom and ability to teach the Dharma. Maudgalyāyana was known for his psychic powers developed in meditation. There were other stories of how not just individuals, but whole groups of religious seekers joined the Buddha's Saṅgha. Later biographies relate that it was also at the time the

Box 1.1

The Authenticity of the Buddha

Buddhism is a religion that does not insist on rituals; and being a Buddhist means something much more than participating in rituals. This is something I had to learn over time.

The very first ceremony I went through as a Buddhist was taking the Three Refuges. I was about eight years old and in the third grade. In my class, there were thirty-seven students, all of whom were Buddhists. The school arranged for us to attend this ceremony at one of the well-known temples in Bangkok.

We arrived at the temple in the afternoon and were guided to the hall with the main shrine. I remember the chief monk led us to recite the Three Refuges three times.

I take refuge in the Buddha.
I take refuge in the Dharma.
I take refuge in the Saṅgha.

This ceremony was a public pronouncement that I am a Buddhist. But I never bothered to think what it really meant to take the Buddha as my refuge until much later in life.

The Buddha was born in fifth century B.C.E. to a princely clan in an area that is now Nepal. He was brought up in a luxurious lifestyle, but when confronted with the problems of old age, sickness, and death, he was concerned and wanted to know how we as human beings can get rid of this cycle of suffering. When a son was born to him, he decided to leave the worldly life and began a serious search for spiritual freedom.

At the age of thirty-five, after six years of practice, he was enlightened and came to be known as the Buddha . . . the fully enlightened one. The truth he discovered was simple yet profound: Life is full of suffering, there is a cause to this suffering, there is a cessation to this suffering, and there is a path leading anyone to freedom from this suffering. During the forty-five years after his enlightenment, the Buddha founded a group of followers (Saṅgha), first consisting of monks and later of nuns.

When I took refuge in the Buddha, how could that historical person truly be my refuge? The historical Buddha passed away some twenty-five hundred years ago, so he cannot really be of any help to me today. But over time, I understood that the Buddha could be meaningful to my life and spiritual salvation because he discovered the Truth that frees one from human bondage. More important than that, he made known his spiritual discovery as well as the path leading to it. That Truth was real for him, and it is real for me also. That salvation was possible for him, and also for me.

With this understanding, I committed myself to putting the Buddha's teachings into practice, and that is how I really became a Buddhist. The authenticity of the Buddha does not lie just in his life, but in the enlightenment which made Prince Siddhārtha the Buddha. That enlightenment is accessible to everyone. It depends on our effort to make it a reality for our lives.

CHATSUMARN KABILSINGH
Professor Emerita
Thammasat University, Bangkok
Now Buddhist nun, Dhammananda Samaneri

Buddha resided at Rājagṛha that he converted Mahākāśyapa. Mahākāśyapa was known for his attainment in meditation, and he appears in the later legends of Zen Buddhism. He was also said to be the person who convened the First Buddhist Council when the Buddha died and who was responsible for organizing the memorization of the Buddha's teachings and precepts.

The later biographies also say that the Buddha went from Rājagṛha to his home town of Kapilavastu. There, he met with his father, stepmother, wife, and son Rāhula. While the rest of the family accepted him and even pledged homage to him, his son and his half-brother, Nanda, actually became ordained monks. It was also during this visit that Upāli became a monk. Among the Buddha's close disciples, Upāli had the greatest memory of the precepts and is said to have recited them at the First Buddhist Council. The Buddha's cousin, Ānanda, became a monk at this time and went on to be the closest companion of the Buddha. Given his extraordinary memory and constant proximity to the Buddha, Ānanda was said to have recited the dialogues and teachings of the Buddha at the First Buddhist Council.

Monasticism

While the early texts do not mention Sudatta, a wealthy merchant from Śrāvastī, the capital of Kosala, later biographies stress the importance of his conversion to Buddhism. It is said that he became a follower of the Buddha when he was in Rājagṛha on business. Later, he bought and donated the Jeta Grove in Śrāvastī to the Buddhist Saṅgha. It was here that Sudatta built the famous Jeta Monastery. From the time of his residing with the five ascetics at Sārnāth, the Buddha had spent the rainy seasons each year in retreat with his followers. For those early years, the biographies relate, the monsoon retreats were held in houses. The Jeta Monastery provided an adequate facility for the retreat gatherings of monks during the rainy seasons. This monastic site would become a model for the building of other Buddhist monasteries.

During the Buddha's life, it became a custom for the monks not to travel and preach the Dharma during the rainy season, but they would instead remain together in spiritual retreat. This custom was institutionalized by the establishment of monasteries that would eventually become centers of Buddhist religion and culture. As monasteries developed, the monastic Saṅgha became a model of ethical, cultural, intellectual, and spiritual life for the larger society. Eventually, Buddhist monasticism provided an extraordinary standard for humankind that was always an ideal for both personal and social fulfillment. For Buddhist monastics, monasteries became a haven for pursuing the spiritual life by being formed in the teachings and discipline of the Buddha. For Buddhist laypeople, the monasteries were thought to model what the enlightened life would be like if it were attained and lived by all society. The monasteries also provided places for moral and spiritual guidance, teaching, and the possibility for merit-making for the laity.

In administering the monastic Saṅgha, the Buddha shared many responsibilities with his enlightened followers. While traditional Indian religious sects reserved their teachings for an elite few, and their teachers retained personal control over their members, the Buddha allowed his representatives to ordain new members and entrusted his local monastic communities to manage their own affairs. The Buddha had great confidence in his enlightened followers and often recognized their expertise in teaching the Dharma. While the Buddha taught a number of "rules of discipline" to the monastic members of the Saṅgha, some of the minor precepts were open to changes and even to being revoked if need be. The members of the Saṅgha were seen as equals, and the governing of the communities was democratic.

Social Concern

The Buddha not only founded his own religious communities but also spoke out about the broader social and political conditions of his time. According to the early texts, he often denounced the injustices of the caste system, and the Saṅgha was open to persons of all castes. The Buddha taught that respect should be earned by moral deeds and spiritual attainment, not given on the basis of one's birth. In terms of social violence, in one early text, after telling a story of a king who did not care for the poor, the Buddha says, "Thus, from not giving to the needy, poverty spreads; from the growth of poverty, stealing increases; when theft becomes more and more common, there is an increased use of weapons; when this happens, there is a greater loss of life" (*Dīgha-nikāya*, III, 68). Elsewhere in that text, there is another story in which a king is advised as to how to deal with such social conflict:

> If your majesty were to increase taxes, that would be the wrong thing to do. If your majesty were to try to get rid of this problem by executions and imprisonment . . . the problem would not be ended. . . . However, with the following policy, you can completely eliminate this problem. To those who are engaged in farming and raising livestock, let your majesty distribute needed grain and fodder. To those engaged in trade, give them the capital they need. To those in government service, assign them a living wage to meet their needs. Then all of those people will be intent on pursuing their occupations, and they will not harm anyone. (*Dīgha-nikāya*, I, 135)

This attitude of compassionate concern for those in need was modeled by the Buddha himself in dealing with people outside and inside the Saṅgha. One story in a later text tells of the Buddha's intervention on behalf of five hundred bandits who were awaiting execution. The Buddha secured their release and gave them, by his teaching, what they really wanted, namely, spiritual as well as physical freedom. Another later story tells how the Buddha tended personally to one of his monks who was suffering from an advanced skin disease. Out of fear of contracting this disease, this person's fellow monks had avoided any contact with him. One day when the Buddha was visiting their community, he discovered the man's plight. Along with his disciple Ānanda, the Buddha took a basin of water and a towel and washed the monk himself. Then he instructed the other monks with these words: "Monks, you do not have a mother or a father here who

Box 1.2

The Gifts of the Buddha

Becoming a Buddhist was a slow process for me that began first with the intellect and only gradually shifted to a personal practice.

Lacking belief and facing death and rational absurdity in my early twenties, I only found consolation in nature, an abiding natural order of existence. Living with this intellectual sense of nature for several years, and supported by the nurturing presence of being part of nature, softened my expectations and judgments. This experience was confirmed and supported by the Buddhist practice of emptying oneself of false hopes and rigid ideas and the Buddhist patient acceptance of our dependent arising with all things. The Buddha's teaching emphasized that misery is created by ourselves and that we need to become aware of the way emotions arise based on how we interpret what is happening to us. Calming ourselves and noticing the interpretations we are giving to events and what expectations are thus being frustrated give a certain distance from our misery and empower us. New and more positive interpretations and emotional responses arise by noticing alternative interpretations and responses. Just by taking time out to notice our emotions and alternative interpretations became a constant source of relief and positive thinking.

Another way that Buddhism has permeated my life has been its method of social reform. As a child of the social gospel and the 1960s, I was eager to save the world but was messed up emotionally. Buddhism taught methods of inner transformation as a basis for changing my sense of the world, and also gave gentler and more inclusive ways to act in the world. Gautama Buddha was a social activist, but he practiced dialogue and compassion, without stridency or righteous indignation. The easy temptation to condemn others, to demonize enemies, and to feel righteous in our militancy was completely absent from the Buddha.

Instead, stories about the Buddha's life show the capacity to find goodness in those who are different from us and to emphasize our interconnections. Until recently, Buddhism has had a weak social gospel. But on looking at the forty-five years that the Buddha taught, one can find many practical ways in which he tried to bring about reform. Even though emperors and kings may have domesticated Buddhism into a passive monastic life, in the stories of Gautama Buddha we find a busy and effective social activist.

The gifts of the Buddha to the world are many. Formally, being a Buddhist means to take refuge in the "Three Jewels": the Buddha, the Dharma, and the Saṅgha. Gautama Buddha is the founder of the Dharma (teaching) that I have found most true and most nurturing, and his life is a model for living this Dharma in compassionate and effective ways. His Saṅgha, the Buddhist community on which I rely, consists, I believe, of people from all religions and cultures who are filled with modesty, compassion, good humor, and appreciation for others, especially for those who are most different from them. And finally this Saṅgha, Dharma, and Buddha become just other names for the infinite mystery of the secret connectedness of all things in the midst of our dying and living.

DAVID W. CHAPPELL

can tend to you. If you, monks, do not tend to one another, who is there to take care of you? Remember that whoever tends a sick person, as it were, tends me" (*Mahāvagga*, VIII, 26).

Women's Ordination

One issue that arose in regard to the monastic life was that of allowing women into the fully ordained monastic Saṅgha. From the beginning, women were welcome as members of the lay community that was associated with the monastic Saṅgha. Then, according to later biographies, five years after his enlightenment the Buddha was visited by his foster mother, Prajāpatī (referred to as Mahāprajāpatī since "māha" means "great"), who was accompanied by a large group of women. They asked to be ordained into the monastic Saṅgha. The Buddha is said to have rejected their request. But after more pleading, and with the intervention of Ānanda, the Buddha accepted the women into the Saṅgha as ordained nuns (*bhikṣuṇī:* Pali: *bhikkhuṇī*).

In his discussions with Ānanda about this issue, the Buddha made it clear that women could attain all the goals of his religion, including full Awakening. So why his initial reluctance to admit women into the celibate Saṅgha? Scholars today surmise that one concern may have been that the relationship between the men and women in the monastic community would have made things more complicated. The men's order needed time to become fully established and mature. Another concern may have had to do with the fact that many non-Buddhists did not like the practice of the celibate life for young men, and such a life for young women seemed even more unconventional and difficult to accept by the broader Indian society. So it would seem that any sudden influx of women into the communities at an early stage of their development would have caused problems both within those communities themselves as well as with the general population. Therefore, according to this interpretation, the Buddha took a cautious approach. Only when he felt that the time was right, when Indian society had accepted the Saṅgha as a valid religious entity, and when the community, represented by Ānanda, was ready for this radical change, did he admit women into the monastic Saṅgha. Yet another explanation is that the nun's order would pose a threat to the monks in terms of competition for resources. Hence, admitting women to the celibate Saṅgha could have been opposed by the monks.

The Buddha gave the women monastics special rules resulting in a certain gender hierarchy. For example, the Saṅgha hierarchy is determined by how long one has been ordained, not by merit or personal attainment. However, in the case of nuns, they must treat all monks as seniors, even those who were ordained after them. Also, whereas any monk can reprove a nun, no nun can reprove a monk. On the other hand, because this hierarchy has nothing to do with attainment, its subordination of women does not indicate spiritual inferiority. Also, to prevent the monks from using the hierarchy to take advantage of the nuns, the Buddha instituted certain rules that safeguard the dignity and independence of the nuns. The monks could not demand work or service from nuns, and the nuns were not to be given any inferior spiritual instructions or ethical rules.

A text entitled *The Verses of the Women Elders (Therīgāthā)* records in seventy-three poems the lives and Awakening of early nuns in the Saṅgha. There are also early records of the Buddha giving high praise to certain nuns. Besides Mahāprajāpatī, who was the senior nun, Uppalavaṇṇā was considered one of the Buddha's chief disciples. Khemā, the former queen of King Bimbisāra, was also respected as a chief disciple of the Buddha. Bhaddā Kapilāni was pledged by her family in marriage to Mahākāśyapa, who became a leading monk in the Saṅgha. Later, Bhaddā Kapilāni became a nun and distinguished herself by her awakened memory of her past lives.

The Rebellion of Devadatta

Another issue addressed by the Buddha was brought about by his cousin, Devadatta, who had joined the Saṅgha. Early texts indicate only that Devadatta was lazy and annoyed the Buddha in various ways. However, in later stories, it is said that Devadatta, stimulated with ambition, wanted to gain control of the Saṅgha when the Buddha had grown older. He, along with an accomplice, actually tried to kill the Buddha, but the Buddha escaped each attempt on his life. For example, a rock intended to crush the Buddha is deflected by mountain peaks, and a wild elephant charging down a narrow street toward the Buddha turns around tamely because of the Buddha's friendly thought. In each case, it is said that the Buddha dealt with Devadatta with gentleness, exhibiting his view that hatred is not deterred by hatred, but by loving kindness.

Later texts that were concerned about distinguishing Buddhism from extreme asceticism claim that Devadatta tried to gain control of the Saṅgha in another way. He attempted to make the precepts of the community more ascetically rigorous. Devadatta was said to have proposed five severe ascetic rules: Monks should dwell all their life in the forest, they should live only on alms that they beg, they should only wear robes made from gathered rags, they should dwell only at the foot of trees, and they should not eat fish or meat. The breaking of any of these rules would lead to expulsion from the Saṅgha. It is said that in the spirit of tolerance, the Buddha decided that all of these rules suggested by Devadatta would be permissible, but not compulsory. He only insisted that the monks not sleep under trees during the rainy season. Devadatta is said then to have tried to draw the monks away from the Buddha to follow his reform movement. However, in the end this attempt to gain leadership by producing a schism in the Saṅgha also failed. Again, throughout these trials brought upon the Buddha, his Dharma, and the Saṅgha, the Buddha maintained an attitude of compassion and loving kindness toward Devadatta.

THE LAST DAYS OF GAUTAMA BUDDHA

Because of his sense of mission to preach the Dharma, the Buddha spent much of his time in or around the towns and cities that were appearing on the Indian landscape. He is said by the early texts to have often resided in or around Śrāvastī in Kosala and Rājagṛha and Vaiśālī in Magadha. One early text tells a rather detailed story about the last days of the Buddha's life. It states that near the end of the Buddha's life, he was residing in the suburbs of Vaiśālī. As the rainy season was approaching, he went to a nearby village where he made his final monsoon retreat with a few of his disciples. During the retreat, the Buddha was struck by an extremely painful illness. In response to Ānanda's concern, the Buddha said, "I have grown old . . . and have traveled down the road of life being in my eightieth year. [I am like] an old cart that can barely manage to hold itself together without the help of leather straps" (*Dīgha-nikāya,* II, 100).

One day after begging alms in Vaiśālī , the Buddha took his midday rest at a sacred tree. There, the story goes, he was visited by Māra, who encouraged him to end his life and attain final Nirvana (*parinirvāṇa*). The text indicates that the Buddha had not wanted to pass away until he had monks, nuns, and male and female disciples who were accomplished in the Dharma, who walked in the path of the Dharma, and who could teach the Dharma to others. Now that this holy life was well established, the Buddha responded to Māra that his passing would come in just three months. The Buddha is said to have at that time renounced his vital "life principle." When this final renunciation occurred, there was a great earthquake accompanied by thunder.

Some time later, taking a final look at Vaiśālī, the Buddha departed and journeyed to the town of Pāvā, where he stopped at the mango grove of a blacksmith named Cunda. The Buddha instructed Cunda in the Dharma, and then took the food Cunda offered to him. The text says that after eating, the Buddha was struck by a severe illness that produced much pain. From the textual description of the illness, scholars conclude that he contracted food poisoning from eating either pork or a mushroom dish. However, the Buddha was able to rise from his illness and even walk to the village of Kuśinagara some distance away. At one point, he stepped off the road and sat under a tree to rest. Ānanda, at the request of the Buddha, brought him some water to drink. At that moment, it is said that a pupil of Ārāḍa Kālāma named Pukkusa approached the Buddha. He engaged the Buddha in conversation about the "lofty powers" of Ārāḍa, and in the end, Pukkusa accepted the Buddha and became his lay follower.

Then the Buddha, along with a number of his monks, went into a nearby river to bathe and drink water. Emerging from the river, the Buddha lay down to rest and spoke to Ānanda about Cunda the blacksmith. The Buddha was concerned that Cunda would feel that it was his fault the Buddha died. So he instructed Ānanda as to what to say to console him. Then the Buddha traveled to another place nearby where he lay down between two sāla trees. The Buddha lay on his right side, with his head to the north and one foot on top of the other (see Figure 1.3). It is said that the trees burst into blossom and sprinkled the blossoms down onto the Buddha. As this happened, the text says that music and song was heard from the sky, and later even the gods gathered weeping over the Buddha's passing. The Buddha acknowledged

FIGURE 1.3. Reclining Buddha at the time of his passing; Luang Prabang, Laos.

this homage but noted that "supreme homage" is given to the Buddha when a disciple practices the Dharma properly.

At this point, the early story goes, Ānanda discussed with the Buddha what to do with his remains. Following this discussion, Ānanda went off some distance and wept with grief. The Buddha called for Ānanda to join him and consoled his grief. He reminded Ānanda, "Have I not already told you that all things . . . are subject to change . . . subject to decay—so how could it be Ānanda that anything should not pass away?" (*Dīgha-nikāya*, II, 144). The Buddha then compassionately praised Ānanda for the loving kindness and wholehearted care Ānanda had always shown to him. He concluded his words to Ānanda by encouraging him to continue to follow the path so that soon he could gain the freedom he was seeking. In his presence, the Buddha also praised Ānanda to the whole assembly of monks for his "remarkable and wonderful qualities," noting that in the past, all Buddhas had such a remarkable chief attendant.

Some of the people from Kuśinagara came out of the town to pay their respects to the Buddha. One person who came to see the Buddha was a wandering religious person named Subhadra. At first, Ānanda would not let Subhadra speak to the Buddha because of concern for the Buddha's condition. However, the Buddha compassionately requested that Subhadra be permitted to speak to him. Subhadra asked the Buddha about the attainment of other famous teachers, but the Buddha would not make such judgments about others. Instead, he taught Subhadra the Dharma. Subhadra converted and became his "last personal disciple." When he finished instructing Subhadra, the Buddha turned to Ānanda and said, "You may think, 'The teacher's instruction has ceased, now we do not have a teacher!' But it should not be seen like this, Ānanda. For what I have taught and explained to you as the Dharma and the discipline will, at my passing, be your teacher" (*Dīgha-nikāya*, II, 154).

Finally, the Buddha asked his monks if they had any doubts or uncertainties about the Buddha, Dharma, or Saṅgha: "Ask monks! Do not later feel remorse thinking, 'The teacher was right there before us and we did not ask him face to face'" (*Dīgha-nikāya,* II, 154–155). When no one asked a question, the Buddha spoke his last words: "Now, monks, I declare that all the conditioned things of the world are passing. Attain your liberation with diligence!" (*Dīgha-nikāya,* II, 156). Following these words, the Buddha entered into meditation and passed away.

After the Buddha had died, members of the Malla clan from Kuśinagara wrapped his body in new cloth and held six days of mourning. On the seventh day, they cremated the Buddha's body. It is said that messengers from seven clans, including the Buddha's own Śākya clan, asked for relics. The Malla clan also requested relics. Those who received relics took them home and built *stūpas* (memorial mounds) for them. The bowl that collected the ashes (see Figure 1.4), along with the ashes themselves, were placed under two other *stūpas.* These *stūpas* became centers for devotion to the Buddha. The Buddha himself is said to have proclaimed shortly before he died, "Whoever lays wreaths of flowers, or puts perfumes, or adds color [to the *stūpas*] with a devout heart will reap benefit and happiness for a long time" (*Dīgha-nikāya,* II, 142). There is also a legend that centuries later, King Aśoka unearthed these relics and further divided them, enshrining them in 84,000 *stūpas* throughout his empire in India.

FIGURE 1.4. Relics of Śākyamuni Buddha and caskets that contain them. Excavated from the Piprahwa relic mound in 1898, the caskets have inscriptions dated to the third century B.C.E. National Museum, New Delhi.

As we can see, much of the Buddha's time for the forty-five years after his Awakening was devoted to teaching the Dharma, founding the Saṅgha, and forming his disciples in the path of the discipline. Even during the very moments before his death, the Buddha was carrying out these tasks compassionately for the good of others. Many people in India during the sixth and fifth centuries B.C.E. were looking for new ideals to guide their lives, new ideas and practices that promised personal transformation, and new social forms of community life. The Buddha offered to the world his own spiritual experience, and he modeled that enlightened and nirvanic ideal with joy, loving kindness, and compassion. His Dharma offered others a path to attain the experience of Awakening and Nirvana and a way of living this ideal in daily life. His Saṅgha provided the spiritual guidance and social support necessary to achieve this ideal and to live out its freedom and peace as a witness to what is possible in human relationships. In the following chapter, we examine the experience of this path and ideal as they are presented in the teachings of the Buddha.

SUGGESTIONS FOR FURTHER READING

Ashvaghosha. *Life of the Buddha*, trans., Patrick Olivelle. New York: NYU Press, 2008.

Carrithers, Michael. *The Buddha*. Oxford, UK: Oxford University Press, 1983.

Cook, Elizabeth, ed. *The Holy Places of the Buddha*. Berkeley, CA: Dharma Publishing, 1994.

Cowell, E. B., trans. *The Jātaka or Stories of the Buddha's Former Births*. 3 vols. London: Luzac, 1969.

Germano, David, and Kevin Trainor, eds. *Embodying the Dharma: Buddhist Relic Veneration in Asia*. Albany: SUNY Press, 2004.

Jones, John Garrett. *Tales and Teachings of the Buddha: The Jātaka Stories in Relation to the Pali Canon*. London: George Allen & Unwin, 1979.

Murcott, Susan. *The First Buddhist Women*. San Francisco: Parallax Press, 1991.

Nakamura, Hajime. *Gotama Buddha*. Tokyo and Los Angeles: Buddhist Books International, 1977.

Nanamoli, Bhikkhu. *The Life of the Buddha According to the Pali Canon*. Kandy, Sri Lanka: Buddhist Publication Society, 1978.

Nyanaponika Thera, and Hellmuth Hecker. *Great Disciples of the Buddha: Their Lives, Their Works, Their Legacy*. Boston: Wisdom Publications, 1997.

Obeyesekere, Ranjini. *Yasodhara, The Wife of the Bodhisattva: The Sinhala Yasodharavata (The Story of Yasodhara) and the Sinhala Yasodharapadanaya (The Sacred Biography of Yasodhara)*. Albany: SUNY Press, 2009.

Penner, Has H. *Rediscovering the Buddha: The Legends and Their Interpretation*. New York: Oxford University Press, 2009.

Schelling, Andrew, and Anne Waldman. *Songs of the Sons and Daughters of the Buddha*. Boston: Shambhala Publications, 1996.

Schober, Juliane. *Sacred Biography in the Buddhist Tradition of South and Southeast Asia*. Delhi, India: Motilal Banarsidas, 2002.

2

The Teachings of the Buddha

An early text relates the story of a Buddhist monk who was especially fond of speculative religious discussions that seem to be never-ending. Once, he approached the Buddha intending to get him to resolve his speculative questions. He asked if the world was eternal or created, if the world was finite or infinite, if the body and soul are the same or different, and whether the *arhat* exists after death. The monk even threatened to leave the Saṅgha and become a layperson if the Buddha did not answer his questions. The Buddha responded that one does not enter the Saṅgha in order to answer these kinds of philosophical questions. If one does so, one can spend all his or her time pondering these questions and never have time for religious practice, namely, for following the path that leads to Awakening and Nirvana. In fact, the Buddha added, a person would not live long enough for the Buddha to explain the truth concerning all of these speculative matters.

To illustrate his point, the Buddha used the following metaphor:

> It is as if . . . a man had been wounded by an arrow thickly smeared with poison, and his friends and companions, his relatives and kinsfolk, were to procure a physician or surgeon for him. And the sick man would then say, "I will not have this arrow removed until I have learned whether the man who wounded me belonged to the warrior caste, or to the priestly caste, or to the agricultural or menial castes." Or he would say, "I will not have this arrow removed until I have learned the name of the man . . . the clan to which he belongs . . . whether he is tall or short . . . the town from which he comes . . . what kind of bow . . . bowstring . . . arrow shaft . . . arrow feathers . . . and arrowhead . . . he used." That man will die without ever having learned all these things. (*Majjhima-nikāya*, I, 428)

After giving this metaphor, the Buddha went on to say that no matter what particular answers one might learn concerning the philosophical questions the monk had raised, the dissatisfactory condition of ordinary, unenlightened life would remain like a poisoned arrow. So the Buddha concluded his reply by saying that there were some questions he would leave unanswered, namely, those that do not lead to religious edification. Therefore, he would only teach about those matters that "tend to aversion, absence of passion, cessation, quiescence, knowledge, supreme wisdom and Nirvana."

The point of this story is that the Buddha did not want to become involved in abstract discussions about religious issues that do not advance spiritual transformation. Some scholars conclude that the questions themselves were ill formed, such that no sufficient answers could ever be given. Others claim that the Buddha only wanted to teach about what directly impacts the existential wounded condition of humankind. Seeing himself as a kind of spiritual physician, the Buddha was concerned with helping humanity understand the nature and causes of its dissatisfactory condition and the path that leads to liberation from this condition. This kind of existential concern determined what the Buddha taught and what the way of life was that he asked his disciples to follow. As for his specific teachings, scholars have always debated about what the Buddha actually taught, since even the earliest texts that record his teachings were written down hundreds of years after his death. However, scholars usually agree that there are certain basic teachings, which, since they are presented in so many places throughout the early texts, must represent at least the kinds of things the Buddha actually taught. In this chapter, we will examine some of these basic teachings that can help us understand more clearly the experience of the Buddha and of early Buddhism.

THE THREE CHARACTERISTICS

One early text quotes the Buddha as saying,

> Whether Buddhas arise, O monks, or whether Buddhas do not arise, it remains a fact that . . . all [the world's] constituents are [1] transitory . . . that all its constituents are [2] dissatisfactory . . . that all its constituents are [3] lacking a permanent self. (*Anguttara-nikāya*, III, 134)

Here, the Buddha is teaching the Three Characteristics of what he calls *saṃsāra*. *Saṃsāra*, literally, "wandering on," refers to the phenomenal world in which one is born, dies, and wanders on to be reborn. All of the world's "constituents," even the constituents of its heavenly realms, are "impermanent" (*anitya;* Pali: *anicca*), are ultimately "dissatisfactory" (*duḥkha;* Pali: *dukkha*), and contain no permanent inner substance or "self" (*anātman;* Pali: *anattā*). Given the earlier answer of the Buddha to the monk's speculative questions, we can assume that understanding the nature of the impermanence, dissatisfactoriness, and selflessness of life "tends to" Awakening and Nirvana. Let us look at each of these characteristics one at a time.

Box 2.1

Impermanence

Ever since inheriting the Lamp of the Dharma and becoming president of Risshō Kōsei-kai, I have wanted more than ever to be a genuine Buddhist and inherit Śākyamuni's enlightenment.

Through studying and learning what has been handed down from the teachings of the Buddha and others, I finally came to understand the "teaching of impermanence." I became confident that this is the supreme and most fundamental of the Buddha's teachings, the basic essence of Śākyamuni's enlightenment.

With this realization, I was released from all clinging and delusion, and felt indescribably refreshed. It was as though a cloud of fog hanging over me had suddenly disappeared in the rays of the sun.

In the second chapter of the *Lotus Sūtra* we find, "It is for this great cause alone that Buddhas, the world-honored ones, appear in the world. . . . The Buddhas, the world-honored ones, appear in the world because they want living beings to open themselves to the Buddha's knowledge and insight, and thus gain a kind of purity." In short, the one "great cause" means that Buddhas appear in the world for one purpose only, to open us to Buddha-knowledge.

Buddha-knowledge is the Buddha's wisdom. Given this knowledge, how do we see this world and human life? We see that all things in this world are dependently arisen, never stopping for a moment, always changing. In short, to open ourselves to Buddha-knowledge is to become aware of the teaching of impermanence.

By opening ourselves to Buddha-knowledge, that is, by being aware of the teaching of impermanence, we can become aware of the importance of living here and now, become mindful of the value of today, and be filled with a sense of dedication. We can spontaneously become joyfully full of life and energy through getting along with others, while giving full play to our individual natural abilities. The infinitely continuous creation of our lives can be developed.

Thus, I have realized that we can be reborn by becoming aware of the teaching of transience, this most precious Buddhist doctrine. I have continued to this day to keep a vow to spread this truth, this Dharma.

PRESIDENT NICHIKO NIWANO
Risshō Kōsei-kai
Tokyo, Japan

Impermanence

The first characteristic of life's constituents is impermanence. For the Buddha, everything except for Nirvana is in constant flux and change. Material things undergo obvious changes, and one's mental-emotional life is also constantly changing. Even the gods, according to the Buddha, are born, experience change, and eventually die only to be reborn in another state of existence.

According to one early text, "All compounded things are impermanent, prone to arise and fall" (*Dīgha-nikāya,* II, 157). The implication here is that all things are impermanent because they are "compounded" by constituents that arise together and then, in time, fall apart. One is reminded of the Buddha's statement near the time of his passing that he felt like an old cart that needed to be held together by leather straps.

Impermanence, as the arising and passing away of the things of life, is sometimes described in the early texts as taking place in three stages. The elements of an object come together so that it "arises" into existence. Then, the arisen object is subject to "decay." This means that once an object has come into being, it changes over time. Finally, the elements of an object change to such an extent that the thing passes away. In this manner, all things are impermanent in two senses: They arise and pass away, and while existing they are in a state of constant change.

Dissatisfactoriness

This characterization of impermanence leads to the second characteristic of phenomena, namely, "dissatisfactoriness" (*duḥkha*). *Duḥkha* has often been translated as "suffering." But that term does not capture the rich meaning of this important notion. The term *duḥkha* connotes the dissatisfactory condition caused by an axle hole that is not properly made. Whether the hole is too big or too small, it causes the axle to wobble or rub in a way that is dissatisfactory. Since the Buddha taught that all the phenomena of this world are also made in ways that produce dissatisfactoriness, the question is, in what ways are things made such that we experience dissatisfactoriness, or *duḥkha?* And what is the dissatisfactoriness that things produce? The Buddha taught that there are three qualities of things that account for *duḥkha* in life. First, physical phenomena are constituted such that they can produce suffering. In the early texts, giving birth, getting sick, growing old, and dying are given as examples of the suffering that one experiences because of how the physical world is constituted. These sufferings, and many others as well, are associated with the changing conditions of physical life.

A second way in which things are dissatisfactory has to do with their impermanence and humanity's search for happiness. The Buddha did not deny that one can find some happiness in the enjoyments of this life. In the early texts, the Buddha mentions the happiness that comes from such things as family life, life in the Saṅgha, and meditative attainments. However, he also points out that these enjoyments are "impermanent, *duḥkha,* and subject to change" (*Majjhima-nikāya,* I, 90). That is, they are dissatisfactory because they cannot provide the lasting happiness that humanity ultimately seeks. In other words, since all things in life must pass away—given their impermanence—so must all the pleasures these things provide be fleeting. Because humanity ordinarily seeks a lasting happiness in things that do not last, or a permanent satisfaction in impermanent things, these things are said to be characterized by *duḥkha.* They leave one with a sense of lack, a feeling that something is still missing that would provide lasting happiness.

A third way in which things are said to produce dissatisfactoriness has to do with the manner in which the human mind is constituted. We have seen that things are characterized as dissatisfactory because they are physically constituted in ways that produce suffering and do not provide permanent happiness. The Buddha also taught that the changing states of human consciousness are constituted such that they produce both personal and social *duḥkha.* Just as an improperly made axle hole functions in a dissatisfactory way, so too the different constituents of one's mind generate such unwholesome states as hatred, anger, greed, and delusion. These unwholesome states of mind, in turn, produce *duḥkha* for oneself and, when acted upon, for others as well. These harmful actions also contribute to such social *duḥkha* as war, poverty, and political repression.

No-Self

Many of the spiritual teachers at the time of the Buddha would have agreed that the world and human nature are constituted in ways that produce suffering and that the true and lasting happiness sought by humankind is not to be found in the fleeting pleasures of the world. However, the Upaniṣadic teachers of the time held that lasting happiness (*ānanda*) could, in fact, be found deep within one's self. They called this inner, permanent, and divine reality the "Self" (Ātman). The Buddha, on the other hand, presented a third characteristic of existence that rejects any such permanent Self. He said that all phenomena lack any underlying and permanent substance; they all have the characteristic of "no-self." This also means that within human nature, there is no permanent self or soul. As we see in the next chapter, this also meant to early Buddhist philosophers that the notion of no-self implied a kind of process philosophy that rejects any type of philosophy based on the notion of substance. What is fundamental to ourselves are processes that can be understood and changed so that one can find freedom from the dissatisfactory conditions of ordinary life and discover the peace of Nirvana.

While this is true, the Buddha always affirmed that persons have an empirical selfhood constituted by a body and a mind. But he also claimed that the various constituents of this conventional selfhood are characterized by impermanence and *duḥkha;* they are always changing, and they ordinarily produce mental and physical processes that are experienced as ultimately dissatisfactory. The Buddha also taught that when one examines these constituents of conventional selfhood, one does not find any permanent substance. Impermanence is not just a characteristic of the phenomena of the external world; it applies to oneself. The Buddha's notion of no-self expresses humankind's radical finitude. It was also the Buddha's view that the belief in a permanent substantial self is not only false but also leads to selfishness and egoism, which, in turn, make the world so dissatisfactory for everyone.

The Buddha found in his own Awakening that the realization of the absence of such a permanent self leads to selfless loving kindness and compassion for others.

In discussing his no-self doctrine, the Buddha did not just deny the existence of a substantial and permanent self behind or within the various constituents of human nature. He also described these constituents and, in so doing, showed that none of them could be considered a permanent substance or self. These constituents of selfhood were called by the Buddha the Five Aggregates (*skandha,* Pali: *khandha*). To understand more clearly just what the Buddha meant by no-self, let us see what these Five Aggregates entail.

THE FIVE AGGREGATES

The first of the Five Aggregates that constitute ordinary human selfhood is material "form" (*rūpa*), or the body that is made up of impermanent material elements. These material elements are said ultimately to be produced by impermanent atoms of different types. The other four aggregates are the mental constituents of the functional self. The second aggregate is "sensation" (*vedanā*), which includes sensations associated with the body as well as feelings. These sensations of felt experience are categorized as pleasant, unpleasant, or neutral. The third aggregate is "perception" (*saṃjñā;* Pali: *saññā*), which includes the cognition and recognition of physical objects and of mental phenomena (ideas or thoughts). The fourth aggregate is "mental formations" (*saṃskāra;* Pali: *saṃkhāra*), which include the various mental states, attitudes, and dispositions that form the character of one's life. These are especially important mental factors because they include all the willful states of mind (*cetanā*) that move one to do good and bad actions, and therefore result in good and bad karma. The fifth aggregate is "consciousness" (*vijñāna;* Pali: *viññāṇa*), which includes mental awareness and discrimination.

Of all the aggregates, the best candidate for a permanent self or soul would seem to be this last aggregate of consciousness. Indeed, the Upaniṣadic tradition claimed that consciousness is of the essence of the Ātman. However, the Buddha taught that consciousness only arises when one of the six sense faculties (*āyatana*) experiences a sense object. For the Buddha, there are six sense faculties, which include the eye, ear, nose, tongue, body, and mind. By "mind" here, the Buddha means a mental faculty that engages mental objects like thoughts and ideas. When any of these six faculties engages its object (visible form, sound, odor, taste, tangible objects, and mental phenomena), a form of consciousness arises. For example, the Buddha gives, in an early text, the following description of the arising of visual consciousness: "Consciousness takes its name according to the conditions in which it arises: on account of the eye and visible forms, it arises and is called visual consciousness" (*Majjhima-nikāya,* I, 250). In the Buddha's view, then, consciousness does not indicate a permanent substance. It simply arises in different forms depending on different factors, so that it is just as impermanent as any other kind of phenomenon.

As these Five Aggregates are constantly changing mental or physical states or processes, none of them can be considered as a permanent metaphysical self or soul. Therefore, in his Second Sermon, the Buddha said that one is not able to point to any constituent within his or her self and say, "This is mine, this I am, this is my self" (*Saṃyutta-nikāya*, II, 68). Another early text explains this idea by using the simile of a chariot for the self. In a dialogue between a Buddhist nun named Vajira and Māra the tempter, the question arises about the nature of the self. Vajira says,

> There is no "being" found here [within oneself], only a heap of karmic constituents. Just as the word "chariot" is used when we come across a combination of parts, so we speak conventionally of a [human] being when the Five Aggregates are present. (*Saṃyutta-nikāya*, I, 135)

A later text uses this same simile in a dialogue between the monk Nāgasena and King Milinda. After describing in some detail how the word "chariot" designates the combination of parts that makes it up, Nāgasena concludes that the word "self" is simply a name that designates the Five Aggregates. Therefore, Nāgasena concludes, "In the final analysis, in the ultimate sense, there is no [permanent] self to be found [within the Five Aggregates]" (*Milindapañha*, 27).

DEPENDENT ARISING

The Five Aggregates give a static view of the conventional self; that is, they describe the various parts that constitute the self. The Buddha also taught the notion of dependent arising (*pratītya-samutpāda;* Pali: *paṭicca-samuppāda*), which gives one a dynamic picture of how these parts interact in ways that generate *duḥkha*, and also bring about the cessation of *duḥkha.* This notion of dependent arising is so important that when the Buddha spoke of his Awakening experience, he said, "I have attained the Dharma, profound and difficult to see. . . . Difficult to see is this contingent or dependent arising. Also difficult to see is this: the quiescence of all composite conditions . . . cessation, Nirvana" (*Majjhima-nikāya*, I, 211–212). The Dharma, or teaching, of the Buddha constantly presents the notion of dependent arising as essential to comprehending the awakened Buddhist experience of life (see Figure 2.1). It is through this teaching that one can understand the way in which *duḥkha* arises in the functioning of the Five Aggregates, as well as how it can be brought to cessation.

Here is how the Buddha described dependent arising in general: "That being, this comes to be; from the arising of that, this arises. That being absent, this is not; from the cessation of that, this ceases" (*Saṃyutta-nikāya*, II, 28). This general principle of conditionality simply states that all things arise and pass away due to certain conditions. When necessary conditions are present to support a thing's existence, it comes to be. As those conditions change and new conditions appear, the thing changes. When the conditions for the

FIGURE 2.1. The Buddha teaching his first five disciples; Luang Prabang, Laos.

thing's existence are finally removed, the thing ceases to be. This principle applies not only to the existence of phenomena but also to the quality of things. For example, the Buddha said that when certain conditions are present, *duḥkha* arises. When those conditions change, *duḥkha* is modified. And when the conditions for *duḥkha* are removed, *duḥkha* itself ceases.

In fact, the Buddha applied this general principle of conditionality to the human condition to explain the arising and cessation of *duḥkha.* That is, he taught a more specific version of dependent arising to explain how certain impermanent constituents of human experience arise such that *duḥkha* itself arises, and also how those constituents can be modified to reduce *duḥkha* until they are fully removed and *duḥkha* ceases. This specific version of the notion of dependent arising can be called the "twelve links (*nidāna*) of conditionality." The twelve conditioning links that produce *duḥkha* include (1) ignorance, (2) mental formations, (3) consciousness, (4) mind and body,

(5) senses, (6) contact, (7) sensation, (8) craving, (9) attachment, (10) becoming, (11) birth, and (12) the whole mass of *duḥkha*. Let us look at these twelve links one at a time.

The following verses from a teaching by the Buddha about these twelve links state how they arise conditionally according to the general formulation of dependent arising, namely, "That being, this comes to be; from the arising of that, this arises":

> On [1] ignorance depends [2] mental formations; on mental formations depends [3] consciousness; on consciousness depends [4] mind and body; on mind and body depends [5] senses; on senses depends [6] contact; on sense contact depends [7] sensation, on sensation depends [8] craving; on craving depends [9] attachment; on attachment depends [10] becoming; on becoming depends [11] birth; on birth depends [12] old age and death, sorrow, lamentation, misery, grief and despair. Thus does this entire mass of *duḥkha* arise. (*Saṃyutta-nikāya*, II, 90)

With this concrete pattern of dependent arising in mind, we first look at the individual links as they contribute to the arising *duḥkha*. Then, we look briefly at how the Buddha says this process can be modified such that *duḥkha* itself ceases. Indeed, most of the rest of this chapter is devoted to the Buddha's teachings on overcoming *duḥkha*.

The first link, *ignorance*, is defined as being ignorant of the Four Noble Truths that we discuss in detail later. In brief, these four truths concern (1) the nature of *duḥkha*, (2) the various causes of *duḥkha*, (3) the possible cessation of *duḥkha*, and (4) the spiritual path that leads to the cessation of *duḥkha*. Ignorance concerning these truths about the dissatisfactory condition of life will condition the second link, namely, one's *mental formations*. These mental formations, as we have seen, are the fourth of the Five Aggregates. While the Buddha taught that the mind is essentially pure and luminous, he explained that it is also defiled by certain mental states that are formed by the mind and that arise dependent ultimately on ignorance. In other words, ignorance conditions negative mental formations, or unwholesome mental states or attitudes. For example, if a person believes that he or she can be satisfied by the passing things of the world, that person will form unwholesome, pleasure-seeking mental states like greed or lust.

The third link is *consciousness*. Its placement at this point means that mental formations condition the state of one's consciousness. For example, if one is always getting angry at people, anger can become a general disposition of one's consciousness. And that disposition of ill will can affect what one is conscious of in others. One may only be conscious of the faults of others, and not their positive qualities. The Buddha also taught that it is this intentional consciousness that, due to karma, continues for a time after death until it sparks a new conscious life, "like one flame lighting another" (*Milindapañha*, 40). Thus, the positive and negative qualities of consciousness follow a person into his or her next life.

The fourth link is *mind and body*, literally, "name and form" (*nāma-rūpa*). That is, the status of one's mind and body, including one's health, is conditioned by the state of one's consciousness. At this point, the body becomes more involved in this process of dependent arising in that one's mental and physical state conditions the fifth link, namely, the orientation of one's *senses* to the world around one. For example, the senses of one's body are drawn toward certain persons and things depending on the orientation of one's mind and body. When one walks into a room, one notices some people and not others because of one's sense orientation toward the people in the room. In this way, one's senses condition the kind of *contact*, which is the sixth link, one has with the world.

Then, because of the positive or negative qualities of this contact, certain *sensations/feelings*, the seventh link, arise. If one contacts something one takes to be positive, one begins to entertain pleasant sensations or feelings. If, on the other hand, one encounters something one takes to be negative, unpleasant sensations or feelings arise. It is based on these emotional responses to persons, things, and events that there is the arising of the eighth link, namely, *craving*. Craving is either a self-centered desire to prolong the enjoyment of a pleasurable feeling or a self-centered desire to get rid of an unenjoyable feeling. This craving conditions the arising of the ninth link, *attachment*. In fact, cravings evolve into attachments. That is, the prior links of ignorance, unwholesome mental formations, and negative orientations toward life all intensify cravings to the point that they give rise to attachments.

An attachment is an active, decision-based clinging to the things of this world, to the pleasures derived from these things, or to an aversion to things one does not enjoy. It is these kinds of attachments that condition the *becoming* of one's life, the tenth link in the process of dependent arising. In other words, one's attachments in life condition the continuing unwholesome process of existence that has arisen from ignorance, negative mental formations, self-centered orientations, and craving. This continuing process of becoming, marked by one's personality-forming attachments, conditions one's *birth*, the eleventh link. This link means how one is reborn after death. However, it can also mean that the way one lives his or her life "gives birth," as it were, to one's personal identity—the kind of person one is. Finally, this birth or identity, because it arises dependent on attachments that are based ultimately on ignorance, conditions the final link, namely, "the entire mass of *duḥkha*."

An example of how these twelve links of conditionality might actually work themselves out in a particular life process would be the following. If we take a person who is born into an abusive situation, because of that person's (1) ignorance, he or she may not understand what is causing the *duḥkha* of that situation. Based on this ignorance, he or she might develop certain unwholesome (2) mental formations, or attitudes, about his or her self, other persons, and the world in general. These attitudes could affect his or her states of (3) consciousness, and thereby his or her (4) mental and physical well-being. This unhealthy condition of mind and body could then affect what he or she (5) senses, (6) contacts, (7) feels, and (8) craves in life. Some of these cravings may develop into unhelpful (9) attachments to people or things that simply continue negative (10) becoming, or patterns of affectivity and behavior. These patterns give (11) birth to the person's identity in ways that produce (12) *duḥkha* for himself or herself and others.

We can see from this example why Buddhists claim that these twelve links of dependent arising should be seen as forming a circle. That is, the conditions of *duḥkha* that a person produces for himself or herself and for others simply contribute to the arising of more ignorance in one's life. Thereby, the circle of negative conditionality continues and deepens. Buddhist art depicts this circle of conditionality as a twelve-spoked Wheel of Life. However, this is not a pessimistic doctrine about life; the Wheel of Life can be broken by the attainment of Awakening and Nirvana. The Buddha expresses this hope by presenting the twelve links in terms of their cessation:

> On the complete fading away and cessation of [1] ignorance ceases [2] mental formations; on the cessation of mental formations ceases [3] consciousness; on the cessation of consciousness ceases [4] mind and body; on the cessation of mind and body ceases [5] senses; on the cessation of senses ceases [6] contact; on the cessation of contact ceases [7] sensation; on the cessation of sensation ceases [8] craving; on the cessation of craving ceases [9] attachment; on the cessation of attachment ceases [10] becoming; on the cessation of becoming ceases [11] birth; on the cessation of birth ceases [12] old age and death, sorrow, lamentation, misery, grief and despair. Thus does the entire mass of *duḥkha cease.* (*Saṃyutta-nikāya*, II, 90)

What is implied here is that the process of dependent arising can also be a process of dependent cessation. We are brought back to the second part of the abstract formulation of dependent arising, namely, "That being absent, this is not; from the cessation of that, this ceases." As we shall see later, the Buddha teaches an Eightfold Path whereby one brings to awareness, pacifies, and even eradicates the ignorance, unwholesome attitudes, craving, and attachments that produce *duḥkha.* The "complete fading away and cessation" of these negative conditioning factors and their resultant *duḥkha* is Nirvana.

KARMA AND REBIRTH

In the center of some of the artistic renderings of the Wheel of Life are pictures of the various realms in which living beings can be reborn through karma. Karma, according to the Buddha, is the result of willful intention: "It is will *[cetanā]*, O monks, that I call karma; for having willed, one acts through body, speech or mind" (*Anguttara-nikāya*, III, 415). In other words, the good or bad willful intentions that motivate the doing of good or bad actions are what result in karmic fruition. Accidental or unintended good or bad actions, like nonmoral actions, do not result in karma. However, all intentional moral or immoral acts condition or mold one's consciousness in ways that, in turn, condition one's life in the future, and ultimately one's rebirth. Remember that it is consciousness that, like a flame in this life, lights the flame of one's next life. In this regard, good or bad rebirths are not to be seen simply as rewards or punishments, but as the resulting effect of one's conscious character molded by lives of good and bad actions that reflect how one ultimately chooses to live.

In defining good and bad actions, the Buddha spoke of wholesome (*kuśala*) and unwholesome (*akuśala*) acts. A wholesome action is one that produces a positive condition of mind and body for the actor and for those affected by the action. A positive condition is one that is ultimately conducive to the attainment of Nirvana. An unwholesome action is one that produces harmful effects and is not ultimately conducive to attaining Nirvana. The Buddha taught that there are three fundamental motivations, or "root causes," of unwholesome actions: greed (*rāga;* Pali: *lobha*), hate (*dveṣa;* Pali: *dosa*), and delusion (*moha*). These are known as the Three Root Evils. Being motivated by greed can mean allowing one's actions to be rooted in longing for something or someone or in more strong desires like avarice or lust. This kind of motivation can also involve clinging to dogmatic views in ways that are not uplifting for oneself or others. Being motivated by hatred can involve irritation with something or someone or strong feelings of aversion, anger, or even wrath. Delusion as a motivation means pursuing actions that result from an active distortion of, or hiding from, the truth in certain matters or from being unclear or full of doubts about things one should make the effort to understand.

On the other hand, the Buddha also taught that one should be motivated by the opposites of these Three Root Evils. Then, one's actions will be wholesome for oneself and others and will contribute to conditions that are conducive to the attainment of Nirvana. For example, motivation from non-greed (*alobha*) implies the positive intentions of generosity or renunciation for the benefit of others. Non-hate (*adosa*) motivations include friendliness, patience, loving kindness, and compassion for others. Non-delusion (*amoha*) motivations include clarity of mind and insight into reality.

Buddhist Cosmology

Good and bad karma, resulting from positive and negative motivations, determine one's rebirth in the cycle of *saṃsāra.* Where this rebirth can take place brings us to the topic of Buddhist cosmology. The early texts describe three types of "realms" in which rebirth takes place: the realms of sense desire (*kāma-loka*), the realms of form (*rūpa-loka*), and the formless realms (*arūpa-loka*).

The five realms of sense desire, the lower of the three realms, include the hell realms, the realms of the hungry ghosts (*preta;* Pali: *peta*), the realms of animals, the realms of humans, and the realms of the lower gods (*deva*). In the hells, everything is repulsive, and one constantly experiences painful states of mind and body. Because no rebirth is for eternity, when the karma that brought one to such an unfortunate state is used up, one is reborn into another realm. The realms of the hungry ghosts are states that overlap the human world. Ghosts are so attached to earthly conditions that they are reborn on earth with a body of "subtle matter" such that they are normally unseen by humans. They haunt this world tormented by their unsatisfied attachments. The animal realms are where beings, because of their karma, have to undergo certain sufferings associated with animal conditions. The human realms are the first sense-desire realms that are seen as a reward for good karma. This is because the human realms are where moral virtue and wisdom can be cultivated, as one's will is not overwhelmed by the pains of the lower states or the pleasures of the higher heavenly states.

The last status in the realms of sense desire is that of certain lower gods. Sometimes proud and fiercesome celestial beings (*asuras*) are mentioned as also existing on this level. They are said to be in opposition to the lower gods because the gods expelled them from their heavens. In any case, the lower gods reside in six levels of existence. In the lowest of these six levels, the gods are more like spirits that inhabit the earth's surface and atmosphere. Sometimes mentioned in this regard are the *gandharvas,* celestial musicians; *yakṣas* and *rākṣasas,* good and evil spirits; *nāgas,* serpents that can assume human form; *garuḍas,* birds with human heads; as well as other minor spirits dwelling in nature. Among the higher celestial levels are found the World-Protectors, the gods of the Vedic religion, and the *Tuṣita* Heaven from where persons are reborn as human Buddhas. It is believed that the next human Buddha after Gautama will be Maitreya, who now resides in the *Tuṣita* Heaven.

The realms of form are inhabited by higher gods, referred to as *Brahmā* deities, who reside in sixteen celestial levels of progressive calmness and purity. The top five levels are attainable by humans who have almost reached Nirvana. In those levels, one will, in fact, complete the path and achieve Nirvana. The other eleven levels are related to the Four Meditations (*dhyānas*) that were practiced by the Buddha in achieving Awakening and have been practiced in Buddhism since the earliest Saṅgha. It is said that these meditations attune the consciousness to such refined states and help one to be reborn in them. In these heavenly realms, the deities are said to have pure forms and to lack the desires that characterize the gods in the realms of desire.

The formless realms consist of the four highest levels of celestial rebirth possible. Here, the *Brahmā* deities have no desire, shape, or form, only pure mental existence. The four formless realms correspond to the Four Formless Meditations. While these meditations have been practiced in Buddhism from the beginning of the Saṅgha as part of the path to Nirvana, they can also lead to rebirth into the formless realms. Rebirth into any of the *Brahmā* realms requires not just meditative attainment but also moral achievement. Of special importance are the virtues called the Four Divine Adobes, or, literally, "*Brahmā* abodes" (*Brahmā-vihāras*). These four virtues include loving kindness, compassion, sympathetic joy, and equanimity. We discuss these meditative and moral practices later. But, it is interesting to note that

Sahampatī Brahmā, the deity who came down to convince the Buddha to teach the Dharma, was from the *Brahmā* realms. Also, one should note that the Buddha did not teach that one should worship these celestial deities. However, the early texts indicate that the Buddha and the Saṅgha respected their karmic attainment.

The earliest texts present the realms of sense desire as constituting a vast number of "world systems" (*cakra-vāla*). The Buddha taught that the beginning of these systems cannot be found, nor can their extent. These world systems have gone through incalculable eons during which they expand and contract. They contract in clusters with the lower realms disappearing, leaving only the upper more spiritual realms. At the center of each world system is the world mountain, Meru or Sineru. It is surrounded by mountains and seas, with continents beyond where humans and animals live, and below which reside hungry ghosts and hell beings. In the shadows of the slopes of Mt. Meru dwell the *asuras,* while on the slopes themselves dwell the lower gods. Above Mt. Meru and beyond the realm of sense desire are the realms of form and the formless realms. Here, the *Brahmā* deities rule over the world systems. As beings "wander" from life to life, they pass from one realm to another, or from one world system to another, until they tread the path of the Buddha and attain the release of Nirvana.

The Wheel of Life

In the Wheel of Life pictured in Figure 2.2, we find a blending of the twelve links of dependent arising, karma, rebirth, and Buddhist cosmology. The outermost ring of the wheel consists of representations of the twelve links that define the manner of causality that result in beings wandering from life to life due to their karma. Inside this ring we find pictures of the six sense realms of existence (lower gods, *asuras,* humans, animals, hungry ghosts, and hell beings). In the next double segment are the two ways: the downward way of rebirth to the lower realms because of the Three Root Evils and the upward way because of the spiritual path. Those monks following the path in the picture are pointed to the goal of Nirvana, depicted in the upper left of the picture, by the Buddha in the upper right of the picture. There is a subtle thread leading from the path to Nirvana that is outside the Wheel of Life. At the very center of the wheel are the Three Root Evils of greed, hate, and delusion symbolized by the cock, snake, and pig. These Root Evils keep the Wheel of Life turning, a wheel that is held in the grasp of the Lord of Death.

THE FOUR NOBLE TRUTHS

We can see from the teachings of the Buddha discussed earlier that for him, the Five Aggregates, namely the five impermanent factors of one's existence, are always changing in certain patterns of dependent arising. No matter what realm one is born into, the patterns of this conditioning process are always in some ways dissatisfactory (*duḥkha*). To seek for a kind of permanent

FIGURE 2.2. The Wheel of Life, painting on cloth, twentieth century, Tibet. Library of Congress Asian Collection.

Self (Ātman), as some Upaniṣadic teachers were proposing, was for the Buddha a mistake. There simply is no permanent substantial self behind or within the mental and physical elements or processes of life. Instead, one should attend to the changing twelve-linked patterns of dependent arising to see how it is that one's life is ultimately dissatisfying. One should examine what the patterns of perceiving and thinking, of decision making and mental formation, of sensing and feeling are like that make life dissatisfactory. Then one should see what the causes of these unwholesome patterns are and how they can be changed and ultimately eliminated.

To make his point, the Buddha taught that all the factors of one's life are "on fire":

> All things, O monks, are on fire. And what, O monks, are all these things that are on fire? The eye, O monks, is on fire. Visible forms . . . eye consciousness . . . impressions received by the eye . . . whatever sensations, pleasant, unpleasant, or indifferent that arise dependent on impressions received by the eye are on fire. With what are these on fire? With the fire of passion, with the fire of hatred, with the fire of infatuation, with the [whole mass of *duḥkha]* are they on fire. (*Mahāvagga*, I, 21)

The Buddha goes on to repeat this claim in regard to the other five senses (including the mind). His point is that all aspects of one's experience are "burning" from an inner "fire" that one must discover and extinguish. As the word *Nirvana* means "to blow out" or "to extinguish," to realize Nirvana, one must discover the hidden "fire" that burns one's life with dissatisfaction and then extinguish it. In his Awakening, the Buddha understood the "fire" causing *duḥkha.* He also discovered how to get rid of that fire to extinguish *duḥkha* and to attain what he called the "coolness" of Nirvana. Moved by compassion for humankind's suffering from the burning of *duḥkha,* it is said that the Buddha sought out the five ascetics with whom he had been friends and delivered to them his First Sermon at Deer Park.

This First Sermon was the "turning of the wheel of the Dharma" (see Figure 2.3) that presented what are called the Four Noble Truths. These Holy Truths are about the dissatisfactory human condition, its cause, its possible end, and the path that leads to this release. These are called "noble" truths because they are morally and spiritually fruitful: When they are realized in a person's experience, they lead to the achievement of Nirvana. They are also noble because it takes a noble person, a person of courage, honesty, and insight, to realize them. It is not easy to face the dissatisfactory conditions of one's own life. In fact, people often do whatever they can to avoid these unpleasant facts. They sometimes turn to worldly diversions, immerse themselves in studies or work, or even lose themselves in mind-dulling drugs or alcohol. But the teaching of the Buddha is that if one truly and courageously faces reality and sees the truth about his or her life, indeed about life itself, with time and guidance, one can find the cause of the discontent, heal it, and realize a new and truly satisfactory life.

The Middle Way

Let us look, then, at the First Sermon of the Buddha (*Saṃyutta-nikāya,* V, 420 ff.) to see what these Four Noble Truths entail. The Buddha begins his

FIGURE 2.3. Dharma Cakra (Wheel of the Dharma) on the hand of the enthroned Buddha; fourth century C.E., India. The Art Institute of Chicago.

sermon by addressing the ascetics' concern that he had given up the rigors of the spiritual life to return to a life of self-indulgence:

> These two extremes, O monks, are not to be practiced by one who has gone forth from the world. What are these two extremes? That one which is joined with the passions, low and vulgar, common, ignoble and useless. And also that one which is joined with self-torture and pain, ignoble and useless. Avoiding those two extremes, the [Buddha] has gained the knowledge of the Middle Way, which gives sight and knowledge, tends to calm, to insight, to Awakening and Nirvana. What, O monks, is the Middle Way . . . ? It is the Noble Eightfold Path, namely, Right Understanding, Right Thought, Right Speech, Right Action, Right Livelihood, Right Effort, Right Mindfulness, and Right Concentration. . . .

The Buddha makes it clear that his Middle Way avoids the pursuit of sensual pleasures on the one hand and the pursuit of ascetic self-torment on the other. He had experienced both the way of life-attachment and life-denial, and found them lacking. What did lead to Awakening and Nirvana was a Middle Way of moral discipline, meditation practice, and penetrating insight that can be found through following the Noble Eightfold Path. It is only after proposing this path that the Buddha goes on to present the Four Noble Truths. In this way, he subordinates conceptions about the truth to moral and spiritual transformation.

The First Noble Truth: Life Is Duḥkha

What are these Four Noble Truths that put one in touch with the reality of the human condition and present one with a religious path that can transform one's life? In the next lines of the Buddha's First Sermon, the first truth is stated:

> Now this, O monks, is the noble truth of *duḥkha.* Birth is *duḥkha,* old age is *duḥkha,* sickness is *duḥkha,* and death is *duḥkha.* Sorrow, lamentation, dejection, and despair are *duḥkha.* Contact with unpleasant things is *duḥkha,* and separation from what one wishes is *duḥkha.* In short, the Five Aggregates onto which one grasps are *duḥkha.*

This First Noble Truth, the truth of *duḥkha,* proclaims that life as ordinarily lived is dissatisfactory. We have already seen what *duḥkha* means when we discussed the Three Characteristics. In this sermon, it is said that *duḥkha* is found in at least four kinds of situations that arise in ordinary life. First are the dissatisfactory conditions associated with physical processes such as old age, sickness, and death. Second are the dissatisfactory conditions, such as sorrow and dejection, that are associated with mental-emotional processes. Third is the particular dissatisfaction one finds with unpleasant things. Fourth is the dissatisfaction one finds in not possessing the things one wants or needs. Finally, the Buddha says that all of these kinds of situations that characterize the human condition point to a simple fact. This fact is that when one "grasps" for lasting happiness in the impermanent physical things and mental processes of ordinary life, distinguished here by the Five Aggregates, one will only find dissatisfaction.

As we saw before, the Buddha is not denying that there is any happiness in life. But, because all elements of life are subject to change, such happiness is not lasting, and therefore not fully satisfying. Certainly most people find some degree of happiness in life, but when one looks around at the world or within oneself, one often finds that things are just not fully satisfactory. Reading this statement of the Buddha into our own times, how many people are living in desperate situations with little or no hope of relief? Even for those who are not directly affected by great tragedies, who is without the experience of "sorrow, lamentation, dejection, and despair?" The Buddha taught that given the dissatisfactory conditions of human life, even in times of relative happiness, within every person there is a sense of lack, a sense that something is missing, a sense of *duḥkha. Duḥkha* is not an abstract idea; every person has his or her personal *duḥkha.* It takes a noble person to realize this fact and to seek the cause of this unfortunate condition shared by all humanity, as well as a possible remedy.

The Second Noble Truth: The Cause of Duḥkha

The Second Noble Truth is the truth about the cause (*samudaya*) of *duḥkha.* Here is how the Buddha describes the cause of *duḥkha* in the next verses of his First Sermon:

Now this, O monks, is the noble truth of the cause of *duḥkha:* that craving which leads to rebirth, combined with pleasure and passion, finding pleasure here and there. This is the craving for sensual pleasure, the craving for continued becoming, and the craving for non-becoming.

The word we translate as "craving" is *tṛṣṇā* (Pali: *taṇhā*), which literally means "thirst." This thirst includes the many forms of desire that seek self-gratification to find happiness. In this sermon, the Buddha presents what he calls elsewhere the "Three Forms of Thirst." The most obvious form of such thirst is the desire for "sensual pleasure." Because all sensual objects of desire are impermanent, the self-gratification that one obtains from possessing them obviously cannot give one lasting happiness. To try to find such happiness in these sensual pleasures only leads to frustration and dissatisfaction, which, in turn, fuel the craving from more pleasures. Also, the search for happiness in the enjoyment of pleasures motivates one to relate to others in self-centered ways that result in negative karma and unhappy rebirths. Here is also a psychological basis for social conflict, injustice, violence, and war.

The second form of thirst is the desire for "becoming." We have already seen in the twelve links of conditionality that craving (or thirst) conditions attachments, which condition becoming, meaning the continuing process of one's life. So this second type of thirst includes the desires to defend or protect oneself and one's possessions and pleasures, to advance one's own life, to enhance one's ego and social status, to gain more power and prestige. On the other hand, the thirst for "non-becoming" includes desires for self-denial in the ascetic life, for the removal of unpleasant people or things from one's life, for self-destructive habits or patterns of behavior. We can see from these Three Forms of Thirst that, for the Buddha, craving is not just a single phenomenon; it has multiple and even conflicting forms.

It is also clear from the twelve links of conditionality that thirst is not the first cause of *duḥkha.* It is conditioned by a deeper source, namely, the ignorance that is referred to as the first of the twelve links. What is this fundamental ignorance? It is a lack of realizing the Buddha's Dharma concerning the real nature of self and world. Using the metaphor from the Buddha's Fire Sermon quoted earlier, the ignorance of such realities as impermanence, no-self, and *duḥkha* produces a very subtle yet powerful self-awareness that is self-centered and burns one's life with craving or thirst. To use another metaphor, this self-awareness is like a "field" in which everything that one experiences is analyzed and judged from a self-centered and ultimately ignorant point of view. It is from this ignorance, this lack of clear insight into the Four Noble Truths about life, that "seeds" of *duḥkha* grow.

In this First Sermon, the craving that causes *duḥkha* implies an ignorant view of the self as an ongoing possessor and enjoyer of the things of life. People are thirsting to be and to possess, to become and to acquire, in ways that produce a dissatisfactory life for themselves and others. This unwholesome lifestyle is based on people's view of themselves as "controllers" or "possessors" and the world as being made up of people and things to be controlled or possessed in ways that cause *duḥkha.* It seems that this inner self-centered vision of self and world "solidifies," as it were, into the kinds of thirsting and often self-destructive states of mind that the Buddha identifies as the causes of *duḥkha.*

Also, this ignorant view of self and world is related to another form of thirst that the Buddha mentions in other sermons, namely, a craving to be right that leads to an attachment to ideas, views, theories, or beliefs. This kind of attachment produces dogmatism, prejudice, and intolerance. When one puts this kind of dogmatic attitude together with the thirst to obtain personal happiness, the thirst to advance one's life (including one's views) by the use of power, and the thirst for self-destructive actions, one finds causes for everything from "verbal wrangling" to ideological warfare. When the Buddha spoke out about the social, economic, and political issues of his day, he taught that these problems that bring about so much *duḥkha* in people's lives are ultimately rooted in the human mind. It is there, in ignorance and unwholesome mental formations, that the root of humankind's *duḥkha* must, in the final analysis, be addressed. For the Buddha, only a deep, insightful penetration into how unwholesome dispositions, attitudes, feelings, and thoughts are produced from ignorance and thirst can enable a person to stop fueling the inner fire that produces the burning of *duḥkha.*

The Third Noble Truth: The Cessation of Duḥkha

The Third Noble Truth concerns the cessation (*nirodha*) of *duḥkha.* In his First Sermon, the Buddha states it in just a few words: "Now this, O monks, is the noble truth of the cessation of *duḥkha.* It is the complete cessation of that very craving, giving it up, renouncing it, release from it, detachment from it." Although in this particular sermon he does not use the word, the cessation he is speaking about here is Nirvana. As we have seen, Nirvana literally means "blowing out" or "extinguishing" and was used to describe the cessation of a fire. In this sermon, the Buddha is saying that the cessation of *duḥkha* is brought about by the extinction of craving or thirst. When craving ceases, its effect, namely *duḥkha,* ceases and the result is Nirvana.

One thing that is interesting about the Buddha's statement of the Third Noble Truth is the few words he uses in comparison to the number used in stating the other three truths. Perhaps the reason is that the Buddha never spoke very much about what Nirvana ultimately is. Up to this point we have been looking at teachings of the Buddha that he explicates at some length. Therefore, there is not a great deal of disagreement among scholars about what those teachings entail. However, this is not the case with Nirvana. In fact, volumes have been written in which scholars have tried to answer the question, "What is Nirvana?" Some claim that it is an absolute Truth. Others say it is a transcendent metaphysical Reality. Still others argue that it is a supermundane experience or a supreme and pure state of mind.

At the conclusion of this chapter, we discuss why the Buddha did not speak about Nirvana in any great detail and also present an interpretation of

Nirvana based just on the early texts. Here, it is enough to say that no matter how Nirvana is interpreted, in the Third Noble Truth it refers to the cessation of *duḥkha* brought about by the letting go of craving. In other teachings by the Buddha, Nirvana is said to entail the cessation of defilements or the cessation of the Three Root Evils of greed, hate, and delusion. However, one should not conclude from these statements that Nirvana is something that is "caused" by the cessation of craving. Nirvana is not produced by anything, and so it is called "unconditioned" (*asaṃskṛta;* Pali: *asaṃkhata*). On the other hand, Nirvana is "realized" by following the Eightfold Path that is proclaimed in the Fourth Noble Truth. That is, the Eightfold Path does not cause or produce Nirvana but leads one to it like a path that leads to a place that is already there to be discovered.

The Fourth Noble Truth: The Eightfold Path to the Cessation of Duḥkha

The Buddha presents the Fourth Noble Truth, about the Path (*mārga;* Pali: *magga*) that leads to the cessation of *duḥkha,* in the next lines of his First Sermon:

> Now this, O monks, is the noble truth of the way that leads to the cessation of *duḥkha.* This is the Noble Eightfold Path, namely, Right Understanding, Right Thought, Right Speech, Right Action, Right Livelihood, Right Effort, Right Mindfulness, and Right Concentration. . . .

In the Four Noble Truths, we can see a method of medical treatment that was popular at the time of the Buddha. First, there is the identification of the disease. Second, there is an analysis of the cause of the disease. Third, this analysis is followed by defining the desired cure that will remove the cause of the disease, and thereby the disease itself, thus producing renewed health. Fourth, there is a specific method prescribed for curing the disease. In the Eightfold Path, the Buddha gave a prescription that will "cure" the dissatisfactory condition of human existence. This Fourth Noble Truth provides a path for the journey from ordinary human living, characterized by *duḥkha,* to a life characterized by freedom, peace, and happiness, namely, to the Nirvana proclaimed in the Third Noble Truth. It is the Middle Way of moral and religious practice that the Buddha mentioned in the introductory passages to this First Sermon.

In the naming of each of these eight steps, we find the word "right" (samyañc; Pali: *sammā*) being used as an adjective. This word is not used by the Buddha to indicate a command. The Buddha is not demanding that his disciples follow these steps as a religious or moral duty. Rather, the word "right" means "skillful." In other words, these eight steps will skillfully help one advance in the religious way that leads to Nirvana. Therefore, the Buddha said that one should not follow these steps simply because he taught them. One should try them in his or her own experience to see if they do indeed lead to Awakening and Nirvana. Also, these steps are not intended to be taken one after the other in the order they appear in the Buddha's listing of them. Rather, they are to be developed more or less together so that they reinforce each other in one's spiritual life. In the next section of this chapter, we look at each of these steps to see how they skillfully advance one's life in the direction of Awakening and Nirvana.

Awakening

In the conclusion to his First Sermon, the Buddha says:

> As long as I did not perceive with knowledge and insight . . . these noble truths, so long, O monks, in this world . . . had I not attained the highest and complete Awakening. But, when I perceived with knowledge and insight . . . these noble truths, then, O monks, in this world . . . I attained the highest and complete Awakening. Thus I knew; knowledge arose in me, insight arose that the emancipation of my mind is unmovable. This is my last existence; now there is no more rebirth.

In complete Awakening, one realizes the end *of duḥkha.* Ignorance, as first in the twelve links of conditionality, is said to entail not knowing the Four Noble Truths. In this passage, Awakening is said to entail knowing these truths with penetrating insight. Thus, the ignorance that conditions the arising of craving is extinguished. By Awakening, achieved through the Eightfold Path, one can find release from the unwholesome factors of mind that produce the dissatisfactory state of ordinary human existence. In short, the Buddha teaches that true "emancipation" from rebirth is Nirvana, and this lasting happiness and peace can be found by attaining Awakening through following the Eightfold Path. At this point, then, let us look more carefully at this path to Nirvana.

THE EIGHTFOLD PATH

The steps of the Eightfold Path (see Figure 2.4) are arranged under three categories. The first two steps (Right Understanding and Right Thought) fall under the category of "proper view"; they present a perspective and way of thinking that orient one skillfully on the path to Awakening and Nirvana. The next three steps (Right Speech, Right Action, and Right Livelihood) fall under the category of "proper conduct"; they define what is required to walk the path in terms of moral purification and living. The last three steps (Right Effort, Right Mindfulness, and Right Concentration) fall under the category of "proper practice"; these practices deepen proper view into the wisdom of Awakening and deepen proper conduct into an awakened life.

These three divisions of the Eightfold Path are also labeled in another way by the Buddha. Proper view is called "wisdom" (*prajñā;* Pali: *paññā*), because its two steps provide the wisdom necessary for Awakening. Proper conduct

FIGURE 2.4. Eight-spoked Wheel of the Dharma between two golden deer: Jo-Khang Monastery, Lhasa, Tibet.

is called "morality" (*śīla;* Pali: sīla), as its three steps define the moral precepts of the Buddhist path. Finally, proper practice is called "concentration" (*samādhi*), because its three steps advance the concentrated states of mind necessary for inner spiritual purification and the attainment of Nirvana. With these general remarks about the Eightfold Path in mind, let us now turn to an introduction of each step on this Holy Path.

Right Understanding

Right Understanding means a "clarity" of understanding that skillfully leads one along the path to Awakening. It involves a clear understanding of the impermanent process of life, the unsatisfactory condition of this process, and the dependently arisen factors of life that make it so dissatisfying. It also entails understanding rightly how the conception of a substantial and permanent self influences one's self-centered dispositions, attitudes, and other mental formations that bind one to this process of dissatisfactory living. On the other hand, it also means to understand well the positive qualities of mind and moral living that can heal this condition and to understand clearly the steps one needs to take to cultivate these satisfactory qualities of thought, word, and action. Right Understanding, in short, means to understand skillfully the Dharma of the Buddha in a way that develops into, to use the words from the Buddha's First Sermon, "knowledge and insight" into the true nature of all things, of how they really are (*yathābhūtam*). In this sense, it is the "seed" of a wisdom that destroys ignorance and becomes complete in the attainment of Awakening and Nirvana.

Right Thought

Whereas Right Understanding entails a "clarity" of insight into the truth about life, Right Thought entails a "purity" of thinking about life. It entails the development of freedom from unwholesome states of mind like thoughts of greed, harm, violence, or ill will toward others. In the development of this freedom, pure or wholesome states of mind such as thoughts of selflessness, goodwill toward others, and compassion are cultivated. These Right Thoughts will, in turn, be expressed in the next steps on the path that have to do with moral treatment of other persons. Without developing wholesome thoughts and attitudes of mind toward others, one's moral actions will only be motivated by an external sense of duty rather than an inner caring attitude. This second step also involves the willingness to relinquish any state of mind that obstructs one's progress on the path. So it includes the right kinds of aspirations for oneself and for others, seeking what is good for all living beings. Therefore, this step is sometimes called "Right Aspiration." It entails thoughts of compassionate aspiration for the well-being of all, tender thoughts of concern for all who are suffering, and the desire to bring goodness and freedom to all living beings.

Right Speech

With the right mental attitudes and aspirations, one can then use his or her speech skillfully for the benefit of all beings. Also, because people speak what they think, Right Speech follows Right Thought. For the Buddha, this third step means that one should refrain from four types of wrong speech: falsehood, slander, harsh words, and idle gossip. Note that besides *refraining* from these forms of wrong speech, one is also asked by the Buddha to *cultivate* forms of Right Speech. For example, one should refrain from telling lies, and instead develop the virtue of truthfulness expressed in what one says. Because slander breaks fellowship with other persons and does violence to their reputation, one should always speak in ways that defend and affirm the dignity of other persons. While harsh words issue from an unkind heart, gentle words, by contrast, issue from a kind and compassionate heart. To engage in harsh language only hardens one's heart and drives out the compassionate virtues of enlightened living. Idle gossip disturbs others in ways that are beneficial neither to the one who is listening nor to the one about whom one is speaking. Such gossip works against peacefulness in relationships and society. Like slander and harsh words, gossip expresses the unwholesome thoughts of ill will and cruelty toward others. One should instead use words that sow the seeds of peace in all relationships. In this regard, the Buddha also advised that if one cannot say anything useful in a situation, one should keep a "noble silence."

Right Action

Right Thought is also expressed in moral actions. The Buddha often presented Right Action in terms of the Five Precepts. Note that just as with Right Speech, whereas each precept presents what one *should not* do, the Buddha also taught what one *should* do. For example, the first precept is "not to kill." The Buddha, in discussing this virtue, says:

> In what ways . . . is a monk perfected in morality? Forsaking the taking of life, he refrains from killing. Having given up stick or sword, he is careful and compassionate, showing concern for the welfare of all living beings. Thus, he is accomplished in morality. (*Dīgha-nikāya*, I, 63)

In other words, one should not only *not* kill any living being, but should also carefully practice compassion with a sincere concern for all. The second precept is "not to steal." Here, too, one should not take what belongs to others, and should practice charity, respect, and generosity in all relationships. The third precept is "not to commit sexual misconduct." Here, one is advised to practice self-control in order to live a life of purity in relationship to others. The fourth precept is "not to lie." Instead of telling falsehoods, one is asked to practice sincerity and honesty in what one says. Finally, the fifth precept is "not to partake of intoxicating drinks or drugs." Here, restraint is practiced to better cultivate one's freedom and develop one's mindfulness. The Five Precepts ask people to preserve life, respect others, develop self-control, express the truth, and attain freedom. To act in these ways deepens compassion, love, and respect for oneself and for others. Acting in ways that destroy life, disrespect others, increase irresponsibility, hide or distort the truth, and lead to addiction decreases one's freedom, enlightenment, and compassionate living.

Right Livelihood

A person who practices Right Action is naturally drawn to a Right Livelihood. This is a step designed for laypersons because the Buddha's monastic disciples relied exclusively on alms. Right Livelihood means that the layperson should only pursue a living that will not cause harm or injustice to others. The Buddha gave as examples of wrong livelihoods the sale of arms and lethal weapons, the slaughter of animals and human beings, and the production of intoxicating drinks and poisons. In pursuing any acceptable form of work, the Buddha cautioned that a layperson's motivation should not be to make more money than one needs. Work should not be done to make money for the enjoyment of luxuries. If work is done for this purpose, then it is a wrong way of making one's livelihood in that it only deepens one's craving for, and attachments to, the pleasures of life. Further, if one is motivated by the desire to become rich for one's own benefit, one may become willing to use deceit or to exploit others to get ahead. If this happens, then any form of livelihood—even an honorable one—becomes a detriment to moral and spiritual living. By working in this "wrong" way, one is becoming more and more bound to what will be a dissatisfactory lifestyle for oneself while harming other persons at the same time. On the other hand, by working in the "right" way, one's work can itself be a vehicle for the development of compassion and loving kindness for others. One will then have the satisfaction of making a living for oneself and one's family, serving humankind, and personally advancing toward spiritual freedom all at the same time.

Right Effort

It certainly takes a great amount of effort to translate one's understanding, thinking, and aspirations into wholesome and skillful forms of speech, action, and work. In doing so, one needs to rid oneself of any unwholesome states of mind that unskillfully compromise one's spiritual journey to Awakening and Nirvana. One also needs to develop wholesome states of mind that skillfully advance that journey. Therefore, there are four types of Right Effort. First is the effort to "prevent" unwholesome states of mind from arising. Second is the effort to "abandon" unwholesome mental states that have already arisen. Third is the effort to "produce" wholesome states of mind. Fourth is the effort to "cultivate" wholesome mental states that are already part of one's mentality. Finally, it should also be noted that Right Effort not only builds a moral foundation for a wholesome life but also aids in cultivating the higher spiritual life. Right Effort can also be used to sustain the spiritual practices of mindfulness and meditation. In short, by Right Effort one's energy can be channeled into the skillful development of all aspects of the Buddhist life.

An example of Right Effort can be seen in the Buddha's advice concerning how to deal with temptations. If one is confronted with unwholesome mental states, such as evil desires, one should practice the second type of Right Effort, namely, the effort to abandon those states of mind. To do so, one should first be mindful of the particular object that is causing those desires. Then one should practice the third type of Right Effort by picturing to oneself, or turning one's attention toward, another object that will produce an opposite mental state, such as loving kindness. This is because the more one focuses on the object of temptation, the worse the temptation becomes. One should simply abandon the tempting object of desire for something that produces wholesome mental states. If the temptation still persists, one should make the effort to look at the broader situation and to visualize the painful consequences to oneself and to others that will happen if one pursues the temptation. If all this fails, one should practice another version of the third type of Right Effort; that is, one should make the effort to change one's environment so that new and more positive sensory input is produced.

Right Mindfulness

Right Mindfulness involves a state of keen awareness with regard to (1) one's body, what one is doing at a particular moment; (2) one's sensations, feelings, thoughts, and impulses at a particular time; (3) one's ideas or views; and (4) the true nature of things, namely, their transience, nonsubstantiality, and dissatisfactory nature. We discuss the actual practice of mindfulness in the next chapter. However, what is essential to mindfulness in all cases is a bare and nonprejudiced awareness that gives one a clear picture of one's dependently arisen mental, emotional, and physical processes and states that are occurring in the present moment. In one case, mindfulness may expose the truth about the impermanent process of one's experience. In another case, it may uncover the sensory, mental, or emotional factors that are interweaving in this process in ways that are either wholesome, unwholesome, or neutral.

The development of mindfulness prevents the person from being led astray in the spiritual journey by bodily sensations or by feelings, desires, thoughts, and ideas that play through the mind. In this sense, being mindful of what one is thinking and feeling can help one know where to direct Right Effort. For example, if one is mindfully aware of a certain desire—say, the desire for vengeance—and is aware of its unwholesome nature and possible consequences, one can see clearly where to use one's Right Effort to free oneself from this negative state of mind. In this way, mindfulness can contribute to one's Right Effort to free oneself from what are discerned to be unwholesome patterns of thought and behavior and from wrong or unjust situations in the world. Not to be mindful of one's own condition is to be moved unreflectively by inner thoughts, emotions, and desires like a puppet on strings. Not to be mindful of the dissatisfactory conditions of the world is not to be aware of how one should live responsibly and compassionately in particular situations. The clarity of mindfulness provides the mental awareness of self and world needed for skillfully changing oneself for the better and for skillfully contributing to bettering the world in which one lives.

Mindfulness practice is also directed toward one's ideas or views. The Buddha taught that the views one uses to understand life can themselves distort one's awareness of how things really are. We have already seen how the Buddha taught that if one believes in a substantial self that must be gratified for it to be happy, that view will blind one to what will, in fact, bring real and lasting happiness. Also, one can misread the facts of a certain situation in an effort to force them to fit one's political or religious ideology. Mindfulness of the conceptual lenses that one uses in viewing oneself and the world can help one see oneself and the world in a clearer, less judgmental, and more compassionate way. Finally, mindfulness practice involves focusing the mind on an object, thus contributing to the next step, namely, Right Concentration.

Right Concentration

By Right Concentration (*samādhi*), the Buddha meant a "one-pointedness of mind" (*cittasyaikāgratā*). It was this concentrated state of mind that helped the Buddha to his full realization of Awakening. His perfect wisdom, arising within the deepest state of concentration, illuminated the true nature of all things such that he realized the Four Noble Truths. Therefore, Right Concentration involves something more than just thinking hard about something. It involves a focused state of mind that supports penetrating insight leading to Awakening. This state of mental concentration also contributes to the healing and integrating of the various aspects of one's being into a pure and unified wholeness leading to Nirvana. Right Concentration achieves these transformative effects by stilling and focusing the mind, by pacifying distracting thoughts, and by purifying unruly emotions and inordinate desires that create *duḥkha.* It thereby brings about mental-emotional "equanimity," "peacefulness," and "harmony," which, in turn, foster the wisdom and mental-emotional integration needed to realize Awakening and Nirvana. The process of transformation achieved through Right Concentration is called "mental culture" (*bhāvanā*).

The Buddha taught specific practices that could be used to cultivate Right Concentration. In the next chapter, we explore a number of these techniques as we examine the original form of Buddhism based on the Buddha's teachings. For now, it is enough to indicate that there are two principal types of mental culture taught by the Buddha. First is "tranquillity" (*śamatha;* Pali: *samatha*) meditation, which is used to develop one-pointed mental concentration. A metaphor for this kind of calming meditation is cleaning a mirror. The ordinary mind is like a mirror covered by dust, in that its inherent clarity is "covered" with mental activity, and therefore cannot reflect reality clearly. With a mind that is made tranquil by meditation, persons can see more clearly what is real about themselves and the world. Tranquillity meditation quiets discursive thoughts and unruly emotions. While the resulting stillness of mind has a healing and integrating effect in and of itself, it also brings forth an inherent inner luminosity that can, in turn, be the basis for deeper penetrating insight into reality. Tranquillity practice also leads to the development of other forms of absorbing meditation, which we discuss in the next chapter.

The second principal type of meditation directly cultivates penetrating insight, and therefore is called "insight" (*vipaśyanā;* Pali: *vipassanā*) meditation. Right Concentration implies not only the concentrating and calming of the mind but also focusing insight into the dependently arisen factors of experience that contribute to, or bring the cessation of, *duḥkha.* For the Buddha, concentration involves turning one's mental focus onto the inner states of mind and processes of life in a manner that brings insight into the real nature of things. It is this insight that builds on mindfulness and cleanses the mind of defilements—of unwholesome states of mind such as worries and anxieties, doubts and craving, hatred and delusion. Insight also aids in cultivating wholesome mental qualities like awareness and knowledge, confidence and joy, leading ultimately to freedom and the wisdom that bring about Awakening and Nirvana. With the clarity of penetrating insight, and with the freedom it brings, one is better able to live in wise and compassionate ways that are of benefit to oneself and others.

Box 2.2

Experiencing What the Buddha Taught

After several years of Zen Buddhist meditation practice, I became curious about the relationship between meditation and the seemingly complex teachings on the self, suffering and the cause of suffering, and dependent arising. I knew from my study that the lists and categories of the early teachings were composed in atmospheres of deep meditation and contemplative investigation, and I was anxious to make this personal link as well.

I arranged to do a month-long retreat in a Tibetan Buddhist retreat center, under the supervision of the resident lama and his students. I found myself in a simple, quiet room under a rule of silence, solitude, and structured practice. Most of the day was devoted to sitting meditation, a simple mindfulness of breathing, which calmed and settled my mind and brought me into the present moment. Several hours of each day I studied the classical texts of the Tibetan Abhidharma, the "Higher Dharma" which comprises these teachings on impermanence, selflessness, and dissatisfactoriness. The lama then suggested structured contemplations in which I would quietly label thoughts as they arose and passed away, identifying how they were painful and looking into their impermanent and selfless aspects. Periodically, he or one of his students met with me, inquiring about my experience.

While I had been familiar with group practice settings, *sesshins* in the Zen tradition, this was my first solitary retreat. The long periods of mindful breathing were simple, naked, and grounding. But I was not prepared for the power of the contemplations, which the lama had given me. I watched the torrent of thoughts, emotions, and sense perceptions rush through my mind and despaired at being able to label them at all. Eventually, the torrent slowed to a river, and I was able to distinguish between thoughts and emotions, between emotions and sense perceptions. Yet they quickly raced by, constantly changing. As I experimented with ways of focusing my mind and labeling, I became more adept at the practice and continued for weeks of focused contemplation.

By the end of the retreat I was astonished—the relevance of the teaching of the Five Aggregates (*skandhas*) came alive! I could no longer regard my concerns, obsessions, and subconscious gossip as weighty and convincing. Instead, I experienced the insubstantiality and constantly changing quality of my experience and felt "myself" dissolve as well. What remained was a constant flow of fleeting vivid moments laced with luminous awareness and steady calm. The liberating message of the Buddha became one of inexpressible simplicity instead of endless numerical lists, compassionate method instead of metaphysics. It is clear why the "Enlightened One" placed so much emphasis upon personal experience in meditation rather than upon intellectual learning.

JUDITH SIMMER-BROWN
Naropa University

FIGURE 2.5. Seated Buddha; c. 475 C.E., India. Museum of Archaeology, Sārnāth, India.

Nirvana → is that freedom from dukkha that one realizes when the causes of dukkha are extinguished

Eightfold Path, we should note two eight steps takes place at different steps at a more elementary level in hat will only be fully dealt with later r example, a beginner may practice Truths at a more intellectual level of r may practice Right Understanding wisdom. The highest practice of the nd the *arhats*. Second, it should now inforce each other in the journey to ight Mindfulness and Right Effort Concentration contributes to Right t Speech, Right Action, and Right

Livelihood give form to Right Thought and also contribute a firm foundation for Right Mindfulness and Right Concentration. All these steps together ultimately lead to the attainment of Nirvana. The Buddha's ability to present the Dharma as a Path to Nirvana is one of the most significant features of the legacy of his teaching (see Figure 2.5).

NIRVANA

As mentioned earlier, because the Buddha himself did not describe Nirvana in any detail, many theories about it have been put forward over the centuries. In what follows, we do not try to present a developed theory about the nature of Nirvana. We only describe what, according to the early texts, its attainment entails in human experience. In most cases, this attainment is described in terms of what is brought to an end, of what ceases or is extinguished in the "blowing out" of Nirvana. For example, the Buddha says that Nirvana is "the complete cessation of craving (thirst), letting it go, renouncing it, being free from it, detachment from it" (*Saṃyutta-nikāya,* I, 136). Or elsewhere, a disciple of the Buddha, when asked about Nirvana, replied: "Whatever . . . is the cessation of greed, hatred and delusion, this is called Nirvana" (*Saṃyutta-nikāya,* IV, 251). We know from the Second Noble Truth that craving, and other negative mental formations like the Three Root Evils of greed, hatred, and delusion, are the cause of *duḥkha.* So in simplest terms, Nirvana is that freedom from *duḥkha* that one realizes when the causes of *duḥkha* are extinguished.

The term *detachment,* used in the quotation in the previous paragraph, often appears in the Buddha's description of Nirvana. For example, "If a monk is freed by turning away, by detachment in regard to things . . . it is fitting to call him a monk who has attained Nirvana here and now" (*Saṃyutta-nikāya,* III, 164). Detachment from things entails freedom from craving for, or clinging to, the things of this world in ways that keep one locked into unwholesome patterns of living. However, this kind of detachment does not mean that a person who enjoys the status of Nirvana does not care about others or about the suffering conditions of the world. Rather, while the Buddha refers to Nirvana as personally "secure" and "peaceful," when he describes the way a nirvanic person relates to others, he often mentions the Four Divine Abodes. Again, these four virtues are the wholesome relational attitudes of compassion, loving kindness, sympathetic joy, and equanimity. The virtue of equanimity means that one lives the virtues of loving kindness, compassion, and joyful affirmation of others equally with everyone, friend and foe alike. So it is clear that when a person is detached, he or she is *free from* reacting to others in unwholesome ways and is thereby *free to* respond to others in wholesome ways. It is said that when a person enjoys the freedom of Nirvana, he or she is like a lotus flower that rises out of the muddy waters. Detached from the unwholesome (muddy) states of mind, a nirvanic person's life flowers with the beauty of wholesomeness.

Besides living the Four Divine Abodes, the person who attains Nirvana is also said to live the Six Perfections that are cultivated in Buddhist spirituality.

These ideals are (1) selfless *generosity,* or charity; (2) benevolent *morality;* (3) *patient endurance* of the difficulties in life that cannot be changed; (4) *energy* to change what one can for the better; (5) the single-pointedness and equanimity of *meditation;* and (6) *wisdom* insight into the truth about existence. Such virtues flow naturally from the mind and heart of the enlightened person enjoying Nirvana. He or she does not have to "struggle" or "toil" to cultivate them anymore.

Note that the last perfection in this list is wisdom. Nirvana thus also entails the cessation of ignorance. In terms of the fire metaphor, the flames of negative states of mind that cause the burning of *duḥkha* are fully extinguished when the fuel that ultimately creates these fires, namely, ignorance, is eradicated. It is because of the cessation of ignorance in the attainment of Nirvana that the Buddha refers to Nirvana as an attainment of "absolute Truth" (*satya;* Pali: *sacca*).

Therefore, with inner freedom, detachment from things, care for all beings, the perfection of virtues, and wisdom realizing the Truth, one is finally free from *duḥkha* and attains the peaceful status of Nirvana. This status of peace and freedom is said by the Buddha to be "unmoved" by the events of life that ordinarily "move" one to negative and unwholesome states of mind. It is said that the person who enjoys this Nirvana is free from any "disturbance" or "oppression" that might limit or compromise his or her nirvanic status. Although the nirvanic person is not immune to such things as sickness, the problems of old age, and even death, in facing these ills one's mind is always "unmoved," "at rest," "peaceful and calm." And one continues to live kindly and compassionately for the good of all beings.

Nirvana is said by the Buddha to be more than just a moral attainment or an insight into the Truth. It is said to be a "supreme status" that is "holy." This supreme holiness, the Buddha said, is a "full consummation," or a "final end," that brings into human experience the "blessedness" of the "highest good." When one reads descriptive terms such as these, one can see that Nirvana is ultimately a sublime religious status. Because our words and concepts are derived from ordinary experience and reflection, language cannot fully convey this sublime status. Nirvana is a blessedness that is ultimately beyond ordinary conceptual understanding and description. Because this is so, the Buddha sometimes used a type of *via negativa* to help people understand something about Nirvana by saying what it is not.

Three negative words he often used are "unborn," "unconditioned," and "deathless." For example, in one text we read, "That monk who here is devoid of craving and passion attains to deathlessness, peace and the unchanging state of Nirvana" (*Sutta-nipāta,* 204). In another text, there is a famous definition of Nirvana:

> There is, O monks, an unborn, not-become, unproduced, not-compounded. Were it not, O monks, for this unborn, not-become, unproduced, not-compounded, no escape from the born, become, produced and compounded would be known. But, O monks, since there is an unborn, not-become, unproduced, not-compounded, there is an escape from the born, become, produced and compounded. (*Udāna,* 81)

That Nirvana is "unborn," "not become," or "unproduced" means that it is not the result of anything; it is not dependently arisen, or "born," like all worldly phenomena. Therefore, it also cannot be produced by the Eightfold Path or even the attainment of Awakening. It is a status that always is—one simply has to realize it in one's own experience. To say that Nirvana is "unchanging," "unconditioned," or "not-compounded" means that it is not like the phenomena of ordinary experience. As we have seen, all such worldly phenomena are dependently arisen, compounded, conditioned, and constantly changing. Only Nirvana is unchanging, uncompounded, unarisen, and not conditioned or moved by any factors of existence.

Finally, to say that Nirvana is "deathless" means that even death cannot condition it or bring it to an end. In this regard, it is important to note that the Buddha spoke of two types of Nirvana. First is Nirvana "with remainder" (*sopadhiśeṣa*), which means Nirvana with the Five Aggregates. This is the Nirvana that is attainable in this present existence. The Buddha himself is said to have lived this type of Nirvana for the last forty-five years of his life. The second type is Nirvana "without remainder" (*anupadhiśeṣa*), which is Nirvana without the Five Aggregates. This Nirvana is also called "Final Nirvana" (*parinirvāṇa*). It is the destiny of the Buddha or *arhat* because he or she, having attained full Awakening and Nirvana in this life, has no more karma to produce a new rebirth. Because this ultimate nirvanic status is "without remainder" of all elements of human experience, what actually happens to such a person after death is one of the questions necessarily left unanswered by the Buddha.

SUGGESTIONS FOR FURTHER READING

Anderson, Carol. *Pain and Its Ending: The Four Noble Truths in the Theravada Buddhist Canon.* Richmond, UK: Curzon Press, 1999.

Bodhi, Bhikkhu, and Nyanaponika Thera, trans. *Numerical Discourses of the Buddha: An Anthology of Suttas from the Anguattara Nikāya.* Lanham, MD: Rowman & Littlefield Publishers, 2000.

Carter, John Ross, and Mahinda Palihawadana. *The Dhammapada: The Sayings of the Buddha.* New York: Oxford University Press, 2008.

Dhamma, Rewata. *The First Discourse of the Buddha.* Boston: Wisdom Publications, 1997.

Gethin, Rupert. *Sayings of the Buddha: New Translations from the Pali Nikayas.* New York: Oxford University Press, 2008.

Gowans, Christopher W. *Philosophy of the Buddha: An Introduction.* London: Routledge, 2003.

Jayatilleke, K. N. *The Message of the Buddha.* New York: Free Press, 1976.

Nanamoli, Bhikkhu, and Bhikkhu Bodhi, trans. *The Middle Length Discourses of the Buddha: A New Translation of the Majjhima Nikāya.* Boston: Wisdom Publications, 1995.

Payutto, Phra Prayudh. *Buddhadhamma: Natural Laws and Values for Life.* Translated by Grant A. Olson. Albany: SUNY Press, 1995.

Pérez-Remón, Joaquín. *Self and Non-Self in Early Buddhism.* The Hague: Mouton, 1980.

Rahula, Walpola. *What the Buddha Taught.* New York: Grove Press, 1962.

Saddhatissa, Hammalawa. *Buddhist Ethics: The Path to Nirvana.* London: Wisdom Publications, 1987.

Sīlānanda, U. *Four Foundations of Mindfulness.* Boston: Wisdom Publications, 1990.

Walshe, Maurice, trans. *The Long Discourses of the Buddha: A Translation of the Dīgha Nikāya.* Boston: Wisdom Publications,1995.

Warren, Henry Clarke. *Buddhism in Translations.* New York: Antheneum, 1963.

3

Early Buddhism and the Way of the Elders

The Buddha said that after his passing, his followers would be guided by the Dharma and the *Vinaya*. This meant being guided by the "teachings" of the Buddha and by the particular "discipline" of the monastic community. Therefore, at the time of the first three-month retreat after the passing of the Buddha, the First Council of Buddhism was held at Rājagṛha to establish the authentic teachings and discipline. Chronicles of this "first recitation of the community" state that 500 *arhats* assembled to standardize an accepted oral record of what the Buddha said about both doctrine and moral and spiritual living.

THE FIRST COUNCIL: THREE BASKETS

In what scholars consider an idealized version, it is said that the Venerable Mahākāśyapa, who had called for the council, first questioned the elder Upāli about the rules of discipline taught by the Buddha. Upāli is said to have stated when and under what circumstances the Buddha taught each of the rules for the monastic order. Then Mahākāśyapa turned to Ānanda and questioned him about the many discourses of the Buddha. As a result of this council, what was recited by the community was said to have been memorized, establishing an oral tradition that was passed down for several centuries before being committed to writing. This oral tradition was divided into two collections, or "Baskets" (*Piṭakas*), that became the earliest form of Buddhist scripture. The collection of discourses of the Buddha make up the "Basket of Discourses," *Sūtra* (Pali: *Sutta*) *Piṭaka;* the collection of the Buddha's rules for the monastic community is known as the "Basket of Discipline," *Vinaya Piṭaka*.

A third collection of canonical teachings concerning the Dharma, called the "Higher Teachings," *Abhidharma* (Pali: *Abhidhamma*) *Piṭaka,* was also said by the tradition to have been recited by Ānanda at the First Council. However, this collection is actually the result of centuries of philosophical systemization based on lists and summaries of topics for discussion that may well have originated with the Buddha and may have been recited at the First Council. The Buddha's original teachings in the *Sūtra Piṭaka* were given in stories, illustrations, anecdotes, and so on, and were not an attempt to present a complete philosophical system. As the early Buddhists explained and defended their views, there developed certain philosophical viewpoints that were more formally and systematically presented in the *Abhidharma Piṭaka*. Centuries after the Buddha's passing, the emerging Buddhist sects added this later scriptural material, thereby producing the more fully developed "Three Baskets" (*Tripiṭaka;* Pali: *Tipiṭaka*), which was the authoritative scripture for much of early Buddhism.

Versions of the *Tripiṭaka* are preserved in the Pali language as well as in Sanskrit, Chinese, and Tibetan. The Pali canon is traditionally said to have been brought to Sri Lanka from northern India in the third century B.C.E., and was written down in the first century B.C.E. Scholars are skeptical that what we have today is the same as what was originally brought to Sri Lanka. What we do have today are a number of Pali texts divided into the three *Piṭakas*. The earliest of these Pali texts include the four primary *Nikāyas* ("Collections") of the Buddha's discourses (*sūtras*), as well as the *Vinaya* texts. The *Nikāya* material as found in the Chinese *Tripiṭaka* is referred to as the *Āgamas* ("Traditions").

The Sūtra Piṭaka

The *Sūtra Piṭaka* consists of the five *Nikāyas*. Using their Pali titles, the older four *Nikāyas* include the *Long (Dīgha), Middle-length (Majjhima), Grouped (Saṃyutta),* and *Numbered (Anguttara) Nikāyas.* It is these four *Nikāyas* that we referred to in the previous two chapters as the "earlier texts." A fifth *Nikāya,* the *Minor (Khuddaka) Nikāya,* contains some famous writings of a somewhat later date. Included here are the *Dhammapada,* a well-known anthology of Buddhist wisdom, and the verses of the *Jātaka,* 547 popular stories about Gautama Buddha's previous lives. In the first two chapters of this volume, we have already presented an introduction to the life and teachings of the Buddha based on the older parts of the *Sūtra Piṭaka*. Here we introduce the *Vinaya* and *Abhidharma Piṭakas.*

The Vinaya Piṭaka

The *Vinaya* has three divisions. First is the "Division of Rules" *Sūtravibhaṇga* (Pali: *Suttavibhaṅga*) that presents the "Code of Discipline" *Prātimokṣa* (Pali: *Pātimokkha*), which contains the precepts of the men's and women's monastic orders along with commentary. Second is the "Sections" *Skandhaka* (Pali: *Khandhaka*) that includes accounts of the Awakenings of the Buddha and his Great Disciples; accounts of the first two councils; rules for ordination and for the Days of Observance when the monastics practice meditation intensely; rules for the governance of the Saṅgha, and personal and social comportment; and rules for addressing offences within the monastic communities. Third is the "Accessory" *Parivāra* that was added later as a supplement and provides summaries, lists, and collections of stanzas.

Taking up the precepts of the *Vinaya* is done in two stages. From the age of eight, a child can take a lower, or novice, ordination. These persons undertake the Ten Precepts and are placed under the care of senior monastics, who become their mentors in the monastic life. The relationship between mentor and student should be, according to the *Vinaya,* like that of father to son or mother to daughter. The following is the typical formula for novice ordination. It includes the Three Refuges repeated three times and the Ten Precepts:

> Praise to the Blessed One, the *arhat,* the completely awakened One. I take refuge in the Buddha. I take refuge in the Dharma. I take refuge in the Saṅgha. . . . I take up the precept to refrain from taking life. I take up the precept to refrain from taking what is not given [stealing]. I take up the precept to refrain from sexual intercourse. I take up the precept to refrain from lying. I take up the precept to refrain from intoxicating drinks, which result in heedlessness. I take up the precept to refrain from eating at the wrong time [i.e., after noon]. I take up the precept to refrain from attending events where there is dancing, singing, music, or shows. I take up the precept to refrain from wearing garlands, perfumes, ointments, ornaments, or cosmetics. I take up the precept to refrain from using high or broad beds. I take up the precept to refrain from accepting gold or silver [i.e., money]. (*Khuddaka Patha,* 1, 2)

At the age of twenty, a person can take full ordination and become a monk, *bhikṣu* (Pali: *bhikkhu*), or a nun, *bhikṣuṇī* (Pali: *bhikkhuṇī*), literally, "almsman," or "almswoman." If one enters the Saṅgha as an adult, he or she must begin monastic life as a novice for a short time prior to full ordination. With this full ordination, the monastic takes on full responsibility for following what is the most important part of the *Vinaya,* namely, the *Prātimokṣa,* or "Code of Discipline." As a development of the Ten Precepts, these rules promote an ordered and peaceful way of life that is conducive to the attainment of Awakening and Nirvana and inspires confidence among the laity. In the Pali canon that is followed today in Sri Lanka and Southeast Asia, there are 227 rules for men, 311 for women.

The *Prātimokṣa* is supposed to be chanted twice a month at a ceremony attended by every monastic living in community. If a monastic has broken a rule, he or she is to confess to the assembly. If not, one is to maintain silence as a sign of purity. If one is ill and cannot attend the ceremony, he or she is to send notice of his or her purity. The prelude to the chanting is as follows:

> Now, I will recite the Prātimokṣa. Everyone should listen and pay close attention. If anyone has broken one of these rules, he should disclose it. Those who have not broken any of these rules should remain silent. . . . A monk who remembers breaking one of the rules but does not disclose it . . . is guilty of deliberately lying. Deliberate lying, Venerable Ones, has been declared by

> [the Buddha] to be an impediment to progressing on the path. Therefore, a monk who remembers breaking a rule and desires purification, should disclose it; for disclosing it will be beneficial to him. (*Mahāvagga*, II, 3, 1–3)

The actual rules themselves are arranged into categories according to the degree of seriousness. For example, in the rules for monks, the first four are the most serious rules, which if broken, lead to expulsion from the Saṅgha: intentional sexual intercourse, theft of something of value, murder of a human being, and false claims to the laity concerning one's attainments. Next are thirteen rules that require the Saṅgha to meet formally to deal with any infractions and to proscribe probation. These rules deal with sexual misconduct other than intercourse, the place and size of one's dwelling, causing or supporting a schism, and having a bad influence on the laity. Then, there are two more rules having to do with proper contact with women. The next thirty rules, which deal with such things as handling money (something that is not permitted) or obtaining articles of value, require confession and possible forfeiture. These are followed by ninety-two rules that only require confession if broken. They deal with issues like lying, verbal abuse, harming living beings, destroying plant life, and drinking liquor. Next are seventy-five rules of deportment that are followed by novices as well as fully ordained monastics. These rules help the members of the Saṅgha cultivate a graceful and dignified presence through the way they walk, beg alms (see Figure 3.1), eat, and so on. Finally, the last few rules outline procedures for resolving disputes.

FIGURE 3.1. Buddhist monks begging for food with alms bowls: Luang Prabang, Laos.

The Abhidharma Piṭaka

While the precepts given in the *Vinaya Piṭaka* formed the discipline of the Saṅgha, the *Abhidharma Piṭaka* evolved in ways that helped to form the philosophy of the Saṅgha. These more philosophical texts were likely beginning to be composed by the fourth century B.C.E. In the fully developed Pali canon, the *Abhidharma Piṭaka* consists of seven texts. Some of the texts, such as *The Enumeration of* Dharmas *(Dhammasaṅgaṇi)*, examine the "factors" *(dharmas;* Pali: *dhammas)* that constitute the physical world and mental experience, and the various mental and physical processes that are produced by them. The many factors of existence analyzed in these texts are refinements of such concepts as the Five Aggregates that were taught by the Buddha. Other texts discuss the process of perception, the working of the mind, the psychology of spiritual attainment, and the types of causal relationships entailed in dependent arising.

We introduce some of these *Abhidharma* ideas later in this chapter. Here, it may be instructive to quote some passages from at least one text, namely, *The Enumeration of* Dharmas. These passages show how a "good thought" can, given dependent arising, generate a series of wholesome mental states *(dharmas)*. Here, we just mention a series of ten of those states that result in Right Concentration, the eighth step in the Eightfold Path. First, the text lists the ten mental states, and then defines each one:

> When a good thought concerning the sense-desire realm has arisen, accompanied by gladness and knowledge, and has as its object a visible form, or a sound, smell, touch, mental state, or whatever [the object of the thought] might be, then there is [1] contact, [2] sensation, [3] perception, [4] volition, [5] thought, [6] application of thought, [7] sustained thought, [8] zest, [9] ease, and [10] self-collectedness.
>
> Born of [1] contact is . . . [2] pleasurable and easeful sensation, pleasurable and easeful feeling. . . . Also born of contact is [3] perceiving with an appropriate element of representative cognition. . . . The [4] volition that is [then] born is purposeful. . . . The [5] thought on that occasion forms ideas in the mind and heart which are clear.
>
> On that occasion, there is [6] an application, fixing, focusing of the mind. . . . [7] Sustained thought is the process, the sustained procedure, the progress and access [of the mind] which on this occasion is the [continuous] adjusting and focusing of thought.
>
> [8] Zest on this occasion is joy, rejoicing at, rejoicing over, mirth and merriment, felicity, exultation, and the transport of the mind. . . . [9] Ease is the mental pleasure, the mental ease, which on this occasion is a pleasant and easeful experience.
>
> [10] Self-collectedness then is the stability, solidity, absorbed steadfastness of thought. Here, there is an absence of distraction, balance, unperturbed mental processes, quiet, the faculty and power of concentration, of Right Concentration. (*Dhammasaṅgaṇi*, 1–11)

The text goes on to show how other wholesome states of mind arise from Right Concentration in this process of consciousness. Those wholesome states include faith, mindfulness, insight, right views, and the absence of the Three Root Evils, namely, hate, greed, and delusion. Here we see one of the central teachings of the *Abhidharma*, namely, that the cultivation of moral thoughts lays the foundation for Right Concentration, which in turn furthers one's advancement on the path to Awakening and Nirvana.

SECOND AND THIRD COUNCILS: MANY PATHS

About 100 years after the Buddha's death, a Second Council was held at Vaiśālī. The council was called because of a disagreement over certain rules in the *Vinaya*. However, problems did not end with this "second recitation" of the tradition. Scholars debate about what the points of dispute were that continued after the Second Council. Most recent scholarship suggests that there was continuing disagreement concerning the *Vinaya* rules. Doctrinal issues, many scholars claim, were not as important at that time, and differences in opinion about them would most likely not have led to schism. In any case, eventually there was a formal division in the Saṅgha. On one hand were the *sthaviras* (Pali: *theras*), or "elders"; on the other hand was the *mahāsaṅghika*, or "great community." The school of the elders is referred to as *Sthaviravāda* (Pali: *Theravāda*), meaning the "Way of the Elders."

As the *Abhidharma Piṭaka* was taking shape during the centuries after the Second Council, the Way of the Elders was also producing different viewpoints about the Dharma. These differences did become important and resulted in a second group splitting off from the Sthaviravādins. This group was called the Pudgalavāda ("Personalist School"). They believed that associated with the Five Aggregates, but not separate from them or identified with them, is an ongoing form of "personhood" *(pudgala)*. They felt that the impersonal analysis of the self, in terms of the many *dharmas*, could not account for the full experience of personhood, the unique identity of oneself as a person. On the other hand, the Sthaviravādins believed that by positing something called a "person," the Pudgalavādins were compromising the Buddha's teaching about no-self *(anātman)*.

Another group to leave the Sthaviravādin fold was the Sarvāstivāda ("All-Exists School"). In particular, the two factions had conflicting ways of understanding the nature of the *dharmas*, the factors of existence discussed in the *Abhidharma Piṭaka*. On the one hand in this debate was the Sthaviravādin sect, the Vibhajyavādin ("Distinctionist School"), and on the other hand was the Sarvāstivādins. The Sarvāstivādins claimed that the factors of existence not only exist in the present but also in the future and the past. They exist in "all" times: past, present, and future. The Vibhajyavādins claimed that the factors of existence only arise and exist in the present, distinct from the past and future. But for now it is important to note that eventually many of the Sarvāstivādins moved to the west and north of India. There, they founded centers that influenced Buddhist thought and practice in India and Central Asia for centuries to come.

The early tradition records that at about 250 B.C.E., King Aśoka called for a Third Council to be held at Pāṭaliputra to resolve another debate that had arisen among the Sthaviravādins. Scholars today are trying to discern what exactly was involved in this debate. Early scholarship taught that the differences had to do with the breaking away of the Sarvāstivādins. But most scholars today believe the debate had to do with another disagreement about the *Vinaya*. In any case, the council seems to have decided in favor of the Vibhajyavāda position within the Sthaviravāda fold.

These two councils give us a glimpse into the first divisions in early Buddhism. Eventually, there would be eighteen Abhidharma schools in the early Buddhist tradition. These schools differed in their interpretation of the philosophical materials found in the *Abhidharma Piṭaka*, hence the name Abhidharma schools. Taken as a whole, they constituted the mainstream of Buddhism in India until its extinction during the thirteenth century C.E. As we see in the next chapter, within that context, Mahāyāna Buddhism was founded and developed as a minority sect of Buddhism. Their doctrines and practices were developed in reaction to the Abhidharma traditions. Therefore, we explore in more depth the teachings of the Abhidharma schools in Chapter 5 when we discuss the full scope of Buddhist thought in India. There, we see how the Abhidharma ideas led to the basic teachings of Mahāyāna. In this chapter, we now turn our attention to one of the early Buddhist schools, namely, Theravāda. It is this form of early Buddhism that spread to Sri Lanka and Southeast Asia, where it has flourished to the present day. This sect of early Buddhism kept its Pali name for "The Way of the Elders" and has remained one of the major branches of Buddhism in the world. To introduce Theravāda, we need to begin with the person who is said by tradition to be responsible for its emergence onto the world scene, namely, King Aśoka (see Map 2).

KING AŚOKA

In 268 B.C.E., King Aśoka inherited the Magadhan empire, which covered most of the Indian subcontinent, except for the far south. Some years later, it is said that he converted to Buddhism but was only a nominal follower. Then eight years into his reign, after the bloody conquest of Kaliṅga in the northeast of India, King Aśoka began to appreciate the true implications of the Buddhist religion. The carnage and destruction of Kaliṅga filled him with remorse, and he began to take the Dharma of the Buddha seriously. King Aśoka recorded his experience in the following edict:

> When [King Aśoka] had been consecrated eight years, Kaliṅga was conquered with 150,000 people deported, 100,000 killed, and many times that number dead. But after that conquest of Kaliṅga, [King Aśoka] began to follow the Dharma, to love the Dharma, and to teach the Dharma. Now, the king feels sorrow over the conquest of Kaliṅga. . . . [He] is depressed even more because among the inhabitants were Brahmins, ascetics, adherents of other sects, and lay people, all of whom were obedient to elders, parents and teachers, who treated [others] . . . with respect, and were firm in their faith. All of these persons were injured, or killed, or separated from loved ones. . . . The fact that all people share in this

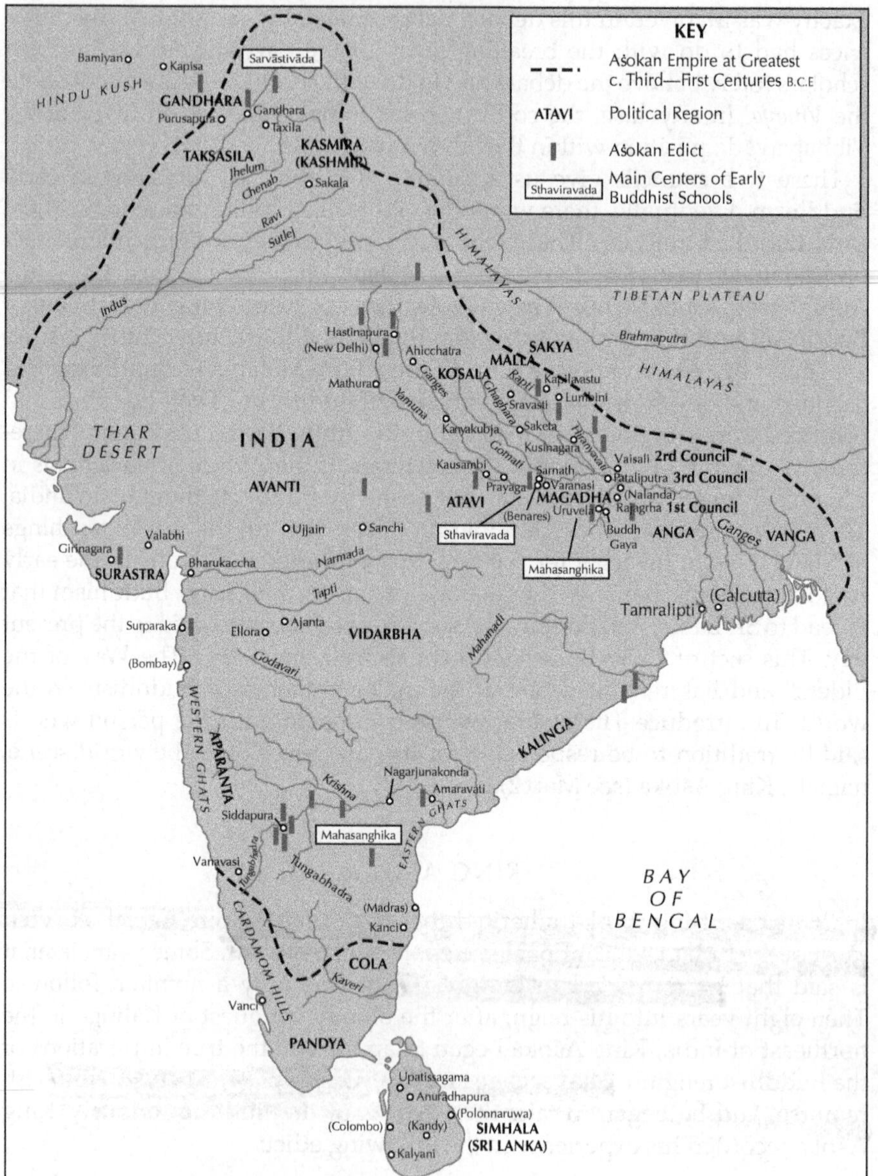
KEY
Aśokan Empire at Greatest c. Third—First Centuries B.C.E
ATAVI Political Region
Aśokan Edict
Sthaviravada Main Centers of Early Buddhist Schools
Bamiyan
Kapisa
Sarvāstivāda
HINDU KUSH
GANDHARA
Gandhara
Purusapura
Taxila
TAKSASILA
KASMIRA (KASHMIR)
Jhelum
Chenab
Sakala
Ravi
Sutlej
HIMALAYAS
TIBETAN PLATEAU
Indus
Hastinapura (New Delhi)
Ahicchatra
Brahmaputra
SAKYA
MALLA
KOSALA
Mathura
Kapilavastu
Lumbini
Sravasti
Saketa
Kanyakubja
THAR DESERT
INDIA
Kusinagara
Vaisali 2rd Council
Kausambi
Sarnath
Pataliputra 3rd Council
Prayaga
Varanasi (Benares)
MAGADHA
(Nalanda)
AVANTI
ATAVI
Uruvela
Rajagrha 1st Council
Ujjain
Sanchi
Sthaviravada
Buddh Gaya
ANGA
VANGA
Valabhi
Girinagara
SURASTRA
Bharukaccha
Narmada
Mahasanghika
Tapti
Tamralipti
(Calcutta)
Surparaka
Ellora
Ajanta
VIDARBHA
Mahanadi
(Bombay)
Godavari
WESTERN GHATS
APARANTA
KALINGA
Nagarjunakonda
Amaravati
Krishna
EASTERN GHATS
Siddapura
Mahasanghika
Vanavasi
Tungabhadra
BAY OF BENGAL
(Madras)
Kanci
CARDAMOM HILLS
COLA
Kaveri
Vanci
PANDYA
Upatissagama
Anuradhapura
(Polonnaruwa)
(Colombo)
(Kandy)
SIMHALA (SRI LANKA)
Kalyani
INDIAN OCEAN

MAP 2. Buddhism in India and Sri Lanka: c. third century B.C.E.–first century B.C.E.

> suffering is grievous to [King Aśoka]. . . . Indeed, [he] desires safety, self-control, calmness of mind, and gentleness for all beings. For, [King Aśoka] considers Dharma-conquest to be the greatest form of conquest. This kind of conquest he has won here [in India] and in all the borderlands up to 600 leagues away. . . . I had this inscription about the Dharma engraved so that all my sons and grandsons may not seek to gain new [military] conquests . . . that they may consider the only true conquest to be the conquest of the Dharma, which is of value both in this world and the next; and that their only pleasure may be in the Dharma. (*The Thirteenth Rock Edict*)

We can see from these words that based on his study of the Buddha's teachings, King Aśoka began to change his personal life and the way he governed the empire. Instead of conquering and ruling by physical force, he began to "conquer" and "rule" by the force of the Dharma. "Dharma-conquest" meant not only preaching Dharma in India but also sending proclaimers of the Dharma to other kingdoms. Some of King Aśoka's envoys were said to have been sent to the rulers of Syria, Egypt, and Macedonia to the west and Sri Lanka and Southeast Asia to the south. Tradition has it that around 250 B.C.E., he sent his own daughter and son—Saṅghamittā and Mahinda—to Sri Lanka. They went as nun and monk and succeeded in converting the whole country to Buddhism.

"Dharma-rule," for King Aśoka, meant to govern in a way that protected and cared for his subjects and also elevated them morally and spiritually according to the Dharma. In fact, he believed that by providing for the physical needs of his subjects, he was laying a foundation for them to follow the moral and spiritual life taught by the Buddha. King Aśoka became famous for his public works, which included providing wells and rest houses for travelers, hospitals for people and animals, care for orphans and the elderly, schools for children, and equal justice for all people. The supreme moral value he preached was *ahiṁsā,* or nonviolence, which he taught by example. He replaced his hunting trips with pilgrimages to Buddhist sites, made his large royal household vegetarian, banned animal sacrifices, and protected nonfood animals. Other values like generosity, mercy, truthfulness, respect for elders and teachers, and chastity were all virtues of the *Vinaya* that he tried to live himself and taught to his subjects.

In his support of Buddhism, King Aśoka convened the Third Council to restore harmony to the Saṅgha. He is said by later legends to have opened the original ten *stūpas,* and then to have distributed the relics of the Buddha to eighty-four thousand new *stūpas* throughout India (see Figure 3.2). In this way, he may have helped popularize devotion to the Buddha in *stūpa* rituals. Also, by using the ideology of Buddhism to support a national sense of righteousness, King Aśoka contributed to the unity of the empire as well as the well-being of his subjects. King Aśoka had his edicts relating to the Dharma, like the one just quoted, engraved on rocks and monolithic pillars around his kingdom.

These activities on behalf of Buddhism did not mean that King Aśoka failed to support other religions. In fact, he tended to the needs of Jain, Brahmin,

FIGURE 3.2. *Stūpa* commemorating the Dharma; c. 500 C.E., Sārnāth, India.

and Ājīvaka communities in his empire. He believed that all religions contribute to the righteousness of the people and should be respected in the spirit of religious toleration. His views were expressed in the following rock edict:

> [King Aśoka] honors members of all religious sects, whether ascetics or lay, by gifts and honors. But more important than gifts and honors is his support of

> the essential message of all sects. The essential message varies from sect to sect . . . [so] one should keep in check praising one's own sect and criticizing another's sect. . . . By doing so, one strengthens one's own sect and helps others too. By doing otherwise, one harms one's own sect, and does a disservice to the others. Whoever honors his own sect and disparages another's, whether from blind loyalty or intending to show his sect in a more favorable light, does the greatest harm to his own sect. Concord is best, where each person listens to and respects the teachings of others. . . . [T]he result is the progress of one's own sect, and the illumination of the Dharma. (*The Twelfth Rock Edict*)

THE WAY OF THE ELDERS

Theravāda, or the Way of the Elders that King Aśoka is said to have introduced into Sri Lanka and Southeast Asia, is based on the original teachings of the Buddha presented in the Pali texts and discussed in the previous chapter. There, we saw that Buddhist monastic experience involves an inner purification of the whole person through moral discipline, the practice of meditation, and the cultivation of wisdom. To appreciate Theravāda's practice of this threefold purification, this Way of the Elders that leads to Awakening and Nirvana, we need to see what it is that they feel requires purification. In other words, we need to understand the Theravāda view of the human condition.

In the previous chapter, we saw that the Buddha taught the Three Characteristics of existence—impermanence, dissatisfactoriness, and the lack of any permanent self. Further, for the Buddha, life is a continuous process of dependent arising in which each aspect of the world and conventional selfhood (the Five Aggregates) arises, develops, and ceases interdependently. We saw an example of this view in the Buddha's teaching about the twelve links of conditionality. We have also seen in this chapter that the *Abhidharma Piṭaka* presents a more detailed analysis of the processes of life. Based on these ideas, Theravāda teaches that human existence is constituted by numerous, dependently arisen, and constantly changing physical and mental factors (*dharmas*).

For Theravāda, this dynamic view of the human person as constituted by changing, interrelated mental and physical factors is not just an abstract theory. In Theravāda experience, the practices of mindfulness and meditation give one an awareness into the changing processes of life and into the various factors that constitute the mental–physical continuum. What one discovers thereby, Theravāda claims, is that these physical and mental factors ordinarily arise and pass away in a manner that is experienced as *duḥkha,* dissatisfactory. Every person's life is in some way dissatisfactory and needs a healing purification of those factors that are causing this condition of life. For Theravāda, the Way of the Elders is a Path of Purification (*visuddhimagga*) that is not only healing, but ultimately leads to Awakening and Nirvana.

The greatest systematizer of the Way of the Elders, the fifth-century C.E. monk named Buddhaghosa (see Figure 5.1 in Chapter 5), composed the classic

Theravāda text entitled *The Path of Purification (Visuddhimagga).* This book has helped define the Way of the Elders over the centuries in Theravāda countries. At the beginning of that text, Buddhaghosa says, "Purity should be understood as Nirvana, which is devoid of all stains, is utterly pure. The Path of Purification is the path to this purity [of Nirvana]" *(Visuddhimagga,* I, 5). Buddhaghosa goes on to situate each of the three divisions of the Eightfold Path in the following order. First is "morality" *(śīla),* which includes Right Speech, Right Action, and Right Livelihood. Second is "concentration" *(samādhi),* which includes Right Mindfulness, Right Effort, and Right Concentration. Finally is "wisdom" *(prajña;* Pali: *paññā),* which includes Right Understanding and Right Thought. The following is Buddhaghosa's rationale for this ordering:

> [One] should, having become well established in morality, develop the serenity and insight that are described as concentration and wisdom. This is how the Blessed One teaches the Path of Purification under the headings of morality, concentration and wisdom. . . . Here the training of higher virtue is shown by morality; the training of higher consciousness by concentration; and the training of higher understanding by wisdom. The system's goodness in the beginning is shown by morality. . . . Its goodness in the middle is shown by concentration. . . . Its goodness in the end is shown by wisdom. (*Visuddhimagga*, 1, 8, 10)

Let us look at each of these three aspects of this Path of Purification as discussed by Buddhaghosa one at a time to introduce the moral, meditative, and wisdom dimensions of the Way of the Elders, of the Theravāda Buddhist experience.

Cultivating Morality

Theravāda Buddhism provides its monastics and laity with high ethical standards. Today, scholars discuss the ways in which these standards for personal moral behavior may have informed social ethics in Theravāda countries. However, here we are not so interested in examining standards for moral and social behavior. Rather, we want to look at how morality plays a part in a purification of consciousness that, in turn, leads to the purity of Nirvana. In this sense, morality is part of the process of mental culture. It is primarily concerned with the inner inclinations, volitions, dispositions, and attitudes that motivate people to perform good or bad actions. The actions that define moral living are the result of ethical choices that are influenced by these motivating dispositions and attitudes. So moral purification, Theravāda teaches, is not just a matter of changing the way one behaves; one must also purify the interior attitudes that motivate one's actions. Therefore, the core of Theravāda morality is, "Refrain from doing evil deeds, perfect good dee and purify the mind; that is the teaching of the Buddha" *(Dhammap* It is precisely this purifying of the mind that brings the inne wholesomeness needed truly to refrain from evil and perfect g

Purification and Wholesomeness

Buddhaghosa emphasizes the importance of this inner moral purification in his ranking of the four ways in which morality is understood in Theravāda:

> [1] Morality as a matter of volition has to do with the kind of volition present in the one who . . . fulfills the practice of the precepts. . . . [2] Morality as a condition of consciousness is the mental states of non-greed, non-hate, and non-delusion . . . [3] Morality as restraint should be understood as restraining oneself in five ways: restraint by the precepts, restraint by mindfulness, restraint by knowledge, restraint by patience, and restraint by energy. . . . [4] Morality as non-transgression is the non-transgression, by body or speech, of the precepts that have been taken. (*Visuddhimagga*, I, 17, 18)

Buddhaghosa has ranked these four meanings of morality in a descending order of importance. At a minimum, morality means to follow the precepts with one's body and speech. More important is to develop an inner moral restraint from doing evil by observing the precepts, by mindfulness and knowledge, and by patience and energetic effort. Even more important is to remove the Three Root Evils of greed, hatred, and delusion from one's consciousness and to replace them with the virtues that are their opposites. Finally, most important is the ultimate moral purification of one's will that is entangled in desires that lead to *duḥkha*. As Buddhaghosa says, "a network of craving . . . arises again and again, up and down among the states of consciousness. . . . [Thus] this order of living beings is entangled in a network of craving, intertwined, interlaced by it" *(Visuddhimagga,* 1, 2). Morality, in its deepest sense in Theravāda, seeks "to disentangle this tangle" by purifying the will *(cetanā)* that determines what one desires in life. With a pure will, one's desire will not be for evil, but for the purity and goodness of Nirvana.

Moral culture at all of these four levels progresses gradually and in ordered stages through Theravāda practice. On the level of moral behavior, lay Buddhists follow at least the Five Precepts taught by the Buddha; the monastic Buddhists add the precepts of the *Prātimokṣa*. As these moral precepts are lived in the context of mental culture, they become internalized. That is, because they are rules that define what one is not supposed to do, as they are lived with "mindfulness and knowledge, patience and energy," they gradually generate inner moral "restraints," which is the second meaning of morality according to Buddhaghosa.

In the previous chapter, we saw that the precepts not only define what one should not do but also define the virtuous ways one should live. So, as the precepts are internalized as inner restraints, one is also developing moral virtues, or wholesome states of consciousness. Here we are at Buddhaghosa's third level of morality, where one's consciousness is purified of unwholesome states of mind, like the Three Root Evils, and wholesome states are cultivated. In the words of Buddhaghosa, "[Morality] is an upholding, meaning a basis that serves as a foundation for profitable states of mind. . . . The abandoning of an [unprofitable state] upholds a profitable state in the sense of providing a foundation for it" (*Visuddhimagga*, 1, 19). An example of this purification of consciousness by morality is when the precept of "not killing" is internalized as a spiritual attitude of compassion for all living beings.

We can now see that in Theravāda, the gradual purification of moral consciousness has two sides to it. On the one hand, the Buddhist begins to let go of unwholesome attitudes or dispositions. On the other hand, he or she begins to cultivate wholesome attitudes or dispositions. What is happening in this transformation of moral consciousness affects one's will, one's power of volition. At this fourth and deepest level of morality, one more and more wills the goodness that these wholesome states of consciousness embody. One therefore not only chooses good thoughts, deeds, and words with a purer mind and heart but also wills to pursue more fully the ultimate goodness of Nirvana.

Releasement for Nirvana

In speaking about volition or the will, we should make it clear that moral purification is ultimately not achieved by just a willful suppression of negative desires and unhealthy states of mind. Rather, in the practice of morality there is a gradual pacification of these unwholesome states through a process of self-understanding and releasement. For example, as one is able to gain insight into why it is that a certain negative desire arises in particular situations—and one is able to see the unfortunate effects that acting on it has on oneself and others—then one finds within oneself a stronger volition not to be controlled by this desire. Also, as one cultivates a virtue that is the opposite of the negative desire—and sees its effect on oneself and others in those same situations—then one develops a stronger volition to live in this more wholesome way. With this strengthened positive volition, there is a pacification of the power of the desire over one's will. That is, gradually with clearer insight, one's will is no longer controlled or "tangled" by the desire but is released from its grip. One freely wills to live in a wholesome way that benefits oneself and others. On the other hand, this does not mean that the Theravādin does not have to make difficult moral choices, and even painful sacrifices. As Buddhaghosa said, restraint is an important part of morality. While pacification develops through gradual growth in insight, there is always need for renunciation.

The purity of the wholesome, disentangled moral will and consciousness then becomes a basis for the next two aspects of the Way of the Elders, namely, the practice of concentration and the attainment of wisdom. In this way, morality's contribution to the Path of Purification produces not only growth in virtue and freedom of the will but also a necessary foundation for spiritual practice. In this regard, Buddhaghosa says,

> Once one's morality is perfected, one's mind then seeks nothing else than the perfection of Nirvana, the state of utter peace. Such is the blessed fruit of morality. . . . So, let the wise person know it well, this root of all the branches of perfection. (*Visuddhimagga*, 1, 159)

Box 3.1

A Message for Everyone

I noticed a young man making his way toward me through the crowd at a Sunday night Meet-Your-Neighbors party at a ski condominium a few years ago.

"My parents just met you," he said, nodding in the direction of a couple I'd talked with earlier,"and they said you were a Buddhist teacher. I'm studying Buddhism in my World Religions class. What kind of Buddhist are you?"

"I teach at Spirit Rock Meditation Center," I replied. "The program there is based on mindfulness and *metta,* loving kindness, the principal meditation practices described by the Buddha in the Pali Canon."

"Oh, I see," he said, "that's *Theravāda* Buddhism, isn't it?"

"Yes, it is," I replied.

"Is it true," he asked, "that those were the selfish Buddhists who were only interested in their own enlightenment and not in the liberation of all beings?" I hope I did not wince at what I recognized as a not uncommon survey textbook, shorthand differentiation of *Hinayāna* and *Mahāyāna* traditions. It is true that the Buddha was a monk and—in keeping with the culture of his time, which considered the renunciate path as ideal for spiritual seekers—he did encourage people to "go forth into homelessness" as a support to their practice. It is also true that he taught laypeople, ordinary householders as well as kings. His message of liberation for "all beings" is that craving is the cause of suffering, that the end of suffering is possible, that peace is possible in this very life, that insight leads to wisdom, which manifests as compassion on behalf of all beings. This message that *Theravāda* proclaims has remained central to Buddhism for the 2,500 years of its evolution through different cultures and different times.

SYLVIA BOORSTEIN
Spirit Rock Meditation Center
Marin County, California

Because the status of Nirvana includes perfected morality, the practice of morality in Theravāda generates a deep seeking for Nirvana, which can only be found by further progress in the Path of Purification. With this questing spirit, one is more inspired to practice concentration and attain wisdom.

Concentration

Buddhaghosa begins his comments on this second aspect of the Path of Purification by saying,

> Concentration is . . . a profitable single-pointedness of the mind. . . . It is concentration in the sense that it entails the act of concentrating the mind . . . the centering of consciousness and the factors of consciousness evenly and rightly on a single

> object. . . . It is the state, in virtue of which, consciousness and its many factors remain evenly and rightly on a single object undistracted and unscattered. (*Visuddhimagga*, III, 2, 3)

Buddhaghosa then goes on to discuss the traditional forty objects on which one can concentrate in meditation. First are the ten *kṛtsnas* (Pali: *kasiṇas*), or objects and concepts used to calm and focus the mind in meditation. These include earth, water, air, and fire, as well as forms of color, light, and a limited space. Second are the ten types of bodily decay used in meditation to develop detachment to material existence. Third are the ten recollections of positive qualities associated with the spiritual life, namely, the qualities of the Buddha, Dharma, and Saṅgha; morality and generosity; faithfulness and peace; and mindfulness of the body, death, and breathing. Fourth are the Four Divine Abodes that also need to be cultivated in meditation. Fifth are the states to be attained in the Four Formless Meditations. And finally, there are certain nutriments and elements that can also be used in meditation practice.

Mindfulness Practice

One example of these concentrating meditations is mindfulness of body and breathing. Actually, the teaching on mindfulness that is most revered by Theravāda Buddhism down to today is contained in an early Buddhist text, *The Establishment of Mindfulness (Satipaṭṭhāna Sutta)*, which is said to be taught by the Buddha. This text describes not only mindfulness of body and breathing but also other forms of mindfulness that contribute to concentration, Awakening, and Nirvana. The following are passages from that text concerning mindfulness in the pursuit of purification:

> There is, O monks, this particular way for purifying beings, for overcoming sorrow and distress, for the extinguishing of pain and sadness . . . for the attainment of Nirvana: The Four Foundations of Mindfulness. What are these four? Contemplating the body as body . . . sensations as sensations . . . the mind as the mind . . . and mental objects as mental objects. . . .
>
> How, O monks, does one contemplate the body as body? Having gone into the forest, or to the foot of a tree, or to a lonely place, a monk sits down cross-legged, holding erect his body and establishes himself in mindfulness. Mindfully he breaths in, and mindfully he breaths out. Breathing in a long breath, he knows that it is a long breath; and breathing out a long breath, he knows it is a long breath. . . . Breathing in a short breath, he knows it is a short breath; and breathing out a short breath, he knows it is a short breath. . . . He trains himself by thinking, "I will breathe in, being conscious of my whole body. . . . I will breathe out, being conscious of my whole body. . . . I will breathe in, calming my whole body. . . . I will breathe out, calming my whole body."
>
> And how is it, O monks, that one abides contemplating sensations as sensations [or feelings as feelings]? When a monk experiences a pleasant sensation [or feeling], he knows that it is pleasant. Then, experiencing an unpleasant sensation, he knows that it is unpleasant. . . . He abides contemplating the arising of

> sensory [or emotional] states, and their passing away. . . . In this mindfulness, he has only a bare awareness of the sensations.
>
> And how is it, O monks, that one abides contemplating the mind as mind? When a monk has a greedy mind, he knows it is greedy; when it is free from greed, he knows it to be so. When a monk has a hating mind, he knows it is hating; when it is free from hatred, he knows it to be so. When a monk has a deluded mind, he knows it is deluded; when it is free from delusion, he knows it to be so. . . . He abides contemplating the arising of mental phenomena, and their passing away. . . . In this mindfulness, he has only a bare awareness that there is mind. (*Dīgha-nikāya*, 11, 290–292, 298–300)

After presenting the mind with its Three Root Evils of greed, hate, and delusion, the text goes on to discuss the arising and passing away of other mental phenomena, both positive and negative, including forms of craving, the experience of the Five Aggregates, various mental factors leading to Awakening, and the Four Noble Truths. The point is clearly made that mindfulness concentrates the mind in a "bare awareness" of the dependent arising of physical, emotional, sensory, and other mental states, as well as the ideas and views one entertains. One gains, thereby, a clearer understanding of oneself and the world as they really are (*yathābhūtam*). Therefore, through mindfulness practice, one can begin to uncover what is often hidden from one's awareness: the dispositions and attitudes that affect moral and spiritual life. This mindful concentration can contribute to purifying one's mind and body of discerned unwholesome patterns of thought and action. Finally, it is important to note that in this mindfulness practice, one is not trying to alter any of the negative states one uncovers, but just to observe them and to gain insight into their nature and effect on one's life. While there are other techniques to alter one's mental-emotional life, the Four Divine Abodes for example, the assumption behind mindfulness is that awareness naturally produces alteration.

Four Divine Abodes

A second example of the forty objects of concentration are the Four Divine Abodes—loving kindness, compassion, sympathetic joy, and equanimity. Loving kindness is an attitude of pure goodwill toward self and others that always seeks the welfare and happiness of all beings. In loving-kindness meditation, one learns to develop this attitude and to extend it to all living beings. Compassion, an attitude of pity or empathy for oneself and others who are suffering, contains the desire to free all beings from pain. Again in compassion meditation, one develops and extends this attitude to all living beings. Sympathetic joy is an attitude of joyful affirmation of the dignity and value of oneself and others. Here, too, in meditation, one learns to develop such joyful sympathy and extend it to all living beings. Finally, equanimity meditation breaks down barriers between oneself and others and generates an attitude of universal embracement of all beings. This type of meditation helps one share the same degree of loving kindness, compassion, and sympathetic joy with all persons, those who are lovable and those who are not, both friends and enemies.

As we saw when we discussed morality earlier, Theravāda teaches that the negative attitudes or dispositions of the human heart, which result in unwholesome thoughts, words, and actions, are gradually pacified with the cultivation of their opposites. Therefore, the development of the Four Divine Abodes is seen as an aid to overcoming such unwholesome states of mind as the Three Root Evils of greed, hatred, and delusion. Buddhaghosa described how loving-kindness meditation can overcome hatred:

> One should seat oneself comfortably on a well-prepared seat in a secluded place. Then one should contemplate the dangers of hate. . . . Thereupon, one should begin to develop loving kindness in order to rid the mind of hate. . . . First of all, loving kindness should be developed only toward oneself by repeatedly thinking, "May I be happy and free from suffering. May I keep free from enmity, affliction, and anxiety, and live happily." . . .
>
> But, does not this attitude conflict with the [teachings of the Buddha]? It does not, because in it one is referring to oneself as an example. . . . One should develop this attitude in this way, "I am happy. And just as I want to be happy and dread pain and death, so too do other beings." Then with one's happiness as an example of what others want, the desire for others' well-being and happiness will arise in oneself. This method was indicated when the Blessed One said, "I visited all parts of my mind, and found none dearer than myself. The self of every other person is likewise dear to them. Who loves oneself will never harm another." . . .
>
> So, one should first, as an example, pervade oneself with loving kindness. Next, in order to proceed easily, one should recollect the kindnesses . . . that inspire love . . . given by a teacher or equivalent . . . thereby developing loving kindness toward that person. . . . If a monk is not content with just that much loving kindness, and wants to break down more barriers, he should develop loving kindness toward a beloved friend . . . then toward neutral person . . . then toward an enemy. If resentment arises when one applies loving kindness toward an enemy, because one remembers wrongs done by that person, one should get rid of that resentment in the following way. Enter repeatedly into the loving kindness for one of the first mentioned persons, and then each time direct that loving kindness toward the enemy. (*Visuddhimagga*, IX, 1–3, 8–12, 14)

After giving more ways of overcoming resentment and hatred, Buddhaghosa says that if one can enter a certain level of meditative concentration, then one should practice the following kind of loving-kindness meditation as taught by the Buddha in *Dīgha-nikāya* (I, 250):

> Now it is by means of . . . meditation that one "dwells focused on one direction [of the compass] pervading it with loving kindness from one's heart. Likewise, one should do the same in the second direction, the third direction, above, below, and all around. Everywhere and equally one dwells pervading the entire world with loving kindness from the heart, abundant, exalted, measureless, free from enmity, and free from all afflictions." (*Visuddhimagga*, IX, 44)

Four Lower and Higher Meditations

Besides mindfulness and the Four Divine Abodes, concentration on the Path of Purification also includes the Four Meditations *(dhyānas;* Pali: *jhānas),* which the Buddha himself used in attaining his Awakening. The first of these four calming meditations achieves an inner peacefulness, free of bother by passions and evil states of mind, while one continues to think discursively, to be joyful, and to feel deep happiness. The second brings about the cessation of discursive thought, while the third brings joyfulness to an end, leaving only happiness or a sense of well-being. In the fourth of these meditations, even happiness is transcended, thus bringing its opposite (unhappiness) also to an end. In this deep state of meditative peace, there is only pure and clear equanimity of mind.

Because this concentrated state of mind is one of equanimity, in this meditation one can understand all things with equal clarity and penetrating insight. Thereby, one is better able to understand the true nature of all life. This is what the Buddha did at the time of his Awakening. The lesson we learn from the fact that the Buddha did not just remain in the quiet peace of this fourth meditation is that such inner absorption is not the final goal of the Theravāda Buddhist quest. The real goal is awakening to the full Truth and the attainment thereby of Nirvana. Therefore, Theravāda continues to use these Four Meditations to calm and integrate the mind, pacify unruly mental-emotional states, and purify one's awareness with luminous equanimity so that one can see reality more clearly (see Figure 3.3).

Among the forty objects for meditation are also the objects of the Four Formless Meditations. The objects of these "higher" meditations are (1) boundless space, (2) boundless consciousness, (3) nothingness, and (4) neither perception nor nonperception. In the first of these Formless Meditations, according to Buddhaghosa, one moves from an awareness of a spatial object to spatiality as such. In the second, one lets go of any awareness of spatiality and gives attention to consciousness as such. In the third, one lets go of any awareness of spatiality or consciousness, so that one is aware of nothing at all. Buddhaghosa explains this third Formless Meditation with the following metaphor: "Suppose a person sees a community of monks gathered together in a meeting hall. . . . Then at the conclusion of their business, they all depart. The man then returns and stands in the doorway seeing the room as empty" *(Visuddhimagga,* X, 35). In the same way, Buddhaghosa says, one finds in the third Formless Meditation that boundless consciousness and space have simply "disappeared."

In the fourth Formless Meditation, there is no perception in the ordinary sense, but only a very subtle perception. Buddhaghosa explains:

> By "neither perception" is meant that perception is not capable of performing its [ordinary] function of perceiving. By "nor nonperception" is meant that perception is still present, but in a very subtle form, as a kind of residual form. (*Visuddhimagga*, X, 52)

FIGURE 3.3. Young Burmese monk meditating: Bagan, Myanmar.

Buddhaghosa says that this very subtle awareness includes not only perception but also all the other states of mind. In other words, this is the highest meditative state of subtle, pure, clear, peaceful, one-pointedness awareness. The value of this meditative experience is that its refined purity, clarity, and subtle peacefulness are a "taste" of the "flavor" of Nirvana.

However, this formless meditative taste is not the same as Nirvana itself because the latter is a permanent condition enjoyed in the midst of the world, not just in a meditative state. Also, Nirvana includes not only peacefulness and purity but also compassion, joy, and loving kindness in relationship to all living beings. On the other hand, this refined meditative state encourages one to continue on the Path of Purification because its subtle awareness gives one an appreciation for the beauty, freedom, and goodness of Nirvana. The Buddha also pointed out that these Four Formless Meditations are impermanent, just like anything else in life. Therefore, those who practice them can gain a better appreciation of the truth of impermanence and the need for nonattachment even to spiritual attainments.

Supernormal Abilities

Associated with these higher mediation practices are five types of supernormal abilities *(siddhi;* Pali: *iddhi)* that can occur in the lives of advanced practitioners. First are certain supernormal powers such as being invisible, walking through solid objects or on water, traveling through the air, and so on. Second is an ability, called "divine ears," by which one can hear both human and divine beings who are far away. Third is the ability to know what is in the hearts and minds of other persons. Fourth is the ability to recall one's past lives. Fifth is an ability, called "divine eyes," by which one can see the passing away and rebirth of beings due to their karma. These abilities are not understood as gifts bestowed by a divine being, but as potentials that all persons could realize if their minds were developed adequately through meditation. Thus, these abilities are *not* signs of holiness and are *not* essential to the attainment of Nirvana.

In fact, although these powers can be used to help others, they can also be hindrances to one's liberation if one becomes attached to them or prides oneself on possessing them. In this regard, we should remember that one of the reasons for expulsion of a monastic from the Saṅgha is boasting about spiritual attainments. This warning about supernatural powers reinforces the Theravāda view that the primary goal of the meditative experience in Buddhism is the fostering of a pure moral consciousness on the one hand, and a penetrating clarity of insight on the other. In Buddhaghosa's words, concentration "cleans the defiling stains and their [moral] pollution" and "provides the benefit of insight by serving as the proximate cause of such insight" *(Visuddhimagga,* XI, 121, 125). Concentration thereby deepens both the moral and wisdom aspects of the Path of Purification.

Box 3.2

Inner Peace, Outer Harmony

I was born into a Buddhist family in a Buddhist country and have spent about sixty years of my life as an ordained monk. Theravāda Buddhist culture is, therefore, deeply ingrained in my being. But I have lived now thirty-three years in the West in countries where Buddhism is either completely unknown or at best a minority faith practiced by a few. Part of my work has been to spread knowledge of the teachings to a wider audience. This has given me the opportunity to assess what it is about Buddhism, and especially about Theravāda Buddhism, which appeals to people who have not been born and brought up with it.

I see one of the key features of the Theravāda tradition as being relatively free of complicated rites and rituals. Its approach is refreshingly simple and straightforward. For laypeople, there are Five Precepts, accepted voluntarily and to be followed in daily life. This establishes a moral platform which gives spiritual meaning to everything Buddhists do and say. Meditation then helps them to develop their characters and personalities and leads them toward contentment and joy.

It is only too easy to allow ourselves to cultivate a frenzied state of mind. This destroys any possibility of being either peaceful or happy and gives rise to further duḥkha. Meditation can help anyone who wants to live a life free from tension, anxiety, and the other forms of contemporary misery. It enables us to experience a life of peace and joy, filled with the kind of understanding which will allow us to observe events as they happen without reacting to them in a way which generates negative thoughts and emotional turmoil.

Meditation ultimately purifies the heart of all its negative emotions, and It encourages a state of mind in the individual in which selfishness is transformed into generosity, hatred into love, cruelty into compassion, and so on. It also deepens the individual's ability to develop warm and meaningful relationships, thereby leading to personal contentment and happiness.

Out of the development of such inner peace and outer harmony, the individual begins to see human existence as it really is. He or she sees not only how suffering is created in the mind of the sufferer but also how that suffering can be overcome and transformed. For Buddhism, wisdom includes the many insights that meditation brings about whereby persons see how they create suffering for themselves and others. It is this wisdom that is at the very core of Buddhism: "Meditation is impossible for one who lacks wisdom, wisdom is impossible for one who does not meditate. One that both meditates and possesses wisdom is near Nirvana" *(Dhammapada,* 327).

I am utterly convinced of the relevance of Theravāda Buddhist teachings to the problems of everyday life in the modern world, and it is my hope that more and more people will come to benefit from hearing the Dharma.

MOST VEN. DR. M. VAJIRAGNANA

Tranquillity Meditation

From this introduction of concentration on the Path of Purification, one can see that various types of meditation seek to produce either tranquillity (*śamatha;* Pali: *samatha*) or insight (*vipaśyanā;* Pali: *vipassanā*). Some of the forty objects of meditation, for example, are used to center, unify, purify, and still the mind in calm abiding or tranquillity. A kind of meditation that produces these results is called "tranquillity meditation." It produces the serene mind that is needed for mental culture, especially for the development of insight that untangles the unwholesome patterns of thought, speech, and action. Insight does so by uncovering and pacifying the negative attitudes and dispositions that cause these afflictive patterns. Meditation practice that generates insight is called "insight meditation."

Insight Meditation

Insight meditation not only gives one a deeper realization of the source of one's own *duḥkha* but also gives one a more profound awareness of the true nature of life itself. One gains insight into the impermanence of life, its dependent arising, and the fact that all phenomena in the process of life are lacking in independent and permanent selfhood. Here, we can see that Buddhist insight meditation links concentration and the final aspect of this path, namely, wisdom. As insight gradually evolves into wisdom, there is greater clarity concerning the Dharma, and the purification of mind and heart continues to grow toward full Awakening. As we will see later, the practice of insight meditation has become popular today both in Asia and more globally due to the crucial role it plays in the growth of Awakening. Theravāda teaches that this growth is possible because the original nature of the mind is pure luminosity. So, when ignorance is removed from the mind by the penetrating insight of wisdom, its nature as pure luminosity becomes the basis of Awakening and Nirvana. Thus, we reach the third and final aspect of the Theravāda Path of Purification, wisdom.

Wisdom

The wisdom aspect of the Path of Purification presents us with the core of enlightened Theravāda Buddhist experience. Here, insight meditation becomes the dominate form of meditative practice. Buddhaghosa says,

> Wisdom has the characteristic of penetrating insight into the essential nature of phenomena. Its function is the abolishing of the darkness of delusion, which conceals the essential nature of phenomena. . . .
>
> How is wisdom developed? Such things as the Five Aggregates, the bases, elements and faculties [of experience], the Four Noble Truths, dependent arising, etc. are the soil of wisdom. The purification of morality and concentration are the roots of wisdom. The Five Purifications . . . are the trunk of wisdom. After

> one performs morality and concentration as the roots of wisdom, then one should fortify wisdom by learning and questioning about those things that are the soil of wisdom. Then one can develop the Five Purifications that are the trunk of wisdom. (*Visuddhimagga*, XIV, 7, 32)

What is meant here is that by practicing the first two aspects of the Path of Purification—namely, morality and concentration—one is establishing the "roots" of wisdom. Then, one can examine the "soil" of wisdom, namely, those things that give nourishment to wisdom's growth. These include the many factors of existence, like the Five Aggregates and dependent arising, that one will need to understand with penetrating insight for wisdom to develop. Finally, the Five Purifications, which we introduce next, can then be used to actually develop wisdom, like the growing of a tree trunk.

Five Purifications

After preparing the "roots" of wisdom by morality and concentration, the first step in the direct practice of wisdom is learning, in some depth, about its "soil." In particular, this means learning about the nature of the Five Aggregates, the factors and faculties that account for human experience, the Four Noble Truths, and the dependent arising of existence. When one's learning about these realities, which we have already discussed in the previous chapter, has reached a certain degree, then one can develop the first of the Five Purifications. This is called "Purification of View." It entails the clarification, by penetrating insight, of the views one has learned about all the various mental and material aspects of life. Next, one develops "Purification by Overcoming Doubt." This involves the purification, again by penetrating insight, of any doubts one might have about what one has learned concerning the cause and effect processes that account for the conditionality of life. In particular it involves insight into the dependent arising of the Five Aggregates in the past, present, and future as influenced by karma. Third, one develops "Purification by Knowledge and Insight of What Is the Path, and What Is Not the Path." Here, one's penetrating insight is focused on what one has learned about the path that leads to Nirvana. In so doing, one is able to abandon any false views or misunderstanding about what leads one to Nirvana.

In the fourth purification, "Purification by Knowledge and Insight of the Way," one develops a deeper wisdom about all of life by moving through a spiritual crisis. One first contemplates the "rise and fall" of the mental and physical elements of life. In so doing, one deepens his or her insight into the Three Characteristics of existence—the impermanence, dissatisfactory nature, and nonsubstantiality of all phenomena. When one focuses one's insight onto the "breaking up" of all phenomena, one is gripped by a "great terror." One experiences the fear over the dissolution of one's own mind and body and cannot find any consolation in the things of this world, because they too will pass away. Thus, one feels a desire to escape from this situation, the desire for freedom from the rising and falling of this impermanent life. Through this desire, one becomes detached from the world; with this dispassionate mind, one again looks at the Three Characteristics of life. Now one's insight meditation is more clear and stable, there is a deeper calm-awareness of life, along with renewed energy, strength, and determination to attain Nirvana. It is said that by this new and more profound wisdom, one enters the "gateway" to liberation.

Finally, one reaches the fifth purification, "Purification by Knowledge and Insight." In the Way of the Elders, the Purification by Knowledge and Insight is the final step on the Path of Purification. In the First Sermon of the Buddha, which we read in Chapter 2, it is said that it was with "knowledge and insight" that the Buddha attained his Awakening. Theravāda claims that this awakening knowledge and insight can be attained through a Purification by Knowledge and Insight that entails what are called the Four Paths.

The Four Paths

The Four Paths are really levels of the experience of Nirvana—direct insight into Nirvana—that at the fourth level includes realization of the goal of early Buddhism, namely, full Awakening and Nirvana. Here again are Buddhaghosa's words about this final segment of the Way of the Elders:

> Next comes a change-of-lineage consciousness. . . . Purification by Knowledge and Insight consists of knowledge of the Four Paths, that is, the path of the Streamwinner, the path of the Once-returner, the path of the Never-returner, and the path of the *arhat*. . . . The thick murkiness that hides the truth has been dispelled. . . . Then when knowledge's repetition [of the aspects of life] has ended, the change-of-lineage consciousness arises which has as its object the signless, unborn, unconditioned, cessation, Nirvana. . . . As one enters into this cessation, Nirvana, one's [consciousness] lineage changes. . . . So is the knowledge associated with the path of the Streamwinner. . . .
>
> A Streamwinner makes it his task to reach the second plane by reducing both sensual desire and ill-will. . . . He works the field of mental formations with the knowledge that they are impermanent, dissatisfactory, and lacking in any permanent self. Thus he embarks on a progressive series of insights. . . . The knowledge associated with this is the knowledge of the path of the Once-returner. . . .
>
> A Once-returner makes it his task to reach the third plane by abandoning, without any remainder, both sensual desire and ill-will. . . . He works over and turns up the same field of mental formations with the knowledge that they are impermanent, dissatisfactory, and lacking in any permanent self. Thus he embarks on a progressive series of insights. . . . The knowledge associated with this is the knowledge of the path of the Never-returner. . . .
>
> A Never-returner makes it his task to reach the fourth plane by abandoning, without remainder, craving for existence in the form-realms, craving for existence in the formless-realms, pride, restlessness and ignorance. He works over and turns up the same field of mental formations with the knowledge that they are impermanent, dissatisfactory, and lacking in any permanent self. Thus he

> embarks on a progressive series of insights. . . . The knowledge associated with this is the knowledge of the path of the *arhat*. . . .
>
> At this point, this *arhat* . . . is one of the Great Ones with all cankers destroyed. He bears his last body, he has laid down the burden, reached the goal and destroyed the fetters of becoming, he is rightly liberated with final knowledge, and is worthy of the highest offerings of the world and its deities. (*Visuddhimagga*, XXII, 1–2, 4–5, 22–23, 25–26, 28–30)

These Four Paths were said, by even the early Buddhist texts, to have been taught by the Buddha. The first of the Four Paths is that of the Streamwinner, whose "stream" or "lineage" of consciousness changes radically as one gains direct knowledge of Nirvana. Buddhaghosa says that this knowledge is not full Nirvana, but more like a "glimpse" of Nirvana because certain defilements still "cloud" the Streamwinner's mind. However, even in this glimpse of insight, the person has destroyed three of the Ten Fetters, namely, *doubt* concerning the Buddha and his teachings, *belief* in the saving power of rites and ceremonies, and *delusion* concerning the impermanence of selfhood. One who has attained this state will not be reborn in a lower realm, such as the hells, the animal realm, or the realm of the hungry ghosts. Also, one is assured of attaining Nirvana in, at most, seven more lifetimes.

As a Streamwinner, one continues to deepen his or her insight, and reduce thereby the other fetters that still obscure full Awakening and Nirvana. Insight, Buddhaghosa says, is focused on mental formations, especially those that are unwholesome. When one's insight develops to the point that two more fetters *(sensual desire* and *ill will)* are reduced enough, one is reborn on the second of the Four Paths, as a Once-returner. A Once-returner will be reborn only one more time as a human or in the realms of the *devas*. Any other rebirth will be in the *Brahmā* realms. The Once-returner continues to "turn over" the "soil" of his or her mental formations, with deeper insight into their impermanence, dissatisfactory nature, and lack of substantial selfhood.

When the Once-returner has, by insight, destroyed completely the fetters of sensual desire and ill will, he or she will attain the path of the Never-returner. On this third of the Four Paths, the Never-returner directs his or her attention to destroying the remaining five fetters by gaining the necessary insight. These five fetters are *craving* for existence in the realms of form, *craving* for existence in the formless realms, *pride, restlessness,* and finally *ignorance*—the last and most entangling of the Ten Fetters. If the Never-returner is successful in destroying these fetters and attaining full Awakening in his or her lifetime, he or she will enter the last of the Four Paths and become an *arhat*. If not, the Never-returner will be reborn in the one of the highest *Brahmā* realms of pure form. There, he or she will mature in insight until becoming an *arhat*.

The *arhat*, or saint, is the person who has finally completed the Path of Purification, who has been made a "worthy one" in the Way of the Elders by following in the footsteps of the Buddha. In the just cited quotation Buddhaghosa says that the *arhat* has completely destroyed not only the Ten

Fetters but also the cankers *(āsrava;* Pali: *āsava).* These include sensual desire, desire for the continuing process of life, and ignorance. Sometimes a fourth canker is mentioned—holding views that are not liberating. Being free from all such hindrances and defilements, one's attainment of Awakening is complete, and one realizes Nirvana. One's task is finished, one's burden is put down, the final goal of the Path of Purification is reached, and with one's death, he or she attains Nirvana "without-remainder."

As a footnote, we should add that Theravāda Buddhism does not call such a person a "Buddha." This is because human Buddhas, according to Theravāda, have not followed a humanly established spiritual path but have discovered Awakening and Nirvana by themselves. An *arhat,* instead, follows the path taught by a Buddha. Finally, it is also recognized that there may be people who make this attainment without following a path taught by someone else but do not communicate this attainment in the form of a teaching. Such a person is called a "Solitary Buddha" *(pratyekabuddha).*

THERAVĀDA BUDDHISM IN SRI LANKA AND SOUTHEAST ASIA

Given the support of King Aśoka, Buddhism became more widely known in India and was proclaimed by missionaries in other countries as well. The first historical account of Buddhism being presented south of India is of King Aśoka's missionaries reaching Sri Lanka around 250 B.C.E. Theravāda Buddhism was quickly accepted in Sri Lanka, and centuries later it became the major religion of much of Southeast Asia (see Map 3). Theravāda continues to this day to be the dominant religion of both Sri Lanka and Southeast Asia. The very early acceptance of Theravāda Buddhism has given Sri Lankans a strong sense of responsibility for the Way of the Elders in the Buddhist world.

Sri Lanka

Tradition states that King Tissa of Sri Lanka, converted by King Aśoka's son and daughter, helped to spread the Dharma throughout the island. He also built the Mahāvihāra, a huge monastery complex in his capital at Anuradhapura (see Figure 3.4). As Buddhism became the state religion, the monastics of Mahāvihāra took on the role of preserving the orthodox practice of Theravāda, especially in the face of early Mahāyāna developments in India (see next chapter). But in the first century B.C.E., a new monastic community formed in Anuradhapura, the Abhayagiri-vihāra. Faced with this division, Mahāvihāra scholars committed the Pali canon and commentaries to writing. However, its final structure was not established until the fifth century C.E.

In the third century C.E., the Jetavana monastic center was established as a third branch of the Saṅgha. It is not completely clear as to how these three traditions differed. Past scholarship proposed that the Mahāvihāra opposed Mahāyāna developments in the other two sects. These scholars also saw this as the main reason that the Pali texts were committed to writing. However, recent scholarship has shown this view to be somewhat problematic. In any

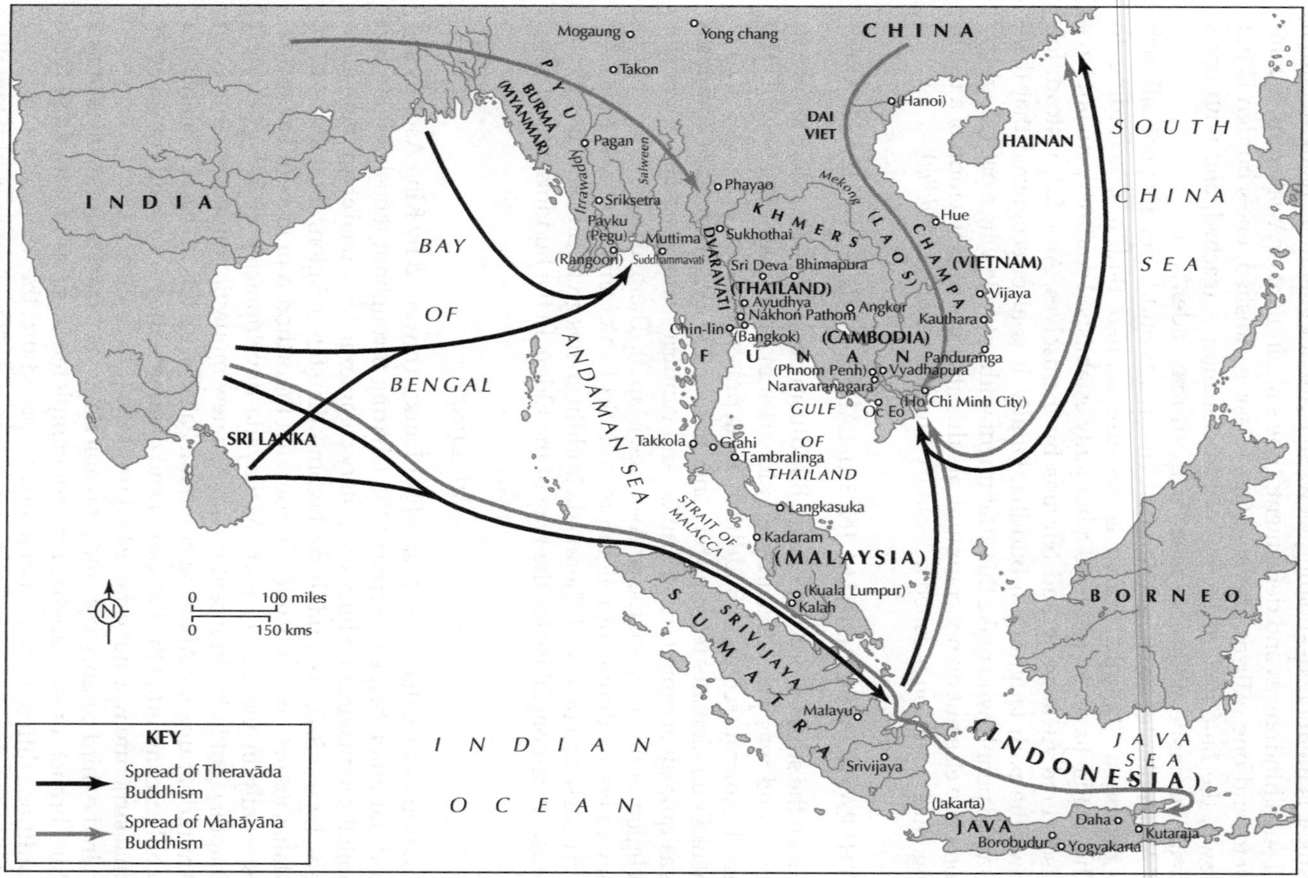

MAP 3. The spread of Buddhism into Southeast Asia: c. first century B.C.E.–tenth century C.E.

FIGURE 3.4. Ruwanvelseya: Great *Stūpa* in Anuradhapura; begun in 149 B.C.E. and finished by King Saddha Tissa (137–119 B.C.E.).

case, during the following centuries, Anuradhapura gained a reputation for scholarship in the Theravāda tradition, and many Indian monastics came to Sri Lanka to study. One such person in the fifth century was Buddhaghosa, whose ideas we have introduced in this chapter.

Sri Lanka was conquered by the Hindu Tamils in the early eleventh century, and the Saṅgha was severely disrupted. Indeed, it seems that the women's order in Sri Lanka died out at that time. Then in the middle of the eleventh century, King Vijayabahu of Sri Lanka, with the aid of Burma, drove out the Tamil forces. The king decided to reestablish Theravāda Buddhism from his new capital in Polonnaruva; this meant that the monastic ordination lineage had to be reestablished. Instead of turning to India, for obvious reasons, the king brought monks and Pali texts from Burma. Unfortunately, the nun's lineage was not reestablished in Sri Lanka. But the new relationship between Sri Lanka and Burma forged a connection in the faith between Sri Lanka and Southeast Asia that remains strong today. Then, during the twelfth century, King Parākrama Bahu I unified the Saṅgha in Sri Lanka under the Mahāvihāra Order. For the next three centuries, a golden age of Theravāda and Pali scholarship in Sri Lanka blossomed.

In 1505, Portuguese colonists arrived in Sri Lanka and controlled the lowland coastal regions. The Sri Lankan kings ruled what they could and supported

Buddhism from their new capital at Kandy in the interior mountains. The Portuguese were replaced by the Dutch in 1658, and finally the British in 1798. The British conquered Kandy in 1815 to rule the whole island. After this defeat, the Saṅgha was weakened significantly. This unfortunate condition of the Saṅgha had also been worsened by the introduction of Western education that replaced the monastic-based education system and by the Christian missions that portrayed Buddhism as backward and superstitious.

In the later half of the 1800s, a movement arose within the Buddhist community to debate Christians and to renew the Buddhist discipline and teachings in ways that were relevant to the modern world. This movement was supported, and in some ways guided, by founding members of the Theosophical Society, Helena Blavatsky and Henry Steel Olcott. In fact, both Blavatsky and Olcott went to Sri Lanka and proclaimed themselves to be Buddhists. When independence was gained after World War II, this spirit of renewal increased and produced a vital and influential Saṅgha along with lay movements dedicated to social reform. We introduce one such movement, the Sarvodaya Shramadana Movement, later in this chapter. The government has continued to support Buddhism and founded the World Buddhist Fellowship in 1950. The Sri Lankan Saṅgha now sends monastics around the world to introduce the Dharma and teach the practice of meditation.

Southeast Asia

King Aśoka is said to have sent missionaries to the area of Southeast Asia that is now part of southern Burma (Myanmar) and central Thailand. This may have been true. However, many scholars argue that Theravāda was more likely introduced into that region from Sri Lanka in the early centuries C.E. In any case, by the fifth century C.E. in the northern part of Burma, it is certain that there was a coexistence of Hinduism, different forms of Buddhism, and the indigenous worship of local spirits. In southern Burma, Theravāda was the dominant form of religion. When the northern Burmese King Anawratha (1040–1077) unified the country, he made Theravāda from the south the main religion of all Burma. It was also this king of Burma who sent monks and Pali texts to Sri Lanka to help reestablish the Theravāda lineage in 1065. Over the centuries, since the time of King Anawratha, Sri Lanka and Burma have enjoyed a close religious collaboration in supporting Theravāda in their two countries.

This Theravādin collaboration was later joined by Thailand. From the eleventh century, Theravāda missions were sent into Thailand from Burma, and the religion enjoyed support from the Thai people. When the Thais won independence from their Cambodian Khmer rulers in the fourteenth century, Theravāda became the official religion of Thailand. At that time, religious connections with Sri Lanka were also established; these ties remain strong today. During the nineteenth century, a number of reforms were made within the Thai Saṅgha; under King Rāma V (ruled 1868–1910), all the Theravāda sects were united under the Mahānikāya (Great Sect). In this century, there have been influential Theravādin leaders in Thailand, such as the Venerable Buddhadāsa (1906–1993), whom we discuss later in this chapter.

It is said that different forms of Buddhism were brought to Cambodia in the second century C.E. It is certain that by the sixth century, Mahāyāna and Hinduism were joined together in a popular syncretistic form of religion. In the eighth century, Cambodia, along with most of the rest of Southeast Asia, was under the rule of Java. Buddhism had been already introduced down the Malay peninsula and into the islands of Sumatra and Java in the fourth and fifth centuries. During the Java empire, around 800 C.E., a huge *stūpa* was build in Borobudur, Java. It remains the largest in the Southern Hemisphere. A Cambodian prince named Jayavarman was a hostage in Java at the time. When he returned home, he proclaimed Cambodian independence and went on to build the Khmer empire covering most of Cambodia, Laos, Thailand, and Vietnam.

It was during this Khmer empire that the great temples and mausoleums were built at Angkor (see Figure 3.5). At first, the complex of buildings were dedicated to Hindu deities. However, in the twelfth century, Burmese missions to the empire won many converts to Theravāda Buddhism, and Buddhist elements began to appear in the Angkor temples. In the fourteenth century, the Cambodian royalty accepted Theravāda, and it has remained a strong tradition in Cambodia ever since. Also, because of Cambodia's influence on Laos, Theravāda became the official religion of that country around 1350. The Khmer empire lasted until the Thais gained independence in 1431.

Māhayāna Buddhism reached northern Vietnam from both India and China as early as the third century C.E. However, the north of Vietnam was

FIGURE 3.5. Towers of Bayon, Angkor Thom; thirteenth century C.E., Cambodia.

most strongly influenced culturally and religiously by neighboring China. Thus, Chinese forms of Pure Land and Thien (Zen) Buddhism were popular from the ninth century on and enjoyed state support from the tenth century. In the south of Vietnam, Hinduism and Mahāyāna were also introduced by the third century. After an invasion from the north in the fifteenth century, the Chinese forms of Māhayāna Buddhism became the dominant religion throughout Vietnam. Although Theravāda Buddhism continued to exist in the south in areas near Cambodia, Vietnamese Buddhism has been most strongly formed by the Chinese Mahāyāna traditions.

Theravāda Monastic and Lay Experience

Buddhist monastics in the Theravāda tradition today follow the rules of the *Prātimokṣa* and live a disciplined life in monasteries. The Buddha allowed them to possess what are called the Eight Requisites: three robes (inner, outer, and heavy for when it is cold), a belt, an alms bowl, a razor, a sewing kit, and a water filter. Today, many monks also have things such as soap, toothpaste, a watch, a flashlight, candle and matches, a fan, and an umbrella. The monastic daily routine, for example in Thailand, includes the following:

- 4:00 A.M.: Waking up, dressing, and meditating for an hour followed by an hour of chanting
- 6:00 A.M.: Going out with alms bowls begging for food in the neighborhood of the monastery
- 8:00 A.M.: Returning to the monastery and sitting together to eat breakfast followed by making a blessing for peace
- Before 12:00 P.M.: Some monastics choose to eat a light lunch, as no food is allowed after noon until sunrise the following morning
- 1:00 P.M.: Attending classes on the Dharma
- 6:00 P.M.: Attending a two-hour session of meditation followed by chanting and blessings
- 8:00 P.M.: Personal study or meditation before retiring for the night

Besides these activities, all monastics have specific roles to play in the morning and afternoon such as maintaining the monastic complex, meeting with laypersons, and carrying out administrative duties. They can also rest in the afternoon.

The layout of a typical Thai monastery has two parts. First is the more public section that includes an assembly hall where the monastics perform rituals, do meditation together, and hold discussions. It is also where the monastics gather to recite the *Prātimokṣa* and discuss consequences for anyone who breaks the rules. Behind the assembly hall is a *stūpa* that serves as a memorial to the Buddha or as a reliquary. Beside the assembly hall is an ordination hall that is also used for monastic activities. There are often other smaller halls housing statues or serving as shrines. There is also a library and study hall. The second part of the monastery includes the living quarters of the monastics.

The monastery, as well as the monastic routine, provides an environment and pattern of living that is conducive to following the Path of Purification leading to Nirvana. This path has traditionally been seen in Theravāda as normally requiring one to be a monastic. Some early Buddhist texts indicate that the Four Paths could be reached by laypersons. But the Theravāda experience was that such a feat would be almost impossible because of the lack of time necessary for proper learning and practice. Recently, however, this view has been reconsidered as lay practice in Theravāda countries has been on the increase. For example, during the twentieth century, Myanmar centers for the lay practice of mindfulness and insight meditation were founded. These centers have developed techniques that have influenced modern Buddhist practice in other Theravādin countries as well as outside Asia. Some persons who use these techniques believe that given this training, and the time that certain laypeople have today for extended retreats, the higher levels of the Path of Purification can be reached by lay practitioners. On the other hand, over the centuries traditional practice of Theravāda Buddhism by the laity has been more focused on moral living, the attainment of this-worldly benefits, and merit for a better rebirth.

As for moral living, the monastic communities of Theravāda in Sri Lanka and Southeast Asia have preached ethical teachings and have provided moral guidance to the laity. We should note that in Theravāda, city monasteries focus on the study of the Dharma, performing rituals, and ministering to the needs of the lay community. Forest monasteries focus on the meditative attainment of their monastics, but sometimes also offer the laity meditative guidance and retreats under the direction of a skilled teacher. The city monasteries have been mainly responsible for providing the teaching of the Dharma and the moral discipline to the larger lay community. More than this, these monastic communities have provided models of moral living for society in general. In their monastic way of life, the monks and nuns present a social ideal for all Buddhists: a community of persons living together with such moral virtues as generosity, forgiveness, loving kindness, and compassion. The monastic Saṅgha gives an example of how people can live together in peace and harmony, with all individuals treated equally and honored not for wealth or power, but for moral and spiritual achievement. Indeed, monasticism has always been at the very heart of the Theravāda Buddhist world.

To carry out their role as moral and spiritual guides for the laity, Theravāda monasteries, especially in cities, contain a complex of halls in which the laity can be educated and can participate in religious ceremonies. There are also monastery schools for children and shrines where statues or paintings of Buddha images are kept for offerings of flowers, food, incense, and the lighting of candles. These offerings are said to bring merit to the laity and to reinforce the values that lay Buddhists try to live in daily life. There may also be *stūpas* where objects for veneration are kept. In fact, Theravāda provides the laity with numerous opportunities for merit-making. Other examples of merit-making possibilities include attending certain rituals, presenting food to monastics when they beg for a meal, listening to a Dharma talk or to monks chanting, making general donations to the Saṅgha, repeating and listening to passages in the Pali texts, and calming the mind in meditation. These and other actions can, Theravādins believe, produce merit that will benefit one in this life and bring a more fortunate rebirth. Therefore, the laity sees the monastic community as a source of growth in the Dharma and moral life as well as a source of good merit that can be obtained, shared with others, and even channeled to the larger society for the benefit of all persons.

Because Hinduism spread south from India along with Buddhism, very early on there were no clear boundaries between these religions. Thus, there developed a popular blending of these religions in Sri Lanka and Southeast Asia that has had a continuing influence on the religiosity of Theravādin laypeople. For example, in Sri Lanka sometimes Buddhist and Hindu religious leaders interacted so closely that they lived in different quarters on a shared religious site. Laypeople consulted the Buddhist monastics about matters having to do with morality, understanding the higher truth about life, and release from the rounds of rebirth. These same people also asked the Hindu priests to pray to the Hindu and local gods for this-worldly benefits such as good fortune, prosperity, and health. Even today, shrines are provided in many Buddhist sites for the worship of both Hindu and local gods. When a young person leaves home, his or her parents may give the following traditional blessing: "May you have the refuge of the Buddha, and the protection of the gods." Another example of this kind of religious interaction is found in Burma, where the ancient belief in local spirits (*nats*) led to accepting Buddhist spirituality along with shamanistic practices, especially for healing sickness. The rationale for this kind of interaction is that the Buddha did not deny the existence of deities that may be interested in helping humans with their needs and may have the powers to do so. He only denied that rites and ceremonies to the gods would aid one in the ultimate journey to Nirvana.

NEW BUDDHIST MOVEMENTS IN SRI LANKA AND SOUTHEAST ASIA

Buddhism in Asia today is experiencing a new growth of innovative reform movements that attempt to address the personal, social, political, economic, and environmental ills that plague their part of the world. Many of these movements have been referred to as "socially engaged Buddhism." And, as we shall see in the final chapter of this book, these movements have spread around the world so that they contribute to the globalization of Buddhism today.

In Sri Lanka, many Buddhist leaders have been concerned with the effect of the capitalist model of economic development on the people and environment of their country since the colonial period. Production-centered development defines the well-being of the country in purely quantitative terms, and thus it creates desires through the media for more consumer goods. Buddhist leaders point out that in working for the wealth needed to purchase these objects, many Sri Lankans forget the well-being of their less fortunate neighbors, as well as the spiritual wealth offered by Buddhism. In part to counter this influence of Westernization on Sri Lanka, A. T. Ariyaratne founded the Sarvodaya Shramadana Movement. *Sarvodaya* is a term first coined by Mahātmā Gandhi to mean "the well-being of all." *Shramadana* is interpreted to mean "the gift of sharing one's time and labor." As a social movement in Sri Lanka, Sarvodaya Shramadana seeks to live the Dharma by sharing both time and labor for the well-being of all to create a society where there is "no poverty and no affluence."

Sarvodaya members live out the experience of no-self (*anattā*) by sharing what they can with all persons in need. They see this selfless service to others as a way of changing their own consciousness into a more awakened and compassionate state on the way to Nirvana. When organized properly, such service can also contribute to social and economic changes that will help those who are served to better understand and live the Dharma. It has been pointed out that the Buddha once did not deliver a Dharma talk until a poor laborer was fed, because, as the Buddha said, no one suffering from hunger can comprehend the Dharma. To guide this work for those in need, Ariyaratne interprets the Four Divine Abodes in the following manner: loving kindness means a love and respect for all persons. This leads to compassion for those persons one loves who are in need. Sympathetic joy comes from seeing how compassionate service to the needy has helped them. Equanimity aids one in continuing this life of service undeterred by praise or blame, gain or loss.

Concretely, Sarvodaya directs village-renewal programs by which members assist villagers in Sri Lanka with their particular problems by applying the Four Noble Truths. First, what is the problem to be addressed? Second, what are the causes of that problem? Third, how can the problem be resolved? And fourth, what are the steps that need to be taken to resolve it? Then, to solve a problem, for example, the need for clean drinking water, villagers join Sarvodaya members in a "project working camp" for a week or so. During that time not only is work done but a positive spiritual atmosphere is created by living together practices and values of Buddhism. Work is both planned and concluded each day in a "family meeting" during which these values are discussed and applied to the task at hand. The work is done in the spirit of the Four Grounds of Kindness: generosity, kindly speech, useful work, and equality. Ariyaratne believes that these four Buddhist virtues can combat the materialism, individualism, and unbridled competition of modern economic life. In so doing, these virtues cultivate spiritual friendship, community, and sharing in ways that foster personal Awakening and social development.

Here are Ariyaratne's own words reflecting on the Sarvodaya experience:

> There was a time in our history when there was total peace and harmony in our country. In modern times, why do children take to violence as they grow to adulthood? Why do we have a society today which is far from peaceful?. . . . One of

> the unique teachings of the Buddha is the theory of dependent arising. Everything is related to every other thing. If there is no peace in a society, there should be a variety of interdependent and interrelated causes that bring about such a situation. All of these causes have to be attacked simultaneously and removed to make a reversal of the processes that have brought about a loss of peace in our society so that we can rebuild a culture of peace. The Sarvodaya Shramadana Movement in Sri Lanka has evolved . . . an integrated self-development approach to counteract the causes that bring about conflicts, crime, and war. . . . People expect quick solutions to the culture of violence that prevails today. They forget that this culture has been caused over a long period of time by multifarious factors. . . . Sarvodaya is patiently and silently rebuilding the foundations of the required new social order. . . . We in Sarvodaya believe that religions should assist human beings and human groups to overcome internal defilements such as greed, ill will, and egotism, and promote internal spirituality so that beneficence, sharing, morality, and enlightenment will evolve within them. The ultimate objective of Buddhists and other religious individuals should be building a critical mass of spiritual consciousness on this planet—which is the surest way to live in a culture of peace.[1]

A second reformer, this time in Thailand, was Buddhadāsa Bhikkhu (1906–1993). At the age of ten, Buddhadāsa entered a temple in his small hometown 600 miles south of Bangkok. There he learned to read and write, celebrate Buddhist ceremonies, and collect medicinal herbs in the forest. Later, he was ordained a monk and took advanced Dharma studies in Bangkok. Missing the peace and simplicity of his hometown, Buddhadāsa returned to the south, where he moved into an abandoned temple and founded *Suan Mokkh*, "The Garden of Liberation." For the first three months, Buddhadāsa remained alone in silence; it was only after five years that three monks came to join him. During those first five years, Buddhadāsa developed a balanced way of Buddhist practice and study. Until that time, it was common for city monks to study the scriptures, while forest monks practiced meditation.

Buddhadāsa taught that personal and social transformation go hand in hand. Both involve cleansing any attachment to self and possessions. The egoism and selfishness that make individuals unsatisfied are the same realities that define social, economic, and political structures and processes in ways that lead to an unsatisfied society. Letting go of egoism and selfishness can quench *duḥkha* for individuals and society. To achieve this letting go, people must find a "right understanding" of life, the first step in the Noble Eightfold Path. For Buddhadāsa, this right understanding involves the experience of emptiness, the voidness of independent selfhood. To see and judge the world in relation to oneself is the "ordinary view" of things. True insight reveals what Buddhadāsa calls "Nature," or the interdependent wholeness of existence in which every being is connected to all other beings. This insight into dependent arising is achieved, Buddhadāsa teaches, by study and strong concentration (*samādhi*) practice. It brings a right understanding that fosters the experience of freedom from self-concern and freedom to live for others in ways that quench both personal and social *duḥkha*. In the words of Buddhadāsa:

> Buddhists aim to penetrate deeply into the inner Nature, the spiritual Nature, the Nature which is the Law of Nature, which is the source of everything. We try to study so that we realize the Nature within which is called "Dhamma—element" (*dhammadhātu*), namely, the law of dependent coorigination or conditionality. If we realize this Nature, we have no way that selfishness can happen.[2]

For Buddhadāsa, Buddhism implies a life dedicated to mutual benefit and support, caring for the needy and the poor, and working together unselfishly for peace and prosperity for all beings. So, following the Buddhist way of wise and compassionate living can bring both social and personal transformation. Buddhist practices, such as mindfulness and loving kindness, can help persons discover their wholesome mind and society regain its healthy peacefulness. By establishing more positive forms of social living, one is not only changing society for the better but is also overcoming the inner egoism that produces personal *duḥkha* and blinds one to the liberating truth about life.

One of Buddhadāsa's students who has sought to build healthy communities based on his teacher's principles is Sulak Sivaraksa (see Figure 3.6). Sulak is especially concerned about the effect of powerful national and international economic interests on Thai cities and villages and on the environment throughout the countryside. These interests have created an economy that has driven subsistence farmers and fishermen from their villages into the cities where they live in slum conditions. These same interests have deforested much of Thailand. Fifty years ago, 80 percent of Thailand was forest; today that number has been seriously reduced. The loss of topsoil by erosion and the destruction of water sources have worsened the plight of those living in the countryside. Some families are driven to sell their daughters to the prostitution industry that is thriving in Bangkok.

As a leading Thai lay Buddhist intellectual, Sulak has founded a number of organizational networks that seek to address these problems. The International Network of Engaged Buddhists (INEB) was founded in 1989 as an international interfaith network for human development among the urban and rural poor. The focus of its human development programs is linking the Thai people together in ways that provide for their economic needs, while conserving their resources, protecting their environment, and promoting cultural values and social harmony. To guide these efforts, Sulak proposes a modern reinterpretation of the principles of Buddhism. One example has to do with the Five Precepts. The first precept, not to take life, is interpreted to mean not to deprive people of a decent living, deplete the soil, contaminate the water, pollute the air, destroy the forests, or consume wastefully while people die of starvation. The second precept, not to steal, is extended to mean opposing inappropriate development that robs people and their land and rejecting economic systems that produce poverty and exploitation of the

FIGURE 3.6. Buddhadāsa Bhikkhu (seated) and Sulak Sivaraksa at *Suan Mokkh*, Thailand (undated).

poor. The third precept, no sexual misconduct, is expanded to mean opposing the widespread exploitation of women in Thailand, especially as prostitutes. The fourth precept, no lying, is said to mean not to use false and misleading statements in the media and hedonistic images in advertising, which generate a consumer culture that believes in the lie that happiness can be found in obtaining consumer goods. Finally, the fifth precept, no intoxicants, is interpreted to mean overcoming social and economic factors, such as unemployment, poverty, and unequal opportunity, which lead to despair and thereby spawn addictive behavior. This restructuring of human consciousness with wisdom, insight, and compassion is also, for Sulak, the essence of Buddhism:

> You don't have to profess . . . faith, you don't have to worship the Buddha, you don't have to join in any ceremonies. What is important is that you grow in mindfulness and awareness. You try to restructure your consciousness to

Box 3.3

A Socially Engaged Buddhist

The Assembly of the Poor in Siam (Thailand) is what we call a "people's organization," a type of movement with increasing influence among NGOs. The Assembly of the Poor unites the villagers, fishermen and women, small-scale farmer families, and crafts folks who lost their livelihood because of a series of dams now obstructing their Pak Moon River. The homes of some 30,000 persons have been flooded. Not far from the point where the Pak Moon River joins the Mekong River, near the border with Laos, the major giant dam has been constructed. At this place, the villagers who organized themselves as the Assembly of the Poor erected a bamboo protest-village.

The World Commission on Dams, an independent commission that scientifically assesses the impact of this type of mega-project, found that the series of Pak Moon dams would not fulfill their purpose, namely, providing energy production for urban-industrial needs and irrigation for chemical farming. Soon after that finding, the protest-village of the Assembly of the Poor was set afire.

But direct violence is not my main worry. My deepest concern is "structural violence." Our world is ruled by anonymous powers systematically manipulating our consciousness to believe that material growth is the ultimate goal in life. Global corporate structures have become more powerful than many nations. Nations have been made to compete amongst each other in seeking ever greater economic development, no matter what the cost to people's lives. The poor nations compete to provide cheap labor in what is called a "race to the bottom." This global development has destroyed most of the traditional, self-sufficient, and sustainable rural community-life on earth. The Assembly of the Poor is but one example.

What can we do? In "Engaged Buddhism," we try to practice interrelatedness or "inter-being." I know that I am part of the struggle of the villagers. Our growing group of spiritual friends attempts to support the villagers. I also know that I am part of the suppressing powers: the rich middle class and elites seeking an increasingly greedy urban lifestyle. So we must try to change minds and seek new and more just alternatives for the good of all people. This can be done through self-critical awareness and dialogue, through critical, direct, spiritual dialogue among human beings across all social and cultural boundaries.

For example, in our Ariyavinaya project, Buddhist monastics (monks and nuns), laypersons, students, artists, media experts, environmentalists, and business people engage in critical dialogue. Together we rethink the *Vinaya* (code of conduct; discipline) within a contemporary perspective and an intercultural context. We also include like-minded friends from other religious traditions in the process.

There are alternatives to what is going on in the world today. We just have to change our minds and hearts through dialogue across all boundaries. Then, we can work to realize our future together.

SULAK SIVARAKSA
Bangkok, Thailand

> become more selfless, to be able to relate to other people more meaningfully in order that friendship will be possible and exploitation impossible. To me the essence of Buddhism is this.[3]

Perhaps the most well-known reformer from Southeast Asia is Thich Nhat Hanh. At the age of seventeen, he entered a Thiên (Zen) monastery in Hue, Vietnam. His training included aspects from both the Theravāda and Thiên traditions with emphasis on mindfulness and *kōan* practice. Nhat Hanh also studied at Saigon University and Princeton. After his studies in the West, he returned to Vietnam and founded the School of Youth for Social Service, which would become one of the primary organizations for Buddhist social engagement during the Vietnam War. In 1965, he founded the "Order of Interbeing" as a new branch of Thiên Buddhism. This order has brought together lay and monastic Buddhists for training in liberating practice and social engagement. Nhat Hanh's work for peace, healing, and reconciliation and his refusal to take sides in the war were seen as threatening by the governments of both North and South Vietnam. While traveling in the West in the late 1960s, Nhat Hanh was advised not to return to Vietnam. So he directed the Vietnamese Buddhist Peace Delegation in Paris until the end of the war.

During the Vietnam War, Nhat Hanh and the Buddhist social movement in Vietnam refused to side with either the North or the South. Instead, they called for a negotiated political, rather than military, solution to the war. This position was embraced by the vast majority of the Vietnamese people in the South, but not by the American government or the government of the South. It was a position that Buddhist leaders took in solidarity with the peasants and masses of people of Vietnam, who were victims of an ideological fight between communism and anti-communism that they did not understand. For example, peasants in villages were told by the Viet Cong to dig caves for their soldiers. If they did not, they were punished. But if they did, they were punished by the South Vietnamese government forces. The Buddhists also saw the American servicemen and servicewomen as victims of the war. For the good of all involved, they felt that the war must come to a negotiated end as soon as possible.

Working for an end to the war, Buddhists practiced many forms of humanistic action. They evacuated villagers caught in cross-fire; they established cease-fire lines outside villages; they worked to reconstruct villages and rebuild buildings destroyed in battles; they cared for orphans and provided basic medical care for everyone. The most dramatic act was self-immolation. Although not sanctioned by any Buddhist group, and not part of any Buddhist program of action, these acts occurred at unexpected moments when a person was unable to bear the suffering of those around him or her and wanted to do something to move the hearts of those causing the suffering.

Since the end of the war, Nhat Hanh continues to share with the world the Vietnamese experience of engaged Buddhist spirituality through his Order of Interbeing. Nhat Hanh has helped people see that experiential insight into the inter-being of life, or the dependent arising of life, frees one from preoccupation with one's own suffering and releases one's loving kindness and compassion for others. This message is expressed in one of the often-quoted poems of Nhat Hanh, "Please Call Me by My True Names":

> Do not say that I'll depart tomorrow
> because even today I still arrive.
>
> Look deeply: I arrive in every second
> to be a bud on a spring branch,
> to be a tiny bird, with wings still fragile,
> learning to sing in my new nest,
> to be a caterpillar in the heart of a flower,
> to be a jewel hiding itself in a stone.
>
> I still arrive, in order to laugh and to cry,
> in order to fear and to hope,
> the rhythm of my heart is the birth and
> death of all that are alive.
>
> I am the mayfly metamorphosing on the
> surface of the river,
> and I am the bird which, when spring comes,
> arrives in time to eat the mayfly.
>
> I am the frog swimming happily in the
> clear water of a pond,
> and I am also the grass-snake who
> approaching in silence,
> feeds itself on the frog.
>
> I am the child in Uganda, all skin and bones,
> my legs as thin as bamboo sticks,
> and I am the arms merchant, selling deadly
> weapons to Uganda.
>
> I am the 12-year-old girl, refugee
> on a small boat,
> who throws herself into the ocean after
> being raped by a sea pirate,
> and I am the pirate, my heart not yet capable
> of seeing and loving.
>
> I am a member of the politburo, with
> plenty of power in my hands,
> and I am the man who has to pay his

"debt of blood" to my people
dying slowly in a forced labor camp.

My joy is like spring, so warm it makes
flowers bloom in all walks of life.
My pain is like a river of tears, so full it
fills up the four oceans.

Please call me by my true names,
so I can hear all my cries and my laughs
at once,
so I can see that my joy and pain are one.

Please call me by my true names,
so I can wake up,
and so the door of my heart can be left open,
the door of compassion.[4]

To foster this insight into inter-being, Nhat Hanh recommends mindfulness as pure observation of the present moment by which one sees through the pain in life to the hidden wonder of interrelatedness. One of the ways to bring one's mindfulness into the present moment with pure observation is, according to Nhat Hanh, by attending to one's breathing. Then, deeper forms of meditation lead one to a fuller insight into one's mind, a letting go of the burdens one finds and discovering there the inter-being of life. Thereby, one is in touch not only with humanity's shared suffering existence but also with an even deeper source of inner peace to give to others. Nhat Hanh, like Ghosananda, stresses that the peace experienced in one's mind and heart is to be lived with one's body. Being peace for others requires inner healing; and that peace given to others is also healing for them.

This journey of healing experience and social ministry is guided in the Order of Interbeing by the Fourteen Precepts, which can be summarized in the following way. First is not to absolutize any belief in a way that blocks growth in understanding and leads to fanaticism. Second is always to continue to learn by observing self and world. Third is not to force anyone to adopt one's own viewpoint. Fourth is to be aware of suffering in oneself and others. Fifth is to live simply and avoid greed, the pursuit of fame, and sensual pleasure. Sixth is to let go of anger and hatred by the practice of meditation and to live compassionately for others, especially those who have wronged one. Seventh is to return to one's true self by breathing practice, meditation, and mindfulness. Eighth is to use language to build unity and not to divide people. Ninth is to purify speech with truthfulness. Tenth is not to use the community for personal gain or for political purposes. Eleventh is to pursue a livelihood that does not harm life. Twelfth is not to kill living beings. Thirteenth is not to possess things that belong to others. Fourteenth is to preserve the vital energies of our body for the realization of the Dharma. These precepts, fashioned from the Noble Eightfold Path in the violent experience of Vietnam, give the world a Buddhist guide for spiritual growth, healing, reconciliation, and peacemaking in the midst of the many difficulties of modern life.

From these examples of new Buddhist movements, we can see that the Theravāda religion has not only provided its monastics in Sri Lanka and Southeast Asia with a spiritual path to follow to the highest state of Nirvanic freedom but has also given its lay members concrete guidance on how to live certain moral values and spiritual qualities taught by the Buddha. Theravāda monasticism has helped to form the values of its societies and has produced an impressive Buddhist culture with art and literature that express the ideals taught by the Buddha. The Theravāda experience of Buddhism has provided a wellspring for the moral, social, intellectual, and cultural life of Sri Lanka and Southeast Asia, while also preserving the Way of the Elders leading to Awakening and Nirvana.

The Cultural Experience of Thai Buddhism Today

Laohavanich Mano Mettanando
President, Hospice Foundation of Thailand

Thailand is known today as a Buddhist country where more than 90 percent of the Thais follow the Theravāda Buddhist tradition inherited from their ancestors. Unlike in most other Buddhist countries, the monarchy in Thailand is central to Buddhist practice and culture. All Thai people are raised to believe and faithfully uphold the "pillars of the security of Thailand": Nation, Religion, and Kings. "Religion" here means Theravāda Buddhism as the national religion of Thailand. The king has to be a Theravāda Buddhist, and he is the patron of the religion and the protector of other faiths. Therefore, the Buddhist religion is integrated into the national life and culture of Thailand.

According to the Buddha, before one attains the goal of liberation, one is subject to a series of rebirths that can lead at times into woeful conditions. Nevertheless, after paying off the bad karma, a person can be reborn again in the human condition. Nirvana is the only eternal resting-place, which is reality when all karmic debt is completely paid off. It is this view of karma that is the backbone of popular Buddhist practice in Thailand. That is, much of popular Buddhist practice and customs have to do with making merit for both spiritual and worldly progress. In this regard, Buddhist monks are seen as the ultimate field of merit-making, so central to the rituals and ceremonies in the daily life of the laity.

In organized Buddhism, such merit-making ceremonies and activities involve revering the Three Refuges: Buddha, Dharma, and Saṅgha. In this regard, the public subsidizes Thailand's 270,000 monks and 90,000 novices at more than 30,000 *wats* (monasteries) by donating food, clothing, and money for necessities. The monastery is a symbolically designed place of worship, meditation, and study. But it can also be a community center, orphanage, hospital, hostel, school, market, playground, meeting place, festival site, foundation, museum, theater, garden, and even zoo. Participating in temple devotions, and in other ceremonies and activities, supports monastic life and enables laypersons to contribute to the Saṅgha and its mission in the world.

On the other hand, modern distractions and global popular culture affect young single men today at an increasing rate. A shortage of monks has caused a sixth of all *wats* to be abandoned. Nevertheless, the Saṅgha refuses to ordain devout white-robed women who follow the eight precepts. Buddha founded an order of yellow-robed fully ordained nuns, but the line faded out before Buddhism arrived in Siam. In 2001, Chatsumarn Kabilsingh, daughter of a Buddhist nun ordained in Taiwan, became a nun in Sri Lanka, and now others have followed her example.

FROM CHILDHOOD TO ADULTHOOD

From an early age, a child is introduced to the Buddhist traditions by his or her parents. Children are often taken to temples and are included in ceremonies and other customs observed by their families. They are taught to pay respect to the monks by giving a *wai*, raising both hands, palms together in front of their chest. Children also see laypeople tending to the needs of monks. Every day at dawn, villages and towns are frequented by serene monks and novices, donned in saffron robes, peacefully going from house to house to receive donations of food and alms offered by faithful laypeople. Thai people, including children, often feel unhappy when they see a monk standing in line, and seats are always offered to monks in a bus or train. In this kind of religious culture, children learn that monks are special people who are endowed with the sacredness of the Three Refuges.

Children mostly learn Buddhism from their parents, at schools, and in temples. Most parents teach their children the basic chants and rituals that they practice at home. Most Buddhist families also have a shrine room at home where Buddha is worshiped on a decorated altar, and children are encouraged to participate in the rituals and in mindfulness and meditation practice. The most popular rituals performed by the laity are morning and evening chanting in the Pali language. The chants were composed by King Monkut, or Rama IV, who reformed Buddhism in the nineteenth century. Besides these standard Pali chantings, lay Buddhist devotees enjoy *Paritta* Chanting, the chanting of certain *sūtras* used for protection and *Jinapañjāra* Chanting, the chanting of certain *sūtras* to conquer defilements and destroy inauspicious influences. Other *sūtras* are chanted to remove fear, regain health, ward off calamities, and so on.

Every government-run school is mandated to teach Buddhism and meditation to students from kindergarten to high school. In addition, many temples in Thailand provide Sunday school for children. All lay Buddhists, including youth, are encouraged to join free meditation retreats offered by various meditation centers. The retreats normally last for a few days to weeks.

To encourage Buddhist practice among the laity, the Ecclesiastical Council of Thailand also provides annual examinations on Buddhism nationwide. There are also Buddhist clubs for youth.

At the university level, there are also Buddhist clubs and societies. Once each year, these clubs organize nationwide examinations on Buddhism at various educational levels. The winners of the national exams are awarded trophies. Each summer, these Buddhist university organizations provide the opportunity for students to participate in a mass temporary ordination program for spiritual training during summer vacation. Besides these more informal religious education programs, the two main monastic universities, Mahachulalongkorn and Mahamakut Royal Monastic University, also offer academic courses in Buddhist studies leading to a bachelor's degree and to a doctorate degree.

In the monasteries themselves, monastic education is classified into two parts: formal Buddhist studies (*naktham*) and Pali language study (*parian*). The former covers four areas: the life of the Buddha, Buddhist doctrines, monastic codes of conduct, and rituals and ceremonies. The latter is divided into nine grades that focus on Pali grammar and the commentaries on the canonical literature of Buddhism. This monastic system of education provides an alternative to youth who wish to engage in religious study but, for various reasons, do not have access to higher education. They can complete the course of study and return to being laypersons.

Thailand is the only country in the world where the Buddhist monastic tradition is maintained by temporary ordination of young laymen coming from all classes of society. They can spend a few months of their life in monastic robes to deepen their spiritual life, strengthen their moral commitment, and broaden their knowledge of the Buddhist religion. They also believe that the merit of the ordination can be passed to their mothers. So each year, from the end of the summer to the beginning of the monsoon, hundreds of thousands of young Thai men are ordained in monasteries all across the country to spend a period of three months practicing Buddhism before they finally disrobe and return to lay life as religiously educated and morally formed men.

MARRIAGES AND FUNERALS

In the past, while a couple might seek a blessing from a monk at a local temple on a day before their wedding, it was considered a bad omen for a Buddhist monk to be present at a marriage ceremony. But in modem times, it is not uncommon to have a Buddhist component to a wedding ceremony. During that part of the service, which may be celebrated at a temple, the couple would bow before the Buddha image, recite basic Buddhist chants, such as the Three Refuges and the Five Precepts, and light incense and candles before the Buddha. The couple might then offer food and flowers to the monks present.

The monks may recite Pali scriptures intended to bring merit and blessings to the couple. A sacred white cord (*sai sin*) may be unwound and held by the monks. The lead monk may place the end of the thread in a bowl of water that will be "sanctified" at the ceremony for blessings and to bring good fortune. The blessed water may also be mixed with wax from a candle from the altar and with other ingredients to form a paste that is applied to the foreheads of the bride and groom. Finally, the highest-ranking monk may say a few words of advice to the couple. The couple would then offer food to the monks, and the Buddhist part of the ceremony is concluded.

In Thailand, most funeral services are performed in a temple. Usually, the body of the deceased is kept in a coffin placed on an altar close to which is an image of the Buddha on a set of ceremonial tables fully decorated with flowers, candles, and incense sticks. Next to the Buddha is a photo of the deceased displayed on a stand for guests to pay their respects. Most funeral services take place every evening for a week before the body is cremated.

After paying respect to the Buddha and the deceased, the guests are invited to sit quietly in the hall to listen to four rounds of chanting from the *Abhidharma* texts by a group of four monks. The ritual is the reenactment of the myth that the Buddha went to preach the *Abhidharma* to his mother in the second heavenly realm for three months during a rainy season. Because it would be too long for the seven books of *Abhidharma* to be chanted, only the first paragraph of each book is used for the chanting. Each round of the chanting lasts ten to fifteen minutes. Traditionally, there is a break for a snack when the monks finish their third round of chanting. The fourth round of chanting is concluded by a merit transfer ceremony whereby the guests of honor and the family members of the deceased are invited to present offerings to the monks.

Cremation is usually conducted in the evening. The ceremony begins when the coffin is transferred onto a cart to circumambulate the crematorium counterclockwise three times. Then it is put on the altar in front of the crematorium. Just before entering the crematorium chamber, the guests of honor are often invited to present gifts of robes to monks who will bless the body for the last time. Each guest will then be invited to participate by putting a small piece of dried incense into the chamber both before and during the cremation. Members of the family of the deceased will gather again the morning after to collect the ashes to be enshrined in their home or scattered on the sea or land, according to the wishes of the family or the will of the deceased.

POPULAR BUDDHIST PRACTICES

Most Thais concern themselves with accruing positive karmic merit through their religious practices. On any given day, besides chanting devotions at home, they can go to the local temple to offer lotus buds, candles, three incense sticks, or even elaborate assemblages. Other actions can be undertaken for merit-making, such as giving donations to the monks or to charities, putting food in monks' alms bowls at daybreak, and performing acts of kindness like freeing caged birds. These kinds of daily practices may also be done on behalf of a deceased relative.

A popular custom for laypersons is the merit-making ceremony performed in the home. A family hosts nine monks, offering them hospitality and food.

Furniture is removed from the main room of the house and cushions are placed along the walls and mats on the floor. A Buddha image is set on an altar by the door along with candles and flowers. A basin of water is set beside the cushion of the senior monk or the abbot to be consecrated by him. A white sacred cord is also draped around the room. The monks chant during the ceremony, and afterward eat the food provided by the family.

In Thailand, *Visākha Pūjā* is the celebration of the Buddha's birthday. It is celebrated throughout the country on the fifteenth day of the sixth lunar month. On *Visākha Pūjā* Day, people put up religious flags outside their houses and also take part in special temple ceremonies. They bring flowers, candles, and three incense sticks to pay respect to the Buddha, Dharma, and Saṅgha. The people take part in candlelit processions in the main hall of the temple, walking around the hall three times. Every layperson carries flowers, three incense sticks, and a lighted candle.

During the seasonal monsoon rains, all Buddhist monks retreat to their monasteries for a period of spiritual renewal dedicated to study and meditation. This retreat lasts for a period of three months—from July to October. Laypersons engage in merit-making during this period by offerings of food and items for daily use to the monks.

Thailand has several religious monuments and pilgrimage sites scattered across the country. Most of these sites are pagodas; some are images of the Buddha made of precious stone, bronze, or gold enshrined in famous temples; and some house popular images in private compounds. According to popular belief, pilgrimages to these sites bring luck and prosperity to the pilgrims. During each visit, Buddhist devotees donate money, flowers, incense sticks, and candles in front of the main Buddha of the shrine hall or at places that have been arranged for donations.

Each holy site also has its own unique history, so Buddhist devotees need to be aware of the specific *mantras*, rituals or favorite items proper to each site. For example, it is unanimously agreed that the most holy object of worship in Thailand is the Emerald Buddha in the Royal Grand Palace. It is magnet to thousands of Buddhists each day who are drawn to pay homage with offerings of hardboiled eggs.

Wat Sothon in central Thailand is also a popular pilgrimage site because of Luang Pho Sothon, one of the most revered Buddha images in Thailand. The huge bronze Buddha image of antiquity was believed to have floated down the river and emerged at the local temple where it is now housed. Therefore, it is believed to have the power to protect one from any danger from water. Amulets of Luang Pho Sothon are worn around the neck of children who live alongside rivers. Each year, thousands of parents present offerings on behalf of their children to the Buddha of Wat Sothon to secure their health and protection from dangers and illnesses. There are two annual fairs, one in April and the other in November, drawing many pilgrims.

Although the Buddhist canon rejects superstitions, each Buddhist country's culture reveals an animist heritage. As can be inferred from this essay, most Thais believe in various superstitions. For example, amulets blessed by monks are thought to heal the sick, bring fortune, boost sexual charm, and protect against injury. Usually worn as a pendant, amulets are commonly encased metal or clay Buddha images, while portraits of King Rama V and famous monks are also popular. More exotic charms include cloths inscribed with sacred drawings, dolls of a beckoning woman representing a spirit that brings money into a household, and tattoos of sacred *mantras* or diagrams.

Animist roots also emerge through spirit worship. On many lots where there are buildings, one finds a spirit house installed at an auspiciously divined location and time. Resembling a mini-temple on a pedestal, it shelters a spirit who is appeased with models of servants, elephants, and dancers, as well as daily offerings. These spirit houses are especially busy the day before lottery numbers are announced.

CONTRIBUTIONS OF THAILAND TO BUDDHIST CULTURE

Because Thailand is the only country in Southeast Asia that has escaped Western colonialism, it has maintained its peaceful and friendly culture and is welcoming to all people. Its many beautiful and elaborate temples and its traditional art forms, from dance to painting, provide the world with recognized cultural treasures. Thailand also offers opportunities for interested Westerners to practice intensive meditation and study Theravāda Buddhism. Most foreign monks from Europe and America who are ordained in the Buddhist tradition of Thailand are well honored by laypeople. These positive characteristics and qualities, cultural expressions, practical opportunities, along with the long and respected monastic tradition of Thailand, contribute to the county's positive Buddhist reputation.

The Thai tourist industry and rapid economic development have made Thai Buddhism better known in the world. Each year, more and more people come to Thailand to experience its Buddhist culture firsthand or to seek spiritual meaning through the study of Buddhism or by attending meditation retreats. However, Buddhism as understood by many Thais is not the religion of radical wisdom, peace, and meditation as understood by people from other parts of the world. Rather, for many in Thailand, Buddhism is a popular religious culture, deeply pervaded by supernaturalism, rituals, omens, and taboos inherited from the distant past.

Today, added to this kind of popular Buddhism, as well as to the traditional monasticism, are more socially engaged forms of Buddhist practice. For example, based on Buddhist moral and social values taught by Ven. Buddhadāsa, Phra Payom Kalyano is an outspoken social activist abbot who oversees large projects for the poor in Thailand. In the early 1990s, Phra Alongkot converted his wat into Thailand's first AIDS hospice, receiving support from the king and the princess mother. These modern figures, and others such as the layman Sulak Sivaraksa, provide the culture of Buddhism in Thailand with a more active, reflective, and compassionate social voice for the benefit of all.

NOTES

1. A. T. Ariyaratne, "Sarvodaya Shramadana's Approach to Peacebuilding," in David W. Chappell, ed., *Buddhist Peacework: Creating Cultures of Peace* (Somerville, MA: Wisdom Publications, 1999), pp. 69–70, 75, 77.

2. Buddhadāsa, *Buddhists and the Conservation of Nature* (Bangkok: Komol Kimtong, 1990), p. 12; trans. Santikaro Bhikkhu in "Buddhadāsa Bhikkhu: Life and Society through the Natural Eyes of Voidness," in Christopher S. Queen and Sallie B. King, eds., *Engaged Buddhism: Buddhist Liberation Movements in Asia* (Albany: SUNY Press, 1996), p. 162

3. Sulak Sivaraksa, *A Socially Engaged Buddhism* (Bangkok: Thai Inter-Religious Commission for Development, 1988), p. 185.

4. Thich Nhat Hanh, *Call Me by My True Names: The Collected Poems of Thich Nhat Hanh* (Berkeley, CA: Parallax Press, 1999), p. 72.

SUGGESTIONS FOR FURTHER READING

Aronson, Harvey B. *Love and Sympathy in Theravāda Buddhism*. Delhi, India: Motilal Banarsidass, 1980.

Bailey, Greg, and Ian Mabbett. *The Sociology of Early Buddhism*. Cambridge, UK: Cambridge University Press, 2006.

Bartholomeusz, Tessa J. *Women under the Bo Tree: Buddhist Nuns in Sri Lanka*. Cambridge, UK: Cambridge University Press, 2008.

Bodiford, William, ed. *Going Forth: Visions of Buddhist Vinaya*. Honolulu: University of Hawaii Press, 2005.

Bodhi, Bhikkhu, trans. *The Connected Discourses of the Buddha*. Boston: Wisdom Publications, 2000.

Bodhi, Bhikkhu, and Nyanaponika Thera, trans. *The Numerical Discourses of the Buddha: An Anthology of Suttas from the Anguattara Nikāya*. Lanham, MD: Rowman and Littlefield, 2000.

Bond, George. *The Buddhist Revival in Sri Lanka: Religious Tradition, Reinterpretation, and Response*. Columbia: University of South Carolina Press, 1988.

Buddhaghosa. *The Path of Purification (Visuddhimagga)*. Translated by Nanamoli Thera. Berkeley, CA: Shambhala Publications, 1976.

Bunnag, J. *Buddhist Monk, Buddhist Layman: A Study of Buddhist Monastic Organization in Central Thailand*. Cambridge, UK: Cambridge University Press, 1973.

Carrithers, Michael. *The Forest Monks of Sri Lanka*. Delhi, India: Oxford University Press, 1983.

Carter, John Ross. *On Understanding Buddhists: Essays on the Theravāda Tradition in Sri Lanka*. Albany: SUNY Press, 1993.

Chakravarti, Uma. *The Social Dimensions of Early Buddhism*. Delhi, India: Oxford University Press, 1987.

Cook, Joanna. *Meditation in Modern Buddhism: Renunciation and Change in Thai Monastic Life*. Cambridge, UK: Cambridge University Press, 2010.

Gombrich, Richard F. *Theravāda Buddhism: A Social History from Ancient Benares to Modern Colombo*. London: Routledge & Kegan Paul, 1988.

Gombrich, Richard F., and Gananath Obeyesekere. *Buddhism Transformed: Religious Change in Sri Lanka*. Princeton, NJ: Princeton University Press, 1988.

Gunaratana, Henepola. *The Path of Serenity and Insight: An Explanation of the Buddhist Jhānas*. Delhi, India: Motilal Banarsidass, 1985.

Harris, Ian. *Cambodian Buddhism: History and Practice*. Honolulu: University of Hawaii Press, 2005.

Harvey, Peter. *The Selfless Mind: Personality, Consciousness, and Nirvana in Early Buddhism*. Richmond, UK: Curzon Press, 1995.

Hoffman, Frank, and Deegalle Mahinda, eds. *Pali Buddhism*. Richmond, UK: Curzon Press, 1996.

Holt, John C., Jacob N. Kinnard, and Jonathan S. Walters, eds. *Constituting Communities: Theravāda Buddhism and the Religious Cultures of South and Southeastern Asia*. Albany: SUNY Press, 2003.

Kalupahana, David J. *Ethics in Early Buddhism*. Honolulu: University of Hawaii Press, 1995.

Keyes, Charles E., Laurel Kendall, and Helen Hardacre, eds. *Asian Visions of Authority: Religion and the Modern States of East and Southeast Asia*. Honolulu: University of Hawaii Press, 1994.

Mannikka, Eleanor. *Angkor Wat: Time, Space, and Kingship*. Honolulu: University of Hawaii Press, 1996.

Miksic, John. *Borobudur: Golden Tales of the Buddha*. Boston: Charles E. Tuttle, 1995.

Nanamoli, Bhikkhu, and Bhikkhu Bodhi, trans. *The Middle Length Discourses of the Buddha*. Boston: Wisdom Publications, 1995.

Nhat Hanh, Thich. *Vietnam: Lotus in a Sea of Fire*. New York: Hill and Wang, 1967.

Seneviratne, H. L. *The Work of Kings: The New Buddhism in Sri Lanka*. Chicago: University of Chicago Press, 1999.

Snodgrass, A. *The Symbolism of the Stūpa*. Ithaca, NY: Cornell University Press, 1985.

Strong, John. *The Legend of King Aśoka*. Princeton, NJ: Princeton University Press, 1983.

Swearer, Donald K. *The Buddhist World of Southeast Asia*. Albany: SUNY Press, 2010.

———. *Me and Mine: Selected Essays of Bhikku Buddhadllsa*. Albany: SUNY Press, 1990.

Tilakaratne, Asanga. *Theravāda Buddhism: The View of the Elders*. Honolulu: University of Hawaii Press, 2012.

Walshe, Maurice O'Clarke, trans. *The Long Discourses of the Buddha*. Boston: Wisdom Publications, 1995.

Wijayaratne, Mohan. *Buddhist Monastic Life According to the Texts of the Theravāda Tradition*. Translated by Claude Grangier and Steven Collins. Cambridge, UK: Cambridge University Press, 1990.

4

The Great Vehicle

There is a collection of stories in the *Sūtra Piṭaka* of the Pali scripture about twenty-four Buddhas who lived before Gautama Buddha. The collection entitled the *Buddhavarmsa* begins with Śāriputra asking Gautama Buddha when it was that he first resolved to become the Buddha and what were the virtues of perfection he achieved to attain this goal. The Buddha then relates how eons ago he was a hermit named Sumedha. One day, he heard that there was a Buddha named Dīpankara teaching in a nearby town. He went to that town and saw Dīpankara Buddha approaching him at the head of a long procession of monks. Sumedha was moved to deep reverence for Dīpankara. He realized that while he could follow this Buddha and become an *arhat*, he could benefit the world more by becoming a Buddha. In that moment, he made a vow to become a Buddha in a future life.

When he did so, Sumedha noticed that Dīpankara Buddha and the Saṅgha following him were approaching a patch of mud. So he lay flat on the mud and invited them to walk over him. Dīpankara read Sumedha's mind and understood that he had vowed to become a Buddha. Dīpankara then predicted that Sumedha would one day attain his goal. Sumedha returned to his hermitage to reflect on how he could achieve Buddhahood. Over time, he came to understand that he would need to perfect ten virtues to achieve this goal. The Pali text lists these ten virtues, later referred to as the Ten Perfections in early Buddhism: generosity (*dāna*), moral virtue (*sīla*), renunciation (*nekkhamma*), wisdom (*pañña*), energy (*vīriya*), patience (*khanti*), truthfulness (*sacca*), determination (*adhiṭṭhāna*), loving kindness (*mettā*), and equanimity (*upekkhā*). Gautama Buddha concludes this story by relating to Śāriputra how he perfected these virtues life after life until his full Awakening in his present life. Here and elsewhere, Gautama refers to himself during his previous lives when he pursued the perfection of the ten virtues as being a "bodhisattva." This title here means "a being who is to become Awakened"; and the Ten Perfections became associated with the life of a bodhisattva.

This story expressed an alternative to the path to Arhatship and Nirvana, namely, what would become known as the Bodhisattva Path to Buddhahood. Indeed, the early schools of Buddhism that we introduced in the previous chapter all recognized this Bodhisattva Path, but taught that it is a heroic path for only a very few. It is best, they argued, to follow the shorter path leading to Nirvana than the more arduous path over eons of time leading to Buddhahood. However, some Buddhist monastics did eventually resolve to follow the Bodhisattva Path. There is very little we know for certain about how, when, and where this happened. But we do know that at some time before the first century B.C.E. there were monastics in traditional monasteries of the early Buddhist tradition who took up the bodhisattva practice of the perfection of virtues alongside their fellow monastics who preferred the original path leading to Nirvana. Scholars note that during the early growth of Buddhism, the literature began to exalt the status of the Buddha, and the worship of *stūpas* and later of images of the Buddha became more and more popular.

By the first century B.C.E., the experience of this bodhisattva practice was expressed in a new literature. New *sūtras* began to appear that claimed to be discourses of Gautama Buddha that presented the wisdom and the practice of the Bodhisattva Path. These *sūtras* taught that the Bodhisattva Path is superior to that of original Buddhism because it leads to a greater attainment, namely, full Buddhahood. The qualities gained in the process of further growth beyond Arhatship could be used to benefit all living beings in ways not possible for an *arhat*. The Bodhisattva Path was therefore referred to as the *Mahāyāna*, meaning "Great Vehicle," "Great Course," or "Great Journey." Followers of Mahāyāna also referred to the earlier forms of Buddhism as *Hīnayāna*, or "Lesser Vehicle," as they do not lead all the way to full Buddhahood. This term carries a negative connotation. In fact, by 200 C.E., there was a split between Mahāyāna and the early forms of Buddhism.

The Mahāyāna *sūtras* were presented as teachings of Gautama Buddha, even though they were unknown from the beginning of Buddhism. One reason given for this historical fact was that the teachings in the new *sūtras* were deeper and more demanding than those originally taught by the Buddha. The Buddha knew that the long and arduous Bodhisattva Path would have attracted only a few followers into the Saṅgha. So he publically presented only the easier Path to Arhatship. He privately taught the Bodhisattva Path to a few followers to be passed on until the Saṅgha was ready for them to be made public. It was also claimed that the *sūtras* were taught to and preserved by certain spirits until the time was right. Others claimed that although the Buddha taught the *sūtras*, they were only "heard" by persons in their dreams when the world was ready for them.

In any case, the task for early Mahāyāna was to define their Great Vehicle from the new ideas presented in their *sūtras*. They considered this task as the "second turning of the wheel of the Dharma." While the different *sūtras* contribute a variety of teachings, there are some fundamental ideas that have become associated with Mahāyāna. Here, we mention four that are discussed in some detail in this and in the next chapter.

THE BODHISATTVA

The first characteristic notion found in developed Mahāyāna is the view that a Buddha, rather than an *arhat,* is the person who can be of most help to people who are suffering and in need of liberation. To achieve this condition of Buddhahood, one needs to follow the Bodhisattva Path. This bodhisattva life begins with what is called the "arising of the thought of Awakening," or *bodhicitta.* This *bodhicitta* is really the altruistic desire, or heartfelt aspiration, to attain Buddhahood so that one can help others gain freedom from suffering. What this means concretely is that one aspires to follow the Bodhisattva Path, or the "Great Journey," rather than the path leading to Arhatship. In fact, Mahāyāna was called the *Bodhisattvayāna,* or "Bodhisattva Vehicle" bringing one to Buddhahood, in distinction from the *Śrāvakayāna,* or "Disciple Vehicle" bringing one to Arhatship. Early Mahāyāna taught Six Perfections that advance this bodhisattva journey to Buddhahood. Later Mahāyāna introduced Ten Stages on the Bodhisattva Path and added four other perfections so that each stage has a particular perfection associated with it. These Ten Perfections vary somewhat from those of the earlier traditions mentioned above. We introduce this path in some detail later in this chapter.

WISDOM AND EMPTINESS

A second characteristic of Mahāyāna teaching is the notion of a "higher wisdom" (*prajñāpāramitā*) realizing "emptiness" (*śūnyatā*). This notion has to do with the awakened experience of the Buddhas and bodhisattvas. For Mahāyāna, what one experiences with awakened consciousness is that all the "factors of existence" (*dharmas*), which we have seen were so carefully analyzed in the *Abhidharma Piṭaka,* are "empty" (*śūnya*) of existing independently, or "on their own." In the language of Mahāyāna, all aspects of existence are "*svabhāva-śūnya,*" that is, "empty of own-being." This means that nothing can exist on its own. In other words, all things in the world, the elementary factors of life and the particular beings that these factors constitute, are seen by a higher wisdom to have this fundamental characteristic of emptiness.

The term *śūnya,* which we translate as "empty," can mean in Sanskrit "hollow," as in something that looks solid but is in fact hollow inside. Thus, "empty of own-being" means that although things seem to ordinary experience as if they are independent entities, deeper insight shows that they are really empty, or hollow, of that independence. This is another way of saying what the Buddha himself taught, namely, that all things arise dependently. To experience this dependently arisen nature of things—their "emptiness" of independence—is the core of wisdom experience according to Mahāyāna. It is this profound Mahāyāna experience of penetrating insight into the emptiness of all things by the awakened consciousness that brings one freedom. It is this profound wisdom realizing emptiness that, coupled with a compassionate motivation to save all living beings, furthers one's Great Journey to the goal of Buddhahood.

LUMINOUS CONSCIOUSNESS

A third characteristic of Mahāyāna teaching concerns the nature of consciousness. We have seen that one view of consciousness found in early Buddhist texts teaches that the mind is naturally pure and clear, having been stained by mental defilements. While in Mahāyāna there are many and sometimes conflicting notions concerning consciousness, we find a similar strand of thought. It claims that consciousness, prior to being affected by defilements, is the luminous clarity and nirvanic status of enlightened Buddhahood. This pure luminosity as the true essence of consciousness gives people the potential for Buddhahood. But ordinary conscious life generates conceptualizations and other mental formations that frustrate this potential. In the end, it is the mind that enslaves people in a life that is untrue and unsatisfying (*duḥkha*); and it is also the mind that can set people free.

CELESTIAL BUDDHAS

Finally, the fourth characteristic notion has to do with the nature of Buddhahood, the goal of the Bodhisattva Path. While the early Buddhist texts claim that the cosmos includes realms of hells, ghosts, gods, and *Brahmā* beings, Mahāyāna expanded this vision of the cosmos by claiming that it also contains countless Buddhas residing in Buddha realms. In following the Bodhisattva Path, one can be reborn in one of these realms, where one can progress toward Buddhahood under the guidance and with the blessings of the Buddha of that realm. When one attains Buddhahood, one will also create a Buddha realm from where one will help others throughout the cosmos. In the meantime, one can receive guidance and blessings in this world, as well as visualize these "celestial" Buddhas and their realms and the advanced bodhisattvas that abide in them in ways that are spiritually transforming. These Buddhas and advanced bodhisattvas develop special skillful means (*upāya*) that they use to appear in the many world systems of the cosmos in order to help other beings become free from suffering and progress in the journey to Awakening and Buddhahood.

As we noted earlier, for many centuries after the beginning of the Mahāyāna movement, indeed perhaps up until the seventh century C.E., members of this newer tradition lived in monasteries side-by-side with Buddhists who chose to follow the original teachings of the Three *Piṭakas*. However, as time passed and some of the *sūtras* became more polemical as they stressed the "superiority" of the Mahāyāna over the older tradition, Mahāyānins began to separate from the other schools. We have seen that the Theravādins spread into Sri Lanka and Southeast Asia. Mahāyāna flourished in various places in India from where it eventually spread into other parts of Asia, especially Central and East Asia. It became the primary form of Buddhism in such countries as Tibet, China, Korea, Japan, and Vietnam. So, with these general comments about Mahāyāna and its teachings, we can now look at some of the individual *sūtras* that have been especially important in defining the Mahāyāna experience of Buddhism.

THE MAHĀYĀNA *SŪTRAS*

The Mahāyāna *sūtras* were written to teach the experiences of Mahāyāna in following the Bodhisattva Path to Buddhahood. The following are some of the major Mahāyāna *sūtras* that introduce the kinds of teachings we have already outlined. We include some selections from these *sūtras* that present (1) the notions of wisdom and emptiness, (2) the nature of consciousness, (3) the transcendent nature of the Buddha, and (4) the existence of Buddha realms. In the next section, we introduce the Bodhisattva Path and its stages and perfections in some detail.

Discovering the Perfection of Wisdom

Among the earliest of the Mahāyāna *sūtras* are the *Perfection of Wisdom Sūtras* (*Prajñāpāramitā-Sūtras*). These *sūtras* began to be written in the first century C.E. Longer versions were written during the next 200 years; more condensed *sūtras* were written from 300 to 700 C.E. (see Figure 4.1). These condensed versions include the famous *Diamond Sūtra* and *Heart Sūtra*. Within some of the Wisdom Literature, the journey of the bodhisattva is defined by the Six Perfections (giving, morality, patience, vigor, meditation, and wisdom). This Bodhisattva Path is lived compassionately for the benefit of others because one's practice of it is motivated by *bodhicitta*, the aspiration to attain Buddhahood to save all living beings. This altruistic attitude leads the Mahāyāna

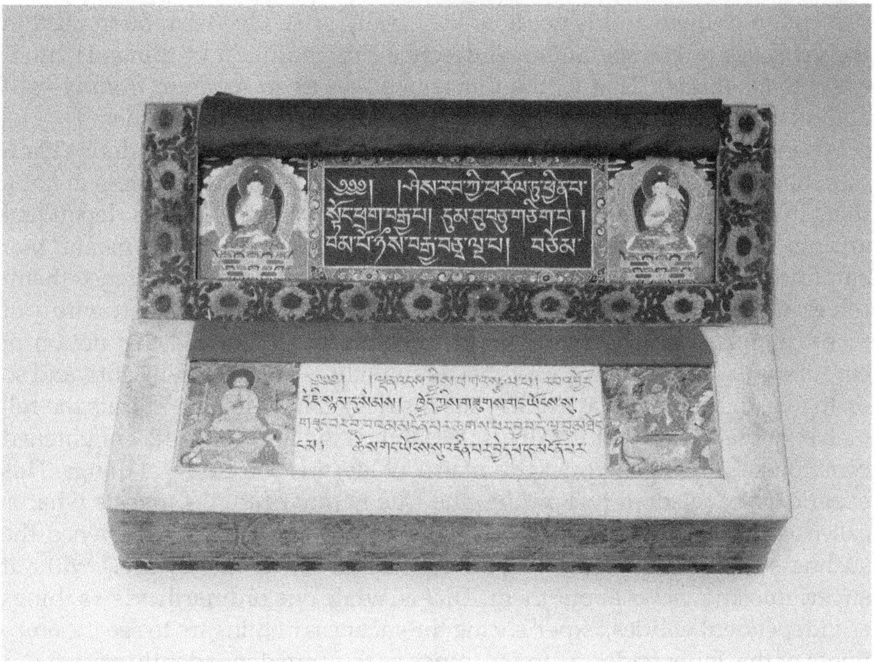

FIGURE 4.1. Illuminated manuscript in Tibetan of the *Perfection of Wisdom Sūtra 100,000 Verses*, eighteenth century, Tibet. Library of Congress, Asian Collection.

Buddhist to renounce any personal attainment of Arhatship and Final Nirvana so as to continue to help others in need. In this regard, the *Perfection of Wisdom Sūtras* depict the *arhats* as selfishly leaving society behind to enjoy the quiescence of Final Nirvana after death.

In following this compassionate path, bodhisattvas can eventually be reborn in celestial Buddha realms where they can gain the powers and skillful means necessary to become Buddhas and help others do the same. As a celestial bodhisattva, and eventually as a celestial Buddha with one's own Buddha realm in the heavens of the cosmos, one will be a more universally active source of blessings for all living beings. Mahāyāna taught that these blessings are possible because of "merit transfer." Because karmic merit can be transferred from one person to another, celestial bodhisattvas and Buddhas—who have accumulated great merit during eons of practicing the Perfections—can transfer that merit to needy sentient beings.

Besides the compassion of the bodhisattva and its implications for religious practice, the *Perfection of Wisdom Sūtras* also expound the wisdom of the bodhisattva. Through the ordinary use of perception and language, one experiences the many things of the world as being separate and distinct entities. But the wisdom of the bodhisattva brings one to the realization that the things of the world are not independent; they lack their seeming inherent existence. Things as normally seen are said to be "like a dream." This does not mean that they do not exist but that they exist like a dream depending on a dreamer. In other words, the many things of the world appear as if they are independent entities; but this appearance of independence depends on one's perception of them and is not how they really exist. One term often used in the *Perfection of Wisdom Sūtras* to describe this condition of things is "non-arising" (*anutpāda*). That is, the things one sees as so separate from oneself and other beings have "not arisen" in such an independent manner.

When one experiences the real status of things, claims the Wisdom Literature, one beholds "emptiness." As we mentioned earlier, emptiness is not a thing in its own right but is precisely the way all things are in their dependent arising, namely, "empty of own-being" (*svabhāva-śūnya*). This means that emptiness is not some ultimate reality beyond the forms of existence themselves; rather, the myriad forms of existence are emptiness—they are empty of own-being. An analogy that is used to help one understand this notion of emptiness is a flower that always needs sunlight, water, soil, nutrients, and so on to live. In a similar way, Mahāyāna is saying that each being needs the full matrix of life to be what it truly is. Wisdom is the insight of the enlightened consciousness that penetrates this matrix of life, this emptiness of things. This experience of wisdom insight into the true nature of things reveals what is called, in many Mahāyāna *sūtras*, "suchness" (*tathatā*). To experience the suchness of things means to experience things "such as they are," without superimposing views about them. That is, while one ordinarily views things as independent entities, experiencing the suchness of things is to see the emptiness of this independence, to see things as they are dependently arisen.

With wisdom insight into suchness, into the empty nature of all beings, there is a liberating effect on the person of wisdom. In experiencing the emptiness of all things, one's attachments to the things of the world are loosened, defilements are brought to an end, and delusion is dispersed. The state of mind that one realizes with this freedom is Nirvana. But because Nirvana is also experienced as empty—as not an independent state separate from the ordinary *saṃsāric* world—one is also free from attachment to this spiritual status. With freedom from the world of *saṃsāra* on the one hand and from Nirvana on the other, one "courses" in the Middle Way. This means that one is free from any attachment to either *saṃsāra* or Nirvana; and therefore one is free to embrace all things as they are in their suchness, while responding to their needs out of selfless compassion. As we shall see in the next chapter, these ideas about wisdom and emptiness presented in the *Perfection of Wisdom Sūtras* became the inspiration for Mādhyamika, one of the major schools of Indian Mahāyāna Buddhist philosophy, as well as many of the schools of Mahāyāna Buddhism in other parts of Asia.

The Heart Sūtra

With these remarks in mind, let us now look at the *Heart Sūtra*, which is said to capture in a few words the "heart" of the Perfection of Wisdom. This is one of the best known of the *Perfection of Wisdom Sūtras* in East Asia. Its teaching is given to Śāriputra, one of the Buddha's chief disciples. Note that the first part of the text begins by saying that the famous celestial bodhisattva named Avalokiteśvara, while engaged in the Great Journey, looks down at the world with his perfection of wisdom. From that vantage point, he sees that the Five Aggregates are "empty of own-being" and that emptiness is not different from the Five Aggregates. Emptiness is their true nature. Avalokiteśvara then sees that all the *dharmas*, analyzed and categorized so carefully by the earlier *Abhidharma* texts, are also empty of own-being. Therefore, from the point of view of emptiness, the *dharmas* are not produced as discrete entities to be characterized by the categories of the *Abhidharma*—they are all the same in that they are all characterized by emptiness.

> Om! Praise to the blessed and noble perfection of wisdom! The noble Avalokiteśvara Bodhisattva was moving in the deep journey of the perfection of wisdom. When he looked down at the Five Aggregates, he saw that they are empty of own-being.
>
> Here, O Śāriputra, form is emptiness, emptiness is form. Form is not different from emptiness, emptiness is not different from form. What is form is emptiness, what is emptiness is form. The same is true for sensations, perceptions, mental formations and consciousness.
>
> Here, O Śāriputra, all *dharmas* are characterized by emptiness; they are neither produced nor cease, they are neither defiled nor pure, they are neither deficient nor complete.

In the next part of the text, it is said that the perfection of wisdom realizing emptiness looks over the Five Aggregates, the six senses and their objects, the eighteen elements that constitute conscious experience, the twelve links of dependent arising, the Four Noble Truths, and the knowledge and attainment, or lack thereof, associated with the *arhat*. In fact, these factors and processes of existence are the ones that Buddhaghosa says are the "soil" to be "turned over" with knowledge and insight to become an *arhat*. However, the *Heart Sūtra* says that when Avalokiteśvara looks at these factors of existence with his higher bodhisattva wisdom, he sees that they do not exist as ordinarily conceived because they are all empty of own-being.

> Therefore, O Śāriputra, in emptiness, there is no form, sensation, perception, mental formation, or consciousness; no eye, ear, nose, tongue, body or mind; no forms, sounds, odors, tastes, objects of touch, or objects of the mind; no eye-element and so on up to no mind-consciousness element; there is neither ignorance nor cessation of ignorance and so on up to neither old age and death nor cessation of old age and death. There is no *duḥkha*, no origination of *duḥkha*, no cessation of *duḥkha*, no path to the cessation of *duḥkha*. There is no knowledge, no attainment, no nonattainment.

The text goes on to say that with this higher insight into the emptiness of all things, including the attainment of Nirvana, the bodhisattva is indifferent not only to worldly things but also to any attainment of Final Nirvana apart from this world. Instead, like all the Buddhas of all periods of time, he or she relies on the perfection of wisdom to be free of any obstacles to becoming a Buddha, and in the end actually realizes Nirvana in this world. The text ends with the great *mantra* that is spoken, as it were, by a personification of the perfection of wisdom. It is implied that while ordinary *mantras* can soothe some *duḥkha*, the perfection of wisdom, like a great *mantra*, conveys the power to bring about a cessation of all *duḥkha* through Awakening inspiring joyfulness. The text concludes with an actual *mantra* in praise of the perfection of wisdom that goes beyond everything to the full Awakening of Buddhahood.

> Therefore, O Śāriputra, because of being indifferent to attainment, a bodhisattva relies on the perfection of wisdom and remains thereby free from mental hindrances. Being free from mental hindrances, he or she is not afraid, overcomes erroneous views, and in the end attains Nirvana. All Buddhas of all times have attained the highest and perfect Awakening by relying on the perfection of wisdom.
>
> Therefore, one should know the great *mantra* of the perfection of wisdom, the *mantra* of great knowledge, the unsurpassed and unequaled *mantra*, the *mantra* that allays all *duḥkha*—it is true, for there is nothing lacking in it. By the perfection of wisdom is this *mantra* spoken. It is the following: Gone, gone, gone beyond, utterly gone beyond; Awakening; O joy! (*Prajñāpāramitā-Hṛdaya-Sūtra*)

A Layperson's Sūtra

Another important Mahāyāna *sūtra* is the *Sūtra Expounded by Vimalakīrti (Vimalakīrti-Nirdeśa-Sūtra)*. Composed in the first century C.E., this *sūtra* tells the story of Vimalakīrti, a rich layman living in Vaiśālī, whose understanding of the Buddha's teaching was so deep that he was accepted as a bodhisattva. Indeed, Vimalakīrti's wisdom was so profound that it surpassed not only the insight of the *arhats,* but even of some of the great bodhisattvas who had come down to visit from their celestial realms. Thus, the Mahāyāna point is made that the attainment of the bodhisattva is greater than that of the *arhat,* and it is not only for monastics but is also open to laypersons.

In this *sūtra,* as in the Wisdom Literature, the doctrine of the emptiness of things is presented. Here, it is said that because of emptiness, the world appears in ordinary experience. However, this does not mean that emptiness is an imperceptible causal force—like a God—that is apart from the things one perceives. Emptiness is instead the hidden "suchness" of all the things one ordinarily experiences with a discriminating mind. In the words of the *sūtra,* emptiness is the "baseless base" of all discriminated things. This emptiness, or suchness, or baseless base of existence is hidden from view by the "dualities" of the discriminating mind. By dualities are meant the perceived differences between self and other, between the senses and objects of sense, between purity and defilement, and, ultimately, between *saṃsāra* and Nirvana. When asked what the nondual condition of life is like, Vimalakīrti "kept silent without saying a word," because words cannot describe it. True understanding of this nondual reality of emptiness must be realized in the direct experience of full Awakening.

In the *sūtra,* there is an instructive dialogue between a goddess taught by Vimalakīrti, and Śāriputra, who represents those who follow the older path of the disciples. This discussion is about how the discriminations emphasized in that earlier tradition, between, for example, wholesome and unwholesome things, cannot capture the real suchness of things. The discriminating mind cannot see the reality that lies beyond its discriminations:

> A goddess . . . listening to the Dharma in Vimalakīrti's room, appeared in bodily form and showered flowers on the bodhisattvas and chief disciples of the Buddha who were present. The flowers that landed on the bodhisattvas fell off and onto the ground. But those that landed on the disciples stuck to their bodies and did not fall off despite all their efforts to shake them off.
>
> Thereupon, the goddess asked Śāriputra why he tried to shake off the flowers. Śāriputra replied, "I want to shake off these flowers because they are not of the status of suchness." The goddess said, "Do not say that these flowers are not of the status of suchness . . . because it is you who gives rise to such a discrimination. . . . But if you no longer make such discriminations, this all will be of the status of suchness. Look at the bodhisattvas whose bodies do not hold the flowers. That is because they have put an end to such discrimination." (*Vimalakīrti-Nirdeśa-Sūtra,* VIII)

As is said in the *Heart Sūtra*, it is by going beyond the discriminations of ordinary experience that one finds emptiness, and the freedom it brings from things "sticking" to one in ways that hinder one's spiritual journey to Awakening. However, it seems that Śāriputra did not understand the goddess's words because later he asks her to change her female body into the form of a man. He is discriminating a man's body as superior to a woman's. The goddess again teaches that in their suchness, all forms are the same in that they are in reality empty of their discriminated characteristics, including those of gender. The goddess points out Śāriputra's attachment to the male gender and chides him for not realizing that the suchness of all forms is the same. Awakening to this truth about the ultimate "sameness" of all things is—the story implies—open to everyone, male and female, lay and monastic.

> Śāriputra asked, "Why do not you change your female form?" The goddess replied, "For the last twelve years, I have been looking in vain for a female form. So, what is it that you want me to change?"
>
> Thereupon, she used her supernatural powers to change Śāriputra into a celestial goddess, and to change herself into a man similar to Śāriputra. She then asked him, "Why do not you change your female form?"
>
> The goddess said, "Like Śāriputra, who is not a woman but only appears in female form, all women are the same. Though they appear in female form, they are ultimately not women. Hence the Buddha said, 'All things [ultimately] are neither male or female.'" (*Vimalakīrti-Nirdeśa-Sūtra*, VIII)

Exploring Consciousness

Whereas the previous two *sūtras* focus more on emptiness, the *Laṅkāvatāra Sūtra* examines the nature of consciousness, its production of ordinary experience, and its potential for Awakening and Buddhahood. The *Sūtra on the Descent into Lanka* (*Laṅkāvatāra Sūtra*) is said by scholars to have been composed around the fourth century C.E. We have seen in the *Perfection of Wisdom Sūtras* and *Vimalakīrti Sūtra* that ordinary consciousness has a role in discriminating people's mistaken experience of independent selfhood and independent objects. The *Laṅkāvatāra Sūtra* explores how the mind creates this false dualistic experience of self and world and how the mind can also escape this misperception of things and attain Awakening and Buddhahood.

The *Laṅkāvatāra Sūtra* stresses the need for an inward journey of meditation to overcome the ordinary workings of the mind, which produce mental discriminations that result in an unsatisfactory life. One's ordinary mental functioning dualistically objectifies an independent self and a world of independent objects in a fashion that leads to unwholesome attachment to things and, thereby, unhappiness. By turning one's meditative attention into the inner field of consciousness itself, one discovers that one's misperception of reality is based in a deeper mental phenomenon, what the *sūtra* calls the "storehouse-consciousness" (*ālaya-vijñāna*). It is this foundation of consciousness that is the ultimate cause of both one's subjective experience of selfhood and one's objective experience of the world. This depth of consciousness is said to create both one's subjective and objective experience like the deep ocean creates waves on its surface. One's experience of oneself and the world—like waves produced by the force of the ocean—is created by the force of the storehouse consciousness. As the *sūtra* says,

> At that time, the [Buddha] recited these verses: "Like waves that rise on the ocean when stirred by the wind, dancing without interruption, in a similar way the storehouse-ocean is constantly stirred by the winds of objectivity such that the multiple waves of consciousness are seen dancing about.
>
> As the waves in all their variety are stirred on the surface of the ocean, so in the storehouse the variety of what is known as consciousness is produced. The mind and its [variety of] consciousness are discriminated as regards their form; [but] the [variety of] consciousness is not separate from the mind. . . . Just as there is no distinction between the ocean and its waves, so in the mind there is no evolution of the variety of consciousness.
>
> "The visible world is discriminated by the [variety of] consciousness. . . . Form with characteristics and status are presented to our consciousnesses as such; they are seen as evolving in the same way as waves." (*Laṅkāvatāra Sūtra*, 46–47)

Whereas the Wisdom Literature and the *Vimalakīrti Sūtra* call for the bodhisattva to experience emptiness, the *Laṅkāvatāra Sūtra* calls for an experience of this ocean of consciousness below the waves of experience. The *sūtra* proposes this experience of the very foundation of consciousness because it recognizes that its storehouse produces the experience not only of selfhood and the world but of Buddhahood as well. How is this possible? The *Laṅkāvatāra* says that if one realizes a "reversion of the foundation of the mind," one can discover its clear, pure luminosity that is the very essence of Buddhahood. Therefore, the storehouse-consciousness is also called the "Womb of the *Tathāgata*" (*tathāgata-garbha*). The term *Tathāgata*—meaning "Thus come" or Thus gone"—is a title given to Gautama Buddha. It indicates that the historical Buddha was one in a series of Buddhas who have come into the world and gone. The word *garbha* means either "womb" or "embryo." So to say that consciousness is like a womb or embryo of the *Tathāgata* means that all people can be part of this series of Buddhas because each person's innermost consciousness is like a womb that holds the embryo of Buddhahood. Here again are the words of the *sūtra*:

> Nirvana is the storehouse-consciousness where a reversion takes place by self-realization. . . . When a reversion takes place in the practitioner of yoga, the [varieties of] consciousness cast off discrimination between [subject and object] in what is realized as the [nature of] mind itself. Here, one enters the *Tathāgata* stage, attaining the realization of noble wisdom; and in this stage, there is no thought of existence or nonexistence. . . . When all these [varieties of consciousness] go through a reversion, I and all the other Buddhas declare that there is Nirvana. The mode and nature of this Nirvana is emptiness, which is the status of reality. . . . [This is because the storehouse-consciousness] is like a great ocean in which waves roll on constantly, but the [depths] subsist unaffected,

> free from the faults of impermanence . . . thoroughly pure in its essence. . . . The storehouse-consciousness is [thus] known by the name of the *Tathāgata-garbha.* (*Laṅkāvatāra Sūtra*, 62, 93, 99, 220–221)

This inner essence of the mind is the original pure, luminous, and nirvanic nature of the storehouse-consciousness that is beyond the dualistic discrimination of its ordinary mental functioning. With this inner realization, the embryo of Buddhahood begins to develop. In the light of the wisdom of developing Buddhahood, one experiences that all forms in emptiness display this luminous essence of the consciousness that produces them like an ocean producing waves. As we shall see in the next chapter, this understanding of consciousness is developed in the Indian Yogācāra School of Buddhist philosophy, which in turn influences many Mahāyāna schools in East Asia.

The Lotus

Another *sūtra* that is one of the most revered in East Asia is the *Sūtra on the Lotus of the True Dharma (Saddharmapuṇḍarīka-Sūtra)* written around 200 C.E. (see Figure 4.2). Like other Mahāyāna texts, the *Lotus Sūtra,* as it is better known, emphasizes the Bodhisattva Path entailing the practice of the Six Perfections leading in the Great Journey to Buddhahood. It also presents the perfection of wisdom's vision of the entire universe, "the world of the triple sphere in all its ten directions," as empty of own-being. In lauding this Mahāyāna experience, the *Lotus Sūtra* also holds out hope that eventually even the *arhats* will reach this higher goal of Buddhahood.

The *Lotus Sūtra* has a special teaching about what it considers the transcendent Buddha. The *sūtra* claims to have been preached at Vulture Peak by a dramatically transfigured Gautama Buddha, who reveals that in reality he had attained his Awakening incalculable, limitless, myriads of eons ago, and resides forever present to the world like a father preaching the Dharma. His human form as Gautama Buddha is a skillful means (*upāya*) to give people confidence that they can attain Nirvana. To display his transcendent power, as the *sūtra* opens, Gautama Buddha enters deep meditation and produces the following effect on his listeners that fills them with awe:

> At that moment, a ray issued from within the circle of hair between the Lord's eyebrows. It extended over eighteen-hundred thousand Buddha realms . . . so that all those Buddha realms were illuminated by its radiance. . . . Likewise, the noble Buddhas staying and living in those Buddha realms all became visible, and the Dharma being preached by them could be entirely heard by all beings. The monks, nuns and men and women lay devotees, practitioners of yoga, those who had attained fruition and those who had not, all became visible. The bodhisattvas, the great beings, in those Buddha realms who follow the bodhisattva's journey with ability due to their earnest faith in many kinds of lessons and ideas became visible too. . . . Then there arose this thought in the mind of the great being, Maitreya Bodhisattva, "O how great a wonder does the Tathāgata display!" (*Saddharmapuṇḍarīka-Sūtra*, I)

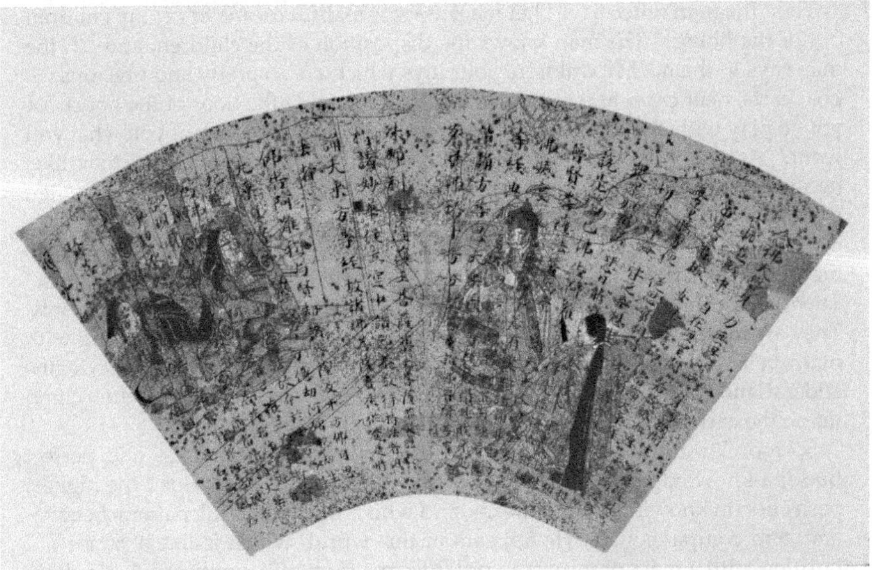

FIGURE 4.2. Mahāyāna Buddhism's spread to Japan: fan-shaped *Lotus Sūtra*; twelfth century C.E., Hōryu-ji Temple, Nara, Japan. Exhibited at Japan House Gallery, New York.

Gautama Buddha goes on in the *sūtra* to say that all Buddhas preach the Dharma of one Buddha-vehicle (*Buddha-yāna*). But because there are different kinds of people in various states of openness to this Buddha-vehicle, Buddhas use different skillful means to reach them. Therefore, there are three vehicles being taught, that of the *arhat*, the *pratyekabuddha*, and the bodhisattva. All who follow these will eventually attain supreme Awakening and become Buddhas. To explain skillful means, Gautama Buddha tells the following parable to Śāriputra. In it, he uses the analogy of three carts for the three vehicles of Buddhism.

> Let us suppose the following, Śāriputra. In a certain village . . . there was a great householder, old . . . and yet wealthy . . . with a grand house that is high and spacious, but built along time ago and now old. . . . The house has but one door . . . and all of a sudden it is being consumed on all sides by a mass of fire.
>
> Let us suppose that the man had many children . . . and that he had come out of the house. Now, Śāriputra, that man upon seeing the house being enwrapped in fire became greatly concerned . . . and made the following reflection, "I myself am able to come out from the burning house through the door . . . but my children are staying in the burning house absorbed in their playing and amusing themselves. . . . They do not perceive that the house is on fire . . . so they are not afraid and have no wish to escape. . . . Therefore, I will warn them."
>
> With this resolution, he calls to his children, "Come, my children, the house is burning with a mass of fire. . . ." But the ignorant children do not believe him . . . for they are not afraid . . . nor understand the word "burning." On the contrary, they run around, walk about, and repeatedly glance out at their father, all because they are so ignorant.

> Then the man reflects . . . "Let me use some skillful means to get my children out of the house." The man knows the disposition of the children, and . . . the man says to them, "My children, your toys which are so pretty and precious . . . goat carts, deer carts, and bullock carts . . . are outside the door of the house for you to play with. So, come out of the house, and I will give each of you what you want." And the children, upon hearing the names of the playthings they like, because they suit their desires, eagerly, pushing and running against each other, quickly rush out from the burning house. . . .
>
> The children each go up to their father and say, "Father, give us those toys to play with that you promised, those goat carts, deer carts, and bullock carts." Then, Śāriputra, the man gives each of his children equally . . . bullock carts only. They are made of seven precious substances, provided with benches, hung with many bells, adorned with rare and wonderful jewels, covered with jewel wreaths and garlands of flowers . . . led by a multitude of servants. . . . The children climb up on the carts with feelings of astonishment and wonder. . . .
>
> So too, Śāriputra . . . the Tathāgata, endowed with boundless and perfect Buddha-knowledge . . . is the father of all worlds, who has attained the highest perfection in knowing skillful means, and who is most merciful, patient, benevolent, and compassionate. He appears in this world, which is like a house . . . burning with a mass of misery, in order to free from affliction, hatred and delusion, all beings who are subject to birth, old age, disease, death . . . and the dark and enveloping mist of ignorance. He does so to rouse them to supreme, perfect Awakening . . . to bestow on them the immense and inconceivable joy of Buddha-knowledge. . . .
>
> Thus, Śāriputra . . . in order to save all living beings from this world which is like a burning house . . . [the Buddha] shows them by his knowledge of skillful means, three vehicles: that of the disciples, the *pratyekabuddhas*, and the bodhisattvas. By means of these three, he attracts all beings forth . . . so that all beings, who are his children, are led to no other vehicle than the One Buddha-vehicle. (*Saddharmapuṇḍarīka-Sūtra*, III)

One is reminded here of the Second Sermon of the Buddha in which he says that the condition of the world of the Five Aggregates is "burning" with "a whole mass of *duḥkha*"—a burning about which humankind is ordinarily unaware. In the *Lotus Sūtra*, it is being said that a Buddha, who is outside and free from the world, uses skillful means to bring people out of this condition by offering different ideals, that of the *arhat*, the *pratyekabuddha*, and the bodhisattva. But in the end all persons escape this condition through one doorway and find one ideal, that of Buddhahood, which is more wonderful than anyone could imagine.

The Land of Bliss

A devotional side of Mahāyāna was also enriched by another set of early *sūtras*, called the *Larger* and *Smaller Land of Bliss Sūtras* (*Sukhāvatī-Vyūha-Sūtras*), which began to be written in the late second century C.E. The main intent of the *Larger Land of Bliss Sūtra* is to tell the story about Amitābha Buddha, the Buddha of Immeasurable Light. In the *sūtra*, Gautama Buddha tells how in

Box 4.1

The Dragon King's Daughter

The *Lotus Sūtra* has two meanings for me: its surface meaning and its deeper "experienced" meaning. Years ago, I decided to practice Nichiren Buddhism, a Buddhist school founded centuries ago in Japan that focuses on the *Lotus Sūtra.* When I first began reciting the *Lotus Sūtra* and chanting its title, *Nam-myōhōrenge-kyō,* I insisted on learning its literal meaning, though I was encouraged to experience it through sound, too.

Since the ancient Chinese characters are complex, there are many translations of the *sūtra's* title. The more suggestive one I particularly liked was "fusion with the mystic law of simultaneous cause and effect through vibration." I was assured I could draw infinite energy from such dynamic fusion for alleviating my own suffering and the sufferings of others. I tucked that away in the back of my mind and began to chant. But, I wondered, what about the rest of the *Lotus Sūtra* recited by Nichiren Buddhists?

The short explanation given to me at the time was that the *sūtra* had two parts. The first part makes the point that all human beings have the potential to attain enlightenment. Buddhahood is latent in the depths of their lives. The second part explains in parables and similes what enlightenment is. This rough sketch was a good start, but I still painstakingly wrote the literal meaning in pencil above each ancient character in my liturgy book.

Before long, as I undertook the daily practice and witnessed exciting changes in my life, the pencil jottings receded from my radar screen. Living the *Lotus Sūtra* and experiencing what my Nichiren society, Sōka Gakkai International (SGI), calls "human revolution" took on the greater importance. It is only now after eighteen years that I've returned again to the surface meaning. SGI President Daisaku Ikeda, through a series of recently published dialogues on the *Lotus Sūtra*, led me back to it.

To me, the most moving part of these dialogues concerned the Devadatta Chapter. In that chapter, Devadatta, who tried to kill Śākyamuni Buddha, receives the assurance that he, too, will attain a great enlightenment. This occurs before a huge assemblage of living beings from all directions of the universe. Perhaps more shocking to the assembly is what happens next.

The Dragon King's daughter, an eight-year-old girl with the body of a dragon, is said to have reached enlightenment in an instant upon hearing the teaching of the *Lotus Sūtra*. Yet Śāriputra, a learned disciple of the Buddha, does not accept the authenticity of her attainment, and cites reasons why women cannot gain enlightenment. Through dramatic acts reflecting wisdom and compassion, the dragon girl refutes all these reasons. This incident affirms the absolute spiritual equality of women.

As a little girl, my biggest fear was to be left out of or put down by a social group. When I reached adolescence, this fear intensified and became a major preoccupation. My mother, trying to help, advised me that whenever I felt left out, I should find someone else on the sidelines and go talk with them. Well, this was good as far as it went, but it didn't change the whole group dynamic: the sad and seemingly inevitable tendency of human beings to cluster and, in the process, exclude others. The *Lotus Sūtra* sets forth a totally different group dynamic, and it does so on a cosmic scale. No one is excluded from Buddhahood.

VIRGINIA STRAUS BENSON
Ikeda Center for Peace, Learning, and Dialogue

another world eons ago, there was a bodhisattva named Dharmākara, who knew that Buddhas have the power to create Buddha realms in the heavens of the cosmos in which they can reside. With the aid of a Buddha who was living at that time, Dharmākara learned about the excellent characteristics of these realms. He then resolved to generate a Buddha realm that would combine these excellent qualities into the purest of Buddha realms. With this possible pure Buddha realm in mind, Dharmākara expressed his bodhisattva resolve for Buddhahood in forty-eight vows. One of the main points of these vows is that Dharmākara promised that he would not become a Buddha until he had gained the powers needed to produce such a pure Buddha realm and to bring all who want to be reborn there to his Land of Bliss. After telling this story in the *sūtra*, Gautama Buddha then commented that this is exactly what happened: Dharmākara Bodhisattva is now Amitābha Buddha (see Figure 4.3) living in a Buddha realm called the "Land of Bliss" (*Sukhāvatī*). In the *Smaller Land of Bliss Sūtra*, this "Pure Land" is then described in some detail.

An important part of this story for Buddhist devotional practice and experience has to do with the power of Dharmākara's bodhisattva resolve to bring to this Land of Bliss all those who seek to be born there. There are differing explanations as to how one can be born in the Land of Bliss. But in general it requires faith in Amitābha Buddha and a sincere desire to be born in his Buddha realm. In some verses, it is said that one must generate the thought of becoming a Buddha (*bodhicitta*), cultivate certain virtues, and chant homage to Amitābha Buddha. As we shall see later, the Mahāyāna schools in East Asia that base themselves on these *sūtras* emphasize the

FIGURE 4.3. Statue of Amida (Amitābha) Buddha at Kōtoju-in Temple, Kamakura, Japan, known as the Great Buddha dated 1252 C.E.

saving grace of Amitābha for birth in the Land of Bliss. Once there—given Amitābha's presence and power along with the purity of his Buddha realm—it will be easier to attain Awakening. At any time in the Land of Bliss, one can hear and understand more clearly the Dharma and practice that lead to Awakening. One will not encounter any evil or hindrances to spiritual attainment. Here is how the Buddha realm is described:

> This Land of Bliss, Ānanda, which is the realm of Lord Amitābha, is rich and prosperous, comfortable, fertile, delightful and full of many gods and people. In this realm, Ānanda, there are no hells, no animals, no ghosts or *asuras*—no inauspicious places to be reborn. That realm of the Land of Bliss, Ānanda, produces many fragrant odors, is rich in the variety of flowers and fruits, adorned with jewel trees, which are visited by flocks of different kinds of birds conjured up by the Buddha's miraculous power. . . . On all sides it is surrounded by golden nets, and covered by lotus flowers made of precious things. . . .
>
> And everyone hears the pleasant sound that they wish to hear. If they just wish it, they may hear about the Buddha, the Dharma, the Saṅgha, the Six Perfections, the Ten Stages . . . emptiness . . . calmness, quietude and peace, great loving kindness, great compassion, great sympathetic joy, and great equanimity. . . . This brings about the state of mind that leads to the attainment of Awakening. Also, nowhere in the realm of the Land of Bliss does anyone hear of anything unwholesome, nowhere are there any hindrances or states of punishment. . . . And that, Ānanda, is the reason for this realm called the Land of Bliss. . . . All the beings who have been born, who are born, and who will be born in this Buddha realm are all fixed on the right method of salvation until they have attained Nirvana. . . .
>
> If any beings, Ānanda, over and over reverently devote themselves to this Buddha, if they plant a large . . . root of goodness, having raised their thoughts to Awakening, if they vow to be born in that realm, then, when the hour of their death approaches, Amitābha Buddha . . . will stand before them, surrounded by hosts of monks. Then having seen that lord, and having died with serene hearts, they will be born in precisely that realm of the Land of Bliss. (*Sukhāvatī-Vyūha-Sūtra*, 15–16, 18, 24, 27)

Finally, it is important to note that the practice of "remembering the Buddha's name" (*buddhānusmṛti*) was popular in early Mahāyāna Buddhism. In this practice, one begins with saying the word *nāmah*, meaning "hail to," and then adds the name of a Buddha. As we shall see later, when Mahāyāna develops in East Asia, the actual chanting of "Hail to Amitābha Buddha" (Chinese: *"Namo Amituofo"*; Japanese: *"Namu Amida Butsu"*) becomes quite popular. With a sincere faith in the power of Amitābha's vow, these devotees hope to be born in his Land of Bliss, or what they refer to as the "Pure Land."

THE GREAT JOURNEY OF THE BODHISATTVA

In Mahāyāna, the Great Journey of the bodhisattva begins with hearing the Dharma of the Buddha and taking up the practice of the Six Perfections.

Box 4.2

Strength for Living, Courage for Dying

I first encountered the Name of Amitābha or, in Japanese, Amida Buddha while I was in the army of occupation in Japan after World War II. Through my doctoral study, I became aware of the spiritual richness and meaning of this Name for countless believers in East Asia. I later became a convert to the Amidist teaching of Shinran, the Japanese founder of Shin Buddhism, after meeting many devoted members in Hawaii for whom it was a vital reality within their lives.

A heart attack made Amida's compassion and wisdom real to me in a deeply personal way through the skill of the doctors and the restorative powers of our bodies. Though I faced death, I was at peace in the experience of Amida's embrace of boundless compassion and wisdom.

Amida Buddha, whose Name means "Infinite," is the Buddha of Eternal Life and Infinite Light. In form and concept, he is the symbol of indefinable and inconceivable reality, which embraces all life and being in Oneness. He is the power of ideals, moving us to higher aspiration, though not a substantial entity. In Buddhist terms, he is empty, but manifest in all forms of existence. His mythic Vows highlight the interdependence of all beings and the cosmos. As the spiritual foundation for all value and meaning, Amida inspires our ideals of love, compassion, and wisdom.

Through intoning his Name in Japanese, *Namu Amida Butsu*, with others or voicelessly in our heart and mind, we are grateful to Life. Expressing our oneness with the Buddha, *Namu* ("I take refuge in") refers to our own ordinary or "foolish" being, and *Amida Butsu*, the Infinite. In quiet contemplation we receive strength for living and courage for dying.

ALFRED BLOOM
Professor Emeritus, Department of Religion
University of Hawaii

These virtues (giving, morality, patience, vigor, meditation, and wisdom) were first advocated in the *Tripiṭaka,* and Mahāyāna agrees with the earlier tradition that one's motivation is what determines the real quality of one's life of virtue. For Mahāyāna, the true aspiration that should motivate the practice of virtue is "the thought of, or aspiration for, Awakening" (*bodhicitta*). In Mahāyāna, after some time of merit-earning practice and with the aid of a teacher, the person on the Great Course experiences the compassionate aspiration to attain Awakening *for the sake of all living beings*. This aspiration inspired by compassion then becomes the motivation of the entire bodhisattva journey.

The altruistic element of this aspiration for Awakening grows stronger as the bodhisattva realizes the truth of emptiness through growth in wisdom. By this wisdom, he or she experiences the ordinary duality between self and the world as a fiction. That is, one experiences that all things arise dependently so that oneself and the universe are empty of existing as independent entities. With this wisdom, one is also enabled to perform the Six Perfections "perfectly," that is, with selflessness. One is able to give to others, for example, without distinguishing between oneself and the others such that the virtue of the giving is "pure," without any self-centered involvement. Therefore, in Mahāyāna practice of the Six Perfections, the sixth virtue, namely the wisdom (*prajñā-pāramitā*) so extolled in the *Perfection of Wisdom Sūtras*, is necessary to practice the other five to the degree that one can attain Buddhahood. With this wisdom base, the bodhisattva goes ahead on his or her Great Journey, cultivating the qualities of Buddhahood for the good of all living beings. The altruistic disposition of the heart is also given particular concrete expression in the bodhisattva "vows," taken by lay and monastic Mahāyāna Buddhists alike. These vows are experienced as being powerful forces in one's psyche, guiding and impelling one toward a deeper level of compassion and practice of the Bodhisattva Path.

Between 100 and 300 C.E., after the Six Perfections had been practiced for centuries, Mahāyāna Buddhism introduced the doctrine of the Ten Stages (*daśabhūmi*) to clarify further the Great Journey of the bodhisattva. Mahāyāna also added four more perfections so that there is one perfection stressed in each of the Ten Stages. These four perfections include skillful means, vows, power, and omniscient knowledge. When one considers the description of Ten Stages, three things become clear about the Bodhisattva Path. First, it is claimed that while the bodhisattva journey takes eons to complete, it enables one to aid many more beings in their pursuit of Awakening than one could by following the path to Arhatship. Second, it is also clearly taught that for a person to journey on this path, he or she requires the aid of celestial Buddhas and bodhisattvas to reach the goal. Third, for this aid to be realized, there needs to be a "transfer of merit" (*pariṇāmanā*) from the bodhisattvas and Buddhas to sentient beings. This kind of transfer of merit was practiced in early Buddhism. For example, a person might give a donation to a Buddhist community and gain thereby certain merit. He or she could then transfer that merit to a deceased relative. The bodhisattvas and Buddhas gain an enormous amount of merit in the Great Journey to Buddhahood that can be transferred to others. Although the merit is not originally a causal force but is the fruit of efforts on the Bodhisattva Path, it can be transformed into a cause of benefit to living beings through being directed toward them by the bodhisattvas and Buddhas. With this in mind, we first look at the original Six Perfections, and then at the Ten Stages, where we also introduce the other four perfections.

The Six Perfections

The first perfection is called *giving (dāna)*. This virtue involves giving of material things, time, the invaluable gift of instruction about the Dharma, even one's own life for the sake of other beings in need. For giving to be a "perfection," it should be practiced with a selfless attitude based on insight into the nonduality of oneself and others. That is, when one has transcended the perceived separation between oneself and another person, then one's giving to that person becomes an action where oneself and the other are united in the pure act of giving and receiving. One should also transform merit gained by this generous action into fuel for one's own eventual Buddhahood and transfer merit for the Buddhahood of others. This dedication of merit is also done in the practice of the other perfections. It helps the person overcome attachments to any immediate material or spiritual gratification.

The second perfection is *morality* (*śīla*), which is the first of the three aspects of the Theravāda Path of Purification discussed in Chapter 3. In fact, the other two aspects of that Way of the Elders (concentration and wisdom) are included under the fifth and sixth perfections. With these inclusions, the Great Journey of the bodhisattva is seen in Mahāyāna as a expansion, rather than a rejection, of the path of the *arhat*. In terms of morality, while some Mahāyāna monastics observe all the *Vinaya* rules, Mahāyāna teaches both lay and monastic Buddhists to practice the Ten Good Actions. These moral actions include (1) not to kill, (2) not to steal, (3) not to engage in illicit sexual behavior, (4) not to lie, (5) not to use harsh words, (6) not to use words that cause enmity between people, (7) not to engage in idle talk, (8) not to be greedy, (9) not to be angry, and (10) not to hold wrong views. It is believed that the Ten Good Actions can begin the necessary moral purification of unwholesome thoughts and dispositions, as well as the actions that arise from such afflictive thoughts and mental attitudes. The result of this perfection of morality is freedom from troubling passions and, thereby, a greater inner balance, mental calm, and equanimity, which are highly valued in all forms of Buddhist spirituality. This freedom and balance provide the basis for deeper spiritual advancement in meditation and wisdom.

The third perfection is *patience (kṣānti)*. This perfection entails the patient endurance of hardships and the forgiveness of those who harm the bodhisattva in those hardships. With wisdom, one can see that the person who harms one is just caught up in negative attitudes and ways of living based on previous causes and conditions. While the perfection of giving helps one overcome greed, patience aids in the conquest of hate, another of the Three Root Evils. Patience also means to be patient with difficult Buddhist doctrines—such at those about emptiness—that can be confusing to persons with little experience on the bodhisattva journey.

The fourth perfection is *vigor (vīrya)*, which refers to the effort, zeal, and energy needed to overcome unwholesome thoughts and attitudes, to cultivate positive virtues, to study the Dharma, and to do good actions. Vigor corresponds to Right Effort in the Eightfold Path taught by the Buddha and includes the four types of Right Effort we discussed when we introduced the Eightfold Path. However, as a perfection in Mahāyāna, it also implies the heroic compassionate effort one should exert to benefit all living beings. Finally, vigor refers to the sustained fervor that is necessary to maintain enthusiasm on the spiritual journey—which at times can seem long and arduous. This vigorous determination is inspired by the deep compassion that arises from seeing others in need of help and realizing that as a Buddha, one can be of most help to all living beings.

The fifth perfection is *meditation (dhyāna)*, corresponding to concentration (*samādhi*), which is the second of the three aspects of the Theravāda Path of Purification. In Mahāyāna, the layperson as well as the monastic is welcome to study and practice meditation. In advancing in meditation practice, the bodhisattva perfects certain forms found in earlier traditions, such as the Four Meditations, the Four Formless Meditations, the Four Divine Abodes, and the practice of tranquillity and insight meditation. However, the bodhisattva does not accept rebirth into the heavenly realms to which some of these meditations lead. Instead, he or she seeks to be reborn only in the Buddha realms where he or she can progress in the Bodhisattva Path to Buddhahood.

It is said that the bodhisattva perfects innumerable other forms of meditation and *samādhi* states, thus opening the Mahāyāna tradition to an acceptance of new types of meditative practices. Also, Mahāyāna stresses three types of meditation from the earlier tradition because they can be used so well to cultivate their experience of emptiness. First is meditation on "emptiness" itself, which is used to realize the lack of independent selfhood of the things one ordinarily perceives. The second form of meditation is on "signlessness." Here, the ordinary cognition of things is transcended so that one does not see their "signs," or perceptible characteristics. This implies the meditative transcendence of the "signs," or characteristics, that distinguish between one's mind and the objects of experience, between subject and object. Thus, one strengthens a "signless" experience of emptiness. The third meditation is on "wishlessness." Here, based on meditations on emptiness and signlessness, one eliminates attachments to, or "wishes" for, the things of the world. The bodhisattva is also free from any wish for liberation from the world as long as there are beings in the world who need his or her help.

The sixth perfection is *wisdom (prajñā)*, corresponding to the third of the three aspects of the Theravāda Path of Purification. In the previous description of three forms of Mahāyāna meditation, we can see that the fifth perfection aids in the attainment of wisdom. The experience of wisdom penetrates the empty, signless, and wishless nature of reality with such power that one finds greater freedom and peace. Therefore, this wisdom is the door to Awakening and Buddhahood. Because of this generative function, Mahāyāna often personifies wisdom as a goddess and refers to her as "the mother of all Buddhas." That is, wisdom—like a mother—"gives birth to" all the qualities of the enlightened character. For example, as we have said, it is by experiencing the emptiness of any independent selfhood with the eye of wisdom that one is able to practice the other five virtues with perfect selflessness.

In Mahāyāna, wisdom penetrates the various factors and processes of life and understands how some of these lead to happiness and others to suffering. It penetrates the dependently arisen nature of life and understands the causes and conditions that make some relations satisfying and others not. In these ways, Mahāyāna wisdom is similar to that of Theravāda. However, the ultimate realization of the bodhisattva's insight is emptiness, the true suchness of life. With this perfection of wisdom, the bodhisattva finds that in living the Dharma, he or she is free from the afflictive thoughts and emotions and the unwholesome words and actions that produce a life of suffering for oneself and others. According to Mahāyāna, this insight into emptiness is such a powerful antidote to *duḥkha* that it overturns ignorance and the attitudes that lead to these negative thoughts, feelings, words, and behaviors. In their place, compassion arises as the spontaneous expression of emptiness and deepens the altruistic attitude (*bodhicitta*) of the bodhisattva toward all living beings.

The Ten Stages

After practicing the Six Perfections for centuries, the Mahāyāna tradition began to teach that there are certain discernible stages (*bhūmi*) of spiritual growth on the bodhisattva's Great Journey. Eventually, Ten Stages became the accepted steps in this spiritual itinerary. In this traditional view, the Six Perfections were related to the first six stages, and four more perfections were added to fit with the final four stages. As we shall see, in the final four stages, bodhisattvas evolve beyond what is possible for human beings. They are born in Buddha realms—such as the Land of Bliss of Amitābha Buddha—to pursue the last four stages. We will introduce these Ten Stages with passages from the *Daśabhūmika Sūtra*, as it is preserved in the Twenty-Sixth Book of the *Flower Garland Sūtra (Avatamsaka Sūtra)*.

A Joyous Choice

The first of the Ten Stages is called *joyous* (*pramuditā*). Here the bodhisattva produces, based on previous good deeds, the "aspiration for Awakening" (*bodhicitta*). Thereby, he or she enters the family of the Buddhas and becomes "joyous." At this stage, the bodhisattva works especially on the first perfection of giving, or generosity. By experiencing with wisdom the emptiness of all things, he or she can give selflessly to benefit others without regret, worry, or desire for praise. Also, by seeing the "nonseparateness" between self and other, the bodhisattva can give to others with the proper attitude of empathy and compassion. Here is how this stage is described in the *sūtra*:

> So, in beings who have developed the roots of goodness . . . who have developed pure intentions . . . who have developed pity and compassion . . . the aspiration for Awakening [*bodhicitta*] is aroused, the quest for enlightened knowledge . . . for the salvation of all beings.
>
> With this arousing, the bodhisattva . . . is born into the family of the Buddhas is established in the lineage of the Buddhas . . . and is certain to attain perfect Awakening. Thereby established in this condition, the bodhisattva attains the first stage of the Bodhisattva Path, that of great joy. . . . One becomes joyful thinking of the Buddhas and the Dharma, of bodhisattvas and their practices, of

> the purification of the Perfections . . . and of the ability they will have to benefit all beings. . . .
>
> Seeing the mass of *duḥkha* suffered by beings . . . the bodhisattva develops great compassion, and seeks to free them from their sufferings . . . to bring them to the everlasting bliss of Nirvana. Thus . . . by sympathy and loving kindness, and by great effort, the bodhisattva relinquishes all things with equanimity . . . for the sake of the salvation of all beings. . . . Of the Ten Perfections, the perfection of giving is foremost . . . so the roots of goodness become more pure and useful.

Purity, Luminosity, and Radiance

The second stage is called *purity* (*vimalā*). This purity is the result of practicing the second perfection, morality. Here the bodhisattva develops the Ten Good Actions and overcomes impure inclinations to engage in unwholesome actions. With wisdom, the bodhisattva's selflessness from stage one is expressed in all the wholesome actions of moral living. With purity of mind, speech, and action, there grows an inner equanimity in the person that is the basis for more profound meditation practice, and a deeper attainment of wisdom. In the words of the *sūtra*,

> Bodhisattvas in the stage of purity naturally develop the Ten Good Actions. . . . By means of these good ways of acting . . . effort is made to achieve the complete purification of all aspects of action. . . . Thus many Buddhas come to be perceived by the bodhisattvas who live in accord with the power of morality. . . . They attend those Buddhas, and they learn the Ten Good Actions from them with great respect . . . thereby they purify generosity and morality.

The third stage is called *luminosity (prabhākarī*). Here, the bodhisattva's luminous wisdom is like the light of the sun as it penetrates the suchness of all things. This same luminous wisdom is like a fire in that its insight into the emptiness of life burns away attachments. It also burns away any perception of duality between oneself and the world during the practice of meditation. This luminous state is strengthened by the third perfection of patience. It is here too that the bodhisattva—with a luminous, patient, and gentle mind—practices with greater success the Four Meditations, Four Formless Meditations, and Four Divine Abodes. The practice of patience helps the bodhisattva overcome anger, hatred, and even annoyance over any harmful acts or words. In luminous wisdom, everything is viewed with patient endurance and compassion. Finally, it is here that the bodhisattva develops the five supernormal abilities (*siddhis*) that are also recognized in earlier Buddhism. Here again are passages from the *sūtra*:

> The bodhisattva in the third stage examines the impermanent nature of all conditioned existence and sees it in its suchness. . . . Seeing all conditioned existence in this way, the bodhisattva's mind is more and more free from attachment to all these conditioned things, and is directed toward gaining enlightened knowledge.

> Bodhisattvas at this stage of luminosity leave behind desires, evil, and unwholesomeness for the realization and practice of the Dharma. . . . With pure mindfulness, they achieve and are established in the fourth stage of meditation . . . the realm of neither perception nor non-perception . . . not for enjoyment, but for the realization and practice of the Dharma. . . . In the same way, their minds are full of loving kindness . . . compassion, joy, and equanimity . . . and experience the five supernormal abilities. . . . Furthermore, the [bodhisattva's] patience and gentleness are purified along with friendliness, freedom from anger . . . and pride. . . . For among the Ten Perfections, the perfection of patience is foremost.

The fourth stage is called *radiance (arcıṣmatī)*. At this stage, the bodhisattva cultivates the fourth perfection of vigor, by which he or she is able to eliminate mental and emotional afflictions. Here, mindfulness and the four types of Right Effort taught by the Buddha are practiced more deeply. With the removal of these afflictive obstructions to the spiritual life, the bodhisattva's wisdom becomes even more "radiant." With this new vigor in the Great Journey, the bodhisattva pursues the traditional Eightfold Path with even greater effort. Thereby, doubts are cut off and the person's disposition becomes more relaxed, kindly, gentle, and peaceful. As the *sūtra* says,

> The bodhisattvas in this radiant stage examine . . . internal and external phenomena with awareness and mindfulness . . . overcoming worldly desire and aversion. . . . The bodhisattvas use vigorous effort to keep unwholesome states of mind from arising . . . to destroy unwholesome states that have arisen . . . to give rise to wholesome states that have not arisen . . . to cultivate wholesome states that have already arisen. . . .
>
> Based on detachment . . . they develop Right Understanding . . . Right Thought . . . Right Speech . . . Right Action . . . Right Livelihood . . . Right Effort . . . Right Mindfulness . . . Right Concentration . . . As the bodhisattvas develop the aspects of the [Eightfold] Path with skillful means and wisdom . . . they attain patience, self-control and peace. Being patient, self-controlled and peaceful, they contemplate the aspects of the [Eightfold Path] in order to purify the higher stages with constant vigor . . . and they produce great roots of goodness, they destroy worldly defilements . . . all doubts are cut off, and they attain joy and inner peace.

Meditation and Wisdom

The fifth stage is called *difficult to conquer* (*sudurjayā*). With great purity and equanimity, the bodhisattva's wisdom is now able more deeply to penetrate the Four Noble Truths about existence. With this indestructible wisdom, the bodhisattva is "hard to conquer" by persons caught in ignorance and evil, but wants to free them from their suffering condition. On this level, the bodhisattva cultivates the fifth perfection of meditation so that he or she is also "hard to conquer" by any inner tendencies toward distractions, as well as temptations or trials. Also at this level, out of compassion for others, the bodhisattva learns about culture, the arts, science, and medicine to help other sentient beings. The *sūtra* says,

> [They] attain concentration that cannot be conquered, and by so doing, they know correctly the truth of *duḥkha*, the truth of the cause of *duḥkha*, the truth of the cessation of *duḥkha*, and the truth of the [path to cessation's] attainment. . . . They know how the mass of *duḥkha* has been caused by ignorance and craving. . . . And it occurs to them, "How strange and sad that these ignorant beings . . . increase the fetters of *duḥkha* . . . do not pull out the arrows of pride and wrong views . . . do not extinguish the flames of hate, greed and delusion, and do not destroy the darkness of ignorance."
>
> Whatever good the bodhisattvas undertake . . . they do so to lead all beings to freedom, to the ultimate Nirvana. . . . The bodhisattvas, thus engaged in helping living beings, practice whatever might benefit these beings, such as writing and teaching, mathematics, the various sciences including medical science . . . song and dance, drama and music . . . these things the bodhisattva undertakes to learn out of compassion. . . . For bodhisattvas in this stage, the perfection of meditation is most important . . . and having attained concentration, they affect a trillion worlds.

The sixth stage is called *face-to-face (abhimukhī)*. Here, the bodhisattva reaps the fruit of the meditative attainments of the fifth stage and realizes the sixth perfection, wisdom. Thereby, the bodhisattva is brought "face-to-face" with reality itself. What he or she sees with wisdom insight is the empty, signless, and wishless nature of things. One comes to this realization by observing the dependent arising of existence. In a way that is similar to how Buddhaghosa described the person on the Four Paths contemplating over and over the dependently arisen factors of existence, the bodhisattva is said to contemplate the dependent arising and dependent cessation of all factors of existence from ten different perspectives. The bodhisattva does so in such a way that he or she overcomes any attachment not only to the world but also to Nirvana. Having practiced all the aspects of the Theravāda Path of Purification that leads to being an *arhat*, the bodhisattva could now enter Final Nirvana after death if he or she wishes. But because of his or her detachment to Nirvana and compassionate aspiration to attain Awakening for the benefit of all living beings, the bodhisattva decides to continue being reborn into the world. As long as there are beings in need, he or she will continue the Great Journey to full Buddhahood to better help others. Here are the *sūtra's* words:

> Based on a meditative understanding of the true nature of all things, the bodhisattva . . . guided by great compassion . . . observes the arising and cessation of the world. . . . Bodhisattvas contemplate dependent arising in ten patterns, and because of contemplating it in terms of . . . its inherent emptiness . . . the door of emptiness and salvation is realized by them. Because of the emptiness of own-being . . . the signlessness of all things is realized by them. For those who have entered into emptiness and signlessness . . . the door of wishlessness and salvation is realized by them. Entering these three doors of salvation, they leave behind the views of self and object . . . of being and nonbeing. Filled with even more compassion, they go ahead in working for the Awakening yet to be achieved. . . . Among the Ten Perfections, the perfection of wisdom is most important to these bodhisattvas, but they also practice the others.

Beyond Arhatship to Buddhahood

The seventh stage is called *going far* (*dūraṅgamā*). Skillful means as a seventh perfection is added to the original six, and is especially practiced at this level of spiritual life. Remaining in the world and perfecting skillful means (*upāya*) to help others gain enlightenment, the bodhisattva is "going far" beyond the *arhat's* attainment. By skillful means, the bodhisattva is able to adapt his or her teaching the Dharma to the needs of different persons. By developing an ability to know the minds and hearts of others, he or she can practice skillfully all the perfections in each moment for the benefit of others. For the bodhisattva to cultivate all the wisdom and skillful means he or she needs at this point in the Great Journey, it eventually becomes necessary that he or she no longer be born as a human being. Therefore, the bodhisattva must be born as a "celestial bodhisattva" in a Buddha realm to develop certain abilities. As *sūtra* says,

> They achieve access to the seventh stage by . . . skillful means, the perfection of wisdom and knowledge. . . . They train their mind well in realizing emptiness, signlessness and wishlessness, but they also collect a great supply of virtue and knowledge. They obtain selflessness . . . but they continue to live loving kindness, compassion, sympathetic joy and equanimity. . . . They become calm and peaceful by removing the fires of afflictions, but they continue to extinguish the fires of afflictive greed, hatred and delusion in all beings.
>
> While the bodhisattvas at this seventh stage have transcended most of the mass of afflictions . . . they cannot be said to be defiled by afflictions, or to be free from afflictions. Why? Because their afflictions do not affect their behavior, they cannot be said to be defiled by their afflictions. Because they are still seeking full Buddha-knowledge . . . they cannot be said to be free from afflictions. . . . [But] by attaining certain concentrations in which skillful means and wisdom are purified, and with the power of great compassion, bodhisattvas go beyond the stages of the disciples [of Theravāda] and the *pratyekabuddhas*. . . . [In this] seventh stage called "going far," most of the bodhisattvas become celestial beings . . . skilled at leading all beings to certainty.

The eighth stage is called *immovable* (*acalā*). The bodhisattva has now gone beyond any false or inadequate conceptualization of the world and is completely established in the Dharma—a position from which he or she is "immovable." It is as though the bodhisattva awakens from a dream and sees the Truth in a new and fresh way. His or her practice now becomes effortless. In this new experience, the bodhisattva's commitment to the Great Journey is also said to be "irreversible." This irreversibility is similar to that of the Streamwinner of the earlier tradition who will never turn back. The difference is that the bodhisattva's Great Journey, Mahāyāna claims, leads beyond the *arhat*'s attainment to full Buddhahood. In this new freedom, the bodhisattvas focus on the eighth perfection of "vows" (*praṇidhāna*), which are the concrete expressions of the aspiration to attain Buddhahood for the benefit of all living beings. Also at this stage, the bodhisattvas gain more advanced forms of skillful means associated with Buddhahood. For example, they obtain the ability to manifest in various emanation bodies throughout the universe to instruct the Dharma to all forms of life. Here we can see why the bodhisattva must be a celestial being rather than a human being—no human could gain such an ability. As the *sūtra* puts it,

> When they attain the eighth stage, called the immovable, bodhisattvas become free from all effort having attained the condition of effortlessness that is freed from mental, physical and verbal striving. . . . It is like a boat . . . that is dragged with great effort to the ocean; but once in the ocean, sails effortlessly by the wind.
>
> They know the ways in which the realm of desire . . . the realm of form . . . and the formless realm [are] constituted. . . . They know the varieties of beings . . . and they apply their knowledge to producing emanations . . . in whatever forms in which beings are born . . . for the purpose of aiding these beings to mature . . . to perfect Awakening. . . . With this knowledge at this stage, not moving from their Buddha-realm, they can appear in . . . untold Buddha realms, taking on the different characteristics of beings . . . according to their attitudes and dispositions . . . with endless forms of emanation bodies for the development and teaching of all beings.
>
> This eighth stage is named "immovable" because the bodhisattvas abiding there cannot be turned back from their journey; thus it is called the stage of irreversibility. . . . These bodhisattvas primarily practice, among the Ten Perfections, the perfection of vows . . . and with the power of these vows, they produce . . . countless emanations of bodies.

The ninth stage is called *good insight* (*sādhumatī*). At this advanced stage, the bodhisattva perfects even more skillful means for bringing others to Awakening and uses them in all the realms throughout the entire cosmos. Here again, we can see why this stage can only be fully practiced by a celestial bodhisattva. At this level, the bodhisattva's understanding of all the "paths" of Buddhism is perfected into "good insight" He or she has clear insight into how people are "entangled," as Buddhaghosa also puts it, in *duḥkha*. Based on this good insight, he or she is enabled to teach the Dharma skillfully, and with a skill and eloquence that even surpasses the abilities of the gods. To do so, the bodhisattva practices the ninth perfection of "power" (*bala*). For example, with one such power, he or she understands and uses all the languages and means of communication of all living things in all parts of the cosmos. Here again are the *sūtra's* words:

> Bodhisattvas at the stage of good insight have penetrating insight into good, evil and neutral conduct . . . the conduct of disciples [of Theravāda], the conduct of *pratyekabuddhas*, the conduct of bodhisattvas, and the conduct pertaining to Buddhahood. . . . With this awareness, bodhisattvas know how all beings get entangled mentally, entangled with afflictions . . . they know the aspects of the mind . . . of the afflictions . . . of weakness and strength. . . . Thus, bodhisattvas know the differences between all living beings' conduct, and undertake to liberate them according to their condition.

Knowing all this, the bodhisattvas give the Dharma to all beings . . . according to their mental dispositions and attitudes . . . their entanglements and afflictions . . . their actions and habits. They apply whatever skillful means may bring liberation by appearing in numerous forms in all worlds . . . knowing the language of all beings . . . with the necessary knowledge to explain the Dharma. . . . Thus, having attained mental power . . . they infuse a billion worlds and teach the Dharma to all beings according to their differences in mentality. . . . Most of the bodhisattvas at this stage become [celestial beings] with great powers, lords of millions of worlds.

The Dharma Cloud

The tenth and final stage is called *Dharma cloud* (*dharma meghā*). Here, the bodhisattva practices the tenth perfection of "omniscient knowledge" (*jñāna*). He or she masters all forms of concentration (*samādhi*) and resides in the *samādhi* of the "knowledge of the omniscient." In this concentration, the rays of wisdom from all Buddhas rest on the bodhisattva's head, sharing their wisdom and consecrating him or her with the qualities of Buddhahood. The bodhisattva is then able to keep in mind this "Dharma cloud," showered on him or her by the Buddhas, from which he or she rains the Dharma throughout the cosmos. However, he or she must be born one more time to undertake the full life of a Buddha and create his or her own Buddha realm. Meanwhile in this tenth stage, the bodhisattva produces limitless emanation bodies throughout the cosmos, raining down the Dharma for the benefit of all beings. As a tenth-stage bodhisattva, obstructions to omniscience are removed, and skillful means, confidence, and power reach their utmost in preparation for birth as a Buddha:

> Those bodhisattvas . . . are said to have attained the stage of consecration with the knowledge of the omniscient in all of its aspects. . . . They realize innumerable millions of concentrations. . . . At the end of innumerable millions of concentrations, he or she realizes a bodhisattva concentration called "receiving consecration by the special knowledge of the omniscient."
>
> Upon the attainment of this concentration . . . the bodhisattva appears seated on a great jewel lotus . . . then as many bodhisattvas as there are other jewel lotuses encircle that bodhisattva on those other jewel lotuses, entering a million concentrations, gazing upon the bodhisattva in the middle of the circle. . . . Then from between the eyebrows . . . of all the Buddhas there come rays of light possessing the knowledge of the omniscient . . . illuminating all worlds . . . causing Buddha realms to quake . . . reaching throughout space, until they return to the encircling assembly, where they disappear into the top of the head of the bodhisattva being consecrated. . . . When the rays of light enter that bodhisattva's head, he or she is said to be consecrated in the realm of the perfectly Awakened Ones. . . . Thus, he or she enters the ranks of the perfect Buddhas.
>
> Thus consecrated, the bodhisattva, mature in virtue and knowledge, is established in the tenth stage, called "Dharma cloud." Bodhisattvas at this stage have complete knowledge of the totality of the cosmos. . . . Since the vast knowledge of the Buddhas is immeasurable, the penetrating knowledge of the bodhisattva at this stage is also considered omniscient. . . . [And] in the arising of just

> a moment of thought, the bodhisattva can now go throughout the universe . . . manifesting infinite embodiments all at the same time. . . . They can also cause the wonderful qualities of the Buddha realms to appear in their own bodies. . . . [Thus] they illumine numerous worlds and cause numerous beings to mature.

THE THREE BODIES OF THE BUDDHA

Now that we have seen what the Bodhisattva Path to Buddhahood entails, this question arises: What exactly is a Buddha in the Mahāyāna tradition? In fact, the notion of Buddhahood developed in Mahāyāna over a number of centuries growing from the notion of the nature of a Buddha taught in early Buddhist traditions. Early Indian Buddhist schools like Sarvāstivāda and Mahāsāṅghika formulated a two-body theory of the Buddha. This included a form body (*rūpakāya*) and a Dharma body (*Dharmakāya*). The Sarvāstivādins claimed that the Buddha's physical form body is born into the world with human limitations and impurities, while the Dharma body of his enlightened realization transcends the world and is always pure. The Mahāsāṅghikins went further in claiming that the Buddha's Dharma body is ultimately omniscient and omnipotent, and has a limitless life span. His physical form body is manifested in the world to liberate living beings and is itself pure. This view of Mahāsāṅghika was the basis for what would evolve into the Mahāyāna notion of the three bodies of the Buddha (*trikāya*).

As we have seen from selections from the Mahāyāna *sūtras*, the teaching of suchness (*tathatā*) claims that the very essence of all beings is pure and nirvanic. This essence may be covered by defilements, but it is never tarnished. It is one, the same for all beings, never changing, unmade and uncreated, and hidden in all things. A living Buddha in his Awakening realizes this true nature of all beings. He realizes it as his "Dharma Body," his *Dharmakāya*. Here, the Buddha is identified in his Dharma Body with the pure and real nature of all things. He is that suchness; it is his true nature. The *Dharmakāya* is the ultimate body of the Buddha, the first of the three bodies of the Buddha according to Mahāyāna. This is true for all Buddhas; they are all in essence the one *Dharmakāya*.

Beyond this more abstract description of the *Dharmakāya*, its realization in individual Buddhas is described as wisdom and compassion filling the entire cosmos. This penetration of the universe by the *Dharmakāya* brings light and compassion to all beings. Here is the religious side to the Mahāyāna notion of *Dharmakāya*. It is the foundation and the support of everything, and it is the source of their transformation through skillful means. While the Dharma Body is eternally quiescent, the transformation of living beings leading to Awakening and Buddhahood is carried out in specific ways by the various Buddhas that manifest the Dharma Body. The *Dharmakāya's* "transformation of support" expresses itself in the two other bodies of the Buddha that together with the Dharma Body make up the *trikāya*. It is through these other two bodies that the *Dharmakāya* delivers sentient beings from suffering and leads them to Awakening and Buddhahood.

The second body of the Buddha is called the "Enjoyment Body" or "Reward Body" (*saṃbhogakāya*). Mahāyāna teaches that a Buddha gains great merit both as a Buddha and as a bodhisattva prior to Buddhahood. This merit produces certain attributes and powers that enable a Buddha to take a celestial *saṃbhogakāya* form as a reward to be enjoyed by that Buddha and others who reside in his celestial Buddha realm (*buddhakṣetra*). A *saṃbhogakāya* Buddha creates this celestial realm by transforming his pure consciousness into the limitless future. In that realm, a Buddha manifests the boundless light and limitless life span of his essence, the *Dharmakāya*. While the *Dharmakāya* is the quiescent one true nature of a Buddha, the *saṃbhogakāya* contains all the Buddha's supernatural attributes and powers as a reward for his practice. These are used by the *saṃbhogakāya* Buddha in teaching, providing blessings, and caring for the needs of all sentient beings. In this regard, the only way a tenth-stage bodhisattva can gain full Buddhahood is by the teachings of a living Buddha. So one of the primary responsibilities of a celestial Buddha is to enable these bodhisattvas who have one more birth to Buddhahood to achieve that goal in his celestial realm.

Finally, we come to the third body of the Buddha, the *nirmāṇakāya* or "Manifestation Body." The ultimate nature of the Buddha is the quiescence of the *Dharmakāya* penetrating the whole cosmos, individual Buddhas can manifest themselves in different forms according to the needs of sentient beings. These forms are *nirmāṇakāyas* endowed with wisdom and compassion to expound the Dharma, to turn the wheel of the Dharma. They may manifest as a human Buddha or as an ordinary person, animal, or even a ghost to liberate different kinds of sentient beings. Gautama Buddha is considered a *nirmāṇakāya*. Manifestation Buddhas like Gautama use their skillful means to mature ordinary people in the paths of both the *arhats* and the bodhisattvas. They all have the *Dharmakāya* as their foundation, wisdom and compassion as their core, and transformation of living beings as their activity.

Celestial Buddhas

The second body of the Buddha, the celestial *saṃbhogakāya*, provides Buddhists with many sources of powerful help. Akṣobhya Buddha is one of the most famous of the celestial Buddhas. When he took up the practice of the Bodhisattva Path, he made a vow never to be angry or have thoughts of malice or hatred toward any living being until he attained Buddhahood. Thus, he was named Akṣobhya, meaning "Unperturbed." Akṣobhya Buddha is perhaps the first of the celestial Buddhas during this eon to be mentioned in the early Mahāyāna *sūtras*. In one of the early *Perfection of Wisdom Sūtras*, Gautama Buddha is said to have enabled his hearers to see Akṣobhya Buddha. In the *Vimalakīrti Sūtra*, it is said that Vimalakīrti revealed Akṣobhya's Buddha realm called *Abhirati*, "Joyous," that is populated mainly by *arhats* and a few bodhisattvas. It is said that with the assistance of Akṣobhya, a person can easily attain Arhatship in his Buddha realm. Scholars see this fact as indicating that Akṣobhya Buddha represents a transitional stage between the goals of Arhatship and Buddhahood.

Certainly the most widely known celestial Buddha is Amitābha, or the Buddha of "Unlimited Light." He is also known as Amitāyus, the Buddha of "Unlimited Life." As we saw earlier in this chapter, the story of Amitābha Buddha is presented in the *Land of Bliss Sūtras*. This Land of Bliss (*Sukhāvati*), also called the "Pure Land," is Amitābha's Buddha-realm. Amitābha Buddha will bring good Buddhists to the Pure Land at death if they arouse the thought of Awakening, meditate with a faithful mind on Amitābha, and desire to be reborn in his Pure Land. Amitābha has the power to bring even an evil person to his Pure Land if that person hears the name of Amitābha Buddha, repents, and seeks to be reborn in the Pure Land. There is a mixture of inhabitants in the Pure Land, including mainly bodhisattvas and some *arhats*. However, the sole practice in this Pure Land is the Bodhisattva Path leading to Buddhahood. We will later explore more about the traditional practices that developed in East Asia around these notions concerning Amitābha Buddha and his Pure Land.

Vairocana Buddha is another of the great celestial Buddhas. His name means "Shining Out" like the sun. The first mention of Vairocana is perhaps in the *Avataṃsaka Sūtra*. There, he is described as being at the center of the cosmos like a cosmic sun radiating the light of the Dharma to all worlds. The luminous rays of his light dispel the darkness of ignorance releasing sentient beings from all obstructions to Awakening. These rays are often represented in Buddhist art. His Buddha-realm was born from the lotus and was purified by Vairocana for eons. Unlike the Buddha-realms of Aksobhya and Amitābha, the Lotus Land of Vairocana is not inhabited by *arhats*, but only by bodhisattvas. Here we see a Mahāyāna development from the Buddha-realm of Akṣobhya where there are mainly *arhats* and a few bodhisattvas, to the Buddha-realm of Amitābha where there are mostly bodhisattvas and a few *arhats*, to the Buddha-realm of Vairocana where there are only bodhisattvas. The *Avataṃsaka Sūtra* also considers Vairocana to be the same as Gautama Buddha, but just different bodies. In later *sūtras*, this relationship is described as Gautama Buddha being the *nirmāṇakāya* of Vairocana.

Celestial Bodhisattvas

Certain tenth-stage bodhisattvas also became celestial persons to be worshiped and venerated. Given their powers gained in the Bodhisattva Path, they too are considered sources of help for Buddhists on the Great Journey. These bodhisattvas are called "Great Beings" (*mahāsattvas*). Different *sūtras* identify these Great Beings in longer or shorter lists. Three of the most important are Maitreya, Mañjuśrī, and Avalokiteśvara. Maitreya, or "Kindly One," is mentioned in the early Pali texts as the bodhisattva who in the distant future will become a Buddha in this world. At the present time, Maitreya is living in the Tuṣita Heaven waiting to be born as the next Buddha after Gautama. In the meantime, he uses his powers and skillful means to respond to the needs of all living beings, especially to those expressed in prayers by worshipers. In tenth-century China, there was a Chan (Zen) monk named Budai. Budai was a happy and rather portly monk who gave presents to chil-

FIGURE 4.4. Stone statue of Budai, 10th century Chinese monk said to be Maitreya Buddha.

dren from a bag he carried with him. After his death, a legend developed in China that he was, in reality, an emanation body of Maitreya. In the West, his image is sometimes called "the Laughing Buddha" (see Figure 4.4).

Mañjuśrī, or "Sweet Glory," is a celestial bodhisattva who resides in many worlds and is so revered for his great wisdom that he is called the "prince of the Dharma." He often appears in dreams and visions and protects Buddhists in times of need with his great powers. Mañjuśrī is known especially for using his great wisdom to destroy ignorance and awaken knowledge.

Avalokiteśvara resides in the Buddha realm of Amitābha Buddha. His name means "the Lord Who Looks Down," indicating that Avalokiteśvara looks down from Amitābha's realm with love and compassion, ready to respond to the needs of living beings (see Figure 4.5). So, while he possesses all virtues, he is especially known for his love and compassion, which he expresses in his limitless forms of skillful means. He often takes on an emanation body to appear compassionately in this world. In Tibet, His Holiness the Dalai Lama is believed to be an emanation of Avalokiteśvara. Later Buddhist art portrays Avalokiteśvara as having many heads and arms, representing his ability to notice and respond to the needs of many beings at the same time. In East Asia, Avalokiteśvara is represented as a female bodhisattva who is widely worshiped. In China she is known as Guanyin, and in Japan as Kannon.

FIGURE 4.5. Avalokiteśvara Bodhisattva statue at Gandan Monastery, Ulaanbaatar, Mongolia, known as "Megjid Janraisig (the Lord who looks in every direction), made of copper and covered with gold leaf.

The celestial bodhisattvas and celestial Buddhas inspire Mahāyāna Buddhists to travel the bodhisattvas course to full Buddhahood. They also encourage Buddhists who are on that way of spiritual transformation to seek the help of those who are more advanced on the Bodhisattva Path and those who have already achieved the goal. This and the other teachings of Mahāyāna present the world with the religious experiences of Mahāyāna Buddhism. Another task of Mahāyāna has been to explain the philosophical implications of these experiences in systematic ways. This led to the founding of certain Mahāyāna schools of thought in India that, together with their Abhidharma counterparts, contributed to the intellectual Indian Buddhist culture that we introduce in the next chapter. As we shall see in later chapters, these Indian Mahāyāna schools would eventually be brought to other parts of Asia where they inspired more recent forms of Mahāyāna Buddhism.

SUGGESTIONS FOR FURTHER READING

Cleary, Thomas, trans. *The Flower Ornament Scripture: A Translation of the* Avataṃsaka Sūtra [With translation of the *Daśabhūmika Sūtra*]. Boston: Shambhala Publications, 1984.

Conze, Edward, trans. *Buddhist Wisdom Books*. London: George Allen & Unwin, 1958.

______, trans. *The Large Sūtra on Perfect Wisdom*. Berkeley: University of California Press, 1975.

Gómez, Luis O., trans. *The Land of Bliss, The Paradise of the Buddha of Measureless Light*. Honolulu: University of Hawaii Press, 1996.

Griffiths, Paul J. *On Being Buddha: The Classical Doctrine of Buddhahood*. Albany: SUNY Press, 1994.

Hurvitz, Leon, trans. *Scripture of the Lotus Blossom of the Fine Dharma (The Lotus Sūtra)*. New York: Columbia University Press, 1976.

King, Sallie B. *Buddha Nature*. Albany: SUNY Press, 1991.

Kiyota, Minoru, and Elvin W. Jones, eds. *Mahāyāna Buddhist Meditation: Theory and Practice*. Honolulu: University of Hawaii Press, 1978.

Lopez, Donald S., Jr. *Elaborations on Emptiness: Uses of the* Heart Sūtra. Princeton, NJ: Princeton University Press, 1998.

Numata Center. *The Three Pure Land Sūtras*. Honolulu: University of Hawaii Press, 2003.

Ohnuma, Reiko. *The Ties That Bind: Maternal Imagery and Discussion in Indian Buddhism*. New York: Oxford University Press, 2012.

Paul, Diana. *Women in Buddhism: Images of the Feminine in the Mahāyāna Tradition*. Berkeley: University of California Press, 1985.

Pye, Michael. *Skillful Means: A Concept in Mahayana Buddhism*. London: Durkworth, 1978.

Ray, Reginald. *Buddhist Saints in India: A Study in Buddhist Values and Orientations*. New York: Oxford University Press, 1994.

Sponberg, Alan, and Helen Hardacre, eds. *Maitreya: The Future Buddha*. Cambridge, UK: Cambridge University Press, 1988.

Suzuki, D. T., trans. *The Laṅkāvatāra Sūtra: A Mahāyāna Text*. London: Kegan Paul International, 1987.

Watson, Burton, trans. *The Vimalakirti Sutra*. New York: Columbia University Press, 2000.

Williams, Paul. *Mahāyāna Buddhism: The Doctrinal Foundations*. London: Routledge & Kegan Paul, 1989.

Wright, Dale. *The Six Perfections: Buddhism and the Cultivation of Character*. New York: Oxford University Press, 2011.

Xing, Guang. *The Concept of the Buddha: Its Evolution from Early Buddhism to the Trikāya Theory*. New York: Routledge, 2005.

5

Indian Experiences of Buddhism

The experiences of Buddhism in India began, of course, with Gautama Buddha. So we have already been introducing the Indian experiences of Buddhism in the four previous chapters of our story. We have seen how they took shape from Gautama's life and teachings. We have also seen how the experiences of Buddhism in India produced two different major expressions in Theravāda and Mahāyāna. In this chapter, we introduce the development of Indian Buddhist schools of thought that present the varieties of Buddhist experience in more systematic and critical philosophies. As we shall see, this means that while this part of our introduction to Buddhism is more philosophically stimulating, it is also more intellectually challenging. However, it is a fundamental part of the story because the Buddhist ideas forged in the Indian context have played crucial roles in the later development of Buddhism throughout the world.

ABHIDHARMA PHILOSOPHIES

In Chapter 3, we saw how different schisms in the early Buddhist community produced such schools as Mahāsāṅghika, Pudgalavāda, Sarvāstivāda, and Theravāda. These eventually were numbered among what are called the eighteen Abhidharma schools because they attempted to explicate philosophically the kinds of ideas presented in the *Abhidharma Piṭaka*. One common feature of these schools was their utilization of the types of analyses that are characteristic of the *Abhidharma* texts themselves. The Abhidharma schools analyzed reality in ways that expanded on the teachings of the Buddha. Their analysis focused on what they considered the fundamental constituents of reality, namely, the *dharmas* (Pali: *dhammas*). These primary elements are either material (*rūpa*) or nonmaterial (*arūpa*). The material elements are said to be earth, air, fire, and water. Here the Abhidharma philosophers are using terms common at the time they were writing. But these fundamental elements of matter were not understood to be substantial atoms as in the Greek tradition. Rather each is a fundamental quality necessary to explain the existence of matter. "Earth" meant the quality of solidity or extension; "air" meant the quality of movement; "fire" meant the quality of heat or energy; and "water" meant the quality of cohesion. These primary elements are not "things" like atoms with qualities; they are particular instances of solidity, movement, energy, and coherence that merge together in different combinations, producing material entities and eventually the objects we perceive.

In terms of the four material elements, they are defined independently, but come together to create material objects. As Buddhaghosa (see Figure 5.1) says, "Matter refers to the four great primary elements and the materiality derived from them" (*Visuddhimagga,* XVII, 187). Material objects derived from the four elements are what they are due to their own internal parts and their particular relationships to other objects, not to the primary elements themselves. Again, Buddhaghosa says: "You should not conclude that difference is to be found in the supporting primary elements. The natures of visible objects are different from each other due to karma, not to any difference in their primary elements" (*Visuddhimagga,* XIV, 45).

As to mental *dharmas,* Abhidharma philosophers identify four kinds of mental elements as states: feelings, perceptions, impulses, and consciousness

FIGURE 5.1. Wall painting of Buddhaghosa offering his writings to the chief monk; Kelaniya Temple, Anuradhapura, Sri Lanka.

itself. Consciousness here is not the same as a mind that has perceptions, feelings, and impulses. It is a *dharma* that always exists with other mental *dharmas* enabling consciousness of mental states. These states (*caitasika*) occur in one's mental processes due to certain internal and external causes and conditions. Some are considered good or beneficial states like faith, mindfulness, and nonhate, nongreed, and nondelusion. Others are considered evil or not beneficial like conceit, worry, envy, and hate, greed, and delusion. A third category includes elements of mental activity like will, reflection, and discursive reason. The moral categorization of some of the mental *dharmas* as positive or negative is important for mental cultivation. For example, states of patience and loving kindness should be identified in one's own mental processes and cultivated, and states of hatred and greed should be identified and eliminated.

Most Abhidharma philosophers considered these elementary factors of existence to be like psychic and somatic "events" that exist only for a few moments in the processes of life. There were disagreements as to how many moments a dharmic event lasts. Sarvāstivāda taught that there are four moments: arising, stasis, decaying, and passing away. Theravāda identified only three moments: arising, stasis, and passing away. In any case, what one finds generally in the Abhidharma traditions is that a doctrine of "momentaryness" was developed out of the Buddha's doctrine of impermanence. As we shall soon see, this led to a number of philosophical problems. The different Abhidharma schools came up with various solutions to these problems, and these positions philosophically divided them even further.

In the doctrine of momentaryness, it is claimed by most Abhidharma schools that even though the elements of existence are momentary events, they are each essentially self-existing. That is, they are said to have *svabhāva*, or "own being," that enables them each to exist. This attribute was important to the Abhidharma philosophers because it meant that they did not need a creator God to account for the existence of these distinct elements. Also, each element has its own characteristic (*svalakṣaṇa*) that accounts for its unique identity. Thus, the popular Abhidharma view of existence was one of radical pluralistic realism. In other words, the world is constituted by many mental and physical elements or events that are real, self-existing, momentary, unique, and distinct from one another.

There are a number of philosophical problems with this Abhidharma view of life. One major problem has to do with causality. If, for example, you imagine a sequence of momentary mental events, how can one momentary event be causally connected with another in that sequence? If there is some causal factor that connects them, as Sarvāstivāda suggested, then you still have the problem of explaining the relation between that causal factor and the two elements it connects. In other words, if all that exists are elements, and if you imagine two elements side-by-side in a sequence and then insert a third causal element between then, how can one explain the actual connection between the causal element and the elements on either side of it? One is here led to an infinite regress.

Another problem with the doctrine of momentaryness has to do with perception. Most Abhidharma Buddhists believed that perception is only possible if an object is present to the senses. They also believed that perception entails a process of momentary mental events that takes some time to complete. But if this is so, how can one perceive an object that exists only for a moment? The object one knows at the end of the process of perception would be different from the object as it was at the beginning of the process. Then there is the problem of explaining memory. If one's knowledge now must have an object, and if the object one remembers is no longer existing, how can one explain the fact that one remembers something that no longer exists?

One of the most influential Indian Abhidharma schools to address these kinds of problems was the Sarvāstivāda School. As we saw in Chapter 3, members of this school attempted to solve the philosophical problems of Abhidharma thought by positing that all periods of time (the past, present, and future) exist simultaneously. This unusual view of time is why the school was called *Sarvāstivāda,* which means "All-Exists School." Although there are variations of this theory in Sarvāstivāda, in general what was taught is that the past, future, and present are like realms where the elements exist. The elements of existence have "own-being" that enables them to always exist in one of these time realms. An element first exists in the future, then appears in the present, and finally resides in the past. Because these three time periods always exist, right now there are elements existing in the future that will eventually exist in the present, and there are also elements existing in the past that had once existed in the present. This being the case, any past element, for example, can continue to be known and can causally affect other elements in the present. This also means, of course, that future elements can affect the present and could be known in the present by supernormal abilities.

A second Abhidharma school tried to avoid this theory concerning time by remaining more faithful to the *Sūtra Piṭaka;* hence the school's name, *Sautrāntika,* or "Adherents to the *Sūtras.*" They also accepted the notion of momentaryness, but understood it more in terms of the Buddha's teaching of impermanence. That is, while life is a series of momentary events, its elements are not separate and self-subsisting, but are interconnected parts of the impermanent flow of existence. One can distinguish the elements, but because they are not really separate from each other, one does not have such a problem with explaining causal relations.

Thus, the Sautrāntikins believed that the Sarvāstivāda theory that all times exist simultaneously was nonsense. Things only exist momentarily in the present, not in the future, and they do not remain existing in the past. This being so, Sautrāntika accepted that in the process of perception, what one knows at the end of this process is not the object as it was constituted at the beginning of this process. They went on to propose a representational theory of perception. In this theory, what one knows in his or her mind is an "impression" or a "representation" of a perceived object. In other words, one does not know objects directly, but only mental representations of them. Finally, as for memory, Sautrāntika introduced a "seed" theory. A momentary event in one's life process can leave a "seed," or potentiality, in the flow of "subtle consciousness" that can manifest as a memory when the mind wills to remember it. As we shall see, something similar to this seed theory would later be advanced by the Yogācāra School of Mahāyāna philosophy.

The Theravāda School approached these philosophical problems from another direction. Instead of trying to find a causal factor that connects the elements of life, they proposed that causality really involves the cooperation of a multiplicity of "conditions." That is, when a number of elements are present, their very presence functions as a set of conditions that entails the arising of an effect, of a new element. This notion goes back to the Buddha's doctrine of dependent arising. When certain conditions are present, there is an arising of something new dependent on those conditions. The Theravādins compiled a list of twenty-four kinds of conditions that influence the process of existence. They were especially interested in the kinds of conditions that account for the arising of *duḥkha* and the types of conditions that contribute to Nirvana.

In dealing with conscious life, Theravāda proposed the existence of a "life-continuum" (Pali: *bhavaṅga*) at the subliminal level of consciousness. This life-continuum supplies a continuing process of consciousness over a period of time. It is also at this level of subconscious activity that "vibrations" from conscious experience continue to remain within oneself. So, when conditions are right, one can remember past events by recalling to mind their traces in the unconscious. It is also at that subconscious level that one's karma matures and affects one's life, even when one is unaware of its presence. Again, this idea of a subliminal level of continuing consciousness, along with the Sautrāntika notion of seeds, will later appear in Yogācāra philosophy.

Theravāda also used its life-continuum theory to explain how a process of many momentary mental events can perceive one momentary physical entity. Theravāda holds that a physical moment is longer than a mental moment. In fact, a physical moment remains long enough for a seventeen-moment process of mental apperception to take place in one's life continuum. Here is how this was explained by Annuruddha, a famous post-Buddhaghosa philosopher:

> How must sense cognition be understood? A single mental moment consists of three phases: arising, stasis, and passing away. Seventeen such mental moments are equal to the duration of one material entity. One mental moment passes as a sense object enters the doors of the senses. When, for example, a visible object enters the door of sight after one mental moment, the life-continuum vibrates and its continuum is interrupted. Then there is one mental moment of an apprehension of sensations, of the visible object. Following this, there are four mental moments: visual consciousness, receiving consciousness, investigating consciousness, and determining consciousness. After [the object is determined] there are seven mental moments of *kāmaloka* apperceptions [apperceptions accompanied by feelings and good, evil and indifferent reactions] dependent on the conditions that evoke them. As a consequence of these apperceptions, two resulting mental moments of retention in the life-continuum take place. After that, the life-continuum subsides. Now is the seventeen mental moments complete. (*Abhidhammattha-Sangaha*, IV, 3)

One other school was rather unique in that it turned its attention from the elements of existence to the person who is seeking Nirvana. This is the Pudgalavāda School. *Pudgala* means "person," and this Personalist School was concerned that in the analyses of life into impersonal physical and mental elements of existence, Buddhist philosophers were forgetting the person who is seeking Nirvana. For the Pudgalavādins, the sense of themselves as "persons," their humanity as persons, is not fully accounted for by impersonal physical and mental elements. Yet the person is not entirely different from the elements either. Personhood is not some entity separate from one's mental and physical life. Also, because it is the person who attains Nirvana, the condition of Nirvana is not different from the elements that constitute his or her life. Based on this view of personhood, Pudgalavāda claimed that it is the person who continues to perceive momentary objects, remember things from the past, and attain Nirvana. What is behind this philosophical position seems

FIGURE 5.2. Bodhgāya *Stūpa* of the Mahābodhi Vihāra erected between the fifth and seventh centuries C.E. at the site of Śākyamuni Buddha's enlightenment. It fell into ruins after the thirteenth century and was rebuilt by the Burmese and British in the nineteenth century.

to be Pudgalavāda's intuition of a personal identity that is distinct but not separate from people's physical-mental life and a Nirvana that can permeate this personal identity in all of its mental and physical states.

The major Abhidharma schools flourished in India for centuries, even after the rise of Mahāyāna Buddhism. They founded their own religious sites (see Figure 5.2) and universities were present in Mahāyāna universities. Chinese pilgrims wrote that members of the Abhidharma schools outnumbered those of the Mahāyāna schools in the seventh century, and Tibetan sources claim that this was true until the thirteenth century, when Buddhism ceased to exist as a viable religion in India. During the early centuries C.E., a Sarvāstivādin work entitled the *Mahāvibhāṣā*, or *Great Option*, was written. This work was highly influential, and in the early fifth century it inspired a person named Vasubandhu to write one of the greatest works of Indian Buddhism. This is the voluminous *Abhidharmakośa*, which is an encyclopedia of Abhidharma thought. Vasubandhu's work has two parts: verses that present the Sarvāstivāda teaching and commentaries that give the Sautrāntika interpretation of those teachings. This work became central to the study of Buddhism in India and East Asia during subsequent centuries. The author is considered by Mahāyāna to be the Vasubandhu who converted to the Yogācāra tradition of Mahāyāna, but modern scholars question this claim. Finally, as we saw in Chapter 3, the Theravāda School spread to Sri Lanka and Southeast Asia, thus being the one Abhidharma school to survive until today.

MAHĀYĀNA PHILOSOPHIES

The Abhidharma schools were concerned with two major philosophical issues: (1) the nature of the things and processes of the world and (2) the nature of consciousness and its knowledge of the world. One Abhidharma school, the Mahāsaṅghika School, presented a view concerning these issues that is similar to those found in Mahāyāna. As we said in the previous chapter, this may actually be due to Mahāyāna influence. In any case, in the Mahāsaṅghika positions, we can find certain ideas that are developed in the two major schools of Mahāyana philosophy. For example, the Mahāsaṅghika philosophers taught that the elements (*dharmas*) of the world are "empty" of any "own-being" (*svabhāva*). Instead, they only exist functionally in the dependent arising of existence. Therefore, the true and "empty" nature of the *dharmas* can only be understood in the relational nexus of dependent arising. As we shall see, this kind of relational view of life plays a central role in the Mādhyamika School of Mahāyāna philosophy.

As for the nature and functioning of consciousness, the Mahāsaṅghika School taught that there is a "base" (*mūla*) consciousness, which, like the Theravāda life-continuum, provides a basis for continuing conscious life at the subliminal level. Also, Mahāsaṅghika taught that consciousness contains "seeds" (*bījas*), good and bad, that condition one's experience of life. Ideas like these about the nature of the mind are also found in the second major school of Mahāyāna philosophy, Yogācāra. As we shall see, both Mahāyāna schools developed their philosophies in response to the philosophical issues being addressed by the Abhidharma schools. With this in mind, we can now introduce the Mahāyāna schools in India. We spend more time discussing these traditions than we did the Abhidharma ones because of their influence on Buddhism in Tibet and East Asia, which we explore in the next four chapters.

The Middle Way

The Mādhyamika, or "Middle Way," School of Mahāyāna was founded by Nāgārjuna (see Figure 5.3), who lived sometime during 150–250 C.E. Nāgārjuna used the forms of argumentation and principles of logic that were widely accepted in India during his day in his major work, the *Stanzas on the Middle Path* (*Mūlamadhyamaka-kārikā*). There, Nāgārjuna articulates the concept of emptiness. Because in that work Nāgārjuna does not mention any Mahāyāna *sūtras*, nor does he even use the word Mahāyāna, some scholars have doubted that he was a Mahāyānist. However, his views are so close to those expressed in the Perfection of Wisdom Literature that most consider him part of the Mahāyāna movement.

Nāgārjuna taught that people are caught in *duḥkha* and the *saṃsāric* chain of rebirth because of the power of karma that arises from unwholesome

FIGURE 5.3. Statue of Nāgārjuna with nāgas, snake beings; Samye Ling Buddhist Center, Eskdalemuir, Scotland.

thoughts, words, and deeds that are motivated by negative mental dispositions. Here, he agrees with Abhidharma Buddhism. But the key question for Nāgārjuna was, from where do these mental defilements come? The answer for Nāgārjuna is that this negative condition is produced by the way people "conceive of" the world in which they live. People misconceive the world, and their "wrong views" lead them to misbehave in ways that bind them to a life of *duḥkha*. One's misconception of the world happens in what Nāgārjuna calls *prapañca*. *Prapañca* means something like "the meaningful conceptualization of the world by the use of language." In other words, it refers to how people use concepts and language to understand the world.

With his concern about *prapañca's* negative effect on people's experience of the world, Nāgārjuna set out to show how the way people use concepts in language produces a "false view" of life. He proposed that when one conceives such entities as an agent of action or a dharmic element, one ordinarily assumes that these entities exist as discrete and independent. Or if one conceives of a process like motion or perception, one again assumes that there are entities that first exist as independent beings and then move or perceive other independent beings. Words like "perceiver" and "perceived object," "mover" and "movement," "agent" and "action," "substance" and "qualities" all imply that the world is constituted by independent entities that engage in relationships with one another.

This assumption of the substantial independence of phenomena is always at work in the human mind, determining how people experience life. By a person's ordinary linguistic use of concepts that imply the existence of independent substantial entities, one actually experiences things as existing independently. This view of life as made up of independent things is, for Nāgārjuna, a "wrong view" that keeps one from seeing the true nature of things. That is, *prapañca* keeps one from seeing that all things are really dependently arisen, they have no "own-being," or substantial independent nature. With this incorrect view of life, Nāgārjuna says, one becomes attached to things in ways that produce the negative dispositions and mental defilements that, in turn, produce *duḥkha*.

What Nāgārjuna did in his writings was to use a very sophisticated logical analysis of concepts such as causality, perception, motion, agency, selfhood, and elements of existence to show that any assumption of there being independent entities involved in these phenomena leads to absurd conclusions. Using this logical method of *reductio ad absurdum* (*prasaṅga*), Nāgārjuna deconstructed the ordinary way of conceiving of reality. In so doing, he proposes that the Buddha teaches the correct view of life, namely, that things are what they are because of the relatedness of life, their dependent arising. If things, including the *dharmas*, arise dependently, then they cannot be independent entities. Because they exist in function of dependent relatedness, they are "empty" of own-being; they are nothing by themselves. This does not mean that things do not exist or that processes like motion and perception do not take place. It just means that this movement, action, or perception does not imply the interaction of any substantially independent entities.

Instead, existence, movement, action, and perception take place because of a relational matrix of dependent arising.

An example of Nāgārjuna's thinking can be seen in his analysis of *duḥkha*, the dissatisfactoriness of life. In the few verses of Chapter 12 of his *Mūlamadhyamaka-kārikā*, he says that ordinarily *duḥkha* is assumed to be either self-caused, caused by another, both caused by self and another, or not caused at all. Nāgārjuna goes on to show that because each of these views assumes a substantial causal agent (either oneself or another) behind the arising of *duḥkha*, they each lead to problems:

> Some people assume that *duḥkha* is either self-caused, caused by another, caused by both self and another, or does not have a cause. Assuming *duḥkha* is such an effect is not justifiable.
>
> If *duḥkha* is self-caused, then it will not have arisen dependently. Indeed, it is dependent on these aggregates that others arise.
>
> If from these [aggregates], others arise, or if from those [aggregates], these arise, then *duḥkha* would be caused by another, for these would be caused by those.
>
> If *duḥkha* is caused by one's own person, then that person can exist apart from the *duḥkha*. What is this [independent] personhood that self-causes its *duḥkha?*
>
> If *duḥkha* is caused by another person, who is that other [independent] person that is without *duḥkha*, but causes it and gives it to another?
>
> Since the self-cause [of *duḥkha]* cannot be established, how can *duḥkha* be caused by another? For indeed, if *duḥkha* were caused by another person, then in relation to that other person, the *duḥkha* would be self-caused.
>
> In fact, there can be no self-caused *duḥkha*, it cannot be caused by oneself. And if another cannot bring about his or her own *duḥkha*, how can *duḥkha* be caused by another?
>
> If *duḥkha* could be caused by both oneself and another, it would have to be caused by each person individually. And where can there be any *duḥkha* without a cause, either by oneself or another?
>
> These four views of *duḥkha* are impossible; it is also not possible to apply these four views to any other elements of existence.

So, if the arising of *duḥkha*, or any other element of existence, cannot be explained by the use of concepts that assume a substantial causal agent, how can it arise according to Nāgārjuna? In Chapter 26 of his *Mūlamadhyamaka-kārikā*, Nāgārjuna analyzes the dependent arising of the "mass of *duḥkha*." In other words, for Nāgārjuna *duḥkha*, like all factors and processes of life, arises dependently. Being dependently arisen, all phenomena are "empty of own-being." This is what Nāgārjuna means when he says, "We declare that whatever is dependent arising is emptiness" (*Mūlamadhyamaka-kārikā*, XXIV, 18). Wisdom, for Nāgārjuna, sees this truth of "emptiness" (*śūnyatā*), that all phenomena are dependently arisen. With this insight into emptiness, one escapes *duḥkha:* "The ignorant person creates mental formations which are the source of *saṃsāra*. While the ignorant person does so, the wise person does not because of his or her seeing the truth" (*Mūlamadhyamaka-kārikā*, XXVI, 10).

Box 5.1

The Flavor of Emptiness

From the very first time I encountered the word in English, "emptiness," I liked the sound of it. Others may find it chillingly abstract, even scary; for me it was a fresh breath of freedom. I chanted the *Heart Sūtra* ("form is emptiness, emptiness is form . . .") every day for years before I ever studied what it meant. I remember once, at the beginning of my practice, walking up and down in a blizzard, snow piled two feet high and drifting, chanting that wonderful text over and over again. Only much later did I plunge into the vast philosophical edifice of Mahāyāna Buddhism, from the *Diamond Sūtra* and Nāgārjuna on, that adumbrates this saving and elusive teaching.

The logic of emptiness is air-tight: Since we know that we are, we know that things affect one another: Unless they do there is no world appearing, but if they do they must touch one another; if so they must have parts: If not they can't touch (they'd melt into one another), and if so there's an infinite proliferation of parts, smaller and smaller, clouds of them. So, if you look closely enough at anything it disappears into a cloud, and the cloud disappears into a cloud, and so on: All is void. The only thing real is connection: void touching void.

I have delighted in this simple but profound teaching, but it is the taste of emptiness in the body, spirit, and emotions that has meant the most to me. Knowing that what happens is just what happens. My body, my thoughts, my emotions, my desires, and hopes—this is the stuff that makes up my life. But it can't ever be desperate because I know it as a cloud. That cloud is all I am: It is my freedom to soar, my connection to all. I can float in it, and watch it form and reform in the endless sky.

This doesn't mean I am disconnected from life: Quite the contrary, I know there is no way not to be connected, no person or place that is beyond my concern.

When I practice meditation, I rest in emptiness: My breath goes in and out, a breath I share with all who have lived and will live, the great rhythm that began this world of physical reality, and that will never cease, even when the earth is gone. It's nice, in the predawn hours, to sit sharing that widely, knowing that this zero point underlies all my walking and talking and eating and thinking all the day through: Is it.

They say that wisdom (the faculty that cognizes emptiness) and compassion are like the wings of a great bird. Holding both in balance against the wafting winds allows you to float, enjoying the day. Really though the two wings are one wing. Where you can appreciate the flavor of emptiness on the tongue you know immediately (without mediation) that love is the only way, and that everything is love and nothing but love. What a pleasant thing to hold in mindl All problems, all joys, all living and all dying—it's love.

ZOKETSU NORMAN FISCHER
San Francisco Zen Center

Wisdom seeing emptiness reveals that all *dharmas*, all elements and processes of life, are empty of the substantial independence people assume them to have in their use of linguistic conceptualizations about them. To be more precise: Wisdom reveals that the many mental and physical elements (*dharmas*) discussed in detail by the Abhidharma philosophers are "empty" of substantial independence. Nāgārjuna uses the term *emptiness* to refer to the lack of any independence to things due to their dependent arising.

What is this condition of "emptiness," this nexus of dependent arising, that is the ultimate truth about existence? Emptiness is not, for example, an Absolute that is separate from the world of ordinary experience. In fact, emptiness does not refer to a thing; it refers to the way all things actually are, namely, empty of the independent way they ordinarily seem to exist. To make emptiness into an entity about which one can have a view is to make the fundamental mistake Nāgārjuna is trying to expose, namely, seeing anything as having a substantial identity. As Nāgārjuna says, "Those who adhere to a view of emptiness are incorrigible" (*Mūlamadhyamaka-kārikā*, XIII, 8).

On the other hand, the proper realization of emptiness, for Nāgārjuna, brings *prapañca* and its wrong views to an end. One sees things as they are in truth. In Nāgārjuna's words, "Beyond conditional [realization], quiescent, without conceptualizations by *prapañca*, not discriminating a variety of meanings, these are the characteristics [of one who has attained] the truth" (*Mūlamadhyamaka-kārikā*, XVIII, 9). With this wisdom insight into emptiness, one's attachment to things and the negative mental formations that result in unwholesome thoughts, words, and actions are also brought to an end. This freedom results in the cessation of *duḥkha* and the attainment of Nirvana.

In Nāgārjuna's understanding of this Nirvana, we find another important aspect of his philosophy. That is, with wisdom, one sees that the ordinary conditioned world of *saṃsāric* bondage is not apart from unconditioned nirvanic freedom. Nāgārjuna says, "Nothing distinguishes *samsāra* from Nirvana; and nothing distinguishes Nirvana from *samsāra*. Between even the extremities of *saṃsāra* and Nirvana, one cannot find even a subtle difference" (*Mūlamadhyamaka-kārikā*, XXV, 19–20). In short, there are not two realities, *saṃsāra* and Nirvana. There is only the "field" of emptiness that is experienced through ignorance and unwholesome mental formations as *saṃsāra* or through wisdom as Nirvana. When one's experience of the world is condihoned by *prapañca*, it is known as *saṃsāra*, full of *duḥkha*. But when by wisdom one experiences the ultimate truth that this same world is empty of own-being, then one finds Nirvana and freedom. In that freedom, one is attached neither to the worldly things nor to the state of Nirvana, which is itself arising in the field of emptiness. With wisdom's penetration into the ultimate truth of emptiness, one is detached from both the world and Nirvana, so that one can freely turn with compassion to address the needs of all living beings.

This nondualism between the freedom of Nirvana on the one hand and the ordinary world of *saṃsāra* on the other brings us to the Mādhyamika doctrine of the Two Truths. Nāgārjuna says, "The teaching of the Dharma by the Buddhas is based on two truths: the conventional truth and the ultimate truth. Those who do not understand the distinction between these two truths do not understand the profound nature of the Buddha's teaching" (*Mūlamadhyamaka-kārikā*, XXIV, 8–9). The "conventional truth" (*saṃvṛti-satya*) is about the world as experienced by ordinary perception and the conceptualization process of *prapañca*. Through this experience, one knows a number of conventional truths about the world, such as the fact that fire is hot, that something is moving, or that a certain person is President of the United States. The "ultimate truth" (*paramārtha-satya*) about existence is that all things are empty of own-being, or are dependently arisen. This ultimate truth is realized in the attainment of wisdom which produces nonattachment and the freedom of Nirvana. The goal of Mādhyamika is to convince people that the conventional truths about things do not give one the ultimate truth about existence.

This ultimate truth does not deny conventional truths; it simply reveals the true nature of what one knows at the conventional level of truth. Nāgārjuna says, "Without relying on convention, the ultimate truth cannot be expressed. Without understanding the ultimate truth, Nirvana cannot be attained" (*Mūlamadhyamaka-kārikā*, XXIV, 10). In other words, first one understands the things and processes of the ordinary world in the conventional way. Then one gains wisdom and sees the emptiness of these things and processes, that they are what they are because of dependent arising. Only in this way can one gain freedom within the dynamic of existence, Nirvana in *saṃsāra*. However, one still experiences conventional truths about the world such as fire being hot, things moving, and a person being President of the United States. By the light of the ultimate truth of emptiness, one reenvisions the ordinary world so that one is no longer attached to things in ways that generate *duḥkha* for oneself or others.

Here, we see why Nāgārjuna's school is called *Mādhyamika*, or the "Middle Way." It does not reject the mundane world for Nirvana. Nāgārjuna takes a middle position where one reenvisions the mundane world from the standpoint of the ultimate truth. In this Middle Way, one enjoys the freedom of Nirvana on the one hand, while dealing compassionately with the conditions of *saṃsāra* on the other. Realizing the emptiness of both *saṃsāra* and Nirvana, one is detached from both *saṃsāric* conditions and the unconditioned status of Nirvana. Thus, one's Great Journey courses in the Middle Way, where one is transformed by the power of the enlightened vision of emptiness, nonattached and free, full of compassion, living for the benefit of all beings.

After Nāgārjuna died, his disciple Āryadeva (c. third century C.E.) carried on his work. These two philosophers were the founders of the "early period" of Mādhyamika philosophy. The "middle period" of the school is marked by a disagreement between two philosophers. The first philosopher of this middle period was Buddhapālita (fifth century C.E.). While Buddhapālita employed the logical method of *reductio ad absurdum* to disprove the views of his opponents, he never attempted to formulate a position of his own. He believed that the ultimate truth cannot be formulated by words, which are always tied to conventional viewpoints. His school of Mādhyamika was later called *Prāsaṅgika* in Tibet because of his *prasaṅga* method of logic. The second philosopher of this middle period was Bhavaviveka (c. 500–570 C.E.). He had a more optimistic view of language's ability to bridge the gap between the conventional and ultimate truths. Influenced by the Buddhist logician Dignāga, whom we introduce later, Bhavaviveka used logic to present positive expositions of emptiness. His school of Mādhyamika was called *Svātantrika* in Tibet because it provided a positive position concerning emptiness by "autonomous" (*svatantra*) logical means.

The "later period" of Mādhyamika was initiated by Candrakīrti (c. seventh century C.E.), who wrote commentaries on Nāgārjuna's and Āryadeva's works that supported the Prāsaṅgika School of Buddhapālita. While a commentator rather than a central figure in Mādhyamika, Candrakīrti's *Clear Words* (*Prasannapadā*) is considered the fullest exposition of Mādhyamika. He clarifies not only Mādhyamika writings but also their spiritual purpose. He shows how the use of concepts and logic cannot reach the ultimate truth, and therefore concludes that only the practice of the Six Perfections in the bodhisattva journey can provide access to ultimate truth and freedom. Here is the way that Candrakīrti explains Nāgārjuna's statement that "Hate, greed and delusion are said to arise from thought-construction" in *Mūlamadhyamaka-kārikā*, XXIII, 1:

> All discursive ideas [which are thought-constructions] without exception are stopped in emptiness, where one sees the emptiness of the own-being of all phenomena. . . . Those who see emptiness do not apprehend the Five Aggregates, the elements and sense-fields, as if they existed as independent entities. Consequently, they do not construct discursive ideas, thought-constructions, about these phenomena with the notions of "oneself" and "objects to be possessed by oneself." Therefore, they do not give rise to a host of defilements, which have the false view of independent individuality as their source. Thus, they do not produce karma, and do not experience *saṃsāra* with [its mass of *duḥkha*]. . . . Hence, one calls emptiness Nirvana, since it stops all discursive ideas [that produce samsaric *duḥkha*]. (*Prasannapadā*, 18)

A famous follower of Prāsaṅgika was Śāntideva (eighth century C.E.). As a philosopher, he proposed a synthesis between Mādhyamika and another school of Mahāyāna called Yogācāra that we explore later. As we will see, Yogācāra taught that existence is derivative from Mind. Śāntideva taught that ultimate reality should be discussed according to the *prasaṅga* method of Mādhyamika. But when speaking about conventional reality, one could use the Yogācāra analysis of consciousness. This kind of synthesis might have been common in Buddhist philosophy at the time Śāntideva was writing.

Besides being a philosopher, Śāntideva was also a poet. This can be seen in his famous work entitled *Undertaking the Way to Awakening* (*Bodhicaryāvatāra*), which became a classic of religious literature. In it, Śāntideva describes the Bodhisattva Path from the arising of the thought of Awakening for the benefit of all living beings (*bodhicitta*) to wisdom's realization of emptiness and full Awakening. Practicing the Six Perfections obtains the mind of Awakening penetrating emptiness, which produces the kind of freedom for which humankind longs. Śāntideva is perhaps most treasured by Buddhists for the following kinds of poetic descriptions of the compassionate heart of the bodhisattva inspired by *bodhicitta*:

> When the thought of Awakening [*bodhicitta*] has arisen in a wretched one bound in existence, he or she is instantly proclaimed to be a child of the Buddhas, worthy of being praised in the realms of gods and humans.
>
> [Adopting the thought of Awakening,] I am medicine for the sick. May I be their doctor and their nurse until sickness does not occur.
>
> Showering down food and drink, may I avert the suffering of hunger and thirst . . . may I become food and drink.
>
> Without any regrets, may I give my bodies, pleasures and goodness . . . in order to achieve the welfare of all beings.
>
> Those who falsely accuse me, harm me, or mock me, may all of these persons share in Awakening.
>
> May as many beings as there are who are suffering pain in body or mind find, through my merits, oceans of happiness and joy.
>
> As long as there is *saṃsāra*, may beings never lose their happiness. May the whole world always receive happiness from bodhisattvas.
>
> May all suffering from the cold be warmed; may all suffering from heat be cooled by oceans of rain from the bodhisattva clouds.
>
> May blind people see forms; may deaf people always hear; and may pregnant women give birth without pain, like the mother of the Buddha.
>
> May the fearful be without fear, and those who are oppressed with sorrow find joy, and those who are anxious be free from anxiety and at peace.
>
> As long as there is space, and as long as there is the world, for that long may I live tending to the sufferings of the world. (*Bodhicaryāvatāra*, I, 9; III, 7–8, 10, 16; X, 2–3, 5, 19, 21, 55)

The Womb of the Buddha

During the period of time between the founding of the Mādhyamika School and the Yogācāra School, a number of Mahāyāna texts were written about the *Tathāgata-garbha*, the "womb" or "embryo" of the Buddha. The earliest of these texts is the *Tathāgata-garbha Sūtra*, composed between 200 and 250 C.E. Most important is the *Sūtra on the Lion's Roar of Queen Śrīmālā* (*Śrīmālā-devī Siṃhanāda Sūtra*), composed between 250 and 350 C.E. Soon after this *sūtra*, the *Analysis of the Jewels and Lineages* (*Ratnagotra-vibhāga*) was written as a summary of *Tathāgata-garbha* thought. These writings did not present a system of

Box 5.2

The Web of Relations

From the day it is born, an animal enters the world of interdependence quite naturally. Food, water, shelter, contact with others—all are central concerns. Almost immediately it becomes obvious that existence depends on others. At minimum, the successful animal learns quickly which beings it must eat or pursue, and which it must avoid in order to survive.

My first insights into the nature of interdependence came from observing the natural world as an ecologist. The science of ecology studies the biological realm of plants and animals to understand relationships within ecosystems. Who eats whom? Which animals or plants are harmful to which others? Why do certain animals prefer only specific host plants? Exploring the ten thousand beings this way, the truth of interdependence is unmistakable, the manifestations endless. The entire life community is nothing but mutually dependent existence continually arising.

When I began to study Buddhism in earnest, I spent a lot of time sitting by the side of a stream, considering the nature of humane existence. Trees, too, provided good companionship in this endeavor. Climbing mountains, walking long beaches, I wondered if Buddhism was another way to understand the natural world. But how to explain the wide range of human behaviors and attitudes toward nature? I found it deeply troubling that some of these behaviors were extremely destructive to plants and animals.

Buddhist practice, in contrast to ecology, emphasizes the study of the conditioned mind as a locus for understanding interdependence. When we observe mental processes, we discover the existential truth of the Buddhist teaching concerning dependent arising. We see that each thought reveals connections to others, each patterned response is a demonstration of relational existence. Fear of predators, exploitation of resources, environmental pollution, all can be linked to patterns of thinking which themselves have historical, causal origins. This central Buddhist teaching permeates not just ecological relations, but all human mental and emotional processes as well.

Human thoughts create and justify human actions, and these have profound impacts on the natural world. In my practice field as a professor of environmental studies, I work with this teaching in all my courses. It provides a grounding point of stability from which to thoughtfully engage the most difficult concerns arising from human impact on the Earth.

STEPHANIE KAZA
Professor of Environmental Studies
University of Vermont

philosophy and did not result in a separate philosophical school like Mādhyamika or Yogācāra. However, while their ideas did not have a great influence on Buddhism in India, they did strongly influence Mahāyāna thinking about the nature of consciousness, Awakening, and Buddhahood in East Asia.

This Mahāyāna literature proclaims that all living beings possess the *Tathāgata-garbha*. This inner reality is like a "womb" in that it contains the potential to become a Buddha, along with the many qualities of Buddhahood. It is also like an "embryo" as it can itself develop into full Buddhahood. It is said to consist of pure and luminous consciousness shining brightly like a jewel. Ultimately the *Tathāgata-garbha* is said to be identical with the Dharma-body (*Dharmakāya*) of the Buddha, the very essence of Buddhahood. Therefore, its condition is always nirvanic, and it responds to the teaching of the Dharma by generating from itself the thought or aspiration to attain Awakening for the benefit of others (*bodhicitta*). It was taught that all living beings already possess this innate essence of Buddhahood; they just do not ordinarily realize that fact. This last claim, about the universality of *Tathāgata-garbha*, was made in response to a debate in India in which some claimed that certain persons, who are "cursed ones" (*iccantika*), have no potential for Buddhahood. This debate would also appear in China, with all versions of East Asian Buddhism accepting the universalist position.

The reason people are unaware of the *Tathāgata-garbha* within them is because it is concealed by defilements like ignorance, hatred, greed, and delusion. These unwholesome mental formations cover over the *Tathāgata-garbha* "like a rag covering a Buddha statue." Once one is free from these defilements, the inner essence of Buddhahood shines forth with its luminous nirvanic nature and pure qualities. In other words, it is not possible for human thought or willfulness to attain Nirvana and Buddhahood any more than a rag can produce the Buddha statue that is wrapped within. Because the *Tathāgata-garbha* is the Dharma-body of the Buddha, it alone is the source of the attainment of Nirvana and Buddhahood. This line of thinking about the generation of Buddhahood is seen by the *Tathāgata-garbha sūtras* to be a positive addition to the Mādhyamika notion of emptiness. That is, when one attains the purification of mental formations and gains wisdom realizing emptiness, one can see this inner Buddha potential shining in all beings, including oneself. One's vision, clarified by the ultimate truth of emptiness, can realize the inner Dharma-body resplendent with Nirvana and the pure qualities of Buddhahood, like a Buddha statue breaking through a rag that had previously covered it. As we shall see, in China this innate and universal potential for Buddhahood came to be called "Buddha-nature" and played an important role in East Asian Buddhism.

The following verses from the *Ratnagotra-vibhāga* express these ideas:

> Because Buddha knowledge is contained in all beings, because it is pure and non-dual in nature, because those who belong to the lineage of the Buddha advance towards it as their goal, therefore all living beings have the *Tathāgata-garbha* within them.
>
> The body of perfect Buddhahood irradiates everything, its suchness is not differentiated. The path to Buddhahood is open to all, so at all times do all living beings have the *Tathāgata-garbha* within them.

> If it did not exist in all beings, there would be no disgust with *duḥkha*, no wish for Nirvana, no striving for Buddhahood, no resolve to gain it for the benefit of all beings [*bodhicitta*].
>
> Like a Buddha in a faded lotus flower, like honey covered by bees, like a fruit in its husk, like gold within its impurities, like a treasure hidden in the dirt . . . like a valuable statue covered with dust, so is this [*Tathāgata garbha*] within all beings.
>
> Nothing can be taken from it, nothing can be added to it. So, it must be seen in its suchness, and seeing the truth, one is liberated. (*Ratnagotra-vibhāga*, I, 27, 28, 40, 96, 97, 154)

Foundations of Consciousness

The writers of the *Tathāgata-garbha* literature were aware of the *Perfection of Wisdom Sūtras* and knew of Mādhyamika philosophy. Today, scholars argue that these writers, like many other Buddhists at that time, were concerned with the negative impression conveyed by the notion of "emptiness." They felt that the notion of emptiness focused just on the *lack* of independent selfhood and did not do justice to the positive and *full* nature of enlightened experience. So their *sūtras* stressed the Awakening to one's Buddha potential that exists within as a luminous treasure waiting to be discovered. The followers of the second Mahāyāna school, Yogācāra, also shared this concern about Mādhyamika. They may well have been influenced by the *Tathāgata-garbha* texts. However, the exact relationship between Yogācāra and these texts is the subject of debate between Buddhist scholars today. In any case, the Yogācāra philosophers were primarily interested in how the mind generates the experience of the dependently-arisen world in which things are empty of own-being.

The Yogācāra School draws its inspiration from certain *sūtras* that began to appear in the third century C.E. Among these are the *Resolving the Underlying Meaning Sūtra* (*Saṃdhinirmocana Sūtra*), the *Mahāyāna-abhidharma Sūtra*, and the *Laṅkāvatāra Sūtra*, which we introduced in Chapter 4. The actual founder of the school was Asaṅga, who lived in the fifth century C.E. Asaṅga converted his half-brother, Vasubandhu, to his school. Both brothers gave a systematic foundation to the Yogācāra School in their writings. Asaṅga wrote, among other things, the *Compendium of Mahāyāna*, the *Abhidharma Collection*, a commentary on the *Saṃdhinirmocana Sūtra, and the Discrimination between the Middle and the Extremes*. Some of the works by Asaṅga were said by Buddhists to have been composed by Maitreya Bodhisattva (see Figure 5.4) and conveyed to Asaṅga either through a semilegendary person who was a manifestation-body of Maitreya, or directly by Maitreya himself. These texts later became known as the "Five Treatises of Maitreya." Some scholars today say that Asaṅga might have attributed these five works to Maitreya due to feeling that the bodhisattva was the inspiration behind them. The important works of Vasubandhu include the *Twenty-Verse Treatise*, the *Thirty-Verse Treatise*, and the *Exposition on the Three Natures*.

FIGURE 5.4. Gandhāran Maitreya; dark gray schist; second–third century C.E., India. The Royal Ontario Museum, Toronto, Canada.

The term *yogācāra* means "practice of yoga." In Buddhism, yoga is understood to be the practice of the Bodhisattva Path, especially the practice of meditation. Because the focus of the school is on the nature and functioning of the mind, Yogācāra was later referred to as *Vijñānavāda*, meaning "School of Mind." As we have seen, the philosophers of the Abhidharma schools taught that consciousness arises when the senses are in contact with objects. Yogācāra turns this commonsense Abhidharma position upside down. What Yogācāra claims is that consciousness actually produces the experience of sensations and their objects. It is not that a subject and an object come together to produce conscious experience, as in the Abhidharma model. Rather, for Yogācāra, there is a fundamental process of consciousness that produces one's experience of subjective selfhood on the one hand and the objective world on the other. One's experiences of both oneself and the world arise dependently from a more fundamental process of consciousness.

Traditionally, scholars of Buddhism have accepted this view as a form of Idealism, the theory that the world is a product of the mind. Today, this interpretation is being debated. Another interpretation claims that the world *as we know it* is produced by the mind; what the world is in itself, we have no way of knowing. Related to this view is an interpretation that approaches the matter from a nondualistic point of view, where the subject and the objects of experience arise together. In any case, for Yogācāra, one's *experience* of self and world is certainly generated by the mind. Given this position, the philosophical task for Yogācāra was to explain how consciousness can be the basis for both the subjective and objective aspects of experience.

To begin with, they claim that all the mental and physical elements (*dharmas*) in experience are arising dependently within a more fundamental process of consciousness. Whereas Mādhyamika emphasized the emptiness of this dependent arising, Yogācāra goes a step further and claims that consciousness is the causal force behind such dependent arising. Consciousness forms itself into the six senses (including the mental faculty that "senses" thought objects) and the objects of these senses. As the *Laṅkāvatāra Sūtra* says, consciousness is like water forming itself into waves. These six senses and their objects arise dependently from consciousness, accounting for the mental and physical elements of one's experience through a process that Yogācāra calls "ideation only" (*vijñaptimātra*).

Behind this ideation process of the six sense consciousnesses is, according to Yogācāra, a seventh form of consciousness that they call "mind" (*manas*). They claim that this more unitary faculty of consciousness is the basis of both inner reflection and self-awareness. Self-awareness arises in the mind as it reflects on, or "follows," the dependent arising of the six senses and their objects. Because of this self-awareness, the mind concludes that it exists as an independent self apart from the objects it experiences. But in fact, both one's self and the world are two dependently arisen aspects of an experiential process that is being produced by consciousness—by ideation only.

Yogācārins also claim that behind the mind of self-awareness and reflection is the ultimate source of this whole ideation process. They call this eighth and final level of consciousness the "storehouse-consciousness" (*ālaya-vijñāna*). In the storehouse-consciousness is the fundamental unity of consciousness that is prior to all its forms. In its use of the above water and waves metaphor, the *Laṅkāvatāra Sūtra* also says that storehouse-consciousness generates from itself all forms of experience like the ocean whose water takes form as waves. In other words, out of its "storehouse," consciousness constructs the subjective experience of one's mind and senses, as well as the objective world of their experience. While one's self and the world seem to be so distinct from each other in experience, they are really just dependently arisen formations from the storehouse-consciousness.

Yogācāra claims that the storehouse-consciousness contains the karmic "seeds" deposited in it from the process of conscious experience. These seeds influence the storehouse's ongoing construction of experience and account for its continuity. The seeds are influenced or "perfumed" (*vāsanā*) by one's positive and negative attitudes. For example, one's negative dispositions, such as the Three Root Evils (hatred, greed, and delusion), condition the seeds of future experience within the storehouse-consciousness in ways that often lead to unwholesome thoughts, words, and actions. These unhealthy thoughts, words, and actions then produce new negative karmic seeds in the storehouse-consciousness that, in turn, will affect one's future experience. Therefore, the storehouse-consciousness accounts not only for one's experience of oneself and the world but also for the moral and spiritual qualities of that experience. This being the case, Yogācāra taught that one must change the karmic condition of the storehouse-consciousness by the practice of the Six Perfections. These perfections cultivate "pure seeds" within the depths of the storehouse-consciousness itself.

On the bodhisattva's Great Journey, mental defilements and afflictions are gradually eliminated, pure qualities are cultivated, and the mind is stilled by meditation. Then, when the inner conditions are right, at the very foundation of consciousness there is a sudden "conversion of the basis" (*āśraya-parāvṛtti*). One's ordinary processes of consciousness stop, and one gains an intuitive insight into the storehouse-consciousness at its basis. Thereby, one attains freedom from all conditioned states of consciousness, Awakening, and Nirvana.

Yogācāra's presentation of this radical and sudden turning over of the basis of consciousness greatly influenced East Asian Buddhism. Some East Asian Buddhist writers read Yogācāra as agreeing with the *Tathāgata-garbha* Literature. These writers believed that both traditions taught that the purity of spiritual life comes from the inherent luminous Buddha-qualities found within one's deepest center. The sudden turning over of the basis of consciousness was thought to reveal a nondual nirvanic nature of luminous and pure consciousness, the unlimited Dharma-body, which is the essence of Awakening and Nirvana. As we shall see, other Buddhist writers disagreed with this interpretation of Yogācāra, and this issue became important to the development of East Asian Buddhism.

Returning now to early Indian Yogācāra, besides its theory of consciousness, the school also presented what are called the Three Natures (*tri-svabhāva*) of experience. First is the "imagined" (*parikalpita*) nature of experience. That is, in one's ordinary experience, oneself and the objects of that experience seem to be independent entities, when, in fact, this independent status is an "imagined" fabrication. For Mādhyamika, this fabrication of the "imagined" independent nature of things in one's experience is made by *prapañca*. For Yogācāra, the imagined nature of experience is generated by the karmic seeds in the storehouse-consciousness, along with the ego-awareness of the mind.

Second is the "interdependent" (*paratantra*) nature of experience. Here, we find the Mādhyamika "ultimate truth" that all entities are arising dependently or interdependently and are therefore empty of "own-being." Yogācāra points out that this interdependent nature of the self and entities of experience is produced by consciousness. That is, although people "imagine" that themselves and the objects of their experience are independent, in fact, they arise in experience interdependently from the processes of consciousness. However, because ignorance leads people to imagine that oneself and the objects of the world are independent, one develops attachments, defilements, and *duḥkha*. Thereby, unwholesome seeds are planted in the storehouse-consciousness, which, in turn, play a part in this dependent arising of experience. Therefore, the "interdependent" nature of experience is both pure and impure, good and evil.

Because of attachment to the imagined independent things of ordinary experience and the resulting impurity of the interdependent nature of experience, Yogācāra posits a third nature. It does so to stress the need to purify oneself from the ignorance that is superimposing the imagined fabrication of independence onto the interdependent nature of things. By this purification, one can cease making this superimposition, see the truth about the dependent arising of experience, and become free from attachment and the defiling of experience. One does so by following the Bodhisattva Path. The result of this purification is the third nature, which is called the "perfected" (*pariniṣpanna*) nature of experience. This perfected nature of experience is ultimately attained by the realization of Awakening, wherein one sees that all ordinary experience is a product of "ideation only" (*vijñaptimātra*). With enlightened wisdom, one realizes Nirvana.

With these ideas in mind, let us now look at some verses from a text by Vasubandhu:

> Since our ideation gives rise to false ideas concerning the self and the [mental and physical] *dharmas* . . . this ideation, which depends on the mind, goes through three different transformations.
>
> First is the storehouse-consciousness, which brings to fruition all of its seeds. . . . It is not affected by the darkness of ignorance or by the memory. . . . It always flows like a torrent. . . .
>
> Second is the mind (*manas*), which depends on the storehouse-consciousness, while, in turn, conditioning it. Its nature and characteristic is reflection. It is always accompanied . . . by ignorance of the self, views of the self, self-pride and self-love. It follows the objects of the mind in their dependent arising.
>
> Third consists of the six senses of discrimination . . . that discriminate objects. Their mental functions include [all the *dharmas*]. . . . Based on the mind, these sense consciousnesses arise dependently with their objects . . . just like waves dependent on water.
>
> Therefore, all the consciousnesses are transformations . . . and for this reason everything is mind-only. As the result of ideation, which renders seeds [in the storehouse], different transformations take place. The influence of these ideation seeds gives rise to different discriminations.
>
> Because of false discriminations, various objects are falsely discriminated. But the objects that are grasped in these false discriminations are empty of own-being. The ultimate truth of all *dharmas* is nothing more than suchness . . . which is the true nature of mind-only.
>
> The state of mind-only is realized when the six senses and their objects are not present. Without grasping and beyond discriminations is perfect wisdom.

Because of the abandonment of energies of the karmic seeds, and the six senses and their objects, the conversion from relative knowledge to perfect wisdom is realized. This is the realm of purity . . . where one finds freedom, peace and joy. (*Triṃśika-kārikā*, 1, 2, 4–9, 15, 17–18, 20, 25, 28–30)

Theories of Knowledge

As Abhidharma and Mahāyāna Buddhism developed in India, there arose the need to train monastics in the many philosophical systems of thought as well as the practices associated with them. Hence, some monasteries evolved into universities. One of the earliest centers of learning, dating back to the second century C.E., was Nālandā (see Figure 5.5) in northeastern India. Nāgārjuna and Asaṅga were said to have taught at Nālandā. Another monastic university was Valabhī in western India. Over time, Buddhist universities like these built vast complexes of libraries and lecture halls, instituted stringent admission standards, and developed curricula that included everything from grammar and linguistics to music, architecture, and science. They became centers of Buddhist culture throughout India. From these universities, missionaries were sent to other parts of Asia, and Buddhist scholars from throughout Asia came to them for advanced education and training.

In this Buddhist university setting, monastic scholars became more and more interested in questions of logic and dialectics. These more critical concerns led to an intellectual Buddhist movement that focused its attention on theories of knowledge. Dignāga (c. fifth century C.E.), said to be a student of Vasubandhu, was the founder of this movement. This movement in

FIGURE 5.5. Ruins of Nālandā University, Bihir, India.

Buddhism started at a time when logic and epistemology (theory of knowledge) were used by Indian philosophers to defend their doctrines. This provided a common ground for the discussion of different religious points of view in India. Dignāga is often presented as a logician, but this is misleading. Although he discussed topics like inference, universals, and so on, he was primarily interested in providing a system for the critical analysis of cognition that Buddhists could use in their search for truth.

Dignāga taught that one needs to distinguish between perception that is free from any conceptual content, and conceptual construction that provides overlays to our raw perceptions. Conceptualization uses inference, language, universals, and so forth to conceptualize what we are perceiving. This means for Dignāga that the real entities that we perceive are themselves not the objects we conceptualize them to be. They are ultimately inexpressible. Dignāga uses the term "particular" (*svalakṣaṇa*) to refer to what appears to us in perception. Our perception of a particular in a moment of preconceptual awareness is all we have to go on in knowing reality. Our perceptions of particulars are themselves unerring given that error arises with the process of conceptualization. But what exactly are these particulars we perceive? This and many other questions about Dignāga's theory of cognition were addressed by Dharmakīrti, who lived during the seventh century C.E.

Dharmakīrti expanded Dignāga's notion of particulars. Particulars for him are real entities that are momentary, exist for an instant; they are inexpressible because they exist prior to conceptualization; and they have a causal effect on us as we perceive them. In this regard, Dharmakīrti accepts some of the ideas of the Abhidharma tradition. He accepts their notion of primary elements of matter. These elements are not perceivable by themselves, but come together in combinations that constitute the particulars we perceive. As in Abhidharma thought about the *dharmas,* it is these particulars that causally interact with moments of perception. In our process of consciousness, these perceptions give rise to "mental images" of the particular. From those images, we mentally construct the physical objects that make up the world. In presenting how this process of consciousness works, Dharmakīrti turns to the philosophy of Vasubandu—namely, Yogācāra.

Dharmakīrti uses the Yogācāra theory of mind to explain how we cognize material objects, like a chair, based on the particulars that we perceive. The four primary elements that constitute particulars are what cause us to produce mental images from the particulars. From that point, it is the mind that weaves together these mental images, or representations, into the experience of the external objects we see around us.

Dharmakīrti goes on to say that consciousness not only brings about *what* we experience but also *how* we experience the world of objects around us. For example, we see a person due to the particulars of our perception. Then through conceptualization we "superimpose" qualities and characteristics on the person. In doing so, we might "view" the person as someone we do not like. We experience that person in a negative way and feel anger or hatred toward him or her. The objective cognition of the person is produced by our consciousness triggered by perceptions of particulars. The negative subjective cognition is also produced by our consciousness triggered by our memories, dispositions, and attitudes. For Dharmakīrti as a Buddhist, one can purify the mind so as to rid oneself of the negative states of mind that react to the world around us. He taught that the true nature of the mind is pure and luminous. Once the "stains" are gone, we Awaken to this purity of mind and find Nirvana.

The Disappearance of Buddhism and the New Buddhists of India

By the seventh century when Dharmakīrti was living, Buddhism was gradually being replaced in the south of India by forms of devotional Hinduism. Because the monasteries depended on popular support, many of them became deserted in that region of India. In the northwest, invasions by the Ephthalite Huns in the sixth century had devastated hundreds of monasteries. In the eighth century there were invasions by the Muslim Turks in northwestern and western India. As these invaders moved south, they pillaged Buddhist monasteries, burned Buddhist *sūtras,* and butchered Buddhist monastics. The famous Buddhist monastic university of Valabhī was destroyed. Buddhist refugees fled to the east, where they found refuge in the Ganges plain. However, the Pala empire which ruled that area was overthrown in 1162, and by the end of that century, the Muslim Turks conquered that region as well. Nālandā was destroyed in 1198. Without the leadership of the monastic Saṅgha and their great universities, the Buddhist communities could not survive. They were assimilated into devotional Hinduism; by the next century, Buddhism in India virtually disappeared. However since the time of Buddhism no longer being a viable tradition itself in India, it has continued to be part of Indian cultural history and its philosophies were accepted as heterodox systems of thought by the Hindu tradition. Then during the twentieth century, a social movement in India led to Buddhism's reemergence in a new form through the efforts of a Hindu leader.

Bhimrao Ramji Ambedkar (1891–1956) was the Hindu leader of the Untouchables in India prior to Indian independence. As a boy, because of his untouchable status, Ambedkar endured terrible persecution at school and in his community. His notebooks could not be touched by his teacher, a drink of water had to be poured into his mouth for fear of polluting contact, and he was beaten when he inadvertently stepped where he was not wanted. However, through his intelligence and perseverance, Ambedkar became only the second Untouchable to graduate from high school in India. Then with support from a liberal Hindu leader, he went on to attend college and gained doctorate degrees from Columbia University and the University of London.

Even as an academic and elected leader in India, Ambedkar continued to experience caste violence. He was evicted from his home and subjected to beatings. Eventually, Ambedkar became convinced that mere reform of the Hindu caste system would never solve the problem of untouchability. So in

1935, he decided to give up Hinduism and thereby his status as an Untouchable by converting to another religion. After exploring a number of religions, Ambedkar decided on Buddhism. On October 14, 1956, during the celebration of the 2,500th anniversary of Buddha's *parinirvāṇa,* he and his wife took vows for the Three Refuges. Six weeks later, Ambedkar died, having opened the way for his Untouchable brothers and sisters to enter and forge a new form of Indian Buddhism. In just five years, over three million Untouchables followed Ambedkar's lead and became Buddhists.

Before his conversion to Buddhism, Ambedkar wrote *The Buddha and His Dhamma,* in which he applies the Dharma of the Buddha to the suffering condition of Untouchables in India. Indeed, Ambedkar saw the teachings of the Buddha as having the precise purpose of eliminating this type of suffering endured by so much of humankind:

> [His] path which is his Dhamma (religion) had nothing to do with God or Soul. His Dhamma had nothing to do with life after death. Nor has his Dhamma any concern with rituals and ceremonies. The center of his Dhamma is man and the relation of man to man in his life on earth. This he said was his first postulate. His second postulate was that men are living in sorrow, in misery and poverty. The world is full of suffering and that how to remove this suffering from the world is the only purpose of Dhamma.[1]

In interpreting this Dharma, Ambedkar set aside certain central teachings of the Buddha such as the Four Noble Truths, karma and rebirth, and the monastic life. The Four Noble Truths, Ambedkar felt, speak only about one's own ignorance and selfishness as the causes of suffering, not the heartless actions of others and the systemic injustice of such social arrangements as the caste system. The idea of karma, he believed, would only accentuate the self-blame of the Untouchables instead of placing the blame on the caste system itself. Also, the monastic life would be of little or no use to the poor masses of India.

On the other hand, Ambedkar believed that the virtues taught by the Buddha do in fact provide a basis for a liberating social life that can uplift those bound by poverty and oppression. The Four Divine Abodes of loving kindness, compassion, sympathetic joy, and equanimity provide the attitudes that lead to working together to address the suffering of poverty. Wisdom enables one to understand one's condition and the steps that one must take to change that situation. The Eightfold Path defines those steps that can bring the self-respect and social-political change needed such that the social structures that produce poverty and suffering are removed. The overcoming of human passions such as hate, anger, and greed can aid in eradicating the roots of class struggle and social inequality, and thereby the suffering they engender.

By converting to Buddhism, the plight of the ex-Untouchables was not changed overnight. There is still much work to be done today to raise their lives out of abject poverty. Therefore, the "New Buddhists" in India, those converts inspired by Ambedkar, founded a number of organizations based on his call for social transformation through Buddhist principles. One such organization is the Trailokya Bauddha Mahasangha (literally the "Buddhist Order of the Three Realms"), or TBM. Lay and monastic members of TBM participate in what is called the "Dharma Revolution," by which New Buddhists can transform their own lives, and work with each other to transform society.

TBM has developed three ways of facilitating this Dharma Revolution. First is through "public centers," one- or two-room huts where Dharma talks and classes are given on Buddhist principles for living and on the practice of meditation. The Dharma is applied to particular problems such as domestic violence, lack of self-esteem, and the effects of poverty. Meditation focuses on mindfulness of breathing and loving-kindness meditation. The second part of TBM work is done at rural "retreat centers" in retreats intended to deepen what is begun at the public centers. The third part of the movement's work is done in "residential communities," where members learn to develop spiritual friendships, live harmoniously with each other, and work together for their common good. To address specific problems of ex-Untouchables, TBM has also set up a number of social projects that include kindergartens, residential schools, women's literacy classes, vocational classes, health-care outreach programs, and outpatient clinics for slum dwellers.

NOTE

1. B. R. Ambedkar, *The Buddha and His Dhamma*, Third Edition (Bombay: Siddharth Publications, 1984), p. 83.

SUGGESTIONS FOR FURTHER READING

Akira, Hirakawa. *A History of Indian Buddhism: From Śākyamuni to Early Mahāyāna*. Honolulu: University of Hawaii Press, 1990.

Ambedkar, B. R., and Valerian Rodrigues, eds. *The Essential Works of B. R. Ambedkar*. New York: Oxford University Press, 2002.

Anaker, Stefan, trans. *Seven Works of Vasubandhu*. Delhi, India: Motilal Banarsidass, 1984.

Brassard, Francis. *The Concept of Bodhicitta in Śhantideva's* Bodhicaryāvatāra. Albany: SUNY Press, 2000.

Conze, Edward. *Buddhist Thought in India: Three Phases of Buddhist Philosophy*. London: George Allen & Unwin, 1962.

De Bary, Wm. Theodore, Ainslie Embree, and Stephen N. Hay, eds. Revised in 1988 by Stephen N. Hay. *Sources of Indian Tradition*. 2 vols. New York: Columbia University Press, 1988.

Dreyfus, Georges B. J. *Recognizing Reality: Dharmakirti's Philosophy and Its Tonetam Interpretations*. Albany: SUNY Press, 1997.

Dreyfus, George B. J., and Sara L. McClintock, eds. *The Svātantrika-Prāsangika Distinction*. Boston: Wisdom Publications, 2003.

Dunne, John D. *Foundations of Dharmakīrti's Philosophy*. Boston: Wisdom Publications, 2004.

Eckel, Malcolm David. *To See the Buddha: A Philosopher's Quest for the Meaning of Emptiness*. Princeton, NJ: Princeton University Press, 1992.

Frauwallner, Erich. *Studies* in *Abhidharma Literature and the Origins of Buddhist Philosophical Systems*. Edited by Ernst Steinkellner; translated by Sophie Francis Kidd. Albany: SUNY Press, 1996.

Garfield, Jay L. *The Fundamental Wisdom of the Middle Way: Nāgārjuna's* Mūlamādhyamakakārikā. New York: Oxford University Press, 1995.

Huntington, C. W. *The Emptiness of Emptiness: An Introduction to Early Indian Mādhyamika*. Honolulu: University of Hawaii Press, 1989.

Jayatilleke, K. N. *Early Buddhist Theory of Knowledge*. London: George Allen & Unwin, 1963.

Jiang, Tao. *Contexts and Dialogue: Yogacara Buddhism and Modern Psychology on the Subliminal Mind*. Honolulu: University of Hawaii Press, 2006.

Kalupahana, David. *Causality: The Central Philosophy of Buddhism*. Honolulu: University of Hawaii Press, 1975.

———. *Nāgārjuna: The Philosophy of the Middle Way*. Albany: SUNY Press, 1986.

Kinnard, Jocob N. *Imaging Wisdom: Seeing and Knowing in the Art of Indian Buddhism*. Richmond, UK: Curzon Press, 1999.

Nagao, Gadjin. *Mādhyamika and Yogācāra: A Study of Mahāyāna Philosophies*. Albany: SUNY Press, 1991.

Napper, Elizabeth. *Dependent-Arising and Emptiness*. Boston: Wisdom Publications, 1989.

Robinson, Richard H. *Early Madhyamika in India and China*. Madison: University of Wisconsin Press, 1967.

Śāntideva. *The Bodhicaryāvatāra*. Translated by Kate Crosby and Andrew Skilton. Oxford, UK: Oxford University Press, 1995.

Schopen, Gregory. *Bones, Stones, and Buddhist Monks: Collected Papers on the Archaeology, Epigraphy, and Texts of Monastic Buddhism in India*. Honolulu: University of Hawaii Press, 1996.

———. *Buddhist Monks and Business Matters: Still More Papers on Monastic Buddhism in India*. Honolulu: University of Hawaii Press, 2004.

———. *Figments and Fragments of Mahāyāna Buddhism in India: More Collected Papers*. Honolulu: University of Hawaii Press, 2005.

Siderits, Mark. *Buddhism as Philosophy: An Introduction*. Hants, UK: Ashgate Publishing, 2007.

Walser, Joseph. *Nagarjuna in Context: Mahayana Buddhism and Early Indian Culture*. New York: Columbia University Press, 2005.

Westerhoff, Jan. *Nagarjuna's Madyamaka: A Philosophical Interpretation*. New York: Oxford University Press, 2009.

Zelliot, Eleanor. *From Untouchable to Dalit: Essays on the Ambedkar Movement*. Delhi, India: Manohar, 1996.

6

Tibetan Experiences of Buddhism

Tibet and Buddhism seem ubiquitous today, but Buddhism arrived rather late in Tibet (seventh century C.E.) in comparison to its neighbors. Buddhism spread along the Silk Road to Central Asian regions west of Tibet from 200 B.C.E. to 100 C.E. and east of Tibet to China in the first to second centuries C.E. Before Tibet embraced Buddhism, it had its own religion. Because the Tibetan historical record begins only after the seventh century C.E., it remains difficult to gain a clear picture of Tibetan religion before Buddhism, but ancient documents attest to the worship of the Tibetan king (Tsenpo) as a divine ruler, complex funerary rites, a certain type of ritual priest called Bön, and the worship of protective divinities *(yül lha)* associated with Tibet's sacred mountains. The latter practice continues to thrive in many parts of Tibet to the present day. The Buddhist conversion of Tibet is a story closely tied to empire, for the two arose together in Tibetan history. From the early seventh through mid-ninth centuries the Tsenpos unified Central Tibet and expanded their reign in all directions through military conquest. At the same time, Buddhist influence percolated into Tibet from India, China, Nepal, and ancient Central Asian kingdoms such as Khotan. What initially attracted the attention of Tibetan emperors was the systematic reasoning, writing technology, and discipline of monastic Buddhism, which provided a model of standardized rule useful to the newly expanded Tibetan empire comprised of diverse peoples. By the second millennium, however, Tibetans would become more fascinated with the occult powers promoted by Tantric Buddhism.

THE EARLY DISSEMINATION OF BUDDHISM IN TIBET

Tibetan historical records remember King Songtsen Gampo (ruled c. 605–650) as the first Tibetan emperor to take a serious interest in Buddhism. Songtsen Gampo inherited a newly unified Tibet from his forefathers. He continued to expand and strengthen Imperial Tibet through violent military expeditions such as overtaking the Zhangzhung Kingdom in the western part of the

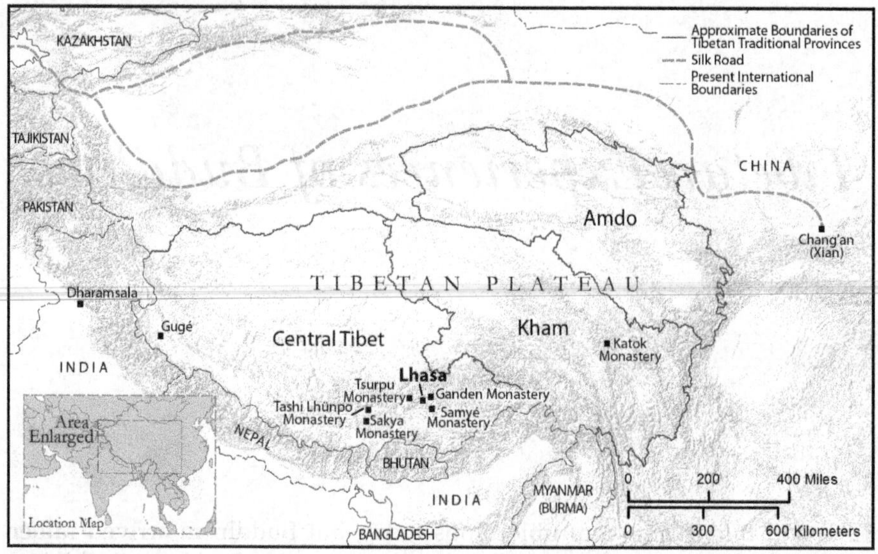

MAP 4. Buddhism in Tibet.

Tibetan plateau and arranging politically advantageous marriages with princesses from Tibet's powerful neighbor kingdoms. Most famously, he created an alliance between the Tibetan Empire and Tang China through marrying the Chinese princess Wencheng, who Tibetans remember for bringing the first Buddhist statue to Tibet, which was an image of the Jowo ("Lord") Śākyamuni. Songtsen Gampo built the first Buddhist temple in Tibet to house this statue, the Jokhang Temple, located in the heart of Tibet's capital city Lhasa. In addition, he transformed Nepal into a Tibetan vassal state and married a Nepalese princess named Tritsün according to later sources. She, too, brought a statue of Śākyamuni Buddha with her to Tibet, for which Songtsen Gampo built another temple in Lhasa called Ramoché. Tibetan historical chronicles credit Songtsen Gampo with making three important cultural contributions, including (1) the first Tibetan writing system, (2) redacting the law code, and (3) introducing the Buddhist religion. Although Songtsen Gampo's foreign brides were Buddhist and Songtsen Gampo supported the building of the first Buddhist temples in Tibet, historical records are less explicit about his own religious beliefs.

Several generations later, his descendant Tri Songdetsen (ruled 755–797) would become the first explicitly Buddhist Tsenpo, with edicts declaring his Buddhist conversion at the age of twenty to prove it. Tri Songdetsen constructed Tibet's first Buddhist monastery named Samyé (c. 779). He invited the great Indian Buddhist monastic scholar from Nālandā University, Śāntarakṣita, to ordain the first Tibetan Buddhist monks at Samyé based on the *Mūlasarvāstivāda Vinaya* code of monastic discipline. Post-twelfth-century Tibetan accounts of Samyé's founding include another important figure, the Indian Buddhist adept Padmasambhava, who would become renowned as the "second Buddha" who succeeded in converting Tibet to Buddhism (see Figure 6.1). In these accounts, Śāntarakṣita was unable to finish building Samyé because demonic local forces obstructed his progress. He called for the help of Padmasambhava, who subjugated the unruly anti-Buddhist elements with his meditative powers and converted them to Buddhism, thus enabling the completion of Samyé. Tri Songdetsen was duly impressed with Padmasambhava's capabilities and became his disciple, offering his guru one of his wives, Yeshé Tsogyel (pictured to the right of Padmasambhava in Figure 6.1), who is revered in the Tibetan Buddhist world as Tibet's preeminent female saint.

Tri Songdetsen's reign was studded with both military and religious achievements. In 763 his Tibetan military forces even briefly took over the capital of Tang China, Chang'an, and during the 780s his armies controlled large swaths of the Silk Road, including the important Chinese Buddhist heartland of Dunhuang. In terms of religion, Tri Songdetsen and Tsenpos

FIGURE 6.1. The Buddhist Trio of Tantric adept, monk, and royal patron: Padmasambhava, Śāntarakṣita (bottom left), and Tri Songdetsen (bottom right). Nineteenth-century Nyingma lineage *tangkha* from the Collection of the Shelley and Donald Rubin Foundation.

following him sponsored a massive translation enterprise consisting of translation committees, including Tibetan and foreign Buddhist scholars, who translated the entire Buddhist canon from Sanskrit and Chinese into Tibetan. Several hundred years later in the thirteenth and fourteenth centuries Tibetans organized these voluminous scriptures into the *Kangyur*, "translated words of the Buddha," and *Tengyur*, "translated commentaries," which together include more than 300 volumes of Tibetan language scripture.

The international scope of the royally sponsored translation project introduced Tibetans to varying interpretations of Buddhism. Tibetan histories remember one result of this as a debate that emerged in the latter part of Tri Songdetsen's reign between a Chinese Chan Buddhist master named Moheyan and an Indian Buddhist master named Kamalaśīla, who was a disciple of Śāntarakṣita. Moheyan's Chan tradition advocated the attainment of sudden Awakening through the practice of meditation. This direct insight into one's "Buddha-nature" triggers that inner nature to express itself and purifies all mental afflictions and defilements. In the following chapter we will examine Chinese Chan Buddhism in greater detail. Kamalaśīla, on the other hand, did not believe that any particular religious experience could eliminate all the mental defilements and afflictions that have been engrained into one for countless lifetimes. Rather, he taught that enlightenment has to be gradually perfected in the Ten Stages of the Bodhisattva Path. One must familiarize oneself with the roots of one's unhealthy thoughts, words, and actions, as well as with the enlightened thoughts, words, and actions of the Buddhas and bodhisattvas. Ridding oneself of the former, and cultivating the latter, involves a long process of growth in wisdom and compassion that no sudden insight can accomplish. Various sources depict different winners of this debate between sudden and gradual interpretations of the Buddhist path to enlightenment. Tibetan records indicate that Kamalaśīla emerged victorious, setting the stage for Tibetans to privilege Indian over Chinese interpretations of Buddhist doctrine. Alternately, Chinese records claim that Moheyan won the debate. In either case, Tibetans looked to India as the motherland of Buddhism and traced their lineages from there, although there is evidence that Chinese Chan teachings also flourished in Tibet.

Tri Songdetsen passed on his faith in Buddhism and patronage of Buddhist monastic institutions to generations of his successors, whose Buddhist expenditures seem to have exceeded royal coffers. Traditional Tibetan accounts remember the fall of their empire as a consequence of the persecution of Buddhism effected by King Lang Darma (r. 838–842), who assassinated his brother who had been king for squandering too much imperial wealth on Buddhism. Lang Darma's budgetary trimming earned him the wrath of the Buddhist Saṇgha, culminating in his own assassination in 842 by a prominent monk. Whether Lang Darma's diminished sponsorship of Buddhism resulted from his alleged faith in Tibet's old religion or from economic necessity remains an open question. It is perhaps more than ironic that many royal houses along the Silk Road suffered an economic depression in the mid-ninth century that not only led to reduced Buddhist patronage but also to their collapse, including both Tibet and Tang China, which fell in 907. A series of uprisings after Lang Darma's death beginning in 869 further unsettled the cohesion of the Tibetan empire, eventually leading to its dissolution, along with that of Buddhist monastic institutions in Central Tibet. Buddhism did not die out in Tibet in the ensuing political chaos, however, but was preserved by lay Buddhist practitioners and by monastics who lived in the relatively prosperous northeastern regions of the former empire.

THE LATER DISSEMINATION OF BUDDHISM IN TIBET

After the fall of Imperial Tibet in the ninth century and the ensuing century-plus of fragmentation, smaller regions of the Tibetan plateau reorganized political authority, regained economic solvency, and renewed their patronage of Buddhism. The revival of Buddhism in Tibet beginning in the mid-tenth century is called the later dissemination (*chidar*) of Buddhism in Tibet, as opposed to its earlier dissemination (*ngadar*) in the seventh and eighth centuries. In this later dissemination period, Tibetan political authority had as much if not more to do with Buddhism than before, for in many cases the local lord or regional king was none other than the Buddhist master himself.

The earliest regions of what had formerly been the Tibetan empire to contribute to the revitalization of Tibetan Buddhism were its far eastern and western extremities. In the mid-tenth century, Central Tibetans traveled to Amdo in northeastern Tibet to return the Tibetan *Mūlasarvāstivāda* monastic *Vinaya* lineage preserved there to Central Tibet, where they founded new monasteries. Meanwhile in the far western kingdom of Gugé, parts of which are located in the present-day Ladakh and Himachal Pradesh regions of India, the king became so devoted to Buddhism that he became an ordained Buddhist monk and took the name Yeshé Ö (c. 959–1036), which means, "the Light of Primordial Wisdom." He founded Buddhist temples and invited Indian Buddhist masters to teach in Gugé. Yeshé Ö and Buddhist enthusiasts affiliated with him perceived the Buddhism that had survived the age of fragmentation after the fall of the Tibetan Empire to be corrupted, infiltrated with Tibetan indigenous practices and moral lapses due to the near dissolution of the *Vinaya* lineage in Tibet. Translators sponsored by the Kingdom of Gugé turned their attention to revitalizing Tibetan Buddhism through traveling to Kashmir, Nepal, and India to study with great Indian masters and translate their sacred scriptures into Tibetan. In particular a Tibetan monastic scholar and expert translator named Rinchen Zangpo (958–1055) played an important role in Yeshé Ö's scriptural translation efforts. Gradually, the new influx of later Indian Buddhist scriptures into Tibet changed the types of Buddhist practice prevalent in Tibet, crystallizing over the space of several hundred years into several distinctive schools of Tibetan Buddhism. Before we embark on a more detailed description of these Tibetan Buddhist schools, a brief introduction to Tantric Buddhism is necessary because of its significant influence on all types of Tibetan Buddhism.

FIGURE 6.2. Tibetan vajra.

TANTRA AND VAJRAYĀNA BUDDHISM

The Buddhism that Tibetans imported from India was a branch of Mahāyāna Buddhism called Vajrayāna, or the "Diamond Vehicle." Vajra can mean either "diamond" or "thunderbolt," connoting the indestructibility and strength of the awakened state of Buddhahood. Modeled on a king's royal scepter, the vajra, shown in Figure 6.2, is an important ritual implement in Tantric Buddhism. Tantra is a notoriously difficult category to clearly define. Etymologically, it is associated with the verb "to weave" and the noun "warp," the lengthwise thread in which a weaver threads the woof. In the context of Buddhism, Tantra refers to a set of scriptures consisting primarily of esoteric ritual manuals. Tantric texts began appearing in India by the third century C.E. and continued until the decline of Buddhism in India in the twelfth century. But it was not until the late seventh century that the term Vajrayāna emerged as a separate vehicle of Buddhism. Vajrayāna Buddhism is therefore not synonymous with Tantric Buddhism, which is a larger category encompassing scriptures that precede the formation of Vajrayāna as a distinctive Buddhist vehicle. However, in the context of Tibetan Buddhism, the two are often used interchangeably because much of the Buddhism that Tibet imported in the first and second dissemination periods was Vajrayāna. Like Mahāyāna Buddhism did not reject but rather incorporated earlier forms of Buddhism into itself, Vajrayāna accepts Theravāda and Mahāyāna scriptures as authoritative in addition to its own Tantric scriptures. We can see this continuation of earlier vehicles of Buddhism in Tibet's Vajrayāna Buddhism in the form of monastic discipline Tibetans uphold, which originates from an early Indian Buddhist school (the *Mūlasarvāstivāda Vinaya*), and in Tibetans' monastic curriculum, in which the study of important Mahāyāna scriptures is foundational for subsequent Tantric scriptural studies. What distinguishes the Vajrayāna Buddhism practiced originally in India and up to the present day in Tibet (as well as other parts of the Himalayas, Mongolia, and certain Buddhist lineages in Japan) from earlier Buddhist vehicles is its emphasis on Tantric ritual techniques. Vajrayāna adherents view these techniques to be so powerful and efficacious that they enable a disciple to attain complete Buddhahood in one lifetime instead of the countless lifetimes of incremental refinement entailed in traversing the Ten Stages of the Bodhisattva Path outlined in Mahāyāna Buddhism.

There is no one standard list of Tantric techniques agreed on by all Tantric Buddhist traditions, but there is a set of features that are found in many Tantric practices to a greater or lesser extent. Tantric Buddhist practices focus on worshipping enlightened Buddhas and bodhisattvas through receiving initiations called *abhiśekas*, reciting incantations called *mantras*, positioning the body in various postures called *mudrās*, visualizing intricately detailed pictorial representations of the enlightened realms of Tantric deities called *maṇḍalas*, and performing various yogic meditation practices involving visualizing oneself as a Buddha (deity yoga) and manipulating subtle forms of energy flowing through the body.

Tantric Buddhism is sometimes called esoteric Buddhism due to the necessity of receiving initiation (*abhiśeka*) from a qualified master (called in Tibetan a guru or lama) to be empowered to invoke a particular Tantric deity. Additionally, Tantric Buddhism is esoteric because of the prevalence of symbolic language in Tantric scriptures that requires elucidation by a guru steeped in the relevant oral commentarial tradition. The existence of symbolic and at times transgressive statements in Tantric scriptures helped to ensure that the meaning remained secret from the uninitiated as well as provided grist for multiple and sometimes contrasting interpretations. Given the complexity of Tantric ritual, a central feature of Vajrayāna Buddhism is the importance of the guru–disciple relationship, without which a Tantric disciple cannot gain understanding and contemplative realization. Disciples cultivate devotion for their guru, perceiving him or her as a fully enlightened Buddha from whom the blessings of their spiritual lineage flow.

A disciple of Tantric Buddhism receives initiation into the *maṇḍala* of a particular Buddha. *Maṇḍalas* are two- or three-dimensional circular diagrams of the realm that particular deity and his or her subsidiary deities inhabit. Often brightly colored and intricately beautiful, depictions of various Tantric *maṇḍalas* cover Himalayan Buddhist temple walls in the forms of painted frescos and hanging canvas scroll paintings called *tangkhas*. Some Tibetan monastics specialize in making detailed *maṇḍalas* entirely out of different colors of sand (see Figure 6.3), which they then sweep away as a demonstration of impermanence and pour into a local water source as an offering. Although often exquisitely crafted, *maṇḍalas* are not art for the sake of aesthetic appreciation but tools to aid Tantric initiates in visualizing the realms of the deities on whom they meditate. By visualizing the *maṇḍala*, the practitioner concentrates on the enlightened attitudes, understandings, and virtues that are symbolized by the deity and his or her realm, which can help her to realize these within herself.

Another essential feature of Tantric practice is reciting *mantras* or oral incantations associated with a particular deity while visualizing that deity in his or her *maṇḍala*. That *mantra* is a distinguishing feature of Tantric Buddhism is demonstrated by an early Sanskrit synonym for Tantric Buddhism, *mantrayāna*,

FIGURE 6.3. Tibetan monk making a sand *maṇḍala*.

or "path of *mantras*," in use prior to its seventh-century emergence as a separate vehicle called Vajrayāna. This association between *mantra* and Tantra persisted in Tibet, where Vajrayāna Buddhism is also sometimes called Secret Mantra (*sang ngak*). When Tibetans translated Indian Buddhist scriptures into Tibetan, they left the *mantras* in Sanskrit because the efficacy of *mantra* is not in the meaning of the words but rather their sound. By reciting the sound frequencies of a deity's *mantra*, the practitioner invokes the enlightened qualities of that deity and deepens his connection to the deity with the goal of becoming inseparable from him or her. The most popular *mantra* in Tibet is that of Tibet's patron saint, the Bodhisattva of Compassion, Avalokiteśvara, from whom Tibetans understand the Dalai Lama to be an emanation. Avalokiteśvara's six-syllable *mantra* "*Oṃ Maṇi Padmé Hūṃ*" resounds from the lips of many Tibetans not only in the midst of dedicated mediation sessions but also in the course of performing daily activities, sometimes with one hand fingering the beads of their *mala* (rosary), which they use to count the number of *mantra* recitations they accumulate.

While the practitioner's mind meditates on a *maṇḍala* and speech recites a *mantra*, she positions her body and hands in a particular posture called a *mudrā* that is identical with that of the deity she is visualizing. Through identifying these three aspects of her being—body, speech, and mind—with the Tantric deity her guru has empowered her to invoke, the practitioner cultivates the enlightened qualities of that deity in herself. Tantra is sometimes referred to as "training in the effect" that one is trying to achieve. Like an architect pays attentive detail to crafting a blueprint of a building he plans to construct, the Tantric practitioner cultivates a visual, aural, and somatic experience of herself as an enlightened Buddha surrounded by a pure realm to gradually embody that awakened state. By not only visualizing a Buddha in his pure realm, but by performing a meditation practice called deity yoga in which the practitioner visualizes herself as that Buddha, replete with divine raiment and accoutrements, the Tantric practitioner gains familiarity with the freedom and joy of the enlightened state, thus enabling her to realize that state within herself more quickly. Behind this practice is the view that within *saṃsāra* is a nirvanic reality, innate in all things, that is the highest joy. This means that all mental and emotional defilements and afflictions are adventitious; they are like mud stains on a jewel that can be wiped away. What one sees in deity yoga is the inherent beauty of what this clearing away produces, namely, the awakened state.

Vajrayāna Buddhism expresses this state as the blissful union of wisdom (Skt. *prajñā*, Tib. *sherap*) and compassion (Skt. *karuṇā*, Tib. *nyingjé*). Compassion is also sometimes called skillful means (Skt. *upāya*, Tib. *tap*), referring to the methods whereby one seeks enlightenment for oneself and others. Wisdom is the last of the six Mahāyāna perfections (*paramitā*) and refers to the wisdom of realizing emptiness (Skt. *śūnyatā*, Tib. *tongpanyi*), or the lack of permanent and stable existence of persons and phenomena. Earlier in Mahāyāna Buddhism as well, skillful means and wisdom formed a pair that together embodied the complete qualities of Buddhahood. For instance, in the *Lotus Sūtra* the Buddha expresses his realization using this dyad:

> Śāriputra, since I attained Buddhahood, I have expounded my teachings through different causes and similes, and have used countless skillful means to guide living beings and cause them to renounce their attachments. Why? Because the Tathāgata fully possesses both skillful means and the perfection of wisdom. (Ch. 2)

What emerges more strongly in Vajrayāna than in earlier forms of Buddhism is a depiction of Buddhahood as the union of compassion and wisdom using symbolism involving gender complementarity in which compassion is male and wisdom female. Vajrayāna Buddhist iconography depicts these male and female qualities in the form *of yab yum* deities, or male and female Tantric deities in sexual union.

Although *yab yum* iconography is symbolic of complete Buddhahood as the inseparable union of wisdom and compassion, sexuality does play a role in certain esoteric Tantric initiations and contemplative practices. This is because a feature common to many Tantric traditions is a conception of the body as containing a subtle architecture made up of channels (*tsa*) in which vital nuclei (*tiklé*) course by means of wind (*lung*). Along the central axis of the body lies a series of wheels (Skt. *cakra;* Tib. *khorlo*), or nexuses of capillary-like channels that emanate outward throughout the body. In ordinary beings who have not yet realized Awakening, the channels that coalesce around each of the *cakras* are knotted together, obstructing the smooth flow of wind and vital nuclei. Tantric practices involving specific forms of sexuality are one of many techniques advanced practitioners use to loosen the channel knots and restore the flow of vital energy throughout the body, resulting in physical health, longevity, and spiritual realization. However, subtle body practices do not necessarily contradict celibate monasticism because the majority of Tibetan Tantric practitioners perform them as Tantric visualizations and not literal sexual encounters with another person. Nevertheless, the existence of esoteric sexual practices in the service of spiritual liberation in later Indian Tantras has earned Tantra a strong association with sexuality in the eyes of those unfamiliar with it, a connection often widely overemphasized and little understood.

In fact, Indian Tantric Buddhist texts contain a wide variety of practices, ritual techniques, and goals, representing more than a millennium of religious developments, most of which do not concern sexuality. As a way of ordering this diversity, some Tibetan commentaries group Tantric scriptures into a four-fold classification. The earliest subdivision is Action Tantra, dating from the second to sixth centuries C.E. Action Tantras prescribe ritual practices using *mantras* and *maṇḍalas*, but unlike later Buddhist Tantra aimed at the realization of enlightenment, the aims of Action Tantra are pragmatic goals such as weather control, protection from danger and warfare, healing illness, and promoting health. The second subdivision of Tantra is Performance Tantras, which encompass a smaller number of texts dating from the seventh to eighth centuries. In these texts, the practice of identifying oneself with the Tantric deity in the center of the *maṇḍala* emerges, although the goals of Performance Tantras remain focused on aims of this world, not on attaining Buddhist enlightenment. The third subdivision is Yoga Tantra, developed by the early eighth century. In Yoga Tantra scriptures, the goal of performing the contemplative practices prescribed within them is to attain the state of Buddhahood.

The final Tibetan classification of Tantric scriptures is Highest Yoga Tantra, which contains two subdivisions: Mahāyoga and Yoginī Tantras, referred to in the Tibetan Buddhist canon (*Kangyur*) as Father and Mother Tantras, respectively. Mahāyoga, or "Great Yoga," had developed by the end of the eighth century, building on the Yoga Tantras. In Mahāyoga Tantras we find initiations and contemplative practices involving sexuality emerging more prominently than in earlier Tantras as well as injunctions to consume transgressive substances such as meat, alcohol, and bodily substances. It remains unclear how practitioners of later Indian Tantra interpreted these antinomian commands, although much of the Indian and Tibetan commentarial writings emphasized their symbolic nature. Mahāyoga Tantras number among the most important Tantras in Tibet, such as the *Guhyasamāja Tantra* and the *Guhyagarbha Tantra*.

By the mid-tenth century, when Tibetans began returning to the Buddhist heartland of India to reimport Buddhism to Tibet, a new group of Tantric scriptures were being formulated, the Yoginī Tantras. These Tantras retained the transgressive elements of Mahāyoga involving sexuality and the consumption of substances deemed impure in Indian culture. In addition, Yoginī

Tantras contain symbolism associated with cremation grounds and a heightened role of female deities, as is evident by the name Yoginī or "female yogi." Some of the most important Tantric scriptures in Tibet are part of this final Indian Buddhist development, such as the *Hevajra Tantra*, the *Cakrasaṃvara Tantra*, and the *Kālacakra Tantra*.

Preliminary Practices

Tibetan Buddhist practice begins with certain preliminary practices. Sometimes these practices are divided into two types. First are the "external" preliminaries, which utilize the basic teachings of Buddhism to help one turn away from attachment to *saṃsāra* and seek Buddhahood. One is to consider that human existence offers one the freedom and opportunity to seek Buddhahood. One is then to consider the impermanence of existence and the defects and sufferings associated with it. With these in mind, one goes on to consider how karma, the principle of cause and effect, applies to all action, so that one commits oneself more fully to avoid negative actions and adopt positive ones. Then one is to consider the means to attain, and the benefits of, liberation from *saṃsāra*. Finally, one considers the importance of following and emulating a guru to attain this goal.

The "internal" preliminary practices are more specifically related to Tantra. Sometimes called the "five sets of 100,000" or *bum nga* in Tibetan, each of the following preliminary practices involves repeating a *mantra* along with a visualization and in some cases other ritual actions to be performed more than 100,000 times each. The first such practice involves taking refuge in the Buddha, Dharma, and Saṅgha and affirming the precepts associated with this "refuge-taking." This is a practice shared with all Buddhist traditions. In Vajrayāna, it is believed that refuge-taking holds a power in itself that plants the seeds of spirituality within the ordinary mind and heart. Along with the refuge-taking is an act of faith in the Three Refuges, the guru, and the practice lineage as essential aids to spiritual growth. One way in which the practitioner cultivates that faith is through performing prostrations. Prostrations may take place before an image, symbol, or altar and must be done with the proper attitude of humble recognition of one's personal need for spiritual aid. In doing prostrations, one recognizes this need and acknowledges the superior wisdom and compassion of the Buddhas and bodhisattvas. One imagines these spiritual beings, along with one's lineage and personal guru, before oneself.

A second internal preliminary practice is the arousing of *bodhicitta*, the intention to gain Buddhahood for the good of all living beings. In this regard, one is to develop *bodhicitta* by different means, and one may express this altruistic aspiration in vows before one's guru or visualized Buddhas and bodhisattvas. One can also train in *bodhicitta*, for example, by extending through meditation good intentions to others, by developing the willingness to exchange oneself for others in need, or by realizing more deeply that just like oneself, all persons seek happiness and freedom from suffering. One can also develop *bodhicitta* by training in the perfections of the Bodhisattva Path. Here, we see clearly the rootedness of Buddhist Tantra in the Mahāyāna tradition.

A third common preparatory practice is Vajrasattva purification. Varasattva is a Buddha associated with the purification of the mind. Different schools have their own ritual methods. But in general, one confesses and reflects on one's past negative actions, vows not to do them again, and seeks purification from Vajrasattva. This latter part of the practice involves visualizating Vajrasattva displacing one's negative emotions, mental afflictions, and other defiling states that resulted from past misdeeds.

A fourth popular preliminary practice is the *maṇḍala* offering. Physical *maṇḍala* offering may involve the use of a round plate and some grains or small grainlike substances. The practitioner pours grains on the plate and moves them in a manner that symbolizes wiping away the Three Root Evils of hate, greed, and delusion or the development of enlightened mind, speech, and body. Eventually, the practitioner uses the grain to form a *maṇḍala* that symbolizes the whole universe. This *maṇḍala* is then offered to the Buddhas, and then the grain is poured into one's own lap. This symbolizes offering everything to the Buddhas and receiving back the blessings of the Buddhas. There is also an "inner" *maṇḍala* offering where one visualizes one's own body as a *maṇḍala* that is pure and can be offered to the Buddhas for the benefit of all sentient beings. Finally, in the "secret" *maṇḍala* offering, one's own mind becomes the *maṇḍala* to be offered for transformation into the mind of enlightenment. It is also common in preliminary practices to offer the merits of one's action for the good of all living beings.

Finally, there is guru yoga. Tibetan Buddhism stresses the need for a qualified guru, or lama, in order to learn and perform Tantric practices properly. This is because Tantra cannot be transmitted by Tantric texts alone, which are often not even understandable without the aid of a guru. Rather, proper transmission comes from a spiritual lineage, and an authentic teacher embodies the transmission power of his or her lineage. He or she is able to apply properly and effectively the Tantric teachings and practices to the life of the disciple. Guru yoga involves visualizing one's teacher as an embodiment of the clear wisdom and pure compassion of Buddhahood. This provides the disciple with a concrete experience of the goal he or she is trying to attain. In this experience of yoga, one receives the teachings and initiations united with their source and their goal. One is led by guru yoga eventually to find this source/goal within the heart of one's own being. That is, one discovers that the guru is an embodiment of one's own innate essence of Buddhahood. Because of the unquestioning faith and devotion associated with guru yoga, the power of the guru can be abused. Thus, one is advised to choose one's guru with great care.

MAJOR SCHOOLS OF TIBETAN BUDDHISM

Versions of the preliminary practices just introduced can be found in all schools of Tibetan Buddhism, but over time the diversity of scriptures Tibetans translated from Sanskrit originals representing all of the classifications of Tantra mentioned earlier led to the multiplication of Tibetan Buddhist schools. In particular, four major schools of Tibetan Buddhism formed during the period of religious renaissance that followed the ninth-century dissolution of the Tibetan Empire: the Nyingma, Sakya, Kagyü, and Geluk. Tibetans divide these into two categories—the old and the new schools—based on their respective geneses in the earlier and later dissemination periods. These were not the only types of Buddhism in Tibet; other schools such as the Kadam thrived in earlier centuries but were later absorbed into these main schools. Additionally, Bön is sometimes listed as a fifth school of Tibetan Buddhism because of its syncretism with post-tenth-century Tibetan Buddhism, although its adherents view it as a separate religion that developed out of Tibet's pre-Buddhist religion. But if Bön is Buddhist influenced, the opposite could also be said: the types of Buddhism formulated in Tibet incorporated elements of Tibet's pre-Buddhist religion.

The "Old" School: Nyingma

The Nyingma School of Tibetan Buddhism traces its origins to the early dissemination of Buddhism in Tibet, and specifically with the miraculous activities of the eighth-century Indian Tantric master Padmasambhava. Other key personages in the sacred history of the Nyingmas include King Tri Songdetsen, the Indian master Vimalamitra, and the Tibetan translator Vairocana. The school's name, *Nyingma,* indicates both that it traces its origin to the "old" or "ancient" roots of Buddhism in Tibet, but also that it formulated itself as such only in response to the "new" schools that arose during and after the later dissemination period.

Nyingmapas, or practitioners of Nyingma Buddhism, recognize two forms of lineage transmission: *kama* and *terma. Kama* is known as the "long" transmission of scriptures from master to disciple in an unbroken lineage spanning back millennia to the historical Buddha. Among other Nyingma Tantras transmitted through *kama* transmission is the Mahāyoga *Guhyagarbha* Tantra. *Terma,* which means "Treasure," is known as the "short" transmission of teachings. Treasure teachings are teachings that Padmasambhava or one of his Imperial Tibetan contemporaries hid for the benefit of future generations to be revealed at the proper times by Treasure revealers, who are incarnations of Padmasambhava's main twenty-five disciples. Although innovative, this idea that Buddhist scriptures were hidden by miraculous means for the benefit of future disciples has Indian precedents. For example, one explanation for how the Buddha taught Mahāyana scriptures that did not materialize until half a millennium after his death is that he entrusted them to the serpentine *nāga* spirits, who held them in their aquatic domain until the right time for their dissemination among humans. Tibetan Treasure teachings come in two forms: as earth Treasures, which are scriptures, statues, or ritual implements discovered in the earth, and mind Treasures, which appear as visualizations in the mind of a Treasure revealer, who then writes them down.

Finding religious Treasures in the Tibetan earth might not have entirely mystical origins, for during periods of Buddhist persecution that occurred during the Tibetan Empire and its aftermath, Tibetans buried scriptures and religious artifacts for safekeeping. Another way of understanding the Treasure tradition is to view it as a Nyingma response to the influx of new Indian Buddhist scriptures during the later dissemination period. That the earliest Treasure revealers such as Sangyé Lama began discovering their Treasures in the eleventh century at the same time as Tibetans were importing later Indian Tantric scriptures that would form the bedrocks of the new schools lends credence to this interpretation.

Another distinctive feature of the Nyingma School is its classification of the Buddhist teachings. Unlike the four-fold division of Tantra into Action, Performance, Yoga, and Highest Yoga Tantra outlined earlier that is characteristic of the newer schools of Tibetan Buddhism, the Nyingma School divides the Buddhist teachings into nine progressively higher vehicles grouped into three main sections. The first section includes the teachings of the Abhidharma and Mahāyāna traditions. The second section includes the three "lower Tantra vehicles," namely Action, Performance, and Yoga Tantra. The third section includes three "higher Tantra vehicles" that encompass what newer schools refer to as Highest Yoga Tantra and culminates in a unique pinnacle teaching called Primordial Yoga (*atiyoga*) or Great Perfection (*dzokchen*). The Great Perfection teachings are contemplative practices geared toward realizing the nature of mind, which is beyond intellect and reasoning. The nature of mind is like a mirror, luminous and clear once one wipes away surface obscurations caused by ignorance. Great Perfection scriptures describe the nature of mind as the basis or ground from which all phenomena in existence manifest. This ground of being is empty in the sense of being insubstantial and lacking in self-nature, but it also has three characteristics: a primordially pure essence, a clear and spontaneously present nature, and an uninterrupted energy. When practicing the Great Perfection, these three characteristics correspond to three aspects of the nature of mind: the calm state in which no thoughts arise, the movement of thoughts, and presence, which is the state of recognizing whether one's mind is calm or moving. A Great Perfection master's instruction is necessary to recognize this latter state of presence. The goal of Great Perfection contemplation is not to cultivate the complex Tantric visualizations that take center stage in Highest Yoga Tantra, nor is it to cultivate the calm state by reducing the mind's movement. Instead, Great Perfection practices aim to recognize both calmness and movement without judgment and while maintaining presence. This state of presence allows whatever arises to self-liberate, or to dissolve back into the ground from which it arose like waves flow back into the ocean.

Over centuries following the second dissemination period, the Nyingma School of Tibetan Buddhism revitalized its monastic tradition and rebuilt major institutions of learning, particularly in the Eastern Tibetan region of Kham such as Katok Monastery (est. 1159; see Map 4). Although it is well known for its contemplative traditions, the Nyingma School also produced several polymath scholar-practitioners who systematized Nyingma doctrine, including Nup Sangyé Yeshé (c. tenth century) and Longchen Rapjampa (1308–1363). The Nyingma's claims to political dominance remains rooted in its ties to the Buddhism that Tibetan kings imported during the Tibetan Empire from the seventh through the ninth centuries. Although subsequent Tibetan rulers would become interested in various aspects of Nyingma Buddhism, after the fall of the Empire it never regained dominance as the main religious lineage of Tibet's rulers.

The "Scripture and Precept" School: Kadam

Among the "new" schools of Tibetan Buddhism, the Kadam School developed as an outgrowth of the religious renaissance initiated by King Yeshé Ö, his royal descendants, and Tibetan translators such as Rinchen Zangpo in far Western Tibet's Gugé kingdom. An important contributor to this renaissance was the Indian Buddhist scholar Atīśa (982–1054). Atīśa had been the abbot of the monastic university Vikramaśīla, and had also studied at Nāropā, where Śāntarakṣita had studied centuries earlier before King Tri Songdetsen invited him to Tibet to help build Samyé Monastery. Atīśa arrived in Tibet in 1042, bearing with him a mature synthesis of Indian Buddhism that integrated Abhidharma, Mahāyāna, and Tantric forms of Buddhism. Atīśa's Buddhism emphasized ethics, textual learning, and proper adherence to the *Vinaya* code of discipline for monastics. We can garner a taste of Atīśa's presentation of Buddhism through excerpts from a work he wrote while in Tibet, *A Lamp for the Path to Awakening:*

> With mind set, never turn back until the attainment of the ultimate Awakening; and with strong faith in the Three Jewels, kneel on one knee and press hands together taking refuge three times.
>
> I go for refuge to the Buddha.
> I go for refuge to the Dharma.
> I go for refuge to the Saṅgha.
>
> Next, with love for all beings . . . and wanting to liberate beings from suffering and the causes of suffering, arouse the irrevocable resolve to attain Awakening . . .
>
> Without the discipline needed to enter into Awakening, perfect aspiration will not grow. Therefore, desiring growth in Awakening, take hold of discipline with strong effort . . .
>
> Moreover . . . celibacy is clearly the most glorious and pure conduct—the discipline of the fully ordained monk . . .
>
> If one desires to practice secret mantras as explained in the ritual activity scriptures [i.e., Action, Performance, and Yoga Tantras], and so forth, then to obtain the spiritual teacher's initiation, one must please the holy teacher with service, gifts, and obedience . . .
>
> Those observing the celibate life should not take the secret wisdom initiation since *The Scripture of the Primordial Buddha* emphatically forbids it . . .

> For one who has obtained the teacher's initiation and has knowledge of suchness, there is no fault in listening to or explaining the Tantras, performing the ritual offerings, or making offerings of gifts.

Atīśa's presentation of the Buddhist path from the beginning point of taking the triple refuge, cultivating the thought of Awakening for the benefit of oneself and others according to the Mahāyāna scriptures, and ultimately entering into Tantric ritual practice emphasizes the supremacy of monastic celibacy. His treatise solves the problem of later Tantric initiations involving sexuality by ruling that only the first Tantric initiation, called the master's consecration, was necessary to be empowered to practice the most esoteric Tantric scriptures. Atīśa's emphasis on ethics and the primacy of monastic discipline cast a reformist tone that had a wide impact on others involved in the later dissemination of Buddhism in Tibet.

Although Atīśa did not set out to found a new school of Tibetan Buddhism, his disciple Dromtön Gyelwé Jungné (1004–1064), who was a layman from Eastern Tibet, founded Reting Monastery north of Lhasa in 1057 and thus instigated the Kadam School. The school's name refers to its central adherence to the Buddhist canonical scriptures (*ka*) of the Tripiṭaka and the precepts (*dam*) of the Mahāyāna. In the late eleventh century, Kadampas founded the college of Sangpu in Central Tibet, which came to be the Tibetan center for rigorous monastic education, including logic and debate. The Kadam tradition did not survive as an independent school after the sixteenth century, but it had a lasting impact on all of the four schools of Tibetan Buddhism, which incorporated various aspects of its teachings into their own.

The "Gray Earth" School: Sakya

The development of the Sakya School exemplifies the overlap between ruler and Buddhist master that came to characterize Tibetan Buddhist institutions in the second dissemination period. Its founder, Könchok Gyelpo (1034–1102), hailed from the powerful Khön family, which descended from Imperial Tibetan aristocracy. Though the Khöns had formerly been adherents of proto-Nyingma teachings, Könchok Gyelpo instead turned towards the new Tantras coming into Tibet from India. To study these, he became a disciple of Drokmi Śākya Yeshé (c. 993–1064), who was a Tibetan monk who spent eighteen years living in the Pala kingdom of northeastern India at Vikramaśila Monastery. Drokmi later returned to Tibet and founded his own monastery and translation center where Könchok Gyelpo became his disciple before setting off to found Sakya Monastery in 1071 (see Map 4). Several generations of his descendants would rise to become the leading scholars and Tantric specialists of their day, setting the tone of the Sakya School as both grounded in scholastic erudition and Tantric ritual expertise based on cutting-edge scriptures fresh from the Buddhist heartland of India.

One of Drokmi's main Tantric lineages stemmed from the Highest Yoga Tantra called *Hevajra*, which he imported from India and translated into

Tibetan. The distinctive teaching of the Sakya School called "path and fruit" (*lamdré*) is based on the *Hevajra Tantra*. The Sakya system teaches that the path to Nirvana and Nirvana itself cannot ultimately be distinguished because of the identity of *saṃsāra* and Nirvana. Following the path in *saṃsāra* is to already have the fruit of Nirvana, but one just does not know it. In the words of the *Hevajra Tantra*, "Then, the essence, being pure and full of knowledge, is where there is no difference between *saṃsāra* and Nirvana. Nothing is produced mentally in the highest bliss, and there is no one producing it" (*Hevajra Tantra*, I, 10.32–33). In other words, when one attains the fruit of Nirvana by walking the path in *saṃsāra*, one has not produced anything that was not there all along the journey. What is found in Awakening is the pure knowledge that has been covered from view by the defilements of *saṃsāra*. Through *lamdré* practice, one comes to recognize mind as an inseparable union of luminosity and emptiness.

The Sakya School gained prominence in Tibet not only for its spiritual insights and monastic institutions but also for unifying political control over Tibet for the first time since the Tibetan Empire. Sakya hegemony over Tibet was unlike that of Imperial Tibetan rulers, however, who consolidated power without the aid and at the direct expense of their neighbors. The Sakyas established their hegemony over Tibet in the thirteenth century through creating an alliance with the rapidly expanding Mongol Empire. At its height in the late thirteenth century, the Mongol Empire controlled everything from Eastern Europe to the Korean peninsula. Given the strength of its empire, Mongol dominance over Tibet was inevitable by the mid-thirteenth century. Rather than ransacking all of Tibet and exerting direct rule over the region, the Mongol rulers became interested in Tibetan Buddhism and sought out Tibet's most prominent monastic leader, who at the time was a descendant of Könchok Gyelpo in the Khön family named Sakya Paṇḍita Künga Gyeltsen (1182–1251). Sakya Paṇḍita established close ties with the Mongols after a favorable meeting with Godan Khan. His nephew Pakpa cemented these ties when he became the priest of Khubilai Khan (1215–1294), who appointed Pakpa as the religious and political leader of Tibet in 1264. This exchange between foreign emperor and Tibetan ecclesiastic hierarch is an early example of what came to be known as a patron–priest relationship, in which a Tibetan priest conferred spiritual blessings on a foreign emperor in exchange for patronage and temporal power over Tibet backed by that emperor's military. The Sakya-Mongol rule of Tibet continued until 1350 shortly before the fall of the Mongol-controlled Yuan Dynasty in 1368. Although the Khön family did not regain temporal control of Tibet, their Sakya religious lineage has continued to thrive to the present day.

The "Oral Transmission" School: Kagyü

The Sakya founder Könchok Gyelpo's teacher Drokmi taught a group of notable disciples, among them Marpa Chökyi Lodrö (1012–1096), who would become the founder of another major school of Tibetan Buddhism. Marpa was a layman from a prominent family in Lhodrak, in southern Central Tibet. Story has it that Marpa was appalled by the high tuition, to be paid in gold, that Drokmi charged to learn the art of Sanskrit-Tibetan translation. Instead of continuing his studies under Drokmi, Marpa journeyed to India several times, where he studied not at a great monastic university, but with noncelibate Indian Tantric adepts residing in cremation grounds and forest retreat centers. Most renowned among Marpa's Indian gurus were Nāropa, with whom Atīśa had also studied, and Maitripa. When Marpa returned to Tibet, he married and began teaching disciples from his home in Lhodrak.

Marpa's most famous disciple was Milarepa (1040–1123). Milarepa had emerged from a troubled family as a great sorcerer, who used black magic to avenge his uncle's cruel treatment of his family after his father's death, causing widespread destruction in his home village. Eventually overcome with guilt for the murder and destruction he had committed, Milarepa turned to Marpa for guidance in how to practice the authentic Dharma. Given the extent of Milarepa's negative karma, his purification was a long and arduous process. Marpa demanded that Milarepa build tower after tower, only to have him tear them down again until his entire back was covered with festering sores. In the end, after Milarepa had endured all of Marpa's privations without ever once losing his faith and devotion toward him, Marpa introduced Milarepa to higher Tantric practices. After twelve years of long retreats, Milarepa attained full Awakening. After his enlightenment, Milarepa spent most of his life as a solitary hermit, living in caves and practicing meditation. Thus, he provided a Tibetan Buddhist model for the renunciate life of strict asceticism and for the miraculous transformative power of the Dharma.

The fifteenth-century biography of Milarepa composed by Tsangnyön Heruka is the most popular saint's biography in Tibet. In addition, folksongs about Buddhist practice attributed to Milarepa are beloved throughout Tibet. The following are verses from two songs attributed to Milarepa:

Homage to the feet of Marpa of Lhodrak
May this hermit be successful in holding fast to solitude.
The principle that sustains life sprouts from the earth;
Ambrosia showers from the blue dome of heaven.
These join together to confer blessings on all living beings;
And in religious life, this happens in the best way.

The transient body is nourished by one's parents;
The sacred Dharma is given by one's holy guru.
These join together to confer the religious life;
And in perseverance lies true success.

The rocky cave provides solitude;
Devotion is zealous and sincere.
These join together and bring success;
Of spiritual wisdom does this consist.

Patience fortifies Milarepa's meditation;
Faith comes from all living beings.
These join together in skillful means;
Of which compassion is the essence.

The hermit meditates in rocky caves;
the layperson provides sustenance.
These join together in gaining Buddhahood;
These merits are offered for the Awakening of all living beings. . . .

Within the temple of the hill of Awakening, my body,
Within my breast where an altar lies,
Within the highest chamber of my heart,
There is the horse of my mind.

What lasso can catch this horse?
What post can it be tied to when it is caught?
What food is it to be given when it is hungry?
What drink is it to be given when it is thirsty?
What enclosure can it be kept when it is cold?
To catch the horse, use the lasso of equanimity.
When caught, it must be tied to the post of meditation.
When hungry, it must be fed the guru's teachings.
When thirsty, it must be given the purity of consciousness.
When cold, it must be kept in the enclosure of emptiness.
(*Jetsün Kabum*, II, 10)

By the end of his life, Milarepa had gained a following of disciples, among whom was Gampopa Sonam Rinchen (1079–1153), who formally founded the Kagyü School based on Kadam's monastic education system along with the particular Tantric practices central to the teachings of Nāropa, Marpa, and Milarepa such as the Highest Yoga Tantra called *Cakrasaṃvara*. An outgrowth of the Kagyü School's monastic institutions was a development unique to Tibetan Buddhism: the incarnation or *trülku* system of determining ecclesiastic succession, which other Tibetan Buddhist schools soon emulated. Reincarnation is a belief common to Buddhism in general, but beginning in the eleventh century the *trülku* system incorporated that belief into a system in which a deceased hierarch's closest protégés could use a combination of divinatory and other methods to locate the rebirth of their deceased master in the form of a young child, who would then inherit the former master's property and religious status. The most internationally famous example of a reincarnation lineage following this *trülku* system is the series of Dalai Lamas, but prior to them and continuing to the present day many Kagyü masters also reincarnate according to this system.

Another distinctive feature of Kagyü practice is the six yogas of Nāropa. Yoga shares a root with the English word "yoke" and means "union." In the context of Buddhist Tantra, yoga is a technique that brings about the union of the practitioner (or *yogi/yoginī*) with the realization of ultimate reality. The Kagyü School attributes six types of yoga to Nāropa. The first is inner heat (*tumo*) practice that generates heat in the body along with spiritual realization by manipulating the energy circulating throughout the channels of the subtle body. The second is illusory body (*gyulü*) practice whereby one cultivates visualizations that lead to realizing the illusory nature of all experience. Third, dream (*milam*) practice aims at cultivating a consistent awareness that one is dreaming, thereby enabling one to realize that waking and dreaming states are equally illusory and allowing one to manipulate the content of one's dreams. The fourth is clear light (*ösel*) yoga aimed at realizing the luminous and radiant emptiness of mind. Fifth, intermediate state (*bardo*) practice prepares one for the moment of death in which subtler aspects of mind manifest and well-prepared meditators can attain liberation in the intermediate state between the end of this life and the beginning of the next one. Finally, the sixth yoga is the transference of consciousness (*powa*), consisting of practices that prepare one to be able to eject one's consciousness from the fontanel of the head at the time of death, thereby ensuring a positive rebirth.

The pinnacle of Kagyü contemplative practice is the Great Seal (Skt. *mahāmudrā*, Tib. *chakchen)*. Analogous to the pinnacle of the Nyingma School, Great Perfection (*dzokchen*), the Great Seal focuses not on cultivating complex visualizations or performing elaborate rituals, but rather on the abstract realization of the nature of mind that is a unity of luminosity and emptiness. Like other advanced practices, to be successful in Great Seal meditation one needs an enlightened guru and a deep and strong compassion for all who are suffering in *saṃsāra*. Great Seal practice includes three parts: basis, path, and result. The basis involves calming and stabilizing the mind through mediation, thereby overcoming negative mental and emotional habitual tendencies that, in turn, condition unwholesome thoughts, words, and actions. The path involves meditating on the nature of mind, and the result is the actualization of realizing the nature of mind. Through Great Seal meditation practice, one realizes that all things are of "one taste" in that they are all empty of own-being. This insight, when applied to one's mind, brings further freedom because one sees that all mental states are not parts of one's real nature. When hatred arises, for example, one understands it for what it really is, empty of substantiality and not an essential aspect of luminous mind. Thus, it loses power over oneself and produces no afflictions. In this freedom, the positive and wholesome states of consciousness are more easily cultivated. Because *mahāmudrā* is the luminous mind with its innate wisdom and its compassion for all sentient beings, it is also the Truth Body (*Dharmakāya*) of the Buddha. Thus, it is the essential basis for realizing the bliss and virtues of Buddhahood.

The Kagyü School began as a contemplative tradition, the highest ideal of which was to renounce the world and live as a mountain hermit like Milarepa, but over time it also became an institutional and administrative power in Tibet. The first Karmapa, the principle reincarnated *trülku* of the Kagyü, established the school's main monastery, Tsurpu, west of Lhasa in

Central Tibet in the twelfth century (see Map 4). But it was not until the fall of the Sakya-Mongol hegemony in the mid-fourteenth century that the Kagyü School became aligned with the main rulers of Tibet. One of the estates that had formerly been part of the Sakya, the Pakmodrupa, ceded from its Sakya overlord and succeeded in gaining power over Tibet in 1350, thus ending Sakya political dominance. Because the Pakmodrupa regime patronized the Kagyü, their influence proliferated. Kagyü masters traveled to the new imperial center of the Han Chinese Ming Dynasty (1368–1644), which patronized them and officially recognized the Pakmodrupa regime as Tibet's official rulers, although unlike the Mongol-controlled Yuan Dynasty, the Ming were never able to incorporate Tibet into their empire.

The "Virtuous Ones" School: Geluk

The last of the new schools of Tibetan Buddhism to take root in the aftermath of the second dissemination of Buddhism in Tibet was the Geluk School. Like Atīśa, who had not set out to establish his own school but rather to reinforce Buddhism in Tibet, the founder of the Geluk School, Jé Tsongkhapa Lozang Drakpa (1357–1419), was a reformer whose disciples later formulated a distinctive and powerful school of Buddhism in his honor. Tsongkhapa (see Figure 6.4) was greatly inspired by the Kadam School that Atīśa's disciple founded, and in particular they shared a commitment to maintaining strict adherence to the *Vinaya* code of monastic discipline and Buddhist scholastics, including logic and debate. Tsongkhapa's genius as a scholar and a religious leader catalyzed major changes in the Tibetan Buddhist landscape of the fourteenth and fifteenth centuries. In 1409 he established Ganden Monastery on a mountaintop near Lhasa, which later became the seat of the Geluk School, as well as the Great Prayer festival performed annually after the Tibetan New Year in Lhasa. He accomplished both of these with the generous sponsorship of the Pakmodrupa ruler of Tibet, thus demonstrating that during Tsongkhapa's lifetime he was not perceived to be a threat to the Kagyü but rather an inspirational reformer within the established religious landscape. In the following decade, his disciples founded two other major monasteries in the vicinity of Lhasa: Drepung in 1416, and Sera in 1419. At its height Drepung would grow to become the largest monastic community in the world with a resident population of 10,000 monks (see Map 4 for locations of Garden and Drepung; Sera is located with in Lhasa).

Tsongkhapa not only founded institutions that would form the mainstays of the Geluk School, but his treatises also became the central foundation of Geluk practice, in particular *The Great Exposition of the Stages of the Path* and *The Great Exposition of Secret Mantra*. In these works, Tsongkhapa set out a gradual set of "stages of the path" or *"lamrim"* through which one traverses the path to Buddhahood. As each stage builds on the insights gleaned from the previous stages, one must move sequentially through each step of the process beginning with *Sūtra* and culminating in Highest Yoga Tantra practices. In framing the stages of the path, Tsongkhapa was influenced by

FIGURE 6.4. Tibetan *tangkha* on cloth of Tsongkhapa, 1357–1419, emanating from the heart of Maitreya, Buddha of the future residing in the *Tusita* Heaven. Date unknown, but was presented by the Thirteenth Dalai Lama to W.W. Rockhill, U.S. Minister to China, on June 21, 1908. Library of Congress, Asian Collection.

Atīśa's *A Lamp for the Path to Awakening* that outlined five paths and ten bodhisattva levels.

He summarized the main stages of the path in his short root text entitled *The Three Principal Facets of the Path.* In that shorter piece, from which we quote some verses below, Tsongkhapa introduces the three stages. First, one develops "renunciation" based on an aspiration to gain liberation from *saṃsāra.* One does so by recognizing that in the impermanence of *saṃsāra* it is rare to be born as a human. It is even rarer to be born as a human who has access to the Dharma, as well as to written texts and teachers who can aid one in the attainment of Awakening. One should therefore resolve to take advantage of this fortunate situation. One should also contemplate the suffering (*duḥkha*) associated with *saṃsāra* to gain an aversion to being reborn in *saṃsāra* and a deeper aspiration to gain liberation.

Second, one realizes that one's renunciation at the first stage of the path is still self-centered. One is seeking liberation to free oneself from *duḥkha.* So one needs to develop *bodhicitta,* the altruistic aspiration to gain Awakening for the good of others. In fact, Tsongkhapa points out, one cannot gain liberation if one's desire for it is selfish because liberation is freedom from such self-centeredness. One can develop *bodhicitta* by contemplating two facts: the first is that all beings are undergoing suffering in *saṃsāra* even though they want happiness and freedom from suffering. The second fact is that given that all beings have been reborn numberless times, in the past each of these beings has been one's own mother. With these two facts in mind, one should consider how all living beings who are now suffering had, in the past, treated one with the utmost loving kindness. This insight will generate the compassionate desire to make all beings happy and free them from suffering. This compassion will, in turn, nourish the development of *bodhicitta.*

Third, even with renunciation and *bodhicitta,* one cannot gain Awakening without the "right view": penetrating insight into emptiness. Wisdom must be added to renunciation and compassion because one's mind contains afflictive states and defilements that hide its innate essence, which Gelukpas call "clear light." It is the "mind of clear light" that is the essential and ultimately nirvanic status of consciousness. Wisdom realizing emptiness destroys the afflictive and defiling states of mind, and gradually one realizes that the innate mind of clear light is "of one taste" with emptiness. It is this realization that results in Buddhahood.

The following verses about these three stages are taken from Tsongkhapa's *Three Principle Facets of the Path:*

> Listen with clear minds, you fortunate people,
> Who aspire to the path that is pleasing to the Buddhas.
> Strive to use well your freedom and opportunity,
> Not attached the pleasures of *saṃsāra.*
>
> All those with bodies are bound by the craving for existence.
> Attraction to the pleasures of *saṃsāra*

Is only stilled by pure renunciation.
So, first of all seek renunciation.

Freedom and opportunity are difficult to get, so there is no time to waste.
Reflect on this fact, and you will overcome your attraction to this life.
Reflect repeatedly on the sufferings of this world,
and you will overcome attraction to future lives.

Renunciation without *bodhicitta*
Does not produce the supreme bliss
Of unsurpassed Awakening.
Therefore, bodhisattvas generate the excellence of *bodhicitta*.

Born over and over in boundless *saṃsāra*,
Ceaselessly tormented by the three forms of *duḥkha*,
All beings, having been your mothers, are in this condition.
Think of them and generate *bodhicitta*.

Though you cultivate renunciation and *bodhicitta*,
Without wisdom realizing emptiness,
You cannot cut the root of *saṃsāra*.
Therefore, strive to realize dependent arising.

One who sees the unfailing causality
Of all phenomena, *saṃsāra* and Nirvana,
And destroys all perception [of own-being],
Has entered the path that is pleasing to the Buddhas.

(*Lamtso namsum*, 2–4, 6, 8–10)

Mastering the stages of the path as outlined in Tsongkhapa's system requires intense years of scholastic study—finishing the Geluk School's highest degree called the Geshé degree takes between fifteen to twenty-five years. The Geluk's strong emphasis on scholastic training is not in lieu of meditation practice, but rather in preparation for it. After receiving thorough training in topics relating to the Mahāyāna Sūtras, Gelukpas engage in Tantric practices, mainly connected to the *Cakrasaṃvara* and the *Kālacakra Tantras*. In addition to their own specialized Tantric systems, Geluks incorporate systems of training from the other schools of Tibetan Buddhism, including the six yogas of Nāropa and the pinnacle contemplative teachings of the Nyingma and Kagyü Schools, the Great Perfection and the Great Seal, respectively.

THE DALAI LAMA

Tsongkhapa and his followers are acclaimed in the Tibetan cultural sphere for their extensive scholastic and contemplative achievements, but they also came to control large parts of Tibet. The Geluks' rise to power is closely

Box 6.1

Trapped in a Suffocating Scream

Recently, I recalled a bothersome incident with my mother.

I had come home during my first year at college and was enthusiastically explaining to her about the fascinating courses I was taking in psychology/anthropology and English and American literature. She bitterly resented the fact that she had not attended college and also had an antipathy to intellectual enthusiasm even though she was intellectually active herself.

Much like my grade-school experiences when I would come home and tell her what was happening and she would start criticizing me bitterly to the point that I shut up, she launched into her invective. We ended up with her in the kitchen on one side of the house and me on the other in the living room in a bright, light-blue rocking chair that she had painted and stenciled. We were literally screaming at each other. I so deeply wanted to get back on the bus and return to college and my studies, but I didn't, remaining in a suffocating scream.

I have often thought, "What would have happened in my life, had I just walked out and gotten on the bus down the road?" And I thought it again the other day when this scene reappeared in my mind.

Then, suddenly it occurred to me that following my Tibetan Buddhist practice, I should reflect within the body of the person screaming from the living room, "Just as I want happiness and don't want suffering, so Mother (that's what we called her) wants happiness and doesn't want suffering." Wow! What a revolution! No need to leave; within that same body, I calmed down within a poignant sense of how she caused so much misery for herself—she'd get so angry on the telephone with her best woman-friend that she would literally hold the phone from her face and scream into it!

I cannot put into words the sense of commiseration. Also, I had found a road out of that scream from the living room without taking the bus back to college. What a relief!

JEFFREY HOPKINS
Professor of Religious Studies
University of Virginia

connected to two major political and religious developments that occurred in the centuries following Tsongkhapa's illustrious career: sectarian conflict between the Kagyü and Geluk Schools inflamed by rival factions of Tibetan rulers, and the rise of the Dalai Lamas aided by Mongolian military and patronage. Just like the Pakmodrupa had originally been an estate that was part of Sakya-controlled Tibet, in the fifteenth century one of the estates within the Pakmodrupa regime called Rinpung began to rival them for control over Tibet. This both caused and escalated tensions between the religious schools the rivals came to patronize, which were the Geluk and Kagyü Schools, respectively. Later the dominant Rinpung were themselves overthrown by another rival, the kings of Tsang, whose antipathy toward the Geluk and support for the Kagyü further fueled sectarian conflict.

Most people who know only a small amount about Tibet have heard of the Dalai Lama and his status as the exiled leader of the Tibetan people. Although the roots of the rise of the Dalai Lamas as leaders of Tibet began with Tsongkhapa's disciples, they only came to dominate Tibetan politics and religion in the seventeenth century. One of Tsongkhapa's foremost disciples was Gendün Drupa (1391–1474), who in 1447 founded what grew to be another major Geluk monastery in Tibet, Tashi Lhünpo (see Map 4). Tashi Lhünpo's *trülku* was Gendün Gyatso (1476–1542), who gained prominence as a great scholar at Drepung Monastery. Only with his *trülku* Sonam Gyatso (1543–1588) did the Dalai Lama incarnation line begin in earnest. Just as Mongol interest in patronizing Sakya hierarchs led to their supremacy as rulers of Tibet during the Yuan Dynasty, another rising Mongolian ruler took interest in the young Sonam Gyatso. When he traveled to Mongolia to visit Altan Khan in 1578, the Khan and the Lama established a powerful reciprocal relationship through exchanging religious and political titles. Sonam Gyatso recognized Altan Khan as an imperial ruler, and in return Altan Khan recognized Sonam Gyatso as his spiritual teacher, in process translating the Tibetan word *Gyatso* of his name, which means "ocean," into Mongolian as "Dalai." Sonam Gyatso became the third Dalai Lama, the first two being his predecessors, even though they were not called by this title during their lifetimes.

The fourth Dalai Lama lived a short life, to be followed by "the great fifth" Ngawang Lozang Gyatso (1617–1682), who was a polymath scholar and shrewd statesman who unified greater Tibet under his rule for the first time since the Sakya-Mongol alliance. The fifth Dalai Lama did not gain the upper hand in Tibet's internal power struggle between rival Kagyü and Geluk supporting Tibetan factions alone, but rather through recourse to his Mongol backers, in particular Gushri Khan (1582–1655). With his help, the fifth Dalai Lama overthrew the Kagyü-affiliated Tsang kings in 1642. The government crafted by the fifth Dalai Lama survived until the twentieth-century incorporation of Tibet into the People's Republic of China (PRC), although actual control over Tibet vacillated over the ensuing 300 years among the Dalai Lama, his Mongol supporters, Tibetan prime ministers, and regents. The fifth Dalai Lama's government combined religion and politics into its administration, with both religious and secular branches of government sharing power. The capital building of the Tibetan government built by the fifth Dalai Lama, the Potala Palace shown in Figure 6.5, survives to this day in the center of Lhasa.

When the Ming Dynasty fell in 1644, the fifth Dalai Lama reached out to the new Manchu Emperor and established congenial relations with the Qing Dynasty (1644–1911), all the while balancing power with his Mongolian allies, who provided the military backing for his dominance. Relations among Mongols, Tibetans, and Manchus did not remain so favorable in the following centuries of Gelukpa rule of Tibet. Mongol kings who affiliated with the Dalai Lamas maintained their hegemony over Tibet to varying degrees, and alliances with rival Mongolian factions led to repeated bloodshed in Central

FIGURE 6.5. The Potala, residence of the Dalai Lama; founded seventeenth century C.E., Lhasa, Tibet.

Tibet. Meanwhile, Tibet became increasingly incorporated into the Qing Dynasty as its colony, and by the eighteenth century the Dalai Lama shared rule with two representatives of the Qing court stationed in Lhasa called Ambans. The Qing never set out to replace the Dalai Lama as head of the Tibetan state, but to incorporate Tibet into its empire following the centuries-old patron–priest pattern, which they did at times with a strong arm and other times in name only. This would all change forever with the fall of Qing Dynasty in 1911, signaling the end of Imperial China.

TIBET IN THE PAST CENTURY

Tibet's entry into the twentieth century brought massive changes and turmoil to the roof of the world. Although Tibet had attempted to preserve its territorial integrity during the nineteenth century through forbidding entry to most foreigners, it nevertheless became the site of imperial ambitions from all sides. Tibet's attractions included its strategic location at the center of the Asian continent and its position as the source of Asia's major rivers, rich with natural resources. At the turn of the twentieth century, Tibet was sandwiched between British India and Czarist Russia, who were locked in a competition for control of Central Asia called the "Great Game." Although Tibet was nominally under the "suzerainty" of the Manchu Qing Dynasty, actual Qing control of Tibet had weakened while the empire was focused on other pressing affairs closer to its imperial center, such as the Sino-Japanese War of 1894–1895 and the Boxer Rebellion of 1898–1901. In 1904 the British Colonel Francis

Younghusband (1863–1942) seized the moment to invade Tibet and force a trade treaty between Britain and Tibet, partly out of fear that the Tibetan government was forming alliances with Russia. The Younghusband expedition slaughtered the Tibetan army it encountered through vastly superior firepower and secured a trade agreement that strongly favored British interests, only to withdraw shortly afterward on command from the British Parliament. After this debacle, the Qing exerted one last attempt to dominate Tibetan affairs by sending General Zhao Erfeng to invade Tibet in 1910. However, the following year the Qing Empire collapsed, leaving Tibet with a new chance to assert its sovereignty.

Through these challenging years, Tibet was controlled by the thirteenth Dalai Lama, Tupten Gyatso (1876–1933), who became head of state in 1895. The thirteenth Dalai Lama was an able statesman who understood the dangers Tibet faced as a result of its former isolationist foreign policy. After Tibet's defeat during the Younghusband invasion, he instigated widespread modernization efforts, including bolstering the Tibetan army, developing agricultural technology, and creating a post office and bank. After the fall of the Qing, the thirteenth Dalai Lama declared Tibet an independent country. Tibet enjoyed a period of what is often called "de facto independence" from 1912 until 1950. During this time the Tibetan government expelled all Chinese military from its territory and managed its own affairs as a sovereign nation, including minting its own currency and distributing its own passports that Tibetans used to travel internationally (e.g., the Tibetan passport of former Tibetan government finance minister Tsepon Shakabpa, 1907–1989, is extant). The thirteenth Dalai Lama improved communication between Tibet and the outside world by installing a telegraph system, and sending a selection of aristocratic boys to be educated in England as well as opening an English language school in the Central Tibetan town of Gyantsé. However, not all Tibetan government officials agreed with the modernization efforts of the "great thirteenth." Conservative factions in the Tibetan government spearheaded by monastic elites resisted the move toward creating closer ties between Tibet and the rest of the world and resisted bolstering the standing Tibetan army for fear that these shifts would compromise their power and inspire anti-Buddhist foreign and secular influences. As the thirteenth Dalai Lama sought to balance military and monastic authority in Tibet, he sensed the challenges in store for his country. In 1932 the thirteenth Dalai Lama wrote a final political testament shortly before his death the following year. In it, he reflected on the destruction of Buddhism by Soviet communists and warned of the dangers that could soon draw near if Tibet did not amass a strong military and maintain friendly relations with India and China:

> It may happen that here in the centre of Tibet the Religion and the secular administration may be attacked both from the outside and from the inside. Unless we can guard our own country, it will now happen that the Dalai and Panchen Lamas, the Father and Son, the Holders of the Faith, the glorious Rebirths, will be broken down and left without a name. As regards the monasteries and the

> monks and nuns, their lands and other properties will be destroyed. The administrative customs of the Three Religious Kings will be weakened. The officers of the State, ecclesiastical and secular, will find their lands seized and their other property confiscated, and they themselves made to serve their enemies, or wander about the country as beggars do. All beings will be sunk in great hardship and in overpowering fear; the days and the nights will drag on slowly in suffering.[1]

His words were later taken to be prophetic in light of the cultural destruction Tibet soon encountered.

By the time that the fourteenth Dalai Lama Tenzin Gyatso (1935–) had reached his teen years in the late 1940s, the question of whether and how to modernize had transformed from a debate into an urgent necessity. In 1949 when Mao Zedong defeated his Republican China foes and established the PRC, one of the new regime's first initiatives was to reoccupy lands formerly held by the Qing, including Tibet. Their mission was to "peacefully liberate" Tibet from an "imperialist" government that shackled its people in feudal serfdom. While the People's Liberation Army (PLA) began taking control of large parts of Tibet's eastern regions, the Tibetan government pronounced the fourteenth Dalai Lama head of state in 1950, when he was only fifteen years old. The Tibetan government appealed to the United Nations, but its members refused Tibet aid. In 1951 the PRC compelled Tibetan representatives to sign the "Seventeen Point Agreement," which formally subsumed Tibet under Chinese rule. The seventeen points of "agreement" were not all deleterious to Tibetan interests, however. For example, Point 7 included religious freedom:

> Point 7: The policy of freedom of religious belief laid down in the Common Programme of the Chinese People's Political Consultative Conference shall be carried out. The religious beliefs, customs, and habits of the Tibetan people shall be respected, and lama monasteries shall be protected . . .[2]

Over the decade of the 1950s, Mao Zedong's preference for a gradualist approach of winning over the Tibetan elite eroded in favor of plunging Tibet into rapid socialist reform. Whatever conciliatory gestures the Seventeen Point Agreement promised toward Tibetan religion and cultural traditions proved elusive. With eastern regions of Tibet under direct attack from communist forces and rumors circulating that the young Dalai Lama would soon be their next target, on March 10, 1959, a spontaneous large-scale Tibetan uprising against Chinese rule erupted in Lhasa. Finally convinced that conditions in Lhasa were unsafe for his continuing survival, the twenty-three-year-old fourteenth Dalai Lama escaped from his summer palace into the Tibetan crowd dressed as an ordinary layman with a small group of companions. He has never been able to return to Tibet.

In the aftermath of the Dalai Lama's escape into exile in India, Mao Zedong's PLA troops severely attacked Buddhist institutions, prohibited

Tibetans from practicing religion at home and in public, and stripped Tibetans' sense of cultural identity by banning traditional customs, beliefs, dress, and social mores. The most severe deprivations occurred during Mao Zedong's disastrous Great Leap Forward (1958–1961) in which agricultural collectivization led to mass starvation in both China and Tibet, and during during the Cultural Revolution (1966–1976), which resulted in countless Tibetan deaths and the destruction of nearly all of the more than 6,000 monasteries in Tibet. After Mao died in 1976, Deng Xiaoping admitted that "mistakes were made" in Tibet. He initiated liberalization reforms that permitted monasteries to be rebuilt in Tibet and for Tibetans to express religious belief, among other important policy changes.

Since the 1980s, PRC policy on Tibetan religion has vacillated between tolerance and repression. Cycles of liberalization followed by Tibetan protests against Chinese rule (the largest being in 1987–1989 and in 2008) have resulted in harsh crackdowns. Today, religious freedom is officially protected by the constitution of the PRC but in fact Tibetan Buddhist institutions and practices are highly regulated by the government due to their frequent association with Tibetan nationalism. In particular, the PRC reserves its utmost contempt for the figure of the fourteenth Dalai Lama himself, who they portray as a "splittist" aiming to separate the Chinese Motherland. Since the 1990s, in many parts of Tibet photographs of the fourteenth Dalai Lama are prohibited in public and private. Routinely, Tibetan monastics are subject to "patriotic reeducation campaigns" during which monks and nuns are "reeducated" in socialist and patriotic values and in some cases forced to denounce their spiritual leader the Dalai Lama or face recriminations.

Despite the challenging conditions, since the 1980s Tibet has experienced a religious revival hard earned by Tibetans who have labored and saved to rebuild their local temples and monasteries. Ironically, this revival has also been financed in part by the PRC government and by wealthy Han Chinese donors from mainland China and Taiwan, where fascination with Tibetan forms of Buddhism is on the rise. Today PRC policy on religious freedom in Tibet is tending more toward repression than tolerance in the aftermath of the widespread Tibetan uprisings of 2008 that coincided with China's Olympic limelight. Most recently, Tibetans have initiated a new form of protest against PRC rule and religious repression: self-immolation. As of January 2013, ninety-eight Tibetans have set fire to themselves inside Tibet since 2009. Widespread self-immolation is virtually unprecedented in Tibetan history due to the Buddhist value placed on the sanctity of human life. It remains to be seen what impact this tragic form of protest will have on the Sino-Tibetan conflict, aside from the increasing levels of government repression it has already garnered.

NEW TIBETAN BUDDHIST MOVEMENTS

As we have seen in India and Southeast Asia, and will see in China, Korea, Taiwan, and Japan, in the twentieth century a number of socially engaged

Buddhist movements have developed. In the final chapter, we will see how these movements have globalized their presence around the world. Given the situation in Tibet, the prominent new Tibetan Buddhist movement is centered around the peace work of the Dalai Lama. Since 1959 when the Dalai Lama crossed the border to India accompanied by a handful of cabinet ministers, armed fighters, and Buddhist masters, he has watched events unfold in Tibet from his exile residence in the northwest Indian Himalayan foothills in Dharamsala, Himachal Pradesh, India (see Map 4). In 1959 the Dalai Lama repudiated the terms of the Seventeen-Point Agreement and founded the Central Tibetan Administration, also known as the Tibetan Government in Exile. Within the first year of his escape from 1959 and 1960, approximately 80,000 Tibetans crossed the Himalayas to follow the Dalai Lama and seek asylum in India and Nepal. Today there are more than 100,000 Tibetans living in exile, mostly in South Asia but also in Europe and North America. Annually between 1,000 and 2,000 Tibetan refugees or "new arrivals" pour into India and Nepal, many of whom walk over dangerous snow-engorged Himalayan passes to avoid detection by Chinese border patrol agents. Some of these refugees seek a new life or a Tibetan education in exile, whereas others come only to have one chance in their lifetimes to meet the fourteenth Dalai Lama, after which they make the arduous return to Tibet.

Over the past several decades, the Dalai Lama has heard reports that over one million Tibetans were killed during the Cultural Revolution; that more than 6,000 Tibetan monasteries were destroyed, their cultural, religious, and artistic treasures pillaged and sold; that Tibetan prisoners, including a large population of monks and nuns, were and continue to be systematically tortured in prison; that Tibetan forests were clear-cut and their wildlife depleted; and that massive populations of Chinese immigrants whom the PRC government incentivized to relocate to Tibet have now surpassed the ethnically Tibetan population of the region. In response to these traumas, the Dalai Lama has formulated policies promoting peace through nonviolent means based on his understanding of Buddhist ethics, in particular his "Five Point Peace Plan" and "Middle Way Approach."

In 1987, the Dalai Lama issued a statement about his Five Point Peace Plan before the U.S. Congressional Human Rights Caucus. Its five parts include:

1. Transformation of the whole of Tibet into a zone of peace.
2. Abandonment of China's population transfer policy, which threatens the very existence of the Tibetans as a people.
3. Respect for the Tibetan people's fundamental human rights and democratic freedoms.
4. Restoration and protection of Tibet's natural environment and the abandonment of China's use of Tibet for the production of nuclear weapons and dumping of nuclear waste.
5. Commencement of earnest negotiations on the future status of Tibet and relations between the Tibetan and Chinese peoples.[3]

FIGURE 6.6. His Holiness Tenzin Gyatso, The Fourteenth Dalai Lama, and Samdech Preah Maha Ghosananda, the Supreme Buddhist Patriarch of Cambodia, at Gethsemani Abbey in 1996, Trappist, Kentucky.

Box 6.2

A Day in the Life of the Dalai Lama

I must say that I am a very poor practitioner. Usually I get up at 3:30 in the morning. Then I immediately do some recitations and some chanting. Following this until breakfast, I do meditation, analytical meditation mainly. Then after each analytical meditation, I do single-pointed meditation. The object of my meditation is mainly dependent arising. Because of dependent arising, things are empty. This is according to the Mādhyamika philosophy of Nāgārjuna and the interpretation of Chandrakīrti, which is called Prāsaṅgika philosophy.

That philosophy is very profound, and, for me, it is really something marvelous. It gives me a kind of conviction about reality, about emptiness, and through that conviction I get the feeling that there is the possibility of eliminating all afflictive emotions. As Nāgārjuna says in his *Treatise on the Middle*, by extinguishing contaminated karma and afflictive emotions through wisdom there is liberation. Therefore, liberation is a state of having extinguished contaminated actions and afflictive emotions. So then, from what is contaminated karma or contaminated actions produced? Contaminated actions are produced from afflictive emotions. Then from what are afflictive emotions produced? They are produced from improper mental conceptuality, improper mental application. And then from what is that produced? It is produced from conceptual elaborations. Those conceptual elaborations are the elaborations of the mind conceiving objects to exist truly in their own right. These elaborations are ceased through meditating on emptiness.

So meditating on this gives me a kind of firm conviction of the possibility of cessation. This is one main object of practice. Another is compassion. These two are my objects of practice. If you ask me about experience in my practice, I think it is better than zero. On that basis, I can assure you that the mind is always changing, so no matter how strong the afflictive emotion, there is always the possibility of change. Transformation is always possible. So therefore, you see, there is always hope. I think that what is really worthwhile is to make an effort.

Then also, in the Tibetan Buddhist tradition, Buddhist Tantrayāna is also involved. So you see, a lot of time is also spent on visualization in deity yoga. This includes visualizing the process of death and rebirth. In fact in my daily prayer or practice, I visualize death eight times and rebirth eight times. This is not necessarily the Dalai Lama's reincarnation, but some reincarnation. These practices I feel are very powerful, and very helpful in familiarizing oneself about the process of death. So when death actually comes, one is prepared. Whether these practices of preparation are really going to benefit me at the time of death, I do not know at this moment. I suppose that even with all this preparation for death, I may still be a complete failure! That is also possible. There is another type of meditation which is like praying. Its purpose is to recollect the various levels and stages of the path by going through something that you have memorized and reflecting on each stage.

So from around 3:30 A.M. until 8:30 A.M., I am fully occupied with meditation and prayer, and things like that. During that time I take a few breaks, including my breakfast, which is usually at 5:00 A.M., and some prostrations. After 8:30 A.M., when my mood is good, I do some physical exercise. One very important thing is that I always listen to the BBC for the news. Then I do office work until noon. And if it is a holiday, I also start reading important texts. Prayer and meditation are usually done without any texts. Then at noon, I have my lunch. Afterward usually I go to the office and do some more work. At 6:00 P.M., I have my evening tea and dinner as a Buddhist monk. Finally, around 8:30 P.M., I go to sleep, my most favorite, peaceful meditation!

HIS HOLINESS TENZIN GYATSO
The Fourteenth Dalai Lama

The following year in 1988, the Dalai Lama publicized his "Middle Way Approach" to solving the Sino-Tibetan conflict before the European Parliament in Strasbourg. The name of this approach is an explicitly Buddhist reference to the Buddha's first sermon in which he described his teaching as the middle way between the extremes of asceticism and self-indulgence (*Saṃyutta Nikāya* 56:11). In the contemporary political context, the Dalai Lama applies this insight to finding a middle ground between Tibet's interest in regaining independence and China's interest in maintaining its sovereignty over Tibet. The Dalai Lama explicitly claims Tibet's independence prior to the Chinese occupation: "And there can be no doubt that when Peking's communist armies entered Tibet (1949–1950), Tibet was in all respects an independent state."[4] However, his Middle Way Approach seeks "genuine national regional autonomy" instead of Tibetan independence from China. This would mean that Tibetans would exert control over the internal affairs of Tibet relating to issues such as religion, culture, education, economy, health, and environment via a democratically elected government, and the PRC would control Tibet's international relations and defense. According to the Dalai Lama, this policy offers "mutual benefit to China as well as Tibet," in the form of safeguarding Tibetan interests in the protection of their culture and Chinese interests in maintaining their territorial integrity.[5]

The international community has responded extremely positively to the Dalai Lama's efforts at finding peaceful compromise with the PRC. In 1989, he was awarded the Nobel Peace Prize, and in 2007, he was awarded the U.S. Congressional Gold Medal. These recognitions in addition to his active international teaching and speaking schedule have earned the Dalai Lama widespread global acclaim, making him a household name for many who otherwise would not know about the plight of the Tibetan people. However, the Dalai Lama's international popularity has not yet translated into real solutions for the Tibetan people, as the recent spate of self-immolations in Tibet underscores. Although representatives of the Dalai Lama and the PRC have engaged in sporadic negotiations over the past several decades, little progress has been achieved, and the PRC continues to accuse the Dalai Lama and his followers of being dishonest, privately pressing for independence while publicly calling only for autonomy. Not only are many Chinese officials suspicious of the Dalai Lama's Middle Way Approach, but a number of Tibetans inside Tibet and in exile have grown frustrated by the persistent human rights violations in Tibet. They question the wisdom of not seeking full independence from China, which from their perspective is a historical fact.

For all its challenges, the Dalai Lama's response to the plight of his people has become a paragon for peace building across the world. His approach is deeply infused by the Buddhist ideals of compassion and the interdependence of all beings. The following are the words of the Dalai Lama regarding traditional Buddhist experience and modern peace building:

> When we rise in the morning and listen to the radio or read the newspaper, we are confronted with the same sad news: violence, crime, wars, and disasters. I cannot recall a single day without a report of something terrible happening somewhere.... According to Buddhist psychology, most of our troubles are due to our passionate desire for and attachment to things that we misapprehend as enduring entities. The pursuit of the objects of our desire and attachment involves the use of aggression and competitiveness as supposedly efficacious instruments. These mental processes easily translate into actions, breeding belligerence as an obvious effect. Such processes have been going on in the human mind since time immemorial, but their execution has become more effective under modern conditions. What can we do to control and regulate these "poisons"–delusion, greed, and aggression? For it is these poisons that are behind almost every trouble in the world.... [C]ompassion is what we must strive to cultivate

> in ourselves, and we must develop it from a limited amount to the limitless [compassion for all sentient beings]. . . . Further, the Tibetan Buddhist tradition teaches us to view all sentient beings as our dear mothers and to show our gratitude by loving them all. For, according to Buddhist theory, we are born and reborn countless times, and it is conceivable that each being has been our parent at one time or another. In this way all beings in the universe share a family relationship. . . . When you train in this sort of outlook, a true sense of compassion—a true sense of love and respect for others—becomes possible. . . . Another result of spiritual development, most useful in day-to-day life, is that it gives a calmness and presence of mind. . . . When faced with a calm and clear mind, problems can be successfully resolved. . . . Thus the practice of compassion and wisdom is useful to all, especially to those responsible for running national affairs, in whose hands lie the power and opportunity to create the structure of world peace.[6]

Instead of flaming anger toward the Chinese, the Dalai Lama and his supporters strive to cultivate compassion for those who are bringing karmic harm to themselves by oppressing the Tibetans. It is easy to feel compassion for those we love, but one's enemies provide an even greater opportunity to expand loving kindness to all beings. Integral to this enterprise of cultivating compassion for others is the realization that they are fundamentally not separate from us, or in Buddhist terminology that we are all empty of independent selfhood. One might distinguish different peoples and their cultures, but we are all equal in that we are diverse parts of the wholeness of life. All people are equally entitled to be free from suffering and to enjoy happiness, whether Chinese, Tibetan, or other. With this insight, the Dalai Lama teaches that one can find the basis for mutual recognition of human rights and mutual cooperation for the good of all persons. A corollary to this view is that any violence against others is to be rejected. Anger-motivated violence may remove the offending party, but it does not produce the ethical mutuality that is needed for reconciliation and peace. Violent action might be a short-term answer to a problem, but violence cannot sow the seeds of peace, just the seeds of resentment and more violence. What can bring a more lasting peace is the right understanding of the problem along with a wise and compassionate program of responsible and just change for all involved. Although this program of the Dalai Lama might take longer to realize, he believes that it will provide a more enduring peace for everyone.

The Cultural Experience of Tibetan Buddhism Today

Geshe Damdul Namgyal
Central Institute of Higher Tibetan Studies, Varanasi, India

The teachings of the Buddha, as summarized in the words of the Tibetan masters, can be stated in the following four lines: If one is attached to this life, one is not a spiritual person (thus unable to avoid unfortunate rebirths in the future). If one is attached to cyclic existence, one lacks the mind of renunciation (thus unable to free oneself from bondage to birth and death). If one is attached to selfish interests, one is not a bodhisattva (thus unable to become a Buddha capable of serving all suffering beings). If one clings to phenomena, one lacks the correct view (thus unable to uproot the obscurations to liberation and omniscience). From this, it is quite clear that the Tibetan Buddhist vision of a genuinely spiritual person ultimately entails transcending the present life. However, this does not mean that the practices in which one engages have no positive effect in daily life and culture. Indeed, Tibetan Buddhism contributes positively to both the everyday life and the culture of its practitioners.

To understand how this is so, we note that popular Tibetan Buddhist practice today can be divided broadly into two categorizes: (1) purification and (2) accumulation. Under purification are all the practices that are directly aimed at the pacification and elimination of miseries and shortcomings, as well as their causes in nonvirtuous actions and in obscurations, whereas under accumulation are all the practices that generate a fresh level of spiritual realization and virtuous attitudes. It is imperative that all Tibetan Buddhist practitioners take up both purification and accumulation practices so that they can hope to achieve the ultimate spiritual goal.

For instance, a practitioner whose main focus is on avoiding unfortunate rebirths in the future must not only expiate the already committed nonvirtuous actions and shun committing them anew so that he or she can bypass rebirths into the three lower realms of existence—that of animals, hungry ghosts, and hell beings. He or she must also cultivate complementary virtuous actions so as to gain rebirth into the three higher realms of existence—that of the gods, demigods, and humans. Similarly, a practitioner whose main concern is to achieve liberation from the bondage of conditioned birth and death must not only work on severing afflictive emotions. He or she should also cultivate wisdom that understands the selflessness of phenomena and develop the complementary positive emotions of the Four Divine Abodes. And a practitioner seeking the state of Buddhahood so that he or she could fully benefit all suffering beings must not only persevere in realizing the selflessness of phenomena. He or she must also develop the complementary attitudes of *bodhicitta*, Universal Love and Great Compassion.

Although many or almost all Tibetan Buddhist laypeople wish to be freed from the shackles of cyclic birth and death once and for all, and even wish to attain full enlightenment for the sake of all sentient beings, they often primarily focus on the more immediate situations in their daily lives with hope for a better rebirth. Their daily situations demand that they discern positive actions and attitudes from negative ones and accumulate the former and purify the latter. Toward this end, they may take up a wide range of practices and customs in their daily routine.

DAILY RITUALS

Almost every Tibetan home has an altar in a separate shrine room or a shrine corner where they have representations of the Buddha's body, speech, and mind. These are symbolized, respectively, by a statue or painting of the Buddha, a scripture or a set of scriptures, and a *stūpa* or a reliquary of blessed objects. These representations also symbolize the Three Jewels—the Buddha, the Dharma, and the Saṅgha. Upon waking up, the first thing the person does is care for his or her altar and the shrine room. He or she would clean the room, dust off the altar items, arrange an array of at least seven water bowls in a particular sequence, and gracefully fill them to the brim with pure, fresh water. Next, he or she may arrange offerings of flowers, incense, lamps, fragrant items, food, musical instruments, and the like, either separately or aligned with the water bowls in a particular arrangement. Those who are trained may perform these actions with the recitation of prayers that facilitate cultivating the proper perspectives and attitudes toward the offerings. For example, one would look at the water as representing fortunate human rebirth, the flowers as moral values, the incense as spiritual perseverance, the lamp as wisdom dispelling ignorance, and so on. After the offerings are all arranged, one would recite a *mantra* to bless the offerings and make them manifold. In the evening, a little before the sunset, the water bowls are emptied into a jar, wiped clean, and stacked aesthetically along the front side of the altar to be again filled the next morning. Likewise, the perishables are taken down before they become stale. All these actions are performed with a sense of admiration and gratitude for the excellent qualities possessed by the Three Jewels and an inspiration to develop these qualities oneself.

One would then sit comfortably on one's meditation cushion, or any regular seat, and recite prayers beginning with that of refuge-seeking, followed by the generation of *bodhicitta*, and several prayers dedicated to the respective Buddhas, bodhisattvas, and deities. This practice also serves for setting the right motivation of appreciation, generosity, and compassion to practice through the entire day. In fact, these attitudes formed in religious ritual and prayer provide a basis for daily living. One, for example, is more disposed to extend generosity to those living beings who are in need—the destitute, sick, and sorrowful—whom one will meet in different situations during the day, both on auspicious occasions and on a regular basis. One especially witnesses these kindly acts at holy sites.

CIRCUMAMBULATION

Often, either before breakfast or a little after, and most invariably in the evening, one might go out for circumambulation, a spiritual practice of slowly walking around and around a place of worship, be it a temple, a monastery, a residence of a high master, or a repository of holy scriptures and images. Except in very special cases, people walk in a clockwise direction as a mark of respect and positivity. While making the rounds, they almost always hold prayer beads, which they finger one bead at a time while reciting prayers and *mantra*-incantations of different Buddhas, bodhisattvas, and deities. The most common *mantra*, among the Tibetans, is the *Oṃ Maṇi Padmé Hūṃ*, the six-syllable *mantra* of the bodhisattva of Compassion, Chenrezik (Avalokiteśvara), of whom, the Tibetans believe, the Dalai Lama is the human manifestation.

So, for example, people on the path around the Dalai Lama's residence are making religious merit; but on a deeper level they are trying to reorient their minds in the direction of greater and more spontaneous compassion, as ultimately they hope to attain the same level as Chenrezik. As they catch glimpses of the residence of Chenrezik's human manifestation, they aspire to become like him. The "*maṇi* walls" (piles of small stones picked up along the circumambulation path and piled one stone at a time with a slab on which *mantras* are carved left on top), *chortens* (small reliquaries in the shape of a *stūpa* containing holy images of deities made of mud beaten with relics of high masters and blessed substances), and rock faces carved with his *mantra* all serve to draw attention to the task at hand. This is done not just to ask some powerful deity for help, but ultimately to become embodiments and work for the betterment of others. As with the religious objects used in daily rituals, those that are associated with circumambulation are works of art that are part of Tibetan religious culture.

Circumambulation is also carried out by a whole community. This communal circumambulation is performed to address an undesirable natural occurrence such as the scarcity of rain. It produces a simultaneous and collective accumulation of merit that affects the undesirable situation. In this kind of circumambulation, members of the whole community would carry an entire collection of canonical scriptures on their backs and walk around the whole area chanting *mantras* and relevant prayers. This kind of event is an important religious and cultural experience for all involved in the community.

PRAYER WHEELS

Many people may have small handheld prayer wheels, also called "*maṇi* wheels," which they spin clockwise while walking and at the same time chanting a *mantra* out loud or silently to oneself. These prayer wheels are filled with rolls of thin paper imprinted with many copies of the *mantra Oṃ Maṇi Padmé Hūṃ*. They are printed in an ancient Indian script or in Tibetan script, wound around an axle in a protective container, and spun around and around as the wheel turns. Typically, larger decorative versions of the syllables of the *mantra* are also carved on the outside cover of the wheel. On a typical path of circumambulation, one would also come across much larger *maṇi* wheels, some even several meters high and one or two meters in diameter. They contain far more copies of the *mantra* and may also contain up to hundreds of sacred texts. There are also *maṇi* wheels mounted in rows on walls next to the pathways to be spun by people entering a shrine.

Tibetans believe that spinning these wheels will invoke the attention and blessings of concerned deities and will also send prayers in all directions for the benefit of one and all. They also believe that reading, seeing, or causing the *mantras* to spin through either a wind-powered or a water-powered device would have similar effects. On a deeper level, the *mantras* symbolize positive virtues and attitudes on which people try to reflect. Through the use of the *maṇi* wheels, they become more and more familiarized with the symbolism so that with time they begin to develop those qualities themselves. For instance, *maṇi padmé* stands for "wish-fulfilling jewel and lotus," the combination of which is an epithet for Chenrezik, the embodiment of Great Compassion, or rather the Great Compassion itself. Like a wish-fulfilling jewel, this Great Compassion can grant our wishes provided we cultivate it within ourselves. Like a *padmé*, lotus rooted in the swamp yet not soiled by it, the Great Compassion will connect whoever possesses it with suffering beings, and yet one will not be susceptible to the miseries himself or herself. With the introduction of Tibetan Buddhism into the West, new types of *maṇi* wheels have come into being. His Holiness the Dalai Lama has said that having the *mantra* on your computer works the same as a traditional prayer wheel. Because a computer's hard disk spins hundreds of thousands of times per hour and can contain many copies of the *mantra*, anyone who wants to can turn his or her computer into a prayer wheel.

PRAYER FLAGS

Occasionally people prepare prayer flags, with short or long prayers printed on them, and sew them onto ropes to be displayed horizontally between poles, trees, or even valleys. Sometimes they are fastened to wooden poles for vertical display. In all cases, the wind flaps them, sending prayers in the direction of the wind for the benefit of others. It is believed that these flags are a means to create an auspicious environment and to accumulate positive karma. Often you will see prayer flags blowing from the top of houses, monasteries, temples, or mountain passes. The colors of the flags symbolize the five elements: yellow for earth, white for water, red for fire, blue for wind, and white and green for space. More often than not, hanging the flags is accompanied by incense burning rituals whereby blessings of the Buddhas, bodhisattvas, and the titular deities are invoked, along with seeking temporary assistance from the local mundane deities. The sewing and coloring of flags along with printing prayers on them, and the hanging and flying of these flags, all add to the unique religious culture of Tibetan Buddhism.

THE RANSOM OF ANIMALS

Every once in a while, people will ransom animals that are destined to be killed by their owners or butchers. Through this ransom, they liberate the animals from being harmed in the future. At a simple ritual ceremony, soon after buying them, the animal would be declared "freed from (unnatural) life-dangers" for the rest of its life. The animal would be marked with colors, normally red, smeared over its mane and back. Multicolored strands of cloth would also be put around its neck or through pierced holes in the ears. We also ransom fish that would be freed deep into the water, hopefully away from the reach of the fishermen. Often, the merit is dedicated for the long life of a beloved master, elder, or any family member who is divined to face risks to his or her life. Related with this practice, almost everyone has an unconditional admiration for vegetarianism, and many take a separate vow from their master to remain a vegetarian. At the very least, those who are not vegetarians try to avoid meat completely on auspicious days.

PURIFICATIONS

Almost all of these practices could be considered in the category of "accumulation," although one would have to look at the motivation behind the actions to be certain. Among the practices for "purification," most lay practitioners would perform prostrations. These can be either a full-length position or a position where the hands, feet, and forehead touch the ground. During the prostration, one reflects on what are called the "Four Remedial Factors": (1) taking refuge and *bodhicitta*, (2) deep felt regret over one's known and unknown wrongdoings, (3) intention to compensate the wrongdoings, and (4) resolution not to revert to the same wrongdoings. While doing the prostrations with these factors in mind, one recites an appropriate confessional liturgy. In so doing, it is believed that one expiates the misdeeds of the body, speech, and mind simultaneously. There can also be corresponding visualizations that one may undertake while making prostrations to reinforce the contemplation and thereby enhance the integrity and potency of the practice.

Another popular purification practice, called *nyungné*, involves the participant taking an eight-precept, one-day vow of fasting and self-discipline at the outset of each day for as long as he or she may decide to carry out the purification practice. The precepts include restraints on the number of times one eats, what quality and type of seats and beds one uses, the nature of the ornaments one may wear, as well as the basic Five Precepts of abstaining from killing, stealing, lying, sexual activity, and intoxicants. The most common form of this practice is to take the commitment for a period of sixteen days (eight pairs of days) during the first half of the fourth lunar month, when several of the major events in Buddha's life took place. The popular custom is to alternate between complete fasting, not even permitting the swallowing of saliva, and silence on one day; and just one vegetarian meal and relaxation of the restraint of silence on the next day. On this second day, the person would engage in group recitations, prostrations, and other such practices spread over the entire day. In this way, one can empathize with the sufferings of *saṃsāra* in general, and that of the hungry ghosts in particular. This empathy can open oneself to several deeper reflections and ponderings on the nature and prospects of cyclic existence, the value of the Great Compassion, and the need to advance to full Buddhahood for the benefit of others.

AUSPICIOUS DAYS

Often, people perform one or many of these practices on what are called "auspicious days." These include the eighth, tenth, fourteenth, fifteenth, twenty-fifth, and thirtieth days of a lunar month; days associated with a particular deity or master; days with astrological significance; and days when the merits accumulated are believed to greatly increase. The dates connected with the life events of the Buddha, such as his birthday and his day of enlightenment, as well as days associated with the Buddha's principal disciples or extraordinary Indian and Tibetan masters, are treated with much reverence. The birthdays of a living master or the death anniversary of a past master are also observed with religious fervor. At special occasions, celebrations can include religious dances by monks accompanied by music, the making of a sand *maṇḍala*, special rituals and liturgies, and other kinds of religious events seen as treasures of Tibetan culture.

On auspicious days, people in the surrounding areas visit the nearest monastery or temple, receiving blessings by touching the statues and holy relics with their foreheads, and making offerings of ceremonial scarves, flowers, or fruits. They may also make contributions for butter lamps or, nowadays, electric lamps. They may also go around pouring a drop of butter oil out of their kettles into the lamps that are already burning. On these visits, they most often make a monetary offering for a propitiation rite to be done in their names, either individually or in common with others, in honor of the protector deities of their choice. This last practice is extremely popular among many people, and they carry it out either themselves or commission others to carry it out for them at the beginning of any major endeavor, business or otherwise. Similarly, they would place requests for special rituals to be performed at the monastery or seek a date for inviting a required number of monks to their homes to perform a particular ritual. In some of these cases, psychic diviners suggest which rituals should be performed to clear away any obstacles in the way of their projects.

There are rituals for almost every human predicament, including death. After a person dies, a grief period of forty-nine days is observed with solemnity and rituals by his or her loved ones. During this time, the dead person's spirit could remain in search of a fresh rebirth into one of the six realms. So the rituals and prayers performed are believed to ease the way of the deceased in his or her search during the period in between lives. Within that period, or even before one's actual death, "birth symbols" in the form of statues of the Buddha, or a *tangkha* (traditional Tibetan painted scroll) could be commissioned, consecrated, dedicated, and installed to influence the selection of the appropriate and positive rebirth.

There are various types of divination by which the Tibetan people seek advice concerning current endeavors or insight into the future. Some are simple and popular, like dough balls with written messages in them. There are also oracles of varying levels within Tibetan communities. Even the Tibetan government-in-exile annually consults the state oracles during the New Year celebrations for insights into the upcoming year, carrying out proscribed rituals with all seriousness to remedy foreseen mishaps and crises. They also ask the Tibetan people for cooperation when it is warranted.

PILGRIMAGE

Pilgrimages are an important part of the life of the Tibetan Buddhist people. In Tibet, people used to spend months at a stretch visiting holy places and engaging in religious activities while living on alms. Sometimes they would travel the entire length and breadth of the country. Ever since the Tibetans went into exile in India, people go on pilgrimages to the holy sites associated with the life of the Buddha and his close Indian disciples. They do so on average almost every other year, and often Tibetan people use the pilgrimage as an opportunity to undertake extensive practices.

The pilgrimage experience gives the pilgrims inspiration in their practices, as well as the natural atmosphere to reflect on the profound teachings and activities of their masters. It also aids the pilgrims in defining their identity as Buddhists, strengthens their connection with the Buddhist community, and focuses their gratitude for and commitment to following the Buddhist path. Surely, this signals spiritual growth and maturation on the part of the practitioner to move on to more advanced practices for seeking personal liberation from cyclic existence, for shouldering the responsibility of working compassionately for the benefit of others, and, in some cases, for preparation to take up the advanced Tantric practices of deity yoga.

WANDERING STORYTELLERS

It is important to note that in the popular culture in Tibet, the general population, especially the illiterate and untrained members of Tibetan society, learned about Buddhism from a people's medium, namely from wandering storytellers. These storytellers presented the Dharma in a simplified, vernacular, singsong kind of language. They imparted ethical codes of conduct, illustrated the moral concept of karma, and encouraged their audiences to feel compassion for all beings. Traditionally, these storytellers were not scholars or members of the religious hierarchy. Instead, they had humble origins and thus easy access to people of all backgrounds. This tradition in Tibet stretches back to at least the twelfth century, but today this storytelling tradition is slowly dying out, both inside and outside Tibet.

Where it still exists, the storyteller travels from place to place with a small shrine and a set of large *tangkhas*, which depict various enlightened world-systems of Buddhas and bodhisattvas, and also those of the unenlightened and less fortunate ones. The latter include the realms of the hell beings, hungry ghosts, and animals, as well as the ordinary humans. In a melodious singsong way, they would lead the audience through the details of the depictions, probing into the beings' backgrounds and suggesting their likely resultant states and conditions. In the setting up and organization of the storyteller's display, one or two of his family members might assist. The audiences consist primarily of laity, many of those who have little or no formal religious training.

The storytelling itself is typically held under a shady tree, under a specially pitched canopy, or beside a wall. It is normal for such storytelling gatherings to go for a full week or more, with the audiences meeting from early morning until evening with breaks for refreshments and meals. Most storytellers are so expert in their art that often the entire audience is moved to tears or to deep faith as the occasion warrants. At the conclusion of the wanderer's story, the audience may make offerings to him in appreciation for the teaching. At the end of a typical day, the listeners make prostrations before the altar and take time to look back at the day to recognize the virtuous and nonvirtuous actions in which they were engaged, to generate rejoicing or regret, and to resolve to do better the net day. A certain particular position, called the position of the sleeping lion (in which one lies on the right side with the left hand on the left thigh and the right hand under the chin) is adopted for lying down. One tries to go to sleep in a positive mental attitude so that the entire sleep period is positively influenced.

THE DEEPER LIFE

So far, we have focused on the devotions and practices of the Tibetan Buddhist laity. It is important to note that these religious activities are related to their experience of and reflection on basic and unfortunate elements of daily life. All persons experience the sufferings and miseries associated with ordinary life in the lower realms of existence, the law of karmic causation in those realms, and impermanence and death. As one becomes more mature in one's understanding of these realities, one may begin to see how he or she is chained by afflictive emotions and their karmic offshoots, and thus liable to sufferings and miseries. This is when one begins to aspire for freedom from the bondage of conditioned birth and death and to search for the root cause of afflictive emotions and their karmic offshoots. Here the devotional life begins to take on a deeper meaning as it points to the path that leads to liberation and the vows that incline one's capabilities in that direction.

Likewise, if one grows further and sees how all sentient beings, without exception, are equal in wanting happiness and discarding suffering just like oneself and how one is related to all beings and has been recipient of their kindness at one point in time or another, one may embrace others in their search for lasting happiness. At this point, one may also add the Bodhisattva Vow and engage in cultivating universal love and compassion as well as overcoming selfishness and self-grasping. Here, too, one's devotional life and daily practices begin to nourish and express a deeper wisdom and ethical life in the Buddha's path.

NOTES

1. Sir Charles Bell, "The Political Testament of H. H. the 13th Dalai Lama," in *History of Tibet*, ed. Alex McKay (London: Routledge, 2003), 511–512.
2. Melvyn C. Goldstein, *A History of Modern Tibet: The Demise of the Lamaist State* (Berkeley: The University of California Press, 1989), 766.
3. http://www.dalailama.com/messages/tibet/five-point-peace-plan, accessed January 20, 2013.
4. Ibid.
5. http://www.dalailama.com/messages/middle-way-approach, accessed January 30, 2013.
6. His Holiness Tenzin Gyatso The Fourteenth Dalai Lama, *A Human Approach to World Peace* (London: Wisdom Publications, 1984), pp. 3, 10–12.

SUGGESTIONS FOR FURTHER READING

Beckwith, Christopher I. *The Tibetan Empire in Central Asia : A History of the Struggle for Great Power among Tibetans, Turks, Arabs, and Chinese During the Early Middle Ages*. Princeton, NJ: Princeton University Press, 1987.

Bell, Sir Charles. "The Political Testament of H. H. The 13th Dalai Lama." In *History of Tibet*, ed. Alex McKay, 509–13. London: Routledge, 2003.

Buffetrille, Katia and Françoise Robin. "Tibet Is Burning: Self-Immolation: Ritual or Political Protest?" *Revue d'Etudes Tibétaines* 25 (December), 2012.

Cabezón, José Ignacio, ed. *Buddhism, Sexuality, and Gender*. Albany: State University of New York Press, 1992.

———. "State Control of Tibetan Buddhist Monasticism in the People's Republic of China." In *Chinese Religiosities: Afflictions of Modernity and State Formation*, ed. Mayfair Me-Hui Yang. Berkeley: University of California Press, 2008.

Davidson, Ronald M. "Atiśa's a Lamp for the Path to Awakening."In *Buddhism in Practice*, ed. Donald S. Lopez, Jr., 290–301. Princeton, NJ: Princeton University Press, 1995.

———. *Indian Esoteric Buddhism: A Social History of the Tantric Movement*. New York: Columbia University Press, 2002.

———. *Tibetan Renaissance: Tantric Buddhism in the Rebirth of Tibetan Culture*. New York: Columbia University Press, 2005.

Goldstein, Melvyn C. *A History of Modern Tibet: The Demise of the Lamaist State*. Berkeley: The University of California Press, 1989.

Goldstein, Melvyn C., and Matthew T. Kapstein. *Buddhism in Contemporary Tibet: Religious Revival and Cultural Identity*. Berkeley: University of California Press, 1998.

Gyatso, Janet. *Apparitions of the Self: The Secret Autobiographies of a Tibetan Visionary*. Princeton, NJ: Princeton University Press, 1998.

Gyatso, Tenzin, The Fourteenth Dalai Lama. *A Human Approach to World Peace*. London: Wisdom Publications, 1984.

——. *The World of Tibetan Buddhism: An Overview of its Philosophy and Practice*. Boston: Wisdom Publication, 1983.

Jacoby, Sarah, and Antonio Terrone. "Tibetan and Himalayan Buddhism." In *Buddhism in the Modern World*, ed. David L. McMahan. London: Routledge, 2012.

Kapstein, Matthew T. *The Tibetans*. Malden, MA: Blackwell, 2006.

——. *The Tibetan Assimilation of Buddhism: Conversion, Contestation, and Memory*. New York: Oxford University Press, 2000.

Klein, Anne C. *Meeting the Great Bliss Queen: Buddhists, Feminists, and the Art of the Self*. Boston: Beacon Press, 1995.

——. *Unbounded Wholeness: Dzogchen, Bon and the Logic of the Nonconceptual*. New York: Oxford University Press, 2006.

Lopez, Donald S. Jr. ed. *Religions of Tibet in Practice*. Princeton, NJ: Princeton University Press, 1997.

Norbu, Chögyal Namkhai. *Dzogchen: The Self-Perfected State*. Ithaca, NY: Snow Lion Publications, 1989.

Powers, John. *A Concise Introduction to Tibetan Buddhism*. Ithaca, NY: Snow Lion Publications, 2008.

Snellgrove, David L. *Indo-Tibetan Buddhism: Indian Buddhists and Their Tibetan Successors*. Vol. 2. Boston: Shambhala Publications, 1987.

Sperling, Elliot. *The Tibet-China Conflict: History and Polemics*. Washington, DC: East-West Center, 2004.

Thondup, Tulku. *Hidden Teachings of Tibet: An Explanation of the Terma Tradition of Tibetan Buddhism*. Boston: Wisdom Publications, 1986.

Thurman, Robert A. E. *The Central Philosophy of Tibet: A Study and Translation of Jey Tsong Khapa's* Essence of True Eloquence. Princeton, NJ: Princeton University Press, 1991.

——. *Essential Tibetan Buddhism*. San Francisco: HarperSanFrancisco, 1995.

Williams, Paul. *Buddhist Thought: A Complete Introduction to the Indian Tradition*. London: Routledge, 2000.

7

Chinese Experiences of Buddhism

It is said that King Aśoka sent Buddhist missionaries to Central Asia, and in fact, Aśokan inscriptions have been found in Afghanistan. Traditional sources also say that Aśoka's son, Kustana, founded the kingdom of Khotan to the northwest of Tibet in 240 B.C.E., some thirty years after the first Buddhist monastery was constructed in Khotan. In the first century C.E., the Kuṣāṇa Dynasty was founded. The Kuṣāṇa empire ruled much of Central Asia, including Afghanistan and parts of northern India, and lasted until the middle of the third century. Members of this dynasty converted to, and supported, Buddhism throughout their empire. This included the Silk Road, which was the major east–west trade route that linked Persia (Iran) to China. It was by way of the Silk Road that Central Asians began to actively export Buddhism into China around the first century C.E. Chinese records indicate that Central Asian Buddhism included both Sarvāstivāda and Mahāyāna sects.

The Silk Road had northern and southern routes, which converged in the city of Dunhuang, China (see Map 5). Dunhuang was a cosmopolitan city, which eventually became a center for translating Buddhist texts into Chinese and for the development of Buddhist art. As Buddhism became more known in China, Dunhuang also became the starting place for Chinese Buddhist pilgrims and scholars to travel on the Silk Road to India to gain more knowledge about their new religion. Much later, in the eleventh century, the Chinese sealed Buddhist texts in the caves at Dunhuang to preserve them from Mongol invaders. In 1900, Wang Yuanlu discovered the caves and some of their contents. He later worked with a British and Indian expedition in 1907, as well as expeditions from France (1908), Japan (1911), and Russia (1914). They discovered 20,000 Buddhist texts and drawings dating from the fifth to the eleventh centuries. This material has given modern scholars a better understanding of the history of Buddhism in both China and Tibet.

Chinese imperial records first refer to Buddhism during the reign of Mingdi (ruled 58–75 C.E.). The Buddhist tradition in China claims that Emperor Mingdi actually brought Buddhism to China. However, historical records

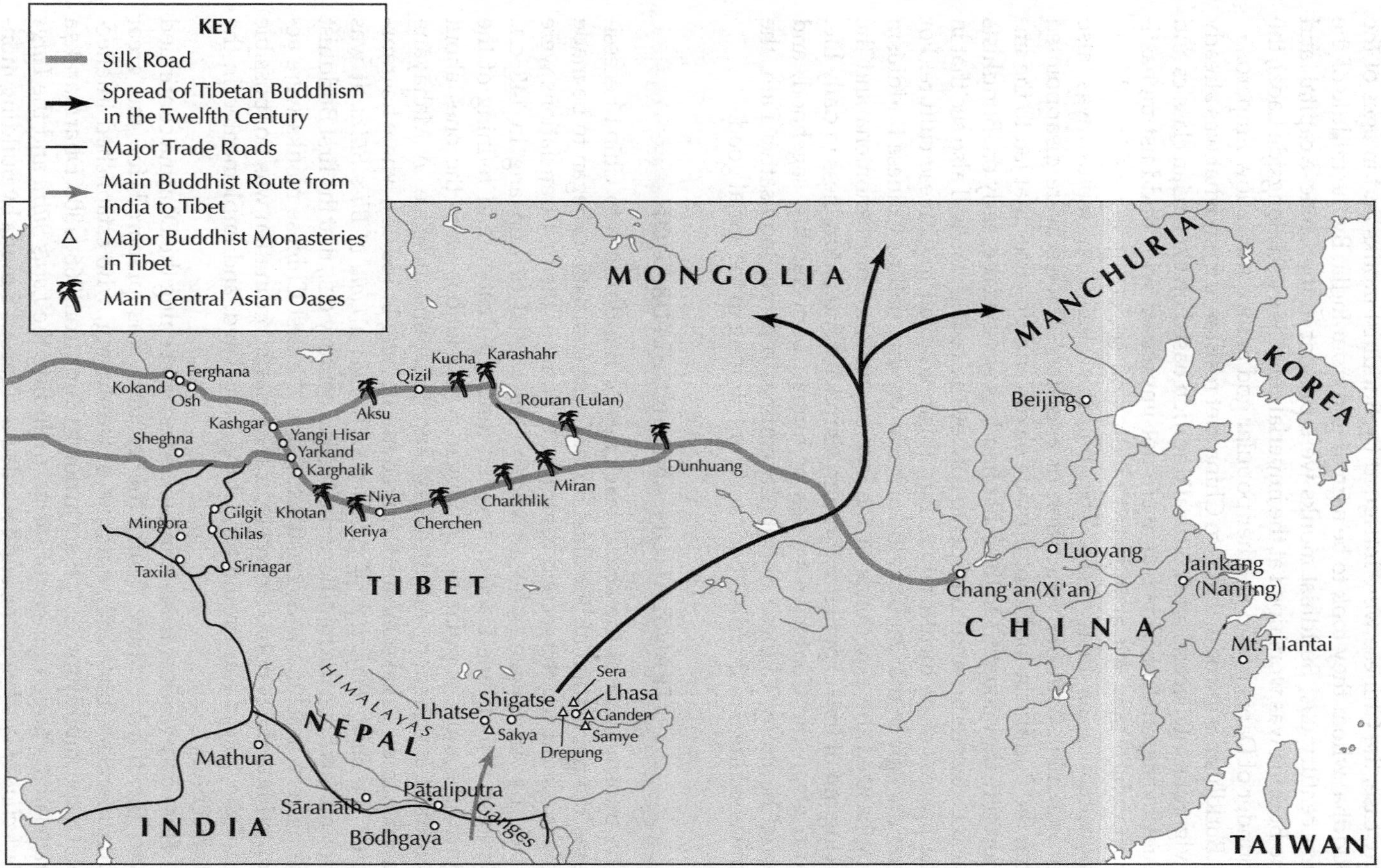

MAP 5. The northern and eastern spread of Buddhism: c. first–twelfth century C.E.

indicate that Central Asian merchants brought Buddhism into the country. In any case, the Chinese were intrigued by Buddhist monks and images of the Buddha, whom they took to be a great god from India. By the middle of the first century C.E., Buddhist monks were present in the Chinese capital, and the Buddha was worshiped at the imperial court as a god alongside Laozi, the founder of Daoism, and another popular god named the Yellow Emperor.

Buddhism's introduction into China met resistance from what was already a vigorous intellectual and cultural tradition based on Confucian classics and Daoist religion. Confucianists were not impressed with Buddhist monasticism, which they felt abandoned family and society, going against the responsibilities of filial piety. The Buddhist belief in rebirth was also incompatible with the veneration of ancestors. Daoists were disappointed that the Buddhists could not provide elixirs and practices that led to the immortality they sought. On the other hand, as we shall see, early on, Buddhists used Daoist terms and concepts to convey their ideas. We will also see that in the process of its inculturation, Buddhism adapted to Chinese culture. For example, given the Daoist value of harmony and nature, Chinese Buddhism emphasized the experience of the interdependence of phenomena and the living out of that experience through simplicity and naturalness in daily life. Also given the Confucian values of human perfectability, sagehood, and social harmony, Chinese Buddhism emphasized the Bodhisattva Path, the universal ideal of Buddhahood, and contributing to the social good.

TRANSLATION AND INCULTURATION

The transmission of the actual teachings of Buddhism into China necessitated the translation of Buddhist texts. These translations began to be made in earnest during the second century C.E. Some of the first translations were made by An Shigao, who arrived in the capital of Luoyang in 148 C.E. Because at that time Daoism stressed inner cultivation and refining of the spirit, the most popular of An Shigao's translations were the ones about Buddhist meditation, mindfulness, and breathing practice. A Mahāyāna monk named Lokakṣema also arrived in Luoyang in 168 C.E., where he translated the *Small Perfection of Wisdom Sūtra* and a *Land of Bliss Sūtra*. It was around this time, the middle of the second century C.E., that the first Buddhist monastery in China was constructed and the first Chinese monks were accepted into the Saṅgha. However, full monastic ordination was not possible until the *Vinaya* was brought to China, translated, and implemented in the fifth century.

This early work of translating texts and preaching the Dharma continued into the third century. Thus, the ground was prepared for the great Dharmarakṣa (born 230), a native of Dunhuang, who established intellectual respectability for Buddhism in north China from 266 to 308. Dharmarakṣa translated a large number of *sūtras*, including the *Lotus Sūtra* and the *Large Perfection of Wisdom Sūtra*, and founded a vigorous Saṅgha by building monasteries, ordaining monks, and expounding the Dharma. Through the efforts of Dharmarakṣa and his disciples, Buddhist monastics gained respect for their wisdom, simplicity, purity of heart, and fellowship with people from all classes of Chinese society. When barbarians sacked the northern Chinese capitals, Luoyang in 311 and Chang'an (Xi'an) in 316, these monks were pillars of strength, compassion, and virtue in a world torn apart by destruction and chaos.

With the loss of north China to the barbarians, many Buddhists from that region traveled to other parts of China, thus spreading Dharmarakṣa's intellectual and disciplined style of Buddhism. In south China, Buddhism developed in peace among the ruling class, and monastics gradually gained influence at the imperial court. With the support of the ruling class, the center of Buddhism in south China was established in the capital city of Jiankang (Nanjing). There, monks produced new translations of Indian texts, lived comfortably, and devoted much of their time to more philosophical pursuits and literary activity. Large monastic estates, supported by the rulers, provided their monastics with both religious education and spiritual formation. There were also smaller monasteries in villages where the less educated monastics provided the populace with devotional services. Finally, forest monasteries were founded for monastics who wanted to devote all of their time to the practice of meditation.

Meanwhile in north China, things were much more difficult. Most Buddhist intellectuals had fled to the south, so the Buddhist community in the north focused more on practice than on theory. Individual monks gained prominence among the barbarian rulers as "holy men" and "wonder workers." For example, around 310, Fotudeng arrived in China, where he witnessed massacres when the capitals fell. By performing what are referred to as "feats of magic," Fotudeng sought to gain the barbarian rulers' admiration to exert a civilizing influence on them. In this way, he hoped to help those innocent people who were suffering under the cruel oppressors. The example of Fotudeng and others like him gave witness to the spiritual power and the moral values of Buddhism. Some modern scholars argue that the real "magic" of Fotudeng was the conversion of the barbarians.

Fotudeng did not pretend to be a scholar like Dharmarakṣa, but stressed the practice of meditation and devotion. His major achievements included his disciplined method of training monks and the foundation of the Chinese Buddhist order of nuns. In 317, Zhu Jingjian (c. 292–361) became the first Chinese woman to take novice ordination. She was soon joined by other women and founded a monastery in Chang'an. However, full women's ordination would not be available in China until 434, when Sri Lankan *bhikṣuṇīs* came for the purpose of establishing such a lineage.

NEW TRANSLATIONS AND SCHOLARSHIP

During the fourth century, some of the more intellectual Buddhist monastics in the south of China were using Daoist and Neo-Daoists terms and concepts to aid in the translation of Buddhist texts and in the understanding of

Buddhist ideas. For example, some Neo-Daoists held, based on original Daoist texts, that the world of phenomena is the "functioning" of the Dao, which is itself Ultimate Reality. All phenomena are the self-determinations of the Dao, formed by the Dao's dynamic functioning. This means that the "essence" of all things is the Dao itself. The Neo-Daoists referred to the phenomena of the world as "being" and the ultimate and formless Dao that is the essence of all phenomena as "non-being." Buddhist scholars used these distinctions in discussing the Mahāyāna notion of emptiness. Emptiness was understood to be, like the Dao, the causal source and formless essence of all phenomena. As essence, emptiness is nonbeing; but in its functioning of dependent arising, it takes form as being.

In time, some Buddhist scholars came to realize that looking at Buddhism through a Daoist lens could be distorting the meaning of Buddhist texts. One such person was Dao'an (312–385), a disciple of Fotudeng who was forced to migrate south due to civil war. In 379, Dao'an returned to Chang'an in the north and began a new translation center. Indian monks were brought to Chang'an to work with Chinese scribes. The most famous monk to come to Chang'an shortly after Dao'an was the great Kumārajīva (344–413). When he arrived in 402, he was already well known in China and was therefore able to gain the ruler's patronage. Kumārajīva, along with a large number of Chinese disciples, undertook a massive translation project. A number of popular *sūtras* were retranslated, and new translations were completed. Kumārajīva's translation of Mādhyamika texts, the Perfection of Wisdom literature, the *Lotus Sūtra*, and the *Vimalakīrti Sūtra* sowed the seeds of a deeper understanding of Buddhism in China. This clearer understanding would later flower in a number of highly creative schools of Chinese Buddhist thought. In this way, the inculturation of Buddhism in China took a giant step forward.

One of Kumārajīva's disciples, Sengzhao (374–414), helped to clarify the central Mahāyāna notion of emptiness. Before Sengzhao, Chinese Buddhists based their understanding of the meaning of emptiness on the previously translated *Perfection of Wisdom Sūtras* in which emptiness is identified with the forms of the world. As we have seen, the Chinese Buddhist understanding of this identity of emptiness and the world had been colored by Daoism. In that Buddhist/Daoist interpretation, emptiness was thought to be a causal force that creates the universe and remains in things as their essence. With the new translation of Mādhyamika texts, Sengzhao was able to explain emptiness in a more orthodox fashion. He used the texts of Nāgārjuna and Āryadeva to show that all phenomena are "empty" of the self-existence we attribute to them through our conceptual understanding of things. The work of Sengzhao contributed to the establishment of the Chinese Mādhyamika School of Buddhism in the sixth century.

Another notion that was of great interest to Chinese Buddhists at the time of Kumārajīva was *Tathāgata-garbha*, a term the Chinese rendered as "Buddha-nature." The *Lotus Sūtra*, and later the *Nirvana Sūtra*, introduced to China the notion that there is within us an innate Awakening that can develop through religious practice into the full Buddhahood. The early Chinese understanding of Buddha-nature was also influenced by Daoism. The Daoists believed that people have an inner spirit of light that manifests the power of the Dao, the creative source of the universe. Dao Sheng (fl. 397–432), another student of Kumārajīva, argued that Buddha-nature should not be understood as a particular spiritual power, but should be understood as one universal reality that is the same in all beings. He also taught that Buddha-nature cannot be grasped gradually, but only all at once, in a single stroke of sudden Awakening. Dao Sheng's teaching about "sudden" Awakening in which one "recognizes one's innate Buddha-nature" contributed to a line of Buddhist thought that was influential throughout all of East Asia.

PERSECUTION AND REFORM

As Buddhism spread in north China during the fourth century, it enjoyed the support of the emperor. Eventually, a monastic "Saṅgha-director" was appointed to establish the government's support and control of the monasteries. While Buddhism flourished under this new system, its prosperity also led to corruption. Much of this corruption was due to the Saṅgha's extensive property holdings. Because of corruption in the Saṅgha, and in response to pressure from Daoist and Confucianist leaders who were afraid that Buddhism was gaining too much temporal power, there was a severe persecution of Buddhism in the north beginning in 446. Many temples and scriptures were destroyed, some of the monks were executed, and others fled to the south. However, with a new emperor in the north, the persecution ended in 452, and Buddhism again enjoyed royal patronage.

While the more philosophically minded monastics like Sengzhao and Dao Sheng emphasized emptiness and the inner essence of Buddhahood, many Chinese lay Buddhists were more interested in worshiping the Buddha according to Mahāyāna's devotional tradition. During the Buddhist revival that began after the persecution in the north ended in 452, Chinese artists glorified the Buddha in a manner that became popular with the masses, and lay worship of the Buddha was reinforced by the architecture of the Buddha-temples. In the temples, the central Buddha statue was the focus of devotion; from this time on, Buddhist art and liturgy offered a strong emotional appeal to the Chinese people. Besides the worship of the Buddhas, by the fifth century there were many popular forms of piety directed to bodhisattvas. One of the most lasting of these has been the devotion to Avalokiteśvara, known in China as Guanyin (see Figure 7.1). Guanyin is worshiped as a female deity in China. Over the centuries, she has remained the most popular deity in all of China, often portrayed as a graceful woman holding a lotus flower. She is considered to be compassionately concerned for the plight of humanity, rushing to the aid of beings in need with her boundless skillful means. In Buddhist temples, a statue of Guanyin has always been a popular site for both lay and monastic devotion.

Another aspect of the Buddhist revival was an early type of social reform in China. Around 470, a Saṅgha leader named Tanyao devised a plan to aid the poor and needy in rural areas. A peasant family could become part of a

FIGURE 7.1. Guangyin Bodhisattva Statue in Fengxian Cave at Longmen Grottos, China dated 672–676.

"Saṅgha household" by donating an amount of grain to the local Saṅgha. The member family could then receive a share of the Saṅgha's grain in times of need. Within this extended Saṅgha family of monks, nuns, and laypeople, the members saw themselves as brothers and sisters supporting each other in the spirit of Buddhist compassion. Another example of social reform was found in the urban areas where the city temples encouraged new types of lay-oriented Buddhist piety. In this system, the monks set aside the monastic contemplative life to be Dharma teachers, supporting and guiding the laity in living their religion in daily urban life. Buddhist householders were taught that the bodhisattva precepts meant that one should generously care for the needy in the community.

In time, a belief developed among Chinese Buddhists in both rural and urban areas that a "Buddha-kingdom" was being built on earth. However, this social vision of a Buddha-centered society disintegrated as the Northern Wei Dynasty fell into civil war and the capital city was sacked and abandoned. Buddhists took both sides in the conflict: high priests supporting the state and lower clerics supporting the peasant uprisings. The disillusionment that rose from this disunity was reinforced when from 574 to 578, the Zhou emperor in the north supported Confucianism and suppressed Daoism and Buddhism. Again monastics from the north fled for refuge to the south.

Some say that the fruit of the persecutions of 446 and 574 was that the monastic migrations south led to a blending of northern Buddhist practice with southern Buddhist scholarship. This blending of theory and practice is said to have influenced the founding of more fully inculturated schools of Chinese Buddhism during the sixth century. The founding of these schools was also influenced by an idea that was strengthened by the disillusionment stemming from the persecution of 574. The persecution that had attacked the sophisticated forms of Buddhist social, intellectual, spiritual, and devotional life meant for many Chinese Buddhists that they were witnessing the degeneration of the Buddha's Dharma. In Indian Buddhist literature, there was a prediction that the teaching and practice of the Dharma would weaken over time. It would be strong and true at first, but then weaken to the point that it would finally fall into a state of degeneration. It was said that this process would take place during three ages: the "age of the True Dharma," the "age of the Semblance Dharma," and the "age of the Degenerate Dharma." Given the situation of Buddhism in China and calculations that were made at that time, it was believed by many that the age of the Degenerate Dharma had arrived. What this meant to many Chinese Buddhists was that Buddhism had to produce stronger forms of practice, since, in the degenerate age, Awakening would be very difficult to attain using only traditional methods that had proven successful during the previous two ages.

INDIAN FOUNDATIONS OF THE CHINESE EXPERIENCES OF BUDDHISM

The Sui Dynasty, founded in 581, reunited China through its conquest of the south in 589. The first ruler of this dynasty was Emperor Wen (ruled 581–604), a devout Buddhist. The capital of Chang'an (renamed Daxing) became the center of Chinese Buddhism as eminent monastics taught in the city with imperial patronage. In this atmosphere of religious freedom and spiritual renewal, various schools of Buddhism emerged. The Chinese have traditionally identified ten principal schools. Of these ten, six were primarily Indian schools in China. They exerted more or less influence on the Chinese experiences of Buddhism but did not last very long as independent schools. The other four, which we introduce in the following section, were more fully inculturated forms of Chinese Buddhism, and defined the lasting spirit and worldview of Chinese Buddhism.

The Abhidharma Schools

After the *Abhidharma-kośa* of Vasubandhu was translated into Chinese by Paramārtha (499–569) from 563 to 567, the Zhushe (*kośa*) School was founded.

Based on Vasubandhu's work and the Sarvāstivāda School that it represented, the Zhushe School held a realistic view of the world. It taught that the elements of existence, the *dharmas*, are real. It categorized the mental and physical elements of life, and it defined the causal forces that structure life and experience. This school's teachings concerning Abhidharma philosophy became a basic part of Buddhist studies in China.

Kumārajīva translated the *Satyasiddhi* ("Establishment of Truth") *Treatise*, which was written in India by Harivarman (c. 250–350 C.E.) and is associated with the Indian Sautrāntika School. The Chengshi (*Satyasiddhi*) School used this text to refute the independent reality of the *dharmas*, thus opposing the Zhushe School. The *Satyasiddhi Treatise* was quite popular during the fifth ana sixth centuries, but eventually the text and its school of thought were absorbed into the Chinese Mādhyamika tradition.

Whereas the Zhushe and Chengshi schools taught doctrines from the Indian Abhidhiarma traditions, another school from that tradition did not transmit any formal doctrinal teachings. Instead, it preached the monastic discipline of the *Vinaya*. Without the *Vinaya*, there was no way to establish ordination procedures or ensure the authenticity of the lineages. This Lu (*Vinaya*) School was successful in China and enjoyed significant influence in the formation of the Saṅghas in Korea and Japan. Founded by Dao Xuan (596–667), the purpose of this sect was to develop a stricter observance of the *Vinaya's* monastic rules. The school was concerned that Mahāyāna placed more emphasis on the spirit of the rules than on the letter. Thus, Lu emphasized a stricter observance of the two forms of Buddhist ordination—novice and full.

The Māhāyana Schools

The fourth school is the Tantric Chenyan ("True Word") School, which developed during this time period but was more formally established later by Amoghavajra (705–774). As a Tantric tradition, the school's name indicates the importance the use of *mantras* has in its practices. In the Chinese context, this school developed from the early Chinese fascination with Tantric masters, who were said to be able to use magic powers and rites for blessings, for averting catastrophes, and for influencing the fate of people after death. Fotudeng was famous for his magical powers and knowledge of Tantric ritual formulas.

As more systematized Tantric texts were introduced into China, the focus of Tantra shifted to meditation involving visualization of Buddhas and bodhisattvas used to aid practitioners in the realization of Buddhahood. Eventually, the Indian monk Śubhākarasiṃha (637–735), and his Chinese disciple Yixing (683–727), translated the *Mahāvairocana Sūtra*, which became quite popular in Tantric traditions in China and Japan. Then the Indian monk Vajrabodhi (671–741) came to China in 719. His disciple from Central Asia, Amoghavajra, is said to be the founder of the Chenyan School. Amoghavajra was also one of the greatest translators of Buddhist texts in Chinese history.

The fifth school was the Sanlun School founded by Jizang (549–623). This school, devoted to Indian Mādhyamika philosophy, is based on the work of Kumārajīva and his disciple Sengzhao. *Sanlun* meaning "Three Treatises," refers to two texts by Nāgārjuna and one by his disciple, Āryadeva. Jizang argued that the Mādhyamika doctrine of emptiness does not imply a dualism between emptiness on the one hand and the ordinary reality of human experience on the other. There is but one reality, namely, this world grasped either by a person's discriminating mind or by the wisdom-mind. By the former, one experiences the ordinary world of things; by the latter, one finds the truth of emptiness. That is, one discovers that the "suchness" (*tathatā*) of the objective world is emptiness; things in their suchness are empty of the independence that the discriminating mind attributes to them.

The sixth school, derived from the Indian Yogācāra tradition, took form in three stages. The first tradition of Yogācāra in China was called the Dilun School, founded in the early sixth century. This school struggled with the question of whether the storehouse-consciousness is pure or defiled. If it is defiled, Dilun taught, then it is in need of purification through the realization of an even higher innate Pure Mind. This school was replaced by the Shelun School, named after a Yogācāra treatise by Asaṅga. Shelun is based on the later writings of the Indian monastic scholar Paramārtha, who arrived in China in 546.

Paramārtha's intellectual work was foundational not only to Yogācāra in China but also to the development of all of Chinese Buddhism. This is because of his role in promoting the *Tathāgata-garbha* tradition. This notion, rendered *Buddha-nature* in China, provided a positive way of depicting ultimate reality. For Paramārtha, Buddha-nature is another name for what he taught was an innate Pure Mind (*amala-vijñāna*) that remains unchanged and undefiled behind the transformations and defilements of the functioning mind. This Pure Mind, he taught, is beyond the storehouse-consciousness. With the realization of the higher Pure Mind, or one's Buddha-nature, all defilements of the ordinary mind are eliminated by its inherent purity, and one lives in the pure freedom of nirvanic Buddhahood.

For Paramārtha, Buddha-nature is not just the essence of consciousness. It is also seen to be the essence of all things. The suchness (*tathatā*) of all existence is Buddha-nature; everything has the Buddha-nature. Because this Buddha-nature is the nirvanic essence of Buddhahood (*Dharmakāya*), then all existence (*saṃsāra*) is the manifestation of the Dharma-body of the Buddha (Nirvana). To see the world with wisdom, which itself is the functioning of Buddha-nature, is to discover the inner Buddha-nature shining with luminosity in all phenomena. Awakening is the "uncovering" of the Pure Mind of Buddha-nature so as to find Nirvana in *saṃsāra*, Buddhahood in all things. It was this positive notion of ultimate reality that the Chinese found to be lacking in Sanlun Buddhism. This notion paralleled the Daoist understanding of the inner "unborn nature." It impressed the Chinese intellectual world and influenced the evolution of Chinese Buddhism.

It is not a coincidence, then, that at around the time of Paramārtha, a text teaching the Buddha-nature doctrine, and claiming to be an Indian Buddhist *sūtra*, was composed in China. This is the famous *Treatise on the Awakening of Faith in the Mahāyāna*, or simply, *The Awakening of Faith*. Written in the mid-sixth century, *The Awakening of Faith* became a seminal text in East Asian Buddhism, influencing such major schools as Huayan and Chan, which we introduce in the next section. This important text taught that Buddha-nature is the "One Mind" which is the source of all the universe. Drawing on Yogācāra, *The Awakening of Faith* states that the One Mind has two aspects. First, it is the always pure nirvanic suchness of existence, the very *Dharmakāya*. Second, it is the basis for the storehouse-consciousness to generate the *saṃsāric* world of experience. The image used by the text to depict this identity is the Yogācāra one of water (Nirvana) within waves (*saṃsāra*).

The third stage in the evolution of Yogācāra in China was achieved by Xuanzang (596–664). Xuanzang was unsure of the Shelun teachings about the nature of the mind, so he traveled to Central Asia and on to India to resolve the question. The teachings of Xuanzang and his disciple Kuiji (632–682) became the basis of the Faxiang ("The Characteristics of the *Dharmas*") School. Xuanzang taught that the experience of one's mind and of objects, of self and world, arise dependently as two sides of an interdependent pattern of consciousness. He says that "both the self and the *dharmas* of the world are constructions based on false ideas, and have no independent reality. . . . How are the self and these *dharmas* produced? They are all constructions based on the . . . transformation of consciousness itself" (*Cheng weishi lun*, 2a). The transformations of the first six forms of consciousness construct one's experience of the world, while the transformations of the seventh form construct the experience of self. Xuanzang says that given that "self-delusion, self-view, self-conceit, and self-love" are associated with these transformations, the eighth consciousness, the storehouse-consciousness, "is defiled" (*Ibid.*, 7).

This means that the strorehouse consciousness contains both pure and impure (moral and immoral) states that then affect one's experience of self and world. One's defiled consciousness can be purified by spiritual practice so that a person can mature in the purity of Awakening and attain Buddhahood. For Xuanzang, there is no innate Pure Mind. While Xuanzang's view on this matter was accepted as the Indian Yogācāra position, it was Paramārtha's *Tathāgata-garbha* notion of a Pure Mind behind the defiled ordinary consciousness that spoke more strongly to the Chinese religious way of thinking.

DEFINING THE CHINESE EXPERIENCES OF BUDDHISM

Although the six schools described in the previous section played foundational roles in the development of Chinese Buddhism, they were essentially schools of Indian Buddhism in China. The four schools described in this section are significantly distinct and creative forms of inculturated Chinese

Buddhism. Because these four schools clearly define the particular Chinese experiences of Buddhism, we spend more time introducing them.

The Heavenly Terrace School

The Tiantai ("Heavenly Terrace") School is named after the mountain in southeast China where it originated. Tradition states that Tiantai was founded by Huiwen (c. 550), who is considered its First Patriarch. Huiwen's disciple was Huisi (514–577), who crafted many of the teachings of the school. However, it was Huisi's disciple who was the real architect of Tiantai. This was the famous Zhiyi (538–597). At the time of Zhiyi, Chinese Buddhists were struggling with how to deal with the diversity of Buddhist texts coming from India. Stressing the Chinese spiritual preference for harmony, Zhiyi sought to reconcile and synthesize different Buddhist teachings by emphasizing the *Lotus Sūtra's* notion of *ekayana*, the "One Vehicle." In so doing, Zhiyi defined one important task of Tiantai as being the reestablishment of the unity of Buddhism.

Zhiyi taught that the differences between the varieties of texts and teachings of Buddhism were due to the Buddha's having accommodated his teaching to his listeners at different times in his life. At the beginning of what Zhiyi called the "Five Periods" of the Buddha's ministry, the Buddha taught the *Avataṃsaka Sūtra*, with the message of sudden Awakening to the Buddha-nature in all things. This message not being understood, the Buddha then taught the *Sūtra Piṭaka*, followed by the early Mahāyāna *sūtras*, and then the Perfection of Wisdom Literature and its doctrine of emptiness. Finally, he taught the *Lotus Sūtra* and the *Mahāparinirvāṇa Sūtra*, both of which again emphasized the sudden realization of Buddha-nature.

Zhiyi taught that the essential message of Buddhism, the notion of the universal Buddha-nature, is most clearly expressed in the *Lotus Sūtra* (See Figure 7.2), the central text of the Tiantai School. However, he also taught that this message is present in all the Buddha's teachings preserved in the variety of Buddhist texts coming from India. Thus, Zhiyi rejected the idea that the teachings of the different texts and schools contradict each other. Instead, they present different perspectives of the One Vehicle; they complement each other and blend into a harmony of different perspectives on the one Buddha Dharma. He also taught that because of the clarity of its presentation of this Dharma, the *Lotus Sūtra* most fully realizes the purpose of the Buddha's advent on earth, namely, to save all living beings. Thereby, Zhiyi recognized the relative validity of the teachings and scriptures of all forms of Buddhism, while at the same time proclaiming Tiantai, given its reliance on the *Lotus Sūtra*, to be the highest form of Buddhism. Other forms of East Asian Buddhism might not have accepted Tiantai's claim to superiority, but many were influenced by the general idea that there is an internal unity in Buddhism and that its highest teaching affirms the universal presence of Buddha-nature in all forms of existence. Here we see the influence of Paramārtha's work, with which Zhiyi and his teachers were familiar.

FIGURE 7.2. *Lotus Sūtra;* gold on indigo; Song Dynasty (960–1279 C.E.), China. Cleveland Museum of Art.

In terms of its teachings, Tiantai presents the oneness of the Three Levels of Truth. The first level is the truth of emptiness, that all things (*dharmas*) are empty of own-being because they are all dependently arisen. The second level is the truth that all things possess a temporary existence due to dependent arising. The third level is that the nature of things is both empty and temporarily existing. This third truth is called the Middle Truth; to behold it, according to Zhiyi is to see all three truths as one.

To behold this identity between emptiness and phenomena is to see the suchness (*tathatā*) of things. This suchness is the true nature of things that Tiantai calls Buddha-nature. Therefore, Buddha-nature is not something that one can see in itself, apart from phenomena. Given emptiness, Buddha-nature is not an independent thing, but is the essence of Buddhahood seen in the phenomena of the world. The metaphor that is used to express this presence of Buddha-nature in phenomena is water in waves. One cannot see water in itself apart from the forms it takes. So, too, the suchness of existence, Buddha-nature, is found when one sees the identity of emptiness and the temporary forms of life.

This identity means that all living beings are embraced by the Buddha-nature, and so can attain Buddhahood. To further emphasize this doctrine of universal salvation, Tiantai points to its understanding of the world and the mind. The cosmos is said to be made up of 3,000 worlds. This is not just an enumeration, but indicates the interpenetration and unity of all worlds. In Tiantai philosophy, it is said that there are ten worlds from the Buddha realms down to the hellish realms. These ten worlds arise dependently, and thus interpenetrate each other, resulting in 100 worlds. Each of these worlds possesses the ten characteristics of suchness, resulting in 1,000 worlds. Finally, each of these 1,000 worlds consists of three distinct worldly conditions, resulting in 3,000 worlds.

Given the interpenetration of these 3,000 worlds, each element (*dharma*) of any world contains the elements of all other worlds. Zhiyi says that this means that the 3,000 worlds are present in one moment of thought:

> Now, one mind contains ten *dharma*-realms, but each of these *dharma*-realms contains ten *dharma*-realms, resulting in 100 *dharma*-realms. One realm contains 30 kinds of worlds, hence 100 *dharma*-realms contain 3,000 worlds. These 3,000 worlds are contained in a fleeting moment of thought. . . . All one can say is that the mind is all *dharmas*, and that all *dharmas* are the mind. . . . It is obscure, but also subtle and extremely profound. Knowledge cannot understand it, and words cannot express it. Therefore, it is called "the realm of the inconceivable." (*Mohe zhiguan*, V)

One implication of this notion of the interpenetration of worlds is that all living beings from the realms of hell to those of the Buddhas are found within the mind. This means that the innate suchness of all beings, Buddha-nature, and all the qualities of the Buddha realms are present in the mind. Therefore, Buddha-nature can be experienced in a moment of thought, a sensation of fragrance, or a perception of color. Each moment of one's experience is united with the dependent arising of all forms of life in the cosmos expressing the suchness of existence, the Buddha-nature in all things. Here again we see the reason why all living beings possess Buddha-nature and are thereby capable of salvation.

Huisi described the mind's relation to its inherent Buddha-nature:

> The mind is the same as the mind of pure self-nature, true suchness, Buddha-nature, and the *Dharmakāya*. . . . Although the mind has always been obscured by *dharmas* based on ignorance, its nature has always been pure; thus it is called pure . . . and is originally enlightened. . . . The Buddhas past, present and future, as well as all living beings have this pure mind as their essence. . . . It is therefore called suchness. . . . This pure mind is called Buddha-nature because "Buddha" means Awakening, and "nature" means the mind. . . . The mind is called *Dharmakāya* because the meaning of *Dharma* consists in functioning, and the meaning of *kāya* [body] consists in establishing. . . . The functioning [of the Dharma] is established on the basis of this one mind. . . . Therefore, the mind is called the *Dharmakāya*. (*Dacheng zhiguan famen*, I–II)

The spiritual goal of Tiantai is to awaken to this identity between the suchness of existence, the interpenetrating unity of life, the inner Buddha-nature, and the innate purity of mind. Therefore, Zhiyi was not only a philosopher but also a practitioner and teacher of meditation. In fact, it was while reading a passage in the *Lotus Sūtra* that he gained the highest *samādhi* in which he realized Awakening. To guide others to this attainment, Zhiyi established an ordination lineage and taught forms of meditation practice that would have great influence on the spiritual practice and experience of all East Asian Buddhism.

The spiritual journey of Tiantai is intended to lead from the unenlightened life, conditioned by blind attachment to the world, to an enlightened vision of the world that brings inner freedom and outer harmony with the universe. To further this ideal, Zhiyi taught meditation methods that fostered both sudden and gradual attainment, tailoring them to the needs of his disciples. For example, he guided his monks in nondual forms of sitting meditation where one moves beyond the distinction between the meditator and the object of meditation to a more sudden experience of Buddha-nature. He also taught forms of quiet walking meditation with focus on one's body and breathing for gradual deepening of concentration. And he taught his disciples how to use the ordinary events of daily life as objects of meditative reflection. All three of these kinds of meditation have enjoyed wide popularity in the Buddhist world of East Asia.

Zhiyi taught a rather unique type of meditation. He believed that since the suchness of the 3,000 worlds is found in all moments of thought, then even blind attachments express suchness. Given the fact that these negative states of mind are common to the unenlightened human condition, they were Zhiyi's favorite objects of meditation. When one realizes the deeper interrelated unity of reality, one sees that the unwholesome states of mind are arising dependently, that they are empty of any substance, and then one finds freedom from any bondage to these negative factors of existence. However, this does not mean that the liberated person is purified of all negative mental factors. Given the interpenetration of all realms, even the hellish ones, these factors can always be found in the mind. While the liberated person is not himself or herself moved or defiled by any negative mental factors, he or she uses them to stay united with all beings in their struggle for liberation and to work as a bodhisattva for their salvation. This meditative use of the negative factors of mental life to penetrate the mystery of their suchness appealed to Chinese Buddhists who believed they were living in the age of the Degenerate Dharma.

Zhiyi also showed how traditional Buddhist tranquillity meditation is harmonious and complementary to traditional Buddhist insight meditation. As when the water is still one can see the bottom of the pond, so too when the mind is still one can see one's innate Buddha-nature reflected in the clear mirror of the mind. Finally, following the teachings of the *Lotus Sūtra*, Zhiyi taught that Gautama Buddha was a manifestation of an ever-present Buddha, thus affirming the value of devotional practice such as the repetition of the Buddha's name. In the end, Tiantai Buddhism emphasized the need in one's spiritual journey to balance study of the Dharma with both appropriate meditation practices and devotionalism. For centuries, this Tiantai balance in religious living influenced the development of the Chinese Buddhist experience.

Zhiyi was regarded as a person of great wisdom, learning, and moral character. He organized Buddhist doctrines, produced an impressive system of philosophy, and trained his disciples in ways that have been respected throughout the ages. His teachings spoke to the minds and hearts of the Chinese Buddhist world, and Tiantai became the first really Chinese form of

Buddhism. A Korean monk named Hyŏn'gwang (fl. 539–575) studied under Huisi and later returned to Korea, where he became famous as teacher of Tiantai. However, it was much later that Ŭich'ŏn (1055–1101) actually founded an independent school of Tiantai in Korea, where it is known as Ch'ŏnt'ae. The Japanese monk Saichō (767–822) studied under a disciple of the Sixth Tiantai Patriarch, from whom he received Tiantai doctrine and bodhisattva ordination. Saichō returned to Japan and founded the Tendai School on Mt. Hiei near Kyōto, which remains active to this day.

The Flower Garland School

The next great school that helped define the Chinese Buddhist experience is the Huayan ("Flower Garland") School, founded by Dushun (557–640). Dushun was a practitioner of meditation and a student of the *Avataṃsaka* (*Huayan*) *Sūtra.* Although Dushun was the First Patriarch of Huayen Buddhism, it was really the Third Patriarch, Fazang (643–712), who was the real architect of the school. Fazang served as preceptor to four emperors and wrote the systematic philosophy of Huayan Buddhism. This Philosophy is considered to be one of the most complex and difficult to understand in the Buddhist world. However, it gives us a glimpse into one of the profound dimensions of the Chinese Buddhist experience.

Box 7.1

Free and at Ease

The strength of Chinese Mahāyāna Buddhism lies in its all-encompassing character and flexibility, enabling it to adapt to all situations and to the needs of those of all capacities and backgrounds. Thus, Chinese Buddhism makes one feel pure, vigorous, and free and at ease under any circumstances.

Take myself for example. I left home to become a monk as a child, and later joined the army. I was ordained once again after ten years and since then have remained a monk. Based on my own Chinese Buddhist experience, all people I have met during these decades I consider friends, never enemies.

For example, when I meet people with different religious beliefs, I always respect them as people appearing in this world with different statuses, assuming different responsibilities, and fulfilling different missions. Although they might not agree with me and become Buddhists, as far as I am concerned, they help me in a variety of ways. To me, they are all bodhisattvas and benefactors. By seeing and treating others in this way, they also become my friends, and do not regard me as an enemy.

This is the beauty of Chinese Mahāyāna Buddhism in my experience.

DHARMA MASTER SHENG YEN
Dharma Drum Mountain, Taiwan

FIGURE 7.3. Statue of Vairocana Buddha in Fengxian Cave at Longmen Grottos dated 672–676.

The Tiantai notion that dependent arising implies the interdependence, or interpenetration, of all phenomena was greatly appreciated by the Chinese people, for whom the harmony of nature and society was so important. Huayan thought also reflects the experience of the dependent arising as interrelatedness. Specifically, Huayan was interested in the interrelatedness of what is called the *Dharmadhātu*, the "realm of all *dharmas*," or the totality of the cosmos. In its devotional writings based on the *Avataṃsaka Sūtra*, Huayan taught that the great *Dharmadhātu* is itself the very body of Vairocana Buddha (see Figure 7.3). Therefore, to realize the true nature or suchness of the cosmos is to discover the Buddha-nature of all existence. In its philosophical writings, again based on the *Avataṃsaka Sūtra*, Huayan taught that the totality of the *Dharmadhātu* arises in an interdependence that is wondrous and harmonious. When one sees this marvelous harmony, one generates a deeper commitment to living the Bodhisattva Path in a way that embodies that harmony in daily life. Huayan sought to explain its experience of this wondrous vision of the cosmos to help Buddhists attain a liberating insight into the harmonious nature of the *Dharmadhātu*.

Huayan teaches that there are four ways of experiencing the *Dharmadhātu*. First is the ordinary experience of existence that reveals the "realm of phenomena" (Chinese: *shi*), or the myriad *dharmas*. According to Huayan, this is the vision of the cosmos with which the early Buddhist tradition, such as Theravāda, works to gain Nirvana by the purification of the negative phenomena in one's consciousness. Second is the experience of existence that reveals the emptiness of all phenomena, the true suchness of all things. This is the "realm of principle" (Chinese: *li*), with which Mahāyāna works to attain Buddhahood. Through this second vision, one realizes that the real and inherent "principle," or nature of things, is always pure. Although phenomena may be either pure or impure, in essence they are empty of the independent nature one conceives them to have. Realizing this emptiness, the dependent arising of existence, reveals the inherent purity as the Buddha-nature of all phenomena. This inherent purity as the principle of existence is likened to a clear mirror. The mirror may reflect pure and impure images, but its essential clarity is never lost. Here again we see the influence of Paramārtha.

Now we come to the third experience of the cosmos, namely, seeing "the realm of the non-obstruction between principle (*li*) and phenomena (*shi*)." This nonobstruction refers to the fundamental Mahāyāna identity of emptiness with phenomena, or Nirvana with *saṃsāra*. For Huayan, these two aspects of reality "interpenetrate" such that the essential purity of suchness is not lost, and the diversity of dependently arisen phenomena is maintained. The two sides of reality do not "obstruct" each other: The essence of things is always pure, while the free expression of phenomena is preserved. This nonobstruction is, as in Tiantai, likened to water and waves. The water (representing the one suchness of phenomena) is always "still," and the waves (representing the diverse phenomena) are always "in motion." The inherent still nature of the water does not obstruct the movement of the waves, and the movement of the waves does not obstruct the still nature of the water. For Huayan, this third vision of reality is at the heart of the Tiantai experience of Buddha-nature in all phenomena.

Finally we arrive at the fourth experience of the cosmos in which one sees "the realm of the nonobstruction between phenomena (*shi* and *shi*)." Here, we are not looking at the relationship between emptiness and phenomena, but at the relationship between the phenomena themselves. For Huayan, the vision of this nonobstruction reveals that the dependent arising of all phenomena exists as a totality of dynamic interrelatedness. It also reveals that the phenomena making up this totality are related to one another by what Huayan calls "mutual identification" and "mutual penetration." To try to understand something about this fourth vision of reality, let us look at these two characteristics one at a time.

The *mutual* identification of all things does not imply a kind of *static* identification by which one might say, for example, that fire is the same as ice. Rather, in the Huayan vision, all phenomena in the cosmos are dependently arising together simultaneously. Each phenomenon provides a condition for the arising of the whole cosmos, and the particular totality of the cosmos is dependent on the conditions provided by all of its parts. If one part, one thing, was different or not present, the totality would itself be different. In dependent arising, each phenomenon plays an identical role in the mutual forming of the universe. Although there may be many differences between phenomena, as between fire and ice, in terms of their mutually conditioning roles, they are identical. Mutual identification refers to the identical way that all phenomena share in the conditioning mutuality of interrelatedness. They are mutually one with each other in providing the conditions for the dependent arising of the totality of the cosmos.

One implication of this idea of mutual identification is that each thing in the world is what it is because of the conditioning effect of all other things in the universe. Therefore, each being one experiences exists due to oneself, due to one's conditioning presence in the universe. For the same reason, one's self exists due to that being. So, despite the many differences between oneself and the beings one encounters, there is a fundamental unity or oneness in which each being finds a mutual identification with all other beings. In realizing this mutual identification, a person discovers that he or she owes his or her existence to countless beings throughout the universe. This discovery gives one a deeper sense of gratitude and respect for other beings. One also feels a deeper sense of responsibility for how one uses his or her existence, given its effect on the universe. This discovery will also give one a greater aspiration to benefit all living beings (*bodhicitta*).

The idea of mutual penetration takes this notion of mutual identification a step further. In the Huayan teaching about the mutual penetration of phenomena, we find the high point of Huayan experience that has been so important to defining East Asian Buddhism. Once, Fazang presented this notion of mutual penetration in a lecture to Empress Wu. In her palace, he used a golden statue of a lion to illustrate his ideas. Later, he used this lecture to compose his famous *Treatise on the Golden Lion*. In what follows, we use passages from that treatise to help explain the Huayan notion of mutual penetration.

At the beginning of his treatise, Fazang clarifies the idea of the mutual arising of the cosmos using the gold of the statue to represent emptiness ("principle": *li*), the lion to represent the totality of the cosmos, and the parts of the lion to represent the phenomena (*shi*) of existence:

> The gold has no self-nature. . . . The arising [of the lion] is due only to dependence, so it is called dependent arising. . . . The lion is empty [not self-sustaining]; there is only the gold. . . . Also, emptiness, having no self-nature, manifests itself through form. . . . This means that since the gold takes in the totality of the lion, apart from the gold there is no lion to be found. . . . This means that when we see the lion coming into existence, we are seeing only the gold coming into existence as form. There is nothing apart from the gold. (*Jin shizi zhang*, 1, 2, 4, 5)

Fazang goes on to present the Ten Mysterious Gates as a way of explaining the mutual penetration of this dependent arising of the cosmos. In the first gate, it is said that the gold (emptiness) and the lion (the totality of phenomena or forms) come into being simultaneously. In the second gate, it is said that the oneness of this dependent arising in which all things condition each other does not obstruct the unique identities of each thing in the cosmos:

> [1] The gold and the lion arise simultaneously, perfectly complete. . . . [2] The gold and the lion arise compatible with each other, the one and the many not obstructing each other. In this situation, emptiness [*li*] and forms [*shih*] are distinct. Whether one considers the one [emptiness] or the many [forms], each entity maintains it own position. (*Jin shizi zhang*, 7)

In the third and fourth gates, Fazang says that even though the forms of life are distinct, they also interpenetrate so that they "contain" each other. By this he means that in dependent arising, the very presence of each phenomenon influences or conditions the other phenomena of the cosmos. The conditioning influence of one phenomenon "enters" into all other phenomena, Fazang says, like reflections of objects enter a mirror. Note here that Fazang does not say that the phenomena physically enter each other. Once, to demonstrate this interpenetration to Empress Wu, Fazang placed a statue of the Buddha with a lamp in the middle of a room with mirrors all around it. He then showed the empress how the image of the Buddha-statue (representing emptiness), while physically remaining at the center of the room, was reflected in each mirror (representing phenomena). He also showed her that each mirror, while physically remaining where it is, was reflected in all other mirrors, and that their mutual reflection (representing mutual penetration) was repeated infinitely. In a similar way, each phenomenon in the cosmos contains the presence of all other phenomena in the cosmos, while at the same time retaining its uniqueness:

> [3] If the eye of the lion takes in the whole lion, then the whole lion is purely the eye. . . . [4] Since the various organs, and even each hair of the lion, takes in completely the whole lion in so far as they are all gold, then each [element of the lion] penetrates the whole [of the lion]. The eye of the lion is its ear, its ear is its nose, its nose is its tongue, and its tongue is its body. Yet, they all exist freely and easily, not hindering or obstructing each other. (*Jin shizi zhang*, 7)

In the fifth and sixth gates, it is said that when one looks at the cosmos (the lion), emptiness (the gold) is hidden; and when one looks at emptiness, the cosmos is hidden. But whether they are hidden or manifest, emptiness and the phenomena of the world "mutually shine," revealing to the enlightened that they are "completely compatible":

> [5] If one contemplates the lion, there is only the lion, and the gold is not seen. The gold is hidden and the lion is manifest. If one contemplates the gold, there is only the gold, and the lion is not seen. The lion is hidden and the gold is

manifest. . . . [6] The gold and the lion may be hidden or manifest. . . . The principle [emptiness] and the jointly arisen [phenomena] mutually shine. Principle and phenomena appear together as completely compatible. (*Jin shizi zhang*, 7)

The seventh gate presents the metaphor of Indra's net. In the *Avataṃsaka Sūtra*, it is said that the Hindu god Indra has a net made with jewels at its knots. Each of these jewels reflects the image of every other jewel and does so on to infinity. Like the mirror example, Indra's net represents the awakened vision of the mutual penetration of the cosmos:

> [7] In each eye, ear, limb, joint and hair of the lion is [reflected] a golden lion. All these golden lions in all the hairs simultaneously enter into a single hair. Thus in each hair, there are an infinite number of lions. In addition, all single hairs, together with their infinite number of lions, enter into a single hair. In a similar way, there is an endless progression [of realms interpenetrating realms] just like the jewels of Indra's net. (*Jin shizi zhang*, 7)

The last three gates relate this vision of mutual penetration to ignorance and insight into suchness, to how all time frames also interpenetrate in the totality of the cosmos, and to how both emptiness and the world of phenomena depend on the transformations of the mind. Note that this final gate presents the Yogācāra position:

> [8] The lion is spoken of in order to demonstrate the result of ignorance, while its golden essence is spoken of in order to make clear its true nature. . . . [9] This lion is a created *dharma*, arising and passing away in every moment. . . . Yet, since the different periods of time are formed dependent on one another, they are merging harmoniously and mutually penetrating together without obstruction in each moment of time. . . . [10] The gold and the lion may be hidden or manifest . . . but neither has any own-being. They are constantly being evolved through the transformations of the mind. (*Jin shizi zhang*, 7)

The treatise ends with the following comments about the attainment of wisdom and Nirvana:

> Wisdom . . . means that when we see the lion, we realize right away that all *dharmas* are produced by causes, and are from the very beginning quiescent and empty. By being free from attachments to the world and from renunciation of the world, one flows along this way into the sea of perfect knowledge . . . [and the] afflictions that result from desires will no longer be produced. Whether one sees beauty or ugliness, the mind is calm like the sea. Wrong views cease, and there are no negative mental formations. One escapes bondage, is free from hindrances, and forever cuts the roots of *duḥkha*. This is called the entry into Nirvana. (*Jin shizi zhang*, 9, 10)

In Huayan practice, tranquillity meditation is used to enable a person to find emptiness as the quiescent nature of all things. This leads to detachment and inner calm in the midst of the world. Then through insight meditation, one sees this emptiness functioning as the forms of the world. This functioning is experienced as an interpenetrating, fascinating, and wonderful matrix of dependent arising. This insight, in turn, leads to a rejection of world renunciation and a compassion for all living beings who fail to see this hidden harmony and are caught in afflictive mental formations. Thereby, one dwells spiritually neither in *saṃsāra* nor Nirvana but courses freely as a bodhisattva in the matrix of the cosmos seeking the benefit of others. Huayan vision of this matrix of mutual identification and penetration, where all things are interwoven in perfect balance and harmony, was very appealing to the Chinese world, which had always appreciated both harmony and nature.

From China, Huayan spread to other parts of East Asia. The Korean monk Ŭisang (625–702) studied Huayan Buddhism along with Fazang under the guidance of Huayan's Second Patriarch, Zhiyan (602–668). Ŭisang, a close friend of Fazang, later brought Huayan Buddhism to Korea. In the eighth century, Huayan was brought to Japan by Korean and Chinese monks, and the Japanese emperor built the Eastern Great Monastery (*Tōdai-ji*) as a sanctuary for the preaching of the Huayan doctrine. *Tōdai-ji*, with its gigantic bronze statue of Vairocana Buddha, still stands near Nara. Huayan thought is studied today in Buddhist centers of learning throughout East Asia.

The Meditation School

The original Chinese word for meditation is *channa*, a rendering of the Sanskrit word for meditation, *dhyāna*. Later, *channa* was shortened to *Chan*. During the sixth century, meditation was just one of many religious activities practiced by the various sects of Chinese Buddhism. In fact, most practitioners of Buddhism would attend lectures, study *sūtras*, participate in devotional rituals, and practice various pious works—often leaving little time for meditation. For those Buddhists who wanted more intense training in the practice of meditation, numerous monastic centers were dedicated to such practice. These monasteries were often located in mountainous areas in central and southwestern China and were led by meditation (Chan) masters. These masters taught powerful meditative practices in ways that were accessible to anyone. Chan techniques were said to be so powerful that they could bring a person to Awakening in the age of the Degenerate Dharma, when this feat was thought to be so difficult.

The manuscripts discovered at Dunhuang have given modern scholars a better understanding of the history of the Chan School that emerged from these early meditation lineages and traditions. These manuscripts indicate that many of the legends concerning the founding of Chan Buddhism are most likely myths. Historically, we know that one of the first Chan masters to gain a wide following in China was Hongren (601–674), master of the East Mountain School. According to the legends about this school, Hongren was the Fifth Patriarch of Chan, the First Patriarch being Bodhidharma. As time went on, this legendary line of transmission was accepted as the founding lineage of the Chan School of Buddhism.

Bodhidharma was a monk from India who arrived in south China about 470 and who was famous for his meditative prowess. According to legend, it is said that the emperor asked Bodhidharma how much merit his building of Buddhist temples, donating to the Saṅgha, and worship offerings had brought him. Bodhidharma is said to have answered that all these acts of piety had brought the emperor no merit at all. The point of this story is that according to Chan, only the direct experience of one's Buddha-nature is truly meritorious. Thus, the whole purpose of Chan is to enable a person to discover his or her Buddha-nature through the practice of meditation. Eventually, the legend goes, Bodhidharma settled in a mountain retreat in north China near Luoyang, where he gathered disciples, guided them in silent meditation, and taught them the *Laṅkāvatāra Sūtra*. It was in this place that Bodhidharma is said to have spent nine years in meditation in front of a wall. This "wall-gazing" meditation demonstrated the power of one-pointed concentration for achieving the goal of Chan.

Legend associates Bodhidharma with the *Laṅkāvatāra Sūtra* as a way of explaining the Chan experience of Awakening. As we have seen, the *Laṅkāvatāra* states that the foundation of the mind is the storehouse-consciousness that contains the *Tathāgata-garbha*, the Buddha-nature. When one attains a meditative state in which there are no thoughts, there can be a sudden "reversion of the foundation of consciousness" whereby the wisdom light of the pure Buddha-nature reveals itself. Chan teaches that to reach this sudden turning over of consciousness that reveals Buddha-nature, one must negate all ordinary distinctions and conceptualizations through meditative stillness of mind. Chan meditation is said to be able to still the mind's functioning in a one-pointed concentration that reaches the ground of consciousness. It is there that the pure wisdom nature of the mind's essence is revealed in a direct and sudden intuition of Awakening.

This goal of Chan practice was stated clearly in a stanza composed around the eleventh century and attributed to Bodhidharma:

> A special tradition outside the scriptures;
> With no dependence upon words and letters.
> A direct pointing into the mind;
> Seeing there one's own nature, and attaining Buddhahood.

The first two lines of this stanza imply that Chan does not emphasize the study of *sūtras* or attempt to harmonize the Buddhist scriptures as did Tiantai. Nor does Chan use words to compose high mystical tracts as did Huayan. Rather, as the last two lines imply, Chan guides, or "points," disciples through the inner levels of consciousness in order to discover their Buddha-nature and attain, thereby, Buddhahood.

In the fully developed legend, the Chan lineage was traced back from Bodhidharma to the historical Buddha himself. In this extended line of transmission, Bodhidharma was said to be the Twenty-Eighth Patriarch in India, and the First Patriarch in China. The legend also states that once when asked about the ultimate truth, Gautama Buddha held up a flower. Among his disciples, only Mahākāśyapa understood this gesture and received "from mind to mind" the "seal of the Buddha-mind." Mahākāśyapa is said to have personally passed this seal of sudden Awakening on in what became an Indian lineage that centuries later was brought to China by Bodhidharma. Legend also states that Bodhidharma brought the martial arts from India to China, where they were taught at a monastery said to have been founded by him, namely, the Shaolin Monastery (see Figure 7.4).

Moving now from legend to history, we come again to Hongren, the Chan master designated in legend to have been the Fifth Patriarch. Hongren was invited by Empress Wu to teach the Dharma at the imperial palace. This gave his East Mountain School some national prominence. It was the disciples of Hongren who claimed that he was the Fifth Patriarch in a lineage dating back to Bodhidharma. These disciples also claimed that one of Hongren's students, Shenxiu (c. 606–706), was the Sixth Patriarch. While the East Mountain School enjoyed some popularity in the capital, in 732 a monk named Shenhui (684–758) attacked the teachings of Shenxiu. Shenhui had been a student of Shenxiu, but when Shenxiu was called to the imperial court, Shenhui went to the south of China to study with another disciple of Hongren named Huineng (638–713).

In his attack on Shenxiu's school, Shenhui claimed that Shenxiu taught gradual Awakening rather then sudden Awakening. In fact Shenxiu taught that a gradual clearing of afflictions and defilements from the "pure mirror mind" was helpful in the attainment of sudden Awakening. Shenhui also claimed

FIGURE 7.4. Shaolin Temple (5th century) on Mt. Song in Henan Province, China, known for its association with the Chinese martial arts.

that Shenxiu's school was the "Northern School" of Chan and that Huineng had founded the "Southern School" of Chan which taught sudden Awakening. Shenhui went so far as to claim that Huineng was the true Sixth Patriarch of Chan Buddhism and that Huineng had Bodhidharma's robe, the symbol of Chan transmission. The result of Shenhui attack on the East Mountain School led to a period of sectarianism among the Chan schools. About a century later, the emperor called a council to settle the controversy, and Huineng was proclaimed the true Sixth Patriarch. The so-called Northern School of Chan continued only until the tenth century, while the Southern School gave life to a number of important Chan schools, two of which continue today.

Before introducing these schools, let us look at some verses from a Chinese text, the *Platform Sūtra of the Sixth Patriarch*. This text purports to convey the teachings of Huineng and provides a famous legend about how Huineng became the Sixth Patriarch. Indeed, partly because of this *sūtra*, Huineng is venerated as one of the greatest Chan figures in Chinese history.

> While I [Huineng] was a child, my father died and my elderly mother and I, her only child, moved to Nanhai. We suffered extreme poverty, and I sold firewood in the market place. By chance, a man bought some firewood. . . . Having received my money . . . I happened to hear another man reciting the *Diamond Sūtra*. Upon hearing it, my mind became clear and I attained Awakening.
>
> I asked the man, "Where do you come from with this *sūtra*?" He answered, "I pay reverence to the Fifth Patriarch, Hongren, at the East Mountain." . . . Hearing what he said, I realized that I was meant to hear him. I took leave of my mother [making arrangements for her] and went to East Mountain.
>
> Hongren asked me, "Where are you from, and why did you come to this mountain to pay reverence to me? What do you want from me?" I answered, "I am from [southern China]. . . . I have come a long distance to pay reverence to you. I ask for nothing but the Buddha's Dharma." The master reproved me saying, "If you are from [Southern China], then you are a barbarian. How can you become a Buddha?" I answered, "While people may be distinguished as northerners and southerners, there is neither north nor south in the Buddha-nature. The bodies of a barbarian and a monk are different; but what difference is there in Buddha-nature?". . . . Then a lay attendant ordered me to the rice-pounding area to pound rice. This I did for more than eight months.
>
> One day the Fifth Patriarch suddenly called his disciples to come to him. When they were assembled, he said, "Let me say this to you. Life and death are serious matters. You disciples are engaged all day in making offerings . . . and you make no effort to achieve freedom from this bitter sea of life and death. If you are still deluded about your true nature, how can these blessings save you? All of you return to your rooms . . . write a verse and present it to me. After I see the verses, I will give the robe [of the Patriarch] and the Dharma to the person who understands the true meaning [of the Dharma], and will appoint him to be the Sixth Patriarch."
>
> At midnight, the head monk, Shenxiu, holding a candle wrote a verse on the wall of the south corridor, without anyone knowing about it. The verse said:
>
> The body is the *Bodhi* Tree,
> The mind is like a bright mirror standing.

> Take care to wipe it diligently,
> Keep it free from all dust.
>
> The Fifth Patriarch said [to Shenxiu], "The verse you wrote shows that you still have not reached true understanding. You have merely arrived at the front gate, but you have not yet entered it. . . . You must enter the gate and see your own nature."
>
> One day, a young novice passed by the rice-pounding area reciting this verse. I knew as soon as I heard it that the person who had written it did not yet know his own nature. . . . I said to the novice, "I beg you to take me to the south corridor, so I can see this verse. . . . " [There], I made a verse and, since I could not write, I asked someone to write it on the wall of the west corridor, so that I might offer my own original mind. If you do not know the original mind, studying the Dharma is to no avail. If you know the mind and realize its true nature, then you will awaken to the true meaning [of the Dharma]. My verse read:
>
> *Bodhi* originally has no tree,
> The bright mirror is nowhere standing.
> Buddha-nature is forever clear and pure,
> Where can there be any dust?
>
> The Fifth Patriarch suddenly realized that I had understood the true meaning. . . . At midnight, the Fifth Patriarch called me into the hall, and expounded the *Diamond Sūtra* to me. As soon as I heard this, I was immediately awakened. That night the Dharma was imparted to me without anyone else knowing about it. Thus the Dharma of sudden Awakening and the robe were transmitted to me. The Fifth Patriarch said, "You are now the Sixth Patriarch. This robe is proof of transmission from generation to generation. But the Dharma must be transmitted from mind to mind. You must help people awaken to themselves. . . . But if you stay here, there are people who will harm you. So, you must leave at once." I set out at midnight with the robe and the Dharma. . . . After taking my leave, I set out for the south. (*Liuzu tanjing*, 2–4, 6–10)

In this story it is said that Awakening can be found within one's own body by gradually purifying the mirror mind by meditation so that no mental "dust" is present. Huineng, on the other hand, is said to have affirmed that Awakening is not something that arises from a mind that is purified, but suddenly from the Buddha-nature, which is inherently pure beyond the duality of mind and body. The *sūtra* claims that Shenxiu's experience of meditative purifying of the mind has brought him to the gate of Awakening. But Huineng's experience of the purity of Buddha-nature is Awakening itself. Elsewhere, the *Platform Sūtra* says more about Buddha-nature being the source of Awakening:

> The nature of humankind is originally pure. It is because of false thoughts that true suchness is obscured. If you are free from delusions, the original nature reveals itself. . . . As the *Vimalakīrti Sūtra* says, "At once, we gain clarity and recover the original mind." Good friends, when I was at Priest Hongren's place, as soon as I heard him [recite the *Diamond Sūtra*], I immediately gained great Awakening as I realized that true suchness was my original nature. (*Liuzu tanjing*, 18, 30–31)

By saying that Buddha-nature must reveal itself, the *sūtra* is not rejecting meditation. It is simply stating that Awakening is possible in any situation since it is not a product of mental purification. Rather, Awakening comes from our original Buddha-nature that can reveal itself anytime and anywhere. Here, Huineng is said to have experienced Awakening to Buddha-nature when he heard the recitation of the *Diamond Sūtra.* This story also indicates that Chan recognizes levels of Awakening and that the private interview with a Chan master is a central element to the process of Dharma transmission from "mind-to-mind."

To clarify the relationship between meditation (*samādhi*) and wisdom (*prajñā*) in light of his notion of Buddha-nature, the *sūtra* uses the distinction between essence and function. That is, meditation is not one thing that precedes and causes another thing called wisdom. Rather, because true meditation is the realizing of one's Buddha-nature, meditation is the very essence of wisdom, and wisdom is the functioning of meditation. This means that meditation and wisdom are not two different things, but a unity of the essence and functioning of Buddha-nature:

> Never mistakenly say that meditation and wisdom are different; they are a unity, and are not two different things. Meditation is itself the very substance of wisdom; and wisdom is itself the function of meditation. . . . Be careful not to say that meditation produces wisdom. . . . How then are meditation and wisdom alike? They are like a lamp and its light. If there is a lamp, there is light. . . . The lamp is the essence of light; and the light is the function of the lamp. (*Liuzu tanjing*, 13, 15)

The eighth century saw the collapsing of the Tang Dynasty, and the more intellectual forms of Chan in the capital cities began to lose their status. Other schools tracing themselves to Huineng began to rise up in rural areas, where a number of innovative Chan masters developed radical techniques to help their disciples awaken to their Buddha-nature. Among the most original of these Chan masters was Mazu (709–788). Mazu was said to have had a "remarkable appearance": He walked "like a bull" and glared "like a tiger." He was the first Chan master to use shouting and hitting mixed with paradoxical dialogue to trigger Awakening in his disciples. While he did not reject meditation, he helped Chan acquire a more practical approach focused on everyday life. In the context of daily living ("drawing water and chopping wood"), it was believed that one could find Awakening with the help of a master. This approach to Chan would later give rise to popular collections of biographies, sayings, conversations, and questions and answers of famous Chan masters. One of the most famous collections was the *Record of the Transmission of the Lamp* (1004).

In terms of Mazu's own Awakening, it is said that one day when he was sitting in meditation, his master asked him what he was doing. Mazu responded, "I wish to become a Buddha." The master then picked up a tile and began to grind it with a stone. Mazu asked his master what he was doing;

to which the master responded, "I am polishing this tile to make a mirror." Mazu replied, "No amount of polishing will ever make a mirror out of a tile." The master then said, "And no amount of cross-legged sitting will ever make a Buddha out of you." In other words, although meditation is valuable for producing a spiritual environment wherein Awakening can take place, this Awakening is the revealment of the Buddha-nature itself. In short, you cannot make yourself *become* a Buddha because you already *are* a Buddha.

As various techniques developed in Chan, the Southern School split into different subschools called the Five Houses. Of these five, two are of special historical importance and continue to be influential today. First is the Caodong School named for its two founders, Dongshan (807–869) and Caoshan (840–901). Instead of practicing unusual techniques, this school emphasizes silent meditation as the best means of fostering enlightenment. This silence is itself understood to be a living expression of the primal stillness of the Buddha-nature. Therefore, sitting in silent meditation is the living manifestation of one's original Awakening. Living one's Buddha-nature in silent meditation allows this original Awakening to gradually show itself in one's complete life. This approach is based on Huineng's own view that wisdom and meditation are really one reality. It is not that meditation leads to wisdom, but that meditation is itself the essence of wisdom. The Japanese Zen master Dōgen (1200–1253) introduced this form of Chan into Japan, where it is known as Sōtō Zen.

The second of the Five Houses that has had continued popularity is the Linji School, named after its founder Linji (died 867). This school aims at a more sudden attainment of Awakening by using various innovations pioneered by people like Mazu. They stress the use of paradoxical sayings called *gong'ans* (Japanese: *kōans*). The term *gong'an* means "public legal case," implying that the sayings used in Linji practice are authoritative "cases" for Chan practice. The *gong'an* stories contain a mysterious question, a paradoxical answer to a question, or an irrational phrase that can be used by the practitioner to set aside rational dualistic thought. By moving beyond conventional reason, and with guidance from a master, the person can become one with the quandary of the *gong'an* itself. Then, in a state of spiritual questing intensified by the *gong'an* practice, the sudden answer to the *gong'an* arises "like the sun from behind a cloud." Since one's very existence is identified with the *gong'an,* in this sudden insight one glimpses one's Buddha-nature as it reveals itself at the depth of one's questing mind. Collections of *gong'ans* became popular in China and the rest of East Asia. A Linji master named Yuanwu Kejin (1063–1135) wrote the famous *Blue Cliff Records* that records one hundred *gong'ans* with his commentary. Later, forty-eight selected *gong'ans* were compiled with commentary by Wumen Huikai (1183–1260) into *The Gateless Gate*, which is held in high regard in Japan.

The Linji sect and its *gong'an* practice had a formative influence on Korean Buddhism. Early on, the Korean monk Pŏmnang (fl. 632–646) studied Chan with Doxin (580–651), considered in legend to be the Fourth Patriarch. Pŏmnang brought Chan to Korea, where it is known as Sŏn Buddhism.

However, it did not really develop in Korea until the Linji sect was later introduced in the ninth century. Since that time, the Linji style has defined all forms of Korean Sŏn Buddhism. The Linji sect was also brought to Japan by Eisai (1141–1215), where it is known as Rinzai Zen.

The Pure Land School

The last of the great Chinese schools of Buddhism is the Jingtu ("Pure Land") School. Pure Land Buddhism, more than any other Chinese school, formed the devotional experience of Buddhism in China and throughout all East Asia. It is considered along with Chan to be a "practical school" because it sets aside more theoretical issues in order to stress practice. Pure Land Buddhism bases its teachings and practices on the *Land of Bliss Sūtras* composed in India. As we saw in Chapter 4, in those *sūtras* it is said that Dharmākara Bodhisattva traversed the Ten Stages of the bodhisattva's Great Journey to become Amitābha Buddha (Chinese: Amiktuofo; Japanese: Amida Butsu). In doing so, Amitābha fulfilled certain vows and gained the power necessary to create a Buddha realm referred to in China as the Pure Land. Through the realization of his vows, Amitābha also gained the power to enable people to be born in his Pure Land, where they can gain Awakening much more easily than in the human realm. Pure Land Buddhism stresses faith in this power of Amitābha to save humankind from rebirth into the realms of ignorance and suffering by bringing those who call on him to his Pure Land.

Pure Land Buddhism in China traces its roots back to when one of the *Land of Bliss Sūtras* was translated into Chinese in the second century C.E. Many scholars believe that the Pure Land tradition in China most likely developed from many sources of devotional practice. However, the tradition itself points, in what may be a more stylistic account, to three patriarchs as the primary founders of Pure Land Buddhism in China. The first acknowledged patriarch was Tanluan (476–542). Tanluan was once convalescing from an illness and had a vision of a heavenly gate opening to him. Inspired by this dream, he began to seek eternal life through the practice of Daoism. However, one day he met the Indian Buddhist monk, Bodhiruci, who arrived in Luoyang in 508. Bodhiruci introduced Tanluan to teachings about Amitābha Buddha and Pure Land piety. Tanluan converted, pursued Pure Land practice, and eventually wrote a book that unified the teachings of the *Land of Bliss Sūtras* with a sophisticated explanation of how to visualize and invoke Amitābha Buddha.

In his writings, Tanluan introduced some of the themes that would become foundational to Pure Land Buddhism. Tanluan was inspired by the Amitābha's eighteenth vow, which stated that "all beings" who think of the Amitābha Buddha for even one thought moment with sincerity and faith when they hear his name will be reborn into the Pure Land. Tanluan interpreted "all beings" to mean that not just saintly bodhisattvas, but even common persons, including sinners, can be reborn into the Pure Land through the help of Amitābha Buddha. With this possibility in mind, Tanluan distinguished between the "difficult" and "easy" paths to Awakening. Given that the human condition is affected by ignorance and defilements, practice based just on one's own efforts is the difficult path. This is especially the case in the age of the Degenerate Dharma. On the other hand, practice becomes the easy path if it is based on one's recognition and acceptance of the power of Amitābha Buddha and one's desire to be reborn in the Pure Land. This inspiration opened the doors to popular Pure Land devotionalism in China.

The task for Tanluan was to define what the "easy" practice should be that depends on the grace of Amitābha Buddha and results in birth in the Pure Land. Studying the Pure Land texts, Tanluan concluded that all beings, even evil persons, can be released from their defilements by reciting the name of Amitābha Buddha. Now, if this "recitation of the Buddha's name" (*Nianfo*) depends just on the efforts of the recitor, the results would be minimal. However, Tanluan believed that the effectiveness of the recitation was dependent on Amitābha Buddha himself. Tanluan claimed that the name of Amitābha Buddha itself embodies the Buddha reality for which it stands. To invoke Amitābha's name is to make present in one's life the Buddha reality it represents. To explain how this name could have the power to purify one's life, Tanluan likened it to a "*Maṇi* gem." Tradition teaches that if you throw such a gem into muddy water, the jewel cleanses the water of impurities. Tanluan taught that as the name *Amitābha* means "infinite light," and since the name embodies the reality it represents, then to recite this name brings its infinite light into one's life. Its brilliance, like with a *Maṇi* gem, penetrates the mind of the recitor, bringing it immeasurable wisdom-light that purifies it of ignorance and defilements.

Finally, Tanluan drew a distinction between "self power" and "Other power," which became fundamental for Pure Land thought. Self power refers to relying on one's own efforts in taking up a discipline and engaging in religious practice. This self-power attitude, Tanluan taught, manifests a certain pride and can actually reinforce the self-centeredness one is trying to overcome. On the other hand, by relying on Other power in one's practice, that is, on the action of Amitābha Buddha, one is humbly allowing oneself to be transformed. Tanluan identified five practices, called the Five Recollection Gates, that he considered helpful to this Pure Land practice: (1) prostration to Amitābha, (2) reciting his name, (3) resolving to be born in the Pure Land, (4) visualizing the Pure Land, and (5) sharing the benefits of the Pure Land. This latter practice means to share one's merit in this world and to be born again in this world to help others after gaining Awakening in the Pure Land.

The next great patriarch of Pure Land Buddhism was Daochuo (562–645). He, like Tanluan, had a deep concern for the plight of the common person. In fact, Daochuo converted to Pure Land Buddhism after visiting a monument praising Tanluan's devotion to spreading the Pure Land faith to the common people. Looking at the sheer numbers of persons who had not gained Awakening, the question that most bothered Daochuo was the following. If all persons have the Buddha-nature, and if they have certainly met a Buddha during their numberless past lives, then why do they continue to be reborn in this world of *duḥkha?* Referring to the image in the *Lotus Sūtra* of children caught in a burning house, Daochuo asked, why have so many people have not found a way to escape?

In answering this question, Daochuo makes a distinction between the Holy Path and the Pure Land Gate. The Holy Path refers to the Buddhist discipline of practicing morality and meditation to still the mind and purify oneself of defilements, and rooting out ignorance by gaining wisdom insight. This path to Awakening and Buddhahood makes for a long and arduous journey, especially in the age of the Degenerate Dharma. On the other hand, the Pure Land Gate can be entered even by a person who is still lost in ignorance and full of afflictions and defilements. Once in the Pure Land, the person can make the journey to Awakening and Buddhahood without any hindrances.

Daochuo concluded that the Pure Land Gate is the only viable way for people to gain liberation. Using the terms "self power" and "Other power," he felt that in the age of the Degenerate Dharma, the Holy Path of self power is not only difficult but is actually useless. The Other power of Amitābha Buddha leading through the Pure Land Gate was the exclusive way to liberation. Of Tanluan's Five Recollection Gates, Daochuo stressed the second, reciting the name of Amitābha Buddha. He is also credited with introducing prayer beads, later used in Pure Land piety throughout East Asia. Besides being known for his own ideas, Daochuo is also honored for being the teacher of the next patriarch of Pure Land Buddhism, Shandao (613–681). Shandao's teachings brought Chinese Pure Land thought to its peak.

When Shandao was twenty-nine, he met Daochuo and was impressed by his lectures. Converting to the Pure Land School, Shandao became its leading exponent in the capital of Chang'an. The foundation of Shandao's thought was his empathy with the sufferings of the common people and his awareness that this suffering is a function of the human condition. This condition, shared by all persons, is marked by defilements, afflictions, and erroneous views that are themselves the result of numerous past lifetimes in which evil actions were committed. Everyone has, during his or her many births, repeatedly killed or injured living beings, stolen from people, treated others unjustly, and spoken to or about others unkindly. Everyone has had evil thoughts, spoken evil words, and done evil actions, breaking all the Buddhist precepts.

Shandao taught that if a person is aware of his or her evil tendencies and actions in this life, even the most insignificant, and repents of these evils, he or she will begin to gain an insight into the shared human condition that is so flawed by the mistakes of past lives. Then, one can better turn with authentic repentance, true humility, and self-knowledge to Amitābha Buddha for his help. This turning to Other power is a matter of faith entrustment. Drawing on Pure Land texts, Shandao defined this faith, or faithful turning to Amitābha, as having three expressions of sincerity: a sincere or honest attitude, a deep mind of sincere faithfulness, and the sincere aspiration to be born in the Pure Land. This faith is nurtured by Pure Land practice. Shandao, following the teachings of Daochuo, stressed the recitation of the name of

Amitābha Buddha as the primary practice of Pure Land piety. All other practices were to be seen as auxiliary.

The following passages are taken from a work by Shandao. It presents his *Parable of the White Path* that illustrates Pure Land spirituality. Shandao first gives the parable, and then his explanation of its meaning:

> [Wishing to be reborn in the Pure Land] is like a man who desires to travel 100,000 *li* to the west. Suddenly . . . he sees two rivers. On the south is a river of fire; and on the north is a river of water. . . . Between the fire and water is a white path barely four or five inches wide, and 100 steps long. . . . The man is in the middle of a wasteland . . . and a horde of vicious ruffians and wild beasts seeing him there alone, vie with each other in their rush to kill him.
>
> [Facing death all around], he is seized with inexpressible terror. . . . Then he hears someone from the east bank call out encouraging him, "Friend, just resolutely follow this path and there will be no danger of death. . . . "And on the west bank, someone calls out, "Come straight on, single-minded and with a fixed purpose. I can protect you, so never fear falling into the fire or water."
>
> Hardly had he gone a step or two, and the horde of vicious ruffians calls to him, "Friend, come back! The way is too perilous, and you will never get across. Doubtlessly you will die. None of us mean you any harm." Though he hears their calling to him, the man does not look back, but straight-away proceeds single-minded on the path. In no time, he is on the west bank, forever far from all troubles. He is greeted by his good friend, and there is endless joy.
>
> The east bank is likened to this world. . . . The west bank is likened to the precious Land of Bliss. The ruffians and wild beasts, which seem to be friends, are likened to the six sense organs, six consciousnesses, six defilements, five aggregates, and four elements. The lonely wasteland is likened to the following of bad companions and not finding good and wise ones. The two rivers of fire and water are likened to attachment, like water, and aversion or hatred, like fire. The white path . . . is likened to the aspiration to be born in the Pure Land, which arises in the very midst of the passions of attachment and aversion. . . .
>
> The man on the path is likened to one who directs all his or her actions and practices towards the west [Pure Land]. Hearing the voices from the east . . . is like hearing Śākyamuni Buddha, who has disappeared from sight, but whose Dharma is still pursued, and therefore likened to "voices." The calling of the ruffians . . . is likened to teachings, practices and evil views that . . . lead people astray. . . . Someone calling from the west bank is likened to the vow of Amitābha. Reaching the west bank, being greeted by a good friend and rejoicing is likened to . . . attaining the Pure Land after death, where one is met by the Buddha, and knows unending bliss. (*Guan jing shu*)

As a footnote to this parable, it should be said that in Pure Land piety, reciting reciting "Namo Amituofo ("Praise to Amitābha Buddha") with the sincerity of a deep faith, attention, and seriousness brings the "infinite light" of Amitābha Buddha into the mind and heart of the practitioner in this world. Therefore, the spiritual journey of Pure Land Buddhism does not just lead through the Pure Land Gate after death. Rather, the Other power of Amitābha Buddha experienced within gives one a taste of the Pure Land even in this life. This experience can also translate into a more compassionate life of humility, gentleness, and kindness toward other beings. By the ninth century, even Chan recognized the positive fruits of Pure Land piety, and began to accept the practice of *nianfo.* Today, recitation of the name of Amitābha Buddha is practiced in Buddhist communities of all types in China. Pure Land practice also spread to Korea and Japan in the seventh century. In Japan, it was instituted into the Tendai (Chinese: Tiantai) School, and later became independent as two major Japanese Pure Land schools through the efforts of Hōnen (1133–1212) and his disciple Shinran (1173–1262).

PERSECUTION AND DECLINE

We can now see that the Tang Dynasty (618–907) is considered to be the high point of Buddhism in China. The great masters of Huayan and Pure Land Buddhism, namely, Fazang and Shandao, lived during that time period. This was also called the "Golden Age of Chan." During this Golden Age, Moshan Liaoran (ca. 800) became the master and abbess of Moshan Monastery. She is the most famous woman Chan master, and she taught both men and women. Her teacher was Gao'an Dayu, who was taught by a student of the great Mazu. Dayu is said to have brought Linji to Awakening. Linji's famous student, Guanxi Zhixian, later studied under Moshan. She is the only woman Chan master to be mentioned in the *Record of the Transmission of the Lamp;* and she was quoted in the *Shōbōgenzō,* written by Eihei Dōgen, the founder of Sōtō Zen in Japan. It was also during the Tang Dynasty that the famous monk Xuanzang (602–644) went on a pilgrimage over the Silk Road to India to find more Buddhist scriptures. He spent seventeen years traveling, and when he returned home translated seventy-five *sūtras* and wrote the *Great Tang Record of the Western Regions* that recounted his journey. This text was the basis for *Journey to the West*, written in 1596, which is one of the great classics of Chinese literature.

While the various schools of Buddhism flourished in China during much of the Tang Dynasty, the Buddhist Saṅgha became quite wealthy. It used national resources to construct huge Buddha statues, and its monastic institutions were exempt from taxation. As the national economy was more and more affected by Buddhist institutions, there was pressure to "purify" the Saṅgha. When the Empress Wu (c. 625–706), who had patronized Buddhism, was driven from the throne, the new emperor, Xuanzong (ruled 712–756), moved against the Buddhist Saṅgha. He laicized about one-fourth of the monastics who were on the imperial rosters. However, the most severe persecution took place a century later under Emperor Wuzong (ruled 840–846). Influenced by Daoism, he attempted actually to destroy Buddhism in China. From 842 to 845, he ordered the destruction of a vast number of Buddhist temples, the confiscation of much of the Saṅgha's property and holy objects, and the laicization of most monks and nuns.

Although this great persecution ended when the emperor died in 846, some schools of Buddhism disappeared and others were greatly weakened.

Of the scholarly schools that depended on monastic libraries only Huayan and Tiantai survived, although severely damaged. Chan was not so badly affected because it did not depend on libraries and was centered in more remote regions of China where the emperor's decrees were less effective. Pure Land also survived with little damage because it was not monastic centered but depended on support of laypeople. After the earlier persecutions, Buddhism had always made a remarkable recovery. But after the persecution of 845, no such recovery was achieved. In fact, even with government support, Buddhism entered a process of decline.

The Song Dynasty (970–1279) began with renewed support for Buddhism. The first Song emperor undertook the Buddhist layperson's vows and encouraged religion in many ways. He ordered the first printing of the Chinese *Tripiṭaka*, which was written on 130,000 wooden printing-blocks; the task took eleven years. Succeeding Song emperors were also helpful to Buddhism. By the thirteenth century, there were almost a half million monks and nuns and around 40,000 temples. Song rulers created monastic estates, which they divided for three purposes. A few were *Vinaya* monasteries for training in the precepts and ordination. A larger number were teaching monasteries dedicated to the formal study of doctrines and texts. The majority of monasteries were for meditation, headed by Chan monastics. This system gave raise to the Three Traditions, whereby a mōnastic was identified by ordination lineage, lineage of meditation training, and doctrinal lineage.

With government support, two Buddhist schools managed to remain active during the Song Dynasty. Pure Land Buddhism increased in numbers as Pure Land Societies sprang up all over China. Chan temples increased in numbers and became involved in the social and political life of the nation. In this way, Pure Land and Chan contributed to Chinese culture, inspiring Chinese art and literature. There were also efforts to develop a closer relation among the existing Buddhist schools. Here, too, Chan played an active role in finding a common ground that would harmonize meditation, devotion, and study. Chan masters began studying the totalistic ideas of Huayan and the unifying teachings of Tiantai. Chan practitioners also saw affinities between mental concentration in meditation and in the invocation of Amitābha Buddha.

It was also during this time that there developed what is known as Literary Chan with its many written collections of *gong'ans.* On the other hand, an important reaction to this literary approach to the *gong'an* came from Dahui Zonggao (1089–1163), who became the dominant figure of the Linji tradition during the Song period. Dahui studied the records of the Five Houses of Chan as well as existing collections of *gong'ans* as a young monk. However, this intellectual understanding did not bring him to Awakening. He began serious *gong'an* practice and on May 13, 1125, he broke through to Awakening. Dahui become abbot of a monastery in the Southern Song capital and his community of monks and lay followers grew to more than 2,000. He became known as the most important Buddhist figure in the Southern Song dynasty. Dahui rejected the practice of silent sitting in meditation as useless to the attainment of Awakening. He taught that to reach Awakening, a "Great Doubt" is necessary in *gong'an* practice. This doubt that is generated by the paradox of a *gong'an* must spread to all life and death prior to sudden Awakening. Dahui is also famous for rejecting the literary study of *gong'ans* as useless to attaining Awakening. To make his point, he had all copies of the *Blue Cliff Record gong'an* collection, as well as the wooden blocks needed to print them, destroyed. It would take 200 years for this famous collection to come back into circulation. Dahui's *gong'an* training method greatly influenced the Linji tradition in China, Korea, and Japan; and his notion of Great Doubt was used some 500 years later by Hakuin Ekaku, the famous Japanese Rinzai Zen master.

Even with government support and these notable accomplishments, Buddhism entered a time of decline in China during the Song Dynasty. Scholars identify two major causes, one internal and the other external. Within the Saṅgha, there was a certain moral and spiritual degeneration caused in part by the government's sale of ordination certificates. The Song Dynasty was threatened by invasions along its northern frontiers. This threat resulted in huge military expenses, as well as annual payments to the northern barbarians. The government had also greatly increased its costly bureaucracy. To meet these expenses, the government decided to sell ordination certificates, which up until that time had been issued to monastics when they were officially ordained and had passed an examination. These certificates exempted the holder from taxation and labor service required of citizens. Under the new policy, even a layperson could purchase such a certificate to avoid taxation or labor service. Others who were criminals or just lazy could use the certificate to seek refuge in monasteries where they would be safe and cared for without any expense or labor service. This policy brought many undesirable persons with no interest in Buddhism into the Saṅgha, contributing to the moral and spiritual decay of the community, which lost respect in the eyes of the Chinese society.

The external cause of the decay of Buddhism in China at this time was the rise of Neo-Confucianism as the unifying force behind Song culture and society. This new form of Confucianism criticized Buddhism for its doctrines as well as its lack of social responsibility. Neo-Confucianism inspired the important thinkers of the age to reclaim China's classical heritage, thus restoring Confucianism to prominence in Chinese culture. Instead of discussing such notions as emptiness and Buddha-nature, Neo-Confucianism focused on reason, the formative forces of nature, the moral potential of the human mind, and the ethical nature of humanness. Because Confucianists eventually controlled the educational system as well as the social service examination system, Buddhism seemed much less attractive to the educated classes in China, and very few entered the Saṅgha.

LATER DEVELOPMENTS

The Yuan Dynasty (1280–1368) of the Mongols, who ruled China from the new capital in Beijing, favored the Tibetan form of Buddhism. The Mongols understood that they needed the cooperation of the masses of China to have a stable government. But they could not embrace either Confucianism or Daoism given the views of those religions concerning Chinese superiority and barbarian inferiority. Buddhism, on the other hand, considered all people as equals, and Tibetan Buddhism had a cultural connection with the Mongolian nation. During this dynasty, Buddhist culture did not advance in China. In fact, secret Buddhist-related societies, such as the Maitreya Society and the White Lotus Society, became quite active. These groups were actually political entities that fomented political rebellions.

One uprising led by Zhu Yuanzhang was successful in overthrowing the Mongols in 1368. Zhu who had formerly been a Buddhist monk, then founded the Ming ("Enlightened") Dynasty (1368–1644). He encouraged Buddhist ordination, and the Saṅgha grew due to this support. Following the pattern of the Three Traditions, the monasteries during the Ming Dynasty were divided into three types: the Chan meditation training centers, the monasteries dedicated to study of the *sūtras*, and the "instruction" monasteries. This last category, an extension of the *Vinaya* institutions, included rituals, prayers, and Tantric ceremonies for the welfare of the common people.

One of the leaders of Ming Buddhism was Zhuhung (1535–1615). Zhuhung, who practiced Pure Land Buddhism and was trained under Huayan, Tiantai and Chan masters, played an important role in a movement to harmonize the different schools of Chinese Buddhism. This movement was one of the significant features of Ming Buddhism. Zhuhang taught that the two major schools of practice, Pure Land and Chan, both focus the mind in meditation or recitation on ultimate reality, which he called "Absolute Mind." This Absolute Mind is ever pure of all passions and defilements, free from all illusions and ignorance, and is the essence of Awakening itself. Zhuhang taught that both Huayan and Tiantai teach about this nature of mind that embraces all phenomena. In this attempt to bring a greater unity between the schools, the common ground included the state of mind that is conducive to advancement in the spiritual life, as well as the foundation of that advancement, namely, the Absolute Mind. In the broader movement toward harmonization, it was not uncommon for Chan practitioners to recite the name of Amitābha Buddha, for Pure Land practitioners to practice meditation, and for both to study the *sūtras*.

Another activity of Zhuhung that contributed to a second feature of Ming Buddhism was his work for the laity. Given its degeneration during the Song and Yuan Dynasties, many people did not wish to join the Saṅgha, but wanted to practice Buddhism as laypersons. This interest led during the Ming Dynasty to the growth of Pure Land piety as well as new forms of lay activities and the printing and distribution of its Buddhist texts. Pure Land devotional experience expressed in the fine arts also made lasting contributions to Chinese culture, especially in literature and poetry. Zhuhung himself supported the formation of lay Buddhists according to Buddhist principles and practices adapted to their daily life.

Under the Manchu emperors of the Qing Dynasty (1644–1912), Buddhism was also supported, especially the Linji branch of Chan and Tibetan Buddhism.

Support of the latter won allegiance from the Mongols and Tibetans. The importance given to Tibetan Buddhism can be seen in the fact that the Beijing Edition of the Tibetan *Tripiṭaka* was completed in 1724, and only later was the Dragon Edition of the Chinese *Tripiṭaka* completed under imperial auspice in 1738, with a Manchu translation completed in 1790.

Activity among the Buddhist laity also continued during the Manchu Dynasty. This was especially true after the Taiping rebellion (1851–1865), during which the rebels destroyed Buddhist images, texts, and temples wherever they went. In response, Buddhist laypersons played crucial roles in reviving the tradition through publishing and disseminating Buddhist literature. Yang Wenhui (1837–1911) brought Buddhist texts from Japan and founded the Chinling Sūtra Publishing Center to print and disseminate Buddhist material throughout China. This kind of publication work was complemented by other Buddhist lay organizations dedicated to social and cultural renewal.

With the fall of the Manchu Dynasty in 1911 and the establishment of the Republic of China, many intellectual leaders saw Buddhism as a part of the premodern Chinese culture that must be set aside to facilitate the modern development of the nation. This opinion was reinforced some ten years later by the introduction of Marxism. To counter this attack on Buddhism, Taixu (1890–1947) inspired a reform movement that had wide-ranging consequences. Taixu promoted an educational program that founded schools where modern secular subjects were taught along with traditional Buddhist scholarship in Western-style classes. He also founded a number of new institutes to educate Buddhist monastic and lay leaders. Taixu's reforms stressed the regeneration of the monastic life and the dedication of monastic structures to aid the needy in society. He developed new contacts with Buddhists in other countries and supported the notion of a closer fellowship of Buddhists around the world. Finally, he supported the study of Buddhist texts and doctrines and the publication of Buddhist books and periodicals.

This kind of Buddhist renewal in mainland China was cut short when communism took control in 1949. In the 1950s, Saṅgha land holdings were confiscated, most monasteries and temples were closed, younger monks and nuns were laicized, older monastics were forced to work, and a governmental Chinese Buddhist Association was established to oversee the remaining Buddhist communities. During the Cultural Revolution (1966–1976), Buddhist buildings and works of art were destroyed. However, the government safeguarded many of the famous Buddhist temples and works of art during the Cultural Revolution, and afterward it rebuilt many other temples and religious sites. More recently, as we see in the essay at the conclusion of this chapter, there has been a renewal of interest in Buddhism in China (see Figure 7.5). Many people in China have been converting to Buddhism, which has had a renewal of its own during the past few decades. This renewal has been inspired by the new Buddhist movements that had been developing in Taiwan during the latter half of the twentieth century that were themselves inspired by Taixu.

FIGURE 7.5. Statue of Amoghasiddhi Buddha at Bolin Monastery, Hong Kong, completed in 1993 and named the Tiantan Buddha since the model for its base is the Temple of Heaven (Tiantan) in Beijing.

Box 7.2

A Nun's Story

When I joined the Buddhist order at the age of twenty, I was still a student in law school. My sudden renunciation was beyond my parents' comprehension; therefore, they opposed my decision.

I recall that my father, whose thinking is strongly influenced by Confucianism, challenged me by asking a question: "Being a nun living in a monastery, how are you going to repay your debt of gratitude to family, school, and society, all of which have raised you and have provided for your education?"

I replied to him that by joining the order without a future family of my own, I could devote myself completely to helping society. My father did not say a word, but I knew that he was wondering how I could be of help to society living as a nun.

Afterward, I did not give up my study of the law; instead, my order supported me in finishing law school and then going to the United States for further education. When I received my doctoral degree from Yale University, my parents, as well as my eldest brother and sister, who both represented my other siblings, flew to the East Coast to attend my graduation. On this occasion, my father told me that he was very proud of me. Due to my accomplishment, my parents received the Father and Mother of the Year Awards in my hometown.

Being a Buddhist nun in Taiwan, especially as a member of Fo Guang Shan, I was fully ordained, received both a clerical and a secular education, and have the opportunity to teach at universities outside the monastery. Through participating in the educational process in Taiwan, I can make a positive contribution to society.

My teacher, the Venerable Master Hsing Yün, advocates "Humanistic Buddhism," a teaching that brings Buddhism into society. Spiritual cultivation is not the sole prerogative of monks and nuns in a monastery, but it is considered a necessary element for humanizing our society. Society should not be seen as just a source of temptation, and thus as an obstacle to spiritual cultivation. On the contrary, society should serve as the soil for nourishing spirituality. From the viewpoint of Humanistic Buddhism, witnessing suffering in society generates compassion. Facing and overcoming temptation in society means not to shy away from desire, but to encounter it without being tainted by It. Training oneself to attain equanimity does not require a solitary place to hide, but rather a peaceful and unmovable mind in the midst of the social turmoil of the world.

Humanistic Buddhism, from which I myself have benefited deeply, provides a philosophy that encourages me to walk into society, keeping social commitment and spiritual cultivation in balance.

VEN. DR. YIFA
Fo Guang Shan Monastery

NEW CHINESE BUDDHIST MOVEMENTS

In 1949, when the Republic of China was established in Taiwan, some of the senior Buddhist leaders in mainland China moved to the island. Since that time, Taiwan has experienced a Buddhist revival. There are now thousands of Buddhist temples and organizations in Taiwan, and many of these organizations have been sending missionaries overseas. More than 10,000 men and women monastics were ordained between 1951 and 1987. Of these new monastics, between 60 and 70 percent are women.

Perhaps the best known of these woman monastics is the Ven. Cheng Yen, founder of the largest charitable organization in Taiwan, the Compassion Relief Tzu Chi Foundation. When Cheng Yen was twenty-three years old, she left home to become a Buddhist nun. Her teacher was the highly revered Dharma Master Yin Shun. Living simply and pursuing a life of helping the poor, Cheng Yen became convinced and taught that the reason there is so much strife in the world is that people have not awakened to an innate and universal love. If they did awaken to and act out that love, this world, she teaches, will become a "Pure Land of peace and joy." Cheng Yen says, "If we remember that all creatures in the universe are one, we will know how to let go of our egotism. . . . We will then return to the true, clear essence of our human nature, and from the depths of our hearts will arise a reverent love for all beings."[1]

In 1966, Cheng Yen founded the Tzu Chi Compassion Relief Association to help the poor. In 1980, she founded the Tzu Chi Foundation with its eight missions. First is charity work, whereby the members provide food and other necessities as well as medical care and spiritual support to those in need. Second, the Tzu Chi medical care network includes hospitals, and a system of mobile free clinics. Their doctors are trained to treat the patients as they would a member of their own family. The third mission is an educational system from kindergarten to graduate schools. Fourth is a cultural mission that publishes books, magazines, and newspapers that bring their values to a broader audience. They also have a cable television station in Taiwan that broadcasts true stories of compassion and service. The fifth mission of Tzu Chi, their bone-marrow donor registry, is now the world's third largest. Tzu Chi has handled transplants worldwide. The sixth mission is their international relief work. They have traveled to Mainland China, Cambodia, Rwanda, Ethiopia, Afghanistan, Kosovo, and more than fifty other countries. The final two mission areas are environmental protection and community volunteerism. In all these eight missions, Tzu Chi members are inspired by the bodhisattva ideal and try to live by the teachings of the Buddha. They seek to change the world by starting with themselves. From just thirty original members in Taiwan, Tzu Chi now includes over four million members throughout the world.

Another large new Buddhist organization in Taiwan is the Fo Guang Shan Buddhist Order. Founded by Grand Master Hsing Yun, Fo Guang Shan has millions of followers and has established temples in Taiwan and other

Box 7.3

Religion and Love

Whenever someone asks me for a definition of religion, I reply that it is an education in the purpose of life. What we call Buddhism is in fact the teachings of the enlightened sage Śākymuni Buddha that guide us along the path toward attaining release, peace, and joy.

Far from stressing the abstruse or esoteric, these teachings instruct us to "actually go and do." While caring for humanity and all living beings we become aware of our own shortcomings and learn bravely to face worldly suffering. From this, love and wisdom arise, and the long-indifferent heart softens.

Therefore, all Tzu Chi people and I make the same wish each year, asking not for good health, but for wisdom and clarity; asking not for a lighter burden, but for greater strength; asking not for everything to go as one wishes, but for perseverance and courage.

Life without love is swathed in darkness. Only love equally and selflessly given can transcend political, racial, cultural, and religious boundaries. Hence, I sincerely want to extend my gratitude and respect to all those who have made contributions and have striven for a better world. Respect for the glory of all life immediately allows every person to become a compassionate living Buddha.

When a drop of water falls in the midst of a desert, it quickly evaporates without a trace. However, were it to fall into an ocean, that same drop of life would never dry up. May the love in each of us converge into a vast ocean of love, which can then be given to everyone in the world without end.

DHARMA MASTER CHENG YEN
Buddhist Compassion Relief Tzu Chi Foundation
Taiwan

countries. In the United States, their central site is the Hsi Lai Temple in Hacienda Heights, California.

Hsing Yun entered Buddhist monastic life at the age of twelve. He went on to become the forty-eighth Patriarch of the Linji lineage of Chan Buddhism in China. When Hsing Yun went to Taiwan, he did not just propagate traditional Chan Buddhism. Given his experience of war and poverty in China, he sought to revitalize Buddhism, making it more responsive to the needs of the modern world. Hsing Yun developed what he calls "Humanistic Buddhism," which seeks to link religious practice with ethical daily living and working for positive social change. The following are Hsing Yun's words about his approach to Buddhist living and its relationship to Humanistic Buddhism. Note his reference to Taixu.

> Living in our bustling, intense, turbulent, and chaotic contemporary society, we need to find something that can set our impetuous minds at ease. . . . Chan reflects wisdom, humor, and compassion. It can prevent the formation of wishful

and vexing thoughts. Guided by the ease, humor, profundity, and liberating nature of Chan, one will not be bothered by unkind words, awkward behavior, or painful memories of the past. They will simply vanish like mist and smoke.

Chan raises life to the level of art. It manifests the perfection of life by revealing the original nature that underlies all phenomena. Chan's exquisite teaching is not confined to temples. . . . It belongs to every family and to every human being. Everyone is in need of its wisdom, spontaneity, freedom, and ethics in his or her daily life.

Chan, if applied in our daily lives, would be like a ship in the sea of suffering. It would be like a bright light in the darkness. At the same time, it would serve as true medicine for the illnesses of our world.

People in the world focus their lives on materialism, personal interests, fame, and power. They do not realize that all such matters are in constant flux. Therefore, how can they dwell in peace?

Chan is not a theory, but rather, it is life. When Chan is implemented into daily life, people will respect and dwell in harmony with each other.

Where is the Pure Land for a Chan practitioner? It is in the performing of lowly tasks. It is in the love for and salvation of others. It is also in the transformation of one's surroundings.[2]

Humanistic Buddhism is not a new kind of Buddhism: it is simply a name used to emphasize the core teachings of the Buddha. The Buddha taught wisdom and compassion. These teachings always lead us back to the lives of other sentient beings. To not understand the unity of human nature and Buddha nature is to not understand the teachings of the Buddha. Humanistic Buddhism encourages us to participate in the world and be a source of energy that is beneficial to others. Our enlightenment depends on others, just as their enlightenment depends of us. Master Taixu said that we can achieve Buddhahood *only* by fulfilling our humanity.[3]

Fo Guang Shan emphasizes the need for Buddhism to meet people's spiritual and physical needs here and now to build the Pure Land in this world. Thus, in Taiwan, thousands of monks and nuns of the order work together with committed and well-educated lay members in a number of projects for the betterment of Taiwan society and for world peace. They have a free medical clinic with mobile units to reach remote villages. They also have founded orphanages, homes for the elderly, social service agencies that provide food and clothing to the poor, and wildlife areas for the benefit of other living beings. Given their belief that education is a way to better people's lives, they have libraries, Buddhist universities, Buddhist colleges, elementary and high schools, as well as Sunday schools, adult education programs, and summer education camps for youths. Through their Buddha's Light International Society (BLIS), they also support human development internationally. This international action is seen by them as a way of contributing to the Pure Land here on earth. To achieve this ideal, BLIS stresses the need to work together with all forms of Buddhism in a kind of Buddhist ecumenism that respects diversity while emphasizing harmony between different traditions and practices. BLIS recognizes that Buddhists can build unity with each other for the good of humankind, but they also need to build unity with other religious traditions that are working for world peace.

We can also see the direct influence of Taixu in the Dharma Drum Mountain organization in Taiwan. One of Taixu's disciples was Dongchu, a prominent Chan monk in China. When Dongchu moved to Taiwan, he founded the Chung-Hwa Institute of Buddhist Culture and the Nong Chan monastery. Dongchu's Dharma heir was Sheng Yen, who went on to found Dharma Drum Mountain, a complex of monasteries and educational centers. The educational complex includes the original Chung-Hwa Institute as well as Dharma Drum Sangha University for monastic training, the Dharma Drum Buddhist College for monastic and lay courses in Buddhist Studies, and the new Dharma Drum University that provides broader educational opportunities and degree programs.

Blending spiritual practice in the Chan tradition with educational programs that teach how to embody practice and knowledge of the Dharma into daily life, Dharma Drum Mountain has developed ethical programs and social campaigns as expressions of humanistic Buddhism. Its Six Ethics of the Mind Campaign teaches how to develop one's character in the context of family, school, environment, workplace, pluralistic society, and daily life. The morality of this ethical training is based on the loving kindness and compassion of the bodhisattva lived in interpersonal relationships in ways that lead to personal growth and to building the Pure Land on earth. Sheng Yent's ideal was also to convey education through concrete acts of charity. The Dharma Drum Mountain Social Welfare and Charity Foundation offers services, including, among other things, emergency relief, home care, and learning assistance for youth.

While these kinds of new Chinese Buddhist movements were growing in Taiwan and spreading globally, Buddhism in China has been going through similar changes. In recent decades, Chinese Buddhist organizations have also been growing and "humanistic Buddhism" has become popular. In the following essay, Dedong Wei describes the traditional Buddhist practices that have long been popular in China, and then presents the new forms of Buddhist social engagement in China.

The Cultural Experience of Chinese Buddhism Today

Dedong Wei
Institute of Buddhism and Religious Theory, Renmin University, Beijing, China

Buddhist rituals in contemporary China form a complex system that is in the midst of change. On the one hand, they carry forward the heritage of a 2,000-year-old tradition, embodying a confluence of Indian Buddhist customs and China's own particular culture. On the other hand, they interact with movements of modernization in contemporary China to give rise to ever-new forms of Buddhist action. We begin by surveying the traditional practices popular in Chinese Buddhist culture, and then look at some newer forms of practice and cultural contributions.

TEMPLE RITUALS

Morning and evening scripture chanting is a Buddhist activity that a monastery's or temple's resident monastics and laypeople must do every morning and early evening. This is the most basic form of self-cultivation for Buddhists, and includes reciting scriptures and *mantras*, worship of the Three Refuges, and chanting of praises. Laypeople from the surrounding communities can attend these daily rituals, too.

Morning recitations are usually held every day between 4:00 A.M. and 7:00 A.M., the actual time varying from one monastery or temple to the next. At the appointed time, all gather in the Great Shrine Hall and recite the *Śūramgama Mantra*, the *Great Compassion Mantra*, the *Ten Small Mantras*, and the *Heart Sūtra* once each, accompanied by Buddhist music and chants at the beginning and the end. Among these, the *Śūramtgama Mantra* is the longest and its recitation becomes a service in itself. The *Great Compassion Mantra* and the *Ten Small Mantras* can be combined into one service as well. So monasteries and temples will usually only do one of these services per day and will rotate these services on alternate days. On festival days, both services will be performed. In all cases, recitation of the *Heart Sūtra* is required.

Evening scripture recitation usually takes place between 6:00 P.M. and 8:00 P.M., and there are three services. The first involves the *Amitābha Sūtra* and the recitation of the Buddha's name for the purposes of seeking rebirth in the Pure Land. The second involves worship of the eighty-eight Buddhas and recitation of the Great Confession and Repentance to give an accounting of one's own past sins and one's intention to repent. This service extinguishes guilt and is generally recited while kneeling. The third is the Meng Mountain Ritual of Offering Food, in which a cup of water and a few grains of rice are offered to other types of living beings. Evening recitation also includes a poetic warning: "This day has passed; and my life is accordingly lessened. Like a fish in shallow water, what pleasure have I? The great mass [of beings] must work diligently and with energy, as if their head were on fire. Only reflect on impermanence, and do not slacken!"

The ritual of Receiving and Reciting the Precepts is an excellent tradition that is of benefit in preserving both the purity and the solidarity of the Saṅgha. Contemporary Chinese Buddhism still follows this ancient system. The monks or nuns gather twice a month and ask those who are perfectly familiar with the *Vinaya* to recite the precepts so that they may compare them to their own conduct. If it is found that they are in violation of the precepts, they should confess and repent their infractions before the assembly to add to their "roots of goodness."

"Passing the Hall" refers to the monastics of a monastery gathering for meals. It is not simply a matter of eating but is seen as a Buddhist worship service, and the whole process is elegant and solemn. After the introduction of Buddhism into China, the Indian Buddhist custom of begging food never went into general practice, and monastics usually took their meals inside their monasteries. The system of Passing the Hall developed from this fact.

During mealtime, talking is prohibited, utensils must be used in such a way as to maintain silence, and one may not make any noise. If one wants more food, one signals by leaning one's chopsticks. After eating, one places one's two bowls at the edge of the table, with the chopsticks in between.

The ceremony of "Worshiping all Buddhas" is a way of expressing wishes for a loved one, or for liberating a deceased loved one. Thus, the ceremony is divided into either "Worshiping all Buddhas for the extension of life" or "Worshiping all Buddhas for the attainment of rebirth [in the Pure Land]." This is an important way that Buddhist temples serve the larger community. The ritual of worshiping all Buddhas for the extension of life expresses the wish that a person might attain good fortune, long life, and good health while avoiding all calamities. The ritual for attainment of rebirth is done for the sake of a person's deceased relatives so that they may turn and enter the Pure Land. In most modern temples, this is done in conjunction with the regular morning and evening scripture recitations. Performing the ritual of Worshiping all Buddhas during regular scripture recitations takes little time, is simple and convenient, and can be done every day. So it is very popular among Chinese Buddhists today and is an important source of temple income.

"Making offerings" at the temples or monasteries is a popular practice for laypeople, too. It means that one places fresh flowers, fruit, or other items before images of the Buddhas and patriarchs as a demonstration of sincere reverence. On some special occasions, like on New Year's Eve, one must go to all of the shrine halls to make offerings to all the Buddhas. On those occasions, the process can take almost half the day. Also in China, Four Famous Mountains (Putuo, Jiuhua, Emei, and Wutai) are considered special abodes for making offerings to bodhisattvas: Avalokiteśvara at Guanyin, Kṣitigarbha at Dizang, Samantabhadra at Puxian, and Mañjuśrī at Wenshu. The desire for pilgrimage to these sites has exerted a powerful influence on the common folk. Thus, the festival days connected with these four bodhisattvas are especially crowded with worshipers.

The Chinese often say, "People are not holy immortals, how can they be without faults?" When one has done wrong, one needs to confess and repent. With regard to oneself, one ought to confess faults; in regard to others, one needs to seek forgiveness. From this sort of repentance and confession, Chinese Buddhism developed a special kind of ritual called the "Service of *Sūtra* Repentance," which is also a service of chanting Buddhist scriptures to avert calamities. Today, this service is done for both monastics and laypeople. When doing this service for laypeople, it is acceptable to collect payment, and so in recent times this has become an important means of income.

BUDDHIST FESTIVALS

The "Festival of Bathing the Buddha" memorializes the day of Śākyamuni Buddha's birth and takes place on the eighth day of the fourth month in the lunar calendar. As is recorded in the Buddhist scriptures, after the Buddha was born, celestial maidens scattered flowers from the sky, and nine dragons spouted water to bathe the prince's body. Accordingly, every year on the Buddha's birthday, all Chinese Buddhist temples hold a celebration. Within the Great Shrine Hall, a basin of water is offered before an image of the baby Buddha, and all the resident monastics in the temple and laypersons also scoop out water in a small spoon and pour it over the image's head, symbolically bathing the Buddha. The image represents a child a few feet tall in a standing position, with the left hand pointing to heaven and the right hand pointing to the earth. When the ceremony is over, the participants dedicate the merit to others, chant the Three Refuges, and conclude by worshiping the Buddha.

The "12-8 Festival" memorializes the day on which Śākyamuni Buddha attained enlightenment. In China, it developed into a major public festival among the common people. The 12–8 Festival takes place on the eighth day of the twelfth lunar month, customarily regarded as the day on which Śākyamuni Buddha attained liberating wisdom. Just as a young woman offered Śākyamuni some milk and millet porridge, so Chinese Buddhists make some rice and fruit porridge and offer it before the Buddha statue on that day. Many temples will cook large quantities of rice porridge in a big pot at the same time that the celebration is taking place, which they then distribute free of charge to the congregation to show how auspicious it is.

The "*Ullambana* Festival" is held on the fifteenth day of the seventh lunar month to liberate ancestors and relatives from the condition of being hungry ghosts. As recorded in the *Ullambana Sūtra*, the Buddha's disciple, *Maudgalyāyana*, through his power of the divine eye was able to see that his mother had been reborn as a hungry ghost. *Maudgalyāyana* filled his begging bowl with rice and sent it to her, but because of her evil karma, the rice turned into fire and she could not eat any of it. *Maudgalyāyana* was distraught and asked the Buddha to teach him a method for rescuing her. The Buddha told *Maudgalyāyana* to gather the monks on the fifteenth day of the seventh lunar month and have them honor the Three Refugees with offerings of many kinds of food and drink. This would rescue parents to seven generations back from being a hungry ghost and enable them to gain rebirth in the realms of humans or gods. Today, Buddhists in China celebrate this festival by making vegetarian offerings to the Buddhas and the monastics as repayment for their parents' kindness in giving them food. At the same time, they make offerings to the hungry ghosts of melons, fruit, noodles, cakes, tea, and rice. The *Ullambana* Festival is today an important temple activity, with scripture chanting during the day and offerings to the ghosts in the evening; many people participate.

POPULAR BUDDHIST PRACTICES

Among the most solemn rites in Chinese Buddhism is the "The Victorious Meeting for Universal Liberation on Water and Land by Sages and Worldlings of the Dharma Realm Through Great Oblations," or for short, the

"Water-Land Dharma Meeting." In the full name, the term "Dharma Realm" indicates the complete equality of the primal nature of both Buddhas and ordinary beings. "Sages and Worldlings" means the four types of holy beings (Buddhas, bodhisattvas, śrāvakas, and pratyekabuddhas) and the six types of worldly beings (gods, humans, asuras, hell beings, hungry ghosts, and animals) and is intended to indicate all living beings in a general sense. "Water and Land" points to all the places where living beings experience recompense for past karma. "Universal Liberation" means the release of all the beings. "Great Oblations" indicates the offering of vegetarian food. "Victorious Meeting" means that both the liberators and those who are liberated all come together in one hall.

The primary reason for holding a Water-Land Dharma Meeting is, through the enormous power of the Buddha-Dharma and by means of offerings of food and Dharma-teachings, to rescue all living beings, especially those who have fallen into rebirth in water and on land where they experience grave suffering. Thus, the goal of this solemn rite is universal liberation. The Water-Land Dharma Meeting, because it produces especially outstanding religious merit, has been one of the most important rituals in Chinese Buddhism. It is very complicated in both the arrangement of its physical space and its liturgy. The ritual space is divided into the "inner altar" and the "outer altar." Images of the Buddhas Vairocana, Śākyamuni, and Amitābha are hung at the center of the inner altar, below which is the main altar, where fragrant flowers, lamps, and offerings of fruit are spread. In addition, there are many implements laid out for the people to use. The outer area has six separate liturgical spaces, within each of which a different ritual takes place. The entire ritual takes seven days.

At the completion of various major festival days or by itself, to liberate wandering spirits, Buddhist temples frequently hold a very large service called "Release of the Flaming Mouths." The Flaming Mouths liturgy is very much like a performance and is both vivid and solemn, including *mantras*, offerings of food, and other elements that are extraordinarily powerful. Because of this, it is very popular among Buddhists. It is done between 7:00 P.M. and 11:00 P.M. in the evening, when ghosts go to feed. The ritual generally requires seven liturgists: a chief celebrant who sits in the middle and six others who sit along the two sides. In front of the chief celebrant are offerings of rice and water to give to the hungry ghosts.

This service is based on a story recounted in Buddhist scriptures. Ānanda, the favorite disciple of Śākyamuni Buddha, is said to have seen in meditation a hideous hungry ghost. The hungry ghost also informed Ānanda that in three days' time his life would be exhausted, and he too would fall into the path of the hungry ghosts. Ānanda, greatly fearful, ran to see the Buddha and begged him for rescue. The Buddha exhorted Ānanda to go and make food offerings according to the teachings of a scripture he preached. In doing so, he would not only be able to present offerings of food and drink to hungry ghosts and sages but would also avoid falling into the path of the hungry ghosts and extend his span of years; furthermore, all the hungry ghosts would come to his support, making whatever he did auspicious.

The phrase "Release of Living Beings" comes from a Mahāyāna Buddhist scripture and has spread all over China and beyond to Japan, Korea, and Vietnam. The ritual is based on the compassion that Buddhists feel, belief in the equality of all living beings, as well as in the concept of rebirth according to the results of karma. When holding a ceremony for the release of living beings, animals are brought into a ritual site, an incense altar will be set up on the site, clear water and willow branches will be prepared, and in the middle, people will make offerings before a statue of the bodhisattva Guanyin. The celebrant will preach a sermon on Buddhist teachings for the benefit of the animals and will transmit the Three Refuges to them. After the ceremony is completed, all of the animals will be taken to a natural setting, there to be restored to a free life.

Finally, funerals are one of Chinese Buddhism's most important activities and, over the past two centuries, its most important social function. After a layperson passes into peace, it is customary to ask both monastics and laypersons to come and recite the Buddha's name to liberate the deceased, in the hopes that he or she might quickly enter into the Western Land of Bliss. Many, many monastics and laypeople are invited, and the time spent in reciting the Buddha's name is quite long.

A funeral service for a Buddhist monastic has three parts. First, the body is bathed and new clothes are put on, after which he or she is sealed into the coffin, which is placed in a special room. Offerings of incense and lamps are placed before the coffin, and the assembly recites scriptures and intones blessings for him or her. Second is the raising of the coffin. The great assembly gathers in front of the coffin, and the celebrant stands in their midst holding a great staff. After preaching, he then strikes the coffin once with the staff and cries: "Arise!" At this, the assembly carries the coffin to the cremation chamber while reciting the Buddha's name. Third is the cremation. The assembly stands on either side of the cremation oven and places incense, lamps, and offerings before it, while the celebrant stands in the middle and says,

> All the elements are impermanent,
> the phenomena of this life are extinguished;
> both production and extinction are now extinguished,
> and the quieting of extinction itself is bliss.

The celebrant then takes a torch and throws it into the oven, saying, "Burn." The assembly recites the Buddha's name. Afterward, the ashes are examined for the presence of relics, to which offerings are presented.

RECENT DEVELOPMENTS IN POPULAR CHINESE BUDDHISM

All of the Buddhist practices described previously basically comprise traditional customs that have come down to the present on the currents of history. Over the last two decades, however, under the influence of Chinese society's modernization and globalization, Chinese Buddhism has either created or promoted many new ways of spreading the Dharma. For example, in attempting to expand Buddhism in contemporary China in a way that makes a significant contribution to the peaceful development of Chinese society, Chinese Buddhism has produced "Humanistic Buddhism." This is an effort to work within the Chinese conditions of modernization with the goal of furthering the public good.

One can see this effort in how Buddhism today has begun modernizing its charitable activities. Primary among Buddhist charities is disaster relief. China covers an extensive area of land, and every year there are disasters in many places, most frequently flooding during the summer and heavy snows in winter. After each such incident, Buddhist temples will solicit contributions for relief efforts and send the supplies and money received to the affected people. In 2003, the SARS epidemic engulfed China, and many Buddhists and Buddhist temples came forward with aid. This left a very good impression within Chinese society.

A second facet of contemporary Buddhist philanthropy involves educational assistance. In mainland China, there are always some young people who, for various reasons, face the threat of losing the opportunity to receive an education. Many Buddhist temples have set up special funds to help students, sometimes providing resources to construct new schools. For instance, the Buddhist Association of the City of Chongqing has for many years supported the Buddhist Hope Project, which sends aid to students who are promising but live in poverty. There are also a few Buddhist temples that disburse college scholarships or give emergency aid to students in trouble.

Besides providing public assistance, Chinese Buddhism has also developed new ways of presenting the Dharma. In 1993, the Bolin Temple in Hebei Province, with the support of Zhao Puchu, head of the Chinese Buddhist Association, held its first "Chan for Life Summer Camp." The temple has continued to host these camps for the last fourteen years. Many other temples have emulated this model, and it has become a new means for propagating Buddhism in mainland China.

The main participants in these summer camps are college students and young adults who have an interest in Buddhism but do not know much about it. Taking the Bolin Temple summer camps as an example, over the past fourteen years 4,000 people have participated, of whom about 60 percent have been college students. The ratio of men to women is 1:1. There are primarily two kinds of activities in these summer camps. One is to experience for oneself the life of a Buddhist follower: going to morning and evening scripture recitations, eating in the refectory, sitting in meditation, sweeping and cleaning, and so on. The other activity is to learn about Buddhist teachings through lectures by well-known Dharma Masters. The activities at the camps are designed for youth; in 2006, more than twenty Buddhist temples hosted this kind of summer camp.

Traditionally, Buddhist temples hosted activities for the laity on the first and fifteenth days of each lunar month and on other festival days. But contemporary lifestyles in China are more and more organized around the

Christian worship schedule. To accommodate this situation, Buddhist temples in China have begun progressively organizing activities on weekends. For example, every weekend the Fayuan Temple in Beijing arranges for a Dharma Master to come and lecture on a scripture, a temple activity that attracts many devotees from the middle class. The Guanghua Temple in Beijing offers weekend classes in Buddhism, which has gone on for seven sessions now and has trained more than 300 people. As an extension service, temples are also publishing more than 100 different Buddhist periodicals and newspapers on the mainland.

The number of people hooked up to the Internet in China reached 538 million in 2012, and the presence of Buddhism on the Internet has developed very quickly to a point where there are approximately 800 Buddhist websites in China, thus creating a new avenue for promoting Buddhism. Temples are the most prominent managers of these websites. For temples, websites mainly function as ways to send out information, circulate publications, and introduce the temple to the broader public. Today, religious activities such as making offerings to the Buddha, worshiping, making charitable donations, and accessing other Buddhist services can all be done by people on the Internet sitting at their computers. Some temples have put their morning and evening scripture recitations online. Also, the canon of Buddhist scriptures is extensive, and it has been difficult for anyone to have them in their entirety. But in digital form, everyone can freely read the canon, and the value of this for the promotion of Buddhism goes without saying.

Another interesting and successful innovation is the Buddhist academy. At present, there are more than fifty Buddhist academies enrolling more than 2,000 people in China. About 70 percent of these Buddhist academies are two- or three-year institutions whose main goal is to train midlevel workers for Buddhist organizations and teachers of the Dharma. The other 30 percent are four-year institutions that also offer graduate studies. The most eminent of these latter institutions is the Chinese Buddhist Academy in Beijing, which has been in operation for fifty years. It has a four-year program at the undergraduate level and a three-year graduate program. Today, all young or middle-age persons working in large Buddhist temples and local Buddhist associations are graduates of a Buddhist academy.

BUDDHISM'S INFLUENCE ON CHINESE CULTURE TODAY

In 2004, at the closing ceremony of the Special Olympics in Athens, a handicapped person from China performed an eight-minute dance with a grace that astonished the global audience. This was the dance of the *Thousand-Armed Guanyin*. A few months later, this performance was judged the best by spectators at an evening gathering during the Spring Festival in China. The reason for this dance's success was its artistic symbolic representation of the Great Compassion of the bodhisattva Guanyin that is so familiar to people in China. The universal appreciation of these symbols of compassion, so valued in Chinese culture, also touched the hearts of people throughout the world. It is a sign of China's social and cultural progress that Buddhist themes can openly take the world stage.

In February 2005, a movie released in China was titled *A World without Thieves*. The film achieved great success, with ticket sales exceeding 100 million. The movie depicted a pair of lovers who are thieves and who encounter a decent young man who believes there are no thieves in the world. To safeguard his belief in a thief-free world, this pair gives up stealing. Why would this pair of thieves change into such good people? The female thief answers that she is pregnant, and "I want to improve my child's karma." This very typical Buddhist thought serves as the foundation for the movie, one that moved its audiences to tears. The male and female protagonists in the movie hope that they themselves might produce some good karma for the sake of their child, so that the child will have a good destiny.

The appearance of Buddhist elements in such cultural forms as the dance of the *Thousand-Armed Guanyin* and the movie *A World without Thieves* is a sign that Buddhism is making positive contributions to contemporary Chinese culture. In past centuries, Buddhism made historic contributions to Chinese culture as well as to the cultures of other Asian countries. Today, Buddhism is contributing to China's cultural renaissance.

The result of all this Buddhist activity in China has been a growing number of conversions to Buddhist organizations by Chinese people looking for a moral and religious foundation to their lives. Today, Buddhism and Christianity are the two fastest growing religions in China. The form of Buddhism that is most popular is Tibetan Buddhism. This is not a political statement, but due to the fact that Tibetan Buddhism has had a historical presence in China, a strong academic and textual tradition, a strong monastic culture, and a rich devotional life.

NOTES

1. Venerable Shih Cheng-yen, "A New Millennium of Goodness, Beauty, and Truth," in Chappell, ed., *Buddhist Peacework*, p. 48.

2. Venerable Master Hsing Yun, *The Lion's Roar: Actualizing Buddhism in Daily Life and Building the Pure Land in Our Midst* (New York: Peter Lang, 1991), pp. xv, 8, 11, 129, 136.

3. Master Hsing Yun, *Lotus in a Stream* (New York: Weatherhill, 2000), p. 154.

SUGGESTIONS FOR FURTHER READING

Chandler, Stuart. *Establishing a Pure Land on Earth: The Foguang Buddhist Perspective on Modernization and Globalization*. Honolulu: University of Hawaii Press, 2004.

Chappell, David. *T'ien-t'ai Buddhism: An Outline of the Fourfold Teachings*. Tokyo: Daiichi Shobo, 1983.

Ch'en, Kenneth. *Buddhism in China: A Historical Survey.* Princeton, NJ: Princeton University Press, 1964.

_____. *The Chinese Transformation of Buddhism.* Princeton, NJ: Princeton University Press, 1973.

Ching, Yu-ing. *Master of Love and Mercy: Cheng Yen.* Nevada City, CA: Blue Dolphin Publishing, 1995.

Cleary, Thomas, trans. *Entry into the Inconceivable: An Introduction to Hwa-yen Buddhism.* Honolulu: University of Hawaii Press, 1983.

Cook, Francis H. *Hua-yen Buddhism: The Jewel Net of Indra.* University Park: Pennsylvania State University Press, 1977.

de Bary, Wm. Theodore, Irene Bloom, and Richard Lufrano, eds. *Sources of Chinese Tradition.* 2nd ed. 2 vols. New York: Columbia University Press, 2000, 2001.

Devido, Elise Ann. *Taiwan's Buddhist Nuns.* Albany: SUNY Press, 2010.

Dumoulin, Heinrich. *Zen Buddhism: A History.* Vol. 1, *India and China.* New York: Macmillan, 1988.

Ebrey, Particia Buckley, and Peter Gregory, eds. *Religion and Society in T'ang and Sung China.* Honolulu: University of Hawaii Press, 1993.

Faure, Bernard. *The Rhetoric of Immediacy: A Cultural Critique of Chan/Zen Buddhism.* Princeton, NJ: Princeton University Press, 1995.

Gregory, Peter N., ed. *Sudden and Gradual: Approaches to Enlightenment in Chinese Thought*. Honolulu: University of Hawaii Press, 1987.

_____. *Tsung-mi and the Sinification of Buddhism.* Honolulu: University of Hawaii Press, 2002.

Gregory, Peter N., and David A. Getz, Jr., eds. *Buddhism in the Sung.* Honolulu: University of Hawaii Press, 2002.

Hakeda, Yoshito S., trans. *The Awakening of Faith.* New York: Columbia University Press, 2005.

Hershock, Peter D. *Chan Buddhism.* Honolulu: University of Hawaii Press, 2004.

Huang, Julia C. *Charisma and Compassion: Cheng Yen and the Buddhist Tzu Chi Movement.* Cambridge, MA: Harvard University Press, 2009.

Jones, Charles Brewer. *Buddhism in Taiwan: Religion and the State, 1660–1990.* Honolulu: University of Hawaii Press,1999.

Kieschnick, John. *The Eminent Monk: Buddhist Ideals in Medieval Chinese Hagiography.* Honolulu: University of Hawaii Press, 1997.

Kirchner, Thomas Yuko, ed., Ruth Fuller Sasaki, trans. *The Record of Linji.* Honolulu: University of Hawaii Press, 2008.

McRae, John R. *The Northern School and the Formation of Early Ch'an Buddhism.* Honolulu: University of Hawaii Press, 1986.

_____. *Seeing through Zen: Encounter, Transformation and Genealogy in Chinese Chan Buddhism.* Berkeley: University of California Press, 2004.

McRae, John M., trans. *The Platform Sūtra of the Sixth Patriarch.* Honolulu: University of Hawaii Press, 2000.

Nattier, Jan. *Once upon a Future Time: Studies in a Buddhism Prophecy of Decline.* Berkeley, CA: Asian Humanities Press, 1991.

Robinson, Richard H. *Early Madhyamika in India and China*. Madison: University of Wisconsin Press, 1967.

Schlutter, Morten. *How Zen Became Zen: The Dispute over Enlightenment and the Formation of Chan Buddhism in Song-Dynasty China*. Honolulu: University of Hawaii Press, 2010.

Sharf, Robert H. *Coming to Terms with Chinese Buddhism: A Reading of the Treasure Store Treatise*. Honolulu: University of Hawaii Press, 2005.

Tsai, Kathryn Ann. *Lives of Nuns: Biographies of Chinese Buddhist Nuns from the Fourth to Sixth Centuries*. Honolulu: University of Hawaii Press, 1994.

Weinstein, Stanley. *Buddhism under the T'ang*. Cambridge, UK: Cambridge University Press, 1987.

Welter, Albert. *Monks, Rulers and Literati: The Political Ascendancy of Chan Buddhism*. New York: Oxford University Press, 2006.

Yampolsky, Philip. *The Platform Sūtra of the Sixth Patriarch*. New York: Columbia University Press, 1967.

Yü, Chün-fang. *Kuan-yin: The Chinese Transformation of Avalokiteśvara*. New York: Columbia University Press, 2000.

Zürcher, Erik. *The Buddhist Conquest of China: The Spread and Adaptation of Buddhism in Early Medieval China*. 2 vols. Leiden, Netherlands: E. J. Brill, 1972.

8

Korean Experiences of Buddhism

Starting in the first century B.C.E., clans vied with one another to gain control of different parts of the Korean peninsula. During the first centuries of the common era, the Koguryŏ clan conquered its neighbors and formed the first of what were to become the Three Kingdoms of the peninsula (see Map 6). The Kingdom of Koguryŏ ruled the northern part of the peninsula and the south central part of Manchuria. By the middle of the third century, the Kingdom of Paekche was consolidated in the southwestern part of the peninsula. And by the middle of the fourth century, the Kingdom of Silla was established in southeastern Korea. With the emergence of the Three Kingdoms of ancient Korea, diplomatic and cultural contacts with China increased through which Buddhism found its way into the peninsula.

THE ADVENT OF BUDDHISM DURING THE THREE KINGDOMS PERIOD

In the fourth century, Koguryŏ became allied with north China against the northern barbarian tribes threatening both of their borders. In 372, the emperor of north China sent the Buddhist monk Shundao with some companions to the Koguryŏ court of King Sosurim (ruled 371–384). It is said that Shundao brought with him a number of Buddhist scriptures and statues. While tradition teaches that Shundao's mission was the first introduction of Buddhism into Korea, there is evidence that the Saṅgha was already present in Koguryŏ when Shundao arrived. In any case, the idea behind this mission was to have these Buddhist monks use their prayers and rites to help protect Koguryŏ from its enemies. The king constructed a temple for Shundao's use, and Buddhism was officially welcomed into the kingdom. Soon the aristocratic leaders of Koguryŏ saw Buddhism not only as offering supernatural protection for the nation but also as a force for internal unification and moral guidance. As the common people adopted the religion, they integrated it with the country's indigenous shamanism.

Meanwhile, Paekche had developed an alliance with south China. Legend has it that in 384, the Indian monk Mālānanda, who had been traveling in south China, came to Paekche by ship, where he was also welcomed and supported in propagating Buddhism. As in Koguryŏ, the Buddhism introduced into Paekche was Mahāyāna. Soon after the introduction of Buddhism into Koguryŏ and Paekche, Korean monastics from both of these kingdoms were traveling to China to study with great Chinese masters like Kumārajīva. When these monks returned to Korea, they brought with them some of the teachings of the Chinese schools of Buddhism. There is evidence that at this time in Korea, the study of Sarvāstivāda, Sautrāntika, the *Nirvana Sūtra*, and other Chinese schools such as Sanlun and Tiantai was taking place. Despite this activity in Koguryŏ and Paekche, the introduction of Buddhism into the Kingdom of Silla was protracted compared to the other kingdoms. Silla was the less developed and most isolated of the Three Kingdoms, and the first Buddhist missionaries to Silla were said to have been martyred. It was not until 527 that Buddhism was finally accepted as Silla's state religion under King Pŏphŭng (514–540).

During the sixth century, Buddhism in Koguryŏ and Paekche developed their own traditions. At the same time, the two kingdoms also sent missionaries to Japan. The Paekche king, Sŏng-myŏng, sent a Buddhist statue, ritual implements, and scriptures to the Japanese emperor in 552, with the result that Buddhist doctrine began to spread among the Japanese aristocracy. Eventually, Korean teachers of the Buddhist scriptural traditions, masters of Sŏn (Zen) practice, as well as temple artisans and architects reached Japan from Korea. Indeed, Korean Buddhists were actively involved in the propagation and development of Buddhism in Japan for over 150 years. This mission included not only the training of monks and nuns in doctrinal study and meditative practice but also the transmission of sophisticated Buddhist art and architecture. During this time, not only were Korean Buddhists traveling to Japan but Japanese Buddhists were also going to Korea for further study.

The Silla monk Chajang (fl. 636–645) journeyed to China for study in 636. Returning to the Silla Kingdom, he worked to import Chinese culture and Buddhism, and he also helped spread Buddhism from the aristocratic community to the general population. Chajang reorganized Buddhism in Silla by issuing four rules of monastic discipline: (1) study of the *sūtras*, (2) seminars on doctrine with examinations, (3) a central temple for ordination, and (4) a government department to maintain temples and other Buddhist property. Chajang helped to establish a solid monastic structure in Korea based on his view that monastic discipline plays a central role in the attainment of Awakening. This strong monastic foundation became a key element in the Korean Buddhist experience, contributed to the eventual success of the Saṅgha, and has been an important reason for the vitality of Korean Buddhism over the centuries. The following passages record some of Chajang's contributions to the monastic discipline of the Korean Saṅgha:

The [Silla] court discussed, "Although the eastern journey of Buddhism has been continuing for hundreds . . . of years, there is a lack of rules concerning its monastic structure. Without them, how can the Saṅgha be kept respectable and pure?" So, by royal decree, Chajang was made the Great National Overseer. . . .

Chajang . . . encouraged each division of the Saṅgha to enhance its training through the following: recite the precepts every two weeks, hold winter and summer examinations, establish an office to make sure the monastics follow the precepts, and send investigators to outlying monasteries to admonish monastics for their faults, and to ensure they carefully and regularly maintain their scriptures and statues. . . . Later, Chajang founded T'ongdo Monastery, where he constructed a Precepts Platform used to ordain those coming from the four directions. (*Samguk yusa*, 4: 192–193)

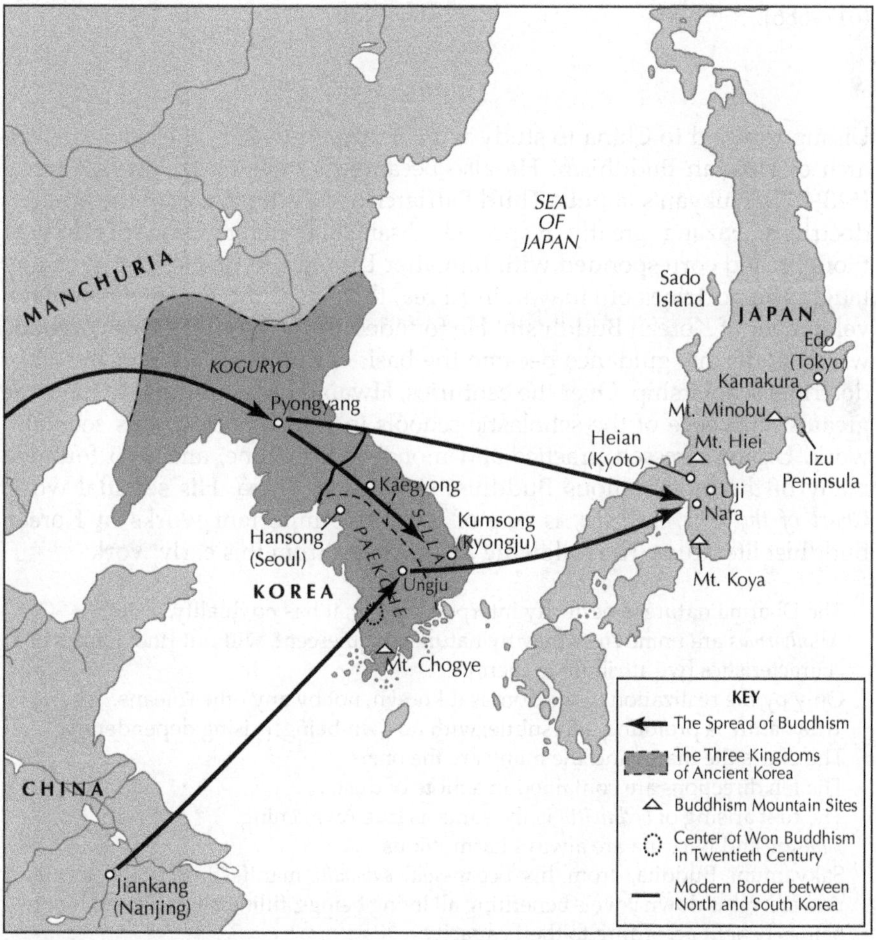

MAP 6. Buddhism in Korea and Japan: fourth–seventeenth century C.E.

BUDDHISM DURING THE UNIFIED SILLA DYNASTY: INNOVATION AND SCHOLARSHIP

Silla conquered Paekche in 663 and Koguryŏ in 668, thus unifying the Korean peninsula for the first time and bringing the Three Kingdoms Period to an end. This unification ushered in the Silla Dynasty (see Figure 8.1), which lasted until 918. During this period, Buddhist scholarship flourished, and major doctrinal developments of Korean Buddhism were made that still define the Korean Buddhist experience today. On the devotional level, the worship of Amitābha Buddha, Avalokiteśvara Bodhisattva, and especially Maitreya Bodhisattva was popular. In regard to Maitreya, the Silla kings claimed to be his emanations to justify their rule, and the common people sought to be reborn with him in the Tuṣita heaven. Within this creative environment, two major figures emerged who made major contributions to the developing uniqueness of Korean Buddhism: Ŭisang (625–702) and Wŏnhyo (617–686).

Ŭisang

Ŭisang traveled to China to study with Zhiyan (602–668), the Second Patriarch of Huayan Buddhism. He also became the lifelong friend of Fazang (643–712), Huayan's famous Third Patriarch and systematizer of the school's doctrines. Fazang greatly respected Ŭisang's understanding of Huayan thought, and corresponded with him after Ŭisang's return to Korea. Ŭisang taught the doctrines of Huayan in Korea, thus inspiring the intellectual development of Korean Buddhism. He founded the Hwaŏm (Huayan) School, which under his guidance became the basis for much of Korean Buddhist doctrinal scholarship. Over the centuries, Hwaŏm has continued to have the greatest influence of the scholastic schools in Korea. Besides this scholarly work, Ŭisang stressed practice and monastic discipline, and also founded many of the most famous Buddhist temples in Korea. His seminal work, *Chart of the Dharmadhātu*, is one of the most important works in Korean Buddhist literature. The following are passages from this early work:

> The Dharma nature is perfectly interpenetrating; it has no duality.
> All *dharmas* are unmoving; they by nature are quiescent, without [the] names or characteristics [we attribute to them]. . . .
> Only by the realization of wisdom is it known, not by any other means.
> True nature is profound and subtle; with no own-being, arising dependently. . . .
> The one is the many, and the many are the one.
> The ten directions are contained in a mote of dust. . . .
> The first arising of *bodhicitta* is the same as true Awakening.
> *Saṃsāra* and Nirvana are always harmonious. . . .
> Śākyamuni Buddha, from his ocean-seal *samādhi* manifesting super-normal powers, rains down jewels benefiting all living beings, filling all space. All living beings benefit according to their capacity.
> Therefore, the one who practices good conduct must also return to the original source, which one cannot attain without ceasing false conceptions.

> By unconditional skillful means, one attains complete liberation, returns home, and receives food according to one's capacity. . . .
> Finally, one is seated on the throne of the ultimate truth of the Middle Way, from which one has never moved. Thus, one's name is Buddha. (*Ilsŭng pŏpkye to*)

Wŏnhyo

The second famous figure of the Silla era was Wŏnhyo. Wŏnhyo, a friend of Ŭisang, is considered one of the great early Korean Buddhist scholars. He was a prolific writer, author of 240 works, and was considered one of the foremost Buddhist scholars in East Asia during his own lifetime. One of his major contributions to Buddhist studies was his attempt to show how the many Buddhist texts and schools reflect in different ways the One Mind that is their true source of inspiration. In this way, he hoped to unite the Buddhist schools in Korea into a new and more comprehensive form of Buddhism. Wŏnhyo was especially concerned about the sectarian friction between the Buddhist schools that were being imported from China. He wanted to produce a new Korean Buddhist ecumenical harmony that reflects the ontological harmony, or mutual penetration, preached by the Hwaŏm School. His work in this regard inspired later and more successful efforts to unify Korean Buddhism. Scholars also see this desire for religious unification as expressing the same spirit that was behind the political unification of Korea in the unified Silla state.

An example of Wŏnhyo's method of "harmonization of all disputes" (*hwajaeng*) can be seen in his use of the essence-function distinction from Hwaŏm Buddhism. In his commentary on *The Awakening of Faith*, Wŏnhyo says that the many doctrines of Buddhism are manifold forms of "unfolding" or "opening" of the Dharma. When these doctrines are traced back to their source, they are "sealed" in the unifying principle of One Mind, the Buddha-nature that is their ultimate basis. In this way, the many forms of Buddhism are the functioning of the essence of the Dharma, namely, the One Mind. Opening the Dharma in its many expressions does not exhaust the essence, and sealing the Dharma in its one essence of Awakening does not diminish its expressions. Wŏnhyo extends this kind of analysis in his discussion of the Three Refuges. There, he defines the Buddha, Dharma, and Saṅgha in terms of the Three Greatnesses (essence, attribute, and function). The Buddha is the very essence of the One Mind, the Dharma is its attribute, and the Saṅgha is its function in the world.

The following are some of Wŏnhyo's comments about unfolding and sealing the Dharma from his commentary on *The Awakening of Faith:*

> The essence of Mahāyāna is described as completely empty and very subtle. But no matter how subtle, how can it be anywhere but in the world of the myriad phenomena? . . . Although it is nowhere but in phenomena, no eye can see its form. . . . One can call it great, but it enters the interior where nothing remains. One can call it small, but it envelopes the exterior without exhausting itself. One might say it is a thing, but everything is empty because of it. One might say it is

FIGURE 8.1. Pagoda at Pulguk-sa Temple; Unified Silla Period (668–935 C.E.), Kyŏng-ju, Korea.

not a thing, but the myriad phenomena arise because of it. Not knowing how to describe it, I call it the Mahāyāna. . . .

Although what is discussed [in *The Awakening of Faith*] is vast, it can be summarized in the following words: By revealing [the suchness and causality] of the One Mind, it comprehends the [many] jewels of Māhāyana doctrines. . . . When the treatise is unfolded, there are innumerable meanings found in its doctrines. When it is sealed, the principle . . . of the One Mind is found as its essence. . . . Therefore, it freely unfolds and seals without obstruction. . . . (*Kisillon so*, 1, 3–4)

Toward the end of his life, Wŏnhyo traveled around the countryside practicing meditation in the mountains and living close to the common people preaching hope in Pure Land devotion. Thereby, Wŏnhyo was instrumental in Buddhism spreading to the general Korean population and the popularity of Pure Land piety in Korea. Wŏnhyo also felt that meditation practice and Pure Land devotion were complementary in Buddhist experience. This view, that both meditation and chanting can contribute to the Buddhist journey to Awakening, became the general opinion in Korean Buddhism. Besides influencing Hwaŏm doctrine and defining the place of Pure Land devotion in Korean Buddhist practice, Wŏnhyo is also considered the founder of the Haedong sect of the Hwaŏm School.

While Wŏnhyo spread Buddhism among the general Korean population, Ŭisang established its centers of scholarship and culture. In many ways, these two Silla monks gave the Korean Buddhist experience its special character of intellectual study, meditative practice, monastic discipline, and personal devotion. Although, as we shall see, there has been tension between these aspects of Buddhism in Korea, they have all played crucial roles in forming the Korean experience of the Buddha Dharma. Also in the writings of Wŏnhyo, we can see the beginnings of the Korean desire to fashion a harmonized form of Buddhism that could unite the Buddhist Saṅgha, as well as contribute to a more united Korean society.

The Five Buddhist Schools

During the Silla Period, the Five Buddhist Schools emerged in Korea. These schools became the orthodox scholastic Buddhist tradition in Korea from the Silla Period onward. Of these Five Schools, three were derived from Chinese schools of Buddhism, and two were unique to the Korean scene. The first variation of a Chinese school was the Kyeyul (*Vinaya*) School. Kyeyul was the Korean version of the Chinese Lu School that propagated the *Vinaya* teachings. As in China, Kyeyul taught that Buddhism is not just a set of doctrines or meditative practices, but must entail a Saṅgha that adheres to monastic precepts. Kyeyul helped in the formalization of monastic education, ordination, and organization throughout Korea. Following the inspiration of Chajang, this school's emphasis on building a well-disciplined monasticism contributed to the vital and enduring Korean monastic Saṅgha that has lasted until the present day.

The second school was the Hwaŏm School, founded by Ŭisang. This rich vein of Chinese Huayan Buddhist thought generated another school in Korea that did not have any counterpart in China. This third school of Korean Buddhism was the Haedong School, based on the teachings of Wŏnhyo. Because Wŏnhyo wanted to produce a unified form of Buddhism in Korea, while this school taught the importance of the *Avataṃsaka Sūtra*, it did not insist on the exclusive use of this *sūtra*. Wŏnhyo, with his desire for unity between the schools, taught that although the *Avataṃsaka Sūtra* was the greatest of all Buddhist *sūtras*, others could also be used to lead a person to Awakening. Both of these early schools show the importance of Ŭisang's and Wŏnhyo's groundbreaking work.

The fourth school was the Pŏpsang ("Characteristics of the *Dharmas*") School. A pioneer of this school was Wŏnch'ŭk (613–696), a Korean monastic scholar who studied and lectured on Yogācāra in Chang'an, the capital of China. While Wŏnch'ŭk espoused Paramārtha's views concurring Yogācāra, he also respected Xuanzang's interpretations. Wŏnch'ŭk's disciples returned to Korea, where they inspired Yogācāra scholarship. From this doctrinal study, the Pŏpsang School was born. This school taught that all phenomena are formed by the mind. Thus, the world *as we experience it* is not the way the world really is. The true nature of all things is found in transcending the duality between mind and phenomena. The Pŏpsang School developed a Buddhist psychology and a theory of knowledge for Korean Buddhism. It also contributed to the Korean Buddhist method of mental purification.

The last of the Five Schools was the Yŏlban (Nirvana) School, based on the *Nirvana Sūtra*. There was no counterpart to this school in China, and it emerged from the popular study of the *Nirvana Sūtra*. The major teaching of this *sūtra* that impressed the Koreans was the *Tathāgata-garbha* doctrine that all beings have Buddha-nature. This doctrine as presented in the *Nirvana Sūtra* strengthened Korean Buddhist faith that all persons can, in fact, experience the happiness of the Buddha through the practice of Buddhist spirituality.

While these Five Schools were being founded, Chinese Tiantai Buddhism also existed in Korea, but not as an independent school. Known as Ch'ŏnt'ae, its first appearance was during the sixth century when Hyŏn'gwang (fl. 539–575) brought it back to Korea after studying with Huisi, the Second Patriarch of Tiantai in China. However, this school did not become fully autonomous until, as we shall see, Ŭich'ŏn (1055–1101), who was considered the real founder of the Ch'ŏnt'ae School.

Tantric Buddhism was also practiced during the Silla Period, especially by the ruling family. A number of Tantric masters in Korea were known for their esoteric powers. Tantra in Korea emphasized ecstatic states of union with celestial bodhisattvas and the use of powerful *mantras* for protection, this-worldly benefits, and healing of diseases. This tradition, based on the Chinese Chenyan School, never became a formal school in Korea and died out with the fall of the Silla Dynasty. Pure Land Buddhism, known in Korea as Chŏng-t'o, was quite popular with the common people, especially due to

Wŏnhyo's influence. Pure Land chanting and piety influenced all the schools of Korean Buddhism and was often expressed in Korean art and literature.

Sŏn (Chan/Zen) Buddhism had appeared just prior to the Silla Dynasty through a Korean monk named Pŏmnang (fl. 632–646). Pŏmnang studied Chan in China under Daoxin (580–651), the person designated as the Fourth Chan Patriarch. Pŏmnang returned to Korea and taught the Chan doctrines and practices as they existed in China prior to the split between the Northern and Southern schools. However, this first phase of Sŏn in Korea did not leave any strong and lasting school. Then in the ninth century, other Chan lineages arrived in Korea. By the tenth century, these lineages had organized themselves, and the Nine Mountains Sŏn School of Buddhism was established. Each of these nine schools took its name from the mountain where its central temple was located (see Figure 8.2). All but two of the nine Sŏn sects were founded by disciples of the successors of the great Chinese patriarch, Mazu.

FIGURE 8.2. Gautama Buddha Statue in the earth-witnessing posture completed in 774 at Seokguram Grotto in Bulguksa Temple Complex, Gyeongju, South Korea.

By the end of the Silla Period, there was a social and economic decline in Korea, and the more intellectual schools of Buddhism were no longer so attractive to the general population. People were looking for a spirituality that helped them deal with hard times. Therefore, both Pure Land and Sŏn Buddhism increased in their appeal. Sŏn Buddhism emphasized that one must remove himself or herself from society to pursue quiet meditation for the attainment of Awakening. Given the social decay at the end of the Silla Period, this message was attractive to many Koreans. However, this approach to Buddhist practice was not appreciated by the more scholastic schools of Korean Buddhism. At odds with these schools, Sŏn attacked its opponents. The following is a dialogue between a Hwaŏm master and a Sŏn master that characterizes this division:

> The [Hwaŏm master] asked National [Sŏn] Master Toŭi, "What other *Dharmadhātu* is there besides the four *Dharmadhātus* taught by the Hwaŏm School?" . . . Toŭi responded, "When the four *Dharmadhātus* you . . . have mentioned are suddenly brought up in the [Sŏn] School of the Patriarchs, their essential principle [Buddha-nature] is experienced directly, just like ice melting [on a hot stove]. When this essential principle of all things is brought up, you cannot find the characteristics of those four *Dharmadhātus*. In the Patriarch's mind of Sŏn, in the original wisdom that cannot be cultivated, no characteristics of those four *Dharmadhātus* can be found." (*Sŏnmun pojang nok*, 2)

In the previous chapter, we saw that the four *Dharmadhātus* are the four ways of experiencing existence according to the Huayan (Hwaŏm) School. They not only provide this school with a way of analyzing experience and existence but also define a gradual growth toward the enlightened vision of the mutual identification and mutual penetration of all phenomena. Here, Master Toŭi is claiming that the original wisdom of the Buddha-nature cannot be cultivated in any such gradual way but actually melts the distinctions so important to Hwaŏm textual study. So, as the Silla Dynasty came to an end, Korean Buddhism was split between the scholastic schools that emphasized textual study and gradual spiritual growth and the Sŏn tradition that stressed meditation and sudden Awakening. Addressing this division would become the primary theme of the next chapter of the story of Buddhism in Korea.

BUDDHISM DURING THE KORYŎ DYNASTY: SEARCHING FOR UNITY

The Silla Period ended with the founding of the Koryŏ Dynasty, which reigned from 918 to 1392. From the beginning of the Koryŏ Period, the kings supported a strong connection between the government and the Saṅgha, maintaining Buddhism as the state religion. The rulers were confident that by so doing, they could ensure the security and prosperity of the nation. The government also instituted a set of examinations for the Buddhist

Box 8.1

The Body and Gesture of Life

The core of Korean *Sŏn* Buddhism is the *mom-momjit* paradigm. *Mom* means "body" in Korean, and *momjit* means "gesture," or more broadly, uses of body. The *mom-momjit* paradigm is complex, but in its simplest form, *mom* is a metaphor for the ultimate and concrete reality, often called "suchness" in Buddhist literature, while *momjit* is the world of karma consisted of thought, language, culture, and history. Our present world is the terrain of *momjit* culture. We live our lives in the world preconceived through language and given rules and values, and we often overlook the "body" that precedes and underlies all words and gestures. The preoccupation with performing and imitating socially accepted *momjit* stifles our awareness of *mom*. Our efforts and worries are mainly geared toward acquiring or bettering certain *momjit*.

Over the course of my life, I experienced the importance of regaining the sense of *mom* in this predominantly *momjit-oriented* culture. For me, breaking this tight reign of *momjit*, recovering the sense of *mom*, and embodying its Life is the heart of Sŏn Buddhist teaching. Here is how I first learned this lesson.

In 1975, I lived through a period of personal crisis. I was a doctoral student at Berkeley and was under a great deal of pressure to finish my dissertation. I had difficult times with my professors since I had different views on certain theoretical matters. At the same time, my wife, who was our sole support at that time, fell ill and couldn't continue working. We had two teenage daughters, and suddenly there was no money coming in.

My emotions were in such turmoil that I made little progress with my thesis, and I became genuinely afraid that I would never finish. Would six years of hard work at Berkeley go down the drain, and would I have to return to Korea a failure?

I had spent years studying Buddhist theory, but nothing I had learned in books helped calm my mind. Without realizing what I was doing, I started to pray, and then an experience I had almost a decade earlier when I was an acolyte living in a Buddhist monastery in Korea suddenly came to life again. In 1966, while a monk at Haeinsa, I spent a year living under a vow of silence. Neither speaking nor communicating by writing, I focused all my energy on meditation, concentrating on the *kongan (kōan* in Japanese) given to me by my teacher. I definitely had a strong feeling during that year that I was drawing closer to a sense of *mom*, the source of Life itself that underlies all life forms.

Experiencing once again the feeling I had at Haeinsa restored me to a larger, more complete sense of myself, and my panic started to subside. I experienced that we are *mom* and the integrity of *mom* is untouched whether we are rich or poor, whether we get our Ph.D. or not, whether we are a success or failure. This is not to say that the world of *momjit* is unimportant. However, when we live our lives in reverence to the workings of *mom*, rather than trying to impose certain "gestures" onto it, the demands we place onto ourselves to fit into certain standards of "gestures" lose their weight.

As my mind cleared, I was able to study again, finish my Ph.D. work, and get a teaching position. I have spent the past thirty years as a professor, teaching and writing about Buddhism. The core of Buddhist practice for me has always been to live from the sense of *mom*, as I experienced during that year of silence in the monastery.

SUNG BAE PARK
Professor of East Asian Philosophy and Religions
SUNY at Stony Brook

priests, thus ensuring that there was always a well-educated Buddhist leadership in Korea. The king could make two important appointments to leading members of the Saṅgha: "the teacher to the nation" and "the teacher to the king."

Under this royal patronage, Koryŏ Buddhism grew in influence and wealth. Some monasteries became huge landowners with many serfs. Others started commercial enterprises such as noodle making or tea production. As happened in China, the government became concerned about this worldly power and its corrupting influence on the Saṅgha. However, the Korean reaction was more moderate than the Chinese. In the tenth century, the government set restrictions on the Saṅgha's involvement in worldly affairs. In the twelfth century, it ruled that any monastic who broke their precepts be laicized.

Ŭich'ŏn

By the eleventh century, there was a clear and pressing need to restore high standards to the Korean Saṅgha. Given the continuing strident controversy between the Sŏn and scholastic (Kyo) schools, there was also the need to restore the spirit of unity within the Saṅgha. This dual task was undertaken by Ŭich'ŏn, another of Korea's great Buddhist scholars. Ŭich'ŏn, a son of King Munjŏng (1046–1083), entered a Hwaŏm monastery at the age of eleven. In 1085 at the age of thirty, he traveled to China, where he studied under renowned teachers of Huayan, Tiantai, Pure Land, Chan, and *Vinaya*. Ŭich'ŏn continued to be influenced by Huayan, but saw in Tiantai a balance between meditation and study that would be ideal for tie Korean situation. Upon his return to Korea, Ŭich'ŏn attempted to bring unity to the Saṅgha by merging Sŏn meditation with the doctrinal study of the scholastic schools in a new and expanded Ch'ŏnt'ae (Tiantai) School. As mentioned earlier, he is considered the real founder of the Korean Ch'ŏnt'ae School.

In addressing the sectarianism of the Korean Saṅgha, Ŭich'ŏn criticized both the Sŏn and the scholastic schools for their reluctance to understand the importance of each other's positions:

> While the Dharma is devoid of words and appearances, it is not separate from words and appearances. If you reject words, you can fall into wrong views and defilements. If you are attached to words, you will not find the truth. . . . Students of the *sūtras* often neglect their inner cultivation and become attached to external pursuits. Sŏn practitioners just ignore helping the world and simply look within themselves. Both positions are biases at two extremes. (*Kang Won'gak kyŏng palsa*, in *Taegak kuksa munjip*, 3, 4–5)

Ŭich'ŏn opposed these biases by teaching the need for *sūtra* study to understand the goal and path of Buddhism and for meditation practice to follow the path and realize the goal. He taught, following Wŏnhyo, that there is an essential unity behind the diversity of Buddhist teachings that is adapted to the capacities and temperaments of disciples. This unity is variously called Buddha-nature, the One Mind, or the *Dharmadhātu*. Sectarian conflict, Ŭich'ŏn concluded, was caused by those who had not realized this essential unity. It would be, he taught, through a combination of study and practice that one could realize this unity and build a more united Saṅgha. Being more influenced by the tradition of study, which he preferred because of his own study of Hwaŏm and Ch'ŏnt'ae, Ŭich'ŏn sought to achieve this unity by incorporating Sŏn into the scholarly side of the Saṅgha. His efforts to merge the various schools of Korean Buddhism in this way were supported by the ruling family and were respected by Saṅgha leaders of all persuasions. Soon, his new school was gaining disciples from all schools of Korean Buddhism. However, his early death brought an end to this experiment with Buddhist ecumenism and added one more school to the Korean Saṅgha.

Chinul

Perhaps the greatest reformer and unifier of Korean Buddhism lived during the twelfth century: Chinul (1158–1210). When Chinul was a child, he had a serious illness and his father vowed to the Buddha that if his son lived, Chinul would become a monk. The child did live, went on to enter a monastery at the age of seven, and received the Buddhist novice precepts at the age of fifteen. Chinul's preceptor was a Sŏn master. But because Chinul did not have a close relationship with him, he did not have a permanent teacher. Lacking personal instruction, Chinul studied the *sūtras* and practiced meditation himself, combining the two sides of the division between Sŏn and Kyo in his own experience. In 1182, he traveled to the capital city to take the Sŏn Saṅgha examinations. He passed the exams but was disillusioned by the worldly state of the Saṅgha. He decided not to pursue a career in the city hierarchy but instead to return to the country to follow the monastic life. In discussing this choice with some fellow students, they decided to form a retreat society in the mountains dedicated to the cultivation of concentration (*samādhi*) and wisdom (*prajñā*).

In attempting to create such a society, Chinul and his friends faced difficulties in finding a site, and Chinul's fellow students went to different monasteries. Chinul decided to travel down the peninsula, and he eventually settled in a monastery in the far southwest region. While there, Chinul had the first of three Awakenings, each of which would affect his teachings about Buddhist practice. Reading the *Platform Sūtra of the Sixth Patriarch* while in the study hall one day, he found a passage that said, "The self-nature of suchness gives rise to thoughts. But . . . it is not tainted by the many images. The true nature is always free and self-reliant." Chinul's reading of this passage brought him to Awakening, and "his heart was satisfied."

After this experience, Chinul continued to study and reflect on the *Platform Sūtra* as well as writings of other Sŏn masters. He became convinced that while he had attained an "initial Awakening" into Buddha-nature, he needed to continue to cultivate both concentration and wisdom to attain "full Awakening." This insight led to his teaching of "sudden Awakening and gradual cultivation," which he adopted from the Chinese Chan patriarch Zongmi (779–840). Chinul taught that in sudden Awakening, one discovers Buddha-nature, one's innate potential for full Buddhahood. This sudden Awakening, Chinul says, is not just a static insight but a realization of a dynamic reality: the *Tathāgata-garbha*, or "embryo" (*garbha*), of full Buddhahood (*Tathāgata*). Growth of this initial realization into the fullness of Buddhahood entails a gradual process of cultivation because of continuing habitual patterns of unwholesome thoughts, words, and actions. In his *Secrets on Cultivating the Mind*, Chinul explains the need for this ongoing cultivation process:

> If in one thought moment a person can trace back the luminosity [of his or her mind] and see his or her original nature, that person will discover that the ground of this nature is innately free of any defilements. . . . It is originally endowed with a . . . wisdom that is not a hair's breadth different from the wisdom of all the Buddhas. Therefore, this is called sudden Awakening.
>
> Even if a person is enlightened to the fact that his or her original nature is not different from that of the Buddhas, beginningless habit patterns are hard to remove suddenly. So, while one relies on this Awakening, one must continue cultivation. Through the gradual permeation of one's whole being by this Awakening, one's cultivation reaches completion. After one constantly nourishes the holy "embryo" [*garbha*] for a long time, one becomes a saint.
>
> While a person must practice cultivation, he or she has already suddenly awakened to the fact that deluded thoughts are originally empty and that the nature of the mind is originally pure. Therefore, one eliminates what is unwholesome without eliminating anything; and one cultivates what is wholesome without cultivating anything either. This is true cultivation and true elimination. (*Susim kyŏl*, Q/A 3, 7)

Chinul defined this cultivation after initial Awakening as the simultaneous development of concentration and wisdom. Concentration in the absolute sense, according to Chinul, is the very essence of one's true nature, the Buddha-nature realized in Awakening. Wisdom in the absolute sense is the very functioning of that *essence*. When one realizes Buddha-nature in initial Awakening, one finds that these aspects of innate suchness are not separate. In the context of cultivation subsequent to initial Awakening, through the gradual permeation of one's whole being by the essence and functioning of Buddha-nature, ignorance and craving are more and more rooted out and the embryo of Buddhahood develops into the full life of Buddhahood. Because this subsequent practice is based on one's prior Awakening, one does not fall into the practice of the gradual school that cultivates concentration and wisdom to gradually attain Awakening. Here again are Chinul's words from his *Secrets on Cultivating the Mind:*

> [F]rom the [absolute] standpoint of the self-nature, [concentration and wisdom] are called essence and function. . . . Concentration is the essence, and wisdom is

> the function. . . . Since wisdom is in concentration, concentration is calm yet always aware. Since concentration is in wisdom, wisdom is aware yet always calm.
>
> On the other hand, even if a person may have initial sudden Awakening, if he or she is affected by defilements, and negative habit patterns are deeply engrained . . . then he or she should use relative concentration and wisdom . . . as countermeasures. . . .
>
> Even if one borrows these countermeasures to bring the negative habit patterns under control, he or she has had sudden Awakening to the fact that the true nature of the mind is fundamentally pure, and that all defilements are empty. Therefore, one will not fall into the degraded practice of . . . the gradual school. . . . In the case of an enlightened person, although one uses these expedients, in every moment he or she is free from any doubts and does not become polluted . . . because one never leaves the true self-nature. (*Susim kyŏl*, Q/A 8–9)

In 1185, Chinul traveled to another monastery, this time on a mountain in the southeastern part of Korea. At that time, it seems that he was especially concerned about the division within the Saṅgha between those monastics dedicated to the practice of meditation (Sŏn) and those dedicated to the study of doctrine (Kyo). Although committed to Sŏn, Chinul was convinced that the experience of Sŏn could also be found in the *sūtras* used by the Kyo schools. So he retired into the mountains to read the scriptures looking for a passage that would indicate something of the Sŏn experience. One day Chinul found what he was looking for in a Hwaŏm commentary on the *Avataṃsaka Sūtra*. This commentary discussed, among other things, the nature of pure wisdom and the interpenetration of phenomena in Indra's net, which we introduced in the previous chapter. Setting aside the text, Chinul breathed a long sigh and reflected:

> The teachings are what the world-honored One said with his mouth. Sŏn is what the patriarchs have transmitted with their minds. The Buddha's mouth and the patriarch's minds certainly cannot be contradictory. How can [disciples of Sŏn and Kyo] not reach the fundamental source, and instead be complacent in their training and ferment disputes, wasting their time? (*Hwaŏmnon chŏryo*, Preface)

From this second Awakening, Chinul understood that the unity of Sŏn and Kyo resided in their common experience of what the Buddha taught and what the Sŏn masters realized. This conviction of Chinul's became the basis for his work to unify the Saṅgha in a comprehensive system of Buddhist spirituality. For Chinul, sudden Awakening and gradual cultivation are possible in the Kyo schools. As the scholastic doctrines of Hwaŏm and the other Kyo schools point the disciple toward Awakening, they can be skillful means to promote enlightened experience. It is just that in the end the doctrines must be set aside in order for Awakening to take place. Although he was a Sŏn master, in his writings Chinul referred to Kyo concepts to explain Sŏn experience. For example, in his *Complete and Sudden Attainment of Buddhahood*, Chinul says that the sudden Awakening of Sŏn entails the realization of what Hwaŏm calls the mutual identification and mutual penetration of the *Dharmadhātu*, or what Wŏnhyo calls *Dharmakāya:*

> We know that the transmission of Sŏn beyond thought is the sudden realization of the *Dharmadhātu*. . . . If . . . sitting quietly in a private room, you can empty your heart and purify your thoughts, then you can trace back the radiance of your mind, returning to its source. You can consider the purity of the sublime mind that appears in that sudden moment of thought to be either original Awakening involved in defilements, or original Awakening of one's pure nature, or the unobstructed *Dharmadhātu*, or the Buddha of complete wisdom, or Vairocana Buddha. . . . [A]ny of these alternatives is acceptable.
>
> The original wisdom of universal brightness [spoken of by the Sixth Patriarch] is the very essence of all living beings and Buddhas. In it, suchness and phenomena . . . are all complete and have faded away. It is likened to the one great *Dharmakāya* taught be Wŏnhyo. . . . [F]rom the standpoint of the meaning of interdependence involved in dependent arising . . . we understand from Awakening that all living beings and Buddhas perfectly interpenetrate in the wisdom of universal brightness. (*Wondon sŏngbullon*, Q/A 3–4)

In 1190, Chinul and some of his fellow monastics who had made the pledge with him to found a Concentration and Wisdom Society finally began their reform experiment. They welcomed all people who were serious about cultivating concentration and wisdom in a secluded environment. By 1197, the community had gained widespread recognition and a large membership. It was said that Chinul's reform was so successful that the number of people who followed him grew so large that his retreat center became "like a city." Needing a larger site for his community, Chinul sent followers to the southwest of the peninsula where a new location was found. Later, the mountain on which this new monastic center was built was renamed *Chogye* (see Figure 8.3), after the mountain on which the Sixth Patriarch lived in south China. Therefore, the order that Chinul's society became was named the Chogye Order.

On his way to this new center in the spring of 1197, Chinul stopped for a time at a monastery for some quiet and solitude. There, he attained his third and final Awakening while reading a passage from the *Records* of the famous Chan master Dahui (1089–1163). Chinul said,

> [Before this Awakening,] I had not yet let go of passions and views, it was like there was something blocking my chest, or like I was living with an enemy. . . . [After this Awakening,] naturally, my chest was not blocked by anything again, and I never again lived with an enemy. I was always at peace from that moment on. (*Pojo kuksa pimyŏng*, *Pulgyo t'ongsa*, III, 338.9–12)

Dahui was a Chinese Chan master in the Linji lineage and a famous popularizer of the *huatou* (Korean: *hwadu*) method of practice. Something of this practice must have been behind Chinul's final Awakening, as Chinul became the first Sŏn master to adopt the *hwadu* method. Through his influence, it

FIGURE 8.3. Songgwang-sa Temple; founded in 1190 by Chinul on Mt. Chogye, Kwangju, Korea.

remains a central practice in Sŏn today. The term *hwadu* literally means "head of speech" and refers to the "critical phrase" in a *kongan* (Chinese: *gong'an;* Japanese: *kōan*). For example, one of the most popular *kongans* in Korea is the following: Once a monk asked Zhaozhou, "Does a dog have Buddha-nature, or not?" Zhaozhou replied, "No!" In this case, the *kongan* would be the whole exchange between the master and disciple. The *hwadu* would be the single word "no."

From the Sŏn perspective, all living beings, including dogs, are said to have Buddha-nature. So, the question is, why did Zhaozhou say "no"? To understand his answer, one has to enter the mind of Zhaozhou at the time he made the remark. In practice, the practitioner can penetrate into the mind of Zhaozhou through the *hwadu* "no" by concentrating on this single word in all sifuations: meditating, walking, eating, working, and so forth. The *hwadu* focuses the mind and its paradoxical content bringing the mind's conceptual functioning to a stop. Behind this progression into the depths of the mind is the force of the questioning "doubt" produced by the *kongan* and intensified in the *hwadu*. When one reaches the innate nature of the mind shared by the practitioner and Zhaozhou, then there can be a "mind-to-mind transmission" of Awakening.

Chinul drew on his three Awakenings in developing his teachings and system of practice. His life and work have done much to define the Sŏn experience in Korea and to unite the Korean Buddhist Saṅgha. Finally, it is also important to note that Chinul wrote a book entitled *The Essentials of Pure Land Practice.* During the Koryŏ Dynasty, Pure Land Buddhism was gaining general popularity with the laity, and Chinul helped ensure that Pure Land piety would continue to be an important part of Korean Buddhism. It is said that Pure Land devotional experience has added a personal dimension to Korean Buddhism that enriches meditation experience and keeps doctrinal study from becoming dry and impersonal. During the Koryŏ Dynasty, this piety also inspired great works of art and the building of many temples around the country.

The Korean Tripiṭaka

One of the greatest feats of Korean Buddhism took place during the Koryŏ Dynasty. In 983, the Chinese completed a Buddhist *Tripiṭaka* that contained not only the early Pali material but also Mahāyāna *sūtras,* scriptural commentaries, and philosophical texts from both the Abhidharma and Mahāyāna traditions. These texts were sent to Korea in 991. Then in 1010, the Khitans invaded Korea, forcing King Hyŏnjong (ruled 1009–1031) to flee his capital. When he did so, the king vowed to carve the whole Buddhist canon in Korean on wooden printing blocks if the invading forces were driven from Korea. It is said that ten days later, the Khitan army withdrew voluntarily. Hyŏnjong therefore initiated the enormous project to ensure continued protection of Korea from foreign invasion. The Korean *Tripiṭaka* was completed decades later and included more than 80,000 wooden blocks.

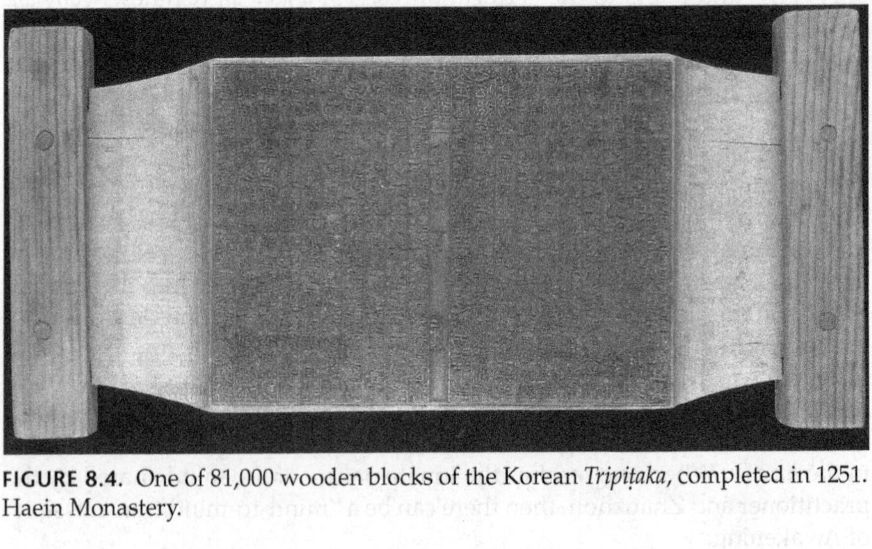

FIGURE 8.4. One of 81,000 wooden blocks of the Korean *Tripiṭaka,* completed in 1251. Haein Monastery.

Unfortunately, whatever protection was afforded by the *Tripiṭaka* was short-lived. The Mongols invaded Korea in 1231, and the ruling family was again forced to flee the capital. The Mongol invaders burned the wooden blocks of the *Tripiṭaka*. However, in 1236, the carving of a new set of blocks was ordered by royal decree. This second set was completed in 1251, and again contained some 1,512 titles carved on over 80,000 blocks. This second *Tripiṭaka* is still preserved today at the Haein Monastery, where it is rightly considered a national treasure (see Figure 8.4). Both the Chinese and Korean *Tripiṭakas* were "open canons" in that they permitted the inclusion of any materials deemed to be appropriate representations of the "word of the Buddha." This methodology allowed East Asians continually to insert new materials. Given its accuracy and comprehensive nature, the Korean text was adopted by the Japanese for their edition of the *Tripiṭaka*, produced from 1922 to 1934.

REPRESSION DURING THE CHOSŎN DYNASTY

By the end of the Koryŏ Dynasty, Buddhism had achieved immense power throughout Korea. Its network of mountain monasteries and city temples became centers where thousands of monks and nuns pursued spiritual and intellectual life and ministered to the needs of the common people. The monasteries were awarded tracts of land that were worked by serfs, who were also given to the monasteries by the government. Some of the monastics developed commercial businesses. However, this power and affiliation with the government was held against the Buddhist religion when the Koryŏ Dynasty fell and was replaced with the Chosŏn (or Yi) Dynasty (1392–1910).

The Chosŏn government turned its support to Confucianism and severely limited Buddhist organizations. The number of monks and nuns in the Saṅgha was restricted, and at times there was a complete ban on ordination. The number of temples was first reduced to 242, but eventually only 36 temples of any importance were allowed to stay open. Monastic lands and serfs were confiscated by the government. The ordination examination system was eliminated, all the city temples were closed, and Buddhist monastics were forbidden to enter urban areas. This meant that the Saṅgha was pushed into the remote countryside, where monastics were isolated from the intellectual and cultural life of the nation. On the other hand, at times conditions did improve for the Saṅgha. During one such period, King Sejong (ruled 1419–1450) united the Sŏn and Ch'ŏnt'e schools into a unified Sŏn School and united the various scholastic schools into one Doctrinal (Kyo) School.

Hyujŏng (1520–1604) was an influential Buddhist monk during the Chosŏn Period. Hyujŏng advocated the use of the doctrinal approach to Buddhism taught by the Kyo School in combination with Chinul's practice of sudden Awakening followed by gradual cultivation as taught by the Sŏn School. In fact, he was appointed director of the Kyo School after taking his monastic examinations, and later was appointed director of the Sŏn School as well.

The following are passages from his *Mirror for Meditation Students* that reflect this ecumenical spirit:

> Here, there is only one thing [the One Mind]. From the very beginning it is clear and holy. It was never born, nor has it ever disappeared. It cannot be grasped by either names or forms. . . . The Dharma has different meanings, and people have different capacities. Therefore, it is necessary to present skillful teachings. [In these teachings,] different names are given, such as "mind," "Buddha," and "living beings." But one must not be attached to names and try to correct each other about them. If their essence is [the one thing/One Mind] right here, then that is what is truly correct. If thoughts are stirred up in the mind, then that is a mistake.
>
> The transmission of mind by the Buddha . . . is the reason for Sŏn. What the Buddha said during his life is the way of Kyo. Therefore, it is said that Sŏn is the Buddha's mind, and Kyo is his words. . . . The Gate of Kyo only transmits the Dharma of the One Mind. The Gate of Sŏn only transmits the Dharma of seeing one's true nature. The mind is one's true nature, and one's true nature is the mind.
>
> Therefore, the students of the [Buddhist] path must first discern through the true words of Kyo that the two principles of suchness and causality are the innate nature and the characteristic of one's own mind. Then they must understand that the Two Gates of the beginning and end of their [Sŏn] practice are the gate of sudden Awakening and the gate of gradual cultivation. Only following this can they set aside the Kyo principles and take hold only of the one thought [*hwadu*] that appears in their mind. Then they can realize what is already right here to be attained. This is called the living path to liberation. (*Sŏnga kugam*, in *Hanguk pulgyo chŏnsŏ*, 7: 619–621)

Hyujŏng also taught that Pure Land recitation and *mantras* from the Tantric tradition could be used in the practice of gradual cultivation. Following Chinul's views about how gradual cultivation can heal negative habit patterns, Hyujŏng especially held Pure Land practice in high regard. He considered it indispensable alongside Sŏn practice. In part as a consequence of the teachings of Hyujŏng and his students, Pure Land practice became quite popular in Korea in the seventeenth and eighteenth centuries, and its practice became the norm in Sŏn monasteries. Another master in the line of Hyujŏng, Sŏngch'ŏng (1631–1700), went so far as to say that in most cases the burden of past karma is so heavy that the vast majority of Sŏn practitioners will end up being reborn into *saṃsāra*. Therefore, Pure Land practice is also important in that it can enable one to be born into Amitābha's Pure Land where there is a greater promise of full liberation.

Toward the end of the Chosŏn Period, Sŏn Buddhism gradually regained prominence, thanks in part to new Sŏn scholarship and the fact that there was a growing collaboration between Confucian intellectuals and Buddhist monastics. Also, there were individual monastics who worked to modernize the Saṅgha and reach out to the laity. One such Sŏn master who was known for his reform work at this time was Kyŏnghŏ (1849–1912). After his Awakening, he encouraged the growth of Sŏn by rebuilding old training centers; offering retreats for monks, nuns, and the laity; and founding Buddhist societies for all people who wanted to take up Sŏn practice. Another reform-minded monk was Han Yŏgun (1879–1944). Han was very concerned with what he saw as the shortcomings of Korean Buddhism after traveling to Siberia and Japan. He proposed a thorough revising of the religion from the education of the Saṅgha to the particulars of temple management. Han also believed that if Buddhism was to contribute to the modern world, it must balance the search for Awakening with a social consciousness. Monks and nuns should not be attached to their religious life in the mountains, but should come down to care for the common people and teach them the Dharma. Here, Han appealed to the bodhisattva ideal that teaches a unity between the attainment of wisdom and the compassionate living of *bodhicitta*.

THE JAPANESE OCCUPATION AND RECENT DEVELOPMENTS

The Chosŏn Dynasty fell when the Japanese annexed Korea in 1910. The new government removed restrictions on Buddhism, and monastics were allowed to enter the cities for the first time in 300 years. At first, this pleased the Buddhist leaders in Korea. However, in the Temple Ordinance of 1911, the Japanese placed control of all Korean Buddhist institutions in the hands of the Japanese governor-general. It soon became clear that the Japanese were planning to place the Korean Saṅgha under the control of the Japanese Sōtō Zen School. Also, the reform proposals of people like Han Yŏgun had included the replacing of the celibate Saṅgha with a married priesthood. The Japanese supported this idea because it would fit the Korean Saṅgha into their own tradition, which accepted married priests. The Japanese leaders in Korea pressured Korean monks to marry and offered Saṅgha leadership positions only to married monks. Gradually, married monks became the majority in the Korean Saṅgha. In 1926, when the Japanese required the Korean monasteries to remove any rules against marriage, there was a serious division in the Korean Saṅgha between its celibate and married members.

In the midst of this crisis and in response to the Japanese threat to control the Korean Saṅgha, the Kyo and Sŏn schools began a series of negotiations in 1928. Seven years later, they reached an agreement and the Korean age-old dream of a united Saṅgha was realized. In 1935, the two schools were united into what was named the Chogye Order. Note that this new order took the name of Chinul's Order that had been founded centuries ago. However, this unity within the Saṇgha was short-lived. When Korea won independence in 1945, the order was split between the minority of monastics who had preserved their celibacy during the Japanese occupation and the majority who had not.

It was not until 1954, after the end of the Korean War, that the South Korean government stepped in to support a celibate order. This led to violent confrontations between members of the two factions. Finally in 1962, a South Korean Buddhist Council recognized two distinct orders in the Saṅgha. First is the Chogye Order, which had been originally founded in 1935 and professes celibacy. Second is the new T'aego Order, which accepts married monks. Today, the Chogye Order is flourishing with virtually all the monasteries of South Korea under its control. The T'aego Order is in decline with few members to staff the small number of temples they have maintained. Meanwhile in North Korea, Buddhism has suffered under the communist government, as has been the case in other parts of East Asia. Even today, the real condition of Buddhism and the status of the Saṅgha in the north are not known.

In South Korea, the Chogye Order has attempted to maintain a blending of Buddhist traditions. This can be seen in the fact that at the four head Chogye training monasteries, there are centers for Sŏn meditation, Kyo study, *Vinaya* discipline study, and Pure Land recitation. As in past centuries, the Sŏn tradition is seen to be the heart of Buddhist monastic training. At the beginning, Sŏn is practiced in the meditation hall dedicated to that purpose. Sŏn today uses the traditional *kongan* practice with emphasis on *hwadu* as taught by Chinul. Twice a year, once in the summer and once in the winter, a three-month meditation retreat is held in the meditation hall. After several years of training at this communal level, the serious student may spend from five to ten years in a hermitage pursuing meditation practice in search of Awakening.

The Chogye Order has also taken steps to reinvigorate Buddhist culture throughout South Korea and to share its experience of Buddhism with the rest of the world. In South Korea, it has developed Sunday schools and private schools for all ages (see Figure 8.5). There are two very active nuns' orders in South Korea, with many of their members active in social work. Numerous lay Buddhist organizations have been founded in South Korea,

FIGURE 8.5. Children celebrating Buddha's birthday in Seoul, South Korea.

and Sŏn masters have opened their training centers to lay Buddhists. Lay-oriented Sŏn meditation centers have been opened around the globe with some success.

Meanwhile since the middle of the twentieth century, there has also been a strong growth of Christianity in Korea. Although Roman Catholicism was introduced in the eighteenth century and Protestantism in the late nineteenth century, only after the Korean War (1950–1953) has the number of Christians surpassed the number of adherents to Buddhism and other traditional Korean religions. During the burgeoning Korean economy in the 1960s, the urban population grew, as did the overall industrial workforce. Christian missions focused on the large cities and the new factories. Also, Christian schools that had been founded earlier expanded and included women, who had previously been excluded from public education. Other factors also contributed to the rising popularity of Christianity in Korea, including the marginalization of Buddhism in the Chosŏn Dynasty and the negative effects of the Japanese occupation on Korean Buddhism, the Christian support of Korean nationalism during the Japanese occupation, the fact that traditional shamanistic Korean religion has the notion of a monotheistic creator God, and the belief by many Koreans that the economic successes they have enjoyed are blessings from God.

WON BUDDHISM: A NEW SOCIALLY ENGAGED MOVEMENT

It is said that in 1916, Pak Chŏng-bin (1891–1943), better known as Sot'aesan, attained a great spiritual Awakening after many years of ascetic practice. Part of his experience was a vision of the future in which he saw many people in the twentieth century enslaved by the power of materialism, turning to violence, and forsaking moral and spiritual living, thus putting modern civilization in danger. Sot'aesan believed from what he saw that there was a need for a spiritual power based on enlightenment, faith, and morality to protect the dignity of humankind and justice in society. Upon reading the *Diamond Sūtra*, Sot'aesan concluded that the Dharma needed to be reformulated to be an effective force for modern spiritual renewal.

Sot'aesan presented an outline of his proposed doctrinal reforms and exchanged ideas about this reform with Buddhist monastics in Korea. Deciding that his reform required a new Buddhist order, the headquarters for such a reform order was begun in Iri, Korea, in 1924. The new order was named "The Research Society of the Buddha Dharma." In 1935, the Great Dharma Hall was built on the grounds of the headquarters, and the *Irwŏn-sang* was enshrined. The *Irwŏn-sang* is a unitary circle symbolizing *Dharmakāya* Buddha, which is seen to be the origin and original enlightened nature of all sentient beings, Awakening, and Nirvana. Branch temples were also established throughout Korea to bring this new movement to the general public. Later, renamed "Won Buddhism," referring to the unitary circle symbolizing the *Dharmakāya*, it became a major religion in Korea with more than 400 temples. Won Buddhism also has more than thirty branch temples in Europe and the United States. Advocating interfaith cooperation between world religions to foster peace and unity, Won Buddhism has been a major contributor to international interfaith activities.

The Won Buddhist experience entails "Four General Platforms" as the bases for dealing with the social ills of modernity. First is "Right Enlightenment and Right Conduct." For Won Buddhism, the essence of the Buddha's enlightened mind, the *Dharmakāya*, is the pure and unchanging essence of all the ordinary and changing things in the universe. "Right Enlightenment" is the realization of this ultimate reality. In "Right Conduct," one reflects this reality that is clear, impartial, and compassionate in dealing with situations that would ordinarily make one greedy, angry, or confused. Thereby, one can use the power of the *Dharmakāya* to escape modern forms of delusion, overcome the temptations of modern materialism, and confront modern types of violence to humanity and the environment.

How does one attain this spiritual experience of *Dharmakāya* and its ethical power according to Won Buddhism? It is suggested that one follow the "Threefold Practice" of spiritual discipline. These three practices relate to the three parts of the Buddha's Noble Eightfold Path: morality, concentration, and wisdom. The first practice, "Mindful Karma Creation," is moral discipline cultivated in daily life and in formal sessions at training institutes. This formal training includes calling on the name of Amitābha Buddha, study of scripture, lectures, discussions, keeping a diary, repentance, and exercise of the precepts. The second practice, "Cultivation of Spirit," is meditation for the development of clear awareness and tranquillity, which are aspects of the essence of one's true mind, the *Dharmakāya*. By practicing Sŏn (Zen) meditation along with chanting to Amitābha Buddha, one can realize this clear and calm reality so as not to be blinded or disturbed by the materialistic desires and violence that attract and attack our modern world. The third practice, "Inquiry into Facts and Principles," is wisdom development that guides proper action. One can gain wisdom by studying the functioning of the *Dharmakāya* in the world. By pondering the seasons; the faces of nature; the realities of illness, birth, and death; and the qualities of goodness and peace, one can discern the *Dharmakāya* and better distinguish truth and goodness in daily affairs.

The second platform is called "Awareness of Beneficence and Its Recompense." Sot'aesan is said to have seen that in the modern world there would be a lack of respect and gratitude for life in its many forms. There would especially be discrimination against people based on social status, age, gender, and race. Won Buddhism teaches that the *Dharmakāya* is the source of the "Fourfold Beneficence" to which one owes his or her life. It says that by recognizing this fact, one can build peace and reconciliation in our modern world. The first beneficence is heaven and earth, which support all life forms with an impartial embrace that cares for all living beings. Gratitude to heaven and earth turns into a practice of grateful care for all people and other living beings. Second is the beneficence of parents, who gave life to their children. Gratitude in this case means to support one's own parents and the parents of all peoples as one would do for one's own. Third is the beneficence of one's

Box 8.2

Who Am I?

Won Buddhism has been instrumental in discovering my identity and value as a person, and maintaining centeredness and balance in my life. Won Buddhist practices of sitting meditation, chanting meditation, and meditation in action have helped me to understand myself and the world around me. Through this process, I have learned to cultivate my own wisdom, inner strength, and beauty.

Won Buddhism helps me overcome many challenges and difficulties, such as sexism, racism, and religious discrimination. Through silent meditation, I have gained the self-awareness that I have an unlimited capacity within myself that is far more powerful than those external difficulties.

I was born in a small village in Korea. Korea is traditionally a kinship-oriented society based on the principle of patrilineal descent. I remember vividly the day I first encountered sex discrimination. In Korea, it is customary to maintain a genealogy in a family lineage book. Once every few years, names of new family members are added. One day, the revised genealogy book arrived at my home. I was very excited to see our family page. On this important page, I saw my father's full name, but not my mother's name. My mother was identified only with her father's name. I saw my brothers' names, even my younger brother's name, but not my name nor my sisters' names.

I felt very awkward. What an outrageous custom! "I am nonexistent according to our genealogy book," I thought to myself. "Women simply do not exist." When I asked my father, he told me that the family lineage book does not include any female members unless they are listed subordinate to their husbands. I realized I lived in an unjust and unequal society. I immediately felt rebellious toward patriarchal values.

From that very young age, I have asked simple questions: Who am I? Why am I here and what value does my life have? How and where do I fit in as a female in our patriarchal society?

It has been a long journey to find some of the answers to these questions, and I am still in the process of searching for the rest of the answers. In this journey, I found Won Buddhism, which practices gender equality. In Won Buddhism, women have an active role and are encouraged to cultivate their full potential since both men and women have the same Buddha-nature. Eventually, I joined the Won Buddhist community and received full ordination.

Through much angst and intense deep inner struggle, I have found strong spirituality, the awakening of the Divine within, the Buddha-nature within myself. It is the way of life that I have chosen to be in touch with my True Self. Won Buddhism helps me to see meaning in my life, in my place in the world, and in Ultimate Reality.

VEN. CHUNG OK LEE
Won Buddhism International

fellow humans, animals, and plants. Gratitude for the support of our life by people, animals, and plants means to share with all living beings whatever one can to better their lives. Finally, the fourth beneficence is the law. "Law" here means religious and moral teachings, the principle of justice, and the particular laws that support a just and peaceful social order. Gratitude in this case means to follow the ways of spiritual and moral cultivation, live justly, and support social harmony and world peace.

The third platform is "Practical Application of the Buddha Dharma." Won Buddhism believes that today Buddhist principles must have practical application to daily affairs for the good of one's self, family, nation, and world. Therefore, Buddhism should become a powerful tool for both personal and social transformation. Finally, the fourth platform is "Selfless Service for Public Well-Being." This means living out the third platform in the spirit of Buddhist compassion embodied in the *bodhisattva* as an antidote for modern egoism, materialism, and consumerism. This bodhisattva-like selfless service is the inspiration for Won Buddhism's social engagement of the modern world.

In his *Scriptures of Won Buddhism*, Sot'aesan presents "The Essentials of Daily Cultivation." They begin with an explanation of how the Threefold Practice relates to the experience of *Dharmakāya*:

> Although there is no disturbance in the mind-ground [*Dharmakāya*] in its original nature, disturbances arise in accordance with the mental spheres; hence, set up the calmness (*samādhi*) of self-nature by keeping disturbances from arising.
>
> Although there is no delusion in the mind-ground in its original nature, delusions arise in accordance with the mental spheres; hence, set up the wisdom (*prajñā*) of self-nature by keeping delusions from arising.
>
> Although there is no defilement in the mind-ground in its original nature, defilements arise in accordance with the mental spheres; hence, set up the precepts (*śīla*) of self-nature by keeping defilements from arising.[1]

This Threefold Practice is complemented in The Essentials of Daily Cultivation with the practice of the Fourfold Beneficence and Selfless Service for Public Well-Being. Failure to pursue or achieve these ideals leads one to personal confession and prayer, and then to a return to further socially engaged practice.

The Cultural Experience of Korean Buddhism Today

Jongmyung Kim
The Academy of Korean Studies, Bundang-gu, Republic of Korea

Korea is a multireligious country, with Buddhism, Protestantism, and Catholicism as the three major religious traditions. Korean Buddhist communities are led primarily by monks and nuns, who in turn are supported by lay followers. Buddhist teachings are gaining greater attention among the educated laity, and Buddhist colleges, run by both monastic and lay organizations, are flourishing. In addition, more Buddhist practitioners, as well as interested non-Buddhists, are engaged in meditative practice.

On the other hand, the actual practice of popular Buddhism in Korea is primarily characterized by devotional activities in pursuit of secular benefits or by the performance of various rituals for deceased family members. As a result, the influence of Buddhism in contemporary Korea appears to be less than in the past, except in political and cultural circles. In terms of politics, the large number of Buddhist followers often makes them the object of interest for politicians, especially during election campaigns. However, Buddhist politicians are few in number. In terms of Korean culture, the richness of the Buddhist heritage attracts the attention of both Koreans and foreigners.

In a strict sense, Korean Buddhist followers are not sectarian. However, it is common for Buddhist laypersons to choose to attend a particular temple affiliated with a specific Buddhist order. More than fifty Buddhist orders are thought to exist today, of which twenty-five are currently registered as members of the Association for Korean Buddhist Orders (*Han'guk chongdan hyŏbŭihoe*). However, the majority of these orders were founded in the past forty years or so and have small followings. The Chogye Order and the T'aego Order are the largest, with their own universities—Dongguk University and Dongbang Graduate University, respectively.

The Chogye Order (http://www.buddhism.or.kr), which is unique to Korea and is run by celibate monks, constitutes the mainstream of Buddhism in contemporary Korea. Although it professes to follow Sŏn in accordance with the teaching of Chinul (1158–1210), the Chogye Order embraces various schools of Buddhist doctrine as well as Pure Land beliefs, making the Korean approach quite different from Chan in China and Zen in Japan. Second to the Chogye Order in influence and governed by married monks, which is a product of Japanese colonial rule from 1910 to 1945, the T'aego Order is characterized by its elaborate performance of Buddhist memorial rituals. Because the Chogye Order of Korean Buddhism (*Taehan Pulgyo Chogyejong*) is representative of the Korean Buddhist tradition today, tlie following discussion of popular Buddhist practice and culture is primarily concerned with lay Buddhist followers affiliated with this order.

TEMPLE RITUALS

Temple rituals in contemporary Korea can be divided into daily rituals and commemorative services held on specific days. As for the performance of daily rituals (*yebul*), temples throughout the Korean peninsula follow nearly identical schedules. Daily rituals are performed in homage to Buddhas and bodhisattvas every morning and evening. There are three daily rituals: the Daybreak Service (*saebyŏk yebul*); the Service at the Watch of the Snake (*sasi Pulgong*), that is, the period between 9 and 11 A.M.; and the Evening Service (*chŏnyŏk yebul*). Both monastics and laypeople participate in these rituals. In the monastic life, these three constitute the core of Buddhist rituals, and among them the Daybreak Service is the most important ritual in that it is most comprehensive in content. Whereas more monks take part in the Daybreak Service and the Evening Service, more laypeople join the service at the Watch of the Snake.

The service at the Watch of the Snake, which takes about an hour, is led by a monk with laypeople following. Lay participants often have difficulty understanding the content of the ritual, possibly because the ritual texts are written in classical Chinese, which is incomprehensible to most laypersons. In addition, *mantras* are an important part of the ritual, and lay followers repeatedly recite the *mantras* in transliteration without recognizing their meaning. On the other hand, homage to the Three Jewels—the Buddha, Dharma, and Saṅgha—constitutes the real essence of the ritual and provides a meaningful experience to the laity.

Commemorative services performed on specific days in which lay Buddhist followers take part include (1) the four main Buddhist commemorative services, (2) the *Ullambana* ritual (*Uranbunjŏl* in Korean), and (3) memorial services for deceased members of the laity. Using the lunar calendar, the four Buddhist commemorative services are the Birthday of Siddhārtha Gautama, celebrated on the eighth day of the fourth month; the Day of Siddhārtha Gautama's Leaving Home, celebrated on the eighth day of the second month; the Day of Siddhārtha Gautama's Attainment of Enlightenment, celebrated on the eighth day of the twelfth month; and the Memorial Day of the Death of the Buddha, celebrated on the fifteenth day of the second month.

Among these commemorative services, the Buddha's Birthday (*Puch'ŏnim osin nal* or *Pult'anil*) is the most important annual Buddhist ceremony in Korea. It is usually celebrated in early May with opulent festivals at all temples throughout the country. This holiday is noted for popular street parades and large displays of what are called "lotus lanterns." The parades and displays of lotus lanterns constitute an important part of contemporary Korean culture, and foreigners also participate in these events. On this day, many Korean Buddhist followers purchase a lotus lantern to make merit for their families. Often the largest lamps inside the main shrine hall at a temple are dedicated to the president of Korea and his wife, as well as other important political figures, thereby indicating the temple's desire to maintain close ties with political leaders. In addition, selling of lotus lanterns to lay Buddhist followers and collecting alms from them make the Buddha's Birthday the most lucrative day of the year for Korean temples.

Following the Buddhist tradition based on the *Ullambana Sūtra*, and engrafted upon native Korean ancestral worship and filial piety, the *Ullambana* ("deliverance from suffering") ritual is performed in Korea on the fifteenth day of the seventh month of the lunar calendar. The ritual includes elaborate offerings made to Buddhist deities for the purpose of releasing from hells those who have died on land or sea. This commemorative service is very popular all over East Asia. In Korea, besides the Ullambana ritual, the monthly schedule of Korean temples contains many memorial services for deceased members of the laity (*ch'ŏndojae*). These services, which constitute an important part of monastic life in Korea, are primarily dedicated to such bodhisattvas as Avalokiteśvara, who is known for her merciful deeds. The most popular of these memorial rituals in Korea is the Ritual on the Forty-ninth Day after One's Death (*sasip kujae*). This ritual is attracting growing attention among both Buddhist and non-Buddhist bereaved family members, even including Korean Catholics. Finally, it is important to note that unlike in Japan or Tibet, Korean Buddhists do not enshrine a Buddhist altar in their houses for devotional and memorial purposes. Therefore, the temple rituals constitute the most significant form of popular religious practice for Korean lay Buddhists.

PRAYER AND PILGRIMAGE

The popular devotional practices that constitute an important part of Buddhism in contemporary Korea are characterized by the term *Buddhism for this-worldly happiness* (*kibok Pulgyo*). The majority of lay Buddhist followers in Korea go to local temples to pray in front of images of Buddhas and bodhisattvas in the hope of fulfilling their wishes for such this-worldly benefits as health, wealth, family needs, their children's success in university entrance examinations, and so on. The visit to the temple often includes devotional practices of lighting incense and/or a candle in front of the altar, presenting flowers at the altar, and bowing before the altar.

At times, many Korean Buddhists also travel to religious sites to perform prayers. One popular site is located on top of Mt. P'algong near Taegu, a metropolitan city in the southeastern area of Korea. There, the *Katbawi* (literally, Capstone Rock) or *Katbawi Puch'ŏ* (Capstone Rock Buddha) is located. It is a gigantic seated Buddha statue, believed to be an image of Bhaiṣajyaguru Buddha, measuring 5.6 meters in height, and presumed to have been built in the seventh century. It is one of the most popular places to perform prayers because it is believed that if a devotee prays with the utmost sincerity, at least one of his or her wishes will be fulfilled. Pilgrims from all over the country, including the leading figures in the fields of politics and business, visit this sacred place in hopes of realizing their wishes. Though the prayer space covers an area accommodating 300 to 400 people, daily visitors often total between 2,000 and 5,000. The number reaches tens of thousands on New Year's Day and on the first and fifteenth day of each month of the lunar calendar.

As in other parts of Asia, Avalokiteśvara Bodhisattva is a very popular personage in Korean Buddhist piety. Lay Buddhists in Korea venerate her through daily practice at local temples, and also go on pilgrimage to venerate her at sacred sites. These sites include Pomunsa Temple on Kanghwa Island, Naksansa Temple in Kangwŏn Province, and Poriam Hermitage in South Chŏlla Province.

All three sites are said to have been built in the seventh century and are known as the Three Sacred Sites for Avalokiteśvara Bodhisattva's miraculous efficacy.

There are currently more than 900 traditional monasteries in Korea that also serve as destinations for pilgrimages. In particular, the Three Jewel Monasteries (*sambo sach'al*) are the most sought-after pilgrimage destinations for Korean Buddhists. The three monasteries are T'ongdosa, representing the Buddha; Haeinsa, representing the Dharma; and Songgwangsa, representing the Saṅgha.

Established during seventh-century Silla and located in South Kyŏng-sang Province, T'ongdosa (http://english.tongdosa.or.kr) is called the Buddha-jewel Monastery (*Pulbo sach'al*). This is because it is believed that the Buddha's relics are preserved in its Diamond Altar behind its main hall. Therefore, unlike other monasteries in Korea, no Buddha statue is enshrined in its main hall. Built in the ninth century as one of the ten temples affiliated with the Flower Garland School (*Hawaŏmjong*) in Silla, and located in South Kyŏngsang Province, Haeinsa (http://www.haeinsa.or.kr) serves as the Dharma-jewel Monastery (*Pŏpbo sach'al*) because it houses the wooden block collection of the *Tripiṭaka Koreana*. Founded in ninth-century Silla and located in South Chŏlla Province, Songgwangsa (http://www.songgwangsa.org) is designated as the Saṅgha-jewel Monastery (*Sŭngbo sach'al*) because it is believed to have produced sixteen National Masters, including Chinul.

THE TEMPLESTAY PROGRAM

The Templestay program in Korea (http://www.templestay.com) provides an opportunity to participate in the daily routine at traditional Korean monasteries. At the hosting of the 2002 World Cup Games in Korea, the Chogye Order opened the gates of its monasteries to both lay Koreans and foreign visitors. This program, in which participants can experience the unique monastic life of Korean temples from early morning to evening, garnered positive response from participants. As of 2006, forty-three temples were included in the program. Although the content of the program is different from temple to temple, it includes meditation, daily rituals, group work projects, monastic meals, the tea ceremony, making of lotus lanterns, and printing and rubbing of a replica of the *Tripiṭaka Koreans*.

BUDDHIST CULTURAL HERITAGE IN KOREA

The Republic of Korea has many "world cultural heritage sites" (http://english.cha.go.kr), as is highlighted by the fact that it holds fourteen items registered on the UNESCO world cultural heritage list as of 2006. Four examples include the Monastery of the Land of the Buddha (*Pulguksa*), the Stone Buddhist Grotto (*Sŏkpulsa*), the Depositories for the *Tripiṭaka Koreana* (*Changgyŏng p'anjŏn*) at Haeinsa Monastery, and the *Chikchi* displayed at the French National Library.

Built in the mid-eighth century and located on the slope of Mt. T'oham in Kyŏngju, the ancient capital of Silla, the Monastery of the Land of the Buddha (http://www.bulguksa.or.kr) is Korea's favorite cultural asset. This monastery, now designated as Korea's most historic and celebrated site, was registered as a world cultural heritage site by the UNESCO in 1995. This monastery is representative of temples that present Buddhist doctrines through their architectural design. The structures of the site symbolize the transformation of the mundane world, the realm of ignorance, to the Lotus World, the Realm of Enlightenment. The monastery itself largely consists of wooden buildings on raised stone terraces. The level below the main temple compound represents the mundane world of the ordinary people, who are motivated by greed, hatred, and delusion. The arches over the bridges that connect this lower level with the upper level symbolize the rivers that, according to early Buddhist cosmology, demarcate the terrestrial world from the celestial realms. The upper level of the stone structure represents the Land of the Buddha composed of three areas: the Land of Śākyamuni Buddha, the Pure Land of Amitābha Buddha, and the Lotus Land of Vairocana Buddha. Among these, the Land of the Śākyamuni Buddha is the most spacious and is considered to be most significant because it emphasizes the original teaching of the Buddha, that is, liberation from sufferings in the mundane world by individual effort.

The Stone Buddhist Grotto, also a product of mid-eighth-century Korea, was registered on the UNESCO world cultural heritage list in 1995. It is a masterpiece of religious art, architecture, and geometry, perhaps unequaled in East Asian civilization. The site is composed of three parts: a rectangular antechamber in the front, a main rotunda with a domed ceiling in the back, and a connecting corridor. The rectangular antechamber symbolizes the earth, that is, the secular world. The main rotunda with a domed ceiling signifies the Buddha's Realm or the Realm of Enlightenment. The corridor represents the Buddhist passageway between this world and the Buddha Realm. The Stone Buddhist Grotto also enshrines an impressive assembly of forty different sculptured images embodying various aspects of Buddhist teaching. All of these sculptures are considered world-class works of art, and a majority of them became models for later Japanese Buddhist sculpture. Like the Monastery of the Land of the Buddha, the Stone Buddhist Grotto is also a representation of early Buddhist cosmology, with an emphasis on the importance of attaining enlightenment to one's True Mind, the source of all existence.

The *Tripiṭaka Koreana*, a complete set of the Chinese translation of the full Buddhist Canon, was printed twice in Korea. The first *Tripiṭaka Koreana* was printed in the eleventh century; the second was printed in the thirteenth century after the first *Tripiṭaka Koreana* was burned to ashes during the Mongol invasions in the early thirteenth century. One of the major achievements of East Asian Buddhism, the *Tripiṭaka Koreana* (http://www.sutra.re.kr) is contained on more than 80,000 wooden blocks. It is characterized by the breadth of its coverage, the accuracy of its content, the precise and exquisite carving technique, its innate ideological and cultural value, and its historical significance for Japan. Its value for Japan resides in the fact that it was the *textus receptus* for the Japanese *Taishō shinshū daijōkyō*, a collection of Buddhist scriptures compiled between 1921 and 1934, as well as for modern Chinese counterparts.

The *Tripiṭaka Koreana* is now available to readers in a forty-eight-volume set of facsimiles published by Dongguk University Press in 1976. This photolithographic reprint edition allows easy access for a large number of readers. In addition, the *Korean Buddhist Canon: A Descriptive Catalogue*, compiled by Lewis R. Lancaster in collaboration with Sung-bae Park and published in 1979, not only facilitates use of the xylograph collection but also serves as a reference work for any of the Buddhist texts that appear in the *Tripiṭaka Koreana*. A complete Chinese translation of Buddhist literature was first digitized in Korea based on the *Tripiṭaka Koreana* in 1993; the Digital *Tripiṭaka Koreana* 2004 is the newest version of it. The *Tripiṭaka Koreana* itself is preserved in the Depositories at Haein Monastery.

The *Chikchi* (http://www.jikjiworld.net) is a Sŏn text with the full title of *Master Paegun's Excerpts from the Buddha's and Patriarchs' Direct Pointing to the Essence of Mind* (*Paegun hwasang ch'orok Puicho chikchi simch'e yojŏl*). This text was published in 1377 and is the world's oldest extant book printed with movable metal type—it was published seventy-eight years earlier than Gutenberg invented movable type in Europe. This book was originally composed of two volumes, but the first volume was lost to history and only the second volume is now preserved in the French National Library. Its contents include recorded sayings of Sŏn masters, focusing on the concept of "no false mind" (*musim* or *munyŏm*) free from attachment to words and letters. The text also includes emphasis on firm faith in enlightenment, sudden enlightenment followed by gradual cultivation, an understanding of *hwadu* as a skillful means in meditation, and characteristic views concerning Buddhist precepts and recitation of the Buddha's name.

THE FUTURE OF POPULAR BUDDHISM IN KOREAN CULTURE

Some Korean scholars of Buddhism have expressed concern that for many Buddhists in Korea, the piety of the religion has been reduced to performing popular devotional practices simply to fulfill secular goals or to provide solace to families who have lost loved ones. A major aspect of the Buddha's teaching was its critique of what he saw as the overritualization of contemporary religion, leading to the loss of spiritual and ethical practice and purpose in life. From this perspective, popular Buddhism in Korea needs to pay more attention to this original spirit of the religion. In fact, Buddhism in Korea is in a period of reform and revival as it addresses the modern world, drawing on the spiritual and ethical heritage that originally inspired Korean Buddhist culture. This positive change is gaining popularity among intellectuals in Korea, while lay Buddhist networks are taking root around the country to promote the reform of Buddhism in the broader Korean society.

An example of such a reform-minded lay Buddhist network is Buddhist Solidarity for Reform (*Ch'amyŏ Pulgyo chaega yŏndae*, http://www.buddha21.org). Founded in 1999, it has forty organizational centers and 600 individual members. Buddhist Solidarity for Reform is a lay community that pursues a peaceful and mindful world based on the Buddha's teachings. Its aim is to promote the reform of the Buddhist orders so as to develop a "Pure Land" in which national unification is realized and human rights, social justice, and peace can be guaranteed. Recently, the Korean government followed the advice of Buddhist Solidarity for Reform and stipulated that governmental organizations should not discriminate against job applicants on religious grounds. It may be that through lay movements such as this one, as well as through the present-day religious renewal of the monastic orders, the spiritual, ethical, and theoretical basis of popular Korean Buddhist culture will be strengthened in the future.

NOTE

1. Bongkil Chung, *An Introduction to Won Buddhism* (Iri, Korea: Won Buddhist Press, 1994), p. 36.

SUGGESTIONS FOR FURTHER READING

Buswell, Robert E., Jr. *Tracing Back the Radiance: Chinul's Korean Way of Zen*. Honolulu: University of Hawaii Press, 1991.

———. *The Zen Monastic Experience: Buddhist Practice in Contemporary Korea*. Princeton, NJ: Princeton University Press, 1992.

———. *The Korean Approach to Zen: The Collected Works of Chinul*. Honolulu: University of Hawaii Press, 1983.

Cho, Eun-su. *Korean Buddhist Nuns and Laywomen*. New York: SUNY Press, 2011.

Chong, Key Ray. *Won Buddhism: A History and Theology of Korea's New Religion*. Lewiston, NY: Edwin Mellen Press, 1997.

Chung, Bongkil, trans. *The Scriptures of Won Buddhism*. Honolulu: University of Hawaii Press, 2003.

Grayson, James Huntley. *Korea: A Religious History*. Oxford, UK: Clarendon Press, 1989.

Kang, Wi Jo. *Religion and Politics in Korea under the Japanese Rule*. Lewiston, NY: Edwin Mellen Press, 1986.

Lancaster, Lewis R., and C. S. Yu, eds. *Assimilation of Buddhism in Korea: Religious Maturity and Innovation in the Silla Dynasty*. Berkeley, CA: Asian Humanities Press, 1991.

———, eds. *Buddhism in the Early Chosŏn: Suppression and Transformation*. Berkeley: University of California Press, 1996.

———, eds. *Introduction to Buddhism in Korea: New Cultural Patterns*. Berkeley, CA: Asian Humanities Press, 1989.

Lancaster, Lewis R., C. S. Yu, and Suh Kikun, eds. *Buddhism in Koryŏ: A Royal Religion*. Berkeley, CA: Institute of East Asian Studies, 1996.

Lee, Peter H., Wm. Theodore de Bary, Yôngho Ch'oe, and Hugh H. W. Kang, eds. *Sources of Korean Tradition*. 2 vols. New York: Columbia University Press, 1996, 2000.

Lee, Peter H., trans. *Lives of Eminent Korean Monks*. Cambridge, MA: Harvard University Press, 1969.

Muller, Charles A. *The Sūtra of Perfect Enlightenment: Korean Buddhism's Guide to Meditation*. Albany: SUNY Press, 1999.

Mullen, Charles A., and Cuong T. Nguyen, eds. *Wonhyo's Philosophy of Mind*. Honolulu: University of Hawaii Press, 2011.

Park, Jin Y., ed. *Makers of Modern Korean Buddhism*. Albany: SUNY Press, 2010.

Park, Sung Bae. *Buddhist Faith and Sudden Enlightenment*. Albany, SUNY Press, 1983.

Pihl, Marshall R. *Koryŏ Sŏn Buddhism and Korean Literature*. Honolulu: University of Hawaii Press, 1995.

9

Japanese Experiences of Buddhism

Buddhism is traditionally said to have been introduced into Japan in 552 by Sŏng-myŏng, the king of the Korean kingdom of Paekche. However, historians point out that there were colonies of Koreans in Japan prior to that date, and most likely Buddhist priests were among them. In any case, Sŏng-myŏng did present an image of Gautama Buddha, some ritual items, and *sūtras* to Emperor Kinmei (ruled 531–571) to foster a political alliance against the neighboring Korean kingdoms of Koguryŏ and Silla. A letter accompanying these gifts said in part:

> This teaching is the very best of all doctrines. However, it is difficult to explain and to understand. Neither the Duke of Zhou nor Confucius could comprehend it. This teaching can produce both happiness and rewards of unlimited quantity and boundless measure. It leads to the full appreciation of Awakening. Imagine a person possessing treasures that content his or her heart, and satisfy all wishes as these treasures are used. This is how it is with the treasures of this teaching. Every prayer can be fulfilled, and nothing is left wanting. This teaching has come from distant India to Korea, where all receive it with great reverence as it is preached to them. (*Nihongi*, II, 66)

The emperor consulted his court as to whether he should accept this foreign religion. The Soga clan, descended from Korean immigrants and responsible for foreign affairs, supported the acceptance of Buddhism. However, the Mononobe and Nakatomi clans, responsible for traditional rituals of what would later become known as the Shintō religion, were concerned that the acceptance of Buddhism into Japan would offend the indigenous *kami*, or spirits. This ancient religious tradition of Japan held the belief that there were many types of spirits residing in Japan. Although the people of Japan did not have a formal organized religious system at the time of the arrival of Buddhism, they did have local customs and ritual forms that were used to relate to and influence the spirits. The spirits were seen as coexisting with people in Japan, especially in the natural environment, so the Japanese people and spirits needed to live in harmony. Bringing foreign deities into Japan and worshiping them could be resented by the spirits and this would break the good relation the people had with the spirits. In the end, the emperor gave the Soga clan permission to adopt Buddhism. The Sogas built a temple to house the Buddha statue and even arranged the ordination of the first Japanese monks and nuns. When a plague broke out, the rival clans charged that the *kami* were in fact angry over this new religion, and they suppressed Buddhism. When this did not affect the plague, Buddhism was again supported.

As the Soga clan eventually dominated the court, Buddhism replaced the indigenous tradition as the state religion within just fifty years. Scholars point out that the acceptance of Buddhism was not so much because of its doctrinal positions or its spiritual practices, but because it was the carrier of an advanced continental civilization. However, most important was the attraction of its rites and ritual formulas, which were perceived to be powerful means for attaining security and prosperity. A major appeal of early Buddhism in Japan was its sacred power expressed in its system of Buddhas, bodhisattvas, temples, rites, and priests that could be called on in times of need.

PRINCE SHŌTOKU

The first Japanese emperor to actually practice Buddhism was Emperor Yōmei (ruled 585–587), who is said to have believed in the teachings of the Buddha while still respecting the way of the national gods. Emperor Yōmei's son, Prince Shōtoku (574–622), is honored by tradition as the founder of Japanese Buddhism. He supported the building of seven temples in Japan. In 593, he built the Shitennō-ji temple in present-day Osaka, which became the center for social welfare activities in Japan. In 607, he also built the Hōryū-ji temple complex at Nara, which housed many fine pieces of Buddhist art and became the center of Buddhist studies. Because many of the temples were built with the guidance of the Korean missionaries, they were crafted in the Paekche style.

In 594, Shōtoku issued an imperial decree that urged all people to accept the Three Refuges of Buddhism as the highest refuge for all living beings. In 604, he issued the *Constitution in Seventeen Articles*, a set of rules for government officials based on Buddhist, Confucianist, and Shintō teachings. In Article Two, he again emphasized the importance of accepting the Three Refuges, or Three Treasures:

> Give sincere reverence to the Three Treasures. These Three Treasures, the Buddha, Dharma and Monastic Orders, are the final refuge for . . . [all living] beings, and are the highest objects of faith in all countries. Few persons are completely evil; so they can be taught to follow it. But if they do not take up the Three Treasures, how can their crookedness be made straight? (*Nihongi*, II, 128)

Prince Shōtoku also saw a profound moral and spiritual philosophy in Buddhism. He is celebrated as the author of eight volumes of commentary on various *sūtras*. From the *Lotus Sūtra*, Shōtoku emphasized the idea of One Vehicle, or *Ekayāna*, and the idea that the highest teaching of this vehicle presents the view that all living beings have the innately pure Buddha-nature (*Tathāgata-garbha*), which is none other than the *Dharmakāya*, the Body of the Buddha itself. So Awakening can be attained by laypersons and monastics, men and women alike. On his deathbed, Shōtoku is said to have quoted a passage from the *Dhammapada* that describes the path to this attainment: "Avoid evil, undertake good, and purify the mind. This is the teaching of the Buddha." Since the time of Prince Shōtoku, this conjunction of moral virtue with the purification of the mind in search for the inner luminosity of one's Buddha-nature has been essential to the Japanese experience of Buddhism.

THE NARA PERIOD (710–784): THE SIX SCHOOLS FROM CHINA

To learn more about Buddhism, Prince Shōtoku initiated diplomatic relations with China and sent official delegations of monastic scholars to China for study. It was because of this initiative that the Six Schools of Japanese Buddhism were founded based on Chinese models. As the pro-Chinese Fujiwara clan replaced the Soga clan as the dominant force in the imperial court, the new Chinese-based Buddhist schools began to grow into an intellectual and political force in Japan. This influence can be seen in the new capital of Japan established in 710 in the present-day city of Nara. The city was modeled on the Chinese capital of Chang'an, and the plan for Nara included Buddhist temples at several strategic places. Emperor Shōmu (ruled 724–749) ordered the building of the famous temple, Tōdai-ji (see Figure 9.1), that enshrined a huge statue of Vairocana Buddha, fifty-three feet tall and made of 450 tons of bronze gilded with gold. This "Great Eastern Temple," dedicated in 757, was the centerpiece of the Nara system of Buddhist temples. It became the headquarters of the Kegon (Chinese: Huayan) School, as well as a place associated with other Buddhist schools. In 741, Emperor Shōmu also ordered the construction of two provincial temples (one for monks and one for nuns) in each province. In this positive environment, the Six Nara Schools flourished.

The Kusha School

The Kusha School, based on the Chinese Zhushe School, originated from the Indian Sarvāstivāda School. The Japanese Kusha School takes its name from the *Abhidharmakośa* written by Vasubandu. The Japanese Kusha School presents a detailed analysis of the elements (*dharmas*) of existence with the aim of helping people eliminate afflictive emotions and clinging attachments that produce obstructions to the attainment of Awakening. By seeing that oneself and the things of the world are products of these dependently arisen elements, one is able to free oneself from defiled states of consciousness (e.g., hate,

FIGURE 9.1. Tōdai-ji Temple; eighth century C.E., Nara, Japan.

greed, and delusion). By the extinction of such defiled mental and emotional elements, one experiences Awakening and reaches the unconditioned freedom of Nirvana. The Kusha School provided the Japanese Buddhist tradition with categories useful for moral, psychological, and philosophical analysis.

The Jōjitsu School

The Jōjitsu School, based on the Chinese Chengshi School, originated from the Indian Sautrāntika School. It also has certain affinities with Mahāyāna and is named after the *Satyasiddhi* (*Jōjitsu*) *Śāstra*. Jōjitsu claims that the Kusha School fails to understand fully the emptiness of the elements it analyzes. Kusha, Jōjitsu says, rightly examines the elements as a way of losing attachment to oneself and the world of things. But one must also discover the emptiness of the elements by experiencing them as impermanent factors in the process of life. However, Jōjitsu also claims that even this experience of emptiness is not enough. One has to transcend the very consciousness of emptiness. Only in this deeper experience of the "completion of truth" (*satyasiddhi*) can the person find the freedom of Nirvana so as to be fully able to live compassionately for others.

The Ritsu School

The third school, the Ritsu School, taught the *Vinaya* (Ritsu) discipline, which would be practiced by other forms of Japanese Buddhism. We saw that in China, there had been a concern that Buddhist monastics were not following true monastic discipline. To counter this tendency, the Lu School was founded to support the *Vinaya* discipline. Emperor Shōmu of Japan also realized that it was essential to have properly ordained and disciplined monks and nuns for Japanese Buddhism to prosper. So he sent two Buddhist priests to China to study the *Vinaya* and bring it to Japan. During their ten years of study in China, they first invited the *Vinaya* master Daoxuan (702–760) to teach the *Vinaya* in Japan. Later, they also invited the *Vinaya* master Jianzhen (687–763), known in Japan as Ganjin, to formally transmit the *Vinaya* lineage to Japan. Jianzhen settled at Tōdai-ji. Two months later, in 754, an ordination ceremony was held at Tōdai-ji, and Emperor Shōmu, part of his family, 440 laypeople, and 80 monastics of various schools received the formal *Vinaya* ordination. The experience of the Ritsu tradition is that the vows taken at the time of ordination constitute a spiritual and moral force that affects one's mind and heart in ways that produce virtuous actions. Also, the mind purified by the *Vinaya* is thought to be more receptive to the teachings of the Dharma and more capable of spiritual progress.

The Sanron School

The fourth school, the Sanron School, is based on the Chinese Sanlun School, itself a transmission of Mādhyamika from India. The Sanron School was the dominant school of thought in the early Nara period, and it has influenced all of Japanese Buddhism with its teachings concerning emptiness. Its first transmission to Japan came by way of the Korean monk Hyegwan, who also brought the Jōjitsu teachings and was the student of the founder of the Chinese Sanlun School. Other transmissions came later, and the Sanron School eventually divided into subsects based on these different transmissions. Given that its teachings concerning emptiness were similar to Jōjitsu's, the latter school was eventually absorbed into Sanron. Sanron taught that the "higher truth" into the real nature of things comes from a spiritual insight that transcends words and concepts. From this higher intuitive viewpoint, one sees that everything in the world is a product of dependent arising or emptiness. Ordinary awareness hides the higher truth of emptiness with its categorizing and conceptualizing mental functioning. Through the meditative cessation of this rational functioning of consciousness, the supreme truth about life can show itself in enlightened experience.

The Hossō School

The Hossō ("Characteristics of the *Dharmas*") School is based on the Chinese Faxiang School, which originates from the Indian Yogācāra tradition with its focus on the nature and functioning of consciousness. As with the Sanron tradition, there were a number of transmissions of Hossō to Japan from Korea and China. Hossō accepted the Sanron position that all things are empty because they are dependently arisen, but sought to understand the way in which things manifest themselves in this matrix to one's consciousness.

The chief concern of the Hossō School in Japan was to understand the nature and functioning of consciousness, because it was believed that the mind is the source of both ignorance and liberation. For the Hossō School, Awakening entails a "reversion" of the deepest level of consciousness so that the mind becomes like a "mirror" and can reflect clearly the truth about oneself and the world. The enlightened mind reflects the true nature of existence, the "suchness" (*tathatā*) of life. This change in one's consciousness transforms the way one thinks and acts. The major contribution of Hossō to the Japanese Buddhist experience was its analyses of human consciousness, the ways in which ignorance hides the truth, and the transformation of mind by which that truth can be found. This contribution helped to make Hossō the predominant school in the late Nara Period.

The Kegon School

The last of the Six Schools is the Kegon School, which is based on the Chinese Huayan School. Bodhisena, a monk from India, is said to have arrived in Nara around 726, and taught the doctrine of the *Avataṃsaka Sūtra*. Then the Chinese monk Daoxuan, who brought the Lu School to Japan, also brought Huayan texts with him in 736. Korean monks were also influential in introducing Huayan ideas. The Japanese government saw the Huayan teachings concerning the harmonious nonobstructed mutual penetration of all phenomena as a model for a unified Japanese society. The Kegon School, therefore, stressed the Huayan Buddhist teachings about the all-embracing interpenetration of the universe and the inherent Buddha-nature in all living beings. These two Kegon teachings are symbolized by the great Vairocana Buddha. Vairocana's radiant body, represented by the sun, symbolizes the luminous unity of all the elements of the universe. Each part of Vairocana's body, containing his Buddhahood, symbolizes the fact that each element of the universe has the Buddha-nature. Emperor Shōmu, inspired by this symbolism, cast the huge Buddha of Tōdai-ji temple in the image of Vairocana and used it to promote the unity of the Japanese nation.

THE HEIAN PERIOD (794–1185): TENDAI AND SHINGON

At the end of the Nara Period, the Buddhist schools had gained immense economic, political, and social power in Japan. Wealthy clans could donate land to monasteries and still receive income from that land. So monasteries came to represent the interests of rich landowners. Also, the government granted rice land and tax-exempt privileges to each of the regional temples. Tōdai-ji itself housed 4,000 families to cultivate its land and had over 100 slaves. The acquisition of such wealth and power brought corruption and the need for reform. This situation is a partial reason why the government moved the capital from Nara in 794 and established its new capital in the city of Heian, known later as Kyōto. In this way, it hoped to escape the influence of the powerful monasteries in Nara. With the seat of political power in Heian, two new Buddhist traditions began to develop near the capital. These are the Tendai and Shingon traditions that produced distinctively Japanese forms of Buddhism, which both drew on and synthesized the ideas and practices of the Nara schools.

Tendai Buddhism

While Tendai is the Japanese version of Chinese Tiantai Buddhism, some major innovations distinguish the Japanese version from its Chinese parent. These innovations are credited to Saichō (767–822), the founder of Tendai. Saichō, born in a village at the foot of Mt. Hiei, left home at the age of fourteen. He received novice ordination at seventeen, and two years later was fully ordained in the city of Nara. After functioning in Nara as a priest, he left the city in 788 to reside in a remote mountain retreat on Mt. Hiei. There, he founded a small monastery and sought to create a more rigorous and purified form of Buddhism. In 794, when the new capital was established in the nearby city of Heian, Saichō met Emperor Kanmu (ruled 781–806). The emperor was impressed with the young monk and his desire to create a new type of Buddhism. Saichō's quest fit with Kanmu's desire for a new form of Buddhism for his new capital. In 798, Saichō presented ten lectures on the *Lotus Sūtra,* which were attended by many scholars from Nara. Given his new fame, Saichō was sent by the emperor to China in 804 to find the best form of Buddhism for the new Japanese capital.

In China, he studied Tiantai at the headquarters of that school on Mt. Tiantai. He also studied Chan, the *Vinaya*, and Tantric forms of Chinese Buddhism. When Saichō returned to Japan, he developed a synthesis of Tiantai doctrine and practice, Chan meditation, Tantric practice and ritualism, Pure Land recitation, and *Vinaya* discipline. Although Saichō stressed the teachings of the Tiantai tradition, the practices of these other traditions were woven into his new school, called Tendai Buddhism (see Figure 9.2). As we shall see, Tendai also provided a religious foundation for the later development of Zen, Pure Land, and Nichiren Buddhism in Japan. Tendai itself became politically involved in Japan as it sought to protect the nation and make it into a "Buddhaland" during what Tendai considered the age of the Degenerate Dharma (*mappō*).

Saichō's Tendai Buddhism stressed the One Vehicle (*Ekayāna*) doctrine of the *Lotus Sūtra* that traditionally had been associated with Prince Shōtoku. Hence, Tendai is referred to as one of the two Heian "One Vehicle Schools," the other being Shingon. Associated with the highest teaching of the One Vehicle is the view that all living beings have the Buddha-nature, and thus partake in the *Dharmakāya*, the Dharma-body or essential enlightened nature of the Buddha. Here is what Saichō says in defense of this emphasis of Tendai in the face of attacks by the older Nara schools:

> I am now establishing the discipline of the One Vehicle for the profit and happiness of all living beings. This essay is being written to initiate this universal discipline. I offer prayers to the everlasting Three Refuges, that they may

> extend their invisible and visible protection so that this discipline will be transmitted without obstruction or harm, protecting the nation for all time. [By this discipline] may all living beings leading worldly or spiritual lives overcome what is incorrect, bring an end to what is evil, and protect their "seed of Buddhahood" [*Tathāgata-garbha*]. May all beings awaken to the universal [Buddha]-nature of all things, and obtain spiritual bliss in the land of peaceful light. . . .
>
> The emperor is equal to the sun and moon in Awakening, and his virtue is not different from that of heaven and earth. . . . The Buddha-sun is shining brightly again, and the Way to inner realization is flourishing. Now is the time for the Mahāyāna discipline of the perfect Dharma to be preached and promoted. . . . The *Lotus Sūtra* says, "Choose the straight Way, and set aside other means. Teach the perfect Dharma." It also says, "Now we should practice only the Buddha's wisdom." At present, however, the six [Nara schools] have so much power that they suppress the Buddha's discipline. . . . How can I remain silent? Instead of speaking, I have used here my brush to express just a few of my thoughts. (*Dengyō Daishi zenchū*, I, 16–17)

To enable people to "awaken to the universal Buddha-nature" and be transformed by it, Saichō taught a comprehensive spiritual journey that synthesized doctrinal and *sūtra* study, meditative discipline, Tantric practice, chanting, and *Vinaya* discipline. On Mt. Hiei, Saichō established two study areas to train his monks for this spiritual journey: One was devoted to study of the *Lotus Sūtra*, and the other was for Tantric studies. Before entering these areas, one had to take the Mahāyāna precepts and make a special vow not to leave Mt. Hiei for twelve years. During those twelve years of seclusion, the discipline of Tendai was rigorous to say the least. The moral, ritual, and *sūtra* training was complemented by a meditation method called *shikan*, meaning "concentration and insight." *Shi* is Japanese for *śamatha*, or tranquillity meditation, and *kan* is Japanese for *vipaśyanā*, or insight meditation. As we have seen, these are the two fundamental forms of Buddhist meditation going back to the original teachings of the historical Buddha.

Four particular types of meditation practice are also used in Tendai to foster the experience of the inner purity of one's Buddha-nature. First is a ninety-day practice during which one does "silent-sitting" meditation in the lotus posture while facing a Buddha image. During that time, one is allowed to chant the name of a single Buddha or bodhisattva to focus the mind. Second is another ninety-day practice that includes "walking" meditation, whereby one circumambulates a statue of Amida Buddha, as Amitābha is called in Japan, and chants repetitions of Amida's name. Third is a thirty-day practice of "half-sitting and half-walking" meditation. At first, one focuses the mind on Tantric images and symbols and chants *mantras* while walking around a Buddha image prior to sitting in meditation. Then one venerates the Buddha, chants passages from the *Lotus Sūtra*, and practices repentance for one's false views about reality. Finally, there is the practice of what is called "non-walking and non-sitting" meditation, which is observed in all of one's daily life. Here, one focuses on *sūtra* chanting and living the *Vinaya* precepts. One reflects on

FIGURE 9.2. Sanzen-in, Tendai garden and temple; Heian Dynasty (897–1185 C.E.), near Kyōto, Japan.

the image of Kannon (Avalokiteśvara) Bodhisattva, the bodhisattva of compassion, as one flavors all daily activities with compassion.

After Saichō's death, Mt. Hiei became the most important monastic center in Japan, with more than 30,000 monks and more than 3,000 buildings. It also began to emphasize more of the Tantric side of the tradition. Saichō himself did not systematize Tendai's esoteric (*mikkyō*) teachings and practices before his death. However, some of his disciples later traveled to China, where they deepened their Tantric studies and training, and returned to Japan to systematize Tantra in Tendai Buddhism. Two monks were especially important in this regard. First was Ennin (794–864), who led the Tendai School after the death of Saichō. Second was Enchin (814–891), who founded a center for Tantric study. Enchin became an abbot on Mt. Hiei, thus creating two lineages in Tendai—one from himself and the other from Ennin. In 933, a succession dispute broke out between the two groups. This split became more violent over the years. In these disputes, and to protect the wealth of Mt. Hiei, some monks became armed and formed the "warrior monk" tradition in Japan. These warrior monks sometimes descended Mt. Hiei and attacked the Heian capital when they disagreed with certain government policies and decisions.

Shingon Buddhism

The second One Vehicle School of Heian Buddhism is Shingon, which is based on the Chinese Chenyan School. The name of this school means "True Word" and refers to the *mantras* used in its Tantric practices. Shingon, then, is a Japanese form of Tantric or esoteric Buddhism. Indeed, because Tendai also uses Tantric elements, Heian Buddhism is sometimes referred to as the "esotericization" (*mikkyōka*) of Japanese religion. The founder of Shingon was Kūkai (774–835). Kūkai entered a state university at the age of eighteen and studied the Confucian classics. At the university, he met a Buddhist monk who showed him a scripture with esoteric passages. This inspired Kūkai to leave the university. He took up the life of a wandering ascetic, and during his travels read Buddhist texts. One text was the *Mahāvairocana Sūtra* from the mature Tantric tradition. Kūkai was attracted to its promise of sudden Awakening to the inner essence of Buddhahood, but he was not able to understand the esoteric use of *mudras, mantras,* and *maṇḍalas* that the text advocated for this attainment. So he decided to travel to China to find a teacher who could teach him this esoteric path. In 803, he became ordained as a Buddhist monk and left for China the next year.

In China, Kūkai received his training from the great Tantric master Huiguo (746–805). Huiguo had received transmission from two Tantric lineages: one based on the *Mahāvairocana Sūtra,* and the other based on the *Vajraśekhara Sūtra.* Under Huiguo, Kūkai received initiation into the meditative techniques associated with both Tantric lineages, and then received ordination as a Tantric master. In 806, Kūkai returned to Japan with *maṇḍalas,* scriptures, and Tantric ritual materials. In 809, the emperor ordered Kūkai to serve at Takaosan-ji, the temple that was the center of the Heian Buddhist world. There, Kūkai systematized Tantric doctrines, organized Tantric materials and *sūtras,* and vigorously propagated Tantric Buddhism. In 816, the emperor gave Kūkai permission to build a monastery on Mt. Kōya, some distance from the capital. Until his death in 835, Kūkai was also in charge of Tō-ji, a temple in the capital that was to be a center for Tantric art and practice.

Unlike Saichō, Kūkai succeeded in systematizing Tantric doctrine and practice within the Shingon tradition through his many writings. Among his writings is his famous *Ten Stages of Religious Consciousness* (*Jūjū shinron*). These stages present Kūkai's evaluation of different religions and forms of Buddhism. The following is from a condensed version of the *Ten Stages* entitled *The Precious Key to the Secret Treasury:*

1. The animal-like consciousness that is goatish in its desires. The common person in a kind of madness does not see his or her faults. This person thinks only of his or her desires and needs, like a butting goat.
2. The ignorant consciousness that is uncultivated yet abstains from evil. Influenced by various external causes, the consciousness is temperate. The will to be kind grows like a seed in good soil. [Confucianism]

3. The uncultivated consciousness that is without fear. The person hopes for rebirth in a heaven, to reside there for awhile peacefully. This person is like a child, like a calf that follows its mother. [Religious Taoism]
4. The consciousness that recognizes the objects of perception, but not the self. This person understands that there are only the *dharmas*, and not any permanent selfhood. [Theravāda Buddhism]
5. The consciousness that is freed from the karmic seeds of causation. Mastering the twelve-linked chain of causation, the consciousness is freed from the seeds of blindness. When rebirth is ended, the ineffable fruit of Nirvana is obtained. [The *pratyekabuddha*]
6. The Mahāyāna consciousness that seeks the salvation of others. When compassion is aroused from within, then the Great Compassion first appears. It views the distinction between self and other as a fiction, and recognizes only consciousness, denying the reality of the external world. [The Hossō School]
7. The consciousness aware of the negation of causality. By the eightfold negations, foolishness comes to an end. With a single thought of the truth, emptiness becomes apparent. The consciousness now empty and quiet knows undeniable peace and happiness. [The Sanron School]
8. The consciousness that follows the true One Vehicle. The whole universe is essentially pure; in this innate purity, knowledge and all phenomena merge. The person who knows this suchness of reality has the cosmic consciousness. [Tendai]
9. The consciousness that completely lacks own-being. Water lacks own-being; when affected by the wind, it becomes waves. The universe has no determined forms; but at the slightest stimulation, it immediately moves forward [into forms]. [The Kegon School]
10. The consciousness filled with the esoteric splendor of the celestial Buddha. With the medicine of the [above] exoteric teachings, the dust and stains of the consciousness are cleared away. Then, the True Words [*mantras*] can open the inner Treasury. When its secret treasures are suddenly displayed, all virtuous qualities [of the Buddha] become apparent in one's consciousness. [Shingon] (*Hizō hōyaku*, I, 420)

The teachings of Shingon are intended to guide people to this tenth stage of virtuous Buddha-consciousness. They do so by stressing that the highest Buddha is the *Dharmakāya*, the essential enlightenment nature of Buddhahood. This Dharma-body is a luminous reality of wisdom and compassion that penetrates and embraces all existence such that the *Dharmakāya* is actually one's own innate Buddha-nature. Kūkai identified this ultimate suchness of the universe with Vairocana Buddha, symbolized by the sun, which radiates its light to all beings in the universe. For Shingon, Vairocana, as the Dharma-body of the universe, preaches and acts continuously throughout the cosmos. Vairocana's presence and activity as the mind, speech, and body of the universe provide a "constant teaching." The purpose of this esoteric teaching is twofold: for

Vairocana's own enjoyment and for the salvation of all living beings. Shingon seeks to experience this teaching through its esoteric methods to realize one's innate Buddha-nature. This direct realization is an esoteric discovery of the very essence of the *Dharmakāya* that Vairocana represents.

Shingon also teaches that the secret and constant teaching of the *Dharmakāya* can actually be communicated to a person through the mysterious words, symbols, and ritual movements of Tantric Buddhism. The *mantras* that one recites bring into awareness Vairocana's speech, the *mudras* that one forms with his or her hands give one a felt sense of Vairocana's body, and the *maṇḍalas* on which one concentrates bring forth Vairocana's states of mind. Thereby, one unlocks the Three Mysteries (*sanmitsu*) of Vairocana: his speech, body, and mind in the universe. With the radiance of the *Dharmakāya* shining through Vairocana's Three Mysteries illuminating the body, speech, and mind of the practitioner, one's innate Buddhahood becomes manifest. Shingon believes that by realizing these mysteries in one's own experience, the long journey to Buddhahood, which in the other traditions might take eons to complete, can be attained in just one lifetime and in one's very mind and body.

In its Tantric empowerment, Shingon emphasizes the power of its *mantras* to open the practitioner to the reality of Buddhahood. Indeed, *mantras* are viewed as "empowerment-bodies" of the Buddha. They embody the power of the Dharma, constantly being taught by the *Dharmakāya*, that brings wisdom to the practitioner, and thereby enables him or her to realize the truth of his or her Buddha-nature. In this *mantra* practice, one focuses on the form, the sound, and the inner meaning of the *mantra* that reveal the form, voice, and mind of the Buddha. In this way, *mantras* are said to embody the very essence of the Three Mysteries. This power of the *mantras* is also "sealed" in the practitioner's body by the *mudras*, so that the practice transforms one's body as well as one's mind. Shingon believes that this dual transformation distinguishes it from other forms of Buddhism.

In Shingon, two *maṇḍalas* have a special place in bringing the virtuous and enlightened qualities of the Three Mysteries into one's experience. First is the Womb or Matrix (*taizō*) *Maṇḍala*, based on the *Mahāvairocana Sūtra*. This *maṇḍala* represents an enlightened view of the universe from the viewpoint of compassion, and implies that the energy of compassion enfolds, protects, and nurtures one's Buddha-nature like a womb holding a child. The many deities of this *maṇḍala* represent the activities of compassion; in Tantric experience, they foster this same compassion in the practitioner. This first *maṇḍala*, symbolized by the lotus, represents the compassionate gentleness of the universe evolving from unity to diversity.

The second *maṇḍala* is the Diamond (*kongōkai*) *Maṇḍala*, based on the *Vajraśekhara Sūtra*. In this *maṇḍala*, the universe is united in the light of wisdom that merges all beings into one. This wisdom concentrates all the universe into the single light of Vairocana Buddha, who is the luminous source of all the *maṇḍala's* deities. Penetrating this *maṇḍala* in Tantric experience is said to infuse the practitioner with the light of wisdom, and transforms his or her life into Awakening. This *maṇḍala* balances the gentleness of compassion in the Womb *Maṇḍala* by representing the diamond hardness of wisdom that cuts through illusion and brings diversity into unity.

By using these two *maṇḍalas* with the esoteric practice of *mantras* and *mudras*, the Shingon practitioner seeks to unite his or her human activities (speech, body, and mind) with the Three Mysteries of the universe—the speech, body, and mind of Vairocana Buddha in all things. The experience of this union with the Three Mysteries brings about a "mutual empowerment" in that both the practitioner and the Buddha are affected. While the practitioner attains Awakening and Buddhahood, Vairocana Buddha actualizes Buddha-nature more fully in the phenomenal world, as every act of the enlightened person is an action of the Three Mysteries. In this transformation process, the practitioner is guided by a Tantric master who alone has the ability to transmit these potent teachings and practices.

Shingon and Tendai both stressed the universal Buddha-nature and the need for moral discipline, study, and practice to realize this true nature of all existence. Both traditions weave together different elements of Buddhist thought and practice to provide more uniquely Japanese forms of Buddhist experience. However, by the end of the Heian Period, their temples held vast land acquisitions, and the tradition of the "maintenance monks" had given rise to the "warrior monks" mentioned earlier. The problem of corruption within Buddhism, coupled with the political chaos and social decay of the times, led many to despair. They concluded that the age of the Degenerate Dharma had overcome them. This conclusion would have an important role to play in the next stage of Buddhism in Japan.

THE KAMAKURA PERIOD (1185–1333): PURE LAND, ZEN, AND NICHIREN

Toward the close of the Heian Period in Japan, the country was divided into estates protected by warriors, and the imperial government was greatly weakened. By 1185, the Minamoto clan defeated its opponents, and its leader, Yoritomo, became the ruling power in Japan. To avoid the corruption found in Kyōto (Heian), Yoritomo established a samurai court in Kamakura far to the east and ruled as the shōgun. The emperor and his court, remaining in Kyōto, never regained any real power in Japan until the nineteenth century. This began the Kamakura Period of Japanese history. It was during this period that three major traditions of Japanese Buddhism were founded: Pure Land, Zen, and Nichiren. All three of the "new" Kamakura forms of Buddhism remain vitally influential today. They were founded by major religious figures who were ordained on Mt. Hiei but found the Tendai tradition to be inadequate. These new types of Japanese Buddhism appealed to the masses, who wanted more simple, independent, and singular forms of Buddhist practice as they faced living in what they considered the age of the Degenerate Dharma. They did not wish to rely on the overly intellectual learning of the Nara schools or on the complex ritualism and combination of practices of the Heian traditions.

Pure Land Buddhism

Mention of the *Larger Land of Bliss Sūtra*, so important in Pure Land Buddhism, was made in writings attributed to Prince Shōtoku. Invoking Amida Buddha was practiced in Nara Buddhism, and also by Tendai during the Heian Period. This invocation chanting practice, called *nembutsu*, was not the exclusive practice for these forms of Buddhism but was considered only one method of concentration. The Tendai abbot Ennin, upon his return from China, established a center on Mt. Hiei where the perpetual chanting of the name of Amida Buddha could occur. From the tenth to the twelfth century, a number of figures began to emphasize such Pure Land piety.

Genshin (942–1017) left Mt. Hiei to devote himself to the practice of *nembutsu* (chanting *Namu Amida Butsu*) and taught that its simple repetition practice was sufficient for rebirth in the Pure Land. Yōkan (1032–1111) stressed the way in which Amida protects his worshipers and also proposed a simple repetition of *nembutsu*. Chingai (1091–1152) founded a branch of Shingon that supported *nembutsu* as a means of reaching the Pure Land after death if it is practiced with sincerity and the desire to save all living beings. Finally, Ryōnin (1071–1132) as a Tendai monk was influenced by the Kegon School's vision of a fully interrelated universe. In that interrelated matrix, each person is united to all humankind in such a way that the action of one person can affect all humanity. Given this matrix, Ryonin believed, the *nembutsu* of one person can purify the whole of humankind.

These ideas provided inspiration for the founder of the Pure Land (Jōdo) School of Japanese Buddhism, Hōnen (1133–1212). Hōnen's father, a local samurai, was killed by an estate manager in a night raid. Hōnen, who was only nine years old, fled to a nearby Buddhist temple, where he spent three years. At age thirteen, he entered the Tendai monastic complex on Mt. Hiei and was ordained two years later. He then retired to a quiet retreat area on Mt. Hiei, where the Pure Land piety of Genshin was practiced. Here, Hōnen joined a group led by the successor of Ryōnin. Also during this time, Hōnen traveled to nearby Nara, where he studied the philosophy of the Six Schools and practiced *nembutsu* based on the writings of the Chinese Pure Land Patriarch, Shandao. In this Shandao inspired practice of *nembutsu*, greater emphasis was placed on the Other power of Amida, and less on the meditative aspects stressed on Mt. Hiei. Inspired by Shandao, Hōnen is said to have eventually attained a spiritual Awakening and inner peace. This attainment led him to leave Mt. Hiei in 1175 and to move to Ōtani on the outskirts of Kyōto. There he began to propagate his Pure Land ideas to people from all walks of life. His new form of Pure Land Buddhism would become known as a "single-practice" school because *nembutsu* was its exclusive form of practice.

Hōnen believed that *nembutsu* chanting would not only bring one to rebirth in the Pure Land after death, but it could purify past sins in this life as well. Therefore, he felt, *nembutsu* should be chanted often. Hōnen was also considered a great ordination master in the Tendai lineage, and even used Tantric rituals. Despite this, his message of single Pure Land practice met opposition from Tendai leaders, who felt that *nembutsu* should only be used in conjunction with other Buddhist practices. In 1206, alleged incidents of improper behavior by some of Hōnen's disciple priests occurred. These priests were beheaded, and Hōnen was exiled for ten months in 1207. He was not allowed to return to Kyōto until 1211, and he died the next year. Among Hōnen's followers, Shōkōbō (1162–1238) is generally regarded as a successor. His sect, which stresses *nembutsu,* is called the Chinzei branch of Jōdo Buddhism. Zennebō (1177–1247) founded the Seizan branch of Jōdo, which stresses *nembutsu* and the intimate relationship between the devotee and Amida Buddha. Although other branches of Jōdo emerged over the years, these two played historic roles in Japan's religious history and are active in Japan today.

The teachings of Hōnen are simple in comparison to the older Japanese schools. Hōnen emphasized Shandao's distinction between the Holy Path (*shōdō*) and the Pure Land (*Jōdo*). The journey on the former path requires reliance on one's own effort, or "self power" (*jiriki*). Reaching the Pure Land requires, on the other hand, a reliance on the "Other power" (*tariki*) of Amida Buddha. Hōnen believed that given the condition of humankind in the age of the Degenerate Dharma, the only real hope for humanity is to be born in Amida's Pure Land. This simple and clear message of hope for all people was very attractive to Kamakura Japan. Also attractive was the whole notion of the Pure Land as a place of joy, purity, and peaceful growth in the bodhisattva journey to Buddhahood. Hōnen taught that with further attainments on the bodhisattva path in the Pure Land, one could again be born in this world as a bodhisattva working for the salvation of others.

In his advice concerning *nembutsu* practice, Hōnen emphasized the three states of mind discussed by Shandao. Hōnen interpreted these to mean that one should recite *nembutsu* with (1) a *sincere* and devoted mind, (2) a mind of deep *faith,* and (3) a strong *aspiration* to attain the Pure Land. *Nembutsu* strengthens these three mental qualities (sincerity, faith, and aspiration) and directs them toward Amida Buddha. For Hōnen, *nembutsu* turns one's mind from worldly experience, evils, and cares to an undivided attention to Amida Buddha and experience of his light, purity, and grace. *Nembutsu* is practiced daily in a way that frees the mind from doubts; disturbing, evil, or idle thoughts; and false ideas. In engenders a growth in virtue and adds a spiritual dimension to one's work, family life, and recreation. In this way, *nembutsu* morally and spiritually enriches the person's ordinary daily experience from the moment it is begun to the moment of death.

One of Hōnen's writings, his *Passages on Selection* [*of the Original Vow*] (*Senchakushū*), is one of the classics of Japanese Buddhism. In it, he argues for selecting the Pure Land over the Holy Path of the other schools of Buddhism. He also expresses his compassion for the many people who sought his solace and healing, urging them to practice *nembutsu* with simple faith in the "Primal Vow" of Other power:

> The way of categorizing the Dharma of the Buddha differs among the various schools and sects. The [Hossō/Yogācāra] School divides . . . it according to existence,

emptiness and the Middle Way. The [Sanron/Mādhyamika] School divides the holy Dharma . . . into two scriptures: that of the bodhisattvas and that of the *śrāvakas*. The Kegon School categorizes the five teachings. . . . The [Tendai] School categorizes the four teachings and the five flavors. . . . The Shingon School categorizes the two teachings . . . the exoteric and esoteric.

Regarding [the categories of] the Pure Land School . . . relying on Master Dúochuo we set up the two gates that encompass the whole [Dharma]: the Gate of the Holy Path and the Gate of the Pure Land. . . . The Gate of the Holy Path is divided into two parts: the Mahāyana and the Theravāda. The Mahāyāna is subdivided into the exoteric and esoteric. . . . The Theravāda . . . is a way of realizing the truth by negating delusions and desires. . . . On the other hand, we find the Gate to birth into the Pure Land. . . . Even though persons may have studied the Gate of the Holy Path, if one wills to learn the Gate of the Pure Land, he or she should leave the Holy Path and take refuge in the Pure Land. Examples of persons who did so are Tanluan . . . and Dúochuo. . . . If these wise scholars of the past did so, then why should we fools in the age of the Degenerate Dharma fail to follow their example?

If the Primal Vow required people to build statues of the Buddha and *stūpas*, the poor and destitute would not have any hope of birth [in the Pure Land]. . . . If the Primal Vow required people to attain wisdom and learning, the unintelligent and foolish would not have any hope of birth. . . . If the Primal Vow required people to follow the precepts and monastic rules, those who have broken them or those who have not taken them would not have any hope of birth. . . . For this reason, Amida Buddha, when in the distant past he was Dharmākara . . . moved by compassion for all and wishing to save all universally, did not choose these many practices . . . in his Primal Vow for birth; but instead chose the single practice of reciting *nembutsu*. . . . "They will be like broken tiles and pebbles that are turned into gold."

If you wish to quickly escape *saṃsāra*, between the two superior methods, set aside the Holy Path and choose to enter the Gate of the Pure Land. . . . The practice that correctly fixes one's birth [in the Pure Land] is to recite the name of Amida Buddha. This is so because of Amida's Primal Vow. . . . *Nembutsu* practice is likened to the moon's reflection in the water, freely rising up and down. (*Senchakushū*, 1, 3, 16)

The most famous disciple of Hōnen was Shinran (1173–1263), who founded another type of Pure Land Buddhism named Jōdo Shinshū, the "True Pure Land School," or, more simply, Shin Buddhism. As a result of a change in the political fortunes of his family, Shinran entered the monastery when he was just nine years old. He went to live and study on Mt. Hiei, where he practiced "perpetual *nembutsu*" according to the Tendai tradition until the age of twenty-nine. During those twenty years of practice and discipline, he was not satisfied with his Tendai life and did not attain what he was seeking. Eventually, his concern over the possibility of his Awakening was so intense that Shinran decided to make a rigorous 100-day meditation retreat in nearby Kyōto. He hoped to receive inspiration for the future of his spiritual journey. The temple where he carried out his retreat enshrined Kannon Bodhisattva. On the ninety-fifth day of the retreat, Shinran had a dream about Kannon. We do not know the whole content of the dream, but it seemed that Kannon promised to come to him in a feminine form to be his helpmate. Also, the dream led Shinran to leave Mt. Hiei in 1201 and to join Hōnen's Pure Land community in Kyōto.

Expressing the deep awareness of his own inadequacies in the spiritual life, Shinran was consoled when Hōnen personally assured him that he was certainly embraced by the compassion of Amida Buddha; Amida cares for even the most evil of sinners. Shinran became Hōnen's favorite disciple; and Shinran always maintained that he was merely transmitting the real meaning of Hōnen's teachings. However, in 1207 certain indiscretions by some of Hōnen's followers led to the disbanding of his community and the exile from Kyōto of Hōnen and some of his followers. This included Shinran. Both men were sent to different places, and they never saw each other again.

Shinran's exile also entailed his being laicized. It was perhaps during this time that Shinran married Eshin-ni. Many speculate that Eshin-ni was, in fact, the helpmate for Shinran foretold in his dream of Kannon. They had six children, and Shinran's decision to marry became the pattern for Jōdo Shinshū clergy. There are also theories about the names and number of Shinran's wives. In any case, Shinran did not wish by being laicized to pursue the worldly life of the laity. So he considered himself to be "neither layman nor monk." Shinran was pardoned in 1211 and moved with his wife and children to the town of Ināda. There, he spent twenty years propagating his form of Pure Land Buddhism to the common people far from the cities of power and culture. He ministered to their needs with sympathy and compassion, quietly developing his spiritual thought and his community of followers. In 1224, Shinran completed the *Kyōgyōshinshō* (*Teaching, Practice, Faith, Attainment*), his major religious writing. Around 1234, Shinran returned to Kyōto, where he spent the final twenty-eight years of his life.

It seems that one of the most formative events in Shinran's life that shaped his understanding of True Pure Land Buddhism was a religious experience he had shortly after moving to Ināda. He had already embraced the single-practice of *nembutsu* and decided to chant a *sūtra* 1,000 times for the benefit of all living beings. After a few days of chanting, Shinran realized that he could not save other beings, that faith in Amida Buddha is itself a gift from Amida. That is, Shinran understood that doing any religious practice on the basis of one's own will, one's "self power," only strengthens one's ego. Relying on self-striving, one has the sense that "I am faithful," and "*I* am chanting." Such practice and any results it may bring are poisoned with ego and selfish desire. True Pure Land Buddhism must be based on the realization that all attempts to progress in the spiritual life through one's own efforts are futile. With this realization, one can then experience the gift of true faith as given by Amida Buddha. Thereby, one's *nembutsu* is no longer an assertion of ego to gain Amida's grace but is an expression of thankfulness for Amida's gift of faith.

This view of faith being a matter of grace does not deny the historical Buddha's admonishment to rely on oneself and one's own efforts. The first step in the Buddhist journey is the choice to enter the Buddhist tradition and take up its practice. However, for Shinran, while this step is essential to begin the journey, attaining the goal is quite another matter. As one advances based on one's own choice and efforts, one begins to realize that the ego is hiding behind all of one's spiritual endeavors. This insight leads to a sense of helplessness, which, according to Shinran, can bring one to surrender to the pure grace of Amida Buddha. This is a very important point. For such a surrender of faith not to be just another act of the will, it must "arise" also due to Amida's grace. So Shinran refers to true faith as *shinjin*, which really means the "arising of faith" from the grace of Amida Buddha. Shinran here is turning the tables on traditional Buddhism, in which faith is preliminary to practice. In Shinran's view, practice is preliminary to faith in the power of Amida's Primal Vow. Indeed, in these ideas, we can see a mirroring of Shinran's own religious life experience.

In this experience of Amida's grace, the True Pure Land devotee realizes what are called the Two Types of Deep Faith. First, one understands the fact that one's human limitations and spiritual defilements entail that one's own "calculated efforts" in the spiritual life are only hopeless attempts. Second, one realizes that the Great Action of Amida Buddha can save one from this condition. In fact, Shinran says that the deeper one's awareness of one's hopelessness and evilness, the greater one's assurance of Amida's compassionate action:

> People often say, "If an evil person can attain birth in the Pure Land, it goes without saying that a good person can." While this saying seems right at first, it is counter to the intent of the Primal Vow, or Other power. This is because those who rely on doing good based on self power, do not entrust themselves fully to Other power. . . . But if they overturn this self-power mentality and entrust themselves to Other power, they will attain birth in the true and real land of fulfillment. [They need to understand that] it is impossible for us, who are moved by blind desires, to free ourselves from *saṃsāra* through any type of practice. [They also need to realize that] Amida, out of pity for us in this condition, made his Vow with the intent of bringing us evil persons to Buddhahood. Therefore, the evil persons entrusting themselves to Other power are precisely the ones who truly possess the cause of birth in the Pure Land. So, such a person says, "If a good person can attain birth in the Pure Land, it goes without saying that the evil person can." (*Tannishō*, 3)

Shinran believed that the three states of mind discussed by Shandao and Hōnen—sincerity, faith, and aspiration—are the qualities of the mind of Amida Buddha. They are not qualities that people can cultivate by *nembutsu* practice based on their own willpower. Rather, Shinran taught, Amida attained these qualities through eons of practice as a bodhisattva, and now transfers them to his devotees. As Amida's mind of "sincerity," or enlightened consciousness, "arises" in the minds of the devotees, this sincerity informs their own minds and hearts. When this quality of Amida's mind forms one's mind and heart, "faith" is graced by the Other power of Amida. Amida thus is present and active in one's life, and one experiences the "aspiration" to be born in the Pure Land and to save all beings. With these qualities, one's *nembutsu* practice is no longer the product of self power, but the Other power of Amida.

Finally, Shinran expresses his ideas concerning Other power with the terms "action, faith and witness" (*gyō-shin-shō*). The overturning of the self-power mind and the entrusting faith to Other power are themselves products of Amida's grace. It is the action (*gyō*) of Amida Buddha that precipitates the arising of faith (*shin*) in the devotee's mind. Amida enables one to realize the Two Types of Deep Faith: one's pitiful condition and the availability of Other power. Faith then transforms one's life in a way that gives witness (*shō*) to the presence and action of Amida Buddha. This living witness is one of freedom and humility, virtue and joy that arises spontaneously from Amida's presence in the devotee's life. In other words, it is the very enlightened life of Amida Buddha itself that makes one able to live its enlightened qualities. One is enabled to live in a way that reflects into daily life the wise and compassionate qualities of Amida and his Pure Land.

So for Shinran, Pure Land Buddhism is not just about being born in the Pure Land. It is about being transformed in this life as well. On the other hand, this life may bear fruit here, but it will also need to be completed in the Pure Land. Then one can return from the Pure Land to help others here find their deliverance. For Shinran, it is this bodhisattva life that is the essence of human fulfillment brought about by Amida's grace. The following passages reflect Shinran's views concerning the human condition, the grace of Other power, and of the growth in virtue:

Although I take refuge in the True Pure Land Way,
It is difficult to have a true and sincere mind.
The self is false and insincere,
I completely lack a pure mind.

Each of us, in our outward appearance,
Makes a show of being wise, good, and devout.
But our greed, anger, perversity and deceit are so great,
We are full of all types of hatred and cunning.

It is extremely difficult to destroy our evil nature,
The mind is like a snake or scorpion.
So, the good deeds we perform are poisoned,
They are called false and useless practice.

Since I lack even a little love or compassion,
I cannot even hope to help living beings.
If it were not for the ship of Amida's Vow,
How could I get across the ocean of this painful existence?

(*Shōzōmatsu wasan*, 94–96, 98)

"Being saved by the inconceivable working of Amida's Vow, I shall certainly be born in the Pure Land!" The very moment that you entrust yourself to the Vow in this way, with the thought of saying *nembutsu* arising within you, immediately you receive a share in the benefits of being always embraced by Amida. You should know that Amida's Primal Vow does not distinguish between young and old, good and evil. Only the arising of faith is essential; for it is the Vow to save persons with deep karmic evil and serious blind desires. So, for persons entrusting themselves to this Primal Vow, good acts are not required because no good action surpasses *nembutsu*. And, one should never despair about their evil deeds, for no evil acts can obstruct the work of Amida's Primal Vow.

Box 9.1

A Child's Caring

One evening as I returned home from work totally exhausted from a demanding day, I slumped down flat on my back on the living room couch. Lying comfortably, almost asleep, I felt a tug on my left sleeve and a murmuring voice calling, "Daddy, Daddy." It was my two-year-old son, Nathan.

I said to myself, "Oh no, it's Nathan. He wants to wrestle with me again. I am in no shape mentally or physically to wrestle with him. Doesn't he see how tired I am? I guess not, and explaining to him won't help." So I pretended to be asleep.

But my son continued to tug at my sleeve with an undaunted, "Daddy, Daddy!" I became more irritated and began conjuring up all kinds of ill thoughts about my two-year-old, saying to myself, "All he thinks about is himself. Doesn't he understand I'm sleeping? His stubbornness must come from my wife's side!" But he kept tugging, "Daddy, Daddy." Finally, totally frustrated, I opened my eyes ready to scold him.

Lo and behold . . . there he stood holding a blanket in his left hand to cover me. He had dragged it from my bedroom all by himself. And neither his mother nor I had ever taught him to do this. This was completely on his own!

This scene has been deeply etched in my memory. I still recall with shame and embarrassment the selfish thought that I had harbored about my two-year-old son. At the same time, I could not but be amazed by my son's caring act, despite my self-centered thoughts. This event is another concrete, everyday example of the myriad compassionate acts and boundless life forces, seen and mostly unseen, that is symbolized as Amida Buddha in my Shin Buddhist tradition.

In response, I utter quietly or in silence *Namu Amida Butsu* ("Amida Buddha and I are one") in amazement and in gratitude for the realization that I am fine, just as I am, in life and in death!

KENNETH KENSHIN TANAKA
Shin Priest and Professor of Buddhist Studies
Musashino Joshi University, Tokyo

> I myself do not have even one disciple. If I made people recite *nembutsu* by my own efforts, then they would be my disciples. But it is wrong to call anyone "my disciple" because they *receive nembutsu* by the working of Amida. . . . *Nembutsu* is not a practice or a good act by its practitioners. Since it is not recited from one's own intentions, it is not a practice. Since it is not something performed from one's own calculations, it is not a good act. For the practitioner, it is not a practice or a good act because it wholly arises from Other power, free from any self power. (*Tannishō*, 1, 6, 8)
>
> The universal Vow, so difficult to understand, is a great ship that carries us across the ocean that is hard to cross. The unobstructed light is the sun of wisdom that disperses the darkness of our ignorance. . . . We know that the auspicious Name that embodies . . . supreme virtues is the real wisdom which transforms our evil into virtue, and that the difficult to accept and diamond-like arising of faith is true reality; it sweeps away doubts and brings one to the attainment of Awakening. . . . The great practice is saying the Name of the Buddha of Unobstructed Light. This practice . . . that possesses the roots of all virtues is the perfect and quick way of bringing them to fullness. It is the Treasure Ocean of Virtues that is suchness, true reality. This is the reason it is called the great practice. (*Kyōgyōshinshō*, I, Preface; II, 1)

Shinran did not designate a successor, and his disciples led sizable communities of followers. His daughter, Kakushin-ni, established a mausoleum shrine where all followers could come to pay respects and where the caretaker of the shrine was to be a member of Shinran's family. This led to a hereditary line of successors. Her grandson, Kakunyo, eventually came to believe that many of the more powerful communities of Shinran's tradition would evolve into independent sects. So he sought to unify them all under the leadership of the shrine, which came to be referred to as *Hongan-ji*, meaning "Temple of the Original Vow." While different branches did emerge due to the powerful military rulers, the Hongan-ji became the unifying center for propagating Jōdo Shinshū.

Zen Buddhism

Zen Buddhism was most likely present in Japan as early as the time of Prince Shōtoku in the seventh century. During that century, Dōshō, the founder of the Hossō School of Yogācāra in Japan, also brought Zen practice from China. He built the first meditation hall in a temple in Nara. Saichō, the founder of Tendai in Japan, also met with a Chan master when in China, and made meditation an important element of Tendai practice. However, none of these early initatives produced a single-practice school of Zen in Japan as existed in China and Korea. It was not until the Kamakura Period that an independent Zen School took root in Japanese soil.

Late in the twelfth century, a Japanese priest named Dainichi Nōnin founded the Sambo-ji Temple in Settsu Provence, where he started teaching Zen. He called his community the Japanese Bodhidharma (Daruma) School of Zen. Nōnin was not trained in Zen but studied Zen texts and practiced meditation on his own and eventually had an Awakening experience. Because he had not received teaching or permission to teach from an authorized Zen master, Nōnin was a controversial figure. So in 1189, he sent two disciples to China, where they obtained authorization for him from the Chan master, Zhuoan Deguang (1121–1203). He then gained a number of followers. However, after his death, the Daruma sect of Zen did not survive, and his disciples joined the Sōtō Zen sect founded later by Dōgen.

The person whom tradition recognizes as the real founder of Zen Buddhism in Japan is Eisai (1141–1215). At the age of eleven, Eisai entered a temple to study Buddhism under a priest who followed the Tantric tradition. Two years later, Eisai went to Mt. Hiei and was ordained in 1154. At Mt. Hiei, he studied Tendai teachings, including esoteric doctrines, and focused on the Tendai practice of meditation. At the age of twenty-eight, Eisai traveled to China for six months, where he observed the popularity of Chan. Upon his return to Mt. Hiei, he decided to do Zen practice as taught by Tendai. He pursued this path, along with Tantric practice, for the next twenty years. On a second visit to China that began in 1187, Eisai practiced in the Linji School of Chan Buddhism. His master also taught him the *Vinaya* tradition, which Eisai would later make the foundation of Zen monastic life in Japan. Eisai finally received the formal approval (*inka*) to teach Zen, and upon returning to Japan in 1191, he built Shōfuku-ji, the first Zen temple in Japan.

Eisai met strong opposition from the Tendai School because they saw in his teachings the possibility for a personal, single-practice form of Buddhism that would challenge their more complex, ritual-based tradition. In 1199, Eisai traveled to Kamakura, where he gained the support of the shogun. With this support, he established a temple, the Jufuku-ji, in Kamakura. Under Eisai's guidance, Jufuku-ji was at first a center for Tantric rituals but later became one of the great centers for Zen practice. In 1202, Eisai was given some land in Kyōto, where he founded another temple, the Kennin ji, in which Tendai and esoteric practices were taught alongside Zen. Because of the resistance of the powerful Tendai School, Eisai was careful to present Zen only in the wider context of the older more accepted Tendai tradition. Therefore, while Eisai is considered the founder of the Rinzai (Chinese: Linji) School of Zen Buddhism in Japan, he was primarily a Tendai priest who tried to reform that tradition. Eisai was also respected for his purity and simplicity, in accord with the Zen style of life, and for his personal kindness and generosity.

The following passages are taken from Eisai's *Propagation of Zen in Defense of the Country*, written in 1198 in an attempt to gain support for Zen in Japan in the face of Tendai resistance:

> The Mind is great. The height of heaven is immeasurable, but the Mind extends itself beyond heaven. The depth of the earth is also immeasurable, but the Mind extends itself below the earth. One cannot outdistance the light of the sun and moon, but the Mind does so. . . . Because of the Mind, heaven covers while the earth produces. Because of the Mind, the sun and moon move, the seasons pass one after the other, and all things come to be. The Mind is indeed great!

We necessarily call it Mind, but it has many other names: the highest principle, the truth of innate wisdom, the one reality, the perfect Awakening.... Gautama Buddha, the greatest of teachers, transmitted the truth of this Mind to [Mahākāśyapa], saying it is a special transmission outside the scriptures. . . . Therefore, with the slightest turning of a flower, a thousand trees broke into bloom. From this single fountainhead, ten-thousand rivers of truth flowed.

Just as in India, this teaching in China has attracted many followers and disciples. Like the Buddha, it propagates the truth . . . transmitting it from person to person.... This vision of the Dharma soon appeared in Korea . . . and the Oxhead School of Zen . . . has made its way to Japan. By studying it, one discovers the essential key to all forms of Buddhism. By practicing it, one's life is fulfilled in the realization of Awakening. In terms of externals, Zen stresses discipline over doctrine; internally, it brings one the highest inner wisdom. This is what the Zen School is all about.

However, there are those who attack this teaching, saying that it is "the Zen of dark Awakening." Others question it saying that it is "utter nihilism." Still others do not consider it suitable for the age of the Degenerate Dharma, saying it is not what our country needs now. Or they express their contempt for our traveling from place to place, and the supposed lack of documented support for our ideas. Finally, some who have a low opinion of their ability to follow our way, consider Zen to be far beyond their power of attainment. In their attempt to uphold the Dharma, these persons are actually suppressing the very treasures of the Dharma. They condemn us without knowing what we are doing. They are not only blocking the Gate of Zen, but they are ruining the work of our great forefather, [Saichō] of Mt. Hiei. What a pity! How sad and distressing! (*Kōzen gokoku ron*, Preface)

Eisai's foundation of Rinzai Zen was later advanced by certain Chinese Chan masters and Japanese disciples in ways that purified the school of Tendai and Shingon elements and produced the great single-practice Rinzai Zen tradition in Japan. This process was aided by the fact that both the shogunate and the imperial court patronized Zen monks. The purification of non-Zen practices from Rinzai happened in the monasteries that were founded by Eisai and by the later Chinese and Japanese developers of his school. One of the greatest of these developers was Enni Ben'en (1202–1280), who studied in China and founded Tōfuku-ji in Kyōto. There, Zen was the major practice of the temple, and all other practices took a back seat. From Tōfuku-ji, a broad Zen movement grew to include more than fifty temples.

Another early Rinzai figure was Muhon Kakushin (1207–1298), who founded the great Kōkoku-ji temple. The Chinese Chan Master Lanxi Daolong (1213–1278), known in Japan as Rankei Dōryū, founded the Kenchō-ji Temple in 1252. Daiō Kokushi (1282–1338) built the famous Daitoku-ji in 1324, as well as the Myōshin-ji in 1337. Kian Soen (1269–1313) established what became the most influential Rinzai temple in Japan, Nanzen-ji. In each of these monastic temples, any mixture of Zen with other forms of Buddhism was avoided, and Zen meditation (*zazen*) was practiced with a strict program of *kōan* study. These temples became the core of more than 300 official Rinzai temples throughout Japan. Today, Rinzai remains famous for its strict monastic discipline and its use of *kōans* in meditation practice to foster the sudden experience of Awakening (*satori*).

The second great Zen innovator of the Kamakura Period was Dōgen (1200–1253), the founder of the Sōtō School of Zen Buddhism. Dōgen's father died when Dōgen was only two years old, and his mother died when he was seven. These difficult early circumstances had a strong effect on the sensitive Dōgen. It is said that while in grief over the death of his mother, Dōgen saw the incense ascending from a Buddhist temple and felt the desire to find Awakening. So, at the age of thirteen, Dōgen went to Mt. Hiei and was ordained a year later. At Mt. Hiei, Dōgen confronted a serious religious paradox in the form of an existential question: If all living beings have an innate Buddha-nature, why does one feel the longing for Awakening and have to engage in spiritual practice? Dōgen did not find a satisfying answer to this quandary on Mt. Hiei, and he left to pursue his spiritual journey elsewhere. First, he went to a disciple of Hōnen, who felt that Dōgen's quest could not be satisfied with Pure Land teachings. So Dōgen was sent to Eisai, because the latter was teaching a strict method of Rinzai Zen that could produce a sudden Awakening in which Dōgen's question might find its answer. At Kennin-ji, Dōgen was trained in Zen by Eisai's disciple, Myōzen (1185–1225).

In 1223, Myōzen took Dōgen with him to China. After trying Linji (Rinzai) and other forms of Chan practice, Dōgen studied under Rujing (1163–1268). Rujing was a master in the Caodong (Japanese: Sōtō) School of Chan, which stressed the pure practice of meditation rather than *kōan* practice. One evening when the monks were sitting in night meditation, Rujing noticed that a monk had fallen asleep. He said, according to Dōgen, "In Zen, body and mind are cast off. Why do you sleep?" Hearing this, Dōgen gained Awakening. After staying for two more years to perfect his understanding, Dōgen returned home to Japan.

Upon his arrival in Japan, Dōgen returned to Kennin-ji, but he was dissatisfied with the mixture of Zen practice and esoteric rituals. So in 1230, he moved to the south of Kyōto, where he founded a meditation center, the Kōshō Hōrin-ji. There, strict Zen meditation practice and observance of the precepts were taught, and Dōgen began to write his greatest work, the *Shōbōgenzō* (*The Essence of the Buddha's True Dharma*). However, because of pressure from the monks on Mt. Hiei, Dōgen retreated to a remote place deep in the mountains of Echizen. He lived in small rural temples until he settled in Eihei-ji, the temple that became known as the headquarters of the Sōtō Zen School. Dōgen lived out his last years teaching the single practice of *zazen* and completing the *Shōbōgenzō*.

While Dōgen recognized the usefulness of *kōan* practice, he emphasized the single practice of "just sitting" (*shikan-taza*). This emphasis reflected the answer to his existential question: Why does one practice meditation if one is originally enlightened? For Dōgen, the answer to that question is found in the experience that all things and actions, including sitting practice, are manifestations of original Buddha-nature. In this regard, practice and attainment are identical. Thus, when one practices sitting meditation, one is manifesting one's Buddha-nature. To realize this fact is to be aware that practice is attainment: One's practice manifests innate Awakening. Dōgen explains this in *A Lecture on Studying the Way:*

> Grass, trees and the land, which this teaching embraces, together radiate a great light. They endlessly teach the inconceivable and perfect Dharma.... This being true, one person's *zazen at* just one moment imperceptibly fits in with all things, fully radiating through all time.... Each moment of *zazen* is itself equally the wholeness of practice and Awakening. It is like a hammer striking emptiness: both before and after, its wonderful sound permeates everywhere.... Things all manifest the original practice from the original face [Awakening], impossible to measure.
>
> It is heretical to think that practice and Awakening are not one. In the Dharma of the Buddha, practice and Awakening are the same. Practice is done in Awakening in this very moment. So, the beginner's practice on the Way is itself the whole of original Awakening. Therefore, when we give instructions for practice, we teach that Awakening cannot be found outside practice, since practice itself is the immediate original Awakening. (*Bendōwa*, 6)

Dōgen felt that just sitting is the best means for nourishing the gradual awareness of this original condition of enlightened Buddha-nature. In just sitting, one gradually sees that one's present condition, no matter what that condition might entail, is already manifesting Buddha-nature. To make this point, Dōgen used the example of a fish swimming in the water without realizing the water is there. Similarly, people are already manifesting their Buddha-nature in each daily activity, like a fish swimming in water, even if they are not aware of that primordial fact. Just sitting quietly in meditation enables one to see what is presently the case, one's originally enlightened Buddha nature reflected in the present moment. As a fish just swims, one just sits until he or she gradually realizes that this sitting practice is a manifestation of Buddha-nature. Therefore, Sōtō is called the "gradual" school of Zen, whereas Rinzai with its intense form of *kōan* practice is called the "sudden" school of Zen.

Further reflecting on his experience, Dōgen claimed, "All beings *are* Buddha-nature." This statement is different from the more traditional claim that all *living* beings *have* Buddha-nature. In the traditional sense, all sentient beings have a Buddha-nature like a Buddha statue covered by a dirty rag. For Dōgen, there are two problems with this traditional statement. First is the distinction or duality between living and nonliving beings. For Dōgen, all states of existence, be they mind or body, mental or physical realities, are manifestations of the one Buddha-nature. Second is the distinction or duality between one's Buddha-nature and one's ordinary mind/body that "has" that original nature within it. The rag/statue analogy implies that there is some eternal and pure spiritual status hidden within, yet separate from, one's transitory and suffering condition. In Dōgen's experience, the search for such a hidden spiritual essence is a misguided example of dualistic thinking. This is because all transient forms of existence are, for Dōgen, Buddha-nature.

All the present forms of life, from mountains and trees to the ordinary states of one's own mind, are manifestations, or self-determinations, of Buddha-nature. To experience this nondualistic fact of true existence is to realize, according to Dōgen, the Buddha-nature that just *is* all beings.

The following passages from Dōgen's *Shōbōgenzō* convey his experience of Awakening. They were placed in the first chapter, suggesting that they are something like his statement of Awakening:

> When all things are [experienced through] Buddha Dharma, there is delusion and Awakening, practice, birth and death, Buddhas and living beings. When the myriad things are [experienced] without self, there is no delusion, no Awakening, no Buddhas, no living beings, no birth and death. Since the Buddha's Way is itself, from the beginning, beyond fullness and lack, there are birth and death, delusion and Awakening, living beings and Buddhas. Though this is so, flowers fall when we are attached to them, and weeds grow when we dislike them.
>
> To bring yourself to the myriad things in order to authenticate them is delusion. For the myriad things to come forward to authenticate yourself is Awakening. . . .
>
> To study the Buddha's Way is to study oneself. To study oneself is to forget oneself. To forget oneself is to be enlightened by all things. To be enlightened by all things is the dropping away of one's mind and body, and the mind and body of others. No trace of Awakening remains, and this no-trace leaves traces endlessly.
>
> When you first seek for the Dharma, you imagine that you are outside its boundaries. But when you see that the Dharma is already conveyed correctly within yourself, immediately you are your original self.
>
> Awakening is like the moon reflected in water. The moon does not get wet, nor is the water broken. Though its light is vast and great, it is reflected in a tiny bit of water. The whole moon and the sky are reflected in dewdrops on the grass, or in just a drop of water. Awakening does not obstruct people, just as the moon does not break the water. A person does not obstruct Awakening, just as the drop of water does not obstruct the moon. The depth of the water is equal to the height of the moon. However long or short is the duration of the reflection, one realizes in the vastness or smallness of the water, the breadth and brightness of the moonlight in the sky. (*Shōbōgenzō, Genjō Kōan*)

After Dōgen's death, Sōtō Zen grew into a mass lay movement that eventually became the largest Zen sect in Japan. This evolution was due primarily to the Fourth Patriarch of Sōtō, Keizan Jōkin (1268–1325). Keizan modified Dōgen's austere Zen style, simplified Sōtō doctrine, and incorporated elements from Shintō and Shingon that were popular with the common and rural people of Japan. Keizan was also concerned with the problems of the common people. His Sōtō priests became involved in social issues and popular projects such as irrigation systems and medical treatment. There was an effort by the Sōtō priests to educate the people as well as rendering them spiritual, ritual, and social services. Some time later, priests of Keizan's tradition took up residence at Eihei-ji and made it the headquarters of the unified national Sōtō School that is today the second largest Buddhist organization in Japan.

Nichiren Buddhism

The third great tradition that began in the Kamakura Period is Nichiren Buddhism, named after its founder, Nichiren (1222–1282). Nichiren was born in a small fishing village associated with the famous Shintō shrine of Ise, far from the cities of political and religious power. Given that the Ise shrine was connected to the imperial family, Nichiren began at an early age to wonder why the emperor had recently suffered disgrace at the hands of an uprising. If the Shintō gods were protecting the emperor, why did this happen to him? Also, by this time Nichiren had observed the many Buddhist sects and wondered which one was the true form of Buddhism. Nichiren carried these two religious questions when he entered the nearby temple of the Tendai School, Kiyosumi-dera, to study Buddhism at the age of eleven.

At Kiyosumi-dera, Nichiren learned the basic Tendai teachings based on the *Lotus Sūtra* and prayed to Amida Buddha and other esoteric deities. But as his faith in the *Lotus Sūtra* grew, Nichiren abandoned his Pure Land piety. At the time Nichiren was studying at Kiyosumi-dera, the temple belonged to an esoteric branch of Tendai. There is a history of "title exegesis" in Tendai whereby one finds the doctrinal essence of the text in the title of a *sūtra* itself. Tendai also divides the *Lotus Sūtra* into two halves. The first half is seen as stressing the teachings of Gautama Buddha, and the second half is seen as more clearly revealing Gautama's eternal nature. Esoteric Tendai stresses this idea of the Eternal Buddha in the second part of the *sūtra*. Also, in esoteric Tendai, *mantras* are used to enable one to realize his or her innate Buddha-nature, and *maṇḍalas* assist one in refining his or her states of mind. In his mature thought concerning the Eternal Buddha and the *Lotus Sūtra*, Nichiren would utilize all of these ideas and practices from the Tendai tradition.

After four years at Kiyosumi-dera, Nichiren was ordained. Two years later, he traveled to Kamakura to further his study. Most likely, he focused on Zen and Pure Land Buddhism. However, he became uncomfortable with the contradictory claims of the schools and with the fact that many *sūtras* were being proclaimed. Eventually, Nichiren decided that the *Lotus Sūtra* taught the truest form of Buddhism, and so rejected Zen and Pure Land. Given his Tendai roots, and the fact that Tendai stresses the *Lotus Sūtra*, Nichiren decided at the age of twenty-one to go to Mt. Hiei. At Mt. Hiei, Nichiren concluded that Pure Land, Zen, Shingon, and the older Nara schools were all inferior to Tendai and that Tendai was the only sect that fully represented "true" Buddhism.

Nichiren became convinced that because the *Lotus Sūtra* was the most perfect presentation of the Dharma, it was the best hope for liberation in the age of the Degenerate Dharma. But more than this, he believed that if people gained liberation, their physical and social life would be so affected that the area in which those people lived would be transformed into a place of peace and prosperity. Reaching this conclusion, Nichiren was able to answer the two questions that led him to take up the religious life. He reasoned that the emperor had been abandoned by the gods because Japan had failed to honor the *Lotus Sūtra*, having instead embraced the lesser doctrines of the other Buddhist schools. Therefore, he felt that it was urgent that the *Lotus Sūtra* be preached to bring people to liberation and to bring peace and prosperity to Japan. With this new conviction, Nichiren left Mt. Hiei at the age of thirty-two to preach his views back at Kiyosumi-dera. However, his ideas irritated Pure Land followers in the region, and within a year's time Nichiren was forced to flee to Kamakura.

In Kamakura, Nichiren taught that he was preaching Tendai doctrine. However, he became more and more convinced that only the *Lotus Sūtra* could offer people true Buddhism, and the Japanese nation peace and prosperity. He concluded that the other schools of Buddhism should not be allowed to exist, and he developed a method of preaching called "confrontational conversion" (*shakubuku*). This method utilized shocking attacks on the other schools of Buddhism. For example, he preached that Zen Buddhists are devils and that Pure Land followers would not reach the heavenly Pure Land after death, but would fall into hells.

To understand Nichiren's radical approach, it is important to note that when he arrived in Kamakura, a number of calamities began: plagues, famines, droughts, earthquakes, and uprisings. There were also eclipses and comets seen in the sky. Nichiren was extremely concerned about the physical, social, and spiritual welfare of the Japanese nation. He also became convinced that only faith in the *Lotus Sūtra* could bring an end to Japan's problems. Because Buddhists were so wedded to their different views, shocking words were needed to get them to reevaluate and change their beliefs. Here are Nichiren's words justifying his approach:

> If a person was about to kill your parents, wouldn't you try to warn them? If a bad son insane with drunkenness threatens to kill his father and mother, wouldn't you try to stop him? If an evil person is trying to burn temples and pagodas, wouldn't you try to stop that person? If your child is seriously ill, wouldn't you try to cure him or her? To fail to do so is to act like those persons who do not try to stop Zen and *Nembutsu* followers in Japan. (*Kaimoku shō*, II)

As one could imagine, the reaction of many Buddhists in Kamakura to Nichiren's words was at first extremely negative. But in time he gathered some disciples. In 1260, Nichiren submitted a document to the government in Kamakura charging that the calamities befalling Japan were caused by its protecting gods leaving the nation because of the popularity of unsuitable Buddhist schools. Nichiren claimed that to save the nation, the rulers must give sole homage to the *Lotus Sūtra*. If not, he predicted that foreign invasions and civil disturbances would occur. The government did not respond, and Pure Land followers in Kamakura attacked Nichiren a year later. When he escaped, they convinced the government to exile him to the Izu Peninsula. During that exile, Nichiren took heart from the story in the *Lotus Sūtra* about a bodhisattva who was persecuted for practicing the *Lotus Sūtra*. Nichiren eventually carne to identify with this bodhisattva, and he saw his sufferings as indicating that his destiny was to make Japan a Buddhist state based on the *Lotus Sūtra* and a springboard for a worldwide *Lotus* community.

When Nichiren was pardoned in 1263, he returned to Kamakura. Drawing on Tendai esotericism, he began to teach his growing group of followers to recite the title of the *Lotus Sūtra* as a *mantra*. This chanting of *Namu Myōhōrengekyō*, he taught, can itself bring realization of one's Buddha-nature. Like *nembutsu* in Pure Land Buddhism, this recitation would become central to Nichiren practice. Then in 1268, Nichiren saw the threat of a Mongol invasion as a confirmation of his prophecy six years earlier. He and his followers stepped up their efforts to convert Buddhists from other schools—efforts that in 1271 led to his second exile, this time to the remote island of Sado in the north.

It was on Sado Island that Nichiren became convinced that he was the emanation-body of Jōgyō Bodhisattva, the protector of the *Lotus Sūtra*. He also came to believe that in the age of the Degenerate Dharma, he was to be a new leader of the Buddhist faithful. While on Sado, Nichiren created the *Gohonzon*, a Great *Maṇḍala* that manifests his Awakening. In this *maṇḍala* are the characters of praise to the *Lotus Sūtra* (*Namu Myōhōrengekyō*) surrounded by figures of Buddhas and bodhisattvas, including Jōgyō. At a lower level are *arhats* and bodhisattvas, and on the lowest level are Shintō gods and names of Tendai masters. For Nichiren Buddhism, this *Gohonzon* became the principal image used in devotions.

During 1274, the year of his return from exile, Nichiren retired to a remote sanctuary on Mt. Minobu, convinced that his message had been ignored by the Japanese nation. There, Nichiren turned his attention to clarifying his philosophy and training his disciples. Meanwhile, two Mongol invasions of Japan were attempted. These were again viewed by Nichiren and his followers as the invasions predicted years ago. However, in both cases the invading ships were struck by typhoons, and the invasions were failures. Then in 1282, the year after the second Mongol invasion, Nichiren became ill. He chose the disciples to succeed him and passed away. His hermitage was enlarged into the famous temple of Kuon-ji. After Nichiren's death, his school spread in different parts of Japan and split into various sects.

Nichiren Buddhism is considered a single-practice school, like Zen and Pure Land, because it teaches that liberation is attainable by chanting the title of the *Lotus Sūtra*. Drawing on Tendai's title exegesis, Nichiren taught that the title of the *Lotus Sūtra*, namely *Myōhōrengekyō*, embodies the power of the Dharma presented in the text. Chanting an invocation to the *Lotus Sūtra*—*Namu Myōhōrengekyō*—concentrates this saving power of the Dharma into the life of the Nichiren practitioner. Along with this *mantra* chanting, Nichiren Buddhism also uses the *maṇḍala* that Nichiren created. This *maṇḍala* is believed to help draw forth from the practitioner the inner qualities of his or her pure Buddha-nature. It is as though the *maṇḍala* is like a mirror that reflects these inner qualities into one's conscious experience.

To explain this experience of personal transformation through chanting, Nichiren taught that the *Lotus Sūtra* contains Three Secret Teachings. First is that the Eternal Buddha, spoken of in the *Lotus Sūtra,* is an image of the innate Buddha-nature, or original Awakening. This enlightened life can be found within oneself by stripping away the layers of ignorance. Second is that the name of the *Lotus Sūtra* carries the reality and power of the Dharma that can overcome ignorance and reveal one's Buddha-nature. Third is that chanting is like an ordination platform. An ordination platform is where one is empowered to live the moral and spiritual virtues of Buddhism. Nichiren believed that as chanting embodies the power of the Dharma, it empowers one with the purity and positive qualities of Buddhahood.

To gain Awakening in this way was, for Nichiren, to realize one's "original Awakening" in the interrelatedness of all existence. Drawing on the Tendai notion that "one thought moment contains the three-thousand worlds," Nichiren taught that in the interpenetration of existence, each moment of life permeates all phenomena. This means one moment of chanting *Namu Myōhōrengekyō,* which embodies the "perfect truth" of one's true original nature, sets one anew in harmony with the positive dynamics behind the interrelated events of life. In this harmony, not only is one's spiritual condition affected but also one's material conditions.

However, more important than these visible signs of the Dharma's power is growth in freedom from afflictive emotions, incorrect views, and unhealthy attachments. This moral and spiritual freedom fosters the more positive qualities of Buddhahood, such as wisdom, courage, purity, and compassion. Nichiren believed that given the interpenetration of life, as these material, moral, and spiritual conditions of people's lives change for the better, society will also change for the better. Thus, Nichiren saw Japan as the center of a world-transforming community of followers of the *Lotus Sūtra.* Following this insight, Nichiren Buddhism has seen itself as working for a more enlightened, peaceful, and happy world civilization. The following words of Nichiren express this kind of experience:

> If you want to be free from the sufferings of birth and death that you have undergone since beginningless time, and if without fail you want to attain supreme Awakening in this very lifetime, then you must realize the inherent, original perfect truth in all living beings. This truth is *Myōhōrengekyō.* Therefore, chanting *Myōhōrengekyō* will enable you to realize the innate perfect truth in all life.
>
> Among the *sūtras,* the *Lotus Sūtra* is king. It is true and correct in both its words and the principle it teaches. Its very words themselves are ultimate reality. This ultimate reality is the ultimate Dharma. It is called the ultimate Dharma because it reveals the principle of mutual interrelatedness of a single moment of life and all phenomena. Therefore, this *sūtra* is the very wisdom of all the Buddhas.
>
> Each moment of life includes body, mind, personhood, the environment of all living beings in the Ten Worlds, the non-living beings in the 3,000 realms from the plants, sky and earth to the tinniest dust particles. Each moment of life permeates the whole realm of phenomena, and is therefore found in all phenomena. Awakening to this principle is itself the mutual interrelatedness of life in each moment including all phenomena.

> However, even if you chant and believe in *Myōhōrengekyō*, if you think that the Dharma is outside yourself, you are not accepting the ultimate Dharma, but an inferior teaching. . . . Therefore, when you chant . . . you must have a deep faith that *Myōhōrengekyō* is your very life. . . . Your practice of Buddhism will not at all free you from the sufferings of birth and death unless you realize the true nature of your life.
>
> The *Vimalakīrti Sūtra* says that when you seek the liberation of the Buddhas in the minds of ordinary beings, you will find that they are enlightened beings, and that the sufferings of birth and death are Nirvana itself. The *sūtra* also states that if one's mind is impure, one's land is impure; but if one's mind is pure, one's land is pure. There are not two lands, one pure and the other impure. The difference is solely found in the good and evil of one's mind.
>
> This is true of Buddhas and ordinary beings. Deluded, one is called an ordinary being. Enlightened, one is called a Buddha. This can be likened to a dirty mirror that can shine like a jewel when cleaned. A mind clouded by the illusions of the inherent darkness of life is likened to a dirty mirror. When this mind is cleaned, it will surely be like a clear mirror that reflects the essential nature of all phenomena, the truth of reality. So, arousing a deep faith, diligently clean your mirror night and day. How should you clean it? Only by chanting *Namu Myōhōrengekyō*. . . . If you chant with deep faith in this inner principle, you will certainly attain Buddhahood in this very lifetime. (*Isshō jōbutsu shō*)

THE MUROMACHI PERIOD (1338–1573): ZEN AND JAPANESE CULTURE

From the end of the Kamakura Period in 1333 to the rise of the Tokugawa Period in 1603, Buddhism faced radical cultural changes in Japanese society, and eventually even tragic religious persecution. From the beginning of the Muromachi Shōgunate (1338–1573), the status of Buddhism was uncertain. The society was becoming more and more secularized, and intellectual interest was turning to China, especially to a popular form of Confucianism called Neo-Confucianism. However, Rinzai Zen held on to a special position in relation to the government that made it a kind of state religion. This relationship was forged by Musō Soseki (1275–1351), who was the religious advisor of the first shōgun. Zen was thus able to affect Japanese culture, in a society that was less open than in the past to direct religious teachings, through certain artistic forms that expressed Zen's subtle spirit.

Zen impacted Japanese culture through a number of different avenues. Zen temples, which were originally inspired by Chinese counterparts, became models for Japanese architecture. Temple gardens, especially the stone gardens of the late Muramachi Period, also created a new style of gardening that spread across Japan. In this artistic style, boulders represent mountains or islands, and planes of moss or sand symbolize the boundless sea of life (see Figure 9.3). But more than this, the gardens themselves have a strong spiritual effect on the viewers. In Zen calligraphy and painting, an enlightened artist can display his or her attainment through a certain vitality expressed in the work of art. The creative brushwork of the calligraphy or ink-painting portrays the spirit of Zen in ways that were appreciated by the

Japanese people. Often the strong personalities of Zen masters could be gleaned from the calligraphy or seen more directly in the ink portraits that seem to stare back at the viewer with extraordinary intensity (see Figure 9.4).

Another avenue of Zen cultural influence is to be found in the Noh drama. The Noh drama was influenced by a subtle Zen aesthetic sensitivity. There is very little external action in these dramas. Rather, what is portrayed are the inner thoughts, feelings, and states of mind and heart that are in the deepest sense unspeakable. The actors' expressions and body movements allow the interiority of life to surface in subtle ways.

Tea gardens provided another unique bridge between Zen and the secular Japanese society, especially in the following Tokugawa Period. A path of irregular stepping stones leads through trees and thick shrubbery to a small teahouse. Walking this way past a stone lantern, water flowing from a bamboo pipe, and a stone water basin for rinsing one's mouth, a person is led from the busy world into a quiet place where worldly cares and concerns are put aside. The quiet tea ceremony, with only little verbal exchange, creates a deep and lasting experience of affirmation, friendship, and peace. The tea garden became a beloved and lasting tradition throughout Japan.

While Buddhism was influencing the broader Japanese culture, the secular nature of that society was also influencing Buddhism. For example, the most important figure in Pure Land Buddhism during this era was Rennyo (1415–1499). Rennyo was known as the "Restorer of Shinshū." He traveled to cities and towns, converting to his ideas not only Jōdo Shinshū followers but also members of other traditions like Tendai and Shingon. In his preaching, a central

FIGURE 9.3. Japanese rock garden at Ryōan-ji Temple in Kyoto Japan, built in the late 15th century.

theme was the distinction between the inner and outer aspects of a person's life. In one's heart, he said, one should hold to a strong faith in Other power. With this inner commitment, one can turn his or her attention to the secular affairs of daily life, such as one's family and occupation. In dealing with everyday issues, the values of one's faith should be guides for how to behave properly. When talking about these values, Rennyo spoke of the Confucian virtues, an ideology that was becoming popular in secular society.

In this and other ways, Rennyo redesigned Pure Land theory and practice in a way that attracted a vast number of common people throughout Japan. Eventually, Rennyo's sect of Jōdo Shinshū Buddhism, the Hongan-ji sect, became a powerful feudal institution popular with the masses. Then in the sixteenth century, the Hongan-ji split into two schools: the Nishi (Western) Hongan-ji and the Higashi (Eastern) Hongan-ji, both headquartered in Kyōto. This split is institutional rather than doctrinal, and both schools combine to form the largest Buddhist school in Japan.

In the fifteenth century, the fabric of Muromachi society was coming apart. The shōgunate was divided by power struggles, and the populace was plagued by civil uprisings. The Ōnin War (1467–1478) brought an end to central government control in Japan, leading to the independence of provincial warlords. In this social chaos, the Pure Land and Nichiren sects created their own feudal states protected by peasant armies. A leader in this Buddhist movement was Rennyo, whose Hongan-ji sect became a powerful force in Japan. Nichiren Buddhist temples in Kyōto held great influence in the southern part of the city. These temples followed the Pure Land example and formed self-defense militias that later developed into armies. After some clashes with armies backed by the Pure Land tradition, a massive army from Mt. Hiei destroyed the Nichiren temples and community in Kyōto. However, this did not stop. Nichiren Buddhism from continuing to grow. Later, it would organize into seven sects and remain one of the important forms of Buddhism in Japan.

Box 9.2

The First Book

Many serious intellectuals had a "first book," which, in a time of youthful crisis, set their lives on course. For some of my friends, searching for meaning in their confused adolescence, it was Thoreau's *Walden*. For Dorothy Day, in anguish over social injustice and an unresponsive church, it was *The Brothers Karamazov*. For me, interned in Japan during World War II, it was R. H. Blyth's *Zen in English Literature*.

That was fifty-seven years ago. I'm a retired teacher of Zen Buddhism now, and looking through those old pages, I find many points where I disagree. Nonetheless, I am still mining the riches of this remarkable work.

Fundamentally, *Zen in English Literature* is not so much about Zen Buddhism, the religion, with its practice of meditation and its course of *kōan* study, as it is about language and the thought and attitudes that produce language.

(Continued)

Blyth quotes Tennyson, speaking of a woman staring hopelessly out of a window:

> Fixed like a beacon tower above the waves
> Of tempest, when the crimson-rolling eye
> Glares ruin, and the wild birds on the light
> Dash themselves dead.

Metaphor vividly exposes the net and indeed the hologram of people, animals, plants, mountains, rivers,the great Earth, sun, moon, and stars in all their infinite variety that is our personal life. Paul Shepard has shown how our language is charged with animal metaphor to describe human qualities and conditions: dogged, foxy, mousey, mulish, owlish, sheepish, and so on. There are countless similar metaphors in daily use from plants, minerals, mountains, the weather, and so on. All expose the net, the unity, the great "cooperative"—In Buddhadāsa's words:

> The entire cosmos is a cooperative. The sun, the moon, and
> the stars live together as a cooperative. The same is true
> for humans and animals, trees and soil. Our bodily parts
> function as a cooperative.

"Great wits jump" to personalize this cooperative. Blyth quotes Shelley's *Skylark:*

> All the earth and air,
> With thy verse is loud.

And comments: "That is, not only the skylark is singing but the trees and stones and rivers, the clouds, winds and air—all is singing, singing with the voice of the skylark."

This kind of example and explication, woven with such genius in my "first book," brought me to Zen Buddhist practice, where metaphor brings forth deepest understanding:

> Yün-men said to his assembly, "Within heaven and earth, through space and time, there is a treasure hidden inside the mountain of form. It takes a lantern and goes to the Buddha hall. It takes the great triple gate and puts it on the lantern.

And it brought me to social action, to sit down squarely in the way of obscene defilements of the cooperative.

ROBERT AITKEN

In the sixteenth century, these Buddhist armies were seen by the warlords as standing in the way of the reunification of Japan. Oda Nobunaga (1534–1582) played a leading role in this reunification effort. In so doing, he was especially ruthless in his drive to strip Buddhism of any political power. His army burnt down all the Tendai temples on Mt. Hiei, attacked the Shingon headquarters on Mt. Hōya, and suppressed the Pure Land and Nichiren armies throughout the countryside. The Zen schools escaped this suppression because they had not formed any kind of armed forces. Nobunaga's successor, Toyotami Hideyoshi (1536–1598), was able to steer a more moderate course because Buddhist political power was essentially broken. Hideyoshi rebuilt temples on Mt. Hiei and aided the construction of the Hongan-ji monastic complex in Kyōto. He also supported the Zen schools to which he felt indebted for their cultural contributions. The full unification of Japan came under Tokugawa Ieyasu (1542–1616), who moved the capital to Edo (modern Tokyo). Thus began the Tokugawa Shōgunate (1603–1868), which is referred to as Japan's modern period.

THE TOKUGAWA PERIOD (1603–1868): STRUGGLE AND REFORM

Japan's "modern period" began with the establishment of the Tokugawa Shōgunate in 1603. This new period advanced the secularization of Japanese society and provided national unity. The government no longer granted Buddhism the leading role in the affairs of the country that it had enjoyed in medieval times. In fact, the shōgunate adopted a Confucian ideology based primarily on the Neo-Confucianism that had successfully contributed to the unity of China achieved during the Ming Dynasty (1368–1644). Although the Buddhist schools were allowed to freely practice their religion if they did not criticize the government, they no longer exercised significant influence over the rulers or the educated classes.

The Tokugawa government did use Buddhism to enforce its tight control over Japanese society. All religious bodies were organized under the state. The Buddhist temples were registered, and all Buddhist schools were associated with either main or branch temples. All families in Japan were also registered with local Buddhist temples for the government to better keep track of the population. The Buddhist schools were forbidden to proselytize because people switching from one temple to another would disrupt the state census. The government did not support Buddhism financially, so the temples had to be financed by their official members.

As Buddhism was stripped not only of its political power but also of its intellectual and moral influence in society, Neo-Confucianism provided Japan with its prevalent worldview and moral code. In presenting their ideas and values, Confucian scholars in Japan also criticized Buddhism for being socially harmful due to its monastic religiosity, which seemed to them to have little social relevance. The Confucian challenge was strengthened by the fact that Buddhism at the time was torn by a sectarianism that had a divisive social impact and by the fact that there was a moral decline among the clergy.

A number of innovative and significant Buddhist responses to this Confucian challenge arose. One prominent example was a Buddhist reform movement founded by Jiun Sonja (1718–1804). Jiun was ordained a Shingon monk but was also trained in Confucianism and Sōtō Zen. As he matured as a Buddhist practitioner, Jiun became more and more aware of the need for a revival of

Buddhist thought, practice, and morality that was not limited by sectarianism. With a small group of disciples, Jiun developed a discipline of study, practice, and strict observance of the *Vinaya*. He called this new reform movement *Shōbōritsu*, or "Vinaya of the True Dharma." Taking the historical Buddha as a model, Jiun proposed that the Buddha's wisdom into emptiness as the interrelatedness of all things shows that all living beings are "one's own body." With this insight, one is inspired to treat all living beings as one would his or her own body. For Jiun, this kind and compassionate treatment of others is best defined in the Ten Good Precepts that are recognized by all forms of Japanese Buddhism.

Jiun believed that this view of the connection of wisdom with morality provided Buddhists with a common ground that transcended sectarian divisions. It also provided Buddhism with a rebuttal to the Confucianist claim that Buddhism is socially irrelevant. Jiun taught that the morality of the Ten Good Precepts gave all people a moral guide for family life, business practices, and government policymaking. Juin did not call for the abolition of the Buddhist sects but taught that each sect should focus on what in its tradition is in accord with the True Dharma and the Ten Good Precepts. They should then live those fundamental aspects of Buddhism shared in common with members of other Buddhist schools.

Another more institutional example of making Buddhist religiosity relevant to the secular world can be seen in the Sōtō School at this time. Many of the Sōtō monks during the Tokugawa Period preached the Buddha's Dharma to the common people in rural areas. They stressed the connection between Zen practice and the daily needs of the people by teaching that secular actions can have religious import if performed in the true spirit of the bodhisattva. When a person has the heart of the bodhisattva and works with that attitude for the welfare of others, then his or her actions are as religious as those performed in the temple.

Besides these kinds of internal Buddhist reforms in Japan, another kind of attempt to renew Japanese Buddhism came from China. Around the beginning of the seventeenth century, an influx of Chinese Chan (Zen) masters brought new inspirations to the Zen world in Japan. Among these masters was Yinyuan (1592–1673). Yinyuan arrived in Japan in 1654, and at first settled in the port city of Nagasaki. He then moved to near Kyōto and was eventually given some property in Uji, also near Kyōto. There he had a new temple built that he named *Mampuku-ji*. He also called the hilly site for the temple *Ōbakusan* after the region in China that he had left behind. This new monastic foundation would become the home of a third school of Zen in Japan: Ōbaku Zen.

Ōbaku Zen combined *zazen* and *kōan* practice with Tantric ritual, *nembutsu*, and the ritual recitation of *sūtras*. Chinese customs of dress and etiquette were also used in everyday monastic life, and the strict monastic rules as observed in China were also introduced. This particular reform was at first somewhat popular. Before Yinyuan died, he had expanded his movement to include some twenty-four Ōbaku monasteries around Japan. However, after a few decades, the growth of Ōbaku slowed because it never became fully inculturated. In 1876, the Ōbaku School was recognized as an independent Zen sect. Today, Ōbaku has about 500 affiliated temples.

The traditional forms of Japanese Zen were not receptive to the complex and sophisticated innovations introduced by Ōbaku. Instead, Japanese Zen often focused on the ordinary, everyday experiences of life, especially those found in nature. For example, Bashō Matsuo (1644–1694) was one of the greatest poets of Japan. Bashō brought the spirit of Zen into the world of poetry with his famous *haiku*. This simple and direct style of poetry provided him with a vehicle for expressing his Zen contemplation of nature. While not a monk, Bashō was a lay disciple, who, from the age of forty, traveled around Japan writing about his aesthetic/spiritual experiences. Certain themes such as solitude and silence, simplicity and ordinariness, seasons and sounds are presented in poems that lack any note of ego. The following poems by Bashō draw on the spirit of Zen:

Only Silence alone!
Into the rock cliff penetrates
The sound of the cicada.

An old pond, Ah!
A frog jumps in
The sound of water.

The light of the moon!
The four gates and four sects
Yet only one.

Another important figure from this period who also stressed the simplicity of Zen was Bankei Yōtaku (1622–1693). Bankei was a Rinzai master who lived and taught in the provinces where he was close to the common people. His message was simple and clear. All people have the innate "Unborn Buddha Mind." It is this innate reality that is the source of enlightenment. In that Unborn Buddha Mind, all things have their proper place and enjoy their true harmony. In discovering that reality, all of one's ordinary daily activities become acts of the Buddha. Instead of quoting the *sūtras* or patriarchs and masters from the past, stressing formal *kōan* practice, or emphasizing the importance of experiences in Zen, Bankei simply directed his followers to become aware of the Unborn Buddha Mind within them. For Bankei, the clarity of this Mind develops in a constant process along the way to Buddhahood.

Although Bankei's Zen was influential and continues to be so, the most famous Rinzai master from this time was Hakuin Ekaku (1686–1769). Hakuin agreed with Bankei about the importance of the process of Zen growth. But unlike Bankei, Hakuin focused on how this process can be nourished by proper *kōan* practice. Hakuin created a comprehensive *kōan* system with 1,700 anecdotes that remains the core of Rinzai training today. There are five types of *kōans* in Hakuin's system. *Kōans* of the first type are designed to bring the Zen student to an initial insight of Zen experience called *kenshō* ("insight into one's True Self"). Hakuin, like Zongmi in China and Chinul in Korea, understood from his own experience that this initial insight must be deepened into full enlightened living. After *kenshō*, this growth is achieved by working with the four other types of *kōans*, which are designed for that exact purpose. In this way, one cultivates freedom, wisdom, and compassion in a process of growth in the Dharma that continues to the end of one's life.

Drawing on his own life experience, Hakuin revitalized Rinzai Zen with his writings, which give us a most detailed description of the process of growth in the Zen experience from beginning to end. He is also known today for his ink paintings (see Figure 9.4). Hakuin discusses his personal struggle in what he calls the "Great Doubt" as it was produced by his *kōan* practice. Based on his experience, Hakuin taught that *kōans* are used initially in meditation and daily life to generate the Great Doubt, or an existential questioning of the suffering condition of oneself and the world. This Doubt is called "Great" because it is not an objective doubt concerning a particular question or some particular phenomenon in the world. Rather, it is a "mass of Great Doubt" in which oneself and the world are no longer separate realities.

This Great Doubt is, Hakuin says, in tension with one's belief in "self power," the power of one's True Self or Buddha-nature to break this mass of Great Doubt and produce Awakening. In this intense process, one works on his or her *kōan* with the guidance of a master. The master moves the disciple beyond thinking about his or her *kōan* in a dualistic and rationalistic way. Eventually, moving beyond such ordinary thought processes, there comes a moment in which suddenly and without willful effort, of itself the True Self realizes itself. One therein finds Awakening in a flash of "Great Enlightenment," or "Great Joy." Here are some of Hakuin's own words about the experience of this Great Doubt:

> A person confronted with the Great Doubt sees in the four directions only wide and empty land, without birth and death, like a plain of ice 10,000 miles in expanse. . . . In his heart, there remains not a trace of desires or concepts, only the word "emptiness" as if one is standing in the wide-open dome of heaven. . . . If one progresses in this Way, without turning back, he or she will suddenly experience something like the breaking of an ice cover, or the collapse of a tower made of crystal. . . . Nothing gives one more joy than to break through the many-storied gate of endless rebirths in *saṃsāra*. This is the inner realization of original Awakening of all the perfected ones in the four directions. (*Orategama*, Appendix)

THE MEIJI PERIOD (1868–1912) AND RECENT DEVELOPMENTS

The Meiji Restoration marked the end of Japan's long period of isolation under the Tokugawa government. Japan opened up to the outside world, and the Tokugawa Shōgunate was replaced with the emperor system. Among the first decrees of the new Meiji government were those that established a new

FIGURE 9.4. Ink on paper painting of Daruma (Bodhidharma) by Hakuin Ekaku, 1686–1769. Indianapolis Museum of Art.

government office for Shintō and separated Shintō from Buddhism. Within the first few years of the Meiji Period, the government also denounced Buddhist traditions and expropriated some temple lands. Buddhist monks serving Shintō shrines had to become Shintō priests or return to the lay state. Another decree permitted Buddhist monks to marry. In fact, today most Japanese monks are married. On the other hand, the women's orders have remained celibate. Fortunately for Buddhism, these policies were soon tempered, and it was clear that the government's intention was not to destroy Buddhism, but to make Shintō the national religion for its political advantage.

Along with the political and economic opening of Japan came an intellectual opening to the modem Western world. After the difficulties of the first few years, Buddhist religious leaders understood that the future of Buddhism depended on adapting to this new intellectual climate. To foster this adaptation, Buddhist institutions expanded the curricula of their monastery schools to include such subjects as modern mathematics and science, Western philosophy and literature, and comparative religions and foreign languages. In some cases, these schools evolved into universities; for example, a Sōtō monastic school became Komazawa University of Tokyo and a Rinzai monastic school became Hanazono Univeristy of Kyōto.

As Japanese Buddhism sought enrichment from contact with Western perspectives, the West was becoming interested in Buddhism. Indeed, Buddhism throughout Asia was being stimulated by Western scholars, who were studying their religion. Many Japanese Buddhist schools sent some of their young monks to study in the West. As they did so, they provided the West with Buddhist teachings as well as the opportunity to practice Buddhism. We will discuss this kind of contact in the last chapter of our story of Buddhism.

Through these kinds of contacts with Western culture, Buddhism produced a new generation of scholars and leaders who sought to redefine their religion in ways that are intellectually respectable, spiritually viable, and socially responsible. This task was at times a real struggle. One example of how this was so is found in the work of Kiyozawa Manshi (1863–1903), commonly referred to by his first name. Manshi was a Pure Land Buddhist educated at the University of Tokyo, where he studied the full range of Western thought. After his education was complete, he settled in Kyōto, where he was an educator. While he valued his modern education, he also treasured his Pure Land faith. The existential problem he faced was how to reconcile the modern view of the world with his personal religious faith. Influenced by German Idealism and Kegon Buddhism, Manshi concluded that the universe is an organic whole in a state of constant evolution and dissolution. Faith that each entity in the cosmos is a dynamic expression of this organic whole brings inner peace as one exercises reason to understand life and live morally. Without this faith, one's rational study and moral reasoning become matters of anxiety and undue exertion.

There were some missteps in this effort to redefine modern Buddhism. During the time of Japan's military expansionism at the turn of the twentieth century, some Rinzai Buddhist intellectuals proclaimed the spiritual superiority of Rinzai Zen. They taught that Rinzai was the highest embodiment of the essence of Buddhism, and of all forms of religion. These Zen writers stressed the tie between Zen and the Way of the Warrior (*bushidō*) with its one-pointed conviction without doubts or questions, fearless discipline, and self-sacrifice for the good of the Japanese nation. Thus, some Rinzai leaders extended the claim for spiritual superiority to one of cultural and racial superiority. This "New Buddhism" was used by the government to bolster national pride, militarism, and the war effort during World War II.

On the other hand, one very positive Japanese Buddhist contribution to the world during the twentieth century was the Kyōto School. As Japan opened to the West, Nishida Kitarō (1870–1949) studied Western philosophy and religion and went on to write highly sophisticated philosophical works drawing on both Buddhist and Western thought. He founded the Kyōto School as an intellectual movement, giving both Zen and Pure Land Buddhism a new and highly respected voice in the international philosophical and theological worlds. The Kyōto School's work was brought forward by such persons as Tanabe Hajime (1885–1962), Nishitani Keiji (1900–1990), Takeuchi Yoshinori (1913–2002), and Abe Masao (1915–2006). Also influenced by Nishida, the great Zen master Hisamatsu Shin'ichi (1889–1980) founded the F.A.S. Society dedicated to the realization of the "Formless Self" (F.) that embraces "All Humankind" (A.) to transform modern society "Superhistorically" (S.), that is, on a spiritual basis. In opposition to New Buddhism, Hisamatsu opposed any kind of racism, nationalism, or any ideology that stands in the way of realizing a more united and peaceful world community.

After World War II, a secular government and society in Japan turned its attention toward rebuilding the nation into one that is technologically and economically progressive. Interest in traditional forms of Buddhism began to wane. However, this meant that certain spiritual needs were left unmet by older religious forms. After the Korean War, new forms of religiosity began to become popular in Japan. What are called the "New Religions" grew in membership as literally millions of Japanese laypeople joined their ranks. More recently, even newer religious groups continue to be founded by charismatic figures. Among the New Religions are a number of influential Buddhist lay movements that have sought to balance personal healing and transformation with social engagement. Some are working in ways that better human society, not only in Japan but also around the world. They see themselves as living and sharing the values of Buddhism for the good of humankind. Two of the best-known of these Buddhist lay organizations are the Sōka Gakkai and the Risshō Kōsei-kaii.

NEW JAPANESE BUDDHIST MOVEMENTS

One of the most successful and yet controversial modern Buddhist movements is Sōka Gakkai (Value Creation Society) of Japan. Tsunesaburō Makiguchi (1871–1944) and Jōsei Toda (1900–1958) founded what would become Sōka Gakkai before World War II, when both men were educators interested in value education.[1] During the war, they were imprisoned for refusing to participate in nationalistic Shintō worship. While Makiguchi died in prison, Toda spent his prison time reading and chanting the *Lotus Sūtra*. During that time, Toda felt that he was being chosen to spread the teachings of Nichiren for the good not only of Japan but the whole world. After the war, Sōka Gakkai was eventually developed as a lay movement associated with one of the smaller Nichiren sects, Nichiren Shōshū. As a lay movement, Sōka Gakkai offered a way of bettering one's life and a new and positive vision of the future to many struggling and disillusioned people in postwar Japan. However, many of the new Sōka Gakkai converts practiced an intense form of proselytizing of other Japanese Buddhists, an activity that contributed to the controversial status of Sōka Gakkai in Japan. Despite this, Sōka Gakkai's membership grew at an incredible rate; today it claims between eight and ten million adherents with more than one million outside of Japan.

Sōka Gakkai uses Buddhism as a foundation for its projects for personal and global betterment. It believes that all persons possess Buddha-nature, but that people's minds and hearts are affected by the fact that they live in the age of the Degenerate Dharma. In other words, the negative karma of the modern age dominates people's lives. People can experience ten levels of consciousness that range from hellish states of anger, hatred, and greed on the one hand, to states of peace and happiness associated with Buddhahood on the other. Although we have the potential for the latter, because of negative karma, our world is full of violent, ignorant, and tragic conditions fueled by the hellish states of people's minds. To build true peace in the world, one cannot just address particular social or political crises; one must also address the problems at their roots, in the human mind. One must free oneself from the lower states of mental bondage and achieve the higher states of mental freedom and Buddhahood by realizing one's Buddha-nature.

The methods of Nichiren Buddhism that Sōka Gakkai believes are strong enough to break this mental bondage include chanting of Nichiren's *mantra* to the *Lotus Sūtra* and using Nichiren's *maṇḍala* (the *Gohonzon*). The *mantra* is said to awaken a spiritual power in one's life that changes the mental and physical conditions in which one finds oneself. The *maṇḍala* is said to bring about an awareness of one's Buddha-nature that is ultimately the source of these positive mental and physical changes. Since one's Buddha-nature is shared by all living beings, its realization brings about a sense of connection to other people and to the natural environment. This sensitivity to others, and especially to the needs of others, impels one to work together with other persons to establish a peaceful and harmonious world in which all can be happy and prosper. This achievement, Sōka Gakkai teaches, will bring an end to the present cultures of division and violence by cutting their roots in the human mind and heart, as well as their expressions in such realities as war, unjust societies, economic poverty, and environmental exploitation.

Sōka Gakkai has attracted many modern urban people who are searching for fellowship in an impersonal secular world and are interested in crafting a better life for themselves and for humankind. Members meet in neighborhood groups that tend to each other's needs, giving advice and support with the problems of daily life. The different official organs of the international Sōka Gakkai movement, Sōka Gakkai International (SGI), present members in many countries with avenues to help build a better world. One such project in the United States is the Ikeda Center for Peace, Learning, and Dialogue, which sponsors programs with world experts on social, political, economic, and environmental problems and publishes materials that explore these problems and possible solutions. In regard to this goal, SGI has established peace education programs to foster face-to-face relations between peoples of opposing cultures and ideologies, programs to address environmental problems such as global warming and deforestation, and humanitarian programs to aid refugees, feed the hungry, and meet the needs of the poor.

In addressing these social and environmental issues, Sōka Gakkai stresses the need to change the way people experience themselves and the world. This personal change, Sōka Gakkai teaches, should lead to structural changes in society. To this end, Sōka Gakkai has entered the world of politics in Japan by forming, for example, the Kōmeitō Party. This move into politics is limited to Japan, and SGI does not become involved in politics in other countries, where it simply emphasizes value education and contributes to public awareness of social issues. In its social thought in Japan, the Sōka Gakkai proposes a "Buddhist Democracy" that affirms the freedom of capitalism but balances it with a "human socialism." This human socialism recognizes the equality of all human beings and seeks to protect everyone from the negative effects of unchecked competitive capitalism. This, they believe, can be done by sharing the wealth of a nation with those in need through providing such benefits as adequate health care and housing and good education and job training. Again, convincing people that sharing with the less fortunate is a social good demands that they begin to experience the world from a less individualistic point of view. Hence the need for spiritual transformation.

The president of SGI, Daisaku Ikeda, describes the experience of spiritual transformation in function of world peace as follows:

> The practice of Buddhism is based on compassion. . . . [I]n Buddhism, compassion signifies the sublime endeavor to share the suffering of another from the stance of our common humanity and to create an expanding network of genuine friendship and trust.
>
> I perceive in Shakyamuni's compassion—elaborated and extolled in the Mahayana tradition as the Bodhisattva Way—a profound and unshakable humanism. The SGI is a body committed to developing activities in the areas of peace, culture and education based on this Buddhist humanism. The bedrock of the Buddhist spirit of humanism is reverence for all life, which discerns an incomparably precious "Buddha nature" inherent not only in humankind but in all living beings. . . .
>
> The bodhisattva, as a world citizen, is someone who is constantly challenging egotism and is engaged in the race to transform what Buddhism refers to as deluded impulses (represented by the three poisons of greed, anger, and stupidity) into enlightenment. Bodhisattvas, refusing to be engulfed in the consumerism and materialism of contemporary society, embrace a noble spirit of serving

> others, and pledge to make this their mission in life. This process sets in motion a fundamental change in life orientation—from egotism to the desire to create happiness for oneself and others.
>
> I believe that every religion should be promoting, according to its own methods, this kind of fundamental change in life from our contemporary materialism to a highly spiritual and humanistic culture. . . . Finally, I strongly hope that the world's religions will use dialogue and exchange to resolve the multitude of problems that threaten the survival of humanity, and stress harmony and cooperation with the aim of creating a culture of peace.[2]

Another important Japanese movement is the Risshō Kōsei-kai (RKK). This lay Buddhist movement was founded in 1938 by Nikkyō Niwano (1906–1999) and Myōkō Naganuma (1989–1957). Its name means "Society for the Establishment of Righteousness and Friendly Relations." While under the guidance of Nikkyō Niwano, RKK emerged from a loose-knit Nichiren reform movement named Reiyukai and has grown into a large international lay organization of more than five million members dedicated to a broader understanding and application of the *Lotus Sūtra*. Niwano felt that the *Lotus Sūtra* presents the culmination of Gautama Buddha's teachings in a way that is universal, and therefore compatible with the world's religions. RKK members conclude that by living the *Lotus Sūtra* in daily life, they can contribute to bringing all humankind to unity and peace. Indeed, Niwano was instrumental in the foundation of the World Conference of Religions for Peace (WCRP), the most important worldwide interfaith organization working for the betterment of humankind. Niwano also established the Niwano Peace Foundation in Japan and the Niwano Peace Prize at the United Nations.

RKK teaches that all persons have the Buddha-nature and can attain Buddhahood through faith and practice. One is enabled through RKK practice to deepen one's experience of wisdom, reflecting the Dharma in one's own life and by compassion into the lives of others. In terms of particular practices, the RKK stresses the Six Perfections and the Bodhisattva Path to liberation. One seeks guidance on this path in the *Lotus Sūtra*. To strengthen this practice, one can turn in faith to the Eternal Buddha. Chapter 16 of the *Lotus Sūtra* states that the historical Buddha was a manifestation of the Eternal Buddha, who has appeared in different forms over the ages to guide and aid beings toward liberation. While some Nichiren groups worship the sacred *maṇḍala*, RKK reserves worship for the Eternal Buddha and uses a *maṇḍala* only for liturgical focus. They also use *mantra* chanting not for obtaining any special power, but as an expression of prayerful gratitude to the Eternal Buddha. RKK believes that the Eternal Buddha fills the universe with his spiritual presence, communicating his mercy to all beings in need.

Community life is central to RKK. As one experiences his or her ignorance and selfish nature, one is led to repentance (*zange*) before the Eternal Buddha and the community. This act of faith entrustment unites the person with both the Eternal Buddha and the community in ways that heal and transform one's mind, speech, and action. The healing and transforming experience of the individual is strengthened by the RKK practice of *hōza*, or "Dharma sitting." People sit in circles to discuss their problems and questions and seek solutions in the principles of Buddhism presented in the *Lotus Sūtra*. Guided by a trained facilitator, the *hōza* circle addresses issues having to do with work, family life, relationships, religion, and ethics. For *hōza* members, the Four Noble Truths are the "key" to this process. All members take on themselves the problem of the troubled person. Then they seek together, from their own experience, the cause of the problem. With the help of the facilitator and the scriptures, they find a path to liberation from the problem, a liberation that brings extinction of the suffering. In the main temple in Tokyo alone, there are more than 200 *hōza* groups that meet each day (see Figure 9.5).

Hōza practice gives people the opportunity to grow in wisdom in the context of compassionate community relationships. By making themselves one with those in need who share their troubles, RKK members move beyond self-centeredness, discover their interrelatedness, and compassionately connect with others. In this manner, they grow in their compassionate awareness of their own Buddha-nature, the Buddha-nature of the troubled person, and the Buddha-nature of all living beings. This communal way of developing enlightened awareness, compassion, and practical insight into solving the problems of modernity has become a model for RKK's activities of social engagement. That is, RKK has sought ways of helping people come together to address national and international problems with wisdom and compassion. This can be seen in the operational style of WCRP as well as in RKK's other projects such as the Overseas Assistance Program, which provides aid to persons in need of food, clothing, or shelter, especially in Southeast Asia.

FIGURE 9.5. The Great Sacred Hall at the Risshō Kōsei-kai headquarters, Tokyo, Japan.

Another good example of communal problem solving is RKK's Brighter Society Movement developed in the late 1960s. This movement is dedicated to bringing together leaders from the worlds of business, government, and religion to promote humanitarian activities. Some of these activities include blood donations, fund-raising for established charities, neighborhood renewal programs, and training for parents in crisis. For RKK, personal faith and practice are linked to collective collaboration for human betterment among religious leaders and all persons who are concerned about the many personal and social sources of suffering in the modern world. Nikkyō Niwano described his personal religious experience and his views concerning peace this way:

> Listening to lectures on the *Lotus Sūtra*, I realized that I had found what I had been looking for. The *Lotus Sūtra* was the perfect net in which to save everyone in the world. Physically and spiritually it could help both the individual and all of society. I was profoundly shaken by what I had learned. The impression made on me was of astonishing, vibrant freshness. It has remained fresh for over forty years. During that time, I have not missed reading the *Lotus Sūtra* a single day. And the text has lost none of its subtlety, none of its ability to reverberate in my heart and sink deeply into my spirit. On the contrary, the more I read the *sūtra*, the more impressive and profound it seems.[3]
>
> The practice of the Risshō Kōsei-kai is to seek to incorporate [the] Eightfold Path into their daily lives and to endeavor to be a motive force in bringing peace to the world. . . . To encourage others to develop peace in their hearts, we must dismantle the armor around our own hearts. . . . When we can face others with an open mind, they will relax . . . and open their hearts to us. Buddhism teaches this in its doctrine that all phenomena lie within a single thought, the doctrine of the Three Thousand Realms in One Mind. The thoughts we embrace, whether good or evil, are transmitted just as they are to others. . . . [T]he doctrine of Three Thousand Realms in One Mind [is] an expression of the essence of the Buddha's teachings in the *Lotus Sūtra*: all sentient beings can attain perfect enlightenment-Buddhahood, and the appropriate goal of believers is to attain enlightenment not only for themselves but for all sentient beings since individual salvation is not true salvation because no individual exists apart from the whole—all things are interconnected. Risshō Kōsei-kai members try to understand at the deepest level the practical doctrine of Three Thousand Realms in One Mind, that is, that it is necessary to improve themselves and practice this doctrine in order to help others.[4]

The Cultural Experience of Japanese Buddhism Today

Tomonobu Shinozaki
Gakurin Buddhist Seminary, Tokyo, Japan

Perhaps the most important characteristic of the Japanese religious culture in general is syncretism. Many Japanese do not feel a commitment to a particular religious sect, or if they do, they do not see any problem with the veneration of deities worshiped by other sects or with performing rituals in temples or shrines of other sects. For example, a person who identifies himself or herself as a Buddhist may venerate Shintō *kami* (gods), and vice versa. Also, Confucianism has never been an independent religious movement or organization in Japan. Rather, it has played an important ethical role within both Buddhism and Shintō. Some ordinary Japanese people do not know to which Buddhist sect the temple they visit belongs, or even whether it is a Shintō shrine or a Buddhist temple. Folk religious practices based on forms of shamanism and animism are also blended into the mix of common rituals.

Given this openness to blending different religious customs, ordinary Japanese people often turn to two Buddhist bodhisattvas in times of need, namely, Jizō and Kannon Bodhisattvas (Kṣitigarbha and Avalokiteśvara). Statues of Jizō can be seen along roads and along the paths to temples. One of the most well-known Jizō figures has a young face and wears a red baby apron. Here, Jizō is believed to be guardian of children and women during childbirth. He is also often prayed to by women who have had miscarriages or abortions. Buddhism in Japan does not strictly enforce a prohibition of abortion, and the Buddhist *mizuko kuyō* ritual service for aborted fetuses is popular. It is a Buddhist way of offering a prayer to Jizō Bodhisattva, and it functions to give a sense of relief.

Kannon Bodhisattva is worshiped by the Japanese people as a very special source of mercy and healing. If people pray to Kannon when faced with various kinds of danger or difficulty, they believe that they can be saved and blessed. They view Kannon as a merciful mother, symbolizing Buddha's compassion. It is often believed that Kannon makes a vicarious sacrifice for those who are suffering like a mother who sacrifices for her children.

In general, given Buddhist and Shintō influences, the Japanese people also have a reverent sense of nature as both beautiful and sacred in its own right. Nature is taken to encompass actual phenomena like mountains, rivers, grasses, rocks, and trees, and is not an abstract reality. The great Buddhist cultural expressions of the past have strengthened this sense through temple gardens of rocks and sand, as well as grass, trees and plantings, and tea gardens. These natural Buddhist treasures of Japan have a strong spiritual affect on the viewers. Also, Buddhist calligraphy and landscape painting, so important to Japanese culture, as well as Buddhist poetry, *Noh* drama, flower arranging, music, and dance, all open a spiritual interiority to nature. They convey an intuitive and emotional sense of the transience of nature and life that produces a powerful kind of spiritual awareness in the Japanese people. This kind of awareness is at the core of the general Japanese philosophy of life. The influence of the arts of Buddhism on Japanese culture cannot be overemphasized.

Kami are considered by many Japanese as part of nature because they dwell within nature; many Japanese believe that when one dies, he or she abides with the *kami* or becomes "like" the *kami* in nature. Many people also believe that the Buddha is something like the great life source within nature, that is, Great Nature, and that when humans die, they return to the Great

Nature. These views imply the idea that spirits of the dead are connected spatially in nature with their descendents. It is in this context that the veneration of ancestors can be understood.

BUDDHIST VENERATION OF ANCESTORS

In contemporary Japan, if people are asked the question, "Do you have a religion?" a large majority responds, "I have no religion." According to a survey of college students, those who have some kind of religious faith of their own are less than 10 percent. Those who believe strongly in the existence of the Buddha and those who strongly disbelieve are both 15 percent; and 30 percent of the students hold either weakly positive or negative views concerning the Buddha's existence.

On the other hand, in terms of life after death, those who strongly believe in an afterlife are 20 percent, and those who strongly disbelieve are only 10 percent. About 40 percent weakly believe and 25 percent weakly disbelieve. Also, more than half of the students say that they visit their family graves during the *O-bon* period; and almost half of the families of the students have a family altar where ancestors are venerated. So, although very few college students have any personal religious faith and less than 50 percent have even a weak belief in the Buddha, well over 50 percent have some level of belief in life after death and participate in ancestor veneration. Ancestor veneration is practiced and accepted today, even by those without any specific religious belief.

The results of this survey of college students mirror the general Japanese thinking molded by Buddhism, namely, that there is some kind of deep interdependent bond between the living and the dead. The Japanese are concerned with the dead partly out of fear of dead spirits and partly out of filial reverence for the dead. They also believe that merit from their good deeds may help the dead, assuring them of an auspicious destiny (karma). Ordinary people think that if they do a good deed, especially by donating money or helping others, they can create merit, which is good both for their ancestors and for themselves. They believe somewhat ambiguously in a certain kind of Buddhist causality whereby doing a good deed creates good merit, and doing a bad deed creates bad karma.

As for Japanese Buddhists themselves, the basis of ancestor veneration performed at contemporary Buddhist temples is the *danka-seido*, the "parish system," which was established around the seventeenth century by the Tokugawa government. Regardless of the differences among Buddhist sects, individuals had to belong to the parish where their family graves were located. Under the control of the government, Buddhist clergy played an administrative role throughout the country. With this, Buddhism began to lose its spiritual influence over the people, and in the more contemporary period the *danka* system has been severely weakened. However, the system was reinforced by the practice of the veneration of ancestors. For example, the founders of the Japanese sects came to be and are still worshiped as ancestral "heroes." Saichō of the Japanese Tendai sect, Kūkai of the Shingon sect, Shinran in the Shin sect, and Nichiren of the Nichiren sect are today revered sometimes even more than the Buddha. Ordinary people are often not so concerned with the doctrinal aspects of Buddhism; rather, temple rituals for veneration of ancestors, both their own and those of their sect, are of primary importance.

When someone dies, the family of the deceased usually requests the traditional custom of having a Buddhist priest give the deceased a posthumous name (*kaimyo*) and conduct a funeral ceremony, which consists mainly of *sūtra* chanting. This custom is so important to Buddhists in Japan that traditional Buddhist sects are often referred to as "funeral Buddhism" (*sōshiki bukkyō*), a name that carries a derogatory meaning. That is, Buddhist temples today have become strongly associated with the performance of funerals and memorial services. However, to change this perception, recently temples have provided attendees at such ceremonies with guidance from the priest on the meaning of life and death from a Buddhist perspective, as well as on the importance of awakening to the Buddhist way of life. Some Pure Land temples have also tried to restore the old Buddhist deathbed ritual for dying persons.

Memorial services are held after someone's death according to a traditional schedule. Usually, these memorial services are occasions for family reunions with relatives of the deceased. These services are held during specific years at a temple and are conducted by priests. *Sūtras* are recited, graves are visited, and after the memorial service people share a meal together. Also, during the weeks of the spring and autumn equinoxes (*Higan*), people visit their family graves at the temples and offer incense and candles at their family altars. Urbanization contributes to a decrease of such customs, but they are still observed. Some people even observe the daily offering of water, flowers, incense, and candles at their family altars or on special family occasions.

O-BON FESTIVAL

A Buddhist memorial service that has become a very popular part of Japanese culture is the *O-bon* festival. *O-bon* is a shortened version of *Ullambana* taken from the *Ullambana Sūtra*. That text tells of a disciple of the Buddha who made an offering for his mother's release from the Realm of the Hungry Ghosts. Upon her release, the disciple danced with joy. From this dance comes the custom of the "*Bon* Dance." It is a time for joyful dancing as one remembers his or her ancestors with appreciation. This festival, which has been celebrated for more than 500 years, is a time when Japanese people take a holiday from work and go back their ancestral homes to participate in an *O-bon* festival or service.

O-bon is celebrated either during mid-July or mid-August depending on the region of Japan. The dance originally was a *Nembutsu* folk dance, but the style of the dance and the music and songs now vary from region to region in Japan depending on local folk customs. In some cases there are only songs;

in others there are only drums or drums with flutes. But in all cases, there is a high wooden structure made just for the festival. People line up around it to dance. Since World War II, there is a new folk dance type of festival where people dance to folk music played in parks or community centers.

During the *O-bon* season, it is believed that family ancestors return home. So some Japanese people prepare to welcome their ancestral spirits. Ways of welcoming ancestors vary from area to area in Japan. A typical custom is to set up a "spirit altar" at home, clean the grave site, and prepare figures of horses or oxen to "carry" the ancestor spirits between grave and house. These horses and oxen are made of straw, cucumber, and eggplant. A family welcomes the spirits with a welcoming fire in front of the house on the thirteenth of either July or August and sends them off with another fire on the sixteenth. These fires signify the illumination of the road between grave and house. Buddhist priests visit the family and recite *sūtras* to welcome the spirits at the family altar

POPULAR BUDDHIST PRACTICES AND HOLIDAYS

It should be noted that in Japanese Buddhist culture, the recitation of *sūtras* and the chanting of *mantras* are popular and are often done for their effect rather than their content. Most *sūtras* are not translated into modern Japanese, and in rituals, most Buddhist priests recite Chinese *sūtras* with Japanese pronunciation. The recitation is thought to have a supernatural or mysterious power to purify one's secular life and one's profane environment, to expel evil spirits, and to invite blessings from the Buddhas and bodhisattvas.

To get rid of impure or unfortunate karma, or to receive the blessing of the Buddhas or bodhisattvas, sacred *mantras* are also chanted, such as *Namu-Myōhō-Renge-kyō* (Hail to the *Sūtra* of the Lotus Flower of the Wonderful Dharma) and *Namu-Amida-Butsu* (Hail to Amida Buddha). Some Buddhists, such as members of the Shingon sect, attend esoteric Buddhist temples for *goma-kuyō* (fire rituals) with recitation of sacred *dhāranī* incantations performed by priests. Along this line of popular Buddhist practices, one also finds the use of *o-mamori* (amulets). On especially important occasions in a person's life (*jinsei girei*), ardent Buddhists visit Buddhist temples to receive blessings. While at the temple, one can purchase amulets that are used for a number of purposes, such as for passing an examination, having a birth free of complications, or safety while driving a vehicle.

Seasonal celebrations, besides *O-bon* and memorial services during the spring and autumn equinoxes (*Higan*), are also popular with Japanese Buddhists. Buddhists commonly visit temples on New Year's Eve. At midnight, every Buddhist temple strikes the temple bell 108 times. There are various reasons for the number 108, but a common one is that it signifies the purification of our 108 human desires. There are TV broadcasts of rituals all around Japan, and people feel the transition from the passing year to the new year.

Setsubun is New Year's Day in the old calendar, usually on February 3 or 4. Buddhist temples, as well as Shintō shrines, draw a lot of people to what are called "bean-scattering" ceremonies. At the ceremony, what are considered to be "lucky beans" that represent good fortune for the new year are "scattered" to the people attending the ceremony. During this day, within the family, soybeans are also scattered inside and outside of the house to frighten away evil spirits. The family chants, "In with good fortune! Out with the demons!" For Buddhists, this activity symbolizes getting rid of the three poisonous "demons" in our minds and hearts: greed, hatred, and delusion.

Finally, Buddhist temples celebrate the Buddha's Birthday on April 8. The celebration is known as Flower Festival (*Hana-matsuri*) because it comes at the time when there are new cherry blossoms. People with children pour a special sweet tea over a statue of the standing baby Buddha. They also parade a cart with an elephant on which the baby Buddha is riding. For many Buddhists, this birthday symbolizes the need to give birth to the qualities of the Buddha in one's own life.

Behind the many Buddhist practices in Japan, be they at the temples or family altars, it is believed that the recitation of *sūtras* or *mantras;* the copying of *sūtras;* the dedication of poems; the writing of devotional literature; the carving of Buddhist statues; and the offerings of flowers, incense, water, or food to the Buddhas or bodhisattvas all affect one's everyday life as well as one's ancestors. These religious activities, in turn, inspire the arts and literature in Japanese culture, as well as a way of religious living. Given this cultural influence, well-educated people in Japan like to study Buddhist ideas and their cultural expressions. They sense a Buddhist spirit in the martial arts, the tea ceremony, flower arranging, *haiku* poetry, or other sophisticated cultural expressions in Japan. This study sometimes leads individuals to taking up Zen meditation practice or Buddhist philosophy, but often without belonging to any specific Buddhist sect.

THE BODHISATTVA FIGURE AND BUDDHIST PRACTICE TODAY

The new Buddhist lay movements in contemporary Japan are largely in the *Lotus Sūtra* tradition. There is an aspect of this tradition that to some extent reflects a new way of thinking about popular Japanese Buddhism. The image of the bodhisattva in this tradition presents an ideal for Buddhist living in which one does not rely so much on external rituals and blessings, but on being disciples of the Buddha through one's own inner conviction and power to spread the teachings to others and transform the world.

The most important image of the bodhisattva in the *Lotus Sūtra* is the countless individual bodhisattvas who emerge from the earth as followers of the Buddha. Their emergence from the earth is not due to rituals and blessings. In this emergence, they change their own destinies by taking responsibility in their situations, instead of blaming others. Their faith and lifestyle involve the effort to overcome hardships, especially those that are self-induced, as a religious exercise and mission. Associated with the image of these bodhisattvas is the lotus flower, which blooms with its pure flower yet is rooted in the ordinary mud for nourishment. All people living ordinary lives are equally considered to be bodhisattvas who can become Buddhas through the way they live their daily lives.

Another characteristic of the bodhisattvas lies in his or her world-orientation (*genseshugi*). They are compassionately concerned with this world, rather than what happens after death. People with such a this-world orientation still believe in seeking worldly benefits, praying to the Buddhas or the bodhisattvas for health, and peace, for example. But they do so with regard to the needs of humanity, understanding that the Pure Land is in our minds or in this world, rather than simply a place we go to after death. Therefore, for example, many new lay Buddhist groups in Japan have been engaged in the peace movement, having as their final purpose achieving world peace. They believe that bodhisattva practice involves helping others and disseminating the Dharma for the good of humanity. Such teachings encourage Buddhists to be more involved in social and political activities, making Buddhist teachings a living tradition that is alive in everyday contexts.

NOTES

1. For contemporary Japanese names, we do not put the last name first.
2. Daisaku Ikeda, "The SGI's Peace Movement," in Chappell, ed., *Buddhist Peacework*, pp. 130, 136–137.
3. Nikkyō Niwano, *Life Time Beginner* (Tokyo: Kōsei Publishing Co., 1978), p. 76.
4. ———, *Some Thoughts on Peace* (Tokyo: Kōsei Publishing Co., 1984), pp. 17–18, 20.

SUGGESTIONS FOR FURTHER READING

Abe, Masao, and Norman Waddell, trans. *The Heart of Dōgen's* Shōbōgenzō. Albany: SUNY Press, 2002.

Abé, Ryuchi. *The Weaving of Mantra: Kūkai and the Construction of Esoteric Buddhist Discourse*. New York: Columbia University Press, 1999.

Andreason, Esben. *Popular Buddhism in Japan: Shin Buddhist Religion and Culture*. Honolulu: University of Hawaii Press, 1998.

Arai, Paula Kane Robinson. *Women Living Zen: Japanese Soto Buddhist Nuns*. New York: Oxford University Press, 2012.

Baroni, Helen J. *Ōbaku Zen: The Emergence of the Third Sect of Zen in Tokugawa Japan*. Honolulu: University of Hawaii Press, 2000.

Berthier, François. *Reading Zen in the Rocks: The Japanese Dry Landscape Garden*. Chicago: University of Chicago Press, 2000.

Colcutt, Martin. *Five Mountains: The Rinzai Zen Monastic Institution in Medieval Japan*. Cambridge, MA: Harvard University Press, 1981.

Cook, Francis H. *Sounds of Valley Streams: Enlightenment in Dōgen's Zen—Translation of Nine Essays from* Shōbōgenzō. Albany: SUNY Press, 1989.

Covell, Stephen G. *Japanese Temple Buddhism: Worldliness in a Religion of Renunciation*. Honolulu: University of Hawaii Press, 2005.

de Bary, Wm. Theodore, ed., with Ryusaku Tsunoda and Donald Keene. *Sources of Japanese Tradition*. 2 vols. (Second Edition of Vol. 1 edited by Donald Keene, George Tanabe, and Paul Varley.) New York: Columbia University Press, 2001.

Dumoulin, Heinrich. *Zen Buddhism: A History*. Vol. 2, *Japan*. New York: Macmillan, 1990.

Franck, Frederick, ed. *The Buddha Eye: An Anthology of the Kyōto School*. New York: Crossroad, 1982.

Groner, Paul. *Saichō: The Establishment of the Japanese Tendai School*. Berkeley, CA: Berkeley Buddhist Studies Series, 1984.

Hakeda, Yoshito S, trans. *Kūkai: Major Works*. New York: Columbia University Press, 1972.

Heine, Steven. *Dogen: Textual and Historical Studies*. New York: Oxford University Press, 2012.

Heine, Steven, and Dale S. Wright, eds. *The Kōan: Texts and Contexts in Zen Buddhism*. New York: Oxford University Press, 2000.

Hirota, Dennis, trans. *The Collected Works of Shinran*. 2 vols. Kyoto, Japan: Shin Buddhism Translation Series, 1997.

Kasulas, Thomas P. *Zen Action, Zen Person*. Honolulu: University of Hawaii Press, 1981.

Kim, Hee-Jin. *Dōgen on Meditation and Thinking: A Reflection on His View of Zen*. Albany: SUNY Press, 2006.

Kitagawa, Joseph M. *On Understanding Japanese Religion*. Princeton, NJ: Princeton University Press, 1987.

Kraft, Kenneth. *Eloquent Zen: Daito and Early Japanese Zen*. Honolulu: University of Hawaii Press, 1992.

LaFleur, William R. *The Karma of Words: Buddhism and the Literary Arts in Medieval Japan*. Berkeley: University of California Press, 1983.

Metraux, Daniel. *The History and Theology of Soka Gakkai: A Japanese New Religion*. Lewiston, NY: Edwin Mellen Press, 1988.

Payne, Richard K., ed. *Shin Buddhism: Historical, Textual, and Interpretive Studies*. Honolulu: University of Hawaii Press, 2009.

Pilgrim, Richard B. *Buddhism and the Arts of Japan*. New York: Columbia University Press, 1999.

Ruppert, Brian. *Jewel in the Ashes: Buddha Relics and Power in Early Medieval Japan*. Cambridge, MA: Harvard University Press, 2000.

Sanford, James H. *Flowing Traces: Buddhism in the Literary and Visual Arts of Japan*. Princeton, NJ: Princeton University Press, 1992.

Seager, Richard Hughes. *Encountering the Dharma: Daisaku Ikeda, Soka Gakkai, and the Globalization of Buddhist Humanism*. Berkeley: University of California Press, 2006.

Senchakushū English Translation Project, trans. *Hōnen's* Senchakushū: *Passages on the Selection of the Nembutsu in the Original Vow*. Honolulu: University of Hawaii Press, 1998.

Stone, Jacqueline I. *Original Enlightenment and the Transformation of Medieval Japanese Buddhism*. Honolulu: University of Hawaii Press, 1999.

Tanabe, George, Jr. ed. *Religions of Japan in Practice*. Princeton, NJ: Princeton University Press, 1999.

Tanahashi, Kazuaki, and David T. Schneider, eds. *The Essential Zen*. San Francisco: HarperSanFrancisco, 1995.

Yampolsky, Philip B., trans. *The Zen Master Hakuin: Selected Writings*. New York: Columbia University Press, 1971.

10

The Globalization of Buddhism

Globalization is the result of a new interdependence of the cultures of the world due to a number of factors such as global transportation, communication, and markets that have resulted in technological, economic, and social networks that transcend national and regional boundaries. The Internet and mass media have strongly influenced these networks as they penetrate the cultures of the world. In the past, cultures with their religions had geographical borders. The Theravāda culture, for example, was primarily limited to Sri Lanka and parts of Southeast Asia. Globalization has allowed cultural boundaries to be penetrated by other cultures, creating global flows and interpenetration of religious ideas, practices, lineages, customs, and overall traditions. In the past, there might have been different religions in a given society, but their relationships were fairly stable. Globalization has brought about new religious phenomena in all parts of the world. A new global pluralism of religions is now commonplace, and in it we see the globalization of Buddhism.

In terms of Buddhism, we have seen how the different Buddhist traditions changed as they entered new cultural settings throughout history. For example, we saw how new forms of Buddhism slowly emerged in China, Korea, and Japan that were culturally compatible, blending into these new forms concepts and values of the cultures of East Asia. However, the globalization of Buddhism during the past half century or so has been rapid and worldwide, with international and interregional flows producing Buddhist networks through which influence and change happens in all directions. What happens in Buddhist communities in one country can influence and shape what develops in Buddhist communities in other parts of the world; and these latter developments can in turn flow back to the country that originated them in the first place. Globalization also enables any Buddhist group to become internationalized, to found temples, Dharma centers, and local communities in countries far from the group's place of origin. In doing so,

Buddhist groups adapt by tailoring teachings to multiple cultures at the same time. This kind of globalization is something new in the history of Buddhism.

When scholars of Buddhism first wrote about the flows of Buddhism outside Asia, they often used the term "West." They spoke about the "Westernization of Buddhism," the "Western transformation of Buddhism," "Buddhism in the West," or just "Western Buddhism." However, the "West" is not a geographical term. It is used to refer to the "First World," namely, Western Europe, North America, and Australia. In a broader sense, it refers to countries that are developed, urbanized, secular, and capitalist. The Second World and Third World are left out. Scholars today note that the globalization of Buddhism actually includes a diversity of non-Asian countries from "first" to "third" with the result being new Global Buddhism. Also, the notion of "Western Buddhism" implied that there are one-directional flows of Asian Buddhism to the West where they were modified to fit Western cultures. However, today scholars have shown that many modern forms of Asian Buddhism have developed due to colonialist incursions into Asia, or later non-Asian influences in Asia. This phenomenon produced a kind of "modern Buddhism" that has been exported to non-Asian countries only to be repackaged and returned to Asia and to other regions of the non-Asian world. For example, books written by Asian intellectuals influenced by the West, like D. T. Suzuki, presented a spiritualized, universalized, and purified Buddhism focusing on meditation and enlightenment, not on specific beliefs, practices, devotions, rituals, rites, and ancestor worship stressed by traditional Asian Buddhism. This modern Buddhism had influence in parts of Asia and became popular in many countries outside Asia. It was also easier to modify to fit different cultural situations.

In this chapter, we explore the diverse experiences of Asian Buddhism in non-Asian countries and regions. We begin with the colonialist encounter with Buddhism in Asia, and the beginnings of Buddhist scholarship in Europe. Then we examine the flows of Asian forms of Buddhism into selected non-Asian countries. We have chosen to expand on Buddhism in the United States because of its large number of Buddhist institutions. This gives us the opportunity to examine in greater detail the Asian Buddhist traditions and modern movements that we have explored in previous chapters. Finally we look at the various issues that have arisen in the globalization of Buddhism as new forms of Buddhist communities and practices are taking shape in non-Asian countries. This also gives us a glimpse into the possible future of global Buddhism.

EARLY EUROPEAN ENCOUNTERS AND SCHOLORSHIP

In the sixteenth and seventeenth centuries, Jesuits in India, China, Japan, and Tibet wrote detailed studies of Asian religions, including Buddhism. Matteo Ricci (1552–1610), the famous Jesuit scholar and missionary in China, used his studies to accommodate Christianity to a Chinese culture infused with Buddhism. However, these writings and experiments never made any significant impact outside Asia. On the other hand, in the eighteenth century,

European Protestant merchants wrote of their travels in Asia in such glowing terms that some European intellectuals began to look more positively at Asian religions. This interest led to the beginnings of Buddhist scholarship in Europe in the early nineteenth century as intellectuals began to translate and study Buddhist texts being brought back from Asia.

Early scholars involved in this endeavor include Michel François Ozeray, Henry Thomas Colebrooke, Brian Houghton Hodgson, Alexander Csoma de Körös, and Eugene Burnouf. Burnouf is often credited with showing that the many forms of Buddhism found throughout Asia are in fact branches of a single tradition going back to the Buddha in India. Burnouf and other European scholars laid the foundations for modern Buddhist studies, and their work also influenced the international intellectual world. Examples of such intellectuals in Europe include Arthur Schopenhauer, Richard Wagner, and Friedrich Wilhelm Nietzsche, while in the United States, there were Ralph Waldo Emerson, Walt Whitman, and Henry David Thoreau. Other important later nineteenth- and early twentieth-century scholars who brought Buddhist studies forward include such people as Thomas William Rhys Davids, founder of the Pali Text Society in 1886 and the Buddhist Society in 1907 in England; Hermann Oldenberg in Germany; Louis de La Vallée Poussin and Étienne Lamotte in Belgium; Theodore Stcherbatsky in Russia; and Paul Carus, Henry Clarke Warren, and Charles Rockwell Lanman in the United States.

One work from this time period that had a significant impact on the non-Asian perception of Buddhism was Edwin Arnold's 1879 poem on the life and teachings of the Buddha, *The Light of Asia*. The following are some verses from that famous work:

As one who stands on yonder snowy horn
Having nought o'er him but the boundless blue,
So, these sins being slain, the man is come
NIRVANA'S verge unto.

Him the Gods envy from their lower seats;
Him the Three Worlds in ruin should not shake;
All life is lived for him, all deaths are dead;
Karma will no more make

New houses. Seeking nothing, he gains all;
Forgoing self, the Universe grows "I";
If any teach NIRVANA is to cease,
Say unto such they lie.

If any teach NIRVANA is to live,
Say unto such they err; not knowing this,
Nor what light shines beyond their broken lamps,
Nor lifeless, timeless bliss.

Enter the Path! There is no grief like Hate!
No pains like passions, no deceit like sense!
Enter the Path! far hath he gone whose foot
Treads down one fond offence.

Enter the Path! There spring the healing streams
Quenching all thirst! there bloom th' immortal flowers
Carpeting all the way with joy! there throng
Swiftest and sweetest hours![1]

Besides the rise of Buddhist scholarship outside Asia and its impact on the intellectual scene, two other events in the late nineteenth century deserve mention. First was the founding of the Theosophical Society in New York City in the 1870s. Its two founders, Henry Steel Olcott and Helena Petrovna Blavatsky, converted to Buddhism and moved to Sri Lanka. There, Olcott helped the Sri Lankan Buddhist community redefine itself in a way that contributed to a Buddhist revival in reaction to European colonialism. The Theosophical Society also helped to disseminate Buddhist ideas outside Asia.

The second event was the World's Parliament of Religions held in Chicago 1893. At this Parliament, articulate Asian spokespeople presented lectures about different schools of Buddhism so that the international audience could appreciate the sophisticated and diverse nature of Buddhism as an attractive living tradition. The interest sparked by the Parliament led to important Buddhist missions in the United States. Anagarika Dharmapala, the Theravāda representative and protégé of Olcott, made a number of lecture tours in the United States after the Parliament. So did the Zen representative from Japan, Shaku Sōen, who later sent some of this students, Nyōgen Senzaki, Shaku Sōkatsu, and D. T. Suzuki. As we shall see, these three figures played major roles in bringing Zen to the United States. The Parliament also fostered interfaith dialogue between Buddhism and other religions, which has aided Buddhists in their efforts to enter the religious mainstream outside Asia.

BUDDHISM IN THE UNITED STATES

Turning to the American scene, a watershed in the history of Buddhism in the United States began during the 1950s. Leaders of the Beat movement such as Jack Kerouac, Allen Ginsberg, and Gary Snyder, along with other figures such as Alan Watts, D. T. Suzuki, and Thomas Merton, began to popularize Zen Buddhism through their writings. For example, the following is from Kerouac's *Dharma Bums:*

> The little Saint Teresa bum [a "thin old little bum" with a prayer by Saint Teresa in his pocket] was the first genuine Dharma Bum I'd met, and the second was the number one Dharma Bum of them all and in fact it was he, Japhy Ryder, who coined the phrase. Japhy Ryder was a kid from eastern Oregon brought up in a log cabin deep in the woods with his father and mother and sister, from the

beginning a woods boy, an axman, farmer, interested in animals and Indian lore so that when he finally got to college by hook or crook he was already well equipped for his early studies in anthropology and later in Indian myth and in the actual texts of Indian mythology. Finally he learned Chinese and Japanese and became a Oriental scholar and discovered the greatest Dharma Bums of them all, the Zen Lunatics of China and Japan. . . .

"Where did you meet Ray Smith?" They asked him when we walked into The Place, the favorite bar of the hepcats around the Beach.

"Oh, I always meet my Bodhisattvas in the street!" he yelled.[2]

During the 1960s, Buddhism in the United States grew into a more diverse phenomenon. Besides turning to Zen, many Americans began to practice other forms of Buddhism such as Pure Land, Nichiren, Tibetan, and Theravāda. Soon, there was a significant growth of new Buddhist communities and organizations not only in a few major cities but also in urban and rural areas across the American landscape. This proliferation of active Buddhist lineages in the United States was aided by the 1965 changes in the U.S. immigration laws that allowed a much larger wave of Asian immigration. During the next decade, it was common to find Euro-American laypersons, men and women, being taught Buddhism by Asian monastic-trained teachers. In the 1980s and 1990s, many of these Western students became teachers themselves. Under both Asian American and Euro-American leadership, the U.S. Buddhist communities had by the end of the twentieth century produced many creative innovations.

As these changes were taking place in the religious culture of the United States, the academic study of Buddhism was also developing in ways that have added not only to the understanding of Buddhism but also to the maturity of Buddhism outside Asia. After the new interest in Buddhism in the 1960s, Buddhist Studies began to be accepted as a significant academic discipline in American universities and by university presses. The University of Wisconsin instituted a formal graduate program in Buddhist Studies. Soon, other graduate programs offering specializations in Buddhism began at such places as the University of California at Berkeley, Columbia University, Harvard University, the University of Chicago, the University of Hawaii, the University of Virginia, and the University of Michigan. At the end of the twentieth century, these and other universities were producing a new generation of Buddhologists that continues to contribute to the objective and critical study of Buddhism as a multifaceted, historical, cultural phenomenon. Meanwhile, Buddhist communities in the United States have recast their Asia traditions in innovative ways.

Chinese Buddhism

Chinese Buddhist temples began to be built in the United States in the nineteenth century to serve Chinese immigrant families. The first such temple was built in San Francisco in 1853. By 1875, there were hundreds of Chinese

Buddhist temples throughout the western states. However, as Chinese people assimilated into American culture, many lost interest in their religious heritage, and temples in Chinatowns were often abandoned. Then came the changes in immigration laws in the 1960s, and Chinese communities experienced an influx of immigrants from mainland China, Taiwan, Hong Kong, and other areas around the Pacific Rim. Along with this change, a number of Chinese Buddhist organizations and individual masters from Taiwan came to the United States to minister in these expanded communities. By 2000, there were more than 200 Chinese Buddhist organizations, temples, and centers in the United States. The result has been a new flourishing of Chinese Buddhism.

Buddhist Pure Land and Chan practices have not been as institutionally separated in China as they were in Japan. So chanting and meditation are taught at numerous Chinese Buddhist organizations. For example, at his New York Chan Meditation Center, the highly regarded monastic of Dharma Drum Mountain in Taiwan teach Chan meditation along with recitation sessions. Chanting or recitation is seen as a powerful means of concentrating the mind and generating peacefulness in a world of distractions. Also, Chinese Buddhist organizations often have *sūtra* study groups to help members understand the teachings of their tradition and to apply them to daily life. They present the Buddhas and bodhisattvas as models of compassion to be emulated in everyday living. Many Chinese Buddhist organizations have

FIGURE 10.1. His Lai Temple; Fo Guang Shan Buddhist Order, Haciend a Heights, California.

taken these models of compassion seriously and have, like their socially engaged Buddhist counterparts in Asia, provided goods for the poor in their cities, health fairs offering free physical examinations, and meditation lessons to prisoners.

The Eastern States Buddhist Temple of America was founded in the early 1960s in New York's Chinatown. It played an important role in bringing Chinese monastics to the United States and has a retreat center in the Catskills named Temple Mahāyāna. Taiwan Master Cheng Yen's Tzu Chi Foundation, devoted to charitable work, now has some 16,000 members in the United States. Master Hsüan Hua (1908–1995) moved to the United States in 1962, and founded the Gold Mountain Dhyana Monastery in San Francisco, and later the City of Ten Thousand Buddhas in northern California. The City of Ten Thousand Buddhas seeks to institute a fully ordained and well-educated monastic Saṅgha. It now has about 350 residents, including 150 monastics. The Buddhist Association of the United States was founded in 1964 in New York City. It has the Temple of Enlightenment in the Bronx and the Chuang Yen Monastery in Kent, New York. The Buddha Hall at Chuang Yen holds 2,000 people and has a thirty-seven-foot statue of Vairocana Buddha.

One of the largest Chinese Buddist global movements in the United States is Fo Guang Shan, which opened the Hsi Lai Temple in Hacienda Heights, California (see Figure 10.1), in 1988. Hsi Lai houses more than 100 monastics and serves as the world headquarters of the Buddha's Light International Society (BLIS). This organization alone has more than 100 regional chapters, and Hsi Lai has branch temples in a number of major cities in the United States. Also developed from Hsi Lai is University of the West, one of the first Buddhist universities in America. While Hsi Lai is a cultural center for Chinese Amercian Buddhists, it also has outreach programs for Euro-Americans. Indeed, nearly all of its meditation students are Euro-Amricans. Some of these students have gone on to take Buddhist precepts, and even to become Buddhist monastics.

Japanese Buddhism

Japanese Pure Land Buddhism came to the United States to minister to the needs of Japanese immigrant communities, and Pure Land temples have been in the United States for more than 100 years. In 1914, Pure Land priests of Jōdo Shinshū founded the Buddhist Mission of North America (BMNA), with twenty-five branch fellowships dedicated to serving the religious and social needs of Japanese immigrants. They provided Dharma schools for children, youth activities, adult education programs, and community support in the face of anti-Japanese attitudes and actions. When during World War II more than 100,000 Japanese living on the West Coast were removed from their homes and taken to inland concentration camps, the BMNA made its headquarters in the Utah Topaz Camp. There, it changed its name to Buddhist Churches of America (BCA), which now has churches and fellowships around the country. The BCA presently offers courses at their American Buddhist Academy in New York City and their Institute of Buddhist Studies in Berkeley, California.

With its focus on faith in the grace of Amida Buddha, on family unity and community support, and on a life of kindness, compassion, and service to others, Pure Land Buddhism has given its Japanese members a link to their spiritual heritage that can also be lived in their adopted country. Recently, young Pure Land members have become interested in addressing pressing social concerns and want to expand the scope of their religion to be more universal to attract more non-Japanese members. The problem now is how to maintain Pure Land Buddhism's traditional and cultural function in the Japanese community, while sharing its experience and values with the broader non-Japanese society. One avenue for achieving this goal has been the Buddhist–Christian dialogue that has involved many Pure Land scholars. This dialogue is said by some to be helping Pure Land Buddhism share its faith and, thereby, to discover a broader mission.

The first Japanese Rinzai Zen master to visit America was Shaku Sōen (1859–1919), who attended the 1893 World's Parliament of Religions in Chicago. Sōen returned to lecture in the United States in 1905, and eventually brought three disciples to teach Rinzai Zen. First was Nyōgen Senzaki (1878–1958), who founded Zen centers in Los Angeles and San Francisco in the 1920s. The second disciple was Shaku Sōkatsu (1869–1954), who lived in the United States twice between 1906 and 1910. When Sōkatsu finally returned to Japan for good, he left behind a lay student named Shigetsu Sasaki (1882–1945). Sasaki eventually became ordained and took the name Sokei-an. In 1930, Sokei-an founded the Buddhist Society of America in New York City, which was later renamed the First Zen Institute of America.

The third disciple of Sōen was by far the best known. He was D. T. Suzuki (1870–1966), who, through his many writings, brought Zen to the awareness of the broader society. Suzuki lectured at different universities, especially at Columbia, and in 1956, the Zen Studies Society of New York was established to support his efforts. Suzuki's younger friend from Japan, Masao Abe, has also traveled and taught Zen philosophy and religion at universities throughout the United States, earning himself the title of Suzuki's heir.

Four more recent Rinzai masters have been active in bringing Zen to the United States. First is Nakagawa Sōen (1909–1983), a friend of Nyōgen Senzaki and a pioneer of Zen on the West and East Coasts. Sōen gave Dharma transmission to another important Rinzai leader, Maurine Stuart (1922–1990), who led the Cambridge Buddhist Association. A third influential Rinzai teacher is Kyozan Joshu Sasaki, who founded the Cimarron Zen Center in Los Angeles in 1966 and the Mt. Baldy Zen Center in 1971. Finally, there is Eidō Tai Shimano, who in the 1960s revitalized the Zen Studies Society of New York, which had been inactive since D. T. Suzuki returned to Japan. Shimano also founded the International Dai Bosatsu Monastery in the Catskills.

Sōtō Zen did not begin to appear in the United States until after World War II. In 1949, Soyu Matsuoka founded the Chicago Buddhist Temple, now named the Zen Buddhist Temple of Chicago. The best-known Sōtō Zen master in the United States was Shunryu Suzuki (1904–1971). He founded the San Francisco Zen Center in 1961 and established the Zen Mountain Center at Tassajara Hot Springs in 1967. In 1972, following the death of Suzuki, the Zen Center opened Green Gulch Zen community in Marin County. Daimin Katagiri (1928–1990) came to the United States in 1964 to assist Suzuki, and then went on to lead the Minnesota Zen Meditation Center with regional centers in the Midwest area. Jiyu Kennett (1924–1996), an English woman, was the first woman since the fourteenth century to be admitted to one of the chief Sōtō training temples in Japan. She came to America in 1969 and founded Shasta Abbey in 1970 for the training of Zen priests.

Shinryu Suzuki's informal Dharma talks in *Zen Mind, Beginner's Mind* have had a great influence on many non-Asian Zen practitioners. The following passages are from one such talk about Dōgen:

> The purpose of studying Buddhism is not to study Buddhism, but to study ourselves. It is impossible to study ourselves without some teaching. If you want to know what water is you need science. . . . It is the same thing with us. We need some teaching, but just by studying the teaching alone, it is impossible to know what "I" in myself am.
>
> When you do not hear anything from the teacher, but just sit, this is called teaching without teaching. But sometimes this is not sufficient, so we listen to lectures and have discussions. But we should remember that the purpose of practice in a particular place is to study ourselves.
>
> Dōgen Zenji said, "To study Buddhism is to study ourselves. To study ourselves is to forget ourselves." When you become attached to a temporal expression of your true nature, it is necessary to talk about Buddhism, or else you will think the temporal expression is it. But this particular expression of it is not it. And yet at the same time it *is* it!
>
> [T]he purpose of studying Buddhism is to study ourselves and to forget ourselves. When we forget ourselves, we actually are the true activity of the big existence, or reality itself. When we realize this fact, there is no problem whatsoever in this world, and we can enjoy our life without feeling any difficulties. The purpose of our practice is to be aware of this fact.[3]

Another strong link between Japanese Zen and the United States has been forged by what is called the Harada-Yasutani lineage of Zen in Japan. Daiun Harada (1871–1961) developed a method of Zen training that tailors both Rinzai and Sōtō practices to students' needs. Harada's student Hakuun Yasutani (1885–1973) established a Zen center near Tokyo that made this training method available to laypersons. Soon, it became a favorite training center for non-Asian and in 1954, Yasutani named this lineage Sanbo Kyodan, "The Order of the Three Treasures." From 1962 until he passed away, Yasutani often taught and led retreats in the United States. In Japan, Yasutani was succeeded by Koun Yamada (1907–1989). Under Yamada's leadership, Sanbo Kyodan has become known for training Christians, mainly Catholic priests

Box 10.1

The Riot Policeman and the Zen Master

My first forty years were greatly influenced by my deep love and admiration of my father. He was a humanist and an atheist, with a passionate concern for the suffering of poverty and racial discrimination so vividly apparent in Alabama, where we lived. When I was forty-two, I had a meeting with a riot squad policemen and a Zen Master which radically changed the direction of my response, but not my deep concern about suffering.

My parents were both professors at the University of Alabama at Tuscaloosa, where we lived until I was eight. My father became more and more concerned about the social injustice all around us, and our comfortable home in the pine woods outside of town became a "rest and recuperation" stop for labor and civil rights organizers who had been beaten up in the course of their organizing efforts. In 1934, he left the university to become a full-time civil rights organizer, and we moved to Manhattan, where he raised funds to support the organizing work he was doing at home. In 1935, he was beaten and left for dead in a field near Birmingham by a group of men working for the leading industrial conglomerate there. When he recovered, we moved back to Birmingham, where he continued his radical social activism.

During the war we moved to California, where my father was serving in the army. After the war, I became very active in efforts to ban atomic bombs and to promote civil rights. I became convinced, as my father had been, that the economic theories of Kari Marx were the most rational and fair way to organize economic life. The communist slogan, "from each according to his ability, to each according to his need," spoke to my idealistic passion for fairness. I became a very self-righteous social activist, "fighting for" peace, civil rights, civil liberties, and economic justice as I understood it.

In 1957, I became very disillusioned with the Soviet Union after the uprising and repression in Hungary, and resigned from the Communist Party. In the same year, my husband was subpoenaed by the House Committee on Un-American Activities and was blacklisted from his profession of more than twenty years. In 1967 my best friend complained of a very bad headache, was diagnosed with a brain tumor, and soon died. She was my age, with small children the age of my children. I was shaken by her sudden and unexpected death. Soon after, I developed an almost fatal septicemia. After my recovery, I realized that my life was changed. All those things about which I had been certain were open to question, and most of all, I was faced with the truth of impermanence.

At this time of deep uncertainty and questioning about the meaning, purpose, and direction of my life, there was a black students' strike at San Francisco State University, where my son was a student. The first day of the strike was described by the newspapers as a "police riot." The riot squad police had arrested and beaten many students. Leaders of the black community called for citizens to come to the campus the next day to interpose themselves between police and students to prevent further violence. I went to the campus and noticed that some of the picketers were harassing some of the students who were entering a classroom building. Some athletic-looking white students were taking pictures and harassing the strikers. Then one of the picketers grabbed the camera and threw it hard on the ground. By this time I had become pretty much a pacifist. I had also become uneasy with the contradiction of "fighting for peace." There was no peace *in me*. As I watched the scene unfolding, I heard myself say," Where's my side?"

In time we all began to congregate on the Quadrangle for a planned rally. A loudspeaker announced, "This is an illegal assembly!" A shoulder-to-shoulder phalanx of policemen in full riot gear emerged from behind some buildings and began to sweep across the Quadrangle with nightsticks extended, poking people who moved too slowly. People were breaking and running behind me in confusion. With no thought I interposed myself between police and students. Just then, someone blew a whistle and the police stopped poking with their nightsticks, and held them horizontal to their bodies with both hands. I looked up and my eyes met those of the policeman in front of me, perhaps eighteen inches away.

At that moment, there was no me, and no policeman. There was only a falling away of all boundaries and a profound experience of identity with the policeman which expanded to include everything. The reality of this experience was stunning beyond any discussion or speculation. Although I had absolutely no conceptual framework with which to understand what I had experienced, I knew that it was more authentic than any ideas I had about the world. I thought, "The world is different than I thought it was; I have to change my life."

Now I had read books on Zen and encountered sayings such as "Self and other are not two." But at the time of the encounter with the policeman, my world was my family, the mathematics and chemistry of my profession, and politics. In my world then, a riot squad policeman was the epitome of "not me." To have such a profound experience of identity with him, together with the previous experiences of impermanence and uncertainty, started me on a search for someone who understood the world in which a riot squad policeman and I are not two.

In the course of my search, I had the good fortune to meet Shunryu Suzuki Roshi, a Sōtō Zen Master then living and teaching in San Francisco. He often used the phrase, "not one, not two," which resonated with my experience. When I met him face to face in a private interview, I knew when my eyes met his, *"He understands my experience with the policeman!"*

I understood that Suzuki Roshi had become the extraordinarily compassionate person I experienced him to be because of his many years of Zen practice. So I began and have never stopped sitting *zazen* (Zen meditation) daily.

ZENKEI BLANCHE HARTMAN
San Francisco Zen Center

and nuns, so that they are able to attain *kenshō* and teach Zen as Christians. In the United States, Yasutaní s heirs include Eidō Tai Shimano, who is also in the Rinzai lineage; Philip Kapleau; Robert Aitken; and Taizan Maezumi.

Philip Kapleau attended D. T. Suzuki's lectures at Columbia and took up formal Zen practice in Japan under Nakagawa Sōen, Harada, and finally

Yasutani. Following this training, Kapleau published *The Three Pillars of Zen*, a American Zen classic, based on his work with Yasutani. Kapleau also founded the Zen Meditation Center in Rochester, New York, in 1966. Robert Aitken was interned in Japan during World War II. There, he met Reginald Blyth, a Zen practitioner and friend of D. T. Suzuki. After the war, Aitken first trained in Zen practice under Nyōgen Senzaki in California, and then with Nakagawa Sōen in Japan. In 1959, he and his wife Anne began a Zen meditation group in Hawaii, which became the Diamond Sangha. Later, Aitken trained under Yasutani and then Yamada, from whom he received Dharma transmission in 1974. The Diamond Sangha has become global and has affiliated Zen centers in many parts of the world. Aitken has been recognized by many as a patriarch of Zen in America for his strong leadership (see Figure 10.2).

Taizan Maezumi was ordained in the Sōtō School but also gained Dharma transmission in Rinzai and from Yasutani. Maezumi came to the United States and founded the Zen Center of Los Angeles in 1956. In 1976, Maezumi established the Kuroda Institute for the Study of Buddhism and Human Values, devoted to furthering Buddhist scholarship. Over the years, Maezumi gave Dharma transmission to twelve of his students, who now have Zen centers throughout the world. They belong to a network founded by Maezumi and his students called the White Plum Saṅgha. One

FIGURE 10.2. Zendō of the Diamond Saṅgha; post-*sesshin* photo taken in 1965 with Philip Kapleau, Katsuki Sekida, and Hakuun Yasutani (front row, left to middle) and Robert and Anne Aitken (back row, far right), Honolulu, Hawaii.

of Maezumi's students is Bernard Tetsugen Glassman, who established the Zen Community of New York. Glassman has created innovative forms of Buddhist social engagement.

Thanks to these and other teachers, Japanese Zen centers have grown up all over the world. For the most part, the focus of the globalization of Zen has not been to create a Zen Buddhist monasticism but to establish Zen centers that mainly train both men and women lay students. These centers offer Zen training on a regular basis and hold *sesshin,* weeklong intensive retreats, during each year. Some of the centers have resident practitioners who follow a daily schedule that involves meditation, rituals, work, study, and community life. A few of these communities are now led by Christian Zen teachers. Ruben Habito, having received Dharma transmission from Yamada, leads the Maria Kannon Zen Center in Dallas. Robert E. Kennedy, a Jesuit priest, received Dharma transmission from Glassman and leads the Morning Star Zendo in New Jersey. Kennedy also has affiliated Zen groups in the United States and Mexico.

Another form of Japanese Buddhism that has been successful in the United States has come from the Nichiren tradition. Inspired by his travels to the West in the 1960s, the president of Sōka Gakkai, Daisaku Ikeda, encouraged his movement to reach out to Westerners. In the United States, the Sōka Gakkai movement was first known as Nichiren Shōshū of America (NSA). It spread rather quickly, attracting people with its promise of giving them the power to change their lives for the better and offering avenues to work together for world peace. While its proselytizing encountered some resistance, by the late 1970s, NSA was said to have had a half-million members in the United States alone.

In the 1980s, NSA began to adapt its structure and activities to non-Asian culture. Some activities were scaled back, more serious regional meetings replaced glitzy national conventions, and eventually its name was changed to Sōka Gakkai International (SGI). In 1991, there was a split between Nichiren Shōshū and Sōka Gakkai in Japan. In the West, this meant that the SGI-run temples were taken control by Nichiren Shōshū. These temples then organized lay communities to replace SGI communities. However, the vast majority of lay members stayed with SGI.

Also, SGI has continued its inculturation by developing a more democratic model of leadership whereby its national organizations are led by executive committees appointed for one-year terms. Local communities have taken over the ministerial tasks once performed by the Nichiren Shōshū priests. Today, SGI sees itself more as a Buddhist lay movement dedicated to serious Nichiren practice for its members and to working with others for world peace. In regard to this latter goal, SGI has recently begun to develop more positive relations with other Buddhist lineages and constructive interfaith relations, both of which were not possible when it was part of Nichiren Shōshū.

The other new form of lay Buddhism in the United States that has emerged from the Nichiren fold in Japan is Risshō Kōsei-kai (RKK). Unlike Sōka

Gakkai, RKK has not sought to convert non-Japanese into its membership. Rather, it has worked within the Japanese American communities in ways that have provided it with a local presence through which it participates in interfaith organizations and activities. This is especially the case with the World Conference of Religions for Peace (WCRP). Recently RKK has developed into a multipractice Buddhist movement more in line with the broader East Asian *Lotus Sūtra* tradition. This provides a unique opportunity to encounter an important traditional form of Japanese Buddhist practice and thought.

Tibetan Buddhism

Beginning in the 1950s and taking root in the 1960s and 1970s, Tibetan lamas brought their traditions to the United States. By the late 1960s, Tibetan lamas and their American students undertook two major efforts to preserve and pass on the traditions of Tibetan Buddhism. First, they collected, translated, and disseminated Tibetan texts. Several presses have aided in this work in the United States including Shambhala Publications, founded in 1969, and Snow Lion Publications, formed in 1980. Second, lamas founded centers associated with the various schools of Tibetan Buddhism throughout the United States and began to draw students who wished to become practitioners of Tibetan Buddhism.

In terms of the Geluk Order in the United States, Geshé Ngawang Wangyal (1901–1983) arrived in 1955. Wangyal lived in Freewood Acres, New Jersey, where he founded the Lamaist Buddhist Monastery of America, later renamed the Tibetan Buddhist Learning Center. Wangyal attracted such students as Jeffrey Hopkins and Robert Thurman, both of whom went on to become Buddhist scholars. Thurman is now the Tsongkhapa Professor of Buddhist Studies at Columbia University. Hopkins founded the Buddhist Studies Program at the University of Virginia. Wangyal also brought a number of important Tibetan scholars to his monastery. One was Geshé Lhündrup Sopa, who later became professor at the University of Wisconsin and founded the Deer Park Buddhist Center in Madison, Wisconsin, in 1975.

The Sakya Order was first represented in the United States by Deshung Rinpoché (1906–1987), who taught at the University of Washington beginning in 1960. One of the first Sakya centers in the United States, the Ewam Chöden Tibetan Buddhist Center in Kensington, California, was founded in 1971. In 1974, the Sakya Monastery of Tibetan Buddhism was founded in Seattle. This latter institution takes an ecumenical approach, hosting lamas from all Tibetan traditions, including the Dalai Lama. On the East Coast, the Sakya Center for Buddhist Studies and Meditation was founded in Cambridge, Massachusetts, in 1980, and the Sakya Phuntsok Ling Center for Tibetan Buddhist Studies and Meditation was founded in Silver Springs, Maryland, in 1986.

The Nyingma Order was introduced by Tarthang Tulku Rinpoche, who arrived in the United States in 1968. With an emphasis on Tantric training,

Tarthang founded the Tibetan Nyingma Meditation Center in Berkeley in 1969. There, he provided rigorous practice but also helped integrate that practice into their normal America life at work and in the family. During the 1980s, Tarthang Tulku began publishing and distributing Tibetan scriptures to Tibetan monks, nuns, and laypeople. In an effort to preserve and promote Tibetan scriptural learning and religious practice, to date he has distributed more than twenty million Tibetan texts to Tibetan Buddhist practitioners. In 1981, Chögyal Namkhai Norbu established the first Dzogchen Community in Italy, and then he opened centers in the United States, Latin America, Russia, and Australia dedicated to giving students greater access to *dzokchen* practice. Another recent Nyingma teacher in the West is Sogyal Rinpoché. Trained in Tibetan studies in India and comparative religion at Cambridge University, Sogyal first founded centers in Europe. Then he established the Rigpa Fellowship with a center in Santa Cruz, California. Giving death and dying an important place in his teachings, Sogyal published *The Tibetan Book of Living and Dying*, from which the following passages are taken:

> So whatever our lives are like, our buddha nature is always there. And it is always perfect. . . . Our true nature could be compared to the sky, and the confusion of the ordinary mind to clouds. Some days the sky is completely obscured by clouds.
>
> So where exactly is this buddha nature? It is in the sky-like nature of our mind. Utterly open, free, and limitless, it is fundamentally so simple and so natural that it can never be complicated, corrupted, or stained, so pure that it is beyond even the concept of purity and impurity.
>
> The purpose of meditation is to awaken in us the sky-like nature of mind, and to introduce us to that which we really are, our unchanging pure awareness, which underlies the whole of life and death. In the stillness and silence of meditation, we glimpse and return to that deep inner nature that we have so long ago lost sight of amid the busyness and distraction of our minds. . . . Meditation is, then, bringing the mind home.
>
> [T]his practice unveils and reveals your essential Good Heart, because it dissolves and removes the unkindness or the harm in you. . . . Through the practice, then, by slowly removing the unkindness and harm from ourselves, we allow our true Good Heart, the fundamental goodness and kindness that are our real nature, to shine out and become the warm climate in which our true being flowers.
>
> That is why in our tradition we see compassion as the source and essence of enlightenment, and the heart of enlightened activity. . . . Compassion is the wish-fulfilling gem whose light of healing spreads in all directions.[4]

As for the Kagyü Order, Kalu Rinpoché (1939–1987), was one of the earliest Kagyü lamas to teach outside Asia. He founded centers in Canada and France and taught in the United States from 1971 until his death. In 1979, the Sixteenth Gyalwa Karmapa, head of the Karma Kagyüs, founded the Karma Triyana Dharmachakra in Woodstock, New York. This center, a monastery with a staff and class offerings for laypeople, has dozens of branch meditation centers in many states. The most famous of the early Kagyü teachers in the United States was Chögyam Trungpa Rinpoché (1939–1987). Trungpa moved to the United States in 1969 and settled at Tail of the Tiger in Barnet, Vermont. Later, Trungpa founded Shambhala International, which has headquarters in Halifax, Nova Scotia and centers around the world. Its main monastic facility is the Rocky Mountain Shambhala Center in Colorado, where students train in Kagyü and Nyingma practice. A network of local centers, called Shambhala Meditation Centers, are also present around the United States. Part of Shambhala's educational branch is Naropa University in Boulder, the first fully accredited Buddhist liberal arts college in the United States.

In Tibet, it is rare for laypeople to pursue in-depth study of Buddhism or to participate in intensive monastic practice, especially Tantric practice. However, the Tibetan orders recently have created ways for laypeople to study Tibetan Buddhism and to be initiated and trained in its practices. Most Tibetan Buddhist centers outside of Tibet offer formal and informal courses of study on Tibetan Buddhism to the general public, sometimes through local universities. In terms of practice, nonmonastic intensive retreats of longer or shorter duration are now offered for laypeople, especially in the Kagyü and Nyingma lineages. Weekend meditation workshops are also offered to the general public with innovative programs of Dharma teaching and guided meditative practice. For example, the Dalai Lama's personal monastery in the United States is Namgyal Monastery in Ithaca, New York. There, the Namgyal Institute offers a traditional Tibetan curriculum to lay students.

In the 1990s, support for Tibet and its culture and religion was galvanized by the Dalai Lama and Tibetan monastics around the world. In New York City, the U.S. Tibet Committee promotes public awareness of Tibet, and the International Campaign for Tibet works with elected officials in Washington, DC. The Students for a Free Tibet grew from 45 chapters in 1994 to 650 in 2012. The Tibet House in New York City was founded as a cultural center to educate the public about Tibet's endangered living culture. Support for the Tibet cause has also been received from the entertainment industry. Adam Yauch of the Beastie Boys sponsored a series of Concerts for a Free Tibet, and in 1997 two films about Tibet were released: *Seven Years in Tibet* with Brad Pitt, and *Kundun,* directed by Martin Scorcese. The public concern for and interest in Tibet, along with serious scholarship and the development of practice and study centers, has made Tibetan Buddhism one of the fastest growing forms of global Buddhism.

Theravāda Buddhism

The first Theravāda temple in the United States, the Buddhist Vihāra Society, was established in 1966 in Washington, DC. By 1996, there were 150 Theravāda temples in more than thirty states, with about 500 resident monastics. Indeed, throughout the United States during the later part of the twentieth century, many Sri Lankan, Thai, Cambodian, Lao, and Burmese immigrant communities founded temples and staffed them with monastic teachers. These temples not only serve the Asian immigrant communities but also provide other Americans with Buddhist study centers, as well as guidance in the practice of mindfulness and meditation.

One of the most influential Sri Lankan monastics to reach out beyond the immigrant community is Henepola Gunaratana, who came to the United States in 1968 to serve the Washington Buddhist Vihāra Society. In 1982, Gunaratana founded the Bhavana Society in West Virginia as a residential retreat center devoted to meditation training and study for Asian and non-Asian laypeople and monastics. Another highly successful Theravādin monastic in the United States was Havanpola Ratanasara (1920–2000). Ratanasara entered the monastic life at age eleven and went on to receive a doctorate from the University of London. He was Sri Lanka's delegate to the United Nations in 1957, the first Buddhist monk to hold such a position. Coming to the United States in 1980, he helped found the Dharma Vijaya Buddhist Vihāra in Los Angeles, the Interreligious Council of Southern California, and the American Buddhist Congress.

Monastic Theravāda has not drawn many Western converts into its monasteries; there are only a few non-Asian monastics in U.S. Theravāda temples as of this writing. Therefore, some Theravāda Buddhist groups have developed lay initiations and ordinations for those people who are interested in participating more fully in the Buddhist way of life, but do not wish to enter fully into the monastic community. These new lay programs provide a unique partnership between Asian monastics and non-Asia converts in the development of Buddhism in the United States. An example of such lay vocations can be seen in the five-level system devised at the Dharma Vijaya Buddhist Vihāra. The first level involves initiation into the Five Precepts. The second level includes initiation into the Nine Precepts, formal daily practice, and training for leadership roles so that one can give Dharma talks and conduct meditation classes. The third level involves more stringent Buddhist precepts. The fourth level carries the status of lay minister and gives the possibility of conducting certain religious services, being a chaplain, and initiating laypeople at the three lower levels. This fourth level involves ordination, taking the precepts of the Ten Perfections, and a more detailed daily regimen. The fifth and final level adds the vow of celibacy.

One important movement in the United States that has grown out of the Theravāda tradition is called the "Insight Meditation" movement. This movement, which emerged in the late 1970s, is now one of the fastest growing forms of global Buddhism. As a loose-knit lay movement, it teaches insight meditation (Pali: *vipassanā)* along with mindfulness and other Theravāda forms of mental culture. The Western founders of this movement were trained mainly by Burmese and Thai meditation masters who refined their methods to be of use to laypeople. A pioneer of this movement is Ruth Denison. She studied Theravāda meditation in Burma in the 1960s and began teaching in the United States in 1973. In 1977, she began what became Dhamma Dena, a retreat center near Joshua Tree, California.

Also in the late 1960s, Sharon Salzberg, Jack Kornfield, and Joseph Goldstein, among others, took training in insight meditation in Southeast Asia and returned to teach in the United States. In 1975, they founded the Insight Meditation Society (IMS), which has retreat centers in Barre, Massachusetts, and, more recently, Spirit Rock in Marin County, California. At these centers, teachers offer short- and long-term retreats focusing on such practices as mindfulness of breathing, insight meditation, and loving-kindness meditation. Today, their practitioners have opened over 150 independent centers around the country. With its practical focus on training, healing, and Awakening, the movement does not emphasize participation in traditional Theravāda institutions. Given this freedom, students of other forms of Buddhism, and even other religions, have trained at IMS centers to complement their own practice with mindfulness and insight meditation. This blending of practice has lessened some of the sharp divisions between schools of Buddhism in the United States and has also fostered positive interfaith relations.

Joseph Goldstein explained the new global attraction of insight meditation:

> We practice the Dharma in order to understand [the way to Awakening], in order to be free. That is the heart of all the effort we make, because from freedom comes connectedness, compassion, lovingkindness, and peace.
>
> The Buddha saw with such clarity how different states of mind and courses of action lead to different results. Unwholesome mind states have certain consequences. Wholesome mind states have results of their own. As we begin to understand the truth of how things are, we see for ourselves what brings suffering in our lives, and what brings happiness and freedom.
>
> Although at first our mind might feel like a whirlwind of activity, the amazing path of Dharma practice helps us begin to sort things out. We establish some stability and focus in our mind and see which elements in it lead to greater peace, which to greater suffering. All of it—both the peace and the suffering—happen lawfully. Freedom lies in the wisdom to choose.
>
> As we walk the way of awareness, we see that the deepest purpose we all have is to perfect the qualities of our heart and mind. The spiritual path transforms our consciousness, purifying it of greed, hatred, ignorance, fear, envy, jealousy—those forces that create suffering in us and in the world.
>
> We all share this most fundamental purpose of freedom. It is the universal potential of the mind itself. . . . Everyone shares the basic commonality of being alive, of having a mind and heart. Our task is to awaken and purify this mind-heart for the benefit of all.[5]

Korean Buddhism

Korean Buddhism has come to the United States through at least two major movements. The first movement is made up of the Korean men and women monastics, who were invited by local Korean Buddhist communities in the 1950s. These monastics serve educational, ritual, and cultural functions in the immigrant communities that allow members of those communities to maintain a connection with their Korean heritage and pass that heritage on to their children. Most Sunday temple services include readings from scriptures, chanting, formal ceremonies, and Dharma teachings. While many of the temples are affiliated with the Chogye Order in Korea, Won Buddhism also serves the Korean communities through their own temples and participates in inter-faith activities and organizations at the local and national levels.

The second movement of Korean Buddhism to the United States involves those Sŏn (Zen) teachers who have opened centers. These teachers have adapted to the diverse cultures of America. They blend such practices as prostrations, Pure Land chanting, and formal liturgies with *sūtra* study and meditation practice. This holistic approach to Buddhist practice is intended to foster a sense of community among its members and to encourage daily living in the spirit of bodhisattvahood. These Sŏn organizations follow the Korean pattern of a head temple with many branch temples. One of the first such teachers in the United States was Kyung Bo Sunim (Korean *sunim:* monk). Kyung Bo came to Columbia University in 1964 and remained in the United States for the next six years lecturing on Korean Buddhism. His disciples founded meditation centers around the country.

More recently, two Korean teachers have been particularly successful. Seung Sahn Sunim arrived in the United States in 1972 and settled in Providence, Rhode Island. He developed a form of Buddhism combining meditation with Dharma talks, chanting, and prostrations that appealed to Western students at what is now the Providence Zen Center. In 1983, Seung Sahn founded the Kwan Um School of Zen, which has globalized with centers worldwide. Samu Sunim arrived in New York in 1967 and moved to Canada the next year. After four years of personal practice, he visited Buddhist centers throughout Canada and the United States. Based on his experience, he eventually founded the Zen Lotus Society, now called the Buddhist Society for Compassionate Wisdom. Centers in this society are located in cities in Canada, the United States, and Mexico. Given his interest in global Buddhism, Samu Sunim and Luis Gómez hosted the landmark Conference on World Buddhism in North America at the University of Michigan and his Ann Arbor temple in 1987. The following reflections of Samu Sunim stress the importance of socially engaged Buddhism in the West:

> [T]he majority of Western Buddhists practitioners pursue their *Dharma* life actively engaging the world while also being seriously involved in Buddhist spiritual practice. . . . *Dharma* work in the world today requires *bodhisattvas* with boundless hearts . . . ordinary persons with "great hearts," who involve themselves enthusiastically in world affairs. . . . With such great hearts, they bring charity to the needy, peace and calm to the troubled, comfort to the afflicted, smiles and forgiveness to the angry, and clarity and wisdom to the confused and perplexed.
>
> Zen is an endless journey where there is no goal aside from the daily living of our life responsibly and full-heartedly. As the new travelers acquire *Dharma* habits and begin to lead a mindful life, an awakening of the "great heart" begins . . . and a new peace of mind and gratitude take hold. . . . The peace and happiness we experience inside through personal transformation must find an

> expression outside through social transformation. . . . We are a universal family, and as such, we depend on one another for peace, harmony and equilibrium. We all participate in the unity of this family. . . . Therefore, the awareness of this unity through Zen awakening also helps us awaken to our global responsibility and planetary consciousness.[6]

Vietnamese Buddhism

After the Vietnam War ended in 1973, Vietnamese Buddhist monastics came to the United States to establish temples in Vietnamese neighborhoods. At first they did so in homes or small storefronts. Today, more traditional temples have been erected, and there are now more than 160 Vietnamese Buddhist temples in the United States. As has been traditionally the case in Vietnam, the temples operate quite independently, with decisions on doctrine and activities made on the local level. Because Vietnamese Buddhism is primarily Mahāyāna, the temples' Sunday services entail chanting *sūtras,* meditation, reciting Buddhas' names, and praying to Amitābha Buddha for rebirth in the Pure Land. While meditation is practiced to some degree, it is felt that Awakening must be assisted by Buddhas and bodhisattvas. Thus, Zen and Pure Land are seen as complementary in typical Vietnamese Buddhist practice. Vietnamese temples in the West also provide Vietnamese language lessons, Dharma classes for children, and adult education. The temples commemorate special Buddhist holidays, perform daily rituals that can be joined by laypeople, and celebrate rituals for funerals and weddings.

While some Vietnamese laypeople take the Three Refuges and even hold bodhisattva vows, few non-Asians have become vowed members of this kind of ethnic Buddhism. However, a number of Vietnamese Buddhist leaders have reached out beyond their ethnic communities. For example, Thich Thien-An (1926–1980), a monk trained also in the Japanese Rinzai tradition, founded the International Buddhist Meditation Center in Los Angeles in 1971. His center is now directed by Karuna Dharma, said to be the first fully ordained American woman. Also, Thich Nhat Hanh has been successful in attracting many non-Asians with his form of socially engaged Buddhism. His books are quite popular and a number of non-Asians have been ordained in his Order of Interbeing. In 1983, the Community of Mindful Living was created in Berkeley, California, to support Nhat Hanh's work and to encourage the founding of retreat centers around the world based on his teaching. Today there are more than 200 such centers. Setting aside the ritual practices of Vietnamese Buddhism, Nhat Hanh's movement balances inner practice with outer action, personal transformation with social change. This balanced style of Buddhist spirituality has made Asian socially engaged Buddhism appealing to many around the world. Nhat Hanh lives in Plum Village in France with 150 monks, nuns, and laypeople. His organization is now under the United Buddhist Church (UBC). UBC retreat centers are around the world with three in the United States.

BUDDHISM IN EUROPE

The 1800s was an era when interest in Budhism in Europe was primarily an intellectual pursuit. At the turn of the century, however, two changes took place. First, a few Europeans became ordained Buddhists. The first to do so was Gordon Douglas in England in 1899. More well known was Allan Bennett McGregor, ordained in 1902, who founded the Buddhist Society of Great Britain and Ireland in 1907. The second change was the foundation of new and highly successful international Buddhist organizations, such as the Maha Bodhi Society in 1891. This society became the first transnational Buddhist organization to spread to the United States (1897) and to European countries (Germany in 1911 and England in 1926).

After World War I, small local and regional societies dedicated more to practice began to develop in Europe. In Munich, Georg Grimm founded the Buddhist Parish for Germany in 1921 with an emphasis on the Three Refuges and the Five Precepts. In Berlin, Paul Dhalke founded the famous Buddhist House in 1924 as a place of practice, study, and residence. In London, Christmas Humphreys formed the Buddhist Lodge in 1924 with a shrine room for celebrating Buddhist festivals. And in Paris, Grace Constant Lounsbery founded Les amis du Bouddisme in 1929. In the vast majority of these cases, it was Theravāda and the Pali Canon that provided the inspiration and foundation of the new societies with focus on philosophical ideas, ethics, and personal practice.

It was after World War II that other Buddhist traditions began to influence the European scene. The agonizing trauma of the war led some Europeans to look for new understandings of life and death. In the 1950s, Pure Land, Zen, and Nichiren Buddhism came to Europe. What is now Sōka Gakkai International (SGI) became popular and remains the largest Buddhist organization in Europe. During the 1960s, Zen meditation and *vipassanā* meditation became especially popular with an increasing number of teachers visiting from Asia. This growth of interest in meditation was followed by the introduction of Tibetan Buddhism in the 1970s. As high-ranking lamas toured Europe (the Dalai Lama's first visit was in 1973), interest spread as Europeans became fascinated by the esoteric nature of Tibetan Buddhist practice and its deep spirituality. With this new influx of Buddhist lineages, the number of Buddhist groups and organizations grew quickly. In Great Britain alone, the number of Buddhist centers expanded from seventy-four to four hundred in twenty years (1980–2000). Similar developments took place in Germany, France, Italy, Switzerland, the Netherlands, and Denmark. More recently, Buddhist groups have been founded in Poland, the Czech Republic, and parts of Russia.[7]

After the Vietnam War, numerous refugees arrived in Europe from Vietnam, Laos, and Cambodia, with many settling in Great Britain, France, and Germany. They founded temples and cultural centers to maintain their cultural and religious identity. These communities were not interested in converting Europeans to Buddhism, nor were their members interested in meditation practice, as were the European convert Buddhist communities. Instead, the temples were and mostly remain primarily places to perform devotional rites, gain merit, listen to the monks teach, perform communal rites like marriages and funerals, and educate the next generations in the cultural aspects of their Asian traditions. Of the estimated 900,000 Buddhists in Europe, the immigrant Buddhist population accounts for about 600,000.

Turning to today, Mahāyāna and Tibetan groups account for about 30 to 40 percent of the European Buddhists, while Theravāda accounts for about 15 percent. The rest of the Buddhist groups are independent. As for national populations of Buddhists in Europe, the figures range from about 16,000 in Austria to around 350,000 in France. In most European countries, Buddhists account for between 0.1 and 0.6 percent of the total population. Although this might be the case, the general impact of Buddhism on European culture is far beyond what these numbers would seem to indicate. This is in part because of the general public's interest in such figures as Thich Nhat Hanh and the Dalai Lama. The growing number of Asian teachers who now live in Europe has also been responsible for public interest in Buddhism. There is also a growing number of Euro-Buddhists who have become priests, monks, and nuns—thus assisting in the inculturation of Buddhism in Europe. Also, as Euro-Buddhist leaders traveled overseas, they founded Buddhist centers that greatly contributed to the globalization of Buddhism.

BUDDHISM IN CANADA

Unlike in Europe, where immigrant Buddhists did not arrive until the 1950s, in Canada Chinese Buddhists arrived on the West Coast in the 1850s to work in the mines. Japanese Buddhists, primarily Pure Land Buddhists, arrived in the late 1880s to work in Alberta and British Columbia. Neither community was involved in proselytizing Euro-Canadians, but as there were intermarriages, especially in the Japanese Pure Land community, some conversions did take place. It was not until 1955 that the Pure Land Buddhists in Canada organized as the Buddhist Churches of Canada. Then in 1959, there was a small influx of Tibetan refugees, followed in 1962 by a much larger wave of Chinese immigration mostly from Hong Kong. By 2000, the Chinese population in Canada reached 600,000, which included immigrants from Taiwan and Mainland China. Also after the Vietnam War, refugees came from Vietnam, Laos, and Cambodia, raising the Southeast Asian population in Canada to about 130,000.

A majority of Japanese Buddhists have continued to be part of the Buddhist Churches of Canada. The Chinese Buddhists, on the other hand, have supported different traditional schools such as Chan and Pure Land. They have also supported contemporary Buddhist masters, including Master Hsing Yun's Fo Guang Shan Buddhist Order and Master Hsüan Hua's Dharma Realm Buddhist Association, which is associated with the City of Ten Thousand Buddhas in California. In this case we see a good example of Buddhist globalization from China to the United States to Canada. The Vietnamese have founded individual temples mainly in Quebec and Ontario, as well as the Union of Vietnamese Buddhist Churches in Canada. They have also supported the engaged Buddhism of Thich Nhat Hanh. The Tibetan groups are also associated with different masters. One such group, begun by Chögyam Trungpa Rinpoché, made substantial headway among non-Asians. This group is Vajradhatu, which has its international headquarters in Halifax and has Shambhala International training centers in countries in Europe, South America, Africa, and Australia.

The non-Asian Buddhist communities in Canada are seen as, in part, a result of the long and distinguished tradition of Canadian academic scholarship in Buddhist Studies that has influenced generations of Canadians. While there is less interest in the Theravāda tradition as practiced by the Southeast Asian communities, the practice of *vipassanā* as made available by Canadian teachers is quite popular. Also popular is Japanese and Korean Zen. However, unlike in Europe where there is a long tradition of Buddhist practice, in Canada this taking up and practice of the Dharma is rather new. Hence, the number of non-Asian Canadians who have converted to Buddhism is just a few thousand.

BUDDHISM IN AUSTRALIA AND NEW ZEALAND

Buddhism was seen substantial growth in Australia. In a 2006 census, almost 2.1 percent of the total population are Buddhists, making up the largest religion group after Christianity. This percentage is much higher than any country in Europe. As in Canada, Buddhism arrived in Australia with the Chinese immigrants who came in the mid-1800s to work in the gold fields. However, the first Buddhist organization is said to have been the Little Circle of the Dharma founded in Melbourne in 1925, and it was not until the 1950s that noted Buddhist teachers began to visit Australia. The first Theravāda teacher came in 1952, followed by Daisaku Ikeda, president of Sōka Gakkai International in 1964. In the 1960s and 1970s, teachers from Theravāda, both Thai and Sri Lankan, and Japanese and Korean Zen traditions as well as Tibetan teachers arrived and established practice and study centers. Later Fo Guang Shan built the now famous Nan Tien Temple complex in the 1990s.

As in Europe and Canada, after the Vietnam War large numbers of refugees arrived in Australia from Vietnam, Laos, and Cambodia. In recent studies, it was estimated that there are 521 Buddhist centers in Australia somewhat equally divided between Theravāda, Mahāyāna (mainly Zen and SGI), and Tibetan. Convert Buddhists make up only about 20 percent of the total number of Buddhists in Australia, which shows the impact of the ethnic Buddhists. Popular among the non-Asian Buddhists in Australia are Zen, *vipassanā* practice, the Thai Forest tradition, SGI, and Shambhala centers as well as other Tibetan Buddhist groups.

Chinese immigrants were the first to bring Buddhism to New Zealand during the gold rush beginning in 1863. As in other non-Asian countries,

Chinese Buddhist temples were built for the immigrant Buddhists. Henry Steel Olcott, one of the founders of the Theosophical Society, spoke in Christchurch in 1897, and the Theosophical movement became active in New Zealand in its support of Buddhist ideas. During the early 1900s, Buddhist teachers visited New Zealand; but the first formal Buddhist organization was the Buddhist Society of New Zealand founded in 1956. Within the next thirty years, the Buddhist landscape greatly diversified. This was especially due to a change in the immigration policy in 1975. It allowed a significant number of refugees from Southeast Asia after the Vietnam War, who founded Vietnamese, Laotian, and Cambodian Buddhist temples. A more open immigration policy in 1987 attracted a large number of immigrants from China, Japan, Korean, and Sri Lanka. This led to the founding of a number of new Chinese, Japanese, Korean, and Sri Lankan Buddhist organizations and centers. In the latest census, 6.6 percent of the population in New Zealand are Buddhists. Of these, 20 percent are Euro-New Zealanders.

If we look at the 100 or so Buddhist organizations in New Zealand, besides the ethnic Buddhist centers that serve immigrant communities, 30 percent of them are Tibetan Buddhist Centers representing all four lineages. About 20 percent of those are from Tibetan organizations founded in the United States. A large majority of the Zen centers are headed by students of American Zen teachers, such as Robert Aitken, Philip Kapleau, Taizan Maezumi, and John Daido Loori. Four of the international Asian Buddhist movements are also present and active: Dharma Drum Mountain, Fo Guang Shan, Sōka Gakkai International, and the Mindfulness Communities of Thich Nhat Hanh. There are also a significant number of nonsectarian Buddhist organizations that appeal to Euro-New Zealanders. Here, as in Australia, we see the effects of globalization where flows from Asia to the United States create Buddhist organizations that fit the American culture and then flow to another country to be recast for that culture. Also, we see the global spread of new Buddhist movements from Asia that blend traditional Asian practice with nontraditional social engagement. And finally, there have developed a few nonsectarian Buddhist organizations that draw on a number of Asian Buddhist traditions integrated in new ways.

BUDDHISM IN BRAZIL

Many countries in Latin America have between twenty and forty Buddhist centers. Some have only between one and ten. However, Brazil has more than 130 centers, making it the country in Latin America that has seen the greatest development of Buddhism, and has become an important source for its spread to other countries in Latin America. Given globalization, flows of Buddhist traditions from Asia, Europe, and the United States into Brazil have led some Brazilian Buddhists to travel to these three regions for further training and then return to Brazil or other parts of Latin America. For example, Claudia Dias de Souza Batista (Zen name: Koen/Coen) studied under Taizan Maezumi in Los Angeles, then traveled to Japan for twelve more years of training, and finally returned to Brazil to become abbess of the major Zen center in the country.

The arrival of Buddhism in Brazil goes back to the 1890s when there was a need for coffee plantation workers. From 1908 to the 1930s, there were nearly 200,000 Japanese immigrants. In the 1920s and 1930s, Pure Land, Zen, Nichiren, and Shingon priests came to Brazil. But it was not until the 1950s that official Japanese Buddhist missions arrived. Soon, there was a large number of Japanese Buddhist temples and centers around the country serving the Japanese Brazilian families. They united in 1958 under the Federation of Buddhist Sects of Brazil. At this time, the non-Japanese Brazilians were learning about Buddhism through books and newspaper articles from the United States and Europe. These books, for example by D. T. Suzuki, presented a spiritual, universal, and pure modern Buddhism that led to the founding of new Budddhist centers devoted to training non-Japanese Brazilians.

Soon, Brazilian scholars and intellectuals began to write about Buddhism and to travel to Buddhist countries or to Buddhist centers in Europe and the United States. Some were ordained as monks, nuns, or lay teachers and returned to Brazil. Then in the 1990s, Buddhism expanded rapidly in Brazil, and from there to other parts of Latin America. Centers for Theravāda, Tibetan, Pure Land, and Zen were established in ways that connected Brazil into the network of globalized Buddhism. Noted Brazilian Buddhist leaders became popular public figures, new Buddhist magazines and books appeared, and famous Buddhists visited and lectured to large audiences (see Figure 10.3). Linkages were made with Buddhist centers in other countries,

FIGURE 10.3. Brazilian Buddhists listen to the Dalai Lama in San Paulo on September 17, 2011.

and new Asian international Buddhist movements entered the country. Today, Buddhism is the second largest world religion in Brazil after Christianity.

As in other countries, Buddhist expansion in Brazil was fueled by the media and technology. Movies dealing with Buddhism, rock groups and celebrities that affiliate with Buddhism, the attraction of the Dalai Lama and Thich Nhat Hanh, virtual international Buddhist communities on the Internet, and attractive websites and CDs with Buddhist music all contributed to the global flows of Buddhism into Brazil in the 1990s and into the new millennium. Another aspect to these global flows is the presence of the new Asian Buddhist movements. Soka Gakkai International began its globalization initiative in Brazil in the 1960s. At first it was made up of Japanese Brazilians who were looking for a modern form of Buddhism to practice. Only later did non-Japanese Brazilians join as SGI–Brazil changed from an ethnic to a universal religious practice focused on ecology and building a more peaceful world. Today, among its 150,000 members in Brazil, 80 percent are non-Japanese. Also today, the Buddhist landscape in Brazil includes about fifty Tibetan Buddhist centers, thirty-five Zen centers, and centers for Pure Land, Nichiren, Shingon, Tendai, Theravāda, and Korean Buddhism. From the United States, there are two Korean Zen centers and three Insight Meditation centers. Dharma Drum Mountain and Fo Guang Shan have three and two centers, respectively.

BUDDHISM IN AFRICA

Many of the countries of Africa have only a few Buddhist centers today. However, there are certain countries with long histories of Buddhist communities that now have new Buddhist organizations. For example, the first Buddhist temple in Africa was built in 1920 in Dar es Salaam, Tanzania. In the early twentieth century, Sri Lankans immigrated to Africa for work. About 450 settled in Tanzania and soon established a Theravāda temple, now called the Buddhist Temple and Meditation Center. In 1956, they build a pagoda and shrine room. Over the years, Sri Lankan monks have served the temple and in 1968, they founded the Buddhist Association that included Thai, Burmese, Chinese, and African members. The abbot of the temple has the title of "Chief Monk of Africa," and since 2008, the position has been held by Ven. Pannaransi. He visits Theravāda temples and communities in ten other African countries where Sri Lankan and other ethnic Buddhists live. For example, Sri Lankan workers arrived in Botswana in 1970 and built a temple with a pagoda, two Buddha statues, and a bronze bell in the 1990s. Given local outreach by these communities, today the Theravāda network includes a good number of African members.

The Theravāda community in Africa that has been most successful in its outreach to Africans is in Uganda. The first African Buddhist monk, Ven. Buddharakkhita, leads the Uganda Buddhist Center (see Figure 10.4). The community is mostly made up of African converts and eleven members

FIGURE 10.4. African Buddhist community at Uganda Buddhist Centre, Kampala, Uganda.

have become monks or nuns. The first African Buddhist nun, Ven. Dhammakami, serves the Ugandan community. Ven. Buddharakkhita himself is a product of the globalization of Buddhism. He traveled and practiced Buddhism in Asia for seven years. Then he went to the United States, where he received higher ordination at the Tathagata Meditation Center in California. Afterward, he trained under Ven. Gunaratana at the Bhāvanā Society in West Virginia. He then returned to Uganda and established the center in 2005.

Zen centers are found in a number of African countries, including Cameroon, Zaire, Ivory Coast, Mali, Burkina Faso, Kenya, Tanzania, and South Africa. One of the most active is the Morosoro Zen Dōjō in Tanzania. It provides Sōtō sitting groups as well as sessions for members who are mainly African. The Dōjō is related to the ZenKenya center where a majority of practitioners are also African. The Morosoro Zen Dōjō is connected to the Zen Buddhist Association of Europe and the International Zen Association also based in Europe. Here we see the global nature of Buddhism in Africa.

Two Chinese Buddhist organizations have a strong, positives, and active presence in Africa. Fo Guang Shan practices "humanistic Buddhism" through social engagement wherever it has centers. In 1992, the Ven. Hui Li visited Africa and decided that the best activity FGS could do was working with orphans. He founded the Amitofo Care Centre organization. First, FGS built the Nan Hua Temple in South Africa as a base for this work in Africa. The first Amitofo Care Centre orphanage was established in Malawi. It has living quarters, a preschool, an elementary school, a medical center, an activity center, and a vocational training center. The children live in "family units" with sixteen to twenty children, a caregiver, and a teacher. Twelve families constitute a "village." New Amitofo Care Centres are now in Zimbabwe, Swaziland, and Lesotho. The activities of the centers are led by African monks trained at the Fo Guang Shan Seminary in South Africa. FGS expects to expand this project to all fifty-three countries in Africa. Also, the Tzu Chi Foundation provides relief supplies, including food and blankets during the winter season to families in South Africa, Zimbabwe, Swaziland, Lesotho, and other countries. They also provide school supplies to children living in orphanages. Tzu Chi established its main center in South Africa in 1992 and another center in Lesotho in 1995 to carry out its missions.

Whereas most countries in Africa have a few Buddhist centers, South Africa has around fifty. Fo Guang Shan has seven centers itself, including the African Buddhist Seminary that has around 300 Africans in training from all over the continent. The seminary offers two- to three-year no-cost monastic residential courses. Theravāda is also strong given the history of Sri Lankan and Southeast Asian workers in South Africa. There are also a number of Korean Zen centers that were founded by the Kwan Um lineage in the United States. The dozen or so Tibetan centers were founded mostly by Tibetan organizations in Europe. There is one Shambhala center from the United States. Nichiren and Sōka Gakkai International are also present. Many of the Tibetan and Zen Buddhist centers include only white South Africans, although it is clear that some reach out to persons of other races. The Theravāda centers mainly serve ethnic groups like the Thai and Burmese. The vipassanā and nonsectarian Buddhist centers are fairly well mixed. Due to the history of apartheid in South Africa, it is clear that the Buddhist landscape there is different from other African countries.

ISSUES FACING GLOBAL BUDDHISM

In the globalization of Buddhism over the past half century or so, Asian traditions have been facing the challenge of adapting to cultures that have already been molded over centuries by other religions and philosophies. Global Buddhist movements and organizations today are in the process of establishing themselves as viable religious institutions that are able to contribute to the societies in which they find themselves. In doing so, it is clear that what is taking shape is not a single religious entity, but a plurality of temples, practice centers, monasteries, fellowships, activist groups, and study facilities. As Buddhism continues to found new communities and reform older ones, a number of issues have arisen. The ways in which these issues are resolved will determine to a large extent what kinds of Buddhism will take shape in the future. We conclude our exploration of the experiences of global Buddhism with a survey of some of the more important issues that will define the future of the globalization of Buddhism.

Ethnicity, Identity, and Practice

Scholars have pointed out that there are certain differences of structure, purpose, and practice between communities founded for Asian Buddhist immigrants and communities created for Buddhist converts. They often distinguish between "immigrant" or "ethnic" Buddhist communities and "convert" Buddhist Communities in non-Asian countries. For example, ethnic temples serve the social, cultural, and educational as well as the religious needs of the community, whereas convert communities focus mainly on religious practice. This means that converts typically identify with Buddhism through a particular single practice, such as chanting, insight meditation, *kōan* practice, or *dzokchen* training, rather than the broad range of doctrinal and cultural aspects of Buddhism so immigrant to Asian Buddhists.

For some in the Asian immigrant communities, there is a concern that this exclusive focus on practice in the convert communities could lead to a certain impoverishment of Buddhist identity. The concern here is that converts might not appreciate the full implications of what it is to be a Buddhist at the moral, intellectual, and social levels of self-understanding. However, for some in convert communities, not appropriating a Buddhist identity as it has been defined in Asia leaves open the possibility of new directions for the development of unique forms of global Buddhism. While there is no real animosity between the immigrant and convert Buddhist communities in this regard, Kenneth K. Tanaka points out the following concerning this issue in the United States:

> Some Asian American Buddhists are offended at the suggestion that [Euro-American] Buddhists are the sole contributors to the creation of American Buddhism, while ethnic Buddhists are seen as having played virtually no role in it. Such perception, in their view, ignores the contributions made by the Asian American Buddhists with much longer history, some entering their second century on American soil. What is often implied, according to Asian American critics, is that Buddhism becomes truly American only when [Euro-]Americans become seriously involved. This form, then, is called "American Buddhism," distinguished from simply "Buddhism in America," as practiced by Asian American Buddhists.[8]

Drawing the distinction between "Buddhism in America" and "American Buddhism" in this way is certainly premature. As we saw in the histories of Tibet and East Asia, the formation of fully inculturated Buddhism is something that takes shape over many centuries, not just a few decades. The United States and other non-Asian countries are still in the first stages of such a process, where there is the need for translations of texts and commentaries, the establishment and stabilization of valid practice lineages and other institutions, and the creation of Buddhist literary, artistic, and other cultural expressions (see Figure 10.5). In this ongoing process both Asian Buddhists and non-Asian convert Buddhists continue to have much to offer.

FIGURE 10.5. Ten Thousand Buddhas Hall at the City of Ten Thousand Buddhas, Talmage, California, at the 2001 Guanyin Bodhisattva Retreat.

In fact, in the United States, for example, Asian American and convert Buddhist communities have provided balance and mutual enhancement for one another in the process of creating viable forms of American Buddhism. For example, Asian American communities tend to hold carefully to the Dharma and its practice as crafted in Asia over many centuries. They feel that Dharma and practice, so defined, have proven themselves by the fact that they produced so many enlightened lives, lasting institutions, inspiring writings, and great cultural expressions. Convert communities have tended to bring the Dharma and its practice to bear on more social and political matters, such as poverty and social injustice, peacemaking and environmental issues, healing, and modern psychology. While the convert groups inspire Asian American communities to take these matters seriously, the latter also emphasize aspects of the Dharma and its practice that could become watered down by pursuing only secular goals.

Women, Ordination, and Authority

During Buddhism's rise in popularity in the 1960s and 1970s, the countercultural influence on some convert Buddhist communities resulted in a disengaging of ethics from spiritual practice. This led to a number of scandals in the 1980s that resulted in crises of leadership. The extent of the scandals is unclear, but it included sexual improprieties and abuse of power. These scandals demonstrated not only the need for ethical standards but also the weaknesses of

Box 10.2

Homecoming

Why would someone born a farm girl in the conservative Christian climate of northern Wisconsin end up not only a Buddhist but someone who publishes widely on Buddhist topics? It is quite mysterious, even to me, or perhaps it is more mysterious to myself than others. People sometimes discuss religious identity as if it were about choices that one makes or does not make. Some people would claim that a person committed to the religion into which she was born was "chosen by the religion, rather than making a personal choice," as a colleague recently put it to me. Her implication was that I, by contrast, had chosen my religion, much as I might choose a dress or a car.

But it doesn't feel that simple and straightforward to me. I did not decide to become a Buddhist. Rather, one day, in the midst of great personal pain, it overwhelmed me that the basic truths proclaimed by Buddhism are, indeed, true. So what should I do? Turn myself inside out trying to find the same clarifying and healing power in the religion I had been observing, as some would claim is the more appropriate course of action? Or follow my heart and my mind into Buddhism?

Obviously, I chose the latter course, and in that sense one could say I chose to become a Buddhist. But the motivation for that choice was not the result of consulting some "consumers' guide" to religions, *but* of something that still feels as if it came to me. In Buddhist language, it would be said that I had a "karmic connection" with Buddhism, so that becoming Buddhist feels more like finally coming home than like choosing a new home. Indeed, many Western converts to Buddhism feel the same way. Granted, I already knew a lot about Buddhism when this experience happened. In fact, I was a college professor teaching university courses about Buddhism. But the fact that I studied Buddhism for so long without ever considering becoming a Buddhist only strengthens my feeling that Buddhism came to me before I came to Buddhism.

Not that this has always been a romantic or an easy journey. I was and am very dissatisfied with the male dominance found in Buddhism throughout its history, even though I know that, in this regard, it is not unlike all other major religious traditions. I have not been silent on this point but have written extensively about Buddhism and gender. Especially important are suggestions for changes that seem, to me and to many others, to be more reasonable, more sensible, and more in accord with Buddhism's basic values. This last point is especially important, for it is hard to justify male dominance on the basis of Buddhism's basic values and teachings. For this activity, I have been criticized by both Asian and Western Buddhists. But many, especially women, have also written to tell me that the work I have done has helped them remain within Buddhism. Such comments have not come only from Western women.

This is all part of the difficult and exciting work of transmitting the Dharma to "the West." At present, there is much controversy over how much Buddhism can or should adopt practices and values common to Western culture. Such controversies are to be expected in this first generation of widespread practice

(Continued)

of Buddhism by people of European and other non-Asian origins. For though Buddhism has *been* practiced in North America for generations by Asian Americans, only in the past thirty years has Buddhism been widely adopted by other North Americans. For us, at least, this is the first generation of what feels like a momentous cultural shift. How better could I have spent my life than to be part of this shift? What fortunate karma!

RITA M. GROSS
Professor Emerita
Department of Philosophy
and Religious Studies
University of Wisconsin–Eau Claire

using an Asian male-dominated authoritarian hierarchy in modern non-Asian society.

In an example of a response to this crisis in leadership, the San Francisco Zen Center established a democratic authority structure and a set of guidelines for proper student–teacher relations. Soon, other Buddhist organizations followed suit. In many communities today, teachers share authority with a lay board of directors. In the case of the San Francisco Zen Center, it now elects its abbot for a four-year term. While Asian monastics continue to be respected for their maturity in the Dharma and play mentor and teaching roles in communities, the unquestioned authority of monastics so common in Asia has given way to models of leadership wherein all persons are held accountable for their actions. Today, scholars refer to this radical change toward a more egalitarian community structure as the "democratization of Buddhism."

Another aspect of this democratization has been an attempt to give men and women equal exercise of authority in Buddhist communities. For example, until recently Zōketsu Norman Fischer and Zenkai Blanche Hartman shared the leadership of the San Francisco Zen Center. Beyond this kind of structural change, some have also been more critical of traditional male-centered practice forms that can produce an atmosphere that is, at times, almost militant. As more women take leadership roles, new patterns of training are being developed. Similar changes are also taking place in communities with regard to gay and lesbian members. Buddhist gay and lesbian practitioners have in recent decades participated more in leadership roles in Buddhist communities. There are also more gay and lesbian practice groups, such as the New York Maitre Dorje and the Hartford Street Zen Center in San Francisco.

In recent decades, many Buddhist women have also taken creative leadership roles in organizations outside their specific Buddhist communities. For example, Paula Green founded the Karuna Center for Peacebuilding, which gives workshops based on Buddhist teachings. Her work has taken her to such places as Bosnia and Rwandan refugee camps in the Congo. Joan Halifax, founder of the Upaya Institute, applies her Dharma teachings to caregiving for the dying. Herself influenced by Buddhist ideas and values, Melody Ermachild Chavis founded Strong Roots, a neighborhood gardening project working with "high-risk" youth. Virginia Straus Benson, once an aide in Jimmy Carter's administration, was the Executive Director of the Ikeda Center for Peace, Learning, and Dialogue in Boston from 1993 to 2009. She is now Senior Research Fellow at the center. Finally, one of the best-known Buddhist activists is Joanna Macy. Her "despair and empowerment" workshops based on Buddhist principles have inspired Buddhist and non-Buddhist activists for decades. The following are her words about the healing of self and world:

> It also helps a lot to remember that each one of us has been called into being at this time. I am convinced of that. We are not here by accident. Is it my imagination to think that we have chosen this? Is it not a privilege to be incarnating at a time when the stakes are really high, at a time when everything we've ever learned about interconnectedness, about trust, about courage, can be put to the test? Each one of us, I believe, is a gift the earth is giving to itself now, a unique gift. Every anguish, betrayal, disappointment can even help prepare us for the work of healing. You don't need to be extraordinary. If the world is to be healed through human efforts, I am convinced it will be by ordinary people, people whose love for this life is even greater than their fear, people who can open to the web of life that called us into being, and who can rest in the vitality of that larger body.[9]

Attention to gender egalitarianism and promoting the position of women within Buddhism are not only American and European phenomena. In many Asian contexts, Buddhists are reexamining the roles of women with the aim of enabling women to partake more fully of the Buddhist experience and give women greater opportunities to contribute to the institutional life of the Saṅgha. For example, Fo Guang Shan has provided equal opportunities to men and women for education, training practice, and leadership. In Won Buddhism, men and women priests have equal status and independently establish and lead local temples.

One of the major current issues facing many Asian Buddhist Saṅghas is the question of whether and how to establish the nuns' full ordination *(bhikṣuṇī)* lineage where it has died out or never been previously established (see Chapter 3 for an introduction to Buddhist ordination). All Buddhist countries offer men the option of taking full ordination vows to become a *bhikṣu,* but only a few maintain lineages offering women the same opportunity. Only women in the Mahāyāna Buddhist traditions of China, Korea, Taiwan, and Vietnam have had continuous access to full ordination. Women in Vajrayāna Buddhist traditions in Tibet, Bhutan, Mongolia, Nepal, and the Indian Himalayas can only receive novice ordination because they have no extant lineage of fully ordained nuns. Women in Southeast Asian countries such as Cambodia,

Laos, Myanmar, and Thailand can receive neither novice nor full ordination as Buddhist nuns, thus effectively barring them from formally joining the Buddhist Saṅgha. This has not stopped them from forming their own renunciate communities modeled on Buddhist monasticism, although they have experienced hardship due to their lower social status and lesser patronage in comparison to their male monastic brethren. For example, in Sri Lanka "Ten-Precept Women" live a celibate renunciate lifestyle, shaving their heads and wearing saffron robes, but are not recognized as part of the Buddhist Saṅgha. Likewise, in Myanmar women take vows to live as "possessors of morality," shaving their heads, dressing in orange and pink colored robes, and living as celibates in nunneries (see Figure 10.6). In Thailand, *maejis* are female renunciates who shave their heads and wear white robes, although they are not accepted as ordained nuns by Thai monks or the Thai government. This relegates some of them to a life of poverty in which they survive by cooking, serving the resident monks, and cleaning the temples in which they live.

In an effort to address these and other issues facing Buddhist nuns, in 1987 a group of Buddhist nuns, monks, and laypeople gathered together in Bodhgāya, India, the place of the Buddha's enlightenment. This gathering was a first on many levels. It was the first ever conference on Buddhist nuns, and since has blossomed into an active international Buddhist women's association that meets regularly in various Asian countries called Sākyadhitā, "daughters of the Buddha." Another "first" that set the 1987 conference on Buddhist nuns and its aftermath apart from previous Buddhist history is that for the first time, a group of *international* Buddhist nuns gathered together to

FIGURE 10.6. Buddhist nuns, or literally "possessors of morality," seeking alms in Myanmar.

share their experiences and ideas about their future. Whereas in previous centuries communication problems and prohibitively difficult travel conditions made it hard for Buddhist nuns from diverse cultures to communicate effectively, today's globalized Buddhism has created new possibilities for international organization.

Although many male and female monastic leaders have expressed support for reinstating the full ordination lineages for nuns and thereby offering men and women equal opportunities within the Buddhist Saṅgha, there are many challenges. For a woman to become a fully ordained Buddhist nun, *Vinaya* rules stipulate that she must undergo a ceremony with a quorum of ten fully ordained female monastics and ten fully ordained male monastics. In places where the lineage of fully ordained nuns has died out, conservative Buddhists claim that it is impossible to reestablish. However, others argue that there are possibilities for reestablishing an extinct nuns' order by either inviting a quorum of nuns from a different country in which the nuns' lineage has been maintained such as Korea or Taiwan, or initially conducting a ceremony in which only monks ordain women, to be followed by ordinations by both quorums of monks and nuns once nuns from that order exist. The problem with inviting fully ordained nuns from another country to ordain those in places where nuns' full ordination no longer exists is that not all Buddhist countries follow the same *Vinaya* lineage. Additionally, Theravāda countries are unlikely to fully accept Mahāyāna ordination ceremonies, as has been a problem in recent years in Sri Lanka. Even within Mahāyāna Buddhist regions, differences in *Vinaya* lineage pose problems, such as the current debate within Tibetan Buddhist communities (who maintain the *Mūlasarvāstivāda Vinaya*) over whether to accept nuns' ordination in the Chinese *Dharmagupta Vinaya* lineage.

Sri Lanka offers an informative example of both the problems and the promises of international Buddhist nuns' organizations. Sri Lanka inherited full ordination lineages from India, where they survived until both monks' and nuns' orders were devastated by war in the eleventh century. When peace returned to the country, the Sri Lankan king reinstated the men's but not the women's monastic order. In the nineteenth century, some women took the ten precepts of novice ordination and lived in women's communities. As part of the Buddhist renewal in Sri Lanka in reaction to colonialism, these "Ten-Precept Women" not only studied and practiced meditation but also opened schools to educate young girls, counseled laypeople, cared for the sick, chanted Buddhist texts for the laity, and assisted at religious ceremonies. Nevertheless, Ten-Precept Women were and continue to be institutionally inferior to Buddhist monastics and as a result receive considerably less funding and less education than do monks.

Recently, the situation of female Buddhist renunciates in Sri Lanka changed dramatically. In 1996 and again in 1998 the first Sri Lankan women were fully ordained in India in ceremonies hosted by Korean and Taiwanese monasteries, respectively. In 1998, these newly fully ordained Sri Lankan women returned home to ordain the first group of Sri Lankan nuns to be fully ordained on

Sri Lankan soil in nearly a millennium. Since then, Sri Lankan monks and nuns have officiated over several more full ordination ceremonies in Sri Lanka. The return of full ordination for Sri Lankan nuns marks a watershed development in Theravāda Buddhist lineage transmission, but its successes have not been without controversies. Not all Sri Lankan monks accept the new full ordination lineage for Sri Lankan nuns because they reject the authenticity of ordination by those who follow a different *Vinaya* lineage, as do the Korean and Taiwanese nuns who reignited the Sri Lankan nuns' lineage. Additionally, not all Ten-Precept Women appreciate the addition of a new community of Buddhist nuns, who pose yet another source of competition for lay Sri Lankan patronage. Some Ten-Precept Women also refuse to take full Buddhist ordination because it entails acceptance of the "eight heavy rules." More information on these eight rules can be found in Chapter 1, but the first of these special rules for nuns specifies that a woman ordained as a nun for 100 years must respect a man ordained as a monk for just one day. This institutional subordination of nuns inscribed in the two-millennia-plus history of Buddhist monasticism complicates contemporary efforts to bolster gender egalitarianism within Buddhist traditions.

Another important event in the international organization of Buddhist nuns occurred in 2007 in Hamburg, Germany, where the Dalai Lama held a conference to discuss the possibilities for how Tibetan Buddhists could incorporate full ordination for nuns. Prominent monks and nuns from diverse Asian countries spoke at the conference, as well as nuns and scholars from Europe and America, further underscoring the globalized dimensions of issues facing Buddhist nuns. Although many conference speakers emphasized the propriety and importance of initiating a full ordination lineage in Tibetan Buddhism, on the final day of the conference the Dalai Lama reaffirmed his support for *bhikṣuṇi* ordination at the same time as he cautioned that more research and discussion is necessary before actually beginning to fully ordain Tibetan nuns. One reason for his caution in moving forward is the importance of maintaining consensus within the already stressed Tibetan exile community. Another reason is the need to carefully determine the best way to go about introducing the new full ordination lineage—whether Tibetan monks should confer this ordination alone as a "single ordination" lineage or whether they should join a quorum of Chinese nuns who adhere to a different *Vinaya* lineage to form a "dual ordination." To date the Tibetan Buddhist Saṅgha is still considering these issues, but given the Dalai Lama and other Tibetans' interest in improving spiritual and educational opportunities for Tibetan Buddhist nuns, it is likely that the Tibetan Saṅgha will find a favorable resolution to the question of how to best introduce full ordination for nuns into its traditions.

In places where the Buddhist women's order does exist in the modern world, it is often flourishing. This is especially true in Korea and Taiwan, where women monastics are given much freedom and education, as well as opportunities to teach, engage in social services, and hold leadership positions. In the words of one such monastic, the Ven. Yifa:

> In Taiwan, Mahayana Buddhist nuns receive higher education, establish temples, give Buddhist lectures, conduct research, transmit Buddhist disciplinary precepts, manage temple economics, as well as manage and participate in various charitable programs such as free medical care, child care and services for senior citizens. These nuns have not only reformed the old traditional Buddhist monastic system, but have also proved to be equal with the male Buddhist practitioners. Consequently, in addition to advancing within the monastic hierarchy, the nuns have made many religious, educational and social contributions to society. Thus, they have helped to propel Buddhism into people's daily lives and thereby to purify Taiwan society.[10]

The lives and work of women like these provide models for those who call for the restoration of the women's order in other parts of the world. Rita M. Gross, a Western scholar and practitioner of Buddhism, makes it clear why the life of a woman Buddhist monastic can be very fulfilling in the modern world:

> Contrary to outsiders' impressions of the limitations of being a nun, most nuns stress the freedom inherent in their lifestyle. . . . [T]hey can develop themselves fully and be available freely and as needed to provide service and support. The emphasis is not on losing an immediate family and a primary relationship, but on taking on a much wider, more inclusive network of relationships that will be healthier and less prone to conflict. Furthermore, nuns live in a supportive community of like-minded and like-spirited companions. . . . Nuns live a lifestyle dedicated to study and spiritual discipline. . . . The opportunity to pursue these goals single-mindedly in a community dedicated to such vocations sometimes seems almost utopian.[11]

The Saṅgha of Buddhist nuns has undergone major challenges since its inception by the Buddha in response to his foster mother Mahāprajāpatī's repeated requests. Warfare, poverty, and social discrimination have threatened Buddhist nuns' survival for more than 2,500, but their communities have proved tenacious and adaptable over time. The dramatic changes of the past twenty-five years made possible by Buddhist nuns tapping into the wider globalized Buddhist network of resources available to them suggest that their best years may be yet to come.

Buddhist Ecumenism

Buddhists from all lineages are today finding various opportunities to meet together in non-Asian pluralistic societies that were not available to them in Asia. For example, we see local and regional Saṅgha councils provide forums in which Buddhists of various traditions can carry out ecumenical discussions, address common problems, and organize cooperative activities in pursuing shared goals. This emerging Buddhist ecumenism opens participants to more productive inter-Saṅgha relationships, resulting in greater mutual understanding. This in turn creates a liberal environment in which historical divisions between Buddhist lineages are sometimes softened, and from which new networks of Buddhism may eventually emerge. Two active eccumenical councils that have made progress in this regard are the Buddhist Saṅgha Council of Southern California and the European International Zen Association.

Besides these kinds of ongoing venues for ecumenical contacts, there have also been Buddhist ecumenical conferences. In 1987, Samu Sunim and Luis Gómez held the aforementioned Conference on World Buddhism in North America at the University of Michigan. At that meeting, representatives of Buddhist traditions in North America crafted the following "Statement of Consensus" in which they agree:

1. To create the conditions necessary for tolerance and understanding among Buddhists and non-Buddhists alike.
2. To initiate a dialogue among Buddhists in North America to further mutual understanding, growth in understanding, and cooperation.
3. To increase our sense of community by recognizing and understanding our differences as well as our common beliefs and practices.
4. To cultivate thoughts and actions of friendliness toward others, whether they accept our beliefs or not, and in so doing approach the world as the proper field of Dharma, not as a sphere of conduct irreconcilable with the practice of Dharma.[12]

This movement toward building Buddhist ecumenism was reinforced by speakers ten years later at the 1997 Buddhism in America Conference in Boston. There the hope was expressed that ecumenical endeavors toward Buddhist harmony and mutual enrichment can provide a rich resource at the local and regional levels for all Buddhist communities facing common issues and problems. Also during the same year, the Buddhist Saṅgha Council of Southern California and the American Buddhist Congress hosted an ecumenical meeting of Buddhist representatives at Hsi Lai Temple. There participants established some guidelines for Buddhist ecumenical consensus-building that respect differences in the spirit of open-mindedness and tolerance.

On a more informal grassroots level, for some time now certain Buddhist teachers from convert communities have been visiting one another and sharing their practices. In this practice-based ecumenism, teachers from one tradition have found that practices from another tradition may be healing or enriching to themselves and to members of their communities. Based on their personal contacts with one another, Buddhist teachers began to meet more formally with each other during the 1990s to discuss the common challenges they were facing. This led to a meeting between non-Asian Buddhist teachers and the Dalai Lama in Dharamsala, India, in 1993. There, participants discussed ways of adapting Buddhism in non-Asian cultures, given their concerns about such issues as integrating the Dharma with psychology, the possibility of a viable monasticism, and the need to emphasize ethical precepts and gender equity. One result of this meeting was the conclusion that Buddhist sectarianism can be countered by ecumenical contacts and discussions, a broader study of Buddhism as a whole, and more opportunities for shared practice.

Interreligious Dialogue

The same pluralistic situation that has brought Buddhists closer together has also brought them into closer contact with persons of other religions. The writings of persons like Thomas Merton in the 1960s led Christians to explore Buddhism while remaining faithful to their own traditions. This interfaith exploration eventually led to persons like Ruben Habito and Robert E. Kennedy, mentioned earlier, gaining Dharma transmission and becoming Christian Zen teachers. Buddhists have also found their interfaith relationship with Christians to be enriching. Many Buddhists have found interfaith dialogue to be an aid to Buddhist inculturation as well as to interreligious understanding, appreciation, and collaboration concerning issues of mutual concern. Havanpola Ratanasara spoke about this interfaith goal in a talk to a group of Christian monastics:

> Religious differences have often been the most deeply rooted and destructive of all. If *we*, as representatives of two of the world's major religions, can show the rest of the world that we can communicate with each other, they just *might* come to realize that there is no reason why they cannot do the same. Here is the real and pressing task of interreligious dialogue today.
>
> In Buddhism, virtuous conduct (*sila*) includes "right speech." And by practicing the virtue of right speech in the context of dialogue, we will be setting an example for the larger world community to emulate. The many problems which beset our communities, indeed all humankind at the close of this century, include: the environment, international terrorism, human rights, urban violence, social justice, and the like. All of our religious communities are affected by these issues and are drawn into the fray. The only question is: Will we rise to the occasion? Will we choose the path of dialogue leading to a more united and peaceful world?[13]

Interfaith dialogue can also provide the context for Buddhism to formulate the Dharma in ways that speak to non-Asian cultural and intellectual traditions. Kitarō Nishida, founder of the Kyoto School mentioned in Chapter 9, crafted his thought in conversation with the ideas of Western philosophers and Christian theologians. One of the recent figures in the Kyoto School, Masao Abe is credited with helping to bring Nishida's philosophy to the attention of scholars in the United States and Europe. Abe's intercultural, interreligious engagement of Buddhist philosophy with Christian theology led him and John B. Cobb, Jr., to found the International Buddhist-Christian

Theological Encounter in 1984. This annual encounter brought Buddhist and Christian scholars together from Europe, Asia, and North America for dialogue on issues of mutual interest. The encounter addressed both theological issues and the contemporary problems of social and environmental violence and their economic roots. The work of scholars like these demonstrates the intellectual promise that dialogue holds for Buddhism in the modern world.

Buddhist and Christian scholars in Asian countries have been engaged in dialogue for decades with very fruitful results. For example, in Japan, based on its dialogue with Buddhism, the Nanzan Institute in Nagoya has produced numerous translations of works by recent Japanese Buddhist scholars who engage Western philosophical and religious ideas in their writings. Also, Japanese Buddhist and Christian scholars involved in dialogue founded what is now named the Japan Society for Buddhist-Christian Studies to carry on their mutually enriching encounter. This kind of academic dialogue in Asia inspired Buddhist and Christian scholars in the United States to found the Society for Buddhist-Christian Studies in 1988. This society now has a large membership, a newsletter, and a respected academic journal entitled *Buddhist-Christian Studies* published by the University of Hawaii. It also holds annual meetings in conjunction with the American Academy of Religion and hosts large international conferences every four years. In 1996, scholars in Europe also founded the European Network of Buddhist-Christian Studies, with their own academic publications and conferences.

In 1977, the Catholic Benedictine monastic tradition established the Monastic Interreligious Dialogue (MID) in Europe and North America to stimulate, develop, and assist in exchanges and dialogues between Buddhist and Christian monastics. During the 1980s and 1990s, Zen and Tibetan monastics traveled to Christian monasteries in North America and Europe, while Christian monastics visited Zen and Tibetan monasteries in Asia. These contacts enabled MID to provide aid to Tibetan monastics in exile during the 1990s. Based on this decades-long friendship, in 1993 the Dalai Lama asked MID to hold an in-depth dialogue on the spiritual life at the Abbey of Gethsemani, home of his friend Thomas Merton. In 1996, MID held the now-historic Gethsemani Encounter with the Dalai Lama and other Buddhist spiritual masters from Sri Lanka, Thailand, Myanmar, Cambodia, Taiwan, Korea, Japan, and India, as well as the United States and Europe. The topics discussed included the practice of prayer and meditation, the stages of growth in the spiritual life, the role of the teacher and the community in spirituality, and the goals of spiritual and social transformation. Beyond the dialogue, Buddhist and Christian participants also practiced meditation together each day and experienced each other's religious rituals. A second Gethsemani Encounter was held in 2002, and a third in 2008.

Another interfaith dialogue that has been fruitful for Buddhism has been with Judaism, due in large part to the many Jews who have leadership roles in Buddhist convert communities. Given this fact, and given that the American Jewish World Service assisted Tibetan exiles in the 1980s, the Dalai Lama met with Jewish rabbis and scholars in 1989. This first meeting led to a group of

Jewish leaders going to Dharamsala, India, to meet with the Dalai Lama in 1990. This meeting was recorded in Rodger Kamenetz's 1994 book *The Jew in the Lotus: A Poet's Rediscovery of Jewish Identity in Buddhist India*. The Dalai Lama was interested in the comparison between Jewish Kabbalah and Tibetan Tantra. He was also interested in how Judaism kept its traditions alive during the Diaspora. In answer to Jewish concern about losing Jews to Buddhism, the Dalai Lama responded:

> In my public teachings I always tell people who are interested that changing religions is not an easy task. So therefore it's better not to change, better to follow one's own traditional religion, since basically the same message, the same potential is there.[14]

More recently, Kamenetz helped found the Seders for Tibet to foster Jewish–Tibetan relations. The Dalai Lama attended one of their seder services in 1997, hosted by Rabbi David Saperstein of the Religious Action Center in Washington, DC. At the closing of the service, those attending recited in Hebrew, "Next year in Jerusalem" and "Next year in Lhasa." Since Kameretz's book was published, other Jews have published books reflecting on their own inner dialogue as Jewish Buddhist practitioners. For example, in 1996, Sylvia Boorstein, a leader in the Insight Meditation movement, published *That's Funny, You Don't Look Buddhist: On Being a Faithful Jew and a Passionate Buddhist*. In that book, Boorstein explains how she has become a more prayerful Jew through understanding more deeply the Buddhist experience of the interdependence of life.

Social Engagement

In 1977, Robert and Anne Aitken hosted a small meeting at their Maui *Zendō* to discuss ways of helping Buddhist practice centers and groups become involved in social and politiçal issues. The result of this meeting was the eventual founding of the Buddhist Peace Fellowship (BPF) as a nonsectarian Buddhist network drawing members from many Buddhist lineages in the United States. Today, that membership includes some 4,000 persons, including persons of other faiths.

Recent literature of the BPF states that while the *duḥkha* that pervades human existence can be addressed through personal practice, its social, political, and economic structures must also be addressed by collaborative efforts. These efforts are to be guided by the Buddhist experience of interdependence and the nonduality between oneself and other suffering beings. To this end, BPF developed a five-point mission:

1. To make clear public witness to Buddhist practice and interdependence as a way of peace and protection for all beings;
2. To raise peace, environmental, feminist, and social justice concerns among North American Buddhists;

3. To bring a Buddhist perspective of nonduality to contemporary social action and environmental movements;
4. To encourage the practice of nonviolence based on the rich resources of traditional Buddhist and Western spiritual teachings;
5. To offer avenues for dialogue and exchange among the diverse North American and world Saṅghas.[15]

In terms of actual projects, BPF has funded such endeavors as medical aid for displaced Burmese people, loans to Tibetan exiles in India and Nepal, and peace walks led by Maha Ghosananda in Cambodia. In the United States, BPF has been involved in disarmament activities, anti–land mine campaigns, and prison work. In the 1980s, BPF sponsored lecture tours by Thich Nhat Hanh. The popularity of Nhat Hanh's engaged Buddhist spirituality led to the founding of the Community of Mindful Living, with its own forms of social engagement. The newest BPF project is the Buddhist Alliance for Social Engagement (BASE), suggested by Robert Aitken in 1992. BASE has organized volunteer corps-type programs responsive to local needs. In its first BASE program, lasting for six months in San Francisco in 1995, volunteers worked in local community programs and attended regular community meditation practice and processing sessions. By the end of the 1990s, BASE had expanded its volunteer program to other parts of the United States. In the mid 1990s, BPF founded the Buddhist AIDS Project (BAP) that supports persons with HIV/AIDS and their families. They now have a Prison Project working with prisioners and their families.

Robert Aitken expressed some of the ideals of BPF's work in relation to the Buddhist experience of dependent arising:

> We can begin our task . . . by meeting in informal groups within our larger sanghas to examine politics and economics from a Buddhist perspective. It will be apparent that traditional teachings of interdependence bring into direct question the rationale of accumulating wealth and of governing by hierarchical authority. What, then, is to be done?
>
> Something, certainly. Our practice of the Brahma Vihāras—kindliness, compassion, goodwill, and equanimity—would be meaningless if it excluded people, animals, and plants outside our formal Sangha. . . . On the contrary, it is clear that we're in it together with all beings.
>
> [The] collaboration in networks of mutual aid would follow from our experience of *paticca-samuppāda,* interdependent co-arising. All beings arise in systems of biological affinity, whether or not they are even "alive" in a narrow sense. We are born in a world in which all things nurture us. As we mature in our understanding of the Dharma, we take responsibility for *paticca-samuppāda* and continually divert our infantile expectations of being nurtured to an adult responsibility for nurturing others. . . . With careful, constant discipline on the Eightfold Path of the Dharma, greed becomes *dāna* [giving], exploitation becomes networking.
>
> *Paticca-samuppāda* is not just a theory but the profound realization that I arise with all beings and all beings arise with me. I suffer with all beings; all beings

> suffer with me. The path to this fulfillment is long and sometimes hard; it involves restraint and disengagement from ordinary concerns. . . . Dharmic society begins and prevails with individuals walking this path of compassionate understanding, discerning the noble option at each moment and allowing the other options to drop away.[16]

A second important Buddhist mode of social engagement was begun by Bernard Tetsugen Glassman upon founding the Greyston Mandala in the 1980s. This organization dedicated to Zen social engagement includes their Greyston Bakery, which provides goods for hotels and restaurants and hires and trains homeless persons and the unskilled poor. Profits are used to purchase and renovate buildings in New York for a housing project for the homeless that also provides child care and job training. In 1998, Glassman and his wife, Sandra Jishu Holmes, also founded the Zen Peacemakers. They now have seventy-three affiliates in twelve country on all five continents. The members of this new order include religious leaders, social workers, and activists who are committed to its three tenets. These are "not knowing," as a letting go of ideas and prejudices; "bearing witness," as a sharing of the pains and joys of others in need; and "healing" oneself and others, as a response to that shared experience. Specifically, the tenets are lived by going into situations of pain that society ignores, being there with openness united with those in need, witnessing to the interrelatedness of life, and finding therein a way to help bring healing to the situation.

Finally, a number of Buddhist prison ministry programs have been founded in the criminal justice system. During the 1960s and 1970s, Hogen Fujimoto of the Buddhist Churches of America presented Dharma sessions at San Quentin and Soledad prisons. Abbot John Daido Loori of the Zen Mountain Monastery in New York founded the Lotus Flower Zendo in Green Haven Prison, and his ministry program now serves a number of New York prisons with meditation training, talks, and other services. In 1992, Kobutsu Kevin Malone and Liz Potter founded what has become the Dharma Song Zendo at Sing Sing. In 1994, Malone established the Engaged Zen Foundation to provide materials and training to Buddhist prison meditation groups. Today, the Upaya Prison Program as part of the Zen Peacemakers teaches mindfulness, meditation, and peace-remaking at a maximum-security penitentiary in Santa Fe.

Ecology and Science

Sometimes called "Eco-centric Saṅgha" or "Green Dharma," Buddhist ecology is a diverse movement that has no organized structure. It includes individuals who address environmental concerns from the standpoint of the Buddhist experience of interdependence and such Buddhist values as mindfulness, compassion, nonharming, and serving all living beings. In 1969, Gary Snyder portrayed the connection between Buddhist practice and ecology in his Pulitzer Prize–winning *Turtle Island*. The following are selections from that book:

> Position: Man is but a part of the fabric of life—dependent on the whole fabric for his very existence. As the most highly developed tool-using animal, he must recognize that the unknown evolutionary destinies of other life forms are to be respected, and act as gentle steward of the earth's community of being.
>
> Situation: The human race in the last century has allowed its production and scattering of wastes, by-products, and various chemicals to become excessive. Pollution is directly harming life on the planet; which is to say, ruining the environment for humanity itself.
>
> Goal: Balance, harmony, humility, growth which is a mutual growth with Redwood and Quail: to be a good member of the great community of living creatures. True affluence is not needing anything.[17]

During the 1980s, BPF began to address the environmental crisis affecting so many living beings. In the 1990s, numerous books and articles were published on Buddhism and ecology, and conferences were held on the topic. One such conference was the Spirit and Nature Conference in 1990 at Middlebury College with the Dalai Lama as keynote speaker. The International Buddhist-Christian Theological Encounter also addressed the factors responsible for ecological violence in its annual meetings.

Concrete Buddhist ecological programs include, among others, Gary Snyder's Yuba River Institute; the San Francisco–based Buddhists Concerned for Animals; the Washington, DC–based Center for Respect of Life and the Environment; and the work done of the Ikeda Center for Peace, Learning, and Dialogue on behalf of the Earth Charter, a set of guidelines for human–earth relations. In most cases, what distinguishes Buddhist environmentalism is the cultivation through practice of the experience of interrelatedness that in turn becomes a basis both for insight into the importance of ecology and for addressing ecological issues. In this regard, Stephanie Kaza says,

> The Hua-yen School of Buddhism . . . placed particular emphasis on this principle, using the jewel net of Indra as a teaching metaphor. . . . To extend this metaphor, if you tug on any one of the lines of the net—for example, through loss of species or habitat—it affects all the other lines. Or, if any of the jewels become cloudy (toxic or polluted), they reflect the others less clearly. Likewise, if clouded jewels are cleared up (rivers cleaned, wetlands restored), life across the web is enhanced. . . . This, then, provides a principle of both explanation for the way things are, and a path for positive action.[18]

While the dependent arising of all things has become a philosophical basis for Buddhist ecology, it has also been a basis for comparisons with modern physics. For example, there have been discussions about how in quantum physics subatomic particles can be understood as arising from a nexus of relations within a field of interaction in ways similar to dependent arising taught by Buddhism. However, in recent decades the focus has turned more to neuroscience and Buddhism. Here too there are speculative theories put forward about the relationship between the mind and the world, but more work is now being done in research on the effects of meditation or mindfulness on the brain. People working in the fields of neurobiology, psychiatry, and stress physiology have been looking at how Buddhist practices actually affect brain function. One example is a 2004 study *(Proceedings of the National Academy of Sciences of the United States of America)* researching high-amplitude gamma-band oscillations in the brain during meditation. When the Tibetan meditators generated feelings of compassion, the result was that these gamma-band oscillations or waves became rhythmic, coherent, and harmonic. These gamma waves were observed as a synchronizing network of high-precision cognitive processes. Also, the gamma wave activity during the baseline state of the meditators' brains after meditation were in accord with what was observed in meditation. This could mean that meditation might alter one's consciousness in positive ways during everyday life.

In a 2003 study *(Journal of Psychosomatic Medicine)*, persons who do mindfulness meditation were found to have significantly higher levels of activation in the part of the brain associated with positive affect than the control group. The findings suggest that mindfulness might change brain function detected in baseline studies as well as during emotional challenges. This study added another dimension by testing the immune function of both the meditators and nonmeditators. Both groups were given an influenza vaccine. The meditators displayed a significantly higher increase in antibody titers compared to the control group. The conclusion of the researchers is that mindfulness meditation may have a positive effect on the immune system.

Buddhists are also finding ways of relating their mindfulness and meditation practices to psychology. As we can glimpse in the earlier quotation from Joseph Goldstein, the Insight Meditation movement has found that in their spirituality of mental culture, the inner journey that faces suffering and its causes in the mind and heart aids in the process of psychic healing and integration. Today, some health care professionals, such as those at the Cambridge Institute for Meditation and Psychotherapy, integrate mindfulness and meditation into their clinical practice. For over twenty years at the Stress Reduction Clinic at the University of Massachusetts Medical Center, Jon Kabat-Zinn has used mindfulness and Zen meditation in programs for pain management and for treating stress-related disorders. More recently, Kabat-Zinn and his colleagues have also founded the Center for Mindfulness in Medicine, Health Care, and Society in connection with the University of Massachusetts in order to apply their work to other settings such as prisons, schools, and the workplace.

Youth and the Internet

The rapid growth of Buddhism in countries like the United States has being going on for just sixty or so years. As we see the "graying" of first-generation Buddhists, we are at the same time seeing the emergence of the second generation. Recently, some scholars have turned their attention to this new generation who have grown up in Buddhist families. One interesting fact is that those of the first generation who converted to Buddhism or who became Buddhist practitioners did so as a free choice. Many of them feel that they need to give their children the same opportunity to choose what they want to believe and practice. On the other hand, Asian Buddhists in non-Asian countries expect their children to attend the temple, take language and culture classes, and be part of family and youth activities at the temple. Of course, here we are not talking just about a second generation because immigrant Buddhist communities have been around for a longer time than convert communities.

Looking at Asian Buddhist youth, one thing that they have in common is that because they belong to ethnic minorities, the temple community is a place where they come to understand more deeply their ethnic identity. They bond with other youth and gain a sense of pride and solidarity, and they can relax and be themselves. In some cases, Asian youth embrace the teachings of Buddhism as they understand it through their community and want to practice it in the temple. In other cases, youth do not want to participate in the religious practices but are what could be called "cultural Buddhists." There are always those who simply leave the temple community; and there are also those who become interested in the convert forms of Buddhism. They see convert Buddhism as offering ways of keeping their Buddhist identity while living it out in ways that are more reflective of the broader culture in which they live.

As different generations of Asian immigrant Buddhists take positions of authority in their communities, new forms of adaption are added. Today, it is not uncommon to find a broad spectrum between tradition and innovation in well-established immigrant Buddhist temples. This often suits the needs of the youth who want to maintain contact with their tradition while practicing it in more creative ways. Finally, it is interesting to note that where there are new global Buddhist movements, many youth get involved in their youth branches. For example, the Japanese Rissho Kosei-kai is involved in global peace building and interreligious cooperation. Many of their events are led by youth who find these activities exciting and in accord with their interests. The Tzu Chi Foundation has relief programs around the world and Buddhist youth participate in large numbers. This involvement brings the youth together with older generations as well as with the movement's leaders, monks, and nuns in activities where they relate on a more equal basis.

Turning to convert Buddhist communities, we find similar responses by second-generation youth. Some simply do not choose to take up Buddhism. Some find that their values and ideals have been formed within a Buddhist environment and want to keep that identity, perhaps with some changes, but do not want to do formal practice. On the other hand, some do take up the practice, and others actually want to take up more rigorous practice. It has been said that aspects of convert Buddhism have been psychologized, watered down as it were. As some in the second generation study Buddhism and come to a deeper appreciation for what practice can lead to, they want to take up a more spiritual practice that leads to life-changing experiences, processes that deepen understanding and compassion, that lead ultimately to Awakening, Nirvana, or Buddhahood.

Thus, convert Buddhist youth find themselves faced with a continuum from simple practices for inner peace and better relationships on the one hand, to more intense monastic practices that truly change one's whole being. Given this situation, during the past decade there have been new youth voices grappling with this continuum and how it relates to their daily life and their aspirations. A popular book has been *Blue Jean Buddha* (2001), which presents reflections, questions, doubts, struggles, and experiences by young persons trying to understand, relate to, and recast the Dharma as formulated by the previous generation. These youth are interested in informal gatherings, not just formal sittings or liturgies. They want open discussions as well as Dharma talks. They want to expand Saṅgha life to include more informal and social opportunities. Also, in 2007, *buddhageeks* appeared on the Internet. The site presents reflections about topics such as Buddhists using social media like Facebook and Twitter, the growing global Buddhist culture, "upgrading" your mind, and video gaming as a contemplative experience. Another site is *Dharma Overground*, where visitors can post their views and experiences on discussion topics such as claims of attainment, humor, morality in daily life, teachers, and retreat centers.

The Internet has also revolutionized global Buddhism in ways that are of special interest to youth. As Buddhist centers, organizations, teachers, and movements in all five continents set up websites, Buddhists can encounter and communicate with the global networks that have been established. They can learn about the creative things Buddhist communities are doing to recast the Dharma in their countries. These virtual linkages contribute to the creative flows of Buddhism around the world. One can see, for example, that in Africa when an African monk leads a Theravāda temple, the Saṅgha community is made up of African families—men, women, and children. Buddhists anywhere can witness the flows of Buddhism from Asia to the United States, back to Asia, and then to another part of the world. They can witness the real-time reality of Humanistic Buddhism as it responds to the needs of the poor and marginalized, as well as find out how to become involved where they live. With this kind of information and connection, Buddhists around the world can network in global ways that were not possible in the past.

THE FUTURE OF GLOBAL BUDDHISM

In previous chapters, we have looked at modern Buddhist movements in Asian countries. We have also seen that these new movements have been globalized and are present and fully engaged in countries around the world. In this final chapter, we have looked at the flows of traditional Asian Buddhism into other countries and the multidirectional flows between global Buddhist communities, both immigrant and convert. By adding to these experiences with examples of some of the important issues that are being addressed today in this globalization of Buddhism, we glimpse some of the directions in which Buddhism is moving today. Traditions and innovations blend in the adapting of ancient lineages to the conditions of contemporary cultures being transformed by globalization. In this recasting of Buddhism into new forms, the global experiences of Buddhism are in flux. Traditions sustain certain experiences that are fundamental to the Dharma, to the gifts of the Buddha to humankind. Innovations enable these gifts to be repackaged in ways that speak the Dharma in new ways to contemporary Asian and non-Asian cultures. This crafting of the future of Buddhism will take time and patience. In the meantime, Buddhism today presents us with a fascinating story of global spiritual, moral, mental, social, cultural, and physical experiences of transformation. At the same time, this story includes inspiring tales of local Buddhist communities and networks of communities in a global Saṅgha bringing healing to the contemporary world. This story is about the weaving of new threads that have rich textures and colors into the 2,500-year tapestry of Buddhism. In so doing, the Dharma takes on a fuller level of global expression, embracing the whole human family. At the beginning of the twenty-first century, the story of this globalization of Buddhism is being written, and in it we can glimpse the future of this great world religion.

A Cultural Experience of Buddhism in America Today

Rev. Heng Sure, Berkeley Buddhist Monastery, Berkeley, California

In previous chapters, contributors have presented the popular Buddhist cultures of Asian countries. In the United States, elements of Buddhist cultures from Asia are replicated by immigrant communities. For example, the *O-bon* festivals of Japan are celebrated in Japantowns in large U.S. cities or at local Japanese temples or cultural centers. Vietnamese temples provide the cultural expressions of Buddhism for their members, including funerals, the celebration of the Buddha's Birthday, and so on. Chinese Buddhists build large temples and monasteries in scenic areas that provide devotees with pilgrimage sites. But these cultural sites, events, and activities are not at all central to American culture today. So, what happens when an American decides to become a Buddhist and to appropriate some of the popular cultural elements of an Asian Buddhist tradition? What is that cultural crossover experience like?

ENCOUNTERING BUDDHIST CULTURE

I grew up in the 1950s and 1960s in Toledo, Ohio, of Scots-Irish ancestry and was president of my high school student council as well as my church's Methodist Youth Fellowship. The culture I grew up in was as mainstream

Midwestern American as corn on the cob. My first encounter with Asian religious culture happened when I took a Chinese language class in high school and picked up a bilingual ancient Buddhist scripture in the local public library. I knew I had to find out why the book's Chinese characters felt strangely familiar and compelling. In college my roommate introduced me to Buddhist meditation. Later, he became a disciple and ordained monk under a Chinese Buddhist Chan Master. One day, I drove to Gold Mountain Monastery to visit my former roommate.

Inside the door of Gold Mountain, my first impressions were physical. I noticed the chill in the air, smelled the sandalwood incense, and marveled at the three large Buddhas seated in full lotus posture on a raised dais with gold-colored dragons curling around the roof. When I heard the tapping of a "wooden fish" drum and the rhythmic chanting of *mantras,* I looked at the Caucasian monks and nuns wearing robes and bowing in the Buddha hall and saw my former college roommate. He was sitting beside Master Hsüan Hua and translating his Mandarin Chinese Dharma talk into English. His head was shaven, and he wore a long robe and a dark brown sash clasped over his left shoulder. If it were not for the audio headphones over his ears, he might have stepped out of a Tang Dynasty court painting. I had an epiphany: I knew I had returned to my spiritual home.

Three years after entering Gold Mountain, I knelt on a platform in a monastery in rural northern California called the City of Ten Thousand Buddhas and professed the many vows taken by Buddhist monastics since the time of the Buddha, 2,500 years ago. Strange to say, promising to live with so many precepts felt not at all repressive. Instead, as I stepped into the lineage of monks and nuns of ages past, my heart felt liberated and joyful. By taking the *bhikṣu* precepts, I set aside the cultural perspective in which I had been raised and entered a new, yet ancient, Buddhist culture. I became a celibate monk, a vegetarian, a mendicant. I vowed to replace my previous cultural lifestyle with the values of the Buddha's Saṅgha. Taking the vows is a ritual process; living in the religious culture those vows express requires bone-deep changes. When I think back to what I went through in making these changes, certain peak experiences emerge from the mist of memory.

BOWING

One of those moments was learning to bow. Bowing is a basic practice in Chinese monastic life and popular Chinese Buddhist culture. My initial experience with bowing was full of hesitation and questions. On Saturday mornings at Gold Mountain Monastery the American monks and nuns lead the newcomers in bowing to an English translation of the repentance liturgy of Medicine Master Buddha. Men and women bowed on two sides of the hall while chanting passages of Buddhist texts and the names of Buddhas and bodhisattvas. When I bowed the first few times, pictures from Sunday school arose in my mind. I recalled stories of God punishing the Israelites for worshiping graven idols. How was bowing to Buddha images any different? For a long time the gesture seemed forced and unnatural, but I stuck with it in large part because there was a vegetarian lunch immediately afterward and I was a graduate student cooking for myself in a studio apartment in Berkeley. After half an hour of bowing and chanting I realized my body felt unusually comfortable. My thoughts slowed down, my breathing was deep and regular, and tension left my shoulders. Bowing felt like yoga, only more spiritually focused.

Bowing also allowed my mind to contemplate the text of the liturgy. The bowing provided a space, and the following words of the Dharma-teaching went deep into my consciousness:

> Therefore the sicknesses of living beings are one single illusory sickness, and the medicines given by the Thus Come One are, likewise, one illusory medicine. . . . So we can know that all the Dharma spoken by the Thus Come One has a single quality and a single flavor. It is the quality of liberation, the quality of leaving [affliction], the quality of cessation, and ultimately, the quality of Nirvana. In the end, it returns to emptiness.

Bowing to this deep insight felt transformative and healing. Master Hua instructed that bowing was not for the purpose of getting anything from a Buddha, for example. Instead, we bowed to get rid of pride and arrogance and to create room for goodness in our minds once pride was gone. This made sense and answered my question as to how my bowing now is different from idolatry. As I adopted this Buddhist practice, it resonated with values that are part of American culture informed by Christianity: the overcoming of pride in the pursuit of goodness. Bowing with my head at shoe-top level, it was more difficult to feel arrogant. I felt humble and soft as I contemplated how many of my mistakes in life had come from loneliness, from a feeling of brokenness and alienation from others. On Saturday mornings at Gold Mountain, when the bowing was over, I felt relieved of a burden, lighter and more connected with the world around me and the people in it. The feeling of connection remained for hours. Bowing became a daily practice I willingly and literally threw myself into.

When I eventually moved over to the monastery from Berkeley, I asked my monk-roommate for an appropriate practice to deepen my cultivation. He suggested I bow to a *sūtra* text, one character at a time. This immediately struck me as a ridiculous notion. I was studying for my master's degree at a prestigious public university, and I had learned to read a number of books, journals, and newspapers at once. Bowing down to one Chinese character at a time in one book simply seemed too slow. He anticipated my reluctance and said, "Don't think about it, don't talk about it, just do it, and tell me later how it felt."

I lit a stick of incense, opened the *Flower Adornment Sūtra,* and, grumbling to myself that this was a waste of time, made the first bow to the first character: *da* for "great," or "large." One hour later, I had bowed my way onto just the second page. But in the process, my mind had downshifted into a slower gear, in tune with my bowing. I contemplated the characters one by one and had another epiphany: While reading great books slowly enhances comprehension and appreciation, bowing at each character in a book moves the mind toward an even deeper level of comprehension and appreciation. This deeper comprehension and appreciation is not only for each word, but it also gradually reduces the inner chatter that had been part of my everyday state. By letting the six senses concentrate on one thing, the *sūtra* text as a sacred object while bowing, I experienced my mind interacting with writing in a whole new way. The practice of bowing to a *sūtra* became my first door into Buddhist spiritual culture.

Since then, I have dedicated years of my monastic formation to bowing, to making ritual prostrations. I made a pilgrimage at one point in my early monastic formation, bowing to the ground once every three steps. It took thirty-three months of steady walking and bowing to travel from South Pasadena, California, up the Pacific Coast Highway to the City of Ten Thousand Buddhas in Ukiah. The pace of bowing and the insights gained from putting my body prone to the ground for those months amended my views concerning such Buddhist practices as bowing and pilgrimage. Using the whole body in practice affects the mind and spirit in unexpected ways; putting the heart and the head on the same physical plane while one is wide awake seems to heal the mind and bring the world around one to life.

TAKING REFUGE AND THE FIVE PRECEPTS

Like many Americans, I first discovered Buddhist thought and concepts through books. I read Kerouac's *Dharma Bums* and found an English translation of the Sixth Patriarch's *Platform Sūtra* in my public library. To step up from being a reader about Buddhist culture to being a participant, the Mahāyāna tradition offers the ceremony for "Taking Refuge with the Three Jewels" and "Receiving the Five Precepts." The Refuge Ceremony is open to laypersons at any stage of practice. The Five Precepts are what distinguishes one as a Buddhist and are common to all traditions, be it Mahāyāna, Theravāda, or Vajrayāna.

I recall the day I took the Three Refuges and the Five Precepts at Gold Mountain Monastery. The Venerable Abbot Master Hsüan Hua said, "Today is your new birthday. You may consider everything you've done heretofore as over and gone. You can consider that everything you will do and who you will become is born anew today as a disciple of the Buddha."

From the point of view of the Chinese Mahāyāna, the act of "Taking Refuge with the Triple Jewel" is the equivalent of a kind of christening in Buddhism. One takes refuge in a ninety-minute ritual, wherein one asks for a teacher to transmit the refuges, invites the "Permanently Abiding" Triple Jewel to draw near and bless the event, repents of past offenses, and then vows to take the Buddha, the Dharma, and the Saṅgha as one's new spiritual affiliation. The elements of popular Buddhist culture are concrete expressions of, and practical ways of living out, this spiritual affiliation with Buddha, Dharma, and Saṅgha.

The presiding Master confers a Dharma-name on the new disciples, and from then on that name represents one's connection to an ancient lineage of Buddhist disciples stretching back to the historical Buddha himself. I felt a weight lift from my heart soon after taking refuge; a fundamental struggle between alienation and belonging had been settled. Clearly the act of taking refuge was more than the ritual itself. It became clear that the answer to my search for identity was a spiritual matter that took me beyond the physical body to which my parents gave birth and beyond my personality, which was shaped in many ways by the culture in which I had been raised.

A next step into the Dharma comes by requesting and receiving the Five Precepts. This ceremony allows one to make a lifelong promise to refrain from taking life, from stealing, from engaging in sexual misconduct (generally interpreted as refraining from adultery and promiscuity, or more strictly, as staying chaste until marriage), from telling lies, and from using intoxicants of any kind. Requesting these precepts required me to make a major change in my thinking about personal freedom and rules. I grew up as a typical American boy, defining freedom as doing whatever I wanted, whenever I wanted. In popular American culture, self-made people and rugged individuals were heroic for taking as much freedom as they could. I asked my monk friend how many precepts a *bhikṣu* observed, and I was shocked at the answer: over 300! I could not comprehend how anybody could live with so many rules. Yet the people who held precepts did not look oppressed or miserable in any way; in fact, quite the opposite. When I observed that monks lived without money, possessions, family, stimulants, newspapers, or television, I questioned how such a lifestyle could survive in the affluent marketplace of North American consumer culture. Perhaps the Buddhist monks were revered in Asian countries and play a role in the lives of laypersons through popular practices. But how could this happen in the West?

BUDDHIST PRACTICE AND WESTERN CULTURE

On Buddha's Birthday in 1972, I drank tea with my monk friend late in the afternoon, after the crowds of disciples had dispersed. He told me his views about the values of the Buddhist monastic culture. He said that the Buddha's monastic Saṅgha is one of the oldest direct democracies in the world, where decisions are made by asking consensus of all the monks. Authority in the Saṅgha comes from virtue and seniority in precepts. The Saṅgha is a democratic community where farmers, scholars, and princes live side by side and share their material goods equally.

In Buddhist cultures in Asia, monks walk with their alms-bowls through towns, but they do not beg. They do not even speak, nor do they accept money. The monks instead serve as "fields of blessings"; that is to say, they make themselves available for laypeople who care to practice generosity by offering food. Supporting the lifestyle of a cultivator of the path to wisdom has always been regarded as meritorious to the giver, hence the name "field of blessings Saṅgha."

Monastics also give to society by preserving literacy and knowledge of the path to spiritual wisdom. They teach school, write, translate, and live lightly on the earth, ecologically speaking, needing only a few vegetables a day to sustain their lives. Their monasteries preserve green space, offering stewardship of nature and refuge for animals. By taking men out of the army, the Saṅgha serves as a counterpoint to a nation's militarization and to rulers' aspiration for armed conflict and political domination through force. In these and other ways, monastics directly contribute to a more peaceful society by modeling the compassionate and nonmaterialistic values that bring true peace to society.

How can Buddhism model these values in American culture, where the marketplace dominates so much of our social identity? One example can be found in convert Buddhist monastics' revolutionary stance of refraining from mercantile activity. For the first twenty-five years of my life as a monk, I held the precept of not touching money. Monks who observe that practice hold no personal assets; they have no savings account, credit cards, or checking accounts. This was only possible because others are willing to pay the bills and keep the monastery's accounts. Monks eat simply, and we wear the same robes year after year, so our needs are simple and easily met.

Not touching money did not restrict my freedom, and the effect on my mind of leaving the marketplace behind was profoundly liberating. I did not need ATMs or banks, catalogs, advertisements, sales, or credit reports. My body rarely went into stores or malls. Most significant of all was that my mind did not go into stores either. I spent no mental effort thinking about things to buy or trade. The amount of time this practice freed up was considerable. The freedom that comes from choosing not to be exposed to the seduction of advertising's manufactured desires that urge one to consume enables one to find one's identity outside the consumer culture in a spiritual-based culture that offers real contentment.

In the nonmaterialistic culture of Buddhism, one learns to pay attention to the desires and thoughts the mind creates, to greed and discontent, and to the forces in popular culture that fuel these thoughts and desires with promises of a satisfaction that never happens. Socially, the impact of a group of people who do not participate in the marketplace can be powerful and wholesome. One learns again the lesson from childhood: Sharing and happiness go together. Living together this lesson provides a wholesome message for people caught in the consumer culture.

By giving his disciples a moral code that was based on wisdom, the Buddha lifted his Saṅgha out of the mundane culture of his time. He thereby provided his followers with an alternative culture, one of equality and democracy, brotherhood and sisterhood, freedom from materialism and consumerism, mindfulness and peace, and sharing and happiness. He offered membership in the Saṅgha to women and men, to outcasts and princes, to poor and rich alike. The patchwork robe and shaven head of the monks and nuns made it possible for people to set aside superficial culture-bound distinctions and to walk the path to spiritual growth and human evolution. For these reasons I feel that Buddhism, seen in this light, can help redefine in positive ways the American cultural values of freedom, equality, and democracy.

NOTES

1. Edwin Arnold, *The Light of Asia* (Boston: Roberts Brothers, 1890), pp. 230–231.
2. Jack Kerouac, *Dharma Bums* (New York: Penguin Books, 1958), pp. 9–10.
3. Shinryu Suzuki, *Zen Mind, Beginner's Mind,* Trudy Dixon, ed. (New York: Weatherhill, 1970), pp. 76–77, 79.
4. Sogyal Rinpoche, *The Tibetan Book of Living and Dying,* Partick Gaffney and Andrew Harvey, eds. (San Francisco: HarperSanFrancisco), pp. 48, 49, 59, 61–62, 189, 198.
5. Joseph Goldstein, *Insight Meditation: The Practice of Freedom* (Boston: Shambhala Publications, 1993), pp. 3–4.
6. Samu Sunim, "Worldly Bodhisattvas: Zen Awakening and Social Transformation," in Donald W. Mitchell and James Wiseman, O.S.B., eds., *The Gethsemani Encounter: A Dialogue on the Spiritual Life by Buddhist and Christian Monastics* (New York: Continuum Publishing, 1997), pp. 143–146.
7. For more precise and comprehensive figures in this section, see Charles S. Prebish and Martin Baumann, *Westward Dharma: Buddhism beyond Asia* (Berkeley: University of California Press, 2002), pp. 94, 96, 123, 142–144.
8. Charles S. Prebish and Kenneth K. Tanaka, eds., *The Faces of Buddhism in America* (Berkeley: University of California Press, 1998), p. 288.
9. Joanna Macy, "Schooling Our Intention," *Tricycle: The Buddhist Review* 3, no. 2 (Winter 1993), p. 51.
10. Venerable Dr. Yifa, "The Woman's Sangha in Taiwan," in Mitchell and Wiseman, eds., *Gethsemani Encounter*, p. 108.
11. Rita M. Gross, *Buddhism* after *Patriarchy: A Feminist History, Analysis, and Reconstruction of Buddhism* (Albany: SUNY Press, 1993), p. 242.
12. Eleanor Rosch, "World Buddhism in North America Today," *Vajradhatu Sun* 9, no. 1 (October–November 1987), p. 28.
13. Ven. Dr. Havanpola Ratanasara, "Dialogue and Unity: A Buddhist Perspective" in Mitchell and Wiseman, eds., *Gethsemani Encounter,* 14–15.
14. Rodger Kamenetz, *The Jew and the Lotus: A Poet's Rediscovery of Jewish Identity in Buddhist India* (San Francisco: HarperSanFrancisco, 1994), pp. 228–229.
15. Buddhist Peace Fellowship mailing, February 11, 1997.
16. Robert Aitken, *Original Dwelling Place* (Washington, DC: Counterpoint, 1997), pp. 138–142.
17. Gary Snyder, *Turtle Island* (New York: New Directions, 1969), pp. 91, 94, 97.
18. Stephanie Kaza, To Save All Beings: Buddhist Environmental Activism," in Christopher S. Queen, ed., *Engaged Buddhism in the West* (Boston: Wisdom Publications, 2000), pp. 166–167.

SUGGESTIONS FOR FURTHER READING

Almond, Philip C. *The British Discovery of Buddhism*. Cambridge, UK: Cambridge University Press, 2007.

Ama, Michihiro. *Immigrants to the Pure Land: The Modernization, Acculturation and Globalization of Shin Buddhism, 1899–1941*. Honolulu: University of Hawaii Press, 2011.

Batchelor, Stephen. *The Awakening of the West: The Encounter of Buddhism and Western Culture*. Berkeley, CA: Parallax Press, 1994.

Boucher, Sandy. *Turning the Wheel: American Women Creating the New Buddhism*. Boston: Beacon Press, 1993.

Chappell, David, ed. *Buddhist Peacework: Creating Cultures of Peace*. Boston: Wisdom Publications, 1999.

Chech, Joseph. *Race and Religion in American Buddhism: White Supremacy and Immigrant Adaption*. New York: Oxford University Press, 2004.

Cobb, John B., Jr., and Christopher A. Ives, eds. *The Emptying God: A Buddhist-Jewish-Christian Conversation*. Maryknoll, NY: Orbis Books, 1990.

Coleman, James William. *The New Buddhism: The Western Transformation of an Ancient Tradition*. New York: Oxford University Press, 2002.

Esposito, John L., Darrell J. Fasching, and Todd Lewis. *Religion and Globalization: World Religions in Historical Perspective*. New York: Oxford University Press, 2007

Fields, Rick. *How the Swans Came to the Lake: A Narrative History of Buddhism in America*. Boston: Shambhala Publications, 1992.

Freedman, Lenore. *Meeting with Remarkable Women: Buddhist Teachers in America*. Boston: Shambhala, 1987.

Gross, Rita M. *Buddhism after Patriarchy: A Feminist History, Analysis, and Reconstruction of Buddhism*. Albany: SUNY Press, 1993.

Hammond, Phillip E., and David W. Machacek. *Sōka Gakkai in America:Accommodation and Conversion*. New York: Oxford University Press, 1999.

Heine, Steven, and Charles Prebish. *Buddhism in the Modern World: Adaptions of an Ancient Tradition*. New York: Oxford University Press, 2003.

Kabat-Zinn, Jon, and Richard Davidson, eds. *The Mind's Own Physician: A Scientific Dialogue with the Dalai Lama on the Healing Power of the Mind*. Oakland, CA: New Harbinger Publications, 2012.

Kabilsingh, Chatsumarn. *Thai Women in Buddhism*. Berkeley, CA: Parallax Press, 1991.

Kaza, Stephanie, and Kenneth Kraft, eds. *Dharma Rain: Sources of Buddhist Environmentalism*. Boston: Shambhala Publications, 2000.

King, Sallie B. *Socially Engaged Buddhism*. Honolulu: University of Hawaii Press, 2009.

———. *Being Benevolence: The Social Ethics of Engaged Buddhism*. Honolulu: University of Hawaii Press, 2005.

Kotler, Arnold, ed. *Engaged Buddhist Reader*. Berkeley, CA: Parallax Press, 1996.

Kraft, Kenneth, ed. *The Wheel of Engaged Buddhism: A New Map of the Path*. New York: Weatherhill, 1999.

Learman, Linda. *Buddhist Missionaries in the Era of Globalization*. Honolulu: University of Hawaii Press, 2004.

Lopez, Donald S., Jr. *Buddhism and Science: A Guide for the Perplexed*. Chicago: University of Chicago Press, 2008.

———. *Curators of the Buddha: The Study of Buddhism under Colonialism*. Chicago: University of Chicago Press, 1995.

Loundon, Sumi, and Jack Kornfield. *Blue Jean Buddha: Voices of Young Buddhists*. Boston: Wisdom Publications, 2001.

McAra, Sally. *Land of Beautiful Vision: Making a Buddhist Sacred Place in New Zealand*. Honolulu: University of Hawaii Press, 2007.

McMahan, David L. *The Making of Buddhist Modernism*. New York: Oxford University Press, 2008.

Mitchell, Donald W., ed. *Masao Abe: A Zen Life of Dialogue*. Boston: Charles E. Tuttle, Co., Inc., 1998.

Mitchell, Donald W., and James Wiseman, O.S.B., eds. *The Gethsemani Encounter: Dialogue on the Spiritual Life by Buddhist and Christian Monastics*. New York Continuum Publishing Co., 1997.

Mohr, Thea and Jampa Tsedroen, eds., *Dignity and Discipline Reviewing Full Ordination for Buddhist Nuns*. Boston: Wisdom Publication, 2010.

Morreale, Don, ed. *The Complete Guide to* Buddhist *America*. Boston: Shambhala Publications, 1998.

Mrozik, Susanne, "A Robed Revolution. The Contemporary Buddhist Nuns Bhikṣunī Movement," *Religious Compass* 3 (2009): 300–378.

Prebish, Charles S. *Luminous Passage: The Practice and Study of Buddhism in America*. Berkeley: University of California Press, 1999.

Prebish, Charles S., and Kenneth K. Tanaka, eds. *The Faces of Buddhism in America*. Berkeley: University of California Press, 1998.

Prebish, Charles S., and Martin Baumann, eds. *Westward Dharma: Buddhism Beyond Asia*. Berkeley: University of California Press, 2002.

Queen, Christopher S., ed. *Engaged Buddhism in the West*. Boston: Wisdom Publications, 2000.

Queen, Christopher, and Sallie B. King, eds. *Engaged Buddhism: Buddhist Liberation Movements in Asia*. Albany: SUNY Press, 1996.

Rocha, Cristina. *Zen in Brazil: The Quest for Cosmopolitan Modernity*. Honolulu: University of Hawaii Press, 2006.

Seager, Richard Hughes. *Buddhism in America*. New York: Columbia University Press, 1999.

Sheridan, Tai. *The Buddha in Blue Jeans Book Collection*. Create Space Independent Publishing Platform, 2012.

Tanaka, Kenneth K. *Ocean: An Introduction to Jōdo-Shinshū Buddhism in America*. Berkeley, CA: WisdomOcean Publications, 1997.

Tonkinson, Carol, ed. *Big Sky Mind: Buddhism and the Beat Generation*. New York: Riverhead Books, 1995.

Tsoma, Karma Lekshe. *Buddhist Women and Social Justice: Ideals, Challenges, and Achievements*. Albany: SUNY Press, 2004.

———. *Sakyadhita: Daughters of the Buddha*. Ithaca, NY: Snow Lion Publications, 1988.

Tweed, Thomas A. *The American Encounter with Buddhism, 1844–1912: Victorian Culture and the Limits of Dissent*. Bloomington: Indiana University Press, 1992.

Tworkov, Helen. *Zen in America: Five Teachers and the Search for an American Buddhism*. New York: Kodansha America, 1994.

Williams, Duncan Ryuken, and Christopher S. Queen, eds. *American Buddhism: Methods and Findings in Recent Scholarship*. Richmond, UK: Curzon Press, 1998.

Glossary of Technical Terms

abhidharma (S) [P: abhidhamma]: "Higher Dharma"; collection of scholastic treatises in the Pali Canon that outline and classify Buddhist teachings; one of the three major divisions of the Pali Canon.
adosa (P): Nonhate; loving kindness and other positive motivations in relation to others.
āgama (S): Canonical texts corresponding to the *Nikāyas* of the Pali texts.
ahiṃsa (S): Nonhurting; nonkilling; nonviolence.
akṣobhya (S): "Immovable"; first celestial Buddha to be mentioned in Mahāyāna texts.
akuśala (S) [P: akusala]: Unwholesome; referring to defiling states of consciousness.
ālaya-vijñāna (S): "Storehouse-consciousness"; Yogācāra concept of a depth of consciousness that contains impure seeds of karmic experience along with pure seeds of Awakening.
alobha (P): Nongreed; positive intentions toward others.
amala-vijñāna (S): Pure consciousness; innate pure consciousness that is identified with the nirvanic nature of reality.
amitābha (S) [C: amituofo; J: amida]: Celestial Buddha of the Western Paradise or Pure Land; Buddha worshiped by Pure Land schools of Buddhism.
amoha (S, P): Nondelusion; clarity of mind in relation to others.
anāgāmin (S, P): Non-returner; third advanced stage in early Buddhist path leading to being an *arhat.*
ananda (S): Happiness, joy.
anātman (S) [P: anattā]: No-self; denial of a permanent self or soul (*ātman*); denial of any permanent substantial nature of phenomena.
anitya (S) [P: anicca]: Impermanence; transiency that is characteristic of all phenomena.
anupadhiśeṣa (S): "Without remainder"; Nirvana without the Five Aggregates; *parinirvāṇa.*
arhat (S) [P: arahant]: "Worthy One"; person who is free from all defilements and has attained Nirvana; fourth and final stage of the advanced Theravāda path.
arūpa-loka (S, P): Formless realm; place of rebirth where deities have no shape or form, only mental existence.
asaṃskṛta (S) [P: asaṅkhāta]: Unproduced; unconditioned; quality of Nirvana.

Note: Sanskrit (S), Pali (P), Tibetan (T), Chinese (C), Korean (K), Japanese (J), Thai (Th).

āsrava (S) [P: āsava]: "Outflow"; mental "canker" that ferments defilements; usually defined as sensual desire, desire for continued existence, ignorance, and, sometimes, holding views that are not liberating.
āśraya-parāvṛtti (S): Yogācāra notion of the reversion or conversion of the basis of consciousness that brings insight into the essence of consciousness.
ātman (S) [P: attā]: Soul; permanent self; central notion in Upaniṣadic Hinduism.
avalokiteśvara (S) [C: guanyin; J: kannon]: Bodhisattva of compassion.
avidyā (S) [P: avijjā]: Ignorance.
āyatana (S, P): Sense faculty.
bhāva (S, P): Being; becoming; existence.
bhāvanā (S, P): Mental culture; mental cultivation through meditation.
bhavaṅga (P): Subliminal life-continuum.
bhikṣu (S) [P: bhikkhu]: Monk; male Buddhist monastic.
bhikṣuṇī (S) [P: bhikkhunī]: Nun; woman Buddhist monastic.
bhūmi (S): Stage on the bodhisattva path to Buddhahood.
bīja (S): Seed.
bodhi (S, P): Awakening; enlightenment.
bodhicitta (S): "Thought of Awakening"; altruistic aspiration to attain Buddhahood for the sake of all living beings.
bodhisattva (S) [P: bodhisatta]: Person who seeks the wisdom and liberation of a Buddha; in Mahāyāna, one who seeks Buddhahood to deliver others from suffering.
bodhisattvayāna (S): Bodhisattva journey, course, or vehicle leading one to Buddhahood for the benefit of other beings.
bön (T): Religion of Tibet that has indigenous and Buddhist elements.
brahmā (S, P): Hindu deity; a type of deity who inhabits the higher heavenly realms according to Buddhism.
brahman (S): Ultimate Reality in Hinduism.
brahmā-vihāra (S, P): Four divine states cultivated in Buddhism: loving kindness, compassion, sympathetic joy, and equanimity.
buddha (S, P): Awakened One.
caitasika (S) [P: cetasika]: Mental states discussed in Abhidharma texts and various schools of Buddhism.
caodong (C): Sect of Chinese Chan Buddhism that stresses silent sitting; known as Sōtō Zen in Japan.
cetanā (S, P): Will; volition; willful states of mind forming karma.
chan (C) [K: sŏn; J: zen]: Meditation; from the Chinese *chan-na,* transliterating *dhyāna,* meaning meditation; school of Chinese Buddhism emphasizing the practice of meditation.
chengshi (C): School of Chinese Buddhism based on Sautrāntika and Mādhyamika; *Satyasiddhi* Treatise.
chenyan (C) [J: shingon]: "True word"; Tantric school of Chinese Buddhism.
chogye (K): Modern Korean Buddhist order.
chŏng-t'o (K): Korean Pure Land Buddhism.
ch'ŏnt'ae (K): Korean Tiantai School of Buddhism.
citta (S, P): Mind.
dalai lama (T): *Dalai* means "ocean," implying the Dalai Lama's wisdom is as deep as the ocean; one of the leading hierarchs of the Geluk School of Tibetan Buddhism; spiritual and temporal leader of Tibetan people.
dāna (S, P): Giving; donations to the Saṅgha; method of making merit.
dao (C): Way; Chinese term for ultimate reality that is the ground of all existence.
daśabhūmi (S): Ten stages of the bodhisattva journey to Buddhahood.

deva (S): Deity; type of Hindu deity; deities that inhabit the lower heavenly realms according to Buddhism.
deva-yoga (S): Deity yoga; type of Tantric visualization practice whereby one becomes familiar with the qualities and consciousness of bodhisattvas, Buddhas, and their realms.
dhāraṇī (S): "That which sustains"; ritual formulas used to sustain religious life, in meditation, or to invoke deities.
dharma (S) [P: dhamma]: Teaching of the Buddha; ultimate truth taught by the Buddha; law that governs things; essence or nature of phenomena; ultimate mental and physical constituents of existence.
dharmadhātu (S): Realm of truth; realm of the *dharmas* as they truly are; totality of all phenomena; absolute foundation for all phenomena.
dharmakāya (S): "Body of the Dharma"; totality of the Buddha's qualities in early Buddhism; luminous and nirvanic essence of the Buddha in Mahāyāna; innate reality of Buddhahood.
dhyāna (S) [P: jhāna]: Meditation; meditative states of consciousness.
dosa (P): Hate; aversion.
duḥkha (S) [P: dukkha]: Dissatisfactory condition of human nature; suffering; the condition of transitory existence; first of the Four Noble Truths.
dzokchen (T): Nyingma meditation practice focusing on the essential pure and free nature of the mind.
ekayāna (S): One vehicle; notion in the *Lotus Sūtra* that refers to the essence or true practice behind all forms of Buddhism.
faxiang (C) [J: hossō]: "Characteristics of the *Dharmas*"; Yogācāra School of Chinese Buddhism.
fo guang shan (C): Modern socially engaged Buddhist order in Taiwan.
garbha (S): Womb; embryo.
geluk (T): "the virtuous ones"; school of Tibetan Buddhism; the school of the Dalai Lama.
gohonzon (J): Great *maṇḍala; maṇḍala* used in Nichiren Buddhism.
gong'an (C) [K: kongan; J: kōan]: "Public legal case"; authoritative, paradoxical sayings and questions used in Chan, Sŏn, Zen practice.
guru (S): Teacher; spiritual master.
guru-yoga (S): Tantric practice of venerating one's guru as embodiment of wisdom and compassion of Buddhahood.
haedong (K): Korean sect based on teachings of Wŏnhyo.
haiku (J): Type of Japanese poetry.
hīnayāna (S, P): Small or lesser journey, course, or vehicle; a pejorative term used by Mahāyāna to denote all forms of early Buddhism that did not accept Mahāyāna teachings.
hossō (J): "Characteristics of the *Dharmas*"; Japanese school of Yogācāra Buddhism.
hōza (J): "Dharma sitting"; communal sharing practice of the Risshō Kōsei-kai in which members search together the *Lotus Sūtra* for aid in daily life.
huayan (C) [K: hwaŏm; J: kegon]: *Avataṃsaka;* "Flower Ornament"; School of Chinese Buddhism based on the *Avataṃsaka Sūtra.*
hwadu (K): "Critical phrase" in a *kongan* used in Korean Sŏn Buddhism to focus the mind in meditation.
hwaŏm (K): Korean school of Hua-yen Buddhism.
inka (J): Formal certification of Awakening and teaching approval in Zen.
irwŏn-sang (K): Unity circle symbolizing the *Dharmakāya* in Won Buddhism.
jātaka (S, P): Birth stories; collection of tales about the previous lives of Gautama Buddha.

jingtu (C) [K: chŏng-t'o; J: jōdo]: Pure Land; Pure Land Buddhism in China.
jiriki (J): Self power; realizing Awakening by relying on one's own effort.
jīva (S): Soul.
jōdo (J): Pure land; Pure Land School of Buddhism in Japan founded by Hōnen.
jōdo shinshū (J): True School of Pure Land Buddhism; Pure Land Buddhism in Japan founded by Shinran.
jōjitsu (J): Japanese school of Chengshi Buddhism; *Satyasiddhi* Treatise.
kadam (T): the "Scriptave and Precept" school; early school of Tibetan Buddhism.
kagyü (T): the "Oral Transmission" School; School of Tibetan Buddhism.
kāma-loka (S, P): Sense-desire realm; realms of hells, hungry ghosts, animals, humans, and lower gods.
kami (J): Spirits worshiped in Japanese Shintō religion.
kangyur (T): "Translated words at the Buddha"; division of the Tibetan Buddhist canon containing what is thought to be the Buddha's teachings.
karma (S) [P: kamma]: Action; intentional act; the effect such actions leave that influence the future of the actor; principle governing cause and effect.
karuṇā (S, P): Compassion.
kegon (J): Japanese Huayan School of Buddhism.
kenshō (J): "Seeing the nature"; enlightened insight in Zen Buddhism.
kleśā (S) [P: kilesa]: Defilement.
kṛtsna (S) [P: kasiṇa]: Devices used as objects in meditation.
kṣānti (S): Patience.
kuśala (S) [P: kusala]: Wholesomeness.
kusha (J): Japanese Sarvāstivāda School.
kyeyul (K): Korean *Vinaya* School.
kyo (K): Doctrinal Schools of Buddhism in Korea.
lama (T): "Guru" in Sanskrit; spiritual teacher.
lamdré (T): "Path and fruit"; meditative practice of the Sakya School of Tibetan Buddhism.
li (C): Principle; inherent pure nature of existence.
linji (C) [J: rinzai]: School of Chan Buddhism that uses *gong'an* practice.
lobha (P): Greed; attraction.
lu (C): Chinese *Vinaya* School of Buddhism.
mādhyamika (S): Major school of Mahāyāna Buddhism in India that stresses emptiness.
mahāmudrā (S): "Great seal"; meditative system of practice associated with the Kagyü School of Tibetan Buddhism and used for the realization of the luminous and empty nature of existence.
mahāsaṅghika (S): "Great Assembly"; early school of Buddhism.
mahāyāna (S): Great vehicle, great course, or great journey; name of one of the major divisions of Buddhism wherein persons strive to become a Buddha rather than an *arhat.*
maitreya (S): Bodhisattva who will be the next human Buddha.
maitri (S) [P: metta]: Loving kindness; friendliness.
manas (S, P): Mind.
maṇḍala (S): Diagram or picture, often circular, used in meditative practice; Tantric diagram used for visualization of a Buddha's qualities and realm.
mañjuśrī (S): Bodhisattva associated with wisdom.
mantra (S): Ritual formula; verse used to invoke a deity or to gain protection; sound used for focus in meditation.
mantrayāna (S): Tantric Buddhism with its stress on the use of *mantras.*
mappō (J): Age of the Degenerate Dharma.

māra (S, P): Tempter; highest deity in the sense-realm, who uses sensuality to prevent people from gaining Awakening and thereby escaping from his realm.
mārga (S) [P: magga]: Path; way.
māyā (S, P): Illusion.
mikkyō (J): "Esoteric practice"; Tantric Buddhist practice.
moha (S, P): Delusion; distortion of the truth.
mokṣa (S): Liberation.
muditā (S, P): Sympathetic joy.
mudrā (S): "Seal"; hand ritual gesture.
mukti (S) [P: mutti]: Freedom; liberation.
nāma-rūpa (S, P): "Name-form"; the mental and physical constituents of existence.
nembutsu (J): "Recollection of Buddha"; Pure Land Buddhist practice of reciting the name of Amitābha Buddha; Japanese translation of the Chinese *nien-fo.*
nichiren (J): School of Japanese Buddhism based on the *Lotus Sūtra* and teachings of its founder, Nichiren.
nidāna (S, P): Link; cause.
nien-fo (C) [J: nembutsu]: "Recollecting Buddha"; chanting the name of the Buddha, primarily Amitābha Buddha in Pure Land Buddhism.
nikāya (S, P): "Collection"; text; group of early *sūtras* in the Pali canon; also called *Āgama.*
nirmāṇakāya (S): Manifestation body of the Buddha; emanation body used by a Buddha to help living beings and teach the Dharma.
nirodha (S, P): Cessation; cessation of *duḥkha* in the Four Noble Truths.
nirvāṇa (S) [P: nibbāna]: "Blowing out"; extinguishing a flame; goal of Buddhism; release from *saṃsāra* by attainment of Awakening.
nyingma (T): the "old" school"; one of the four major schools of Tibetan Buddhism.
ōbaku (J): School of Japanese Zen Buddhism.
paramārtha-satya (S): Ultimate truth; truth found in wisdom insight into dependent arising of existence according to Mādyamika.
pāramitā (S, P): Perfection; virtue, of which there are six or ten traditionally in Buddhism.
paratantra (S): Interdependent nature of experience; experience of all phenomena as arising interdependently; category in Yogācāra Buddhism.
parikalpita (S): Imagined nature of ordinary experience; ordinary experience of phenomena as independent entities; category in Yogācāra Buddhism.
parinirvāṇa (S) [P: parinibbāna]: Complete or final Nirvana; utter release from *saṃsāra* achieved by a Buddha or *arhat* at the moment of death.
parinispanna (S): Perfected nature of experience; purified consciousness recognizing that all phenomena are in essence consciousness only; category in Yogācāra Buddhism.
pŏpsang (K): Korean Yogācāra School of Buddhism.
prajñā (S) [P: paññā]: Wisdom; knowledge of truth associated with Awakening; liberating wisdom into the true nature of existence.
prajñā-paramitā (S): Perfection of wisdom; designation for early Mahāyāna *sūtras,* the Wisdom Literature.
prapañca (S): "Play of words"; meaningful conceptualization of the world through use of language; important notion in Mādyamika Buddhism.
prāsaṅgika (S): Sect of Mādhyamika Buddhism founded by Buddhapālita.
prātimokṣa (S) [P: pātimokkha]: Code of monastic precepts.
pratītya-samutpāda (S) [P: paticca-samuppāda]: Dependent arising; dependent origination; dependent co-arising of all phenomena.
pratyekabuddha (S): "Solitary Buddha"; person who attains Awakening with no help and never preaches to others.

preta (S) [P: peta]: Hungry ghost.
pudgala (S): Person.
pudgalavāda (S): Personalists; early school of Buddhism in India.
rinzai (J): School of Zen Buddhism that uses *kōans,* based on the Chinese Linji School.
risshō kōsei-kai (J): Modern Buddhist lay movement in Japan based on the *Lotus Sūtra.*
ritsu (J): Japanese *Vinaya* school of Buddhism.
roshi (J): Zen master.
rūpa (S, P): Form; material element of existence.
rūpakāya (S, P): Form or material body of a Buddha.
rūpaloka (S, P): Realm of form; place of rebirth as higher Brahmā deity.
sādhana (S): Esoteric or Tantric practice.
sakṛdāgāmin (S) [P: sakadāgāmin]: "Once-returner"; second advanced stage of early Buddhist path leading to being an *arhat.*
sakya (T): One of the four major schools of Tibetan Buddhism.
sakyadhītā (S): "Daughters of the Buddha"; association dedicated to Buddhist women's issues, especially full ordination of women monastics in Theravāda Buddhism.
samādhi (S, P): Concentration; Right concentration in the Noble Eightfold Path; deep state of meditation.
śamatha (S) [P: samatha]: Tranquillity; calmness; serenity; cessation of thoughts and desires in meditation.
sambhogakāya (S): Enjoyment or reward body of a Buddha; body of a celestial Buddha.
saṃjñā (S) [P: sañña]: Perception; one of the Five Aggregates.
saṃsāra (S, P): "Wandering"; process of birth, death, and rebirth; world of suffering.
saṃskāra (S) [P: saṃkhāra]: Mental formation; volition; one of the Five Aggregates.
saṃvṛti-satya (S): Conventional truth; truth given by ordinary sense perception and conceptualization according to Mādyamika.
saṅgha (S, P): "Community"; orders of men and women monastics; all Buddhist persons, lay and monastic.
sanlun (C): "Three treatises"; school of Mādhyamika in China.
sanron (J): Mādyamika School of Buddhism in Japan.
sarvāstivāda (S): All-Exists School of Buddhism.
satori (J): Awakening; sudden enlightenment in Zen Buddhism.
sautrāntika (S): "Adherents to the *Sūtras*"; early school of Buddhism.
sesshin (J): Intensive Zen retreat.
shakubuku (J): Confrontational method of evangelizing in Nichiren Buddhism.
shih (C): Phenomena; phenomenal *dharmas.*
shikan-taza (J): "Just sitting"; quiet sitting practice in Sōtō Zen.
shingon (J): "True Word"; school of Tantric or esoteric Buddhism in Japan.
shinjin (J): Arising of faith; trust in the saving action of Amida Buddha.
shintō (J): "Way of the spirits"; indigenous religion of Japan.
shōdō (J): Holy Path; Pure Land Buddhist name for the path to liberation that demands one's own effort, and not relying on the grace of Amida Buddha.
siddhi (S) [P: iddhi]: Supernormal power or ability.
śīla (S) [P: sīla]: Precepts; morality.
skandha (S) [P: khandha]: Aggregate; the five kinds of constituents of existence: material form *(rūpa),* sensation *(vedanā),* perception *(saṃjña),* mental formation *(saṃskāra),* and consciousness *(vijñāna).*
smṛti (S) [P: sati]: Mindfulness; part of the Noble Eightfold Path.
sōka gakkai (j): Modern Nichiren lay movement.
sŏn (K): Meditation; Chan Buddhism in Korea.
sopadhiśeṣa (S): "With remainder"; Nirvana with the Five Aggregates.

sōtō (J): School of Zen Buddhism in Japan founded by Dōgen.
śramaṇa (S) [P: samaṇa]: Renunciate status present in India during the time of the Buddha.
śrāvaka (S): Disciple; term for disciple of the Buddha seeking to be an *arhat.*
śrāvakayāna (S): Term for the early Buddhist path leading to being an *arhat.*
Srotāpanna (S) [P: sotāpanna]: "Streamwinner"; first of the advanced stages of early Buddhism leading to being an *arhat.*
sthavira (S) [P: thera]: Elder.
sthaviravāda (S) [P: Theravāda]: Way or teaching of the elders; school of early Buddhism.
stūpa (S, P): Memorial mound for the bones or remains of the dead; used as a shrine for the Buddha.
sukhāvati (S): Land of bliss; Pure Land of Amitābha Buddha.
śūnyatā (S): Emptiness; lack of substantial independence; fundamental Mahāyāna notion of ultimate reality.
sūtra (S) [P: sutta]: Text; scripture; collection of discourses by the Buddha in the Buddhist canon.
svabhāva (S): "Own-being"; substantial self-existence; that which enables a phenomenon to exist independently; attributed to the *dharmas* by some early Buddhist schools.
svabhāva-śūnya (S): "Emptiness of own-being"; notion in Mahāyāna that denies own-being of all *dharmas* in favor of emptiness, the dependence of existence.
svalakṣaṇa (S): "Own-characteristic"; distinguishing characteristic of a *dharma.*
svātantrika (S): Sect of Mādyamika Buddhism founded by Bhāvaviveka.
tantra (S): Esoteric tradition in Buddhism; esoteric texts in Buddhism.
tariki (J): Other power; relying in Pure Land Buddhism on the power of Amida Buddha to gain liberation.
tathāgata (S, P): One who has "thus come" or "thus gone" to Awakening; epithet for the Buddha after his enlightenment; title for all Buddhas in Mahāyāna.
tathāgata-garbha (S): "Womb or embryo of the Buddha"; innate potential for Buddhahood; Buddha-nature.
tathatā (S): Suchness; thusness; true reality; such as things truly are.
tendai (J): Japanese school of Buddhism based on the Chinese Tiantai School and additional teachings by Saichō.
tengyur (T): Division of the Tibetan canon that contains commentaries.
terma (T): Hidden treasure; entities or teachings hidden in Tibet by spiritually advanced persons and discovered when helpful to the community; Nyingma practice.
tertön (T): Treasure finder; one who finds a *terma.*
theravāda (P): Way or teaching of the elders; early Buddhist school that became the major form in Buddhism in Sri Lanka and Southeast Asia.
tiantai (C): "Heavenly terrace"; Chinese school of Buddhism based on the *Lotus Sūtra.*
trikāya (S): Three bodies of the Buddha: *Dharmakāya, Sambhogakāya,* and *Nirmāṇakāya.*
tripiṭaka (S) [P: tipitaka]: Three baskets; three divisions of the Pali canon: *Sūtra, Vinaya,* and *Abhidharma;* three parts of the Tibetan and East Asia comprehensive collection of Buddhist texts.
tṛṣṇā (S) [P: taṇhā]: Thirst; desire or craving; a root cause of *duḥkha.*
trisvabhāva (S): Three natures of experience; Yogācāra's three ways in which one experiences existence: *parikalpita, paratantra,* and *pariniṣpanna.*
upādāna (S, P): Attachment; clinging.

upaniṣad (S): Texts from early Hinduism that posit the existence of an absolute ultimate reality *(Brahman)* and its identity with the soul *(Ātman).*
upāya (S): Skillful means.
upekṣā (S) [P: upekkhā]: Equanimity; equal treatment of all beings.
vairocana (S): "Shining out"; celestial Buddha associated with the totality of the cosmos.
vajra (S): "Diamond" or "thunderbolt"; Tantric symbol for the power of Tantrism, and the basis of Buddhahood.
vajrayāna (S): Diamond journey, course, or vehicle; path to Buddhahood based on Tantric practice.
veda (S): Early texts of Hinduism that teach about the many gods.
vedanā (S, P): Sensation; feeling; one of the Five Aggregates.
vibhajyavāda (S): Distinctionalist School of early Buddhism.
vihāra (S, P): Monastery.
vijñāna (S) [P: viññāna]: Consciousness; mental awareness and discrimination; one of the Five Aggregates.
vijñānavāda (S): School of mind or consciousness; Yogācāra Buddhism.
vijñaptimātra (S): Ideation only; mind or consciousness only; according to Yogācāra, the basis of physical and mental experience.
vinaya (S, P): Precepts; rules for proper conduct; monastic discipline; one of the Three Baskets of the Pali canon.
vipaśyanā (S) [P: vipassanā]: Insight; meditation that produces insight into reality.
visuddhimagga (P): Path of Purification associated with Theravāda Buddhism.
wat (Th): Monastic temple complex.
won (K): One; symbol of unity and the *Dharmakāya;* new movement in Korean Buddhism.
wu (C) [J: mu]: Nothingness; emptiness; void.
yathābhūtam (S): "Things as they truly are"; what one discovers in Awakening.
yogācāra (S): "Practice of yoga"; major Mahāyāna school of Indian Buddhism that emphasizes the nature of consciousness.
yoga-tantra (S): Tantric practice involving visualization of oneself as a Tantric deity.
yŏlban (K): Nirvana; school of Buddhism in Korea based on the *Nirvana Sūtra.*
zange (J): Repentance.
zazen (J): Seated meditation in Zen Buddhism.
zen (J): Meditation; Japanese School of Buddhism based on the Chinese Chan school.
zendō (J): Zen meditation hall.
zhushe (C): School of Chinese Buddhism based on Sarvāstivāda.

Index